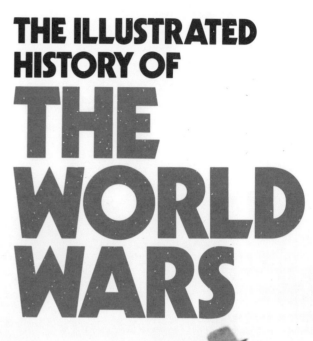

THE ILLUSTRATED
HISTORY OF
THE
WORLD
WARS

THE ILLUSTRATED HISTORY OF THE WORLD WARS

Editor-in-Chief

AJP Taylor

octopus

CONTENTS

THE GREAT WAR

This edition first published 1978 by
Cathay Books Limited
59 Grosvenor Street
London W1

ISBN 0 7064 0660 5

© 1968/69/70 BPC Publishing Limited
© 1973/74/78 Phoebus Publishing Company

Produced by Mandarin Publishers Limited
22A Westlands Road, Quarry Bay
Hong Kong

Printed in Singapore

This book is adapted from "The History of the 20th Century".
It has been produced by Phoebus Publishing Company in co-operation
with Octopus Books Limited.

WORLD WAR II

THE GREAT WAR

Introduction

For those who lived through the First World War, it was known as, and is still considered to be, the Great War. It was the cataclysm of a century, perhaps of all time. That is certainly the way it seemed then. A great war among the European powers had been feared for decades, but it was assumed that at the final moment, they would stop short of the brink, and major war could be averted.

In July 1914, however, it was different. When the diplomats stumbled and armies mobilized, the long dormant fear of a major war rose and, surprisingly, was welcomed on all sides. Within every European state social forces were pressing for change. In Russia, electoral, industrial and social reform on a broad front was being demanded by every stratum of society, from the nobility right through the middle classes and the peasantry. In Britain the Irish question was tearing at the fabric of the nation and causing great rifts among the politicians of the majority party, the Liberals. Trade unions were demanding shorter hours, higher pay and better working conditions throughout Western Europe. Women were demanding the franchise. By 1912 the Social Democratic Party had become the majority party in the German lower house, the *Reichstag*. The monarchs of Central and Eastern Europe had held back the tide of nationalism in Poland and the Balkans for decades. The more democratic, more highly industrialized states of Western Europe had held off the demands of the working classes in the factories for decades too. All demanded change. Each group thought that a war might bring about these changes faster. Thus, even those parties which had previously been anti-militaristic, like the German social democrats, now accepted and supported the war, for the call of nationalism was too strong to resist.

Ironically, those who resisted social change also supported the idea of war, as they believed it would divert attention from social, economic and electoral reform in a great national effort that would unite, rather than divide, class against class. When war came, therefore, it was accompanied by an outburst of enthusiasm and relief from every social class in every major European nation. German helmets were festooned with flowers, placed there by the women who cheered as their troops, their husbands and sons, marched off to the front. French and British soldiers who boarded the trains taking them to war, and many to their deaths, were cheered with equal enthusiasm. An outburst of nationalistic pride and fierce chauvinism gripped Europe in August 1914. It would, of course, be a short war. The boys would be home by Christmas.

It is difficult to pinpoint the reasons why war, which had been feared and avoided for so long, should break out because of the killing of an Austrian archduke and his wife. Why should world war have broken out over the Sarajevo Incident, and not over the many, seemingly more important crises, which had taken place earlier? The answer lies in the power of Great Britain relative to her European rivals. After the defeat of Napoleon, Britain was unrivalled as a major world power. On the seas Britannia ruled without peer; her colonial empire expanded when and as British interests determined it should. But in the most important area of all, industrial power and technological superiority, Britain was decades ahead of even France, potentially her greatest continental rival. As the 19th century went on, however, this once yawning industrial and technological gap perceptibly narrowed.

By 1870, when Prussia had expanded to create the German Empire, the Second Reich, proclaimed in the Hall of Mirrors of the Palace of Versailles after the defeat of France in January 1871, Britain still maintained her once seemingly insurmountable lead. But now a rival worthy of her potential loomed across the North Sea, then called the German Ocean. Although never a serious rival as a naval or colonial power in the 19th century, Bismarck, the German Chancellor, sought to pit Britain against France and Russia in a naval armaments race and a scramble for colonial territory which heretofore Britain had been content to influence, but not necessarily rule. Meanwhile, Bismarck saw to it that Germany's industrial strength increased in the only continent which mattered to him, Europe. By 1900 it was clear that the industrial gap had narrowed markedly between Britain and Germany, and at this stage Kaiser Wilhelm II, who had sacked Bismarck ten years before, sought to challenge Britain in a naval arms race as well. Although most of the Eastern Hemisphere had been divided into colonies or spheres of influence between Britain and France and a few other states, the Kaiser sought to provoke Britain in the colonial world, demanding a 'place in the sun', more colonial influence, and above all, greater prestige for Germany in consonance with her increased industrial strength.

Britain took this challenge seriously. But by 1914 Germany had passed Britain in many crucial areas. Certain key indices pointed to a German supremacy which had already been established. German production of pig iron was 40 per cent greater than Britain's; in steel production Germany was far ahead, her annual total over double that of Britain. Germany was almost an equal to Britain in coal production. Furthermore,

Germany was far more self-sufficient in foodstuffs than a Britain which had increasingly come to depend on her colonies and the United States for the food she consumed. Markets which had once been British for industrial goods—the Low Countries, Scandinavia—were now increasingly within German orbit. Given time, Germany would surely have outstripped Britain in the rest of Europe.

Given time, Germany's increasing naval strength would have been a major challenge on the seas which Britain had come to regard as her own. If Germany was to be stopped, the time was now—in 1914. Britain could not afford to give Germany more time. The Kaiser's bellicose pronouncements, his aggressive stance, his celebrated or infamous blank cheque to Austria to do with Serbia what she would, made it easy for Britain, urged on by France, to meet the German challenge. Diplomacy failed in 1914 because the Great Powers deliberately let it fail. Ironically, the Kaiser, who most stood to gain by maintaining a fragile European peace, did more than most to provoke the war which could deny Germany the hegemony in Europe which Bismarck and Wilhelm II had sought for so long.

But even the Kaiser realized that only a short war could bring victory to Germany. Britain's command of the seas would bring her the foodstuffs and industrial supplies from abroad which she would require in a long conflict. Thus, for many years Germany planned on striking a knockout blow against France within the first six weeks of the war, before France's ally, Russia, had time to mobilize her armed forces. Then German military might could be brought to bear upon Russia, thereby forcing a peace on her two greatest continental rivals regardless of what Britain did. So it can be argued that the war was lost for Germany at the First Battle of the Marne in early September, when the French and British Expeditionary Force stopped the great German sweep across Belgium and France short of Paris.

By the end of the autumn a line of trenches was dug from the English Channel to Switzerland. The war of attrition on the Western Front had set in. The boys would not be home by Christmas. It was going to be a long war.

On the Eastern Front Germany did rather better. After the humiliation inflicted upon Russia at Tannenberg, German soldiers slowly pushed into Russian Poland. By the end of 1914 German troops had occupied practically all of Belgium, much of northern France, and parts of western Russia. The Allies had been driven from German soil. The Allies, like the Germans, still hoped to bring an end to the war by one sudden breakthrough, even though it became increasingly apparent, to the men at the front at least, that such a breakthrough would

cost too many lives and was, in the circumstances, impossible.

Unable to win on the Western Front, the Allies hoped to achieve victory by starving Germany to death through a blockade of her coasts and seizing colonial territory from Germany and her ally, the Ottoman Empire. By 1915 the German flag had been rung down over the few colonies she possessed in Africa and Asia, save in Tanganyika, German East Africa, where von Lettow-Vorbeck fought on, clinging to a part of the colony by an intensive and cleverly fought semi-guerrilla campaign. Japan and Australia had partitioned German possessions in Asia, and France and Britain and her dominion of South Africa had taken what Germany once held in Africa. The pressing concern for the Allies in early 1915 was to bring assistance to Russia, who was unable to maintain a line of defence against Germany and Austria-Hungary, who continued to press the Russians back. The Gallipoli campaign, the purpose of which was to force the Dardanelles and bring Turkey to her knees, thereby giving the Allies access to the Black Sea to bring arms to Russia unharassed on a year-round basis, was one of the major disasters of the war for the Allies. The landings on the Gallipoli peninsula south of Constantinople were mishandled. Turkish forces, aided by German arms and military advisers, like Liman von Sanders, stiffened. Partly due to Allied errors, partly to Turkish resistance, the Allies were thrown back. Gallipoli was a fiasco.

The time had come for the Allies to seek further assistance. A deal was struck with Italy, heretofore neutral in the war and to one extent or other allied to both sides, to give her portions of Austrian and Turkish territory if she declared war against the Central Powers. It was hoped that Italian pressure on Austria-Hungary would sap the strength of the Central Powers, thereby stopping the advance into Russia and preventing a German breakthrough on the Western Front. The Italian declaration of war in the spring of 1915 did not accomplish this aim. First of all, Italy declared war only against Austria-Hungary. She did not declare war against Germany until 1916, and in any event, could do nothing directly against German territory. The war in Italy went badly for the Allies, who ironically had to send troops and munitions to prevent a collapse of the Italian front.

It was clear that further help was needed for an Allied breakthrough. By now most of Europe was in the war, and those nations that were not were not terribly significant in broad terms. Although the Scandinavian countries and the Netherlands remained neutral, the British blockade saw to it that few goods from the Americas and elsewhere were able to filter through these states to Germany as they had done at the outset of

the war. Of the Great Powers in the world, only one remained outside the conflict by 1915; the United States. There was little fear that the US would enter the conflict, if they did so at all, on the German side. But if America could be brought into the war in support of the Allies, it could make all the difference. The sinking of the British liner *Lusitania* helped Allied propaganda in the United States immeasurably. Although the Germans had warned any Americans travelling aboard the *Lusitania* that they were travelling at their own risk into a war zone around Britain which Germany had filled with submarines in order to break the Allied blockade, the American public reaction was one of shock and horror when it became known that 128 Americans, some of them quite prominent, had lost their lives when the liner was sunk off the coast of Ireland.

President Woodrow Wilson insisted that the unrestricted submarine warfare the Germans were waging be brought to an end. Otherwise Germany ran the risk of bringing the US into the war. Unrestricted submarine warfare did end after a time, but a significant shift in American public opinion had taken place. Although it is now known that the *Lusitania* carried considerable amounts of arms and other contraband, and therefore Germany was within her rights under international law to sink her, British propaganda in the States utilized this event to the full. Like the death of Edith Cavell, a British nurse who was acting as a spy behind German lines in Belgium and who, when caught, received the treatment that any captured spy in wartime can expect, the sinking of the *Lusitania* made Americans feel that the Germans were brutes, inhuman and worthy of contempt, outside the community of civilized nations. It has even been argued that Winston Churchill, the driving force behind Gallipoli, who was sacked because of its failure, contrived to have the *Lusitania* sunk because it would bring the United States nearer to intervention on the Allied side. But America steadfastly remained neutral, although she did loan Britain billions of dollars and continued to ship foodstuffs and other goods to Britain even though she was now virtually unable to trade with Germany. If an Allied breakthrough was to take place in 1915, it would have to be without American help.

The diplomatic illusions of the old Europe were shattered when the troop trains started rolling in August 1914. The military illusions of the general staffs had expired in the bloody trenches of Gallipoli and Neuve-Chapelle. The first two chapters take us to that point where the combatants realized that Europe's 'Great War' was a conflict far beyond the confines of any previous experience. The stage was set for the mass battles of 1916, the waging of Total War . . .

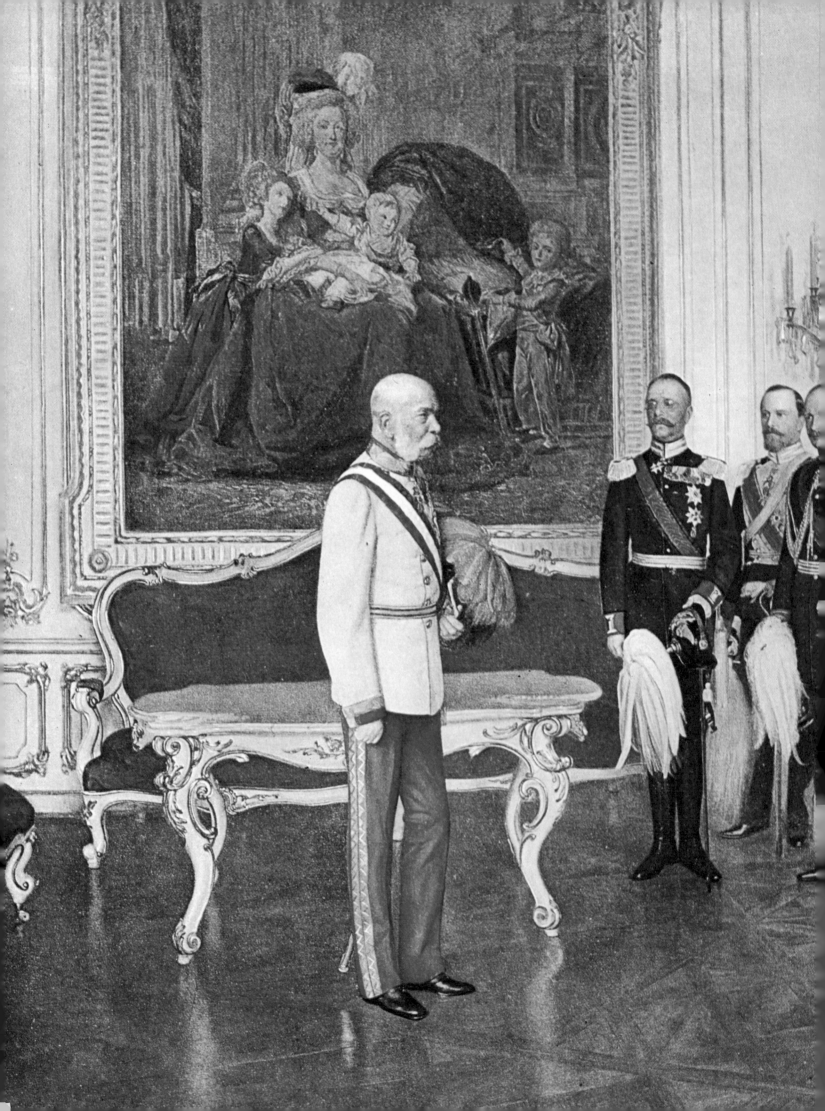

1 THE GREAT WAR BEGINS

Why Europe Went to War

In 1911 G. P. Gooch, an English historian who had, until the previous year, been a Liberal MP, published a little book called *History of our Time 1885-1911*. It is still worth reading, not least because its closing sentences show an optimism about international affairs which has now all but disappeared. Although, the author noted, five million men were at that moment under arms in Europe, nevertheless he said, 'we can now look forward with something like confidence to the time when war between civilized nations will be considered as antiquated as a duel, and when the peacemakers shall be called the children of God'.

In those words spoke the proud, confident, liberal, humanitarian Europe which had been built over the previous half-century. Less than three years later it was blown to the winds, and we have never quite recovered it.

It is worthwhile to recall just how great a blow was given to this confidence by the scale of what followed. The war which began on 1st August 1914, when Germany declared war on Russia, was the first of several wars which were later to be lumped together as one—the 'Great War'. The struggle between Austria-Hungary and Serbia—the expression of a deeper conflict soon to erupt between Austria-Hungary and Russia—and the war between France and Germany which quickly followed had little logic to connect them: what had Vienna to do with Alsace, or Frenchmen with the fate of Serbia? That the British, too, should then join in seemed odd to many people on both sides of the Channel. And this was only the beginning. Japan, Tur-

key, China, Siam—the list of those at war was to grow until it included every major state and left unrepresented no part of the globe. Thirty-two 'victorious' nations were to be represented at the Peace Conference in 1919; some of them did not even exist in 1914 and twenty-two of them were non-European. By then, Baluchis and Vietnamese had been brought to fight in France, Americans and Japanese had gone to Vladivostok, Canadians to Archangel and Australians to Palestine, while Germans and British had slaughtered one another across the oceans of the world from the coasts of Chile to the Western Approaches. The fighting only ended when, in 1922, Greeks and Turks at last made peace.

This extraordinary explosion of violence was hardly foreseen in 1914. Though many people by then feared war, few envisaged so colossal a holocaust. In part, this was because, once started, the struggle developed its own, unforeseeable logic. The two sides were nearly balanced in strength at the outset and this led to efforts to mobilize a margin of superiority which would guarantee victory and to find new allies: this intensified and spread the war. Yet much of what followed was implicit in the state of the world and, above all, of its centre, Europe, on the eve of the outbreak.

The shock of the war soon provoked a hunt for those who were guilty of starting it. This was the earliest form of the search to explain so astonishing an event. It was to go on for many years. It came out most crudely in popular catch-phrases: 'Hang the Kaiser' in Great Britain had its equivalents in other countries. But some looked for guilty men at home. Even before 1914 radicals and pacifists were attacking the Liberal government and its foreign secretary, Sir Edward Grey, for

committing the country to the side of France without authorization from Parliament. Another personal, but different, criticism was made of Grey by Germans: if only he had been more explicit (it was said), if only it had been made clear that Great Britain would enter a war between France and Germany, the German government would not have gone to war.

Some people preferred to blame whole groups of men. Germans blamed the British who, they said, grudged them their place in the sun; the British detected in Germans and German history a domineering tendency. Radicals and socialists attacked rather vaguely defined 'capitalists' who, it was alleged, either by so manipulating foreign policies as to safeguard their overseas investments and trade, or by encouraging the armaments which kept their factories working and paying large dividends, had pushed the world towards war. Whatever plausibility such arguments once had, historians have swung away both from them, and from large, schematic interpretations of the origins of the war in terms of economic interest.

We now prefer to place less emphasis on personal responsibility and policy except in the case of a few, clearly identifiable and delimited, crucial decisions. We need not go so far as to say that no one was ever personally responsible for anything decisive; the actions of Wilhelm II and his military advisers would by themselves make nonsense of such a view. Nevertheless, we admit that statesmen often have less freedom to act than they think, and that circumstances are as important in shaping their decisions as their own view of what they want. If we approach the world of 1914 in this way, what was there in its nature and structure which now appears,

Left: Franz-Josef of Austria-Hungary – symbol of the old order

The Great War Begins

first, to have made war likely, and then so disastrous when it came?

The diplomatic 'system'

The international system itself has been blamed. In an age of so much quarrelling and bickering, it may seem paradoxical to speak of a 'system'. Yet there was enough awareness of common principles and practice to make it possible to use this term. Diplomats everywhere understood one another in a sense in which, perhaps, they do not today, when deep ideological differences may separate them on fundamentals. The concept of national self-interest was the accepted basis of their business. This was tempered by a broad agreement that only vital threats to a nation's self-interest or a violent outrage to its dignity (whose preservation was a part of the national interest) could justify war between great powers. If war came, it was assumed, no power would ever seek to modify fundamentally the institutions of another – there would be, that is to say, no appeal to revolution as a weapon, and peace would eventually be made on the basis of a new adjustment of enduring interests.

This framework of common assumptions was reinforced by the fact that diplomatic business was then almost exclusively the affair of professional diplomats, who had evolved a very effective *esprit de corps* and skill. In 1914 they could look back to a long succession of tragedies averted and crises survived as evidence of the success of their methods. One towering fact stood out above all: since 1871 there had been no war between two European great powers and in this sense the Continent had enjoyed its longest period of peace since the Reformation.

The 'concert of Europe', as it had been called in the 19th century, was still a reality in that the European great powers had recently still tended to act in concert to avert threats to peace. They had done this successfully many times and, of course, to most statesmen it was only the European great powers which really mattered. This was not unreasonable. Portents of a very different future could already be discerned: there *had* been a war between Russia and Japan, and the United States *had* stripped Spain of her Caribbean and Pacific possessions. But these hints of a new era of global politics did not invalidate the achievement of the diplomats in Europe, because in 1914 it was still Europe which determined the fate of the world.

Yet this traditional diplomatic system has itself been blamed for the disaster. In one sense, this is a truism: war did break out in 1914 and the old diplomacy did not stop it. Many students of the crisis have concluded that the statesmen who were trying to deal with the crisis were too much

imprisoned by their conventional assumption and too unwilling to step outside their usual framework of ideas to be able to dominate affairs as, perhaps, a Bismarck might have done. This is a charge which it is easier to make than to prove or disprove. What may fairly be observed is that conventional diplomacy assumed that the aims of the great powers were rational and moderate enough for negotiation to bring about their reconciliation one with another – and this was no longer possible when some of these powers had come to believe, as they had done by 1914, that their very existence was at stake.

Yet it is not usually on this basis that the old diplomacy has been attacked. More usually, it has been asserted that there was a defect in the international machine itself which made conflict in the end inevitable,

and this has been identified as the 'nightmare of alliances' which Bismarck had so feared and which was an almost all-embracing reality in 1914. It had by then long been pointed out that the alliances introduced a dangerously mechanical and deterministic element into international life: once one cog began to turn, would not, in the end, the whole machine have to follow? Those who feared this thought mainly of two alliances: the Franco-Russian, signed in 1894, and the Triple Alliance of Germany, Austria-Hungary, and Italy, formed in 1882 and later modified and adhered to by Rumania. By them, it was said, Europe was divided into two armed camps, and the chance of war was immeasurably increased.

This is too simple. Qualifications are needed. The Triple Alliance, for example, was far from firm. Italy was not to enter the war on her allies' side in 1914 and by then it was well known in Vienna and

Berlin that Rumania could not be depended upon. Both countries eventually went to war – but on the other side. The Franco-Russian treaty, too, had originally been made as a basis for co-operation against Great Britain. Its terms, so far as they concerned Germany, were consequential upon German action. Only if Germany attacked Russia was France to come to the aid of her ally; in the end the alliance never came into action at all because the Germans settled the question of France's involvement by attacking her. Similarly, the *entente cordiale* by no means pointed irresistibly towards a Franco-British alliance against Germany. In 1911, Agadir had certainly aroused feeling and had strengthened the informal ties between London and Paris. Yet this, too, was a paradoxical outcome, since the French government of the day

Europe's heads of state in 1914. 1 Franz Josef of Austria-Hungary at a family wedding. 2 Kaiser Wilhelm II with the French General Foch. 3 Kaiser Wilhelm and George V of Great Britain. 4 President Poincaré (centre) of France visits Russia in 1914

was one which had hoped to cultivate better relations with Germany. By 1914 the British had got over their alarm at the Germans' battleship-building, and down almost to the eve of the war Anglo-German relations were better than they had been for twenty years.

Nor did European alliances determine the extent of the conflict. Although the Great War was to be focused on Europe and make its impact on world history through the damage it did to Europe, it was to be a world-wide war. Great Britain's participation made this inevitable, but there were other reasons for it, too. Tradition, geography, and domestic politics all made it inconceivable that the United States should join in European quarrels in 1914, but two other non-European states—Japan and Turkey—did become involved.

Japan's position in 1914 cut right across the pattern of European alliances. She was the only formal ally of the British, who had turned to her because of their traditional fear of Russia in Asia and the threat to their interests posed by the seeming break-up of China. The alliance was crowned by the Japanese victory over Russia in 1905. Two years later, an Anglo-Russian convention attempted to clear up some of the delicate problems which still divided London and St Petersburg. Yet by 1914 the two states were bickering over Persia much as they had always done. It was not, in other words, formal alliances which brought about the paradoxical situation at the end of August 1914 in which Great Britain, Japan, and Russia stood on the same side as allies against Germany.

Struggle for the Balkans

Turkey, too, was involved fundamentally and perhaps inevitably in the war, but hardly because of formal diplomacy. One possible name for the Great War would be the last war of the Turkish succession; eastern European history since the 17th century had been the story of attempts to allocate the booty and fill the vacuum left behind by the slow rolling-back of a Turkish power which had once embraced Hungary and lapped at the very walls of Vienna. The last stage in the dissolution of Turkey's European empire had opened in the Balkan Wars of 1912. The second Balkan War made it clear that among the claimants to the Turkish succession—the 'new nations' which had appeared in the Balkans in the 19th century—quarrels were just as likely as between the Habsburg and Romanov dynasties which had for so long suspiciously watched one another's advances at Turkish expense.

Here, indeed, was a true seed of the war. Two great states sought power and influence in an area abandoned to feeble and bickering small states by the Turkish retreat. Inevitably, they had favourites and satellites. But Vienna and St Petersburg managed to co-operate or avoid conflict until the annexation of Bosnia-Herzegovina in 1908. Thereafter, to concern about prestige and influence in the Balkans was added fear for the Habsburg empire itself. Serbia, a Russian protégé, drew like a magnet the loyalty of the South Slav subjects of the Dual Monarchy in the recently annexed provinces. A reckoning with Serbia would have to come, it was felt

in Vienna, and felt all the more strongly when Serbia gained more than a million and a half new subjects in the Balkan Wars. If the reckoning came, Russia would not be likely to leave Serbia unsupported in a second humiliation like that of 1909, when she had to recognize the Austro-Hungarian annexation.

Yet, Turkey's involvement at this level was remote and indirect: she was only to enter the war for very different reasons. Since 1900 German commercial and military influence had grown greatly in Constantinople. The Russians became more and more alarmed at the prospect of a re-invigorated Turkey under German influence. The old historic link between Berlin and St Petersburg, based on their common guilt in holding down the Poles, had begun to give way when Bismarck's successors decided to support the Dual Monarchy unconditionally against Russia (a crucial specific decision). It was killed by the fear of German power at the Straits. Russian hostility led the Turks to an alliance with Germany on 2nd August, 1914, the day after Germany declared war on Russia. It still took two months and the arrival of a German battle-cruiser (which guaranteed naval supremacy in the Black Sea) before Turkey took the plunge. And that meant the extension of the war to Egypt, Mesopotamia, and the Caucasus—theatres far from the provinces of Alsace and Lorraine, which had once seemed the greatest threat to European peace.

Thus, the part played in 1914 by formal alliances was small. The striking fact about the actual outbreak of war was the extent to which policy, in the end, was subordinated to questions of technique. What mattered were military plans and time-tables. In the end, the Franco-Russian alliance never came into operation at all, the entente proved too weak to take Great Britain into the war without the German invasion of Belgium, Germany's allies, Italy and Rumania, felt greater grievances against Vienna than against the entente and so stayed out, and, by a crowning irony, the contingency upon which the German-Austrian alliance had rested – a war between Russia and the Dual Monarchy – was the last and most superfluous link of all in the main chain of events. It was not until 6th August that those two empires went to war.

The failure of the diplomats, therefore, though real enough, was not pre-determined by the irresistible working of an alliance system which trapped them. Much in the traditional system, indeed, worked in precisely the opposite way in the twenty years before 1914. Not only had the well-tried resources of diplomacy avoided war over Fashoda, Morocco, Bosnia, and Agadir; they had also partitioned Africa peacefully and demarcated the interests of the powers in China. Even the aftermath of the Balkan Wars had again shown how the great powers could, if they wished, impose their will on the troublesome small.

The failure of Liberalism

If we accept the fact that the alliances did not lead men willy-nilly into conflict, but that many different forces brought about this, we have a problem at a different level. When we have isolated the facts which made the last crucial decisions probable, and can understand the logic of the military and logistical planning which dominated the last weeks, it still remains astonishing that so many Europeans dreaded war so little and did so little to avert it. We have to explain why the comparatively few people who worked the machine should have felt so confident that their action would be endorsed by the millions they commanded.

This is all the harder to understand because the first years of this century were, for many people, the culmination of an era of liberal civilization and idealism. It had been marked by great optimism about the progressive enlightenment of international society. It was evidence of this which encouraged such men as Gooch – and there were many like him. The Hague Conferences had seemed to be the first steps towards disarmament and they had actually done something to regulate the conduct of war between civilized nations. An international peace movement existed and carried on a vigorous propaganda. The practice of international arbitration of disputes between two states had become more and more common. And even those who felt sceptical about such things could still comfort themselves with the thought that

commercial and other economic ties made the disruption of international life by war between two major states almost unthinkable. Even the socialists felt confident: did not governments know that the workers of all countries would act, if necessary by strike action, to stop them going to war?

Or so it was hoped. Little attention was paid to what factors might qualify this optimism. The Second International, for example, could not actually organize collective action against war. All it could do was to conceal divisions between the socialists of different countries by vague formulae. In 1914 they meant nothing. One British socialist minister left the government and the Serbian and Russian socialists condemned the war. But that was all. As the German chancellor, Bethmann Hollweg, had hoped, Russian mobilization swung the SPD into line behind the imperial government. The socialist failure was, in a measure, symptomatic; it was only the most disillusioning of all the evidences of the helplessness of the pacifist and progressive forces so confident only a few years before. The force which overwhelmed them was old-fashioned patriotism.

This century, much more than the last, has been the great age of nationalism. More new countries have appeared since 1914 than ever before, and have been accepted as possessing the right to exist. The Great War was in this sense a great triumph of nationalism; it broke up historic and dynastic Europe to provide the new nations of the 1920's. But national feeling had already played a big part in mobilizing the psychological and emotional support which in some cases sustained and in some cases trapped governments in 1914. In every capital immense crowds greeted with enthusiasm the news that many of them were to be sent off to be killed.

Of course, the actual outbreak was a moment of excitement. Clearly, too, they did not know what was to come. By 1916 'war-weariness' and casualties would take the steam out of patriotic enthusiasm everywhere. Yet even then there was little support anywhere for a peace that was less than victory. In retrospect this seems astonishing; no nation, after all, faced in the Great War what seemed to face Great Britain or Russia if they were defeated in 1940 or 1941. The explanation of desperation born of fear, therefore, is not enough. The strength of nationalism is the key to the inner nature of the Great War, the most popular war in history when it started, and the most democratic yet seen in the efforts it called forth as it went on.

This had not been easy to foresee. The behaviour of representative bodies is not a clear guide. The attitude of the Reichstag is not good evidence for the views of the German people and it is notable that the

elections of 1914 in France (the only European great power where universal male suffrage actually worked) produced a chamber very hostile to the law of 1913 which imposed three years military service. On the other hand, the British Liberal government had more trouble with its internal and parliamentary critics than with the electorate when it undertook its great ship-building programmes.

The difficulty of knowing how to interpret such evidence as there is of mass opinion before 1914 has led to some attempts to blame the more strident examples of nationalism at that time on conscious propaganda. Some weight can be given to this, it is true. The British Navy League and the German *Flottenverein* had done much to excite popular interest in naval rivalry, for example. Winston Churchill's account of the years before 1914 in *The World Crisis* shows how wide an influence this exercised. Germans were encouraged by the publicity campaigns of their admiralty to believe that only a fleet could guarantee them British respect. This made Englishmen who had hardly given a thought to naval strategy uneasy; figures of comparative battleship strengths seemed easy to comprehend and were easy to dramatize. In turn, British spokesmen used violent language which aroused in Germans fear of an attempt to 'Copenhagen' (the modern expression would be 'Pearl Harbor') the German fleet: that the British Admiralty might have similar fears was neither here nor there. Fear, indeed, some of it consciously inspired, must come high on the list of explanations of what happened in 1914. Fear of the consequences of a Russian victory provided the excuse German Social Democrats needed to fight for capitalist and imperialist Germany in 1914. But fear need not be the only source of acts of collective madness.

National feeling and xenophobia were, after all, not new. They had been shown more violently by the French against the British at the time of Fashoda and the Boer War than they were by the British against the Germans in 1914. What was new – or comparatively new – was the social context of nationalist feeling before 1914. Patriotism and jingoism were now widely shared, thanks to new technical and institutional facts. One of the most fundamental, paradoxically, was the immense spread of popular education since the mid-19th century. This had two important results. The first was that most education, because it was provided by the state, led to the spread of common attitudes and assumptions, many of them intimately linked with the nation and its symbols. Whether elementary education brought to the mass of the population the reading of patriotic poems and the singing of patriotic

Below: This was, at its outset, perhaps the most popular war in history. Here, a German crowd greets the declaration of war by singing a patriotic song. Was one of the most enthusiastic members of the crowd Adolf Hitler (see inset face)? Certainly, like many others, he lost himself happily in a surge of warlike enthusiasm

songs as in France and Germany, rituals about the national flag as in the United States, celebration of royal birthdays or glorification of the national past as in Great Britain, it was probably the most single powerful agency in spreading a conscious sense of national identity. And nations, traditionally, glorified their prowess in war.

The second important result was the spread of the ability to read. It is no accident that the sensational newspaper appeared in about 1900 in most western European countries as well as in the United States. Its pre-condition was a mass readership, and by that time this had been created by mass education. It was quickly associated with a stridently patriotic style of journalism, whose first-fruits were the excitement of American opinion against Spain in 1898 and the British hysteria over Mafeking. They could arouse popular excitement over international affairs, which had previously interested only a relatively small governing class.

One curious reflection of changing popular mentality was the growth of a new class of popular books about imaginary future wars. An able recent study has shown that between 1900, when there appeared *How the Germans Took London*, and 1914, when Conan Doyle's *Danger* gave a prescient account of the threat unrestricted submarine warfare would pose to Great Bri-

tain, there were something like 180 books published in the main European languages on this topic. This was roughly double the rate of the fourteen years before 1900. They were enthusiastically received everywhere. In Germany, *Der Weltkrieg* (1904), which depicted a German conquest of Great Britain, was a best-seller. The greatest success of all was the English book of 1906, William Le Queux's *The Invasion of 1910*, which sold a million copies.

These books had great influence in forming the stereotyped ideas which filled most people's minds when they thought about international affairs. Many were zealously pushed by interested parties; Lord Roberts endorsed Le Queux's book as valuable support for the plea for compulsory military service. They also reflect shifts of opinion. In 1900 the 'enemy' in English books of this sort was still usually French. In 1903 came Erskine Childer's description of a German plan to invade England in *The Riddle of the Sands* and thereafter Germany was usually the danger which threatened. Such books prepared the popular mind for the fears and excitements which were first to sustain the big armament programmes and later to feed the hatreds used by the professional propagandists of the war years.

Another dangerous feature of pre-war society was its familiarity with violence.

Most people saw something of it, if only by report. We must beware of being selective as we look back at the golden age which the years before 1914 sometimes appear to be. As J.M.Keynes, the economist, was to remark when the war was over, and the truth of his observation was obvious, the crust of civilization was very thin. In many countries there was a deep fear of revolution, which was strengthened by the social violence so common in the decade before the war. A great individual disturbance like the *Semana Trágica* in Barcelona in 1909, or the massacres attending the Russian revolution of 1905, did much to encourage such fears, but they were fed almost every day by a running current of social unrest and violence. Giovanni Giolitti, the liberal Italian prime minister, was accounted a great humanitarian idealist (or, alternatively, a poltroon) because he suggested that there might be some better way of dealing with Italy's social troubles than by force. Clemenceau made himself hated by French socialists by his ruthless strike-breaking long before he was famous as the saviour of France. Even in Great Britain, the use of soldiers in support of the civil power was common in the years before the war.

Nor did all the violence or potential violence which faced governments come from social or economic grievance. The

The Great War Begins

terrorism which broke out at Sarajevo had been for years a threat to the Habsburg empire. In Poland young revolutionaries held up post offices to obtain money for their cause. Nationalism, wherever state and nation did not coincide, was a far more violently disruptive force than class hatred. In 1914 the most striking example, indeed, was in Great Britain where the irreconcilability of two communities, the southern Irish and the Ulstermen, brought the country to the verge of civil war in 1914 and presented the world with the astonishing spectacle of leaders of the Conservative Party abetting armed resistance to laws made by Parliament.

Fear of revolution

It has sometimes been suggested that fears and tensions arising from such sources led some people to welcome war as a means of avoiding revolution. There is something in this; certainly the Ulster crisis evaporated almost overnight when the outbreak of war removed the threat of Home Rule. It is also true that many people welcomed war through ignorance of what it would mean. This is not merely a matter of ignorance of what the results of the war would be but also of what its nature would be while it was going on. Soldiers, sailors, civilians alike all assumed, for example, that war would be short. Hardly any foresaw the destructive power of modern weapons and the casualties they would impose. That the internal combustion engine, barbed-wire, the machine-gun, and the aeroplane might revolutionize tactics was almost equally unforeseen. Above all, as the literature of imaginary wars shows, the inhumanity of 20th-century war was undreamed of. Only one writer, a Swiss, I.S.Bloch, correctly outlined the nature of the next war (one other writer, a man of genius, H.G.Wells, saw even farther ahead, and in 1913 already wrote about 'atomic bombs'). Most people assumed that war would be a sharp but short struggle of the armies and fleets.

Such ignorance made it easier for politicians to think war a simplifying release from problems otherwise almost insoluble. Revolutionaries in eastern Europe, too, sensing the damage war could do to the great empires they hated, thought the same. But it was not only ignorance of what war would bring that prepared people to accept it. One of the most surprising features of the reception of the news of the war was the enthusiasm shown not only by the half-educated and xenophobic masses, but by intellectuals, too. It was a German economist and future minister of the Weimar republic, Walter Rathenau, who, even in 1918, remembered the outbreak as 'the ringing opening chord for an immortal song of sacrifice, loyalty, and heroism' and a great historian, Meinecke,

who later looked back on it as a moment of 'profoundest joy'. A famous English example was the poet, Rupert Brooke. His enthusiastic and second-rate poem, 'Now, God be thanked Who has matched us with His hour', expresses an attitude shared by many of his contemporaries in all countries. In Italy many felt dismay at the prospect of neutrality.

Running through such responses to the war was a significant trait in pre-war culture which has too often been ignored. When it has been recognized, it has been explained as the creation of, rather than part of the background to, the Great War. This is the deliberate cultivation of values and qualities directly opposed to those of the dominant liberal civilization of the day. To the belief in reason inherited from the Enlightenment was opposed the glorification of unreason as the source of man's greatest triumphs; to liberal eulogies of the virtues of co-operation and negotiation as social techniques was opposed the teaching of those who saw conflict and violence as the dynamo of progress.

The roots of such cultural currents are very deep. The teachings of Karl Marx and Charles Darwin about the social and biological role of conflict must be counted among them. The much misunderstood but also much quoted writings of Friedrich Nietzsche were another. Some of the pioneers of the irrationalist wave, too, were not themselves aware of all the implications of what they were doing: Sigmund Freud's great onslaught on the primacy of reason was conducted in the name of scientific enquiry and therapeutic technique, and William James, whose philosophy of 'Pragmatism' won admirers in Europe in the early years of this century, was pursuing a healthy attempt to bring philosophy down to the firm earth of commonsense experience. Yet such sources fed a current deeply destructive of the assumptions of liberal civilization which made their work possible.

This came out clearly and explicitly in attempts to justify violence and irrationalism in moral or aesthetic terms. One spectacular example was the French engineer-turned-philosopher, Georges Sorel. His work, *Reflections on Violence* (1908), justified industrial action by the workers by a view of history which attributed all great achievements to violence and the heroic attitudes which were fed by struggle and myth. He despised the intellectuals and parliamentarians of his day who emasculated their civilization by directing its attention to material goals and to the rational settlement of disputes. In this he was like the Italian poet, Gabriele d'Annunzio, later to be identified by Lenin as the only true revolutionary in Italy. D'Annunzio had himself done very well out of the material goods of bourgeois society,

but had joined the violent Italian nationalists to urge forward his countrymen to the invasion of Tripoli in 1911 as a step towards national regeneration by heroism and sacrifice.

A taste for violence was shared by other Italians. One of the oddest was the painter and poet, Marinetti, leader of the 'Futurists', who had already begun that attack on accepted aesthetic standards which culminated in Surrealism. The Tripoli adventure of 1911, he claimed, showed that the Italian government had at last become Futurist and his cultural pre-occupations increasingly drew him towards political themes. One Futurist's invention of the early weeks of the war, 'anti-neutralist' clothing, was, perhaps, only comic, but even such gestures as this registered the bankruptcy of traditional culture and traditional authority in the eyes of many of the young. The great liberal platitudes seemed to them to be cramping and stifling: they could not believe in them and strove to smash them. *'Merde à Versailles Pompei Bruges Oxford Nuremberg Toledo Benares!'* proclaimed the French poet, Apollinaire, in a Futurist pamphlet. Cultural revolutionaries, like political ones, welcomed a war that promised to destroy the *status quo*.

Many middle-class people had expressed dissatisfaction with the materially satisfying but morally uninspiring world of the early 20th century. William James once said that humanity needed to find a 'moral equivalent of war'—an experience which promised the same demand for heroism, the same possibility of release from the humdrum and the conventional. In 1914 the behaviour even of thinking men throughout Europe showed how little progress had been made towards this elusive goal. The tiredness and the stuffiness of liberal civilization turned men against it, just as, paradoxically, did its material success.

It is not, therefore, in the diplomatic documents or the plans of the war offices that the whole story of the origins of the war can be found. When they have been ransacked, there still remain important questions about mass psychology and spiritual weariness to be answered before we can confidently say how so great a cataclysm came about. One participant, Winston Churchill, sketched briefly his own diagnosis in 1914 when he wrote: 'There was a strange temper in the air. Unsatisfied by material prosperity the nations turned restlessly towards strife internal or external'. It is only in this context that the automaton-like movements of the great military machines in the last crucial days can be understood, for it was only this temper that had prepared men, slowly, subtly, to accept such machines at all.

Sarajevo

No other political assassination in modern history has had such momentous consequences as the shooting of Archduke Franz Ferdinand, heir apparent to the Habsburg empire, in Sarajevo, the capital of the turbulent provinces of Bosnia-Herzegovina, on 28th June 1914.

The Sarajevo murder was an incident which, under more normal international circumstances, could not have provoked such historical upheavals. But in the early summer of 1914 relations between the great European powers were so tense that the killing of the archduke by a Bosnian student, named Gavrilo Princip, led to the outbreak of the First World War through a series of quick and irreversible steps—the Austrian ultimatum to Serbia on 23rd July, her declaration of war on 28th July, Russian mobilization, Germany's declaration of war on Russia on 1st August, and on France on 3rd August, and Great Britain's declaration of war against Germany on 4th August.

The murder in Sarajevo was one of the most amateurish assassinations carried out in modern times. The assassins were students, most of them in their teens. They belonged to a secret society called *Young Bosnia,* one of the many clandestine organizations among the South Slavs within the Habsburg monarchy. Although between 1910 and 1914 there had been six attempts against the lives of the Habsburg dignitaries, organized by the South Slav revolutionary movement, and a dozen conspiracies which did not materialize, the plot of 28th June 1914 was very badly conceived. It succeeded only through sheer luck and the negligence of the authorities.

Precautions left to providence

The Habsburg police did not take any serious measures to protect the archduke and the imperial party when they entered Sarajevo. However, warnings against the archduke's visit to Sarajevo had been numerous and they had come from all sides, from Sarajevo, Vienna, Budapest, Berlin, and even from the United States (the secret societies of the Americans of South Slav descent plotted for years against Archduke Franz Ferdinand, and the secret agents of the Habsburg police in New York suspected a distinguished professor of the Columbia University of Serbian origin of being a member of the leading group among the conspirators).

The archduke was a brave man and sometimes had a fatalistic attitude towards the warnings he had been receiving. Two

months before his violent death, while he was at Miramare, near Trieste, he decided on the spur of the moment to take a short excursion. Somebody mentioned the question of security and the archduke answered: 'Precautions? Security measures? . . . I do not care the tiniest bit about this. Everywhere one is in God's hands. Look, out of this bush, here at the right some chap could jump at me . . . Fears and precautions paralyze one's life. To fear is always a dangerous business.'

The archduke's wife, the Duchess of Hohenberg, was in great fear for his life on the journey to Sarajevo and she expressed doubts on the necessity of the visit on several occasions. The archduke persuaded her, however, that they should go to Bosnia. According to the memoirs of the archduke's eldest son, Dr Max Hohenberg, even Emperor Franz Josef tried to convince the archduke not to go to Bosnia: 'The High Command decided that the great manoeuvres should take place that year in Bosnia. The choice of this country, recently annexed by Austria, where a muffled rebellion persisted, was deplorable. We were distressed to learn that the old Emperor Franz Josef—who only by a miracle escaped an attempt on his life during the visit to Sarajevo—advised our father against going to the great manoeuvres. Would we thus be deprived of this treat? Our joy returned when we learned that our father had scoffed at the Emperor's prudent advice. One evening he said at the table: "I am Inspector-General of the Austro-Hungarian armed forces. I must go to Sarajevo. The soldiers would never be able to explain my absence." '

The Emperor Franz Josef had many reasons to be afraid for the life of his heir apparent. The resentment at Habsburg rule in Bosnia-Herzegovina was strong, particularly among the Serbs. The archduke had deliberately chosen to visit Sarajevo on 28th June, the greatest Serbian festival, St Vitus' Day, *Vidovdan.* This day has been celebrated among the Serbs since 28th June 1389, when at the battle of Kosovo, an Ottoman army commanded by Sultan Murad annihilated the Serbian feudal army led by Prince Lazar. Both warlords were killed—the Ottoman Sultan by a Serbian nobleman called Miloš Obilić who penetrated by ruse into the Turkish ranks and ripped the Sultan's stomach with his dagger. The Serbians lost the battle, and this defeat marked the end of the independence of the medieval Serbian state, and the beginning of more than four

Above: Front page of a special edition of the Bosnian Post. *The headline was: 'The Attacks'. The cross-headings read (starting in the left-hand column): 'Messages of sympathy'; 'To the second attack'; 'An unexploded bomb'; 'The assassination the work of a long arm?' (meaning Serbia); 'The effect of the catastrophe'. **Left:** Archduke Franz Ferdinand—victim of one of the most amateur assassinations of modern times*

centuries of harsh rule by the Ottomans over the Serbs and South Slavs.

The archduke's decision to visit Sarajevo on the Kosovo day festival, 28th June, 1914, was as bold as if, for instance, King George V had decided to visit Dublin on St Patrick's day in 1917!

Despite this explosive situation, the security precautions on the day of the archduke's assassination were almost non-existent, particularly in comparison with the police protection provided for Emperor Franz Josef on his visit to Sarajevo in June 1910. For the Emperor's visit the route through which he was passing had been lined with a double cordon of soldiers, while for the archduke there were no soldiers on the streets, although 70,000 of them were just outside Sarajevo. When the Emperor came, hundreds of suspected citizens were ordered not to leave their homes, but no such measures were taken on the occasion of Franz Ferdinand's visit.

The police officials of Sarajevo defended themselves and put the blame on General Oskar Potiorek, the military governor of Bosnia, and on the military committee for the archduke's reception. They prepared a special report on the activities of the Young Bosnians, but were rebuked 'for having a fear of children'. On the eve of 28th June they again warned that the archduke should not visit Sarajevo on St Vitus' Day. However, the chief of the committee, an army officer, rejected the warning by saying: 'Do not worry. These lesser breeds would not dare to do anything.'

'Security measures on 28th June will be in the hands of Providence' was the answer of one police official. On their own initiative, the police issued orders to their 120 men, reinforced by a few detectives from Budapest and Trieste, to turn their faces toward the crowd during the passage of the imperial party. But 120 could not do much on a route of about four miles.

The deed is done

In the activities of the local police there was a lot of *Schlamperei* (sloppiness). Most of the policemen, seeing six automobiles with the Habsburg noblemen, lost their heads. They were overwhelmed by the sight of the great spectacle. But the conspirators stuck to their job. Nedeljko Cabrinovic asked a policeman who was standing by him to tell him which car the archduke was in. The excited detective pointed in the right direction, and a few seconds later the assassin knocked the cap off a hand grenade and hurled it at the archduke's car. The bomb wounded twenty people, among them three of the imperial party. The Duchess of Hohenberg was slightly injured, too: the skin of her neck was grazed.

After the first attempt, the fateful decision was made that the archduke should continue his drive through the streets of Sarajevo. General Potiorek lost his head and not only issued new orders for security on the streets, but to the explicit question of the archduke, 'What about these bombs, and will it happen again?' answered: 'Your Imperial Highness, you can travel quite happily. I take the responsibility.'

Princip (front row, centre) and other conspirators on trial

The only change in the route of the imperial procession was made at the wish of the archduke so that he could visit one of the wounded officers, but no one informed the drivers of the cars. Who made this mistake, and whether it was deliberate or accidental, is a controversial point. The Czech driver of the archduke's car was about to follow the first two cars in which were detectives and local chiefs, when General Potiorek shouted angrily at him: 'What is this? Stop! You are going the wrong way!'

Stepping hard on the brake, the driver stopped the car just in front of a shop, close to the crowded pavement, where the chief assassin Gavrilo Princip, the best sharp-shooter among them, was waiting. At that very instant he took out his revolver. A policeman saw the danger and was on the point of grabbing his hand, when he was struck by someone standing nearby, presumably a friend of the killer. Pistol shots were heard. Princip was only a few steps from the target. The duchess died first. A bullet aimed at General Potiorek had penetrated the side of the car, her corset, and her right side. The archduke outlived her for a few moments. A bullet had pierced the right side of his coat collar, severed the jugular vein and come to stop in the spine.

All was over at 11.30 am 28th June 1914. The imperial couple lay dead in the governor's residence, the *Konak*, a building dating from Turkish times. The archduke's collar was open, and a gold chain from which hung seven amulets, with frames of gold and platinum, could be seen. Each of them was worn as protection against a different type of evil. His sleeves were rolled up, and on his left arm could be seen a Chinese dragon tattooed in colours. Around the neck of the duchess was a golden chain with a scapular containing holy relics guarding her from ill health.

The gift from Mars

For the Viennese war party, the tragic event in Sarajevo was a godsend, a gift from Mars. Although this powerful group lost its leader, Archduke Franz Ferdinand, its grip in Vienna was strengthened. General Franz Conrad von Hötzendorf, the chief of the Austro-Hungarian general staff, and the late archduke's right-hand man, had for years advocated aggression against Serbia. According to his own memoirs, in the seventeen months from 1st January 1913 to 1st June 1914 he had urged a war against Serbia no less than twenty-five times. For Conrad and other members of his group the Sarajevo assassination was the long-sought excuse for the settling of the accounts with Serbia. He wrote: 'This is not the crime of a single fanatic; assassination represents Serbia's declaration of war on Austria-Hungary . . . If we miss this occasion, the monarchy will be exposed to new explosions of South Slav, Czech, Russian, Rumanian, and Italian aspirations . . . Austria-Hungary must wage war for political reasons.'

On his return from Sarajevo, Conrad found that the foreign minister, Count Leopold von Berchtold, and the Austrian government shared his opinion. The Hungarian prime minister, Count Stephan Tisza, had some scruples about a rash punitive action against Serbia. Conrad and Berchtold at first had the idea of attacking Serbia without warning. Tisza's attitude forced them to prepare an ultimatum to Serbia, which was purely a formality since the decision to declare war on Serbia had already been taken in the first days of July.

Germany's attitude in the crucial days after 28th June was decisive. Of all the great powers Germany had the most advanced military preparations. Since October 1913 a common understanding had grown up between Berlin and Vienna over the Balkan policies of the two Germanic empires. After 28th June 1914 Berlin gave Vienna the green light to settle accounts with Serbia by force, and on several occasions in the first weeks of July urged that Austria-Hungary should not lose this opportunity. As the documents from the German state archives show, Berlin was aware that the Austro-Hungarian attack on Serbia might drag Russia into the war.

However, Great Britain's behaviour in the decisive weeks of July was rather ambiguous. Berlin's interpretation of this was that London was not much interested in the conflict between Austria-Hungary and Serbia. It is true that the mutiny of the militant Protestant settlers in Ulster threatened the unity of the British armed forces and that Sir Edward Grey, the foreign secretary, had to take the wishes of the pacifists within the Liberal government into account, but there was an overall impression that Grey's attitude encouraged German aggressiveness.

In fact London was well informed about Vienna's real intentions against Serbia since the very beginning of July. The first warning to Belgrade about Vienna's warlike preparations came from the Serbian minister in London!

During the previous two great international confrontations, over Agadir in 1911 and the First Balkan War in 1912, for instance, the British government made its position to Berlin very clear by stating that in the case of a general conflict, Great Britain would come to France's aid. But for the first three weeks of July 1914 Sir Edward Grey was noncommittal.

Vienna, however, did its best to hide its preparations for the aggression against Serbia. Berchtold told Conrad that 'it would be a good thing if you and the minister of war would go on vacation for a time. In such a way an appearance would be kept up that nothing is going on'.

The Black Hand

What at that time was the Serbian government's position and was it in any way involved in the Sarajevo conspiracy?

As has already been mentioned, the Young Bosnians were one of the many South Slav secret societies operating against the Habsburg rule. They had contacts with similar organizations in Slovenia (the secret society *Preporod)*, Croatia, and Dalmatia as well as with secret societies in Serbia, particularly with the *Ujedinjenje ili smrt* ('Union or Death', better known as the *Black Hand)*. It was headed by Colonel Dragutin Dimitrijević-Apis, the chief of the intelligence department of the Serbian general staff.

Although the Sarajevo assassins were Bosnians and Austro-Hungarian citizens, and although they had plotted against the Habsburg dignitaries for years, three leading members of the conspiracy, Princip, Čabrinović, and Grabež came to Sarajevo from Belgrade, armed with pistols and bombs which they had obtained through some Bosnian youth from Major Vojislav Tankosić, a leader of the Black Hand.

The common goal of the Young Bosnians and the Black Hand was national liberation. Despite this they differed in

their philosophy and in their approach to the internal problems of South Slav society. Colonel Apis was a militarist and a pan-Serb, who wanted for Serbia among the South Slav lands a privileged position, something like Prussia's position in the German empire. The Young Bosnians were rebels not only against a foreign rule, but against their own society. They were a kind of anarchist group, atheists; they were for a South Slav federation in the fullest sense of the word.

On the eve of 28th June 1914 the Black Hand was in a life and death struggle with the Serbian government. Prime Minister Pašić regarded Colonel Apis and his group as a sort of praetorian guard that was threatening the whole political system of Serbia. Colonel Apis had planned a *coup d'état* against the government in the spring of 1914, but the conspiracy was discovered in time to prevent it.

The Serbian government had no reasons to provoke any conflicts with Austria-Hungary in 1914. After two Balkan wars and an uprising in neighbouring Albania which, when the insurgents raided Oebar and Ohrid, compelled the Serbs to mobilize and invade, the Serbian army was decimated and had neither enough weapons nor ammunition. The country badly needed peace. The Serbian government did its best to stop any incident during the archduke's visit to Bosnia, as recently discovered Serbian documents prove. The Serbian government was informed by the civilian authorities at the border that some members of the Black Hand were smuggling arms into Austro-Hungarian territory. An investigation was opened at once against Colonel Apis, but he denied that his men were involved in these operations.

There is a theory that it was the power struggle between Pašić and Apis that led Apis to approve Tankosić's delivery of the arms to the Sarajevo assassins. It seems that Apis did not expect that Princip and his accomplices would succeed in killing the archduke, but that he did think their efforts might further strain relations between Pašić and the Vienna government and that such complications would further weaken Pašić's position in relation to Apis. This thesis was strengthened by Tankosić's statement when he was arrested after the delivery of the Austrian ultimatum to Serbia. A general present at the arrest asked: 'Why have you done this?' Tankosić replied: 'To spite Pašić.'

The investigation in Sarajevo provided no proof of the Serbian government's responsibility. A special emissary of the Viennese foreign ministry, Friedrich von Wiesner, went to Sarajevo on 10th July 1914 to study the investigation material and find out whether the Serbian government had in any way been responsible for the

Top: Austrian stamp commemorating the victims. Above: Uniform (with blood-stains) worn by the Archduke at Sarajevo

assassination. On 13th July Wiesner telegraphed: 'There is nothing to show the complicity of the Serbian government in the direction of the assassination or its preparations or in supplying of weapons. Nor is there anything to lead one even to conjecture such a thing. On the contrary, there is evidence that would appear to show complicity is out of the question . . . If the intentions prevailing at my departure still exist, demands might be extended for:

(a) Suppression of complicity of Serbian government officials in smuggling persons and material across the frontier; (b) Dismissal of Serbian frontier officers at Šabax and Loznica in smuggling persons and materials across the frontier; (c) Criminal proceedings against Ciganović and Tankosić.'

It is interesting that German authorities came to a similar conclusion. The former chancellor Bernhard von Bülow wrote in his memoirs: 'Although the horrible murder was the work of a Serbian society with branches all over the country, many details prove that the Serbian government had neither instigated nor desired it. The Serbs were exhausted by two wars. The most hot-headed among them might have paused at

the thought of war with Austria-Hungary, so overwhelmingly superior especially since, in Serbia's rear, were rancorous Bulgarians and untrustworthy Rumanians. Thus at least did Herr von Griesinger, our minister in Belgrade, sum up the position, as also did the Belgrade correspondents of every important German newspaper.'

Nevertheless, in its note and ultimatum to Serbia, on 23rd July 1914, the Austro-Hungarian government chose to draw quite different conclusions and asserted that the Serbian government had tolerated the machinations of various societies and associations directed against the monarchy, unrestrained language on the part of the press, glorification of the perpetrators of outrages, participation of officers and officials in subversive agitation, and so on.

The Austro-Hungarian government asked the Serbian government to undertake specifically these ten points:

1. To suppress all publications inciting to hatred of Austria-Hungary and directed against her territorial integrity;

2. To dissolve forthwith the *Narodna odbrana* society and to 'confiscate all its means of propaganda'; to treat similarly all societies engaged in propaganda against Austria-Hungary, and to prevent their revival in some other form;

3. To eliminate from the Serbian educational system anything which might foment such propaganda;

4. To dismiss all officers or officials guilty of such propaganda, whose names might be subsequently communicated by Vienna;

5. To accept 'the collaboration in Serbia' of Austro-Hungarian officials in suppressing 'this subversive movement against the monarchy's territorial integrity';

6. To open a judicial inquiry against those implicated in the murder, and to allow delegates of Austria-Hungary to take part in this;

7. To arrest without delay Major Tankosić and Milan Ciganović, implicated by the Sarajevo inquiry;

8. To put an effectual stop to Serbian frontier officials sharing in the 'illicit traffic in arms and explosives', and to dismiss certain officials at Šabac and Loznica who had helped the murderers to cross over;

9. To give explanations regarding the 'unjustifiable' language used by high Serbian officials after the murder;

10. To notify Vienna without delay of the execution of all the above measures.'

The fateful telegram

The Serbian government informed the Austro-Hungarian minister on 25th July that it accepted all the demands, except point 6, which would be a violation of the Serbian Constitution and of the Law of Criminal Procedure. The Serbian govern-

ment stressed also that if the Austro-Hungarian government was not satisfied with the reply, it was 'ready, as always, to accept a peaceful agreement, by referring this question to the Hague Court, or to the great powers which took part in drawing up the declaration made by the Serbian government on 31st March, 1909'.

The Serbian government made this decision despite the fact that the Russian government advised Serbia that it should not offer any resistance in the event of an Austro-Hungarian invasion and place its future in the hands of great powers. But the decision of the Russian government to mobilize its troops in military regions close to Austria-Hungary gave hopes to the Serbs that Russia would defend them if Austria-Hungary attacked.

Although, even in some circles in Berlin, the Serbian answer was regarded as favourable, Austria-Hungary declared war on Serbia, on 28th July, at 11 am. The Viennese foreign office for the first time in history sent a declaration of war by telegram, which reached the Serbian government in Niš, a town in central east Serbia, at about 1 pm. At that very moment, the Serbian prime minister, Pašić, was at lunch. Sibe Miličić, a poet from Dalmatia, and a junior official in the Serbian ministry of foreign affairs, described thus the historical event of the receipt of the Austro-Hungarian declaration of war:

'I was having lunch in Hotel "Europa" in Niš. The dining-hall was crowded with people from Belgrade. Between twelve and one o'clock a postman entered and handed something to Mr Pašić, who was eating not far from me, about two tables away. Pašić read what the postman handed to him, and then stood up and said in a deadly silence: "Austria has declared war on us. Our cause is just. God will help us!"'

When Pašić hurriedly returned to his office, he learned that the Serbian supreme command had received an identical telegram from Vienna. He started doubting the authenticity of the telegram. His suspicion was further strengthened by the fact that at 3 pm, on the same day, when he asked the German minister for news, he was told that the German legation knew nothing. Pašić immediately sent cables to London, Paris, and St Petersburg about the strange telegram, asking whether Austria-Hungary had really declared war on Serbia.

However, his doubts were cleared even before he got the answers to his cables. The news came from Belgrade that the Austro-Hungarian guns had started bombarding the capital of Serbia. The last hopes that war would be avoided were shattered; the biggest slaughter in the history that mankind had yet experienced was beginning.

War by Time-table

It was often said before 1914 that one day the weapons of war would go off by themselves. In 1914 this happened. Though there were no doubt deep-seated reasons for disputes between the great powers, the actual outbreak of the First World War was provoked almost entirely by the rival plans for mobilization. Events moved so fast that there was no time for diplomatic negotiations or political decisions. On 28th July the great powers were at peace. On 4th August all except Italy were at war. They were dragged into war by their armies, instead of using the armies to further their policies.

The great powers had been elaborating plans for mobilizing mass armies ever since the Franco-German war of 1870-71. As usual, men prepared for the last war instead of for the next one. The general staffs all assumed that the coming war would be decided by the first engagements on the frontiers, as had happened in 1870, and each general staff aimed to get its blow in first. Yet they were all terrified that the other side might beat them to it. Each one of them attributed to others a speed and flexibility which they knew they did not possess themselves. The deterrent of the overwhelming blow put the generals in a panic instead of giving them security. Such is the usual way with deterrents.

The plans for mobilization were all based on elaborate railway time-tables, precisely calculated over the years. The moment the signal was given, millions of men would report at their barracks. Thousands of trains would be assembled and would proceed day after day to their allotted places. The time-tables were rigid and could not be altered without months of preparation. Germany and France both had only one plan for mobilization — each directed, of course, against the other. Russia and Austria-Hungary had alternative plans: the Russian either for general mobilization against both Germany and Austria-Hungary or for partial mobilization against Austria-Hungary alone; the Austrian against Serbia, Italy, or Russia. If one of these plans began to operate, it would make the switch to an alternative plan impossible. The time-tables could not be changed overnight.

None of the plans had been rehearsed. No great power had mobilized since the Congress of Berlin in 1878, except for Russia during the Russo-Japanese war, and that was irrelevant to European conditions. The plans existed only on paper and were the more rigid on that account. No general staff had the experience of extemporizing plans as it went along. Moreover the plans had been worked out in academic secrecy. The generals did not tell the statesmen what they were doing or, if they did, the statesmen did not take it in. Count Leopold von Berchtold, the Austro-Hungarian foreign minister, thought he could threaten Serbia without losing his freedom of action against Russia. Sergei Sazonov, the Russian foreign minister, thought he could threaten Austria-Hungary without losing his freedom of action against Germany. Bethmann Hollweg, the German chancellor, thought he could threaten Russia without losing his freedom of action against France. Sir Edward Grey, the British foreign secretary, thought that he could protect Belgium without becoming necessarily committed to France. They were all wrong. When they learned their respective mistakes, they surrendered helplessly to the dictates of the military time-tables.

The statesmen had not been unduly alarmed by the assassination of Archduke Franz Ferdinand at Sarajevo. They were used to troubles in the Balkans and assumed that this trouble would end as earlier ones had done — with alarms, threats, and ultimately negotiations. They recognized that Austria-Hungary had grievances against Serbia and believed in any case that, as a great power, she was entitled to get most of her own way. Even Sir Edward Grey held that Serbia, being a small country, must pay the price for peace, however unjust that might be. But there was nothing Europe could do until Austria-Hungary formulated her demands. These demands, when they came, were excessive. For this very reason, they seemed to offer all the more opening for negotiation and compromise.

The Austrians, however, were determined not to be dragged before a European conference. They wished to keep their dispute with Serbia as a private quarrel. Hence they first broke off relations and then on 28th July declared war. Even now the other European statesmen were not dismayed. Bethmann Hollweg, Sazonov, and Grey all arrived independently at the same solution. This was the Halt in Belgrade. The Austrians would occupy Belgrade and thus vindicate their military prowess. Then they would declare their willingness to halt and would hold Belgrade as a pledge during negotiations. There would be a compromise, very much at Serbia's expense, but she would remain an independent country, and hence the prestige of Russia, Serbia's patron, would be vindicated also.

THE "SCRAP" OF PAPER

These are the signatures and seals of the representatives of the Six Powers to the "Scrap of Paper"—the Treaty signed in 1839 guaranteeing the independence and neutrality of Belgium. "Palmerston signed for Britain. "Bülow for Prussia.

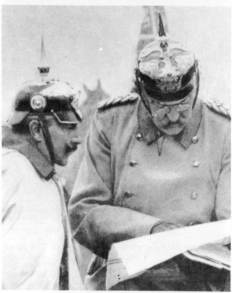

Top: British poster illustrating the treaty that guaranteed Belgian neutrality, described by Bethmann Hollweg as a 'scrap of paper'. ***Above:*** *Kaiser Wilhelm and Moltke pore over plans for the invasion of the west*

The Great War Begins

Belgian relics of Germany's assault: a page from a book of mobilization records and a pistol, now in the Royal Army Museum in Brussels

This ingenious proposal broke down for an unexpected and most extraordinary reason. Though Austria-Hungary claimed to be a great power, her army was in no condition to occupy Belgrade and so could not halt there. Mobilization, even against Serbia, would take some weeks. In any case, the Austrian general staff dared not mobilize against Serbia unless it were first assured of Russian neutrality, for, if it did so, it could not switch over to the alternative plan for mobilizing against Russia. Hence the Austrian general staff preferred to do nothing. As a little extra twist of irony, the Serbs had decided not to defend Belgrade, which could therefore have been occupied by a single Austro-Hungarian company, and the Halt in Belgrade would really have been possible after all.

Just as the Austrians knew nothing of the Serbian plans, so the Russians knew nothing of the Austrian plans, or lack of them. The tsar and his ministers assumed that Austria-Hungary would attack Serbia almost at once. The Russians were resolved that they would not leave Serbia in the lurch as they had done during the Bosnian crisis of 1908-09. Somehow they had to assert Russia's interest in the Austro-Serbian conflict. They could no longer claim to be included in negotiations. These, as between Austria-Hungary and Serbia, were over. Direct negotiations between Russia

and Austria-Hungary could be initiated only if Russia answered the Austro-Hungarian gesture of declaring war against Serbia by some corresponding gesture of her own. Sazonov, the Russian foreign minister, thought he knew the answer. The Russian army should begin a partial mobilization directed solely against Austria-Hungary. In this way, he imagined, there would be no Russian challenge to Germany. Now the time-tables interfered again. The Russian generals were horrified at Sazonov's proposal. A partial mobilization, they insisted, would rule out any general mobilization against Germany for months to come. Russia would be helpless, at Germany's mercy.

Sazonov might have persisted if he had been confident of German neutrality. Exactly the opposite was the case. Bethmann Hollweg and Kaiser Wilhelm had promised to support Austria-Hungary against Russia and believed that threats were the best way of doing this. Moreover the German generals took alarm at the rumour of even a partial Russian mobilization. Far from recognizing that this would cripple Russia in any activity against Germany, they believed that it was a preliminary to general mobilization and thus a sinister device for stealing a march on the German time-table. On 29th July therefore the German ambassador warned Sazonov that any Russian mobilization, however partial, would provoke German mobilization – and war. Sazonov believed the first part of the warning. He still could not believe that any power would proceed from threatening gestures to the real thing.

Decision lay with Nicholas II, the Russian tsar. By nature, he was a retiring family man, who preferred tennis and sea-bathing to the affairs of state. But he had inherited a unique position as an absolute monarch, and he dutifully discharged his trust. Now he had to show that Imperial Russia was a power of the first rank. Throughout 29th and 30th July he debated with Sazonov and with the minister of war. Or rather he sat lackadaisically by while the two ministers argued. The orders for partial and for general mobilization both lay on his desk. Really there was little to discuss. The only object of partial mobilization had been to appease Germany, and, now that the Germans had refused to be appeased, there was no sense left in it. The only alternatives were general mobilization or nothing, and to do nothing would be to abdicate as a great power.

In the evening of 29th July the tsar agreed to general mobilization. Half an hour later he changed his mind. The order was cancelled. The next day the discussion began again. One of the generals said: 'It is hard to decide.' Nicholas II was provoked. He answered roughly: 'I will decide,' and

signed the order for general mobilization. This time there was no going back. The red notices of call-up were soon displayed all over Russia. The troop-trains began to gather. Nicholas wrote in his diary: 'I went for a walk by myself. The weather was hot. Had a delightful bathe in the sea.' The decision had been made without consulting either France, Russia's ally, or Great Britain, Russia's friend. Later on, British and French statesmen were criticized and condemned for failing to warn Russia against this grave step. What held them back was fear that, if they did so, Russia might break with them and go over to the German side. As well, the British and French statesmen, just like the Russian, did not realize exactly how grave the consequences would be. They appreciated that a general Russian mobilization would increase the tension, but they also supposed that for this very reason it would speed up the opening of negotiations between the great powers. They still envisaged some sort of European conference and had no idea that in German eyes Russia's mobilization made war inevitable.

Here was the strongest factor in 1914, and one which proved catastrophic. All the great powers had carefully-prepared plans for general mobilization which would put them in a better position for fighting a great war. These plans would take some time to mature, and even then the mobilized armies could be held on the frontiers in suspense. For all of them there was a margin, though a thin one, between mobilization and war. For all of them, that is, except Germany. The Germans had no plans for general mobilization as such. The German general staff had wrestled for twenty years with the problem how they were to win a two-front war against France and Russia with one army. Their answer was to defeat France before the Russian army was ready. The French frontier itself was too strongly fortified for a successful attack to be possible. Hence Count von Schlieffen, who had been chief of the German general staff from 1891 to 1908, devised a plan for encircling the French armies by marching through Belgium.

This was a difficult operation. There were only eighty miles between the supposedly-impassable Ardennes and the Dutch frontier. Through this gap four armies, 840,000 men, had to be pumped. All of them had to go through the single railway junction of Aachen. The troop trains could not pile up at Aachen, however much its marshalling yards were extended. They had to go on so as to clear the lines for more trains behind. Hence, in the German plans for mobilization, there was no stopping at the frontier. The advance into Belgium was an integral part of the mobilization. Schlieffen never reflected that Germany might want to make a show of strength without actually starting a war. He was a technician pure and simple. Helmuth von Moltke, his successor, had no gift for strategy. He accepted the plan just as Schlieffen had left it. Or rather he gave no thought to the question until the news of Russia's mobilization. Then he opened the drawer of his desk and followed Schlieffen's instructions.

Kaiser Wilhelm and Bethmann Hollweg, with whom the political decisions rested, had no idea how restricted they were by the military plans. They never asked, and the general staff never told them. They went on dreaming that they could rattle the sword, as other European rulers did, without actually drawing it. Now on the morning of 31st July, Moltke appeared with the news that Russia was mobilizing. He insisted that the German armies must mobilize at once and invade Belgium. Bethmann Hollweg asked whether there were no lesser alternative. There was none. Bethmann Hollweg bowed to the dictates of strategy. The preliminary orders for mobilization were sent out. An ultimatum was dispatched to St Petersburg, demanding that Russia should arrest her mobilization within twenty-four hours.

The demand was of course refused. On 1st August the German ambassador handed to Sazonov Germany's declaration of war. The Kaiser, wearing full Guards uniform, drove in an open carriage from Potsdam to his palace in Berlin. Surrounded by glittering generals, he was keyed up to sign the order for general mobilization. Bethmann Hollweg appeared with startling news from London. Sir Edward Grey had stated that Great Britain would remain neutral, if Germany would refrain from attacking France. The Kaiser was delighted: 'This calls for champagne. We must halt the march to the west.' Moltke changed colour. Eleven thousand trains would have to be stopped in their tracks. He said in a trembling voice: 'It is impossible. The whole army would be thrown into confusion.' Once more the time-tables dictated policy. Wilhelm acquiesced and signed the mobilization orders.

The streets were crowded with cheering people. It appeared to simple Germans that they were threatened with attack by Russia's Mongol hordes. Until this moment the German Socialists had been contemplating, somewhat glumly, their pledge to declare a general strike against war. Now they rallied to the defence of European civilization against the barbaric East. The Reichstag passed the war-credits unanimously. The parties declared a political truce for the duration of the war. Inspired by this unity, Wilhelm declared: 'I see no parties any more. I see only Germans.'

War had started between Russia and Germany, though neither power was in a condition to fight it. All Germany's offensive power was directed against France, with whom as yet she had no ostensible cause of quarrel. A pretext had to be found. On 1st August the German ambassador called on René Viviani, the French premier and foreign minister, and demanded a promise of French neutrality. If Viviani had agreed, the ambassador would have gone on to demand the surrender of Toul and Verdun as a pledge. Viviani cut the discussion short: 'France will act according to her interests.' The Germans did not renew their demand. It occurred to them that France might agree and then their offensive plans would be ruined. Instead German aeroplanes dropped a few bombs on Nuremberg. The Germans announced that these aeroplanes were French, and with this pretext declared war on 3rd August. The French statesmen had been somewhat worried how they were to explain their secret obligations under the Franco-Russian alliance. Now they did not need to do so. France, too, was fighting a war of national defence. The French troops' trains also began to roll towards the frontiers.

Thus Germany, Russia, and France were brought to war by Schlieffen's time-table. Two great powers, Great Britain and Italy, were not included in the schedule. Italy, though allied to Germany and Austria-Hungary, was determined not to fight on their side. She badgered her allies for approval that she should remain neutral. At the same time, she badgered them for the rewards she would have received if she had not stayed neutral. This complicated double-play ended by missing on both counts.

The British government was technically uncommitted. It had friends, but no allies. Some Englishmen, mainly Conservatives, believed that Great Britain should at once rush to the aid of Russia and France. Others, mainly radicals and Labour, thought that Great Britain should remain strictly aloof. As one radical paper said: 'We care as little for Belgrade as Belgrade does for Manchester.' Grey, the foreign secretary, felt that he was committed to France, but tried to avoid saying so. He waited for his hand to be forced. As he wrote later: 'Circumstances and events were compelling decision.' On 30th July he refused to give Russia any promise of support. On 1st August he even suggested that Great Britain would stay neutral if France were not attacked – though it is uncertain whether he meant what he said. On 2nd August the leaders of the Conservative opposition delivered a letter to Asquith, the prime minister, urging support for France and Russia. The Liberal cabinet took no notice. Instead they resolved that they would not allow the German fleet to enter the Channel and attack the French

Britain's French (1); France's Lanrezac (2), Galliéni (3), and Franchet d'Esperey (4)

Germany's Ludendorff (1), Hindenburg (2) and Kluck (3); and Serbia's Putnik (4)

Russia's Duke Nicholas (1), Rennenkampf (2); Austria's Conrad (3), Potiorek (4)

The Great War Begins

ports. This was not a decision for war. It was a decision for armed neutrality, and the Germans were delighted with it: keeping out of the Channel was a cheap price for keeping Great Britain out of the war.

The crux – Belgian neutrality

The British government had one little worry. It was determined to protect the neutrality of Belgium, as its great predecessor Gladstone had done in 1870. Then a request that both France and Germany respect Belgian neutrality had kept Great Britain out of war. So why not now? On Sunday, 2nd August, the cabinet resolved that 'any substantial violation of Belgian neutrality would compel us to take action'. The neutralists in the cabinet regarded this as a victory. Like everyone else, they did not grasp that Germany's strategy revolved on the invasion of Belgium. The Belgian people also did not grasp this. They spent that Sunday enjoying a sunny neutral afternoon. The same evening the German ambassador presented the demand that German troops should be allowed to pass through Belgium. The Belgian government deliberated until the early morning and resolved that the German demand should be refused. It still hoped that resolute opposition would deter the Germans and therefore appealed to the British government only for 'diplomatic intervention'.

Monday, 3rd August, was a Bank Holiday in England. There were cheering crowds in the streets of London, as there had been in Paris and Berlin. Lloyd George, the chancellor of the exchequer, who had previously been against the war, was much affected by the display of wartime enthusiasm. In the afternoon, Grey explained to the House of Commons the equivocal entanglements with France and Russia into which he had drifted. Fortunately, he was able to tack on the news about Belgium, and this united practically all the members of the House of Commons. Later in the evening, the cabinet decided that a polite message should be sent to the Germans, requesting them to leave Belgium alone. Grey apparently did not think there was any urgency. At any rate he did not send the message until the next morning, when German troops were already in Belgium.

About midday, the news reached London, though there was as yet no Belgian appeal for help. However, the news stirred Grey into firmer action. Without consulting the cabinet, he sent off an ultimatum to Germany, demanding by midnight a promise to respect Belgian neutrality. At 7 pm Bethmann Hollweg refused to make any such promise. He complained that Great Britain was going to war 'just for a scrap of paper'. Did he use these very words? Did he speak in English or German? We shall never know. But a fortnight earlier there had been amateur theatricals at the British Embassy in Berlin. The piece by Sardou was entitled *A Scrap of Paper*. No message from Berlin reached London. Asquith and other cabinet ministers sat round, perhaps still half-hoping for a favourable reply. Someone unknown ingeniously pointed out that midnight in Berlin was 11 pm in London. Hence they could declare war an hour early and get off to bed. The declaration of war was in fact handed to the German ambassador at 11.5 pm. The time-tables had won another triumph.

There was a final twist. The British had gone to war in order to protect Belgian neutrality. But when Asquith met his generals on 5th August, he learned that time-tables dictated even to the small British army. There was a prepared plan for placing this army on the left flank of the French. There was no plan for sending it to the aid of Belgium. Thus Great Britain found herself a full ally of France after all.

The British declaration of war committed the entire British Empire also, including the Dominions and India. Only the Canadian parliament subsequently expressed independent approval. The one country still tailing behind was the one which had started the race: Austria-Hungary. On 6th August Austria-Hungary declared war on Russia. On 12th August, after complaints from Russia, Great Britain and France declared war on Austria-Hungary. Every country claimed to be fighting a war of self-defence, and so in a sense they were. But all of them believed that attack was the only form of defence. Hence, in order to defend themselves, they attacked each other. The general staffs, who had given the signal for war, proved wrong on every count. The war was not short; there were no quick victories; defence turned out to be the best form of defence.

THE DAILY MIRROR

"THREE CHEERS

FOR BELGIUM!"

The Military Balance

George Stephenson and General Lazare Carnot could well be called the grandfathers, or perhaps the great grandfathers, of the European military system of 1914. From the French Revolution and from Carnot, who had built the armies Napoleon used, came the concept of the nation in arms—so-called, though it would be more accurate to call it the concept of 'the whole manpower of the nation in the army'. Under Napoleon this system had overwhelmed the armies of the old regime. To save themselves the other great continental powers had been forced to adopt it, but once peace was re-established, a military as well as a political reaction had set in, and armies had reverted to traditionalism and long-service professionalism.

In 1857 Prince Wilhelm, Regent of Prussia, appointed General Helmuth von Moltke chief of general staff of his army, and, in 1859, another reforming general, Albrecht von Roon, minister for war. Meeting bitter political opposition to army reform, Roon suggested the appointment of Bismarck as minister-president. Under these four, Wilhelm, soon King of Prussia, Bismarck, Moltke, and Roon, the nation in arms idea re-appeared in Prussia and there reached its prime. In 1866 the Prussians quickly and decisively defeated the old-style Austrian army, then, in 1870 at the head of the North German Confederation, overwhelmed the French.

Roon in 1870 put 1,183,400 officers and men into the field. Moltke had been a pupil of Clausewitz, but he could not have handled effectively and rapidly an army of this size if there had not been two vital technical advances. First, the development of agriculture and industry had provided the means to feed, arm, and equip great numbers, and indeed produced the larger populations from which they sprang. Second, railways could now assemble this massed manpower along frontiers, supply it, and effect further strategic movements as needed. Deeply impressed by the events of 1866 and 1870, the armies of continental Europe made haste to imitate the Prussian model.

The weapons of 1870 were a marked advance on those used in the Napoleonic Wars. By 1914 weapons had been further developed. Not at the pace to which we are accustomed today, but faster than at any previous time in history. The magazine rifle, the machine-gun, and the breech-loading quick-firing field gun, especially, had been perfected since 1870. But, partly because the internal combustion engine was still in its childhood, and much more because soldiers and statesmen in power are inherently prejudiced against change, no new military system had appeared. Strategy remained a strategy dependent on railways. Movement at the 15-20 mph of the troop train became movement at the age-old 15-20 miles a day, normal march for men and horsedrawn transport, as soon as contact with the enemy became likely. Tactical theory, recoiling from the ugly lessons of 1870 and of the American Civil War of 1861-65, had gone into reverse, and reflected ideas that had already started to be out of date in the days of muzzle-loaders.

The German Aufmarsch

The German empire, proclaimed in the Hall of Mirrors, Versailles in 1871, had in 1914 a population of over 65,000,000. In theory, except for the small number required by the navy, all fit men of military age belonged to the army. Called up each year, from the age of seventeen to twenty they were enrolled in the *Landsturm,* Class I. At twenty those who were fit joined the active army for two-years' service, or the cavalry and horse artillery for three. Afterwards they went into the Reserve for five years (in the case of the cavalry and horse artillery for four years). In practice, the active army could only take about half the annual call-up, and the surplus, together with those excused for other reasons, was enrolled in the *Ersatz* Reserve, receiving, at best, very limited training. From the age of twenty-seven to thirty-nine, all served in the *Landwehr,* then from thirty-nine to forty-five in the *Landsturm,* Class II.

The active army of twenty-five and a half army corps—each of two divisions—and eleven cavalry divisions was maintained at fifty to sixty per cent war strength. In addition, there were thirty-two reserve, seven *Ersatz* reserve and the equivalent of sixteen *Landwehr* divisions.

Mobilization was a vast and critical operation, during which the army would be largely ineffective as a fighting machine. Nor did it end there, for the army must be deployed, which in 1914 meant deployment by rail. This operation, the *Aufmarsch,* was vital and planned with at least as much care as mobilization itself, for on it would hang the success of the opening campaign and, it was thought, of

Top: Troops of Belgium's neglected and poorly trained army. Above: Austrian cavalry officers, the 'élite' of the Habsburg army. Left: Kaiser Wilhelm II (fourth from right), surrounded by German generals

the war. Mobilization must be ordered in time so that the enemy could not establish a lead, and once ordered it led inevitably to the *Aufmarsch*. The armies could perhaps then be halted on the frontier, but the possibility was not seriously canvassed, and in 1914 mobilization spelled war.

Schlieffen's strategy

To this pattern, almost standard in Europe, the Germans had made two exceptions. Seeking to achieve crushing superiority for a quick victory against France in a war on two fronts, General von Schlieffen, chief of the general staff from 1892 to 1905, had planned to use reserve and *Ersatz* reserve divisions in the opening battles, relying on the well-trained regular and reserve officers and on strong cadres of regular non-commissioned officers to make good the reserves' deficiencies of training. Secondly, six infantry brigades with attached cavalry, artillery, and pioneers were maintained in peace at war strength and quartered close to the Belgian frontier, ready to seize the Liége forts and open the way through Belgium to northern France as soon as war was declared.

The peacetime strength of the army in 1914 was 856,000. On mobilization, trained reserves would bring it up to 3,800,000, but in emergency a maximum of 8,500,000 could be called to the colours. Against France seven armies would be deployed, totalling thirty-four army corps—of which eleven were reserve formations—and four cavalry corps. In the east, the VIII Army—four army corps of which one was a reserve corps with cavalry and some *Landwehr*—comprised some 200,000 and would hold off the Russians as best it could. There were other garrisons, depots, and reserves, and in Schleswig-Holstein a reserve army corps was held back in case the British attempted a landing.

Despite their defeat in 1870, the French had given the Germans more than one sharp lesson about the power of the breech-loading rifle against men in the open, and in their training afterwards the Germans took modern fire power seriously. When the machine-gun was perfected, the Germans took it up more seriously than other armies. Schlieffen's strategic plan to envelop the French armies by a massive advance through Belgium stemmed from his realization that frontal attack would be costly and indecisive. Watching the German manoeuvres of 1895, an expert British observer wrote that the soldiers '. . . act like intelligent beings, who thoroughly understand their duty, and the fact speaks volumes for the way in which even privates are taught to use their initiative'.

But as the years passed, memories of 1870 faded and traditionalism and arrogance asserted themselves. The Germans remained good soldiers, but of the manoeuvres of 1911, Colonel Repington of *The Times* wrote, 'there is insufficient test of the initiative of commanders of any units large or small . . . The infantry lack dash and display no knowledge of the ground . . . offer vulnerable targets at medium ranges . . . are not trained to understand the connection between fire and movement and seem totally unaware of the effect of modern fire'.

In theory the vain and unstable Wilhelm II would be commander in war, and until 1908 he frequently spoke of actually doing so. He lacked his grandfather's serious interest in military affairs, revelling in display rather than warlike efficiency. Schlieffen pandered to him with military spectacle, cavalry charges, and unrealistic victories in manoeuvres and war games. General von Moltke, nephew of the great Moltke and also a Helmuth, who became chief of general staff at the beginning of 1906, refused to do so. Artistic, doubting his own military ability, obsessed by fear of revolution, he had accepted the appointment in the belief that he would not be called upon to command in war. Lacking the conviction and force of character needed to carry through the Schlieffen Plan, he tampered with it, weakening the enveloping right wing, strengthening the holding left and the Eastern Front. In war games he accepted frontal offensives as practicable. In 1914 he was sixty-six, in poor health, past the work to which he had never been equal.

Below him came the army commanders: on the vital right wing, commanding the I, II and III Armies respectively, a trio of sixty-eight-year-olds, Generals von Kluck, von Bülow, and von Hausen, hard men, drivers—especially Kluck, brutal, a little brittle in crisis. Next came a trio of royals: the Duke of Württemberg commanding the IV Army; the Crown Prince, the V; Prince Rupprecht of Bavaria, the VI; then finally von Heeringen, sixty-four, ex-minister for war, the VII. In the Prussian tradition their chiefs of staff supported them with authority almost equal to theirs. Commanding the VIII Army in East Prussia was General von Prittwitz und Gaffron, sixty-six, fat, self-important, indolent, with connections so far proof against Moltke's wish to remove him. Major-General Ludendorff, forty-nine—his name was unadorned with the aristocratic von—was assistant chief of staff of the II Army, having lost the key post of head of the deployment section under Moltke for too much insistence on increasing the intake of the army.

The populations of France and the North German Confederation had in 1870 been approximately equal, but by 1914, while the population of the German empire had risen to over 65,000,000, that of France was still under 40,000,000. The disparity dominated French strategic thinking, and, with tragic irony, led in the end to a military creed savagely extravagant of human life.

France had astonished the world with the speed of her recovery after 1870. She had re-organized her army on the Prussian model with short service and a powerful general staff. Where the loss of Alsace and Lorraine had laid open her eastern frontier, she had built a strong fortified line stretching from Belfort to Verdun. At the turn of the century the army had been racked and discredited by the Dreyfus Affair's outcome. In 1905 military service had been cut down to two years. Confronted with the rising menace of Germany, the prestige of the army and willingness to serve in it recovered, and in 1913 service was restored to three years. After that men served in the Reserve, the Territorial Army and the Territorial Reserve for varying periods up to the age of forty-eight.

In July 1914 the peace strength of the French army was 736,000. On mobilization it rose to 3,500,000, of which some 1,700,000 were in the field army of five armies, in all twenty-one army corps, plus two colonial, three independent, ten cavalry, and twenty-five reserve divisions, the rest in territorials, garrisons, and depots. The five armies stretched from the Swiss frontier, where the 1st Army had its right at Belfort, to a third of the way along the Belgian frontier, where the left of the 5th was near Hirson. Beyond that was a cavalry corps of three divisions. A German offensive from Metz would thus be covered, but one through Belgium would meet only a weak cavalry screen.

French élan

The French, however, had no intention of waiting for any offensive to develop, for the army had persuaded itself that the disasters of 1870 had been due to lack of offensive spirit on their side. Looking back to Napoleonic and even earlier battles, the army had become imbued with mystical faith in the attack, pressed home regardless of cost, as the answer to all military problems. To ensure its *élan,* when the Germans went sensibly into field grey, the French had retained the traditional long blue coats and bright red trousers of their infantry. More practical matters were neglected, and the French infantryman wore his long coat and heavy military underwear even in the heat of August, his boots were hard, and a load of sixty-six pounds was piled on him compared to the German's fifty-six.

For fire power, the French relied on the rifle and the 75-mm field gun, an outstanding weapon produced in large numbers. Machine-guns were neglected. As for tactics, 'Success depends,' said the

	Great Britain	France	Russia	Germany	Austria-Hungary	Turkey
Population	46,407,037	39,601,509	167,000,000	65,000,000	49,882,231	21,373,900
Soldiers available on mobilization	711,000[1]	3,500,000+	4,423,000[2]	8,500,000[3]	3,000,000+	360,000
Merchant fleet (net steam tonnage)	11,538,000	1,098,000	(1913) 486,914	3,096,000	(1912) 559,784	(1911) 66,878
Battleships (built and being built)	64	28	16	40	16	
Cruisers	121	34	14	57	12	
Submarines	64	73	29	23	6	
Annual value of foreign trade (£)	1,223,152,000	424,000,000	190,247,000	1,030,380,000	198,712,000	67,472,000
Annual steel production (tons)	6,903,000	4,333,000	4,416,000	17,024,000	2,642,000	
Railway mileage	23,441	25,471	46,573	39,439	27,545	3,882

[1] Including empire [2] Immediate mobilization [3] Emergency maximum

manual of 1913, 'far more on forcefulness and tenacity than upon tactical skill.' Luckily the French soldier was not only brave but also adaptable and able to learn quickly, while the colonial empire, which during the war would supply 500,000 men, was available to replace some of the first shattering losses.

General Joffre, sixty-two, was vice-president of the war council, earmarked as commander-in-chief on an outbreak of war. He had been appointed in 1911, largely because the disciples of attack wished to get rid of his predecessor. Ponderous, very taciturn but a good listener, veteran of colonial service, he had no strong views on strategy or tactics, but was an engineer, and expert in military movement. He was to prove imperturbable and able in crisis, but did nothing before the war to check the ideas and plans that made crisis inevitable when war came. Galliéni, Joffre's superior in the colonies, more alert and realistic, had refused the appointment, and was now without military employment.

Of the army commanders, Lanrezac of the 5th Army, brilliant, pessimistic, impatient, and outspoken, was thought of by many as Joffre's eventual successor. Foch, responsible as commandant of the staff college for spreading the doctrine of attack, was a corps commander. Like Joffre he would be strong in crisis, and had in Weygand a chief of staff who could translate his wishes into clear orders. Pétain, out of favour for his realistic belief in fire power, commanded a division.

Neutral Belgians: British 'mercenaries'

Standing in the path of the main German thrust, Belgium deployed a field army of six infantry divisions totalling some 117,000 men, and three fortress garrisons, Antwerp, Liége, and Namur. Because Belgium was neutral, two infantry divisions faced France, one at Antwerp, Great Britain, one at Liége, Germany, with the rest in central reserve.

Relying on her neutrality, Belgium had neglected her army. Service in it was unpopular, training severely limited, morale poor, the officer corps seriously disunited. The fortresses were obsolete, improvements planned in 1882 were still incomplete and had by now been themselves overtaken by weapon development. There was one bright spot, however. King Albert, thirty-nine, was intelligent and brave, and he had great personal integrity. He did not control the army in peace, but when war came he was obliged by the constitution to command it.

The British, as is their habit, were in two minds about sending an army to the Continent at all. In 1908 Haldane had reorganized the British army, forming the units at home into an Expeditionary Force,

six infantry and one cavalry division totalling some 160,000 men, capable of supporting either the garrisons of the empire or a Continental ally. In 1905 staff talks with the French had been authorized, but had languished until, early in 1911, the francophile Major-General Henry Wilson had come to the War Office as director of military operations. That August the crisis over Agadir had revealed an alarming divergence of war plans between the War Office, where Wilson had made detailed arrangements with the French for the deployment of the Expeditionary Force on the left of the 5th Army, and the Admiralty, which strongly opposed continental commitment of the army, though it did not have a properly worked out proposal to put in place of Henry Wilson's. The Council of Imperial Defence had deferred formal decision, but allowed the War Office to continue planning with the French.

When in 1914 war was declared, there were those who thought that the Expeditionary Force should remain in Great Britain, or should go direct to Belgium in fulfilment of the British guarantee of neutrality, but it was too late now to change, and on 6th August the cabinet decided that it should go to France as planned, but without two of its divisions which would for the present remain in Great Britain.

Although small, the British army was well-trained and equipped. On the South African veldt Boer bullets had taught it something of the reality of fire power. Now the marksmanship of the infantry was in an entirely different class from that of continental armies. The cavalry, too, were armed with a proper rifle, not the neglected carbine of continental cavalry, and knew how to use it, but there peacetime reaction was setting in and the glamorous, futile charge coming back into fashion.

Called by the Germans an army of

mercenaries and, more flatteringly, a perfect thing apart, the British army was recruited from volunteers, who enlisted for seven years followed by five in the reserve. Each battalion at home found drafts for another in the overseas empire, so that its men were often raw and its numbers short. There were experienced men in the divisions that went to France, but to see them all as hardened professionals is a mistake; some were young soldiers, others reservists grown soft in civil life.

Continuing an old tradition in modern shape, the Territorial Force and the Yeomanry had been organized by Haldane into a second-line army of fourteen divisions, far from fully trained or equipped, but a good deal more effective than many realized. Beyond that there were the older reservists and the militia for replacements, and the distant imperial garrisons and armies of India and the dominions.

Field Marshal Sir John French, commander-in-chief, British Expeditionary Force, had been a successful cavalry commander in South Africa, but at sixty-two was showing his age. Lieutenant-General Sir Douglas Haig, commanding the 1st Corps, French's chief-of-staff in South Africa and Haldane's assistant in the subsequent reforms, was able and ambitious, but inflexible and wedded to cavalry doctrine. Kitchener, now secretary of state for war, a tremendous national figure, had flashes of insight amounting almost to

1 The imperturbable, ponderous, and taciturn Joffre—the French commander-in-chief. 2 Moltke—the German commander-in-chief. He was artistic, lacked force of character, and doubted his military ability. 3 French military dress of 1914: cavalry helmet, bayonets, képis, and bright red trousers

genius but little appreciation of staff organization or civilian control. In general, British officers were efficient and devoted but narrow in outlook. However, a far higher proportion of them than of officers in France and Germany had experienced the reality of war.

The armies in the East

With the main German strength committed in the west, the clash in the east would be between Austria-Hungary and Russia. Austria had been worsted by the French in 1859, and in 1866 trounced by Prussia. Since then the army had been reformed on the Prussian model, but not for forty-eight years tested in war.

The population, 50,000,000 in 1914, was a complex racial mixture. Germans were the ruling group in Austria, Magyars in Hungary; Poles in Austria and Croats in Hungary had special privileges; Ruthenes, Czechs, Slovaks, Slovenes, Serbs, Italians, and Rumanians were potentially disaffected. Languages, literacy, religions, and racial characteristics differed widely. Slav races formed two-thirds of the infantry, and the Germans in charge notoriously lacked the high martial seriousness of the Prussians. Yet, if the sottish chaos described by Jaroslav Hašek, a Czech writer, in *The Good Soldier Schweik*, typified one side of the coin, there was another: to many the army was an ideal of the empire as a supra-national society.

At the beginning of 1914 the peace strength of the Austro-Hungarian army was some 450,000. On mobilization it rose to over 3,000,000, of which some 1,800,000 formed the field army of six armies, in all sixteen army corps—mostly of three divisions, some of them reserve divisions—and eleven cavalry divisions. In a war against Serbia, the III, V, and VI

Armies would be deployed in the south, according to Plan B (Balkans); but in a war against Russia and Serbia, Plan R, the III Army would be deployed northeast with I, II, and IV in the Galician plain beyond the Carpathian mountains. By ordering partial mobilization on 25th July the army was committed to Plan B, until the III Army could be recalled from the Serbian front.

General Conrad von Hötzendorf, chief of general staff, sixty-two, a cavalryman, hard working, spartan, a writer on tactics and training, was, like Foch, a firm apostle of the offensive. His recipe for victory against Russia was an early attack before the vast manpower of the enemy could be brought into action, but that plan was now seriously compromised by partial mobilization. Conrad would command the northern armies, General Potiorek, another spartan, keen, vain, incompetent, with powerful court connections, responsible for the muddle that had given the Sarajevo assassins their chance, would command against Serbia.

Although Russia went to war to rescue Serbia, the Serbian army, under Marshal Putnik, 190,000 strong, organized in three armies each little stronger than an Austrian corps, was in grave danger of being overwhelmed before help could become effective. Leaving delaying detachments on the frontier, it assembled in north Serbia, ready to deploy wherever the attack came. It had fought in the bitter Balkan Wars of 1912 and 1913. Its men were seasoned, inspired by fierce patriotism, and looked back undaunted on generations of relentless warfare. The prospect of engaging it in its native mountains might have given pause to better soldiers than Conrad and Potiorek.

The Russian masses

For Russia, whose population numbered 167,000,000, manpower seemed the least of her problems. Bad roads, scant railways, low industrial capacity, poor standards of education and literacy, and a grudging treasury limited the size and effectiveness of her army. Later it would appear that so much of the Russian economy depended on sheer manual labour, that it would suffer disproportionately from withdrawal of manpower. For the moment, the great distances and bad communications slowed mobilization. Officer and non-commissioned officer cadres were weak in numbers and education, weapons, and equipment were in short supply, ammunition reserves set low, manufacture severely restricted.

Russia had fought Japan in Manchuria in 1904-05 and been badly worsted. Since then efforts had been made with the aid of large loans from France to modernize the army, but the combination of vast numbers

and restricted resources had prevented it reaching the standard of Western armies of the day. In such choice as there was between quantity and quality, Russia had chosen quantity, instinctively believing that sheer numbers would bring victory. While a Russian division had sixteen battalions against a German division's twelve, its fighting power was only about half that of the German.

The peace strength of the Russian army was 1,423,000. On mobilization, three million men were called up at once, with 3,500,000 more to follow before the end of November. There were thirty-seven corps, mostly of two divisions, and in all seventy first-line divisions, nineteen independent brigades, thirty-five reserve divisions, twenty-four cavalry and Cossack divisions with twelve reserve.

It was planned to deploy thirty corps—ninety-five infantry and thirty-seven cavalry divisions, some 2,700,000 men—against Germany and Austria, but of these only fifty-two divisions could appear by the twenty-third day of mobilization (22nd August). Two armies, the 1st and 2nd, would face East Prussia; three, the 5th, 3rd and 8th, Austria. Another, the 4th, would deploy against Germany (Plan G), if the main German strength came east, or against Austria (Plan A), if it struck west against France. Two more armies watched the Baltic and Caucasian flanks. General mobilization was ordered on 29th July, and on 6th August, deployment on Plan A.

General Sukhomlinov, minister for war since 1909, had been an energetic reorganizer, backed by the Tsar; he was corrupt, possibly pro-German, and a military reactionary, boasting that he had not read a manual for twenty-five years. Grand Duke Nicholas, commander-in-chief, fifty-eight, an imposing figure six-foot-six tall, was a champion of reform and opposed by Sukhomlinov. The jealousy of his nephew, the Tsar, had kept him from the Russo-Japanese War, depriving him of the chance to prove his worth as a commander, but also keeping him free of blame for the defeat. General Zhilinsky, commanding against East Prussia, had visited France in 1912 when chief of general staff, and had absorbed Foch's military beliefs, while also becoming personally committed to Russia's undertaking for an early advance against Germany.

Almost from the moment of declaration of war, France began to urge Russia to make this advance quickly and in strength. Russia responded gallantly, sacrificing her chance of massive deployment before action. Perhaps it need hardly be added that in Russia, as elsewhere, progressives and reactionaries were agreed on one thing, their faith in the offensive.

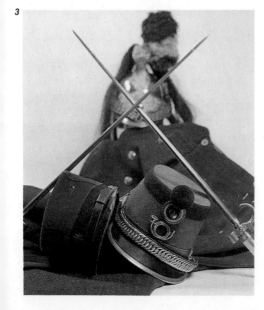

3

2 THE SHOCK OF ARMS

The Battle for Northern France

At the outbreak of the First World War both the German and the French general staffs looked forward to a quick war – 'home before the leaves fall'. After all, the last two major European wars, the Austro-Prussian (1866) and the Franco-Prussian (1870-71), had been quick, decisive wars of 'movement'. Few foretold anything different on 3rd August 1914. And, indeed, the opening phase of the war, the struggle for northern France, began in traditional style. For Germany a knock-out blow, as prescribed by the Schlieffen Plan, was essential if she were to avoid a two-front war against France and Russia. The French hoped that the pattern of offensives called for by Plan 17 would bring a quick recovery of the lost provinces, Alsace and Lorraine.

But the battle did not proceed according to plan. That was hardly surprising in so far as France was concerned, since Plan 17, based on wishful thinking, made assumptions which were wholly unjustifiable. It was considered that even should the Germans violate Belgian neutrality, they would not be able to extend their offensive dispositions north of Luxembourg. This deduction led the French to concentrate their five armies between Belfort and Mézières (see map, p. 39), leaving a gap of 125 miles between their left and the sea. Nor can this be excused by saying that they counted on the British Expeditionary Force and the Belgians to hold this gap, for no arrangements could be made with neutral Belgium, while the BEF was to arrive in France in total ignorance of its allies' intentions. In defence of Plan 17 it should be pointed out that a move westward to the Sambre, about

Left: The Canadians at Second Ypres

eighty-five miles from the sea, was envisaged in the plan – and anyway, a concentration of forces on the Belgian frontier would have looked very curious in peacetime. Even so, at the tactical level, the French doctrine was thoroughly unsound. The '*offensive à outrance*' – all-out attack with the bayonet – was the ideal, but it was a system which had not even worked in the days when Wellington's line used to shatter Napoleon's column by its concentrated fire. There had been no war with Germany for forty-four years and it is understandable that training should have become unrealistic. Still, a careful study of the South African and Russo-Japanese campaigns might well have saved the lives of many of the 300,000 Frenchmen who fell in August 1914. But whatever their disadvantages the French had one great asset: the monumental calm of their phlegmatic commander, General Joffre.

The German plan, calling for a great enveloping movement round the French left wing, seemed far from being unrealistic. By including twelve reserve corps in their order of battle the Germans were able to deceive the French as to their numbers, and had the younger Moltke, the chief of the general staff, had anything of the genius for war displayed by his uncle, the victor of 1866 and 1870, the campaign of 1914 might well have ended in the fall of Paris and the rout of the French armies. The unprincipled decision to invade Belgium added the BEF and the Belgian army to Joffre's order of battle and went some way towards redressing the balance of numbers. But these reinforcements were far from being sufficient to turn the tide against the Germans. In truth, they had no worse enemy than their elderly commander, who besides continually tinkering with the

Schlieffen Plan, never had that firm control of the battle which is the hallmark of military greatness. It may also be that the Germans paid insufficient attention to the problem of supplying their strong right wing.

At the tactical level the Germans were certainly superior to the French, handling their machine-guns and heavy artillery to much better effect. Their infantry were rather inclined to bunch, a fault which had not been sufficiently checked at manoeuvres, and therefore paid a heavy price for their advances.

Army commanders on both sides, except for the princes among them, were rather elderly by modern standards, and two at least – Moltke, and French, in command of the BEF, who had suffered a mild stroke – should never have passed the doctor.

The strategic moves of both sides were governed by their relative slowness once they were beyond the railways. When a corps could make only fifteen to twenty miles in a day, and had no motor transport to lift it, it behoved the staff to see that they really marched them to the right place. False moves were paid for by the exhaustion of the men, and a decline in morale. To many the *pavé* roads of northern France were far more terrible than a brisk skirmish.

Few military plans survive the opening phases of a battle, since commanders have to improvise as their opponents' moves interfere with their cherished combinations. In 1914 the Germans managed to adhere to their plan for considerably longer than their enemies, for the French plan came unstuck in about five days.

The Germans were first off the mark. On 5th August Kluck's I Army attacked the Belgian fortress of Liége, whose reduction

Left: German Infantry advance through Belgium

was a necessary preliminary to the deployment south and south-west across Belgium of the two northernmost German armies. The Belgian garrison under Lieutenant-General Leman put up a spirited resistance. Unfortunately, however, the forts, built twenty years earlier, had not been connected by a trench system as planned by their constructor, the famous engineer, Brialmont. As a result the Germans penetrated the line by a night attack and took the city. This daring exploit very nearly went wrong, but General Ludendorff took command of a lost brigade and seized the citadel on 7th August. The forts had still to be reduced, but they were smashed by the huge Austrian 42-cm. Skoda howitzers, and by 14th August the German columns were pouring through the city. The last fort fell on the 16th.

The French wings had begun to probe forward as early as 6th August. On the left General Sordet's cavalry corps got within nine miles of Liége, but did little to dispel the fog of war, because the area was as yet unoccupied by the Germans.

By 16th August it was clear at Joffre's headquarters that seven or eight German corps and four cavalry divisions were pushing westwards between Givet and Brussels 'and even beyond these points'. It was thought that there were six or seven corps and two or three cavalry divisions between Bastogne and Thionville. South of Metz the Germans appeared to be acting on the defensive. While this intelligence was not inaccurate the presence of reserve corps had not yet been discovered.

Joffre now planned to take the offensive, intending to break the German centre, and then to fall upon their advanced right wing. His plan was decidedly optimistic. He had no reason to suppose that his centre outnumbered Moltke's and, therefore, he should not have counted on a break-through.

The French offensive opened in the south where for several days Prince Rupprecht of Bavaria fell back according to plan, until early on the 20th he counter-attacked in the battles of Sarrebourg and Morhange. The French 2nd Army was driven back and the 1st conformed to its movement, though it struck back on the 25th and checked the pursuit. Eventually the front became stabilized just inside the French frontier.

The ill success of his right wing was not enough to alert Joffre, whose early service had been in the engineers, to the shortcomings of French infantry training. On 21st August the 3rd and 4th Armies crossed the frontier and after an advance of some ten or fifteen miles the heads of their columns ran broadside on into the German armies of the Crown Prince and the aged

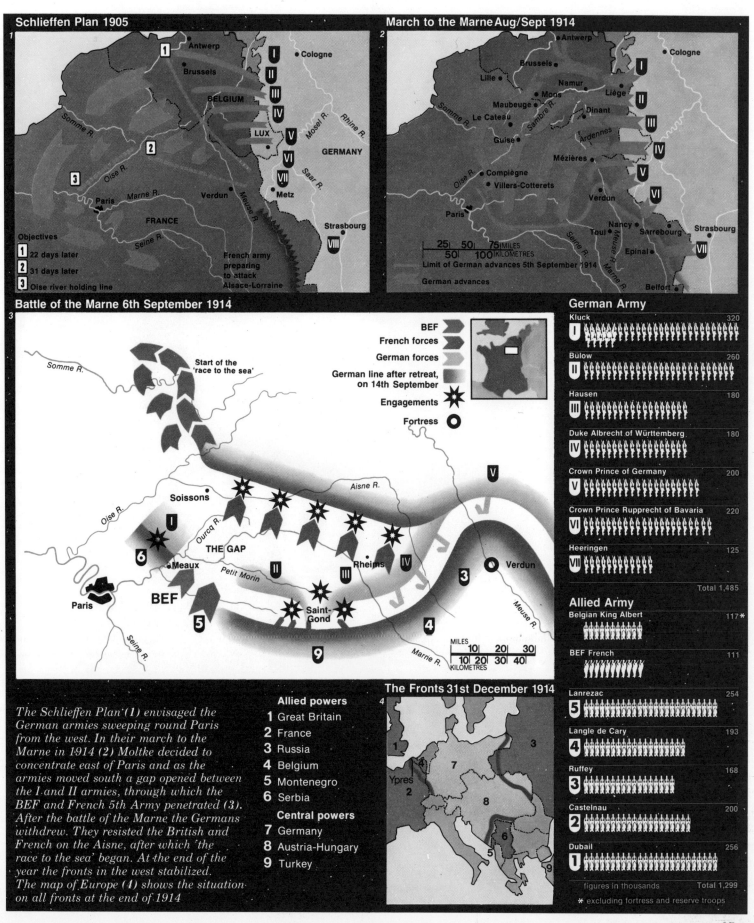

Schlieffen Plan 1905

Antwerp
Cologne
Brussels
I
II
BELGIUM
III
IV
Somme R.
LUX
V
Mosel R.
Rhine R.
VI
GERMANY
Oise R.
VII
Saar R.
Paris
Marne R.
Verdun
Metz
Meuse R.
FRANCE
Seine R.
Strasbourg

Objectives
1 22 days later
2 31 days later
3 Oise river holding line

French army
preparing
to attack
Alsace-Lorraine

VIII

March to the Marne Aug/Sept 1914

Antwerp
Cologne
Brussels
I
Lille
Namur
Liège
II
Somme R.
Maubeuge
Mons
Dinant
III
Le Cateau
Sambre R.
Ardennes
IV
Guise
Mézières
V
Oise R.
Compiègne
Verdun
VI
Villers-Cotterets
Paris
Nancy
Sarrebourg
Strasbourg
Toul
Seine R.
Epinal
Meuse R.
Marne R.
VII
Belfort

25 50 75 MILES
50 100 KILOMETRES
Limit of German advances 5th September 1914
German advances

Battle of the Marne 6th September 1914

BEF
French forces
German forces
German line after retreat,
on 14th September
Engagements
Fortress

Somme R.
Start of the
'race to the sea'
Aisne R.
Soissons
V
Oise R.
I
Ourcq R.
6
THE GAP
Meaux
II
Rheims
IV
Petit Morin
III
3
Verdun
Paris
BEF
Saint-Gond
Meuse R.
5
4
9
Marne R.
MILES 10 20 30
10 20 30 40
KILOMETRES

German Army

Kluck	I	320
Bülow	II	260
Hausen	III	180
Duke Albrecht of Württemberg	IV	180
Crown Prince of Germany	V	200
Crown Prince Rupprecht of Bavaria	VI	220
Heeringen	VII	125
	Total	1,485

Allied Army

Belgian King Albert		117*
BEF French		111
Lanrezac	5	254
Langle de Cary	4	193
Ruffey	3	168
Castelnau	2	200
Dubail	1	256
figures in thousands	Total	1,299

* excluding fortress and reserve troops

The Schlieffen Plan (1) envisaged the German armies sweeping round Paris from the west. In their march to the Marne in 1914 (2) Moltke decided to concentrate east of Paris and as the armies moved south a gap opened between the I and II armies, through which the BEF and French 5th Army penetrated (3). After the battle of the Marne the Germans withdrew. They resisted the British and French on the Aisne, after which 'the race to the sea' began. At the end of the year the fronts in the west stabilized. The map of Europe (4) shows the situation on all fronts at the end of 1914

The Fronts 31st December 1914

Ypres

Allied powers
1 Great Britain
2 France
3 Russia
4 Belgium
5 Montenegro
6 Serbia

Central powers
7 Germany
8 Austria-Hungary
9 Turkey

1914: on all fronts
a war of movement

*In both east and west during 1914, the
fortunes of the war ebbed and flowed to an
extent perhaps unparalleled except in 1918.
The Germans, having reached the Marne,
were driven back into northernmost France
and this was matched by the short-lived
inroads of the Russians onto the 'sacred
soil' of East Prussia and the unsuccessful
Austrian attack on Serbia.*

*1 A panorama (in which the perspective has
been distorted) of the battle of the Marne. In
the left-hand panel, the BEF (in three
wedges in the centre of the picture) can be
seen advancing through the gap between
Kluck's and Bülow's armies. The long
column (in the upper right section of the
panel) is Kluck's retreating army. The
centre panel shows Foch's army (bottom
left) recouping to attack the German III
Army. The right-hand panel shows Langle
de Cary's army shelling the German IV
Army in the Argonne. 2 German troops on
the Eastern Front. 3 Austro-Hungarian
troops attacking a village in Serbia*

Duke of Württemberg in slightly superior force, which were crossing their front. In the actions at Virton, Tintigny, Rossignol, and Neufchateau they were defeated with heavy loss especially in officers—it was a point of honour with the latest 'promotion' from St Cyr to wear white gloves and their full-dress shakos for their 'baptism of fire'. It is understandable that, caught in the narrow wooded defiles of the Ardennes, the French had been unable to employ their artillery to much purpose. They fell back to the Meuse. Joffre's bid to break the German centre had collapsed.

The real trouble was that the infantry ignored the basic tactical principle known as 'fire and movement', by which, even in those distant days, sub-units helped each other forward, engaging the enemy with aimed fire. Here the unreasoning belief in the bayonet took its toll of French manhood. Had it not been for a premature attempt at an enveloping movement by the Crown Prince the disaster to the French might have been still worse. German casualties were also heavy, especially when their columns exposed themselves to the fire of the 75s.

BEF goes into action

On 21st August the BEF, which had begun to mobilize on the 5th and had crossed the Channel without the least interruption from the German navy, was approaching the Mons-Condé Canal. By this time the situation was that the Belgian field army had been driven back into the fortress of Antwerp, though not before inflicting considerable delay on the Germans, notably in the action at Haelen on 18th August, a check which may account for the undue caution of the German cavalry in the fighting that followed.

Of the Allied armies only those under Lanrezac and French had so far escaped a mauling. The Allies' strategic situation was hardly brilliant at the moment when the BEF stepped upon the stage. The Schlieffen Plan was unrolling itself with something like clockwork precision. The only real hitch had been the failure to drive the Belgian field army away from Antwerp. This had compelled them to employ two corps in investing that city. Victory was within Moltke's grasp. Without the four divisions of the BEF which lay that night (21st August) with its outposts overlooking Marlborough's old battlefield of Malplaquet (1709) Joffre, for all his iron nerve and relentless will, could never have turned the tide which was running so strongly against him.

The BEF was in action next day. From the first, British musketry asserted its superiority. In a skirmish that same afternoon the Scots Greys inflicted thirty or forty casualties for the loss of one officer

wounded. This superiority was to be a factor of prime importance until the campaign died out in the damp November woods round Ypres.

While the BEF was moving up French had on 17th August visited Lanrezac to confer as to their future co-operation. Neither understood the other's language, Lanrezac, tense with anxiety, was needlessly rude, and the interview, so far from doing good left the two army commanders in a state of profound mutual distrust. Lanrezac told Joffre that the British would not be ready until the 24th at the earliest, that their cavalry were to be employed as mounted infantry and could be counted upon for no other purpose. More significant still, he raised the question of possible confusion if the British used the same roads 'in the event of retirement'. It was a considerable shock to Joffre to find that Lanrezac, who, in peacetime had been 'a veritable lion', not only had made no attempt to join in the great French advance, but was now thinking of withdrawal.

On 23rd August the long-awaited storm broke over Lanrezac's army when Bülow attacked him with four corps on the line of the Sambre. 'It rained shells,' was all that one French soldier could remember of that day's fighting. An Algerian battalion, 1,030 strong, charged a German battery, bayoneted the gunners, and returned, it is said, with only two men unhit! Everywhere the French suffered terrible losses especially in officers. One corps was compelled to fall back.

During the night Hausen brought four corps, supported by 340 guns against Lanrezac's line on the Meuse, gaining bridgeheads west of the river. Here they were up against a great soldier General Franchet d'Esperey ('desperate Frankie' to his British allies), the commander of 1st Corps. D'Esperey had actually made his men dig in, but this was simple prudence not over-caution. His corps counterattacked and pitched the Saxons back across the river.

Through the long day Lanrezac remained at his headquarters, Philippeville, a 'prey to extreme anxiety'. Well he might be. He received no guidance from Joffre, merely demands for his opinion of the situation. At noon came the well-nigh incredible news that the Belgians were evacuating Namur, the great fortress hinge of the Sambre-Meuse line. He received no information from Langle on his right, but on his left French, while declining to attack Bülow's right, guaranteed to hold the Mons Canal for twenty-four hours. While Lanrezac watched the endless column of Belgian refugees drifting through the square at Philippeville, his staff opportuned him with vain demands for a counter-attack. Lanrezac ordered no

such thing. Perhaps he was pusillanimous as his critics assert: he was certainly correct. Late in the day came news of Langle's retreat, which left the Meuse unguarded between Lanrezac's right and Sedan, where the French had met with disaster in 1870, as they were to do again in 1940. The day ended with another splendid counter-attack on d'Esperey's front, when General Mangin's brigade drove the Saxons out of their bridgehead at Onhaye. But this did not alter the fact that Lanrezac's position was untenable. At the risk of being taken for a 'catastrophard' he ordered a general retreat. To one of his staff he remarked 'We have been beaten but the evil is reparable. As long as the 5th Army lives, France is not lost.'

Mons and the retreat

This was the situation when on 23rd August the BEF fought its first serious action in the coalfields round Mons, on a line about nine miles northward of Lanrezac's main position and with both flanks in the air. For a loss of about 1,600 casualties and two guns the 2nd Corps, under General Smith-Dorrien, delayed Kluck's advance for a whole day and inflicted very severe losses on three of his corps (III, IV, and IX). A German account frankly describes the fighting: 'Well entrenched and completely hidden, the enemy opened a murderous fire . . . the casualties increased . . . the rushes became shorter, and finally the whole advance stopped . . . with bloody losses, the attack gradually came to an end.' The XII Brandenburg Grenadiers (III Corps) attacking the 1st Battalion Royal West Kent lost twenty-five officers and over 500 men. The 75th Bremen Regiment (IX Corps) lost five officers and 376 men in one attack. Frontal attack was worse than useless against British troops dug in in such a position. Only a flanking movement could turn them out and this—belatedly—Kluck realized.

Lanrezac neither consulted nor warned French before retreating, and it was not until 11 pm on the 23rd that Sir John was told of it by his liaison officer, Lieutenant Spears. With the BEF left in the air its temperamental commander was beset with gloom, and in a letter to Kitchener next day hinted that he was contemplating departure, 'I think immediate attention should be directed to the defence of Havre.'

By this time the BEF, to the astonishment of the Brandenburger captain, Bloem, who had seen his men slaughtered the previous day, was in full retreat. By the 24th even the placid Joffre recognized that his army was 'condemned to a defensive posture' and must hold out, making use of its fortified lines, wear down the enemy, and await the favourable moment for a counter-attack. The evident lack of success so far he attributed not to any fault of his own, but to 'grave shortcomings on the part of commanders'. That some had broken cannot be denied. During the Ardennes battle one divisional commander had actually committed suicide. Joffre sacked the weaklings ruthlessly. There was some recognition of French tactical failings and on the 24th Joffre issued a training instruction emphasizing the need for collaboration between infantry and artillery in the capture of *'points d'appui'* ('strongpoints'): 'Every time that the infantry has been launched to the attack from too great a distance before the artillery has made its effect felt, the infantry has fallen under the fire of machine-guns and suffered losses which might have been avoided.

'When a *point d'appui* has been captured it must be organized immediately, the troops must entrench, and artillery must be brought up.'

'Reign of terror'

Joffre's lesson on tactics would have seemed pretty elementary stuff to the officers of the BEF—or to the Germans for that matter. But they, too, had their troubles. The British after long marches up the *pavé* in the August sun, had won a victory, and were now, incomprehensibly, invited to march back the way they had come. They felt they were being 'messed about'. The Germans had a special nightmare of their own: the *franc tireur* (guerrilla). Captain Bloem records that on a day when his company marched twenty-eight miles not a man fell out: 'the thought of falling into the hands of the Walloons was worse than sore feet.'

To orderly German minds the thought of civilians intervening as snipers, albeit for

hearth and home, was utterly repugnant. Princess Blücher was told that there were thirty German officers in hospital at Aachen, their eyes gouged out by Belgian women and children. Atrocities, even imaginary ones, breed reprisals, and *Shrecklichkeit* (Frightfulness) was a matter of deliberate policy with the German high command which did not mean to detach strong forces to guard the lines of communication. Had not the great Clausewitz laid it down that terror was the proper way to shorten war? Only by making the civilian population feel its effects could the leaders be made to change their minds, and sue for peace. In Belgium the first important massacre was at Andenne where Bülow had 211 people shot on 20th and 21st August. At Tamines, sacked on the 21st, 400 were executed in the main square. The Saxons pillaged and burnt Dinant on the 23rd, leaving their aged commander, Hausen, 'profoundly moved', but indignant against the Belgian government which 'approved this perfidious street fighting contrary to international law'. The sack of Louvain—sparked off, apparently by German soldiers firing on each other in panic after a Belgian sortie from Antwerp—was the worst episode of this reign of terror. If anything these atrocities served to stiffen the resolution of the Belgians and their allies.

The retreat continued, but with five German armies carving their way into France, Joffre never despaired of resuming the offensive. By this time he had realized that the forces of his left wing were insufficient to stop the German onrush. On 25th August he ordered the formation of a new French army, the 6th under Maunoury. Its divisions were to be found from the now static front in Lorraine, and it was to take its position on the left of the BEF.

Moltke's fatal error

On the 25th Moltke also was taking men from the Western Front, not, however, from Lorraine where they could perhaps have been spared, but from his right wing! And this at a time when Kluck was detaching one of his corps to invest Maubeuge. Moltke was worried by the Russian threat to East Prussia and determined to reinforce the latter with two corps, though, ironically enough, they were not to arrive until the Germans had won their decisive victory at Tannenberg. Beyond question this was fatal alteration to the Schlieffen Plan at a moment when decisive victory lay within his grasp. The trouble was that by the 24th the Germans thought that they only had beaten men before them. That this was not so was forcibly demonstrated by the BEF at Le Cateau on the following day. Late on the night of the 25th Smith-

Dorrien (2nd Corps) realized that, with some of his units only just coming in, and with many scattered and exhausted, it was not possible to carry out French's orders to continue the retreat. He decided to stand and fight.

Battle of Le Cateau

Kluck had nine divisions within reach of the battlefield at dawn, but only managed to bring two of them, with three cavalry divisions, into action against Smith-Dorrien's three. Kluck had, however, a tremendous concentration of artillery, and it was really this which made the British stand difficult. The German infantry came on in bunches, firing from the hip, and suffered severely. Kluck's strong right wing (two corps) allowed itself to be engaged by Sordet's cavalry corps and a French territorial division. The corps on his left, marching and counter-marching, covered eleven miles without intervening in the fight. In consequence Smith-Dorrien managed to extricate himself with a loss of some 8,000 men and thirty-eight guns. Mons and Le Cateau left Kluck with a profound respect for the BEF—'it was an incomparable army', he told British officers after the war. Its rapid rifle fire had convinced many Germans that the BEF had twenty-eight machine-guns per battalion when in fact they had two.

While the battle of Le Cateau was in progress Joffre held a conference with French and Lanrezac at St Quentin in order to explain his latest plans. General Order No. 2 had reached GHQ the previous night, but there had not yet been time to study it. Joffre was shocked by French's excited complaints. He was threatened with envelopment by superior numbers and his right had been left in the air by Lanrezac's sudden withdrawal. His men were too tired to go over to the offensive. After this uncomfortable meeting Joffre departed, suspecting that the BEF had lost its cohesion. The truth was that GHQ had lost touch with the army it was supposed to control, and things were not as gloomy as French thought. Kluck for his part saw things in much the same light as Sir John. On the 27th he hoped to 'cut off the British who were in full flight westwards'. With Namur in his hands and Bülow pressing Lanrezac's broken troops Moltke was feeling the 'universal sense of victory' that now pervaded the German army. But already things were going wrong. In three days furious fighting (24th-27th August) Rupprecht's twenty-six divisions had been hurled back from Toul, Nancy, and Epinal by Castelnau and Dubail. On the Meuse Langle held up the Duke of Württemberg from the 26th to the 28th.

GOUVERNEMENT MILITAIRE DE PARIS

Armée de Paris, Habitants de Paris,

Les Membres du Gouvernement de la République ont quitté Paris pour donner une impulsion nouvelle à la défense nationale.

J'ai reçu le mandat de défendre Paris contre l'envahisseur.

Ce mandat, je le remplirai jusqu'au bout.

Paris, le 3 Septembre 1914.
Le Gouverneur Militaire de Paris,
Commandant l'Armée de Paris,

GALLIÉNI

Above: Galliéni's pledge to defend Paris 'until the end'

The Shock of Arms

On the 29th Bülow's army, astride the river Oise, blundered head-on into Lanrezac's columns, which were crossing their front, and suffered a severe check. In the battles of Guise and St Quentin Lanrezac was counter-attacking, most reluctantly, on direct orders from Joffre, who stayed with him and watched him for three hours of the battle. Had French permitted Haig's corps, which was still practically intact, to co-operate, the Germans might have suffered a severe defeat. Once more a counter-attack by d'Esperey's corps sustained the right wing at the moment of crisis. It was a magnificent spectacle. Bands playing, colours flying, the French infantry, covered by the fire of the 75s, swept eagerly forward and the Germans gave way. That night the 5th Army withdrew unimpeded.

The pursuit continued, though thanks to the absence of five corps — practically the equivalent of an army — awkward gaps were beginning to appear in the German right wing. On 31st August Kluck abandoned his pursuit of the British who had disappeared south of Compiègne, and wheeled south to strike at Lanrezac. On 1st September he crossed the Oise reaching Crépy-en-Valois and Villers-Cotterets, a bare thirty miles from Paris. The same day a stormy interview took place in the British embassy in Paris, when Kitchener, in his field-marshal's uniform, made it clear to the sulking French that he was to keep the BEF in the line and conform to the movements of his allies.

'We must strike'
Moltke was now attracted by the idea of driving the French south-east and thus cutting them off from Paris. He ordered Kluck to cover this movement in the direction of Paris, 'remaining in the rear of the Second Army'. The independent-minded Kluck, whose army was the farthest forward and the best placed to attack the French 5th Army, did not see this. Nor did he anticipate any danger from Paris. On the evening of the 2nd he gave orders to cross the Marne next day, leaving only one weak corps as a flank guard. That night the French government left Paris for Bordeaux. Next morning General Galliéni, the governor, still thought the Germans were marching on the capital. When at noon an airman reported their columns moving east towards the south-east, Maunoury's staff refused to credit it, but at 7 pm it was confirmed. 'We must strike!' cried Galliéni, and having given warning orders, asked Joffre's permission. At 8 am on the 4th one of his officers reached Joffre's headquarters at Bar-sur-Aube, and the intelligence staff traced Kluck's latest moves on the wall map. 'But we have

them,' they exclaimed. 'We must stop the retreat and seize our heaven-sent chance at once.'

Joffre himself appeared. 'A remarkable situation,' was his comment. 'The Paris army and the British are in a good position to deliver a flank attack on the Germans as they are marching on the Marne.' It remained to convince Sir John French.

D'Esperey, who had replaced Lanrezac, was ready with proposals for an attack on the 6th. These he had drawn up in concert with Major-General Wilson, French's deputy chief-of-staff. Galliéni pointed out that by the 7th the Germans would have

German cartoon, October 1914. Grey, the British foreign secretary, having buried Belgium, is now burying France

scented the danger threatening them from the direction of Paris.

Meanwhile, Moltke's mood of elation was deteriorating through a period of deepening panic towards complete nervous breakdown. Despite the pictures painted by his generals, there were still no masses of prisoners, no parks of captured guns. The French and British had refused to admit defeat, Kluck was following his own devices, and French reinforcements were approaching Paris from the east. At 6 pm on the 4th he sent out the following order

by wireless: 'I and II Armies will remain facing Paris, I Army between Oise and Marne, II Army between Marne and Seine.' This order did not reach Kluck until next day, by which time he had crossed the Marne. He gave the order to advance towards the Seine on the 5th, leaving only one corps behind the Marne.

On the afternoon of the 5th Joffre visited French's headquarters at Melun in order to ensure British co-operation. Later he wrote: 'I put my whole soul into convincing French that the decisive hour had come and that an English abstention would be severely judged by history. Finally, striking the table with my fist, I cried: "Monsieur le Maréchal. The honour of England is at stake!" French blushed, and murmured with emotion, "I will do all that is possible", and for me that was the equivalent of an oath.'

The battle of the Marne
The battle of the Marne was in effect a series of disjointed combats. It began on the afternoon of the 5th when the French 6th Army moving up to its start line on the river Ourcq unexpectedly ran into Kluck's flank guard, IV Reserve Corps, in the hills north of Meaux.

During the evening an emissary from Moltke, who was still running the campaign by remote control from Luxembourg, arrived at Kluck's HQ. This was Lieutenant-Colonel Hentsch, chief of intelligence branch, whose mission was to explain the real situation and in effect to bring him to heel. Kluck resigned himself to a withdrawal, but as yet unaware of the action on the Ourcq, contented himself with a leisurely retrograde move which left most of his army south of the Marne.

The three armies on the Allied left made a little progress on the 6th. Until the previous day the BEF and the 5th Army had continued the retreat, and the sudden change left them in cautious mood. The 6th Army was held up some six miles short of the Ourcq. The River Marne and a gap of eight miles separated its right from the BEF. In the south the 1st and 2nd French Armies successfully resisted the German VII and VI under Rupprecht, and on the 8th Moltke finally abandoned the unprofitable Lorraine offensive. The 3rd French Army, now under General Sarrail, and the 4th Army held their own well against the German V and IV Armies. But where Hausen's Saxons threatened Foch's much weaker 9th Army there was serious cause for disquiet.

On the 7th, Gronau reinforced by two more of Kluck's corps recalled from farther south, had little difficulty in holding Maunoury west of the Ourcq. The aggressive Kluck now conceived the notion of attacking the 6th Army from the north, hoping to drive it back on Paris and enter the capital on its heels. For this master-stroke he switched his two remaining corps with astonishing speed from south of the Marne to his northern wing. By so doing he opened a gap of some twenty miles between himself and Bülow, a gap which was masked by a fairly strong screen of nine infantry battalions (eight being *Jäger*) and two cavalry corps on the Petit Morin.

German retreat

If the British were slow to exploit this advantage the fault lay with GHQ rather than the men, who were in good spirits now that they were going forward once more. D'Esperey's progress on the 7th was comparable with that of the BEF, but by this time Foch, under severe pressure, was being driven south from the marshes of Saint-Gond. It was on the 8th that he sent the legendary report to Joffre: 'My centre is yielding, my right wing is giving way. An excellent situation. I attack tomorrow.' But the Germans no longer hoped for a break-through; rather it was their aim to extricate Bülow and close the gap. Shortly before 9 am on the 9th an aviator reported to Bülow that there were five British columns with their heads on or across the Marne. Another had already reported that there were no German troops in the path of the BEF's advance. Warning Kluck of his intention, Bülow issued orders for a retirement. Almost simultaneously Kluck also gave orders for a withdrawal in the general direction of Soissons. It was about 5.30 pm before it became evident to the British that the Germans were abandoning the battlefield. Their success had not been particularly costly; between 6th and 10th September the BEF's casualties numbered no more than 1,701.

The battle of the Marne, in which, it has been calculated, some fifty-seven Allied divisions (eight cavalry) turned back fifty-three German (seven cavalry) was over, and with it died the famous Schlieffen Plan. Tactically its results were disappointing, for it was not fought to the bitter end. Strategically it was of profound importance, for it meant that all hope of a swift knockout blow was over. As in 1940 the Germans counted on a swift *blitzkrieg* to defeat their semi-mobilized enemies and win the war. Could they have won? The two corps sent to East Prussia would have been more than sufficient to close that famous gap.

Joffre is not generally numbered among the great captains, but he had won one of the strategically decisive battles of all time.

By the morning of the 10th the Germans had vanished, Kluck retiring to the Aisne

at Soissons and Bülow to the Vesle at Rheims. In general it cannot be said that the pursuit was vigorous, though much transport, some forty guns and about 14,000 prisoners were taken. Bad weather prevented air reconnaissance and the French, whose men and horses were tired, could only average six or seven miles a day. There was still a gap between the German I and II Armies, but this was not evident to the Allies. On the 13th the VII reserve corps, released by the fall of Maubeuge, arrived in the nick of time to close the gap. By a forced march of forty miles in twenty-four hours it just succeeded in forestalling Haig's corps.

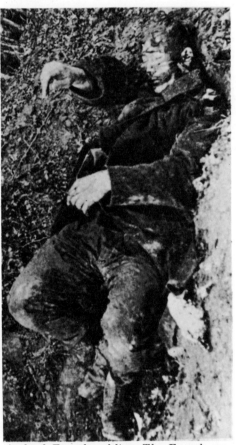

A dead French soldier. The French soon found that élan *was of very little help against the enemy's concentrated firepower*

The offensive had left one-tenth of France, with much of her coal and iron, in German hands. The failure of the Schlieffen Plan had brought Moltke's secret replacement by General Erich von Falkenhayn, the minister of war, who at fifty-three was a mere boy compared to most of the army commanders on the Western Front. Neither he nor Joffre quite despaired of a speedy decision in a war of movement. When the battle of the Aisne began to crystallize into the trench warfare of the next four years, both improvised

plans to outflank the other's northern flank, between the Oise and the sea. With the Belgian field army, 65,000 strong, ensconced in Antwerp, the Allies had some hopes of a success in Flanders. Winston Churchill, the First Lord of the Admiralty, did his best to stiffen the garrison with a naval division, 12,000 strong (30th October), but two-thirds of these men were neither well-trained nor properly equipped. The Germans began to bombard the city on the 7th and General Deguise, the fortress commander made no attempt to hold out to the last. The north-eastern forts were tamely surrendered without bombardment or attack, but the field army escaped westwards to the River Yser.

Meanwhile, Joffre had agreed that the six British divisions on the Aisne should be transferred to Flanders and they began to detrain near Abbeville on 9th October. On the same day the 7th Division landed at Ostend, and, since Antwerp had fallen, became part of the BEF.

First battle of Ypres

With Antwerp in his hands Falkenhayn had a fleeting chance of a break-through, for he had five reserve corps available for instant action. They were not the best troops in the world for 'the men were too young and the officers too old', but they showed the most determined bravery in the first battle of Ypres, which raged between Arras and the sea in that autumn (12th October to 11th November).

The fighting opened well enough for the Allies but by 21st October the Germans had won the initiative, and battered away at the Allied line for the next three weeks. The Kaiser himself appeared in the battle area to witness the break-through. The climax of the battle came on the 31st when the Germans broke into the British line at Gheluvelt.

In an astonishing counter-attack, inspired by Brigadier-General Fitzclarence, the 368 survivors of the 2/Worcestershires threw them out. Eventually, the storm died out with the repulse of the Prussian Guard on 11th November.

The BEF had, it is estimated, lost over 50,000 men, and the Germans at least twice as many, including about half the infantry engaged.

The Western Front now ran from Switzerland to the sea, following the line of the Vosges, the Moselle, the Meuse hills, the Argonne, the Chemin des Dames, the Aisne, until by way of Armentières and Ypres it reached Dixmude. There were still those who believed that with the spring would come the return of open warfare. But the line was not to move more than ten miles either way for the next three years.

The Eastern Front

Within a week of the German invasion of Belgium, 800 miles to the east the battle lines of the 'Eastern Front', running from the gloomy East Prussian marches in the north to the high Carpathians in the south, were already drawn up and the several armies swarming on them, the Russian, the Austro-Hungarian and the German, were on the point of being set in full motion. The Russians, though mobilization had so far brought only one-third of their available manpower into the field, were intent on breaking into East Prussia: the Germans concentrated to defend it. In southern Poland and Galicia the Austro-Hungarians, their army a multi-national patchwork stitched out of Germans, Slavs, and Magyars, prepared to strike at the Russians, while the Russians proposed to launch their main attack against Austria-Hungary. The result was soon a whirlpool of battles which sucked in whole armies to destruction, crippling the Austrians, battering the Russians, and straining the Germans. Wild as the fighting was, with the masses of Austrian and Russian peasant soldiers lumbering about, the Eastern Front impinged directly on operations in the west when, at a crucial stage in the flailing German offensive against 'the Franco-English Army', the German command drew off men and speeded them eastwards to hold sacred German soil, the sanctum of Prussia, against the Slav intruder, the historical image of whose 'frightfulness' fevered the German mind. The rival armies in the east each played their special supporting parts: Russia marched on East Prussia at France's urgent request, Austria-Hungary, battling with Serbia, lunged across the Russian frontiers at Germany's prompting. For Germany, the two-front war had materialized, not in military mathematics, but as gunfire on its own frontiers.

The armies which rolled upon each other in the east did so in accordance with the war plans upon which the respective general staffs had prepared long before the actual clash. German planners wrestled with the intractabilities of a two-front war; early planning variants (relying on the lengthy period which they presumed Russian mobilization would take) stripped East Prussia of men, but subsequent signs of waxing Russian strength caused a revision; according to the new plan the VIII Army was to be stationed in East Prussia, its role essentially defensive. Austria-

Hungary nurtured two war plans. The first, Plan B, envisaged war against Serbia only, against whom three armies would be committed while the other three held Galicia against the Russians; the second, Plan R, related to war with Serbia and Russia: two armies would march on Serbia and four against Russia. Russia, meanwhile, developed two war plans of its own, one defensive, Plan G, the other offensive, Plan A. Plan G assumed a primary German effort against Russia, in which contingency the North-Western and South-Western Army Groups would first retire, and then the Russians would make a counter-offensive. Plan A prescribed an offensive when the German blow was directed against France: Russian armies would strike at East Prussia and Galicia, the bulk of Russian strength (four armies) falling on the Austrians, with two driving into East Prussia.

This military calculus was based, not only upon guesses about what would happen, but also upon the possibilities (and the restrictions) of the supposed 'front'. Overshadowing all else was the giant Russian salient – Russian Poland – which jutted out to the west, its tip not 200 miles from Berlin. The salient was both a springboard and a trap for the Russians; from it they could leap into Silesia, but they could be militarily entombed if German troops from East Prussia and Austrian troops from Galicia struck from north and south to crumple the salient. East Prussia was unmistakably exposed but, thanks to German attention to interior communications, eminently defensible. In terms of plans, Germany determined to hold East Prussia: Russia, at France's insistence, opted for Plan A: Austria-Hungary, having first set in motion Plan B, suddenly switched to Plan R (which meant pulling the whole II Army back from Serbia).

The Russians take the field

At daylight on 12th August 1914, under a calm morning sky, the first units from Rennenkampf's 1st Army – cavalry squadrons and a rifle regiment – crossed the frontier into East Prussia. The Russian invasion had begun, a converging attack mounted with two armies of General Zhilinsky's North-Western Group: Rennenkampf's 1st Army was to strike from the east, Samsonov's 2nd Army from the southeast, two claws digging into East Prussia

Left: Russian machine-gunners bitterly resist the German advance at the battle of Tannenberg. A realistic film-still.
Above and below: *The campaign and orders of battle on the Eastern Front, August to December 1914*

German and Russian order of battle: East Prussia, August 1914	
German	**Russian** (North Western Group)
VIII Army (Prittwitz Hindenburg)	1st Army (Rennenkampf) 2, 3, 4, 20 Corps
I, I Reserve XVII, XX Corps	2nd Army (Samsonov) 1, 6, 13, 15, 23 Corps

Austro-Hungarian and Russian order of battle: Galicia, August 1914	
Austro-Hungarian	**Russian** (South Western Group)
I Army (Dankl)	4th Army (Salza)
IV Army (Auffenburg)	5th Army (Plehve)
III Army (Bruderman)	3rd Army (Ruszki)
II Army (moved from Serbia) (Ermolli)	8th Army (Brusilov)

German, Austrian, and Russian order of battle: late November, 1914 (battle of Łódź)	
German	**Russian**
VIII Army	10th Army
IX Army	1st Army
	2nd Army (Łódź)
Austrian	5th Army
I Army	4th Army
IV Army	9th Army
III Army	3rd Army
II Army	8th Army

to crumple and destroy it. On the German side, Lieutenant-General von Prittwitz had already begun to deploy the four corps of the VIII Army assigned to defend East Prussia: to block the Russian drive from the east, three corps took positions along the line of the river Angerapp and a fourth was deployed to the south, amid the lakes and forests of Tannenberg, barring the way to the Russian army moving from the south-east. Deliberately, taking advantage of excellent internal communications – and with substantial knowledge of Russian movements, thanks to an appalling carelessness shown by the Russians in transmitting orders *en clair* for much of the time – Prittwitz drew up his corps and made his plans: he would deal with one Russian army at a time, striking first at Rennenkampf and then at Samsonov. Though the alarm bells were beginning to ring through Prussia, there seemed to be a margin of time and therefore an assurance of safety.

Certainly the Imperial Russian Army was – at France's entreaty – rushing into the attack; as a consequence it was incompletely mobilized. Yet this was not its basic weakness. The real defects lay deeper. To shortcomings in organization, training, equipment, and supply were added the fatal flaws of a corrupt, ruinously inefficient society where no institution could respond to 'the concentrated demands of wartime'. In addition, the Russian army was fearfully short of fire-power: even where the guns did exist, the available ammunition often ran out. The Russian Plan A nevertheless went into operation, and the attack on East Prussia slowly ground into gear. On 17th August Rennenkampf's 1st Army moving from the east, its columns separated and its northern flank dangerously bare, crossed the frontier in force. Samsonov in the south-east was not due to move off for another five days.

Meanwhile, farther south, Austro-Hungarian troops had crossed the Russian frontier on 10th August. Following the dictates of Plan R, Field-Marshal Conrad von Hötzendorf launched the Austro-Hungarian armies from Austrian Poland (Galicia) towards the north to engage the main Russian forces, which he assumed lay in this direction. The field-marshal's assumption proved to be totally wrong; Russian strength lay in yet another direction, to the south-east, and this again was due to the mistaken anticipation by the Russian command of Austrian intentions. General Ivanov, South-Western Group commander, expected the Austrians to strike from the direction of Lemberg (Lwów) and it was here that he proposed to make his own maximum effort. These initial misconceptions, therefore, played a

major role in producing a lop-sided battlefront, with the Austrians flailing away in the north and the Russians loosing a massive attack in the south.

At first, Austrian and Russian armies blundered into each other along the Austrian line of advance to the north (in the direction of Lublin-Kholm), though after 23rd August heavy fighting developed. Vastly encouraged by the first results, Conrad reinforced his left flank and ordered the III Army into the attack east of Lemberg – where the Russians were ready and waiting: and having switched from Plan B to Plan R, Conrad brought II Army shuttling up from Serbia. On 26th August Ivanov opened his own offensive with two armies (3rd and 8th) which smashed into the depleted, struggling Austrian III Army: the III Army fell back in disorder on Lemberg. Late in August Conrad was facing a confused though by no means desperate situation – the gleam of success in the north, the spurt of danger in the south. The field-marshal decided to fight for his Lemberg front, not of itself a disastrous decision, but the manner in which he implemented it finally provided Ivanov with the opportunity to rip the whole Austrian front wide open.

The Russians are trapped

Though Russian armies were on the verge of a vast triumph in Galicia, the invasion of East Prussia had come to terrible grief. From its first set-piece arrangement, the battle for East Prussia rapidly developed into a rolling, lurching, savage affair, pitching into violent motion when the impetuous commander of the German I Corps, General François, brought Rennenkampf to battle ahead of the line chosen by Prittwitz. But the undiscerning Rennenkampf ploughed on, thereby helping to restore reality to German plans. On 20th August Samsonov began his advance from the south-east, a signal for Rennenkampf to halt calmly so that Samsonov might catch up in time and space. Prittwitz determined to act, proposing to launch a counterblow at Rennenkampf, much to the disgust of his chief operations officer, Max Hoffmann, for it meant unravelling the German line. General François once again led the I Corps against Rennenkampf and other corps engaged in the 'battle of Gumbinnen', a wild, swirling encounter in which the German XVII Corps was badly mauled. News of this, intelligence of Samsonov's advance, and panic that the Russians might burst through the Insterburg Gap, splitting the VIII Army apart, caused Prittwitz to lose what little nerve he possessed. He decided on precipitate retreat to the Vistula, to the consternation of his commanders. Adamant about withdrawal, Prittwitz proceeded to petrify the high

Top: Postcard illustration of Austro-Hungarian artillery men. Above: Russian howitzer – primitive looking weapon, but the Russians could have done with more

command with the details of disaster he retailed by telephone to Helmuth von Moltke (the German chief of general staff) at Coblenz – the Vistula it had to be, and Prittwitz doubted that he could hold this line without reinforcement.

This wailing from the east cut across the gigantic battle raging in the west. Moltke wasted no time. He despatched Major-General Erich Ludendorff as chief-of-staff and General Paul von Hindenburg (hitherto on the retired list) as the new commander of the VIII Army. Prittwitz was brushed aside. The idea of hasty withdrawal had already been abandoned in the east and Hoffmann devised a plan to draw off troops facing Rennenkampf to pit them against Samsonov. Rennenkampf failed to follow through after Gumbinnen; he hung poised in the north, an undoubted threat but a stationary one. Samsonov inched his way along, arguing all the way with Zhilinsky. The VIII Army command faced one crucial question: was there time to knock out Samsonov before Rennenkampf came down from the north? On the morning of 25th August that problem received swift, if startling resolution; uncloaked by code, Rennenkampf broadcast his line of advance and its distance. The Russian 1st Army would not, on this evidence, strike into the rear of the VIII Army. As for Samsonov, imagining himself to be pursuing a broken enemy, he proposed to rest his troops on 25th August. It seemed as if the Russians were inviting their own destruction. Further news from their own command, however, brought disquiet to the Germans; at Coblenz, Moltke had decided to pull out three corps and a division from the Western Front—where every unit was needed—as reinforcement for the east. Two corps and a cavalry division were already detached on 26th August, an action Moltke justified by arguing that 'the decision' in the west had already been gained. Yet three corps, loaded as they were on troop trains and trundling over Germany, could not 'save' East Prussia and remained lost to the German right wing on the Western Front.

Meanwhile the VIII Army, speeded along internal railway lines, shifted its weight to the south. The Russian 'pincers' waved in the air: at the *Stavka* (Russian GHQ) concern mounted at Rennenkampf's dawdling. Zhilinsky did nothing to urge Rennenkampf to close with Samsonov, whom he thought to be in no danger. On 26th August Samsonov's 2nd Army resumed its advance, the Russian centre moving all unsuspecting into a German trap ringed with four corps: the full weight of VIII Army —all but one division, which was holding Rennenkampf in the north crashed on Samsonov's hungry, ill-clad men. The 'battle of Tannenberg', running its course for three agonizing days, snared three Russian corps (13th, 15th, and 23rd) in the German net: German guns lashed the Russian divisions, the Russians broke and the fight continued in the woods and across the marshes. On 29th August Samsonov knew the extent of the catastrophe; that evening he spent huddled in a clearing in the forest. Shortly after midnight he drew aside and shot himself. The Germans took over 100,000 prisoners and large quantities of guns. Two Russian corps (13th and 15th) were obliterated, another (23rd) drastically thinned, and the two flank corps reduced to the strength of mere divisions.

With the defeat of Samsonov, the killing was but half done. Rennenkampf in the north was now marked down for destruc-

tion and the VIII Army, coiling across East Prussia like a spring and strengthened by reinforcement arriving from the west, regrouped to attack once more. On 5th September the German drive on Rennenkampf's left flank opened, and 'the battle of the Masurian Lakes' began; at the centre Rennenkampf held off the German assault, but in so doing weakened the whole of the 1st Army. On 9th September Rennenkampf ordered a general withdrawal to pull the 1st Army out of the trap closing on it, and also launched one stabbing attack with two divisions—enough to slow down the German right wing. The Russian infantrymen trudged eastwards: Rennenkampf made the journey in the comfort of his car, back to and over the Russian frontier. His army did escape, but had suffered a grievous mauling, with 100,000 men lost. The invasion of Prussia, which cost the Russians almost a quarter of a million men, had failed. Zhilinsky tried—unsuccessfully—to unload the blame on Rennenkampf: Rennenkampf (whose conduct incurred suspicions of treason) stayed and Zhilinsky was dismissed.

The rout of the Austrians

9th September 1914: the Germans had failed on the Marne: Samsonov was dead, Rennenkampf in retreat: the Russians were defeated in East Prussia, and almost triumphant in Galicia. Conrad, in trying to cover himself at Lemberg, opened a gap in the north and the Russian 5th Army came bursting through. To escape encirclement, the Austrian command ordered a general withdrawal, and withdrawal degenerated into pell-mell flight. The whole Austro-Hungarian front quivered and collapsed, caving in to a depth of a hundred miles and immolating over 300,000 men in the Galician catastrophe. Russian troops took Lemberg and swept on to cut off the great fortress of Przemyśl, bottling up 100,000 more men. In this whole *débâcle,* the Austro-Hungarian armies suffered a loss not even suggested by numbers, for many of the cadre 'Austrian' officers, the hard core of the army, were lost or captured. The rout of the Austrians in Galicia, for it was nothing short of that, brought fresh dangers to Germany: the Russians were already opening a pathway into Silesia. The situation called for German troops, but Erich von Falkenhayn (who replaced Moltke after the first battle of the Marne) would let none go from the Western Front. Hindenburg therefore stripped East Prussia of four of its six corps to form a new German army in the east, the IX, which began to deploy at Czestochowa late in September, closing with the Austrian I Army. Both sides—Russian and German—were at this stage planning to attack and a phase of fierce,

formidable battles in the east was about to begin. The Russians found themselves once more under pressure from the French to mount a major attack, this time in the direction of the German industrial base in Silesia; the Russian threat to Cracow did itself involve the security of Silesia—and Hindenburg had hurried to close the most staring gap—but an offensive along the Warsaw-Posen axis by Russian armies would mean great and growing danger for Germany. Towards the end of September, Russian armies were regrouping for this new offensive.

Hindenburg, however, struck first, using his new IX Army and aiming straight at the huge Russian base of Warsaw, the attack for which the Austrians had pleaded at the end of August. For the first time the Russians learned of the existence of the IX Army and rushed every available man to the Vistula to hold off the German advance: Austrian troops also started an attack towards the line of the river San. Late in September the IX Army rolled forward and by 9th October Hindenburg was on the Vistula. Three days later German troops began their advance on Warsaw. To hold the city the Russian command speeded up the movement of Siberian regiments from the Far East, troops released for service in European Russia at the end of August when Japan entered the war against Germany and Russia had no further fear of a clash with Japan. At the end of a month's journey, the Far Eastern regiments detrained in Warsaw and went straight into action, fighting savage bouts with the bayonet under the walls of the city.

By mid-October, with two Russian armies (1st and 2nd) piling up on his northern flank, Hindenburg deemed it prudent to withdraw; the IX Army began to fall back, the Austrians were floundering to the south and by the end of the month German and Austrian troops were back in the positions they had occupied towards the close of September. It was now the turn of the Russian command to take the offensive, to launch an invasion of Silesia with four armies while a fifth (1st Army, still under the command of Rennenkampf) protected the Russian northern flank from its positions on the Vistula. Once again, with staggering negligence, the Russians blared their movements over the air and once again the Russian command failed to take speedy German redeployment into account. The German IX Army, formidable and efficient, was already on the move, speeding along good rail communications to its new concentration area, a blocking position between Posen and Thorn; the place of IX Army in the German-Austrian line was taken by the Austrian II Army which had been moved up from the Carpathians.

1△

The scene was almost set for the fiercest round fought so far, without the grand tragedy of East Prussia or the massive confusion of Galicia, but a test of arms of a very decisive nature, itself connected with a subtle but profound change which was overtaking the war in the east—at least from the German side. Hindenburg and Ludendorff now assumed over-all command of German troops in the east. They were already the inseparable martial pair, twinned by the triumphs of East Prussia and set upon that rise which took them finally to supreme military control of Germany's destiny. In the east the German army fought a war of mobility and also in the east Ludendorff sought to realize Schlieffen's idea of victory—not attained in the west—that true victory must be wholly and utterly decisive. Ludendorff was therefore embarked on his search for 'a decision' in the east, which inevitably brought a clash over the claims of the west: it meant conflict with Falkenhayn, and it required reinforcements, the addition of strength to mobility.

To fend off the Russians, the German command determined to pre-empt their attack. With the IX Army drawn up in its new operational area, now under General von Mackensen's command, the German plan envisaged an operation timed for 11th November and designed to crumple the

Russian drive into Silesia by driving between the 1st and 2nd Russian Armies. On the Western Front Falkenhayn was fighting the last great battle of 1914 at Ypres, and having broken through the British lines to the south-east, he espied eventual victory: no men could be spared for the east. Hindenburg and Ludendorff, however, could not afford to wait, being persuaded—correctly—of the gravity of the Russian threat. On 11th November, as planned, the IX Army attacked on a front west and north-west of Łódź, closing on the 1st and 2nd Russian armies. This did not prevent the Russians from loosing their armies in a westerly drive towards Silesia three days later, but within forty-eight hours the Russian offensive was brought to an abrupt halt. The German IX Army had crashed straight into the junction of 1st and 2nd Armies—and the fault this time lay unambiguously with Rennenkampf in charge of the 1st Army. On 16th November the enormity of the situation finally broke over the Russian command, who had been waiting for the IX Army to be crushed between the two Russian armies—a Russian Tannenberg where the IX Army would march to its doom. But Mackensen tossed Rennenkampf's corps aside—badly strung out as they were—and then ripped into the right flank of the Russian 2nd Army, which the Germans intended to

encircle, the second time that this unfortunate army was to be done to death.

With the grip of winter tightening each day, the fight for Łódź and for the life or death of the 2nd Army lasted until early in December. Furious fighting flared as the Germans closed in and as the Russians beat them off. The Russian 5th Army was ordered to close with the 2nd: two Russian corps, driven along in forced marches, managed to press the right flank of the IX Army back. The left flank of the IX Army lapped right round to the south-east of Łódź, giving the Russians the chance to spring a trap of their own, though late in November the German corps fought its way out. In the end neither the German nor the Russian trap had closed fully, but early in December Russian troops began withdrawing from Łódź, whereupon German troops immediately entered the city in their wake. After his showing in these battles, Rennenkampf was finally dragged out of his command of the 1st Army; the new commander, General Litvinov, quickly ordered a withdrawal to the Bzura and Rawka river lines where the army wintered. The battle of Łódź, even if it enjoyed none of the fame of Tannenberg, nevertheless had a decisiveness all its own: frustrated though they were in their tactical designs, Hindenburg and Ludendorff had throttled completely the Russian offensive.

1 and 2 German and Russian troops (right) in action during the fighting on the Eastern Front. 3 General Samsonov, who shot himself after the battle of Tannenberg. 4 After the battle, Samsonov's wife searches for her husband. 5 Austro-Hungarian troops in Galicia tend one of their wounded. The early months of the war brought a shattering defeat for Austria-Hungary

Russia licks her wounds

For the rest of December the Eastern Front remained quiet. Four months of fighting, however, had wrought some fearful changes. Russian armies had been dreadfully mauled in East Prussia: Austria-Hungary suffered calamitous losses in Galicia and a motley army lost much of its irreplaceable 'Austrian' cadre. The Russian triumph in Galicia could momentarily blot out disaster in East Prussia, but Tannenberg inflicted a deep and terrible wound: worse, it stood as a sinister portent. The Russian infantryman, ill-equipped and under-fed, performed prodigies of endurance and raw, unflinching courage, but manpower could not continually match a murderous enemy firepower: German superiority in artillery mangled the Imperial Russian Army. Within a month of the opening of the war Russian armies were chronically starved of ammunition and the gun-batteries, insufficient as they were, remained all but bereft of shells. The war minister, Sukhomlinov, 'an empty and slovenly man', bore most of the responsibility for this disgraceful state of affairs, but it was the regime itself which allowed men like Sukhomlinov to grow fat on inefficiency and to flourish on calamity. The Russian high command showed mostly its ineptitudes: the Imperial Army took the field inadequately trained, indifferently and incompetently led, badly supplied—and for all this the peasant soldier had to pay in blood.

At the end of 1914, though Russian losses were already grievous—shocking enough to promote feelings that a settlement with Germany would be the best course, or that again Russia was shouldering an unfairly heavy burden—Russian armies still covered Warsaw, the front was advantageously shortened in western Poland and much of Galicia was in Russian hands. The Russian command had plunged from the outset into the offensive in fulfilment of their agreement with the French, even though only a third of the Imperial Army was mobilized and deployed: Tannenberg and then the disaster at the Masurian Lakes had followed. 'The first days of war were the first days of disgrace,' branding a sense of helplessness, of ineradicable inferiority into Russian consciousness in the face of a German war-machine which clicked, whirred, and roared to command. The German success in the east was huge and enlarged by the developing myth of Hindenburg-Ludendorff; the German command waged a relentless, fierce war, applying the principle of mobility and maximum concentration against the weakest point with devastating effect.

It was also a brutal war: if 'the flames of Louvain' blazed in the west, so did 'the flames of Kalisz' crackle in the east. For a moment, when the fat, trembling Prittwitz had the telephone to Moltke in his hand, disaster seemed to loom, but massed German guns, the speeding German trains, the tactical ingenuity of the command swept this away. Yet, almost ironically, the very magnitude of German successes in the east conjured up problems of a singular order for the military leaders; the critical issue was not that some German formations had moved from west to east during a particular battle, but that the idea burgeoned of winning the war by actions in the east. German victory in this theatre itself contributed directly to sustaining hopes for speedy, 'total' victory—and the prospect of knocking an enfeebled, bumbling Russia out of the war seemed glittering. General Falkenhayn was not so very greatly impressed (nor, for the moment, was Russia's military prospect utterly critical); Falkenhayn, committed to guarding the gains in the west and launching limited offensives to tear at the enemy, was firmly of the opinion that 'no decision in the east . . . could spare us from fighting to a conclusion in the west'. Hindenburg and Ludendorff perforce argued that Germany could not afford—if for no other reason because of the need to hold up a tottering Austria-Hungary—to defer or avoid seeking a decision in the east.

The Spreading War

On a fine autumn day of 1914 Colonel Hankey, secretary of the British pre-war Council of Imperial Defence and now of the smaller War Council, crossing the South Downs near Lewes, stopped to watch the men of Kitchener's army marching and drilling, scattered across the usually deserted downland. Still in civilian clothes, for uniforms and rifles could not yet be provided for them, they had in hundreds of thousands answered the call for voluntary enlistment, overwhelming the creaking military machine. That winter, as Hankey listened to ministers, admirals, and generals, he was to think of that scene and the drilling men, the flower of Great Britain's manhood. It was their fate that had to be decided.

On the Western Front the German army had been stopped on the Marne. After that had come the so-called race to the sea, as the opposing forces tried to outflank each other to the north, only to crash head-on again, as each attempted the same manoeuvre. When in mid-November the last desperate German attacks failed against an equally desperate defence at Ypres, no vulnerable flank remained. Frontal attack, then, it must be, but frontal attack had already failed repeatedly with shattering losses. By the spring the armies would be firmly entrenched, with deep barbed-wire entanglements and ever growing numbers of machine-guns.

On the Eastern Front the Germans had crushed the Russians invading East Prussia at Tannenberg and the Masurian Lakes, but in the great, complex series of battles around Lemberg (Lwów) – which happened almost at the same time as that of the Marne – the Russians had thrown the invading Austro-Hungarians back to the Carpathian passes. Here, too, November had seen a second round as the Germans came to the aid of their allies, defeating the Russians at Łódz. Halted by the eastern European winter, the battered armies licked their wounds, but here, in the vast eastern plains, as no longer in the west, room still remained for armies to manoeuvre against each other.

In the south the heroic Serbian army still surprisingly survived, having inflicted galling defeats on the Austro-Hungarians. Now it was exhausted, weakened by casualties, short of supplies. Typhus raged in its ranks. Bulgaria, nursing deep injuries from the Second Balkan War but still undecided, threatened its flank. Austria-Hungary, too, was threatened by new enemies, for Italy and Rumania were discussing with the Allies the terms on which they might join them.

At sea the German High Seas Fleet, having refused to give battle to the stronger British Grand Fleet, was penned in the south-eastern corner of the North Sea. Raiding cruisers, a serious nuisance in the wide Atlantic and Pacific, had, by the end of 1914, mostly been rounded up. Submarines had given the Grand Fleet a scare, but so far they had hardly threatened the laden merchant ships whose protection or destruction is, in the last analysis, the purpose of fleets.

Turkey – the ramshackle empire

At the beginning of November Turkey entered the war against the Allies. The ramshackle Ottoman empire had been crumbling for fifty years when, in 1908, the revolutionary Young Turks Committee had seized power, getting rid of Sultan Abdul Hamid with startling ease. Further defeats had followed: in 1911 by Italy in Tripoli, and in 1912 in the First Balkan War. Although the Turks regained some territory in the Second Balkan War, the army, exhausted by six years' fighting, was by then close to collapse, often hungry and in rags, its pay in arrears, its administration broken down. Since then a strong German mission had been at work, energetically organizing and training. The Turks knew, at least, the realities of war, and in the Turkish units – some of the divisions were Arab and resented Turkish dominance – there burned a fierce, resentful, wolf-like pride, which would on the battlefield make Turkish soldiers as stubborn and bitter fighters as any in the world.

Cut off by Bulgaria, still neutral, from her northern allies, Turkey could receive from them the much needed military supplies only by subterfuge. Within her own territories, the new railway being built by German engineers still had breaks either side of the Gulf of Alexandretta, where it crossed the Taurus and Amanus mountains on its way to Aleppo. There it branched one way towards Baghdad, but stopped 380 miles short of the Tigris, and the other towards Amman and Medina. It was 250 miles from the Russian Caucasus frontier at its nearest point.

The army, something over a million strong with thirty-six regular divisions, was distributed in the I, II, III, and IV Armies, which were respectively in Turkey-in-Europe, western Anatolia, Erzurum near the Russian frontier, and Syria. In addition there were two regular divisions each in the Yemen, central Arabia, and Mesopotamia (modern Iraq).

Above: Prisoners of a world strategy – Germans under guard in distant East Africa. Although a colonial 'sideshow', the war the British Empire fought to eradicate von Lettow-Vorbeck's German guerillas cost her three times the lives that she had lost in the Boer War, and the campaign left the Germans undefeated in November 1918.
Left: Field Marshal Lord Kitchener.
Below: The East African campaign. The British advanced from British East Africa, South Africa, and Rhodesia (as the arrows show). The Germans withdrew, making a brief stand whenever there was an opportunity to inflict heavy casualties. By September 1916 the British and South Africans had cooped the Germans up in fifteen per cent of the territory – but the army remained for another two years

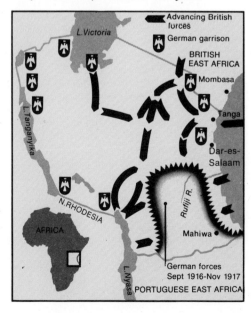

L.Victoria

Advancing British forces

German garrison

BRITISH EAST AFRICA

Mombasa

Tanga

L.Tanganyika

Dar-es-Salaam

N.RHODESIA

Rufiji R.

AFRICA

Mahiwa

L.Nyasa

German forces
Sept 1916-Nov 1917

PORTUGUESE EAST AFRICA

The Shock of Arms

Enver Pasha, minister for war, who with Talat Bey, minister for the interior, dominated the cabinet, took command of the III Army, about 150,000 strong, and in mid-December sent his ill-equipped soldiers across the mountains into the Caucasus against the smaller Russian 7th Army. Overtaken by winter blizzards, the timing of the arrival of the three corps was thrown out, and they attacked piecemeal. But the hungry, exhausted soldiers fought fiercely, and the Russian command was alarmed. Then, defeated around Sarikamish, the Turks faced the choice of surrender or retreat through the icy passes. Only 12,000 got back to Erzurum. One entire corps laid down its arms, and the Russians counted 30,000 frozen bodies in the mountains.

In February the IV Army sent 20,000 men across the Sinai peninsula to cut the Suez Canal. Egypt, still in 1914 nominally a part of the Ottoman empire but since 1882 controlled and occupied by Great Britain, had been declared a British protectorate when Turkey entered the war. It was garrisoned by one British Territorial and two Indian divisions, and the two-division Australia and New Zealand Army Corps was assembling and training there. The Turks were thrown back with ease. In the years that followed, the British turned to the attack across Sinai, at first clumsily and tentatively, then in 1917 under Allenby brilliantly and overwhelmingly, taking Jerusalem in December 1917.

Farther east the British took the initiative early against the Turks. A brigade from India landed at the head of the Persian Gulf in October 1914, followed by the rest of a division intended to guard the Anglo-Persian oilfields and prevent enemy incursions into the Indian Ocean. It quickly took Basra and gained some distance up the Euphrates.

By far the most important Turkish contribution to the Austro-German cause was, however, the immediate one, made in October 1914 by closing the Dardanelles and Bosphorus to Allied shipping. This, by cutting off Russia's Black Sea ports, brought her great corn exporting trade to an end, and closing her most important gateway for supplies from the outside world. At a blow her exports fell by ninety-eight per cent and her imports by ninety-five per cent, figures crippling to any nation, likely to be fatal to Russia with her vast population and flimsy industrial base. It imposed powerful strategic and moral obligations on her Allies to come to her aid.

Germany's empire seized

On the African coast of the Indian Ocean lay German East Africa (modern Tanzania), bordered to the north by British East Africa (Kenya) and to the west by the Belgian Congo, 400 miles from north to south, 600 miles inland to Lake Tanganyika, mostly uncultivated bush, varying from grassland to deep jungle. Here von Lettow-Vorbeck successfully resisted the British attempts to dislodge him.

Across equatorial Africa, on its western coast, were two more German colonies. The Cameroons, 200 miles of coastline, extending 500 miles inland and reaching a width of 600, bordered by the British colony Nigeria and French Equatorial Africa, was garrisoned by 200 German and 3,300 African soldiers and armed police. A small Franco-British force landed from the sea and took the port, Douala, on 27th September 1914, but the Germans withdrew inland across the swampy coastal belt to the capital, Yaoundé. Columns sent across the undeveloped grass hinterland from Nigeria and French Equatorial Africa took Yaoundé on 1st December 1915, and the garrison slipped back through the coastal belt to internment in Spanish Guinea. Togoland, with ninety miles of coastline, 300 miles deep, between the British Gold Coast and French Dahomey, was quickly occupied in August 1914.

Finally, between the South Atlantic and the Kalahari Desert lay German South West Africa (subsequently mandated to South Africa), with 800 miles of coastline, reaching in the north 600 miles inland, mostly high, sandy desert. It had two harbours, Lüderitz Bay and, facing the British enclave at Walvis Bay, Swakopmund, with the capital and wireless station at Windhoek. It was garrisoned by 2,000 German soldiers backed by 5,000 male German civilians. Its African population had risen in 1904 and had been brutally suppressed.

Now the Germans hoped for a rising of the South African Dutch against the British, but South Africa had become a self-governing dominion in 1910, and on 10th August 1914 the last British troops left Cape Town for France, leaving South Africa, under the general cover of British seapower, to handle her own defence. A small South African force took Lüderitz Bay, but then a rising of some 11,000 pro-German South Africans brought operations to a standstill until the end of January 1915. After that Swakopmund was quickly occupied. Windhoek fell on 12th May 1915, and on 6th July the German commander capitulated, freeing South African forces for German East Africa and for France.

Of the scattered islands and harbours of the Pacific, the second area where her belated colonial activity had taken her, Germany held the Marianas Islands, the Marshall Islands, the Caroline Islands with Yap and Truk, the Palau Islands, the Bismarck Archipelago with Rabaul, the eastern half of New Guinea with Port Moresby, and Samoa — names familiar in the Second World War as the scenes of battles between American and Japanese fast carrier groups, amphibious forces, and island bases — and, on the Chinese mainland, a concession on the Shantung peninsula, Kiaochow Bay, with the port of Tsingtao. Such strategic value as these had was, in 1914, as potential lying-up places for raiders and as bargaining counters in peace negotiations.

At the outbreak of war, small Australian and New Zealand forces took German New Guinea and Samoa, while the Royal Navy destroyed the wireless stations at Yap and Nauru. On 23rd August 1914 Japan declared war on Germany and occupied the Palaus, Carolines, and Marshalls, then, early in September, landed a division, to which one British and one Indian battalion was attached, to take Tsingtao. On 31st October Japanese 11-inch howitzers began to bombard the recently completed fortifications, and on the night of the 6th November the infantry assault went in with the determination that characterized the Japanese in a later war. Early next morning the Germans surrendered.

Back in London, in 1914 at the turn of the year, the choices still lay open which, wisely taken, could shape the war. On Boxing Day Hankey submitted a long and able paper to the war council. It began: 'The remarkable deadlock which has occurred in the western theatre of war invites consideration of the question whether some other outlet can be found for the employment of the greater forces of which we shall be able to dispose in a few months' time.' It suggested the development of new armoured devices to overcome the siege warfare conditions of the Western Front, and went on to recommend the use of British seapower to open a new flank or front. Discarding attack on the German coast as requiring the violation of Dutch and Danish neutrality, Hankey turned to the Mediterranean to suggest that an attack on Turkey, or through the Balkans on Austria-Hungary should be considered, and to the German overseas empire, already, as we have seen, being taken over.

Almost simultaneously, on New Year's Day, Lloyd George, chancellor of the exchequer and a member of the war council, circulated a memorandum, which reasoned similarly. He suggested either an attack on Austria-Hungary in conjunction with the Greeks and Rumanians, who might be rallied to the Allied cause, and Serbia, or an attack on Turkey by a landing in Syria after the Turks had got themselves involved in Sinai. 'Unless we are prepared for some project of this character, I frankly despair of our achieving any success in this war,' he wrote. 'Germany and Austria have between them 3,000,000 young men quite as well trained as the men of the Kitchener Armies, ready to take the place of the men now in the trenches when these fall.'

Winston Churchill, first lord of the Admiralty, had during the autumn conferred with Sir John French on the possibility of an amphibious operation against the German northern flank. On 29th December he wrote to Asquith, the prime minister: 'I think it is quite possible that neither side will have the strength to penetrate the other's lines in the Western theatre . . . although no doubt several hundred thousand men will be spent to satisfy the military mind on that point.' He still mentioned the Admiralty's pre-war plan to seize islands off the German coast and open the Baltic, but his mind was turning to the Dardanelles. Admiral Lord Fisher, first sea lord, still thought of the Baltic, but the reality of war and its risks were beginning to make him cautious.

Kitchener, who had for some time been sounding French, wrote to him on 2nd January that if the French army could not break the German front, 'then the German lines in France may be looked upon as a fortress that cannot be carried by assault, and also cannot be completely invested—with the result that the lines can only be held by an investing force, while operations proceed elsewhere'. Sir John replied, claiming that, given more guns, more shells and, of course, more men, the Germans could be beaten in France in 1915. At this juncture a message came from the British ambassador in Petrograd forwarding an urgent appeal from Grand Duke Nicholas for a naval or military demonstration to relieve Turkish pressure in the Caucasus.

The War Council met under Asquith on the 7th and 8th January to consider the situation. Sir John's project for an attack along the Flanders coast met a chilly reception, but it was agreed that he should be allowed to continue his preparations and be sent additional divisions, subject to final approval for the attack itself. Consequently when, on the second day, the council turned to the situation in the eastern Mediterranean, Kitchener had to inform it that the Anzacs in Egypt were not yet trained and he had nothing available for any action there. As the council, stale from two days discussion, contemplated this unwelcome information, Churchill introduced the idea of a naval attack on the Dardanelles, which would require no considerable military force, and could be easily abandoned if it did not succeed.

The idea caught on, and it was finally agreed that in addition to French's offensive in Flanders, preparations should be made for a naval expedition in February 'to bombard and take the Gallipoli peninsula, with Constantinople as its objective'. A final proviso said that 'if the position in the western theatre becomes in the spring a stalemate, British troops should be despatched to another theatre and objective'.

The sentence of death

This, although it perhaps reads like an attempt to please everyone, was at this stage sound enough, calling as it did for full investigation of two of the proposed operations, and leaving the way open for others. In 1915, however, nothing comparable to the chiefs-of-staff committee and joint planning staff of the Second World War existed, and the necessary staff studies and reference back for considered decision were not undertaken. Kitchener, with whom Churchill continued to confer, and Fisher, who after momentarily backing the Dardanelles increasingly gave way to rather senile fits of temperament, would by later standards have been responsible for this neglect, but both had spent their lives in the days of arbitrary decision by senior officers and no argument.

So the protagonists pursued their separate projects, and Churchill was able to push through the ill-fated naval attack on the Dardanelles.

The Balkan project put forward by Lloyd George found, rather surprisingly, influential support in France. By coincidence Galliéni had on 1st January made a similar proposal to M.Briand, the war minister, and M.Viviani, the premier. 'One cannot break through on the Western Front,' he said; 'therefore we must find another way.' Joffre, who on 20th December had begun another attack which was to cost him 90,000 casualties to little advantage, had supported French against Kitchener. When Galliéni's proposal was referred to him, he said it was unsound and refused to part with divisions for it. Two were, however, scraped up, and sent to take part in the Gallipoli expedition, and later others were found to form with the British the Army of the East under the French General Sarrail. On 5th October 1915, one British and one French division landed by secret agreement with the Greek prime minister, Venizelos, at Salonika—a Greek port recently acquired from Turkey in the Balkan Wars—to go up the Vardar valley to Serbia. By then Bulgaria was mobilizing against Serbia, King Constantine of the Hellenes was ready to dismiss Venizelos, and the chance to rally the Balkans to the Allies, if it ever existed, had passed.

French's offensive, meanwhile, began in March; as might have been expected, it had little result other than to create new and higher piles of bodies between the trenches, at greater and greater cost.

At the beginning of 1915 Germany, too, faced an east versus west decision. In September 1914, when it became clear that the battle of the Marne was lost, General Falkenhayn, minister for war, was called by the Kaiser to take Moltke's place as chief of general staff, retaining his old appointment as well. Realizing, after the battles of November, more clearly than the French and British generals opposed to him, that the war had become static, he gave orders to husband German strength by the systematic application of trench warfare methods, by intensifying the manufacture of guns, machine-guns, and ammunition, and by improving railways by which reserves could be quickly moved where required. By these means, and by raising four new corps with experienced cadres, he planned to have available in the spring of 1915 a powerful central reserve, to strike a concentrated, decisive blow in the west.

Ludendorff v. Falkenhayn

Like the Allied statesmen, however, the German chancellor and foreign minister called for action in the east, where they were working to bring Bulgaria, Rumania, and Italy into the war on their side. Rather desperately the Austrians supported them. Conrad von Hötzendorf telegraphed Falkenhayn on 27th December: 'Complete success in the eastern theatre is still, as hitherto, decisive for the general situation and extremely urgent.'

The German general staff was quite capable of turning a deaf ear to the chancellor and Conrad, but now Falkenhayn was faced with a powerful opponent within his own military system. On the favoured Western Front the events of 1914 had been indecisive and bitterly disappointing, but in the east, starved of means, Hindenburg and Ludendorff had won a series of spectacular victories. They now confronted Falkenhayn with the proposition that the war could be won in the east, if a great new effort were made, but not in the west, and demanded that he send them the central reserve. On New Year's Day Falkenhayn, Conrad, and Ludendorff met in Berlin, and Falkenhayn gave his decision for the west. Hindenburg then approached the chancellor asking for Falkenhayn's removal. On the 4th Conrad, hearing that Italy was about to join the Allies, telegraphed Falkenhayn and Hindenburg for German divisions. Falkenhayn refused them, only to find that Hindenburg, without consulting him, had promised them to the Austrians.

As chief of general staff and minister for war, Falkenhayn was Hindenburg's superior, and this was defiance, but the prestige of the Hindenburg-Ludendorff combination was far too high for them to be dismissed. It had to go to the Kaiser, and he decided for the east, but kept on Falkenhayn. So in 1915 the Germans would defend in the west, and attack in the east with disastrous results for the Allies.

The Sea-raiders

Until at least the 1890's, as an Englishman once said to Grand Admiral von Tirpitz, Germany 'was not a sea-going nation'. Plans for a navy, inspired as much by nationalism as by strategic needs, stagnated in disputes between the competing authorities, the admiralty, executive command, and the naval cabinet, between the Kaiser and the general staff. Even after Tirpitz gained the Kaiser's favour in 1892 and began to create the nucleus of the German navy, there remained the dilemma of what sort of force it should be. Was there to be a High Seas Fleet to wear down Great Britain (because there was never any doubt of the ultimate naval enemy) from a strong centralized position as Great Britain herself had done in the Napoleonic Wars? Or should they build fast cruisers, like 18th-century privateers, to destroy the enemy's trade and distract their main fleet as well?

German naval authorities argued about this crucial decision for ten years after 1895 —the year in which Tirpitz resigned because his battle fleet was being subordinated to the political arguments for cruiser warfare. Colonial ambition was proving a strong argument in favour of a far seas strategy. Not only were the new fast cruisers to fly the German flag in every port of the world, reinforcing pro-German sympathies in South America, Africa, and Asia, but they provided the defence of the scattered islands and territories proudly called the German 'empire'. Frequently they were the reason for acquiring them: Tirpitz himself negotiated the acquisition of the last of the treaty ports in China, Tsingtao, as a base for the East Asia Squadron.

The primacy given to cruiser warfare faded after Tirpitz returned. The second Navy Bill of 1900 outlined the need for a strong home fleet. But as a *quid pro quo* to the cruiser strategists, it also attempted to define an important role for the warships in the far seas: 'to represent the German navy abroad . . . and to gather fruits which have ripened as a result of the naval strength of the Reich embodied in the Home Battle Fleet'.

Until 1910 this policy backed a programme of building fast, well-armed cruisers and light cruisers, capable of from 24 to 27 knots and fitted with 4·1-inch and 6-inch guns which were, at that date, the most accurate for their size in the world. When, under the pressure of the race to build larger and larger capital ships, the emphasis changed, and all new cruisers

were kept for the battle fleet, it was the cruisers of the period 1905-10 which were assigned to foreign stations. They were superior both in speed and gunnery to the equivalent British ships, although this was not obvious to either side before hostilities began. They were intended, however, not for direct action against warships, but to draw away vital units from the British Grand Fleet and leave the North Sea open to a blow from the German North Sea Fleet.

British strategy did not rely òn a counterpart to the German cruisers. It was hard enough to get money to build battleships— even the dreadnoughts—and only enough new cruisers were laid down for home waters. This left a fair number of County Class cruisers, built in a period of bad naval design between 1895 and 1905, too costly to scrap, whose failings in speed and armaments were not shown until they were actually under fire. To make up these deficiencies, and to guard her immensely long trade routes and communications, Great Britain relied on the alliance with Japan— whose fleet could blockade Tsingtao, Germany's only effective Asiatic port—and on the combined forces of Australia and New Zealand, which were to neutralize Germany's Pacific colonies. No specific defences were provided for the Indian Ocean, which was felt to be a British preserve.

When war was declared, the main German strength lay in the East Asia Squadron, commanded by Vice-Admiral von Spee, which consisted of the heavy cruisers *Scharnhorst* and *Gneisenau* and three light cruisers *Emden*, *Leipzig*, and *Nürnberg*. In the Caribbean were two of the fastest light cruisers, *Karlsruhe* and *Dresden*, and in the Indian Ocean, based on German East Africa, *Königsberg*. In the Mediterranean there was *Goeben*, one of the finest battle-cruisers in the German navy, and *Breslau*. Finally, mainly in American or German ports, there were the great liners of the passenger fleet, ships of over 20,000 tons, capable of 25 knots, fitted with gun mountings, waiting for the signal to rendezvous with warships and collect their armaments.

The Allied defences appeared far greater on paper than they were in practice because of the immense distances to be covered. Eastern command was based in Hong Kong and Singapore and combined with the small, but modern, Australian fleet. The North Pacific was left to the Japanese; three cruiser squadrons and one French squadron defended the Atlantic; two obsolete squadrons in the Indian Ocean

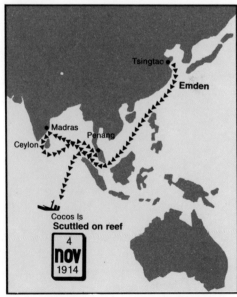

Top: Karlsruhe *and* Dresden *terrorized the coast of Brazil. When Spee summoned* Dresden *to meet him in the Pacific,* Karlsruhe *turned north. She was making for the rich British colony of Barbados, when, unaccountably, she blew up.*
Above: Emden *wrought havoc in the Indian Ocean, once regarded as a British preserve. She sailed from Tsingtao through the Sumatra channel, sank nine ships, bombarded Madras, sank another ten ships near Ceylon, sailed into Penang harbour to sink more ships. Eventually, chased by* Sydney, *her captain ran her aground off the Cocos Islands.*
Left: The Emden *ablaze*

completed the preparations in the far seas. Churchill, the first lord of the Admiralty, and his staff were aware that the line was thin – they did not realize how severely it was to be tested.

Impressive initial successes

Immediately after the declaration of war, Germany chalked up an impressive list of successes. *Goeben* bombarded the French bases of Bône and Philippeville in North Africa and, with bewildering speed, evaded the French and British fleets in the Mediterranean. She succeeded in reaching Constantinople where she was sold to the ostensibly neutral Turkish government. The persuasive force of her presence in Constantinople and, even more, the intrigues of her powerful commander Admiral Souchon, helped materially to bring Turkey into the war on the side of Germany in the autumn of 1914. Meanwhile, in early August, *Königsberg* sank the *City of Winchester* with most of the Ceylon tea crop on board, off the coast of Aden, and threatened the safety of the Suez route to India. Two armed liners escaped through the North Sea and another, *Kronprinz Wilhelm,* ran the blockade of the American ports, while *Karlsruhe* sank her first merchant ship in the Caribbean.

Before the British Admiralty had time to react to these threats, the necessities of the war on the Western Front made the job more difficult. After the retreat from Mons the demand for more power rose dramatically. As the front extended itself from the Channel to Verdun, Kitchener, the secretary of state for war, summoned the reserves, subordinating the Admiralty's other plans in order to escort home the vital battalions of the British army in India. Added to this were the divisions from Australia and New Zealand which, with *Königsberg* at large, would need to be escorted at least through the Red Sea. For weeks half the far seas squadrons were diverted from chasing the German cruisers.

But what might have been a great opportunity for the raiders was lost. One of the decisive battles of the war, the minor engagement in the North Sea off Heligoland on 28th August, in which the Germans lost three light cruisers, so disturbed the Kaiser that he shrank from endangering his cherished fleet again. A defensive strategy took the place of that worked out before 1914; a defective one as far as cruiser warfare was concerned. Instead of ordering immediate strikes at vulnerable points, German planning took account of the imminent loss of her Pacific bases, Samoa, Nauru, New Guinea, and Tsingtao, and the difficulties of supplying and coaling

The Königsberg, *which was to prove her superior speed and guns in the Indian Ocean*

the raiders, rather than of their immense potential. Tirpitz wanted to order Spee home, but such was the atmosphere in Berlin that no orders were sent at all: Pohl, the chief of naval staff, said: 'it is impossible to tell from here whether the squadron will be able to choose against whom it will deal its dying blows'. Within a month of hostilities, the German admiralty had entirely abandoned the preparation of years, the network of colliers and supply ships, communications, and neutral sympathizers. The successes of the raiders in the autumn were obtained without even moral support from home.

The raiders harried two main areas, both vital to the British war effort: the mid-Atlantic and the Indian Ocean. The most vital British interests in August were the troop convoys from India through the Suez Canal. None of these were safe until the whereabouts of *Königsberg* were known. But Captain Looff and his ship had disappeared; he had gone back to German East Africa and did not emerge until 20th September when at dawn he attacked the quiet harbour of Zanzibar, shelled the port, and sank the British light cruiser *Pegasus*. In these anxious months, the calm of the waters between Australia and India, so long a British preserve, was shattered by the foremost raider of all, *Emden*.

'There are great prizes to be won'
Admiral von Spee had left Tsingtao on manoeuvres before war broke out and he was soon deprived of his base by the Japanese blockade. He foresaw the dilemma of his squadron: that if he stayed in the Pacific he must ultimately run out of coal or be destroyed by the Singapore and Japanese squadrons. Instead, he chose to sail round Cape Horn, break through the Atlantic defences, and run for home through the North Sea. But Karl von Müller, captain of *Emden*, asked permission to raid in the Indian Ocean. Spee wrote: 'A single light cruiser can coal from captured vessels and maintain herself for longer . . . as there are great prizes to be won there, I despatched the fastest light cruiser.'

Heavily disguised, with a false funnel, *Emden* crept through the Sumatra channel and began her raiding career on 7th September by sinking nine ships in a week. When the news reached London it produced consternation and a steep rise in insurance rates; and Australia and New Zealand demanded a strong escort for the Anzac troop convoy. Nothing could be given because of the war office priority for the Indian convoys endangered by *Königsberg*. On 21st September Müller carried the war on to enemy territory and bombarded the city of Madras by night, setting fire to the great oil tanks and, by the light of the blaze, destroying the harbour installations. He

then turned south and in the seas around Ceylon, impudently within range of the defences of Colombo, captured or sunk another ten merchant ships. Loss of confidence and prestige caused bitter questions—what was the Admiralty doing? Australia and New Zealand bluntly postponed the convoy for three weeks.

Emden did not strike again until mid-October—just when the convoy, with an escort, was ready, and at a time when the war in South Africa against the German-backed rebels under Christian de Wet was at its most dangerous. Several more sinkings preceded one of the boldest strokes of the war: Müller sailed into the harbour of Penang on the Malay peninsula and sank the Russian light cruiser *Zhemchug* and a French destroyer. Combined with the steady toll taken in the Atlantic by *Karlsruhe* and the armed liners, and Spee's attack on the French colony of Tahiti, the raiders were achieving their object of distracting the enemy. By the end of October they had captured or sunk more than forty Allied ships.

Karlsruhe alone had accounted for nearly 100,000 tons of shipping. She had nearly been caught by Admiral Cradock's squadron in the Caribbean in early August, but she refuelled from the armed liner *Kronprinz Wilhelm* and escaped to Puerto Rico with almost empty bunkers. But thereafter Captain Kohler could easily evade pursuit in his 27½-knot ship, as Cradock wearily traversed the mid-Atlantic. In concert with *Dresden* during August and September, the two raiders terrorized the waters off the coast of Brazil where all the trade routes to South America converged. They held up cargoes of frozen meat in Argentine ports and gave a strong stimulus to pro-German feeling among neutral Latin American countries.

Then Spee summoned *Dresden* to meet him in the Pacific, luring Cradock south and leaving the West Indies open to *Karlsruhe* — a chance which Kohler did not miss. He drew his information about the sailings of merchant vessels from German intelligence in Brazil, the Argentine, and Chile, and waited for them to arrive. Working with *Kronprinz Wilhelm* he sank twenty ships in late September, taking what he needed from their cargoes.

The extent of this damage was only realized when he landed 400 prisoners, and the pursuit was not fully organized until 14th October, when Admiral Stoddart was given overall command of the mid- and North Atlantic and the modern cruiser *Defence*. But Kohler was warned in advance; he sank two more rich cargoes and turned north, planning a spectacular blow to Allied morale in the heart of the West Indies, by destroying Barbados and Fort de France in Martinique.

So far, the only British successes had been the sinking of two armed liners, *Kaiser Wilhelm der Grosse* on the African coast, and *Cap Trafalgar* (by another armed liner, the Cunard *Carmania*) which disrupted supplies of coal to *Karlsruhe*. In the Pacific, all the German bases had been captured by combined operations with the dominions and Japanese. But the main danger was the unknown, powerful squadron of Spee, of which Admiral Cradock, now commanding the South Atlantic, was more aware than the British Admiralty. No one could know that Spee had decided to bring his ships home, if possible, intact. If he passed Cape Horn, Cradock reasoned, he could attack Capetown or even cross to head off the Anzac convoy. It was this which led him, at loggerheads with the Admiralty, to seek out Spee on the Pacific coast—and to the disastrous battle of Coronel. The first British naval engagement for a century ended on 1st November in almost total disaster for the British.

At once the strategic picture changed. Spee must be destroyed. Two battle-cruisers were withdrawn from Jellicoe's Grand Fleet and despatched with such urgency that the fitters were left on board. A great concentration took place off the Brazilian coast and a net of steel was stretched on either side of Cape Horn. The Japanese and Australian fleets cut off the retreat to the Pacific. The urgency of the war in Europe was at last transferred to the far seas and finally ended the careers of the raiders: only as a result of a major humiliation was Pohl's gloomy prophecy fulfilled.

End of the 'Swan of the East'
After two months of unparalleled havoc in the Indian Ocean, pursued by the game but ineffective Captain Grant in *Yarmouth*, *Emden*'s luck changed. Müller decided to attack the wireless station in the Cocos Islands to cut the trunk cables to Australia and South Africa, and ran straight into the path of the Anzac convoy which, heavily escorted, had at last left Perth. HMAS *Sydney*, under Captain Glossop, was detached in pursuit, and after a long running battle, Müller ran the ruined shell of *Emden*, the 'Swan of the East', on the coral reefs of the Cocos Islands. He was taken prisoner and, in unusual recognition, allowed to keep his sword.

Captain Kohler was meanwhile steaming towards Barbados. With all the Atlantic warships to the south, nothing could have saved the unsuspecting colony, but on a clear day, for no known reason, *Karlsruhe* suddenly exploded and was torn in two, sinking at once with the loss of her captain and most of the crew. It was ironic that, on the same day, the German admiralty cabled: 'Return home, your work is done.'

The end of a glorious career – Emden, the 'Swan of the East', now a battered shell, on the coral reefs off the Cocos Islands

The danger of armed liners was also largely over. They had been, at best, an extravagant form of raider, fast but requiring immense quantities of coal. An organization for supplying them existed, run by Captain Boy-Ed of the German embassy in Washington, but the British warships waiting outside US territorial waters were too great a deterrent and the majority were interned. Only *Kronprinz Wilhelm* had a successful raiding career, sinking in six months some 60,000 tons of shipping. But although her speed was 25 knots she had to spend valuable weeks coaling at sea from captured colliers and, after November, was largely disregarded by the British forces concentrating on the threat at Cape Horn.

On 9th December came the news of the battle of the Falkland Islands in which Admiral Sturdee destroyed the whole of Spee's squadron except the raider *Dresden*. This was, practically speaking, the end of the war in the far seas. *Dresden* escaped along the myriad inlets of the Chilean coast but remained a hunted vagrant, finally tracked down and scuttled at Juan Fernández. The German colliers still slipped out from Brazilian ports to supply *Kronprinz Wilhelm* and another armed liner, *Prinz Eitel Friedrich*, which had escaped before the battle of the Falklands. Between them they took eighteen merchant ships during the winter but in March, for lack of coal, unable to undertake the long voyage home, they both ran in to Newport harbour in the United States and were interned. Six months later the recall of Captain Boy-Ed was demanded by the American government. His activities probably did more to swing American opinion against Germany than to create any lasting advantage for German seapower.

Königsberg alone remained. After the successful raid on Zanzibar Captain Looff had returned to his secret base, charted before the war, in the intricate muddy channels of the Rufiji river in German East Africa where he was tracked down and bottled in by a strong British squadron commanded by Captain Drury-Lowe. But *Königsberg* was out of range and hidden behind the forests and mangrove swamps, while her men were entrenched in efficient land defences. Supplies reached them from the interior. One of the channels was blocked by sinking an old collier, but others were open: *Königsberg* posed a unique problem and tied down three modern cruisers.

Primitive aircraft brought by ship from Capetown were able to locate her, but tropical rain and heat made them unusable. Both sides settled down to stalemate and nothing happened until March, when the German admiralty sent the collier *Rubens* to refuel the raider and give Looff the chance to break for the open sea and return home. After circling the north of Scotland and running down past the Cape, *Rubens* was sunk within a day's sail of the Rufiji. Looff sent half his men inland to help General von Lettow-Vorbeck in the war on Lake Tanganyika and abandoned hope of escaping. But *Königsberg* was still indestructible. More aircraft were sent out, and finally two monitors—flat gun emplacements, drawing only five feet of water. In the first air-sea operation ever mounted they steamed up river, firing indirectly at *Königsberg*, the fall of shot spotted from the air. At the first attack they were withdrawn, severely damaged. But the Germans were short of ammunition and the next assault, a week later, succeeded. The last of the German raiders was left, a riddled hulk on a mosquito-plagued shore, nearly a year after the start of the war.

The daring of the privateers
The raiders inherited the tradition of 18th-century privateers. Their orders debarred them from attacking warships except in emergency. German planning of bases, supplies of coal, and repairs was as efficient as the scattered nature of her colonies and the benevolence of neutrals would allow. But because of reverses in Europe, there was no subsequent strategy except, at the end, the order for recall. Yet, in the North Sea, few of the raiders would have had a use comparable to their value abroad. Events called in question the whole conception of far seas strategy. The German cruisers were superior in speed and gunnery to their British counterparts. *Karlsruhe* could have taken on Cradock's whole squadron and escaped—and if Spee, instead of turning away to preserve his ships had sailed straight into Port Stanley itself, he would have caught a fleet half at anchor, and sunk or severely damaged some of the best units in the British fleet, 6,000 miles from a British port. The German admiralty seems to have been dominated by calculations of sheer number. If the staff really believed the cruisers were doomed, they could have sent them down in crippling attacks on troop convoys or even harbours like Hong Kong. The courage and dash came from the raiders themselves, Müller and Kohler, not Berlin.

The war of movement took both sides by surprise. The effectiveness of the raiders, the daring of *Emden* and *Karlsruhe*, had not been foreseen. The needs of the army in Flanders overrode naval advice and it took Coronel to galvanize the British defences. Then the truth became clear: surface raiders had only a limited life. Submarines, two years later, were needed to bring Great Britain to the edge of starvation.

But the raiders meant something more. They pointed the contrast between war in the far seas and the struggles on the Western Front and the stagnation of embittered fleets facing each other across the North Sea. The raiders hit the headlines and the imagination. The gamekeeper's pursuit of the poacher did not. To German soldiers in Europe and in the snowbound trenches of the Russian Front the names of *Emden*, *Karlsruhe*, *Dresden*, and *Königsberg* brought pride and, above all, hope for the future, as operations contracted, grimly, to the war of attrition.

Revenge at Sea

At the outbreak of war, the German East Asia Squadron under Vice-Admiral Graf Maximilian von Spee had been widely dispersed; but by 12th October all the most powerful ships, the *Scharnhorst, Gneisenau, Nürnberg* and *Leipzig* were gathered at Easter Island where they were joined by the light cruiser *Dresden,* which brought news of the British reaction to Spee's exploits to date, and thus gave him some idea of the forces being ranged against him.

These did not amount to much. If what *Dresden*'s captain told Spee was correct, the only British ships west of Cape Horn were the old armoured cruiser *Monmouth,* the modern light cruiser *Glasgow,* and the armed merchantman *Otranto,* while just east of the Horn at the British coaling base at Port Stanley on the Falkland Islands, the admiral commanding this tatterdemalion collection of ships, Vice-Admiral Sir Christopher Cradock, waited—presumably for more effective reinforcement—in the armoured cruiser *Good Hope.*

If this were all the naval opposition ranged for the moment against him, there was obviously no point in further delay; Spee coaled his squadron from colliers carefully collected beforehand at Easter Island, and on 18th October left—first for Más Afuera and then for the Chilean coast. He and his ships were forty miles off Valparaiso late on the afternoon of 30th October, and the following evening he learned that the British light cruiser *Glasgow* was at Coronel, 250 miles to the south.

Detaching *Nürnberg* to pick up mail in Valparaiso, Spee took his squadron south in order to cut off the British cruiser, and perhaps to meet other British ships in company. By 1600 on Sunday, 1st November 1914, his ships were off Coronel, and at 1625 his lookouts sighted two ships away to the south-west; they were *Glasgow* and *Monmouth* and shortly afterwards these two were joined by *Good Hope* flying the flag of Admiral Cradock, and the armed merchantman *Otranto.* The two forces had found each other at last, and the first battle began in which ships of the German navy were ranged in line of battle against ships of the Royal Navy.

Everything favoured the German ships.

By 1800 the two battle lines were formed, and briefly there did appear some small advantage for the British: the setting sun was behind them, blinding the German gunners but lighting up the German ships into perfect targets. But the range was not close enough for the out-dated British guns, so at 1804 Cradock turned his ships four points towards his enemy—who with superior speed and room to manoeuvre turned away and kept out of range. Grimly, the British re-formed their battle line and assessed the odds against them—now shown up with ominous clarity; *Scharnhorst* and *Gneisenau* riding powerfully over the seas, the details of their high-placed heavy armament picked out by the westering sun, the seas racing along the towering sides and occasionally sweeping the foredecks.

Behind them came the light cruisers *Leipzig* and *Dresden,* and radio signals warned that *Nürnberg* was coming down fast from the north—but most fatal of all for the British, evening slowly crept over the sea from the east and touched the German battleline, greying it into the sea and the sky beyond. As twilight thickened, the moon came up behind heavy clouds, to show fleetingly through them, briefly outlining the German ships—and at last it seemed that *Scharnhorst* and *Gneisenau* were closing in. To the west, the afterglow of the sun made a fiery, yellow-shot tapestry of the windswept sky, against which the British ships now stood out in black, hard-edged clarity; nothing would help them tonight but their courage and the long tradition of the Royal Navy.

The massacre begins

At 1904 on Sunday, 1st November 1914, the 8·2-inch guns of the German East Asia Squadron at last opened fire on the British ships, at a range of 12,000 yards.

From the bridge of *Glasgow* were seen two lines of orange flashes from *Scharnhorst* and *Gneisenau,* and as the thunder of *Good Hope*'s 9·2s answered, grey-white mushrooms blossomed from the sea 500 yards short of the British ships, beautifully aimed, beautifully grouped.

Glasgow's pair of modern 6-inch guns fired experimentally into the darkness, but even while the gun controller was vainly searching the east for fall of shot, the orange lines sparkled again and then again—lengthened now as *Leipzig* and *Dresden* opened fire. Shell splinters whined shrilly overhead, the seas erupted around the British ships, *Monmouth* steamed ahead through a forest of water and *Good Hope*'s foredeck exploded in a sheet of flame which twisted the forward 9·2-inch gun into a hopeless knot of steel protruding from a turret like a blazing cauldron, and abruptly halved the British chance of

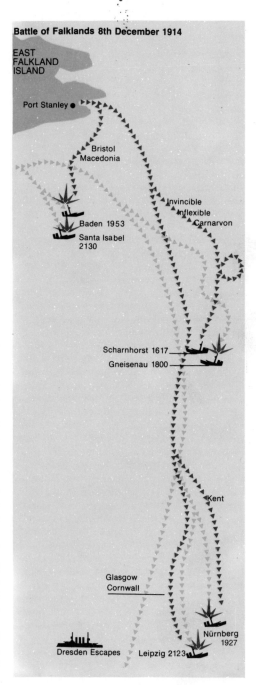

The battle of the Falkland Islands, showing when the German ships sank. *Baden* and *Santa Isabel* were supply ships mopped up during the battle

harming the enemy at anything but short range. Before the mind could react, the next salvo arrived.

Monmouth's foredeck flared in hard-edged flame and black smoke billowed from sudden, sharp fires along her starboard side; *Good Hope*'s deck amidships threw up a fan of sparks, her upper bridge, mast-head, and foretop glowed redly as *Scharnhorst*'s high-explosive burst between them, and as the glow faded cordite flared on the deck, and stacked ammunition exploded whitely along the gun-flats.

Intent on closing the range and thus bringing his secondary armament into action, Cradock now led the British ships directly towards the German line—but Spee expertly held the range to his own advantage so that his ships remained unscathed while Cradock's took a dreadful punishment. *Monmouth*, especially, received the full attention of the guns of the *Gneisenau*—which had won the Kaiser's Gold Cup only months before—and began slowly to sag out of line as though beaten away by sheer weight of metal. Flames belched from her quarterdeck, water flooded through gaping holes in her bows, she listed badly to port and as darkness increased she disappeared to the south and her guns lapsed into silence.

Except for the endless flashes from their batteries, the German ships were now quite invisible from the British decks. Not so *Good Hope*; she flared like a beacon.

Since action had commenced the British flagship had received the undivided attention of the gunners aboard *Scharnhorst*, who were to prove as efficient as their colleagues aboard *Gneisenau*. At 1940, *Good Hope* was seen to slow and stagger under the rain of blows; her foredeck was ablaze, clouds of steam and smoke billowed around her, glowing sullenly, and her ports glowed redly from the fires in her crowded flats.

Then at 1942, as if in contempt for her own condition, *Good Hope* seemed to gather up her remaining strength, turn directly towards her antagonists and charge them. Abruptly, *Scharnhorst* and *Gneisenau* changed course slightly and shortened range to bring their full broadsides to bear—and, blanketed under a dreadful fire, *Good Hope* was at last brought to a halt and her last desperate throw defeated.

As though stunned, she drifted down silently between the lines.

Then the fires reached a main magazine and at 1953—fifty minutes after the first salvo had been fired at her—*Good Hope* was shattered by an explosion which still lives in the memories of those who witnessed it. A broad column of flame rose upwards from between her main and after funnels until it towered two hundred feet above her decks, and in its awful light jagged and incongruous shapes soared up

and away into the darkness, twisting and weaving in the blast, tumbling in the sudden vacuums.

Then the waves took the blazing hulk farther off into the darkness, the flames dwindled and all that now remained of Cradock and his men drifted out of the battle. This was virtually the end of the battle of Coronel. *Otranto* had already left the battle-line—ordered away by Cradock—and now *Glasgow*, after a vain attempt to succour *Monmouth*, fled to the south. At 2035, *Nürnberg* found *Monmouth* painfully making her way towards the Chilean coast and as the British ship made no attempt to strike her colours, had little choice but to reopen the action and finally sink her. At 2058 the waves finally closed over the stern of the British cruiser. There were no survivors—and none from the *Good Hope*, which was never seen again after she drifted from the battle. In two hours the Royal Navy had lost two ships and over 1,000 men and boys.

When the news reached Great Britain, the reaction was immediate and drastic. The first lord of the Admiralty, Winston Churchill, learned of the disaster at 1900 on 4th November, and immediately convened a meeting with the sea lords. As it happened, the position of first sea lord had just been taken over (for the second time) by Lord Fisher, and this doughty old man

Dresden, *tracked down, shows the white flag*

had no time for half measures—a characteristic which endeared him to Churchill.

Within a week the two battle-cruisers *Invincible* and *Inflexible* (as superior in speed and armament to *Scharnhorst* and *Gneisenau* as the German ships had been to *Good Hope* and *Monmouth*) had sailed from Devonport for the Falkland Islands, and they were joined on their voyage south by the County Class cruisers *Carnarvon*, *Cornwall*, and *Kent*, and the light cruisers *Bristol* and *Glasgow* (hurriedly patched up after her escape from Coronel in the dry dock at Rio). The squadron was under command of Vice-Admiral Sir Frederick Doveton Sturdee, and as it moved farther and farther south—searching all the time for Spee's ships in case they had already come around the Horn—his search line was lengthened every day by the addition of a

host of colliers together with the armed merchantman *Orama*, and eventually by another cruiser, *Macedonia*.

Sturdee's augmented squadron reached the Falkland Islands on 7th December, and he ordered concentration in Port Stanley and the outer bay at Port William for coaling. After their long voyage, some of the ships needed to draw their fires for boiler examination, but *Glasgow* and *Carnarvon* coaled through the night, *Macedonia* patrolled outside the harbour, and at dawn on 8th December the colliers went alongside the battle-cruisers to begin filling their enormous demands for fuel.

To Sturdee, it thus seemed that within ten or twelve hours—twenty-four at the most—his entire squadron would be ready for sea again, to take up the search for the elusive German ships. This, of course, was his great problem, for with the enormous power at his disposal, there could be no doubt as to the outcome of a battle with the East Asia Squadron, once they were sighted. It was a problem rapidly solved.

Shortly after 0830 on the morning after his arrival at Port Stanley—while his capital ships were still coaling and two of his cruisers carrying out boiler examination—Sir Frederick was interrupted while shaving with the news that *Gneisenau* and *Nürnberg* were approaching the island and about twenty miles off, and the smoke from the other ships of Spee's command was visible on the horizon astern of them. It says much for the Vice-Admiral's *sang-froid* that his only comment was the classic 'Then send the men to breakfast'.

Spee's critical error

There is no way of being certain why Spee chose to attack the Falkland Islands, but there is little doubt about the fact that had he ordered an immediate attack on the British squadron as they lay at anchor in the two bays, he could have inflicted on them a defeat of staggering proportions—though probably at the cost of his own ships and certainly at the cost of using up all his remaining ammunition.

Fortunately for Sturdee, however, as soon as the captain of the *Gneisenau* reported the presence of a large number of British warships, Spee issued the order: 'Do not accept action. Concentrate on course east by south. Proceed at full speed.'

In doing so, the German admiral signed his own death-warrant and condemned his squadron to annihilation—though this fact did not become apparent to him or his men until 1000 when, to the dismay and astonishment of the observers aboard *Leipzig*, two pairs of tripod masts—the recognition mark of battle-cruisers were seen above the low-lying spit, proceeding towards Port William harbour.

From the British point of view, every

advantage favoured them. A long summer day stretched ahead, visibility was at its maximum, the sea calm, the sky clear and pale. By 1048 the whole squadron was at sea in a long line stretching eastwards from Port William – *Glasgow* in the lead, *Inflexible* and *Invincible* three miles astern, *Kent* two miles astern of them and *Cornwall* and *Carnarvon* as much again. The squadron's speed was 19 knots, the enemy were some twelve miles ahead and their calculated speed was only 15 knots.

The distance between the two adversaries inexorably lessened and at 1257 *Inflexible* fired the first shot of the battle of the Falkland Islands – at *Leipzig*, the lame duck of the German squadron. The shell fell well short, and only occasional sighting shots were fired during the next thirty minutes; then at 1320, Spee hoisted the signal: 'Light cruisers part company and endeavour to escape.' And the two armoured cruisers bravely turned to accept action from their formidable opponents.

As at Coronel by six o'clock in the evening, the main forces were now ranging broadside against broadside – but this was half past one in the afternoon, there were still eight hours of daylight left, and no mounting seas or storm clouds to complicate the hazards of war. *Invincible* opened fire against *Gneisenau*; *Inflexible* against *Scharnhorst*.

By this time, the British light and County Class cruisers had swung away from the main battle to chase the escaping German light cruisers, and Captain Allen aboard *Kent,* later wrote this description of the scene:

'With the sun still shining on them, the German ships looked as if they had been painted for the occasion. They fired as if they had but eight minutes in which to make a record battle-practice score and never have I seen heavy guns fired with such rapidity and yet with such control. Flash after flash travelled down their sides from head to stern, all their six and eight-inch guns firing every salvo.

Of the British battle-cruisers less could be seen as their smoke drifted from them across the range and not only obscured their own view but also the spectator's view of them. Nevertheless, they seemed to be firing incessantly, their shells hitting the German ships at intervals whereas all that could be seen of the German fire was that it straddled the British ships. Four or five times in the first twenty minutes the white puff of bursting shell could be seen among the clouds of brown cordite smoke in Gneisenau, *and she was seen to be on fire near her mainmast, but this soon disappeared.* (By permission of *Naval Review.)*

In addition to the greater weight of broadside and greater range of guns, the battle-cruisers had a further advantage – they were firing, for the first time in a naval battle, lyddite shell, and this new explosive wreaked dreadful havoc aboard the German ships. However Spee might seek to twist and turn, hoping for some sudden squall or mist patch in which to escape, the British battle-cruisers hung grimly on, unhurried but implacable, inexorably smashing his ships to pieces. All through the afternoon the battle continued, and aboard the British ships great admiration was felt for the perfect timing and grouping of the German gunnery, despite the chaos visible on the German decks.

By 1545 clouds of steam gushed upwards from *Scharnhorst's* decks, the first and second funnels were leaning against each other, an enormous livid rent had been torn in the side plating below her quarterdeck and she was blazing fore and aft – but still her starboard batteries fired.

Her masts were gone, her bridge was wrecked, her magazines must have been almost empty, but still her ensign fluttered from a jury mast above the after control station. Then suddenly, just before 1600 her batteries ceased fire as though they had been switched off, and she was seen to turn eight points to starboard and come staggering across the seas towards her powerful antagonists. Behind her, *Gneisenau* swung across still firing rapidly, and as *Inflexible* re-engaged the farther ship, *Invincible* turned and headed for Spee's flagship. Less than 10,000 yards separated the two admirals, but it was soon evident that they would never meet, for *Scharnhorst's* decks were a sea of fire, her speed fell away and she listed badly.

Just before 1610 her list took her deck-rails under, water flooded inboard to quench the flames and she rolled on to her beams end. Through rents in her plating a few figures climbed laboriously and stood on her side-plates watching the battle-cruisers and the cold, impartial sea. Seven minutes later, *Scharnhorst's* bows suddenly dipped, her stern came up, steam and smoke wreathed about her and with her flag still flying, she slid quickly under water and was gone, leaving only a huge yellow patch on the surface of the sea.

Fifteen minutes later, *Carnarvon* reached the spot and steamed directly through the stained waters. Neither survivors nor wreckage were visible.

By this time, *Invincible* had rejoined *Inflexible* and the two battle-cruisers turned their attention on *Gneisenau*.

The end was now a foregone conclusion, and as Sturdee had no intention of sustaining avoidable damage to either of his ships, he ordered them to stand off and take their time. Thus *Gneisenau's* agony was protracted for another hour, by which time the destruction aboard beggared description.

Between the masts, her decks were beaten down to the armoured deck, and soon even this was torn open by plummeting shells. Her after-turret was jammed at ninety degrees, all the starboard casemate guns blown into the sea or pounded into shapeless masses of metal. Half her crew were dead or wounded, and shells had ended much suffering by exploding in the sick-bay and in the stokers' bathrooms where an emergency bay had been set up.

Then a shell from *Carnarvon* caused jamming of *Gneisenau's* helm so that she slowly came round and, almost for the first time, the port batteries could come into action – though there was little enough ammunition left to fire. But there was some – enough to sting the battle-cruisers into re-opening fire and finishing *Gneisenau* as a fighting ship. Just before 1730 she lay almost motionless in the water, listing so badly that the seas flooded inboard through the lower gun ports.

Yet she was not sinking – and in order to ensure that nothing of value would fall into British hands, her captain gave the order for explosive charges between the inner and outer hull skins to be blown, and the stern torpedoes to be fired with the sluice gates left open. At a few minutes to six in the evening, *Gneisenau* seemed to shake herself and come fractionally out of the water; then she lay over at about ten degrees and began to settle. Her crew – what was left of them – gave three cheers for the Kaiser and then clambered across the decks to drop down into the icy waters alongside; and at two minutes after six, *Gneisenau's* bows came up, keel uppermost, then slid down out of sight, leaving the seas littered with debris and struggling men. Only 187 of these, including seventeen officers but not *Gneisenau's* captain, were picked up by British boats.

Of the remaining ships of Spee's command, *Nürnberg* was chased, caught, and sunk by *Kent* at 1927, *Leipzig* fought gallantly until 2123, against both *Cornwall* and *Glasgow*; and *Dresden* escaped for the moment. She reached Punta Arenas three days after the battle, passed through the Magellan Straits and played hide and seek with British pursuers until the morning of 14th March 1915, when she was found by *Glasgow* and *Kent* sheltering in Cumberland Bay on Juan Fernández Island.

But there was no battle. Tamely, her captain ran up a white flag, evacuated the crew ashore and then blew up the main magazine – and *Dresden's* wreck still lies in the bay. After the fire and fury of the two battles, this was something of an anticlimax, but it should be remembered that *Dresden* was not an original member of the East Asia Squadron. Spee's captains all fought to the end, and went down with their ships.

Italy Goes to War

In July 1914 Italy had for thirty years been allied (by the Triple Alliance of 1882) to the central European empires of Austria-Hungary and Germany. Ten months later Italy, forced by circumstances, entered the war against Austria-Hungary. No one in July could have foreseen this.

Italian Nationalists were ever ready to theorize on the inevitability of war, but even after the fatal revolver shots of Sarajevo, they still predicted that there would be a long period of peace for the Habsburg monarchy, troubled though it was by its own domestic problems.

If the Nationalists thought this, there were others who thought so too. On the morning of the 25th July, just after the news broke that Austria-Hungary had delivered her ultimatum to Serbia, there was much excitement among the passengers on the Milan-Venice express. On board the train was the president of the Trento and Trieste Irredentist Association. (Irrendentism was a movement which worked for the union of various Italian-speaking districts, mainly those ruled by Austria-Hungary, with Italy.) In the course of their conversation the president's travelling companion, Giuseppe Volpi, authoritatively declared that 'everything will be settled as usual by an international conference . . . And so, no war? No, certainly not. Europe has other things to think about. . . .'

Volpi was a high financier, a diplomat, and an expert in Balkan affairs. But Claudio Treves, one of the leaders of the Italian Socialist Party, reasoned along nearly the same lines as Volpi. On the eve of the war he placed his hopes for peace in two forces: 'high finance and socialism, the bank and the proletariat'. Above all he pinned his faith on Great Britain, in particular on the diplomacy of Sir Edward Grey, the 'spokesman of capitalist preoccupations'. Treves belonged to the moderate wing of the party; the revolutionaries, however, echoed his words, or else trusted completely in a rebellion of the masses who might be dragged to the slaughter. Luigi Luzzatti, the former prime minister (1910-11), believed that 'the destruction of lives, wealth, culture, civilization, whoever was victorious and whoever was conquered, would debase and debilitate Europe, so benefiting another continent, America, and would provide a pretext for a future Asiatic invasion'. Giovanni Giolitti, the most influential man in Italy, the Liberal 'dictator' of Italian politics, was, in the vital last weeks of July, abroad. He too, right up to

the end, refused to believe that the governments of civilized Europe could fall prey to the folly of war. It took the German ultimatum to Russia and France to make him change his mind. He was afterwards frequently to recall his extremely bitter disappointment at the 'monstrous war'.

In this atmosphere of dismay it was clear that if Italy had to take up a position in favour of one side or the other, she would follow the policy mapped out in the past. Besides, after the Libyan affair, the introduction of universal suffrage, and the bloody disturbances of the 'Red Week', Italian political parties were divided into two great blocks. There were the parties of law and order (in fact, of the 'establishment'): Liberals, Liberal-Conservatives, Catholics, and Nationalists; and there were the popular parties: Radicals, Social Reformists, the Italian Socialist Party (PSI), Republicans, Syndicalists, and Anarchists. This very division strengthened the tendencies of the parties of order (who had a majority in parliament) not to stray from traditional paths in either foreign or domestic policy.

The 'irredentists' and the Triple Alliance

In Trieste itself and in several small towns in Venezia Giulia many Italian irredentists (supporters of the Liberal National party and of Nationalist currents) thought along similar lines. On 29th July 1914 the Italian consul in Trieste reported that 'last night a great procession of Austrian patriotic societies and constitutional elements marched on the consulate, cheering Italy, the war, and the Triple Alliance'. From the end of the 19th century the Italian irredentists had seen Slav pressure grow, politically, economically, socially, and culturally. They could not disregard it. They wanted to become part of Italy; but they were, nevertheless, also willing to fight a war for the Triple Alliance.

When it became certain that there would be a European war the Nationalists, therefore, had few doubts. They wanted Italy to enter the war on the side of Austria-Hungary and Germany. They admired Germany and considered the Habsburg empire a great bulwark against the Slav advance. And they were concerned more about the Mediterranean and the colonies than about the Balkans. The real enemy for them was Italy's 'Latin sister', France, who had usurped the position of a great power, while she was becoming ever weaker on account of her democratic misgovernment.

The Liberals supported the Triple

Top: The right-wing Salandra who committed Italy to her Adriatic war.
Above: General Cadorna who was to command her army. He favoured a war against the French in a German alliance. Although he undertook war against the Central Powers enthusiastically he was later dismissed for incompetence.
Left: 'The Intervention', an ironic painting by Aldo Carpi. The red flag of socialism and the white flag of reaction greet Italy's entry into the war against her former partner in the Triple Alliance

*Headlines of two Italian socialist papers—
November 1914—show the political struggle
developing around the defence of neutrality.
Benito Mussolini, founder of Italian
Fascism, starts his political journey to the*

*extreme right wing by quitting as editor of
the socialist* Avanti! *(below) and founding
the interventionist* Il Popolo d'Italia
(above). In the headline shown above,
Avanti! *attacks its former editor*

Alliance for rather different reasons. The
Liberals, who still considered themselves
the true 'governing party', prided themselves on being cautious and realistic,
and for that very reason were unwilling to
break old ties. One could see this simply by
reading their mass-circulation newspapers, whether Giolittian or anti-Giolit-
tian, northern or southern. *La Stampa, La
Tribuna, Il Giornale d'Italia, Il Mattino,*
and *Il Resto del Carlino,* all predicted, or at
least admitted, that Italy would intervene
on the side of the Central powers. They may
have been frightened at the prospect of
Great Britain entering the war, but what
they feared more was isolation. They regarded the Triple Alliance as a means by
which Italy could assert itself. There were
some exceptions, but even Luigi Albertini,
editor of the *Corriere della Sera,* who regretted the Austrian ultimatum and its
result, did not exclude the possibility of
Italy entering the war on the side of her
ancient allies.

Then there were the Catholics who, for
the most part, made the arguments of the
Liberals their own. They felt a special
sympathy with Austria, the great Catholic
state and bulwark against the Orthodox
Christian Slavs. Everyone—Nationalists,
Liberals, Catholics, at any rate—severely
judged the popular parties which, at a
moment's notice, organized meetings and
demonstrations against the war. The
government alone had the right to the last
say: the state must be strong and dis-
ciplined. Memories of the 'Red Week'
lingered on, aggravating the differences
between the parties.

The view of the popular parties

Even among the popular parties there were
some who, like Arturo Labriola, the tire-
less spokesman of revolutionary syndical-
ism, were in favour of Italy's intervention
on the side of the Central powers. Some
influential Radical parliamentarians were
of the same opinion but, on the whole, the
popular parties were against war. They
revived their past preoccupations: opposition to the Triple Alliance, sympathy for
France, distrust for the monarchy, the anti-
militarism which had been growing since
1911, internationalism and pacifism. They
organized demonstrations and took up
again their traditional catchphrases
'against Austrian militarism which had
erected gallows and gibbets in Italy'.
'No blood, no money, no complicity with
the Habsburgs'. 'Let governments of all
Europe set light to the fuse; the explosion
will blow them up and them only'. But
events took the popular parties by surprise
and their various moves were badly co-
ordinated. News from beyond the Alps
of the international proletariat's trial of
strength (to prevent war) was dishearten-
ingly bad. Moreover, there was bad blood
between revolutionaries, Social Reformists,
and Radicals. The popular parties, while
seeking a decision in favour of neutrality,
were already showing their weaknesses.

These party divisions gave the government a fairly free hand, but it did not find it
easy to orientate itself. The right-wing
Liberal-Conservative, Antonio Salandra,
had replaced Giolitti as prime minister in
March. Giolitti cabled from Paris in
favour of neutrality, but Sidney Sonnino,

the old political friend of Salandra, the
real leader of the Liberal-Conservative
wing, insisted on fighting with Italy's
allies. And for his part the chief of general
staff, General Cadorna, had on 29th July
already taken military measures to
strengthen defences against France. Two
days later he even suggested to the King
that half the Italian army should be transferred to the Rhine to help the Germans.
Nevertheless, the government was increasingly favouring the course of neutrality and on 2nd August the Italian government declared itself neutral. Nothing in the
Triple Alliance compelled Italy to mobilize,
and Austria-Hungary was opposed to any
discussion on the 'compensations' foreseen
by the treaty. The Italian government
therefore reasserted its freedom of action.
But there were many alternatives. San
Giuliano, the foreign minister, was soon
to consider war against Austria, though
without excluding other eventualities: 'it
suits us to make every effort to maintain
good relations for after the war with the
allies', he wrote to Salandra on 4th August.
Later he confided to his friends, 'The ideal
for us would be for Austria to be defeated
on one side and France on the other'.
Despite everything, the legacy of the Triple
Alliance was still strong. And it is here
that we have the key to our understanding
of the events.

Only a few days after the declaration of
neutrality the Nationalists made a *volte
face.* They now argued that Italy should
enter the war against Austria-Hungary.
The leap was certainly enormous. Nevertheless, the Nationalists did not try to
disclaim the attitude they had held earlier.
They still wanted Italy to become a really
great power. But the Central powers, they
argued, had left Italy in the lurch, and the
Triple Alliance no longer served any purpose. It was better, therefore, to gain
supremacy in the Adriatic. Italy had to
wage 'her own war', the 'Italian War', and
conquer Trento, Trieste, and Dalmatia.
Italy had no interests in common with
France, Great Britain, or Russia. Her
natural alliances were not with these
powers; and once the war was over she
would have to reconstruct them. Austria-
Hungary, the Nationalists thought, should
be reduced but should not disappear, Germany would be conquered but still powerful. Some time in the future, Italy would
march again hand in hand with the Central powers for the great conflict, which
would take place in the Mediterranean.

For the Nationalists in particular, an
alliance between Italy and Germany,
nations who had come recently into being
as unified states at the same time inspired
by the same national enthusiasm, obeyed
the laws of history.

The Nationalists (Corradini, Federzoni,

Rocco, and others) were few in number, and had only three representatives in parliament (ten if one includes their allies). But they spoke a great deal and got themselves talked about even more. They had the sympathy of many Liberal-Conservatives and Catholics. In order to strengthen their position, they were prepared to come to an agreement even with the interventionists from the popular parties. The Nationalists intended to use them, not to serve them. The war, they thought, would mark the triumph of the authority of true values: tradition, hierarchy, discipline, 'in place of the three false ideals—innovation, equality, and liberty'. The Nationalists, in fact, wanted as always to drag in the other parties of order, and, unfortunately, they met no insuperable obstacles.

The Liberal reaction
The Liberals remained the largest party, but now they seemed unequal to the gravity of the situation. They were split into neutralists and interventionists. Perhaps it was not so much this that mattered but rather that they no longer shared the ideas of the Nationalists, without managing to find any realistic alternatives. Whether neutralists or interventionists, it was on the whole difficult for them to go beyond their programme: to negotiate with

Right: Giolitti, 'the old wizard', who for once misjudged the situation and lost control. Below: Mussolini, arrested after an intervention rally which became a riot

Austria-Hungary (for Trentino and part of Venezia-Giulia) or to declare 'our war'.

The Liberals were also deeply reluctant to abandon completely the July 1914 position. Those who tended to favour war wanted first to discover whether Vienna would concede any of the Italian districts in Austrian possession. Those inclined towards neutrality wanted to be sure that it would not imperil Italy's position. They would stay neutral, but only at a price—which they were prepared to make Austria-Hungary pay. In other words, they were prepared for a purely 'Italian War', one that would not involve them too much with the Entente powers and would not, if possible, mean an irreparable break with

Germany. They had their own views undoubtedly; but it was almost impossible to stand in the way of the Nationalists.

Giolitti, 'the old wizard' of Italian politics, was for once in danger of failing to produce the magic formula to calm the tempest. He was still the head of the majority party, but he brushed aside the advice of friends to bring down the Salandra government. He preferred to influence affairs from the outside. Salandra, prime minister mainly because of Giolitti's support, was a Liberal-Conservative, and an old enemy; but the Liberal-Conservatives in fact were hesitating, inclined towards neutrality, but neutrality 'with profit and with honour'. This almost coincided with Giolitti's policy. With his experience, with his hidden but deep faith in the liberal state, Giolitti tried to study the problem deeply, but he did not this time manage to find a clear-cut solution. All too often he measured events with a pre-war yardstick. He thought, in spite of everything, that the real friction was between Great Britain and Russia in the Dardanelles and in Asia, and that in any case the Entente between Great Britain, France, and Russia was not stable.

In the spring of 1915 *La Stampa,* the great Giolittian newspaper, let it be understood that Italy's real hope for the future would consist in an Anglo-German-Italian agreement. Italy, as long as she could, would have to move between Great Britain and Germany.

Certainly, for the moment at least, it was hard to separate Germany from Austria-Hungary. Giolitti felt that hostility against Austria-Hungary would automatically mean hostility against Germany, and this seemed to him a very strong argument in favour of neutrality. But at moments Giolitti appeared to share the idea that Germany would leave Austria at her hour of need to her own destiny and that Italy could declare war against Austria with Germany's agreement or connivance. Just as in May 1915, one of his followers was later to reveal, Giolitti still hoped that some secret factor would be found which could justify the government's decision—that secret factor being an agreement with Germany at Austria-Hungary's expense. Giolitti considered that Italy was still too weak, and that one had to weigh things carefully before exposing her to war.

In January 1915 Giolitti published a famous letter, in which he declared himself in favour of negotiations with Vienna. Giolitti, as usual, was thinking of Trentino, of part of Venezia-Giulia, of Trieste Free City—all territories he seriously wanted to obtain. 'If the war ends without our gaining any advantage there will be trouble. Even present neutralists will throw stones,' he confided to his friends.

Giolitti was a relative neutralist; and so, in the main, were the business community and the organized Catholics. So too was the Holy See, which took it for granted that Italy should obtain part of the unredeemed territory from Austria—otherwise intervention was inevitable. Such was the predominant mood in Italy.

The popular parties and intervention
No serious guarantee of neutrality was possible. The PSI, a number of Syndicalists, and Anarchists tried to ensure it, but in vain. The masses, in particular the large peasant masses, were calm. As many Prefects reported, they were quite resigned. In the event of intervention against Austria-Hungary, there would be no serious disorders.

The defence of neutrality did not allow any effective political initiative. Many revolutionaries (Socialists, Republicans, Anarchists, and Syndicalists) were soon convinced of this. Benito Mussolini, editor of the Socialist newspaper *Avanti!,* was one of these.

Those of the revolutionaries who favoured intervention on the side of the Entente powers considered that, from the beginning, the government's position of neutrality had been equivocal. The parties of order, they thought, were beating about the bush, were still aiming at some kind of compromise with the feudal authoritarian Central powers. The revolutionary interventionists felt that the war was a 'revolution of the people'—against the establishment, against the old ruling class, against the monarchy, and for a revolutionary cause and for international democracy. They wanted to bring to a happy end the *Risorgimento* (the 19th-century

The debates of the politicians ended.
For thousands of Italians it meant farewell to their families and off to the war

wars in which Italy threw off the Austrian yoke), and secure the triumph of a vague 'proletarian nationalism'.

In reality there was a great deal of confusion in these ideas. Popular leaders like Bissolati, Salvemini, and Battisti tried to clarify the situation. They were the leaders of another form of interventionism, which was openly democratic. They wanted to see the disappearance of Austria-Hungary and the triumph of the principle of 'nationality'. Intervention, participation in the 'democratic war', had, they thought, become a duty as well as a necessity. But they failed to convince even all their own followers; and they succeeded even less in convincing the parties of order.

In fact, as when Italy declared herself neutral, in August, the final word was again left to the government, which had to resolve the dilemma: negotiations with Austria or an 'Italian war'.

Giolitti was in agreement; but this time he had committed two errors: he had not taken into account Austria-Hungary's habit of always arriving 'an hour late' at the appointments of history. Furthermore, he had not fully realized what leaving a free hand to the government in power, principally to the key men, might involve—particularly when the key men were men like Salandra and Sonnino, who became foreign minister in November 1914, after

San Giuliano's death. The consequences of these two errors, when added to one another, were irreparable. Salandra and Sonnino, of course, started serious negotiations in Vienna, and also in Rome with Bülow, the former German chancellor. But when Austria hesitated and procrastinated about considering territorial concessions, Salandra and Sonnino, much more readily than Giolitti, embraced the idea of war. Salandra and Sonnino were not warmongers; they suppressed mass demonstrations of the interventionists. But as good Liberal-Conservatives they reasoned differently from Giolitti. In Italy they thought there was a need to reinforce the authority of the state, to strengthen traditional institutions, to improve the prestige of both crown and army. A victorious war—which, as many thought at the time, would last six months or a year at the most—could be just what was needed.

At the beginning of March they opened negotiations with the Entente powers; on 26th April 1915 they signed the Treaty of London. Sonnino, who in 1914 had so decisively supported intervention on the side of Austria-Hungary and Germany, had now taken the plunge. But he did not abandon all his ideas. By the treaty Italy was to obtain south Tyrol (Trentino), Trieste, Venezia-Giulia, and northern Dalmatia together with several islands, in order to guarantee Italian supremacy in the Adriatic against the Slavs. In short, the treaty corresponded to the 'Italian War' concept. Moreover, the treaty did not say in so many words that relations with Germany would irreparably be broken off. At least that is what Salandra and Sonnino relied on. And it was not to be until the middle of 1916 that Italy declared war against Germany.

Nevertheless, there was more than enough in this treaty to trouble Giolitti and the majority of Liberals and Catholics. When the news broke there were also several Liberal-Conservatives who thought that Salandra and Sonnino had jumped the gun. Giolitti returned to Rome, and soon afterwards, on 13th May, the ministry resigned.

It was the last but one act of the drama. Salandra and Sonnino were really quite willing to cede power or to accept Giolitti's advice: to re-open negotiations with Vienna. They interpreted the Treaty of London as an agreement between governments and not between states, especially as military plans were still unsettled. And the recent Austro-German victory at Gorlice-Tarnów (2nd May) caused anxiety. But it was now too late to reappraise the situation.

Passions had been roused little by little; interventionists, once united, organized demonstration after demonstration at which d'Annunzio made his inspiring calls

to rebellion, to war, and to violence; the neutralists, uncertain and passive, were as usual not keeping up with events. Giolitti himself did not want to take back the reins of power. The situation was getting too hot to handle, and the risk of failure after having advised resumption of negotiations, was too great.

Italy declares war

The King had, meanwhile, refused to accept the resignation of the Salandra ministry. On the 24th May 1915 Italy entered the war against Austria-Hungary, Salandra invoking what he called *sacro egoismo*—the sacred demands of self-interest—to justify this action. But the situation was by no means clear. The old ruling class was by now split. The interventionists once again started squabbling among themselves. The Socialists had lost the initiative. Economic preparations were inadequate, and were arranged from day to day. Moreover, the country in a large measure was passive. This assuredly was not a good start for the terrible ordeal to come.

Foreign policy encountered far more serious difficulties. During the negotiations with Austria-Hungary, and during those which led up to the Treaty of London, the aims of national unity for the 'unredeemed territories' had certainly established the directive throughout. But between *realpolitik* and nationalism the liberal aim of the 19th century had now dispersed itself. In 1914-15 the myth of the 'last war of the *Risorgimento*' was still alive, but had little or at least only indirect, influence on the ruling classes.

What is more, with Italy's intervention, the problem created by the Habsburgs' rule over many widely differing nationalities had been put into the 'melting pot'. But Italy, under the Treaty of London, could not co-operate with the other oppressed nationalities of the Habsburg empire. The possibilities of a happy solution were more remote than ever.

The army was also in difficulties. Much money had been spent on it, but military preparations had followed old-fashioned methods. Moreover—it is the only conclusion which could be deduced from the fighting which had already taken place in the war—tactical and strategic plans were based on the theory that frontal attack on the enemy troops would be the best method of fighting. The battles and the massacres of the Isonzo were not far off. That the chief of staff, the army commander in the war, should be the very same Cadorna who in July 1914 had made the suggestion that half the Italian army should be mobilized on the Rhine against France, seemed at the moment only an ironical symbol of the troubled thinking which had led Italy into the war.

The Dardanelles Campaign

It is doubtful whether any single campaign of either of the two World Wars has aroused more attention and controversy than the ill-fated venture to force the Dardanelles in 1915. 'Nothing so distorted perspective, disturbed impartial judgement, and impaired the sense of strategic values as the operations on Gallipoli,' Sir Edward Grey has written. Lord Slim—who fought at Gallipoli, and was seriously wounded—has described the Gallipoli commanders in scathing terms as the worst since the Crimean War. The defenders of the enterprise—notably Winston Churchill, Sir Roger Keyes, and General Sir Ian Hamilton—have been no less vehement and there have been other commentators who have thrown a romantic pall over the campaign. 'The drama of the Gallipoli campaign,' wrote the British official historian, 'by reason of the beauty of its setting, the grandeur of its theme, and the unhappiness of its ending, will always rank amongst the world's classic tragedies.' He then went on to quote Aeschylus's words: 'What need to repine at fortune's frowns? The gain hath the advantage, and the loss does not bear down the scale.'

Today, more than fifty years later, the Gallipoli controversies still rumble sulphurously, and the passions that the campaign aroused have not yet been stilled.

Amateurs in council

Few major campaigns have been initiated under stranger circumstances. The opening months of the war had imposed a strain upon the Liberal government from which it never really recovered. Asquith's leadership at the outbreak of war had been firm and decisive, but subsequently—whether from ill-health, as has been recently suggested by Lord Salter, or from other causes is immaterial in this narrative—his influence had been flaccid and irresolute. The creation of a War Council in November had not met the essential problem; the council met irregularly, its Service members were silent, and its manner of doing business was amateurish and unimpressive. As Winston Churchill commented in a memorandum circulated in July 1915: 'The governing instrument here has been unable to make up its mind except by very lengthy processes of argument and exhaustion, and that the divisions of opinion to be overcome, and the number of persons of consequence to be convinced, caused delays and compromises. We have always sent two-thirds of what was necessary a month too late.'

The military situation itself played a crucial part in what developed. The first fury of the war had been spent, and the opposing lines writhed from the Channel to the Swiss frontier; Russia had reeled back from her advance on East Prussia; everywhere, the belligerents had failed to secure their primary objectives. Already, the character of the battle on the Western Front had become grimly evident, and by the end of 1914 Churchill (first lord of the Admiralty), Lord Fisher (first sea lord), Lloyd George (chancellor of the exchequer), and Sir Maurice Hankey (secretary to the War Council) were thinking in terms of using British force—and particularly sea power—in another sphere.

It was Churchill who emerged with the most attractive proposal. Since the early weeks of the war his restlessness had been unconcealed, and he had already proposed, at the first meeting of the War Council on 25th November, a naval attack on the Dardanelles, with the ultimate object of destroying the German warships, *Goeben* and *Breslau,* whose escape from British squadrons in the Mediterranean in August had been a decisive factor in bringing Turkey into the war at the beginning of November on the side of the Germans. The suggestion had been shelved, but the idea had been put forward, and Hankey is not alone in stressing the significance of this first airing of the plan.

Impatience with the lack of progress on the Western Front was now buttressed by an appeal from Russia for a 'demonstration' against Turkey, after a large Turkish army had advanced into the Caucasus. (By the time the appeal was received, the Turks had been defeated, but this was not known for some time in London.) Churchill at once revived the idea of an assault on the Dardanelles, and telegraphed to the British admiral—Carden—in command of the squadron standing off the western entrance of the Dardanelles about the possibilities of a purely naval assault. Admiral Carden replied cautiously to the effect that a gradual attack might succeed; Churchill pushed the issue, and Carden was instructed to submit his detailed plans; when these arrived, Churchill put the matter before the War Council.

The extent to which Churchill's service colleagues at the Admiralty were alarmed at this speed was not communicated to the ministers on the council, a fact which to a large degree absolves them from their collective responsibility. Churchill's account was brilliant and exciting, and on 15th January the War Council agreed that 'the Admiralty should prepare for a naval ex-

Top: Assault by British Royal Naval Division on the Turkish lines. Above: HMS Cornwallis in action

pedition in February to bombard and take the Gallipoli peninsula, with Constantinople as its object'. Churchill took this as a definite decision; Asquith, however, considered that it was 'merely provisional, to prepare, but nothing more'; Admiral Sir Arthur Wilson, a member of the council, subsequently said that 'it was not my business. I was not in any way connected with the question, and it had never in any way officially been put before me'. Churchill's naval secretary considered that the naval members of the council 'only agreed to a purely naval operation on the understanding that we could always draw back – that there should be no question of what is known as forcing the Dardanelles'. Fisher, by this stage, was very alarmed indeed.

Quite apart from the matter of whether the navy had sufficient reserve of men and ships – even old ships, which was a major part of Churchill's scheme – to afford such an operation, the forcing of the Dardanelles had for long been regarded with apprehension by the navy, and Churchill himself had written in 1911 that 'it should be remembered that it is no longer possible to force the Dardanelles, and nobody would expose a modern fleet to such peril'. But Churchill – as his evidence to the Dardanelles Commission, only recently available for examination, clearly reveals – had been profoundly impressed by the effects of German artillery bombardments on the Belgian forts, and it was evident that the Turkish batteries were conspicuously sited, exposed, and equipped with obsolete equipment. And Churchill was not alone in rating Turkish military competence low. The admirals' doubts were put aside, Fisher swallowed his misgivings, and Carden prepared for the assault.

All this represented a considerable

achievement for Churchill. There is no doubt that he forced the pace, that the initiative was solely his, and that his subsequent account in *The World Crisis* must be approached with great caution. A case in point is his version of the negotiations to persuade Lord Kitchener (secretary of state for war) to release the Regular 29th Division for the Eastern Mediterranean. The recently revealed minutes of the War Council make it plain that Churchill had no intention of using the troops for the attack on the Dardanelles, but to employ them subsequently 'to reinforce our diplomacy' and garrison Constantinople. It was not surprising that Kitchener did not agree to send the division until March 10th.

The plans for the naval attack continued, and the British and Dominion (Australian and New Zealand) troops in Egypt were put on the alert. Carden opened his attack on 19th February, and had no difficulty in suppressing the outer forts at Sedd-el-Bahr and Kum Kale. The difficulties really began when the warships entered the Straits.

The intermediate and inner defences consisted of gun emplacements on the Gallipoli and Asiatic shores. These were supplemented by batteries capable of causing damage only to lightly armoured ships, and by mobile batteries. The Straits had been mined since the beginning of the war, but it was only in February and March that the lines of mines represented a serious menace. The attempts of the British minesweepers – East Coast fishing trawlers manned by civilian crews and commanded by a naval officer with no experience whatever of minesweeping – ended in complete failure. Marines went ashore at Kum Kale and Sedd-el-Bahr on several occasions, but early in March the resistance to these operations increased sharply.

Bad weather made the tasks of the warships and the hapless trawlers – barely able to make headway against the fierce Dardanelles current, operating under fire in wholly unfamiliar circumstances – even more difficult. Carden was an ailing man. The warships – with the exception of the brand-new battleship *Queen Elizabeth* – were old and in many cases in need of a refit. The standard of the officers was mixed. The Turkish resistance was more strenuous with every day that passed. The momentum of the advance faltered.

Urged on by Churchill, Carden decided to reverse his tactics; the fleet would silence the guns to allow the sweepers to clear the minefields. On the eve of the attack Carden collapsed and was replaced by Rear-Admiral Robeck.

By now, the soldiers were on the scene. Lieutenant-General Birdwood, a former military secretary to Kitchener now commanding the Anzacs in Egypt, had been sent by Kitchener to the Dardanelles to report on the situation. His reports were to the effect that military support was essential. Slowly a military force was gathered together, and General Sir Ian Hamilton was appointed commander-in-chief of what was called the Mediterranean Expeditionary Force, and which consisted at that moment of some 70,000 British, Dominion, and French troops. Hamilton was informed of his new appointment on 12th March; he left the next day – Friday, 13th March – with a scratch staff hastily gathered together, a series of instructions from Kitchener, and some meagre scraps of information about the area and the Turks. He arrived just in time for the *débâcle* of 18th March. Robeck lost three battleships sunk, and three crippled, out of nine; the minefields had not been touched.

Much ink has subsequently been spilled on the subject of what Robeck ought to have done. He did not know, of course, that the Turkish lack of heavy shells made their situation desperate. Even if he had, the fact remained that it was the mobile and minor batteries that were holding up the minesweepers. Roger Keyes's plan of using destroyers as minesweepers and storming the minefields was the only one that had a real chance of success, and it would have taken some time to prepare them.

The soldiers, however, were very willing to take over. On 22nd March Hamilton and Robeck agreed on a combined operation, and Hamilton sailed off to Alexandria to re-organize his scattered forces. 'No formal decision to make a land attack was even noted in the records of the Cabinet or the War Council,' as Churchill has written. '. . . This silent plunge into this vast military venture must be regarded as an extraordinary episode.' It was, however, no more extraordinary than the events that had

Hamilton – 'He should have really taken command, which he has never yet done'

Liman von Sanders – he committed several major errors which might have been fatal

The landing at Suvla Bay, Gallipoli, 1915, painted by subaltern R.C.Lewis during the action, using the dye from cigarette packets

preceded the crucial conference of 22nd March. Attempts by Hankey to obtain better information and an agreed assessment of the situation made no progress. 'The military operation appears, therefore, to be to a certain extent a gamble upon the supposed shortage of supplies and inferior fighting qualities of the Turkish armies,' he wrote in one of a series of prescient memoranda. But the War Council did not meet from the middle of March until two months later.

What subsequently happened was the direct result of the manner in which the British drifted haphazardly into a highly difficult amphibious operation. No calculation had been made of whether the British had the resources to undertake this operation. As Hankey wrote at the end of March: 'Up to the present time . . . no attempt has been made to estimate what force is required. We have merely said that so many troops are available and that they ought to be enough.' The state of affairs was subsequently well summarized by Sir William Robertson: 'The Secretary of State for War was aiming for decisive results on the Western Front. The First Lord of the Admiralty was advocating a military expedition to the Dardanelles. The Secretary of State for India was devoting his attention to a campaign in Mesopotamia. The Secretary of State for the Colonies was occupying himself with several small wars in Africa. And the Chancellor of the Exchequer was attempting to secure the removal of a large part of the British army from France to some Eastern Mediterranean theatre.'

One can sympathize with the cry of the GOC Egypt, Sir John Maxwell: 'Who is co-ordinating and directing this great combine?'

Furthermore, there was divided command in the eastern Mediterranean. Maxwell was in command in Egypt; Hamilton had his army; Robeck his ships. Before the campaign ended, there were further complications. Each commander fought for his own force and his own projects, and the limited supplies of men and material were distributed on an *ad hoc* and unco-ordinated basis.

To all these difficulties, Hamilton added some of his own. His refusal to bring his administrative staff into the initial planning – and, indeed, into anything at all so long as he was commander-in-chief – had some easily foreseeable results. Security was non-existent. 'The attack was heralded as few have ever been,' the Australian military historian has written. 'No condition designed to proclaim it seems to have been omitted.' This was not Hamilton's fault, yet his protests were wholly ineffective.

His plan for landing on Gallipoli – Asia he ruled out entirely, over the strong arguments of Birdwood and Hunter-Weston, commanding the 29th Division – was imaginative and daring. The 29th Division was to land at five small beaches at the southern end of the peninsula; the Anzacs were to land farther to the north on the western shore, just above the jutting promontory of Gaba Tepe, and then to push overland to the eminence of Mal Tepe, overlooking the narrows. There were to be feint landings at Bulair, at the 'neck' of the peninsula, and (by the French) at Besika Bay, opposite the island of Tenedos. The French were also to make a real, but temporary, landing at Kum Kale, to protect the landing of the 29th Division.

Meanwhile, the Turks had been having their own problems. Until March the Turkish forces in the area had been scattered and few in number. In spite of the urgency of the situation, the Turks acted lethargically. When, on the morning of 26th March, General Liman von Sanders arrived to take command of the troops at the Dardanelles, the situation that faced him was grim indeed. In short, his task was to defend a coast-line of some 150 miles with a total force of 84,000 men, but an actual fighting strength of only about 62,000. His army had no aircraft, and was seriously deficient in artillery and equipment. The men themselves, for so long used to defeat, were the despair of the German officers, and it would have been difficult to see in these poorly equipped and ragged formations the army that was to rise to such heights of valour and resource.

Sanders has been fortunate to have been treated at his own valuation by the majority of British commentators. In fact, he committed several major errors which might have been fatal. He placed two divisions at the neck of the peninsula, two on the Asiatic shore, one to defend the entire southern Gallipoli peninsula, and a final division in reserve near Mal Tepe. The entire area south of the bald, dominant height of Achi Baba was defended by one regiment and one field battery, with the reserves placed several hours' marching away to the north. To the dismay of the Turkish officers, Sanders drew his forces back from the beaches and concentrated them inland. This, the Turks argued, overlooked the fact that on the whole of the peninsula there were barely half a dozen beaches on which the British could land; Sanders, like Hamilton, over-estimated the effects of naval bombardment on well dug-in troops. He was saved by the epic courage of the Turkish troops, good luck, and mismanagement by the enemy from losing the entire campaign on the first day.

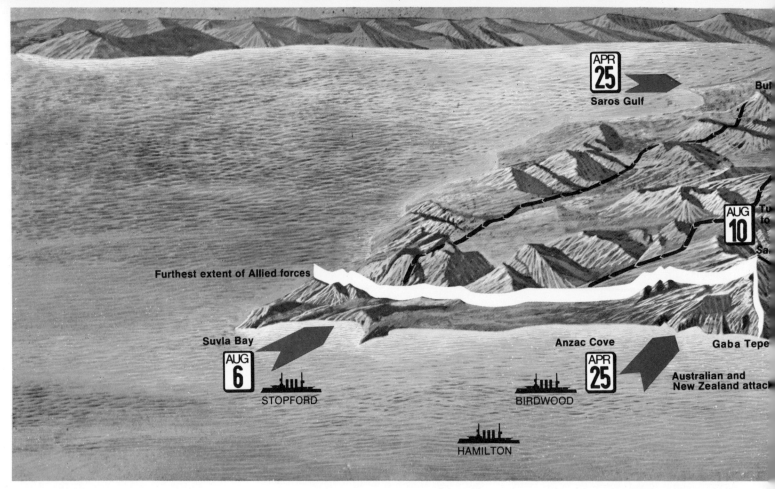

APR 25 Saros Gulf

AUG 10

Furthest extent of Allied forces

Suvla Bay

AUG 6 STOPFORD

Anzac Cove

APR 25 BIRDWOOD

Gaba Tepe

Australian and New Zealand attac

HAMILTON

The Gallipoli peninsula, seen from the west. On the map are marked the naval attack on 18th March, the landings on 25th April, the landing at Suvla Bay on 6th August, and the farthest extent of the Allied advances. The broken black lines show the direction of the Turkish thrusts against the Allies. The generals directed operations from ships offshore

It is impossible, even now, to contemplate the events of 25th April 1915, without emotion. The British and Dominion troops sailed from Mudros Harbour, in the island of Lemnos, in a blaze of excitement and ardour. 'Courage our youth will always have,' Lord Slim has written, 'but those young men had a vision strangely medieval, never, I think, to be renewed.' It was the baptism of fire for the Anzacs. It was also, in a real sense, the day on which Turkey began her emergence as a modern nation.

Three of the British landings at Helles were virtually unopposed. One was resisted, but the enemy defeated. But the fifth, at Sedd-el-Bahr, was a catastrophe. As the British came ashore, a torrent of fire was poured upon them as they waded through the water or sat helplessly jammed in open boats; others who attempted to land from a converted collier, the *River Clyde,* fared no better. In this crisis Hunter-Weston did not show himself to advantage. He was in a cruiser, barely five minutes' sailing from the disastrous beach, yet it was not until the day was well advanced that he was aware of what had occurred. The day ended with the British, exhausted and shaken, clinging to their positions.

The Anzacs had had a day of very mixed fortunes. They had been landed over a mile to the north of their intended position, in some confusion, to be faced with precipitous

cliffs and plunging, scrub-covered gorges. As the first men moved inland, congestion built up at the tiny beach—Anzac Cove—which had to cope with all reinforcements and supplies. Only one battery of field artillery was landed all day, and units became hopelessly intermingled. As in the south, the maps were dangerously inaccurate. By mid-morning the Turks had begun to counter-attack and, spurred on by the then unknown Colonel Mustapha Kemal, these attacks developed in fury throughout the day. By evening, the Anzacs were pushed back to a firing-line which extended only a thousand yards inland at the farthest point; casualties had been heavy, and Birdwood's divisional commanders advised evacuation. In the event, although Birdwood reluctantly agreed, Hamilton ordered him to hang on. This was virtually the only initiative taken by Hamilton—on board the *Queen Elizabeth*—throughout the day. As Birdwood wrote—some months later, 'he should have taken much more personal charge and *insisted* on things being done and really taken command, which he has never yet done'. Thus began the epic defence of Anzac, a fragment of cliff and gorge, overlooked by the enemy.

Hamilton pressed on at Helles, but although a limited advance was made, it was apparent by 8th May that the initial effort of his troops was spent. Casualties had been horrific—over 20,000 (of whom over 6,000 had been killed) out of a total force of 70,000—and the medical and supply arrangements had completely collapsed under the wholly unexpected demands. The arrival of a German submarine and the sinking of three battleships—one by a Turkish torpedo-boat attack—deprived the army of the physical and psychological sup-

port of the guns of the fleet. Thus ended the first phase of the Gallipoli Campaign.

A week later the Liberal government fell, the first major casualty of the campaign, although there were other important contributory causes. Asquith formed a new coalition government in which Balfour, the former Conservative leader, replaced Churchill as first lord of the Admiralty. An inner cabinet, from 7th June called the Dardanelles Committee, took over the conduct of operations, and a ministry of munitions was established. The new government resolved to support Hamilton, and more troops were dispatched. Hamilton continued to batter away at Helles throughout May and July until, in the memorable words of a British corporal, the battlefield 'looked like a midden and smelt like an opened cemetery'. Achi Baba still stood defiantly uncaptured, and the army was incapable of further sustained effort. To the shelling, the heat, and the harsh life of the trenches was now added the scourge of dysentery.

Hamilton now swung his assault north. A daring scheme for capturing the commanding heights of the Sari Bair range had been worked out at Anzac. Unfortunately, as in April, other schemes were added to this basic project, until it developed into a joint operation as complex and dangerous as the first. The Anzacs, with British and Indian reinforcements, would break out of the Anzac position to the north, and scale the incredibly tangled gullies and ridges to the summit of the Sari Bair range by night after diversionary attacks at the south of the Anzac position and at Helles. At dawn on 6th August, a new Army Corps would be landed in Suvla Bay, which was thought to be sparsely defended and which lay to the north of Anzac, and,

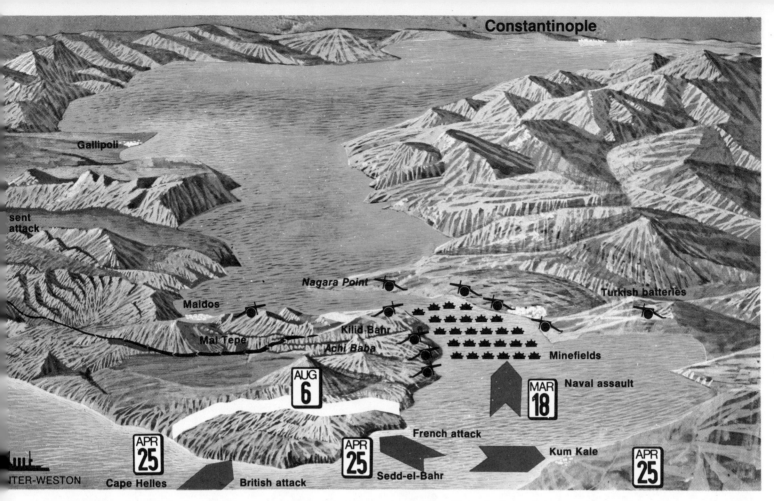

Constantinople

Gallipoli

sent attack

Nagara Point

Maidos

Turkish batteries

Mai Tepe

Kilid Bahr

Achi Baba

Minefields

AUG 6

MAR 18 — Naval assault

APR 25

Cape Helles

APR 25

British attack

French attack

Sedd-el-Bahr

Kum Kale

APR 25

ITER-WESTON

at first light, the Turkish positions at Anzac would be assaulted from front and rear. Some 63,000 Allied troops would be attacking an area defended by well under 30,000 Turks.

This time, the veil of secrecy that descended on the operation was so complete that senior commanders were not informed until very late. Sir Frederick Stopford, the commander of the 9th Corps, which was to land at Suvla, was allowed to amend his instructions so that his task was merely to get ashore and capture the bay. There was no co-ordination between General Stopford and Birdwood at Anzac, either before or during the action. Hamilton stayed at his headquarters for two vital days.

In the circumstances, the marvel was that the operation came so close to success. Sanders, once again, was outwitted by Hamilton. The night march from Anzac was a chaotic and frightening business, but by dawn on August 7th the New Zealanders were within a fraction of seizing the vital summit. The Suvla landing, although opposed by small units and something of a shambles in other respects, was successful. By the morning of August 7th the Turkish situation at Sari Bair was desperate, but the heat, the exhaustion and inexperience of the British, and dilatoriness by their commanders, saved Sanders; the Turks, as always, fought with frenzy and unheeding valour. It developed into a weird, ghastly battle. At Suvla, 9th Corps remained glued to the shore, and advanced only with timidity. At Anzac, the failures in advance planning and command meant that everything depended on the courage and initiative of the troops and their immediate officers; neither were lacking, and the fighting was intensely bitter, even by Gallipoli standards; but they were insufficient. Sanders gave

command of the entire area to Kemal, who checked the British at Suvla just as they were making a positive forward movement on the urgent commands of Hamilton, and at Sari Bair he launched a desperate attack at first light on August 10th that swept the Allies from the positions that had been won and held at a severely high cost. One British officer, commanding men of the 1/6th Gurkhas, had a glimpse of the Dardanelles.

The rest was aftermath. Hamilton launched one last abortive attack at Suvla which was in terms of numbers the biggest battle of the campaign, but the issue had already been decided. At home, the many opponents of the venture became more vociferous and urgent; a new army was sent to Salonika; the Gallipoli fronts subsided into trench warfare; the weather got colder, and the decision of Bulgaria to enter the war meant that Austrian guns began to shell the exposed British lines with a new accuracy. In October Hamilton was recalled. His successor was Sir Charles Monro, a man of a very different stamp, who recommended evacuation. Bluntly faced with the grim implications, the government became irresolute again. Kitchener went out to investigate, and was eventually persuaded of the necessity of withdrawal. Birdwood was in charge of the evacuation of Suvla and Anzac, which was brilliantly conducted, without a single casualty, on 19th-20th December.

The evacuation of Helles was now inevitable, and this was accomplished on 8th-9th January, again without loss of men, although that of stores and equipment was extensive. Thus, the campaign ended with a substantial triumph, an indication of what might have been achieved earlier.

The casualties were substantial. The

first was the Asquith government, and, in particular, Churchill, whose removal from the Admiralty in May was a *sine qua non* for Conservative participation in the new coalition; it was many years before the shadow of Gallipoli was lifted from his reputation. Asquith's own prestige and position were badly shaken, as were those of Kitchener. The dream of a Balkan alliance against Germany was shattered, and Italy was the only Mediterranean nation that—in mid-May—joined the Allied cause. The British had acquired another vast commitment in Salonika. The Russian warm-sea outlet was irretrievably blocked. Compared with this last strategical disaster, the actual losses in battle or through disease—which are difficult to calculate on the Allied side but which were certainly over 200,000 (the Turkish are unknown, but must have been considerably greater, with a higher proportion of dead)—were perhaps of lesser significance. But, at the time, these loomed largest of all, and what appeared to many to be the futility of such sacrifice when the real battle was being fought almost within sight of the shores of Great Britain had an enduring effect. On 28th December the cabinet formally resolved that the Western Front would be the decisive theatre of the war. The stage was set for the vast killing-matches to come.

Had it all been loss? The enterprise came near to success on several occasions, but it is questionable whether even the capture of Gallipoli and the Straits would have had the decisive effects that appeared at the time. The entire operation grimly justified words written by Lloyd George before it had even been seriously considered: 'Expeditions which are decided upon and organised with insufficient care generally end disastrously.'

1915: Disasters for the Allies

A majority of the Allied leaders, both military and political, suffered in the opening months of 1915 from the delusion that the war would be won that year.

The generals, British and French, believed that this victory would follow from a reversion to 'open' warfare. They had seen their enemy elude them (as it appeared) by 'digging in' after the battle of the Marne. If the key could be found to unlock this barrier the character of the fighting would alter, and the Allies would have the advantage.

The first of these propositions is incontestable, the second highly dubious. The science of military analysis was not much heeded by the French generals, still less by the British, both preferring the doctrine of their own infallibility—which was good for morale. It seems that they interpreted the German adoption of trench warfare as an admission of weakness, a form of cowardice it could be said, by an enemy who feared the outcome of a 'real' battle. It is probable also that they drew encouragement from the east, where a combination of space, limited firepower, and enormous bodies of cavalry endowed the campaign with the appearance of something in a different epoch from that of the close-fought positional battles in the west.

But if the setting was different, the principles of grand strategy were immutable, and in due course the Russians had been caught by their application. The bloody defeat of Samsonov's army at Tannenberg effectively halted the Russian steamroller, and eliminated the threat to East Prussia. Furthermore, it showed to Falkenhayn, the chief of the German general staff, that although the Schlieffen plan had failed its purpose might still be attained because the scale of forces needed to defeat the Tsar was not—on account of the tactical clumsiness and ineptitude of the Russian commanders—irreconcilable with an active, though necessarily defensive, Western Front.

Accordingly, in his appreciation for 1915, Falkenhayn recommended a defensive posture in France and concentration of strength in the east. After some vacillation the Kaiser had agreed and the necessary redeployment (which also entailed taking divisions from Hindenburg and Ludendorff in Silesia) was put in motion. Headquarters, and the imperial train, moved to the east, carrying the German centre of gravity with it.

All this took time, and during those weeks the southern wing of the Russian armies continued to batter away at the Austro-Hungarians, taking the famous fortress town of Przemyśl in March. Friction began to develop between the German commanders. Ludendorff had his own, more radical scheme for defeating the Russians by a wide outflanking stroke from the north, and resented being held in check while Falkenhayn concentrated for a direct approach on the Galician front.

To the Allies, therefore, appearance augured better than reality. The Germans appeared to be standing on the defensive in France from fear of their opponent, while in the east they were still in retreat. Considerations of grand strategy vied with those of national—and personal—prestige to make a Western contribution to this giant 'pincer' urgently desirable.

Joffre was intending to mount the French offensive in May. But there were private reasons which made the British commanders in the field keen to stage a 'demonstration' at a much earlier date. Lord Kitchener, the secretary of state (who enjoyed poor relations with the commander of the British Expeditionary Force, Sir John French), favoured using the new units which had been formed during the winter for an amphibious assault on Ostend and Zeebrugge in Belgium. Both Sir John, and Douglas Haig, his subordinate, saw that this would entail restricting the size and resources of the BEF—perhaps indefinitely—in favour of a new army which would come under the command of Kitchener or his nominee. Accordingly they planned to attack the enemy themselves as soon as weather permitted.

The area selected was the German salient which protruded around the village of Neuve-Chapelle. It was lightly defended, by some six companies who disposed of twelve machine-guns between them, set out in a line of shallow sand-bag breastworks (the ground was too waterlogged for a proper trench system). Against this 'position'—in effect little more than a screen—Haig threw no fewer than forty-eight battalions supported by sixty batteries of field artillery, and a hundred and twenty heavy siege pieces. In several places the attackers broke right through, into open country—a feat which they were not to repeat for two and a half years. But the expected 'open' warfare never materialized. To hesitant leadership, at every level, was added poor communications and a cumbersome chain of command.

During the night the troops who had broken through milled about aimlessly on the edge of certain natural barriers that were very lightly held by some scratch

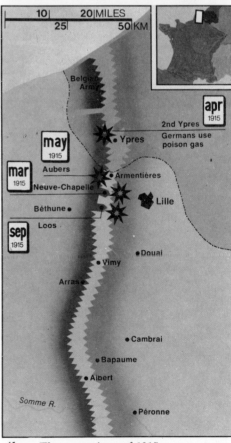

Above: The campaigns of 1915. In the west it was a story of failed offensives, and in the east of massive German victories and advances. *Left:* Two French grenadiers wearing gas masks. Poison gas, used for the first time this year, had added a new horror to warfare

groups of enemy infantry, in the belief that it was the German 'second line'. In fact, the Germans had no second line, but they energetically improvised one, with two companies of bicycle-mounted sharpshooters, during the early hours of the morning. On the second day less than a dozen machine-guns held up the whole British army, whose artillery had practically no ammunition left to deal with them. However, the British numerical superiority was still more than seven to one and Haig, the army commander, ordered that 'attacks are to be pressed regardless of loss'. Loss, not surprisingly, was the only result.

The battle of Neuve-Chapelle exemplifies the way in which the relation of attack to defence remained constant – though the degree of force applied on either side was to escalate violently throughout the war. Ammunition shortage had lulled the Germans into underestimating the power of the British artillery, hence their feeble, lightly-manned defence works. If the British had disposed of the firepower which the French enjoyed they might well have broken through at their second attempt; if the German line had included the deep concrete *Wohngraben* shelters which they began hastily to dig after digesting the shock of the Neuve-Chapelle attack, the British would never have got across no man's land – as was to be painfully demonstrated in the Aubers offensive two months later. In point of fact the two forces remained in balance (which meant of course that the defence prevailed) all the way up to the ten-day barrages and concrete pill-box chains of Passchendaele in November of 1917.

Both sides drew their conclusions from the failure to exploit the initial breakthrough at Neuve-Chapelle. Falkenhayn expressed the view that 'the English troops, in spite of undeniable bravery and endurance on the part of the men, have proved so clumsy in action that they offer no prospect of accomplishing anything decisive against the German Army in the immediate future'.

But the British staff took a different view. A GHQ memorandum, dated the 18th April, concludes the 'lessons' of Neuve-Chapelle with the assertion that '. . . by means of careful preparation as regards details it appears that a section of the enemy's front line can be captured with comparatively little loss'.

And this was a judgement which Joffre regarded as needlessly conservative. Of his own prospects, he confided to Sir Henry Wilson (the liaison officer at French HQ) that 'he was bringing up even more troops and really thought he would break the line past mending, and that it might be, and ought to be, the beginning of the end'.

The new German soldier. A cartoon drawn by Raemaekers in 1915, shortly after the experimental poison gas attack at Ypres

Poison gas

Meanwhile, time was running out for the Russian armies in south Poland, as Falkenhayn gradually accumulated fresh German divisions behind the depleted Austrian line in readiness for his counter-offensive. The Germans planned to reinforce their local numerical superiority (fourteen divisions against two) by tactical surprise (the use of a new weapon – poison gas). However, the commanders responsible for mounting the gas attack had insisted that the new weapon should first be tried under actual battle conditions, and it was decided to stage the dress rehearsal in the west.

The area selected was a quiet four-mile stretch of front at the northern corner of the Ypres salient. The line was held by French colonial troops whose erratic tactics and discipline had been a source of friction between the British and French commanders for some weeks. Ill-fitted to resist a determined conventional attack, they collapsed immediately under the impact of this new and frightening weapon. This time it was the Germans who broke right through the trench line (they, too,

would have to wait almost three years before they could repeat the performance) and it was their turn to be surprised by the opportunity which offered. The gas had been used without any particular objective, even at tactical level, in mind. The German Corps commander quickly tried to improvise an operation which might pinch out the whole Ypres salient from the north, but he was frustrated by his own meagre resources and by the extraordinary heroism of small detachments of Canadian and British troops who placed themselves across his advance.

Once the German impetus had died away Sir John French staged a series of ill-managed and extravagant counter-attacks against the new enemy positions (the British troops were told to protect themselves against gas by dipping their handkerchiefs in a solution of water and Boric acid, and tying them across their mouths). These achieved little except the destruction of two brigades of the Indian army and the dismissal of Sir Horace Smith-Dorrien, the first – and last – senior commander to protest against the cost in casualties of repetitive frontal attacks.

The experience of 'Second Ypres' (as the April battles in the salient were called) confirmed the lesson that the fighting soldier was fatally vulnerable to accurate – but remote – artillery and isolated machine-gunners under conditions of 'open' warfare. In fact, his only defence was to dig, as fast and as deep as he could. But the senior Allied commanders continued to regard a break-up of the trench system as their goal, and held the view that this could be attained by the application of the same formula; though in heavier and heavier concentrations. In any case it was now too late to alter the plans for the next British offensive, to be launched against the Aubers ridge on the 9th May, timed to coincide with Joffre's own, delayed, attack farther to the south.

This time the British artillery was weaker than at Neuve-Chapelle, the German defences stronger. As the first wave went over the top the Germans were amazed to see that '. . . there could never before in war have been a more perfect target than this solid wall of khaki men side-by-side. There was only one possible order to give – "Fire! Until the barrels burst!"' The attack was stopped dead. But the men who had been moved up to 'exploit' it now congested the forward trenches, and they too were ordered to attack – in exactly the same place, and with the same result. There could be no thought of working round the enemy flank. It was a point of honour to advance directly on to his guns. Two days later there were no shells left, and very few men. In some gloom (and unusual candour) an officer at Haig's headquarters wrote that '. . . Our attack has failed, and failed badly, and with heavy casualties. That is the bald and most unpleasant fact.'

Soon after the failure at Aubers news began to seep back to the western capitals of a terrible disaster in Poland. Falkenhayn's long delayed offensive had burst upon the Russian right flank, and four German Army Corps were pouring through the gap. Within a week they had advanced seventy miles; a fortnight passed and the San, the great river barrier in the Russian rear, had been forced at Jaroslaw; a month, and Przemyśl had been recaptured—all those fortress towns whose fall had cheered the Allied press in the winter months of 1914 were now abandoned by the fleeing Tsarist armies.

The Russian collapse

There was much to distract the British public—the Dardanelles, the 'Shells Scandal' (the British lack of shells was fiercely attacked in the press), the cabinet changes. But the hard facts remained. While the Allies licked their wounds impotently on the Western Front the Russian collapse became daily more serious. If she should be forced out of the war, the German strategic purpose—the original motive of the Schlieffen plan—would be achieved and the whole weight of the German army could be shifted to France.

How was it that the front, on either side, could so often be broken in the east, so seldom in the west? Why was it that gains in Poland were measured in hundreds of miles, in France in yards?

The force-to-space ratio (force being an amalgam of numbers and firepower) was widely different between the two theatres. In France the ratio was very high and steadily increasing. But in Russia the front was four times as long, the number of men engaged little higher than in the west, their scale of armament very much lower. Wheeling cavalry formations encountering the odd machine-gun could simply gallop off into the steppe, out of range. The Russians were short even of rifles, and those equipped with them seldom had more than twenty rounds per man. Many of the Austrian rifles were not even magazine-fed.

Across this sprawling, under-manned battlefield the well-led, well-equipped Germans cut a deep swathe: following his victory at Gorlice-Tarnów on 2nd May, Falkenhayn at last allowed the impatient Ludendorff to debouch from East Prussia and seize the vital rail junction of Bialystok in July. Under this double threat the Russian armies, plagued by desperate munition shortages, stumbled back to the shelter of the Dvina and the Pripet. By the middle of August they had lost 750,000 prisoners.

Now the Allied motives swung right round; so far indeed, that the solution, seen from the opposite pole, seemed identical. Massive attacks in the west were urgently necessary, no longer as part of a victorious pincer movement but as succour for the failing Russian strength, a desperate attempt to draw the bulk of the German army back across Poland to the west.

Joffre, as always, was optimistic; his British colleagues less so. The French were to attack in Champagne, the British at Loos. The British did not yet have enough artillery to support the whole of their attack frontage and so Haig decided to use gas on a large scale. This immediately put

The first gas masks—respirators which were issued in May 1915. When gas was first used the British troops were told to protect themselves by dipping handkerchiefs in a solution of water and boracic acid and tying them across their mouths. A German wrote: 'The effects of the successful gas-attack were horrible . . . All the men lie on their backs, with clenched fists; the whole field is yellow'

his men at a disadvantage as gas depends for its effectiveness on a favourable prevailing wind (which could not, naturally, be guaranteed at H-hour) nor, by itself, will it cut barbed wire. In addition, the British and French sections were too far apart to give mutual support. For some weeks the British procrastinated and all the time the news from the east got worse. Finally, the date was fixed, for 25th September—ironically, a week after Falkenhayn had ordered that offensive operations in the east were to be halted, and the divisions transferred to France.

No one had much confidence in the prospects. The ground had been selected, not by the British themselves, but by Joffre. As the hour approached Sir John French's nerve began to fail and he sent a message (effectively calling the whole operation off) that he '. . . would assist according to ammunition'. There was uproar at French HQ. 'Sir John had better walk warily,' growled Henry Wilson into his diary. Joffre himself complained to Kitchener, darkly hinting that he had been made personally responsible for securing English cooperation and that if he should be sacked the politicians might make a separate peace. Haig, meanwhile, had recovered his own confidence and believed that the attack would be successful. Under this double pressure, from above and below, Sir John could do nothing but go along with the plan. All that could be hoped was that by committing everything, including two raw volunteer divisions that had just arrived in France, something might be achieved—even if it was only to impress our Allies with our 'sincerity'.

Winston Churchill has described how, back in London, '. . . The Private Secretary informed me that Lord Kitchener wished to see me. He ('K') looked at me sideways with a very odd expression on his face. I saw he had some disclosure of importance to make, and waited. After appreciable hesitation he told me that he had agreed with the French to a great offensive in France. I said at once that there was no chance of success. He said that the scale would restore everything, including of course the Dardanelles. He had an air of suppressed excitement, like a man who has taken a great decision of terrible uncertainty, and is about to put it into execution'.

In the event, the battle of Loos was a miserable defeat. Like Neuve-Chapelle in its clumsy repetition of frontal attacks and disdain for the indirect approach, it differed when the attackers came to the enemy second line. This time they were ordered straight at it, without any preparation, artillery or reconnaissance or even—in the case of the two fresh volunteer divisions—being given a meal. A German Regimental war diary records how: 'Ten columns of extended line could clearly be distinguished, each one estimated at more than a thousand men, and offering such a target as had never been seen before, or even thought possible. Never had the machine-gunners such straightforward work to do nor done it so effectively. They traversed to and fro along the enemy's ranks unceasingly. As the entire field of fire was covered with the enemy's infantry the effect was devastating . . .'

Nothing, at either strategic or tactical level, was achieved by the Loos offensive. Nor can anything be said to have been learned from it. But its effects were highly important. Sir John French was dismissed; Haig was promoted; Robertson, a close personal associate of Haig's, was transferred to London where, as chief of the imperial general staff, he controlled the strategic direction of the war.

Kitchener, whose deep Imperial vision and gloomy assessment of the Western Front obstructed all those commanders whose ambition resided there, was left without real power and henceforth the strategic decisions were taken by the Haig-Robertson duumvirate, a combination irrevocably committed to the continental strategy, the massive land force on the Western Front, and to a rejection of the imperial strategic principles of William Pitt, which had stood inviolate for a hundred and fifty years.

German cartoon, 1915. Russia's commander-in-chief, Grand Duke Nicholas, is depicted as Macbeth 'in blood Stepp'd in so far that, should I wade no more, Returning were as tedious as go o'er'

The Sinking of the Lusitania

The New York passenger dock was more than usually crowded with newspaper reporters, cameramen, and sightseers when the *Lusitania* sailed on 1st May 1915. Their interest was prompted by an advertisement in the travel pages of the morning editions warning Atlantic travellers that British and Allied ships on route from the United States were liable to be attacked if they entered the European war zone. The notice was paid for by the German embassy and in some papers it appeared next to a Cunard list of departure dates which included a prominent reference to the *Lusitania,* the 'fastest and largest steamer now in Atlantic service. . . .'

The newshounds quickly added two and two together and came up with the obvious answer. Cunard's proudest vessel was marked as a potential victim of Germany's submarine patrol. By sailing time the rumour had strengthened to the extent that many passengers were receiving anonymous telegrams urging them to cancel their bookings. Yet few were noticeably perturbed by the excitement on shore. After all, the *Lusitania* was known to have the steam power to outpace almost any vessel above or below the water. But more important was the irresistible feeling that a floating luxury hotel could not be regarded as a worthwhile target for a German

The last of the Lusitania, *drawn by an Englishman who survived the disaster. He was fortunate. 1,198 of the* Lusitania's *passengers and crew, 128 of them American, were swallowed up by the waves*

1 The nurses on board the Lusitania. *Few of those who travelled on her were alarmed by the German warnings. 2 Captain Turner: 'What in God's name have I done to deserve this?' 3 A medal struck by a German craftsman. It was intended as a satire on the Anglo-American cupidity which allowed the* Lusitania *to sail despite German warnings, but the British reproduced it in large quantities as proof that the German government was exulting over the death of the passengers. One side (left) shows 'The great steamer* Lusitania *sunk by a German submarine, 7th May 1915'. The inscription above reads 'No contraband'. The other side of the medal shows Death selling tickets in the Cunard office under the motto 'Business before everything'. 4 British poster on the sinking of the* Lusitania. *The sword of justice is proferred to America*

U-boat – particularly when it was crowded with neutral Americans whose good will the Kaiser could not lightly afford to lose. Any last-minute doubts were finally settled when the celebrities came on board. Their names read like an extract from an American *Who's Who.* There was Alfred Vanderbilt, multi-millionaire; Charles Frohman, theatrical producer; George Kessler, wine merchant and 'Champagne King'; Rita Jolivet, actress; and Elbert Hubbard, whose mid-west brand of homespun philosophy made him one of the best known newspaper and magazine writers in the United States. Surely, said the humbler passengers, if there was any danger these VIPs would know enough to save their valuable necks. There were one or two cancellations, but no more than were normal on any voyage.

The Lusitania sets out

As the 32,000-ton liner edged its way out of New York harbour, and its occupants turned their attention to the pleasures of an ocean cruise, unpleasant stories of the European conflict were forgotten. A British girl later recalled: 'I don't think we thought of war. It was too beautiful a passage to think of anything like war.'

A more realistic attitude might have prevailed, if the travellers had known that the cargo list included an item that could be regarded only as war material. Stacked in the holds of the *Lusitania* were 4,200 cases of small arms ammunition – not, perhaps, a vitally significant contribution to a campaign in which millions of rounds were expended in a single battle, but the Germans, who were already suffering from a blockade that seriously impeded their military supplies, were in no mood to make allowances for a minor breach of the rules. All ships carrying war contraband were legitimate naval targets if they were caught in the waters surrounding Great

Britain and Ireland. As if to underline the warning, the *Gulflight,* a tanker flying the American flag, was torpedoed on the day the *Lusitania* sailed from New York. Three Americans, including the captain, were killed.

In May 1915 there were about fifteen German submarines on the prowl, out of a total force of not more than twenty-five. Their captains, like contemporary aeroplane pilots, were a small, select company, publicized as larger-than-life heroes whose spirit of gallantry somewhat humanized their destructive powers. For instance, it was customary to warn crews on merchant ships to get clear before the torpedoes were launched and, later in the war, one U-boat captain even provided a tow for two lifeboats stranded some distance from land.

The underwater pirates were immediately successful and, faced with the prospect of greater losses, the British Admiralty ordered merchant ships to be armed, and worked out a procedure for ramming U-boats if they surfaced. The rate of destruction of cargo vessels continued to increase, but submarine commanders were inclined to act less generously towards their potential victims.

The *Lusitania* crossed the half-way line on the night of 4th May. A few hours later the U 20 appeared off the Old Head of Kinsale on the south coast of Ireland. Kapitänleutnant Schwieger had not achieved a single kill in the five days since he and his crew had sailed from Emden. He attacked one merchant vessel, but allowed it to escape when he saw that it was flying the Danish flag.

Ireland offered slightly better prospects. An old three-masted schooner on its leisurely way to Liverpool with a small cargo of food was halted by the U 20. As the crew pushed away in their life-boat, shells splintered the brittle timbers and she

slumped over on her side. It made a pathetic sight: the latest and most terrible weapon of war exercising her superiority over a tired veteran.

On 6th May the U20 sank the *Candidate,* a medium-sized liner bound for Jamaica, and the *Centurion,* on route to South Africa. In neither case were there any casualties among the passengers or crew, who managed to get clear despite Schwieger's natural refusal to give advance warning. At 7.50 pm Captain Turner, on board the *Lusitania,* received the first Admiralty confirmation of U-boat activity off the south coast of Ireland. Forty minutes later an urgent radio message advised all British ships in the area to avoid headlands, pass harbours at full speed, and steer a mid-channel course. The appeal was repeated at intervals throughout the night. Safety precautions were checked, the life-boats swung out, and some of the watertight bulkheads closed. Shortly after midday on 7th May, when the morning fog had dispersed, the *Lusitania* was in sight of the Irish coast. Turner was disturbed by the total absence of patrol boats or, for that matter, any other type of vessel. His concern might have been all the greater had he known that twenty-three merchant ships had been torpedoed in the area during the past week. At 1.40 pm he sighted a friendly landmark – the Old Head of Kinsale. Kapitänleutnant Schwieger, who at that moment was searching the horizon through his periscope, experienced the same thrill of welcome discovery. He had sighted the *Lusitania.*

The torpedo was fired at 2.09 pm. A starboard lookout was the first to see it. Captain Turner heard the warning shout and caught a glimpse of the trail of white foam on the water. At 2.10 pm Schwieger noted: '. . . shot hits starboard side right behind bridge. An unusually heavy detonation

follows with a very strong explosion cloud. . . .'

The passengers did not know it, but they had only eighteen minutes to escape from the sinking liner. A general feeling of security, based on the knowledge that the coastline was within ten miles, gave way to near panic as the ship listed sharply to the starboard side. The first life-boats were swung out, but even without engine power the *Lusitania* was moving too fast for a safe launching. The order to stop lowering was immediately obeyed but not soon enough to save one boat which had dropped heavily at one end, spilling its occupants into the water. By this time the starboard list was so pronounced that boats on the port side either fell on the deck when released or were gashed open as they slithered down the ship's plates.

Passengers rushed this way and that, searching for their lifebelts and fitting them with inexpert hands. One or two jumped overboard and more followed as the water inched up to the starboard deck. A few of the remaining boats plopped safely into the sea but many others were left dangling uselessly at the end of their ropes. Women screamed, children cried, seamen swore, and three Irish girls sang 'There is a Green Hill Far Away' in cracked voices. Chairs, tables, crockery, trunks, and all objects not fastened to the boards slid across the ship in destructive confusion.

From his unique vantage point, the commander of the U 20 recorded in his log: '. . . great confusion on board . . . they must have lost their heads.' Schwieger was convinced that the *Lusitania* was about to capsize.

In fact the massive liner tilted down at the bows and, as the remaining passengers and crew scrambled up the deck, the propellers and rudder—which moments before had been hidden beneath the water

—rose steeply into the air. Briefly the ship remained in this position as her bows penetrated the mud three hundred feet below the surface. Then her stern gradually settled and with a roar that to some survivors sounded like an anguished wail, the *Lusitania* disappeared. Bodies, debris, swimmers, and boats covered an area half a mile across. As the rescue ships steamed into sight those who stayed afloat must have silently expressed the bewildered sentiment of Captain Turner, who was holding on to an upturned boat: 'What in God's name have I done to deserve this?'

'Piratical murderers!'

One thousand, one hundred and ninety-eight passengers and crew drowned with the *Lusitania*. One hundred and twenty-eight of them were Americans. The *Frankfurter Zeitung* described the sinking as 'an extraordinary success' for the German navy, but Allied journals referred to 'piratical murderers' who attacked 'innocent and defenceless people without fear of retaliation'. It is often thought that the torpedo which destroyed the *Lusitania* was chiefly responsible for bringing the United States into the war, and certainly a flood of propaganda was directed to this end. Commemorative medals said to have been issued by the German government were reproduced by the Foreign Office who distributed them at home and abroad to show what devilish practices the enemy were happy to approve. A *Times* editorial was directed at the 'doubters and indifferent' who ignored 'the hideous policy of indiscriminate brutality which has placed the whole German race outside the pale'. With his readers across the Atlantic very much in mind the writer continued: 'The only way to restore peace to the world, and to shatter the brutal menace, is to carry the war throughout the length and breadth of

Germany. Unless Berlin is entered, all the blood which has been shed will have flowed in vain.' But the United States remained neutral for two more years and by that time other factors, including the German offer to help Mexico reclaim New Mexico, had robbed the sinking of the *Lusitania* of its dramatic impact.

If the propaganda experts failed to win a powerful ally for Great Britain, they could at least congratulate themselves on effectively smothering those features of the story that might have set a limit to anti-German feeling. The official inquiry skirted the fact that the *Lusitania* was carrying war material and concluded that a second explosion was caused not by the ammunition but by a second torpedo. Leslie Morton, an able seaman on the *Lusitania* who is now a retired captain, maintains that he saw two torpedoes running right into the point of contact between numbers 2, 3, and 4 funnels. But all other evidence, including the submarine log, suggests that the damage caused by one shot from the U 20 was greatly aggravated by the accidental detonation of the war cargo. That is why the *Lusitania* sank in eighteen minutes.

Other embarrassing questions were left unanswered. For instance, why was the *Lusitania* not diverted around the north coast of Ireland when submarine activity was first detected? At the very least, why was she not provided with an escort? Why did the patrol boats remain in Queenstown harbour until it was too late for them to do anything except lend a hand with the rescue work?

The sinking of the *Lusitania* was a stupid error of judgement which the Germans could ill afford; but those who died were perhaps the victims of Admiralty carelessness as well as the victims of ruthless fighters.

3 TOTAL WAR

Introduction

The second and third years of the war were trying for both sides. The myth that the war would be short was finally laid to rest. But many misconceptions, born in the enthusiasm of the summer of 1914, were still maintained. The dream of imminent breakthrough on the Western Front alternated with the despair born of mass slaughter and the impasse which led some to believe that breakthrough was impossible; either peace must be secured with no decision either way, or victory, out of the grasp of the Allies and the Central Powers, could be obtained some other way. For the Germans and Austrians, the impasse in Flanders and France led them to hope for either a breakthrough on the Eastern Front and in the Balkans or victory at sea. The conquest of Serbia, after almost a year and a half of conflict, came at last to Austria-Hungary. Further advances into Russian territory by the German army gave only temporary hope to the Kaiser.

It became clear by 1916 that victory in the Balkans would have only a peripheral effect on the fighting capacity of Britain and France, and no matter how much Russian territory was occupied, the Russians had an age-old advantage; they could sell space to gain time. And there was a lot of space. True enough, one of the principal German war aims, as announced in Chancellor Bethmann Hollweg's September Programme in 1914, was to create a series of puppet states in Eastern Europe economically, and thus, ultimately, politically tied to the Second Reich. That end was clearly being accomplished. A nascent Polish state was being created, and as the German armies pushed into the Baltic provinces of Russia, efforts toward creating Lithuanian and Latvian

states were similarly made. But these advances brought the end of the war no nearer. Thus, any effort to win the war for Germany outside Western Europe had to be made on the seas.

Britain's lifeline had always been her sea routes, protected by the superiority of the British fleet. As early as 1915 this superiority was being challenged by Germany in a new way. Submarine warfare plagued Allied shipping. For Britain this was a matter of life or death. Food was required in Britain, and something like half of it had to come from overseas, particularly wheat and other grains, mostly from Canada and the United States. Germany estimated that by sinking an average of 600,000 tons of shipping per month for five or six months they could bring Britain to her knees. The upshot of the *Lusitania* disaster was the suspension of unrestricted submarine warfare. Even at that, caused by Woodrow Wilson's insistence that it stop, an average of 300,000 tons of shipping per month was being sunk. If British naval superiority could effectively be challenged, Germany could win the war. The greatest sea battle of the war, the Battle of Jutland in 1916, helped to destroy this dream.

Jutland was the meeting of giants, the heavyweight championship of the naval world, when the two giant navies clashed for the one and only time during the war. The German High Seas Fleet, equipped with more modern dreadnoughts and submarines than the British Grand Fleet, was, on the whole, numerically far inferior. From 1915 on it had languished in port, bottled up by the Allied blockade.

The Germans decided to mass their forces in the North Sea off the Danish peninsula of Jutland. When the battle was over it was clear that in numerical terms, the Germans

had won. The British lost almost twice as much tonnage and over twice the number of men. But the High Seas Fleet was a spent force. It was a classic example of winning the battle and losing the war. Never again did the High Seas Fleet venture far from harbour. The threat of German naval power was swept from even the North Sea. If Germany was to break the blockade it would have to be done through submarine activity, made all the more difficult now because of the fear that a renewal of unrestricted warfare would bring America into the conflict on the British side, perhaps tipping the finely balanced scales of power against the Germans. The introduction of the convoy to safeguard the seaways across the Atlantic reduced the effectiveness of submarine warfare as well. Throughout 1916 Germany was frustrated, unable to break through on either the Western Front, the blockade, or the Eastern Front. The Brusilov Offensive indicated that Russia was not quite a spent force, and these albeit temporary setbacks for Germany in the East did not increase the confidence of the Central Powers in 1916.

It was becoming clear to both sides that if the war was to be won or lost, it would have to be done the hard way, on the trench-lined Western Front. Throughout 1916 two battles were fought which must be considered among the greatest blood-lettings in history. The German attempt to seize the fortress of Verdun and the British attempt to relieve the fortress by an attack on the Somme literally cost hundreds of thousands of lives on both sides. The French, British and Germans were still labouring under one of the great myths of the Great War: that with one gigantic effort, with sufficient élan, a breakthrough could be achieved if only one persevered and continued to throw more troops into the fray. Both sides were

War in the trenches: Germans have occupied an Allied trench and auxiliaries run up to strengthen its defences against counter-attack

less convinced of this after Verdun and the Somme. On the first day of the Somme offensive, 1st July 1916, 60,000 British lives were lost. Although General Haig was still convinced that with just one more push the 'Boche' would cave in, some of his superiors in London were less willing to sacrifice the lives of a generation. It was as true in Britain as it was in France, Russia and Germany: how much longer could this slaughter go on without the most disastrous social upheavals at home? But how could any government face its people with a peace without victory, merely the cessation of hostilities, which Woodrow Wilson and even the Pope called for?

Yet, although the situation looked increasingly grim for Germany and Austria-Hungary, by 1916, deprived of the charismatic leadership of their old Emperor Franz Joseph who finally died after 68 years of rule over the Habsburg Empire, it was not remarkably better for the Allies. The social upheavals which the war was supposed to postpone or prevent began to break out when the Irish, who had pressed for home rule for two generations, decided to take matters into their own hands in the Easter Week rebellion of 1916, which began a civil war within the United Kingdom for the next six years. Forced to introduce conscription for the first time in its modern history in 1915, with women earning their right to vote by filling the empty places in factories and offices vacated by men in France and elsewhere, the British government now had to divert some of her troops to quell the Irish rebellion, while continuing to conduct the European war. Nationalism was as dangerous a movement to unleash in the British Empire as it was in the Habsburg domains. If the Habsburgs ruled over at least ten different language groups and nationalities, the British ruled over hundreds. While Ireland was in turmoil, India began to question British imperialism. Yet Britain herself used anti-imperialist sentiments when, through the intercession of T.E.Lawrence, she championed Arab

nationalism against the Ottoman Empire in the Arabian peninsula and the Levant.

Implying that national self-determination would be granted to the Arabs if they supported the British invasion of Palestine and Mesopotamia, while at the same time partitioning the area with France in the Sykes-Picot agreement of 1916, the British placated influential Jewish families like the Rothschilds, who helped to underwrite the costs of the war effort, by promising the Jews a 'national homeland' in Palestine after the war was over.

These conflicting promises did not prevent Britain from gaining the support she needed to destroy the Turkish Empire from the Arabs, and from 1916 on steady progress was made in overthrowing Ottoman power in the Levant and replacing it with British troops. While British imperialism was being questioned in Ireland and India, it was clearly on the march in the Middle East.

While neither side was capable of breaking the impasse which the war had reached in 1916, both sought the aid of new weapons which would bring the breakthrough which men could not achieve. Three new weapons were introduced, but none of them was able to achieve victory. Submarines harassed but did not break the blockade. Planes, first used for reconnaissance, later for bombing and dog-fighting in the skies over France, were colourful yet ultimately ineffectual in winning the war. Aerial bombing of Britain by Zeppelins frightened the British population but caused little fundamental damage either to the British fighting spirit or British industry, against which they were aimed. But the introduction of the tank into the fighting on the Western Front in 1916 was the development that was hoped would win the war. Like the introduction of gas warfare into the trenches in 1915, tanks tended to neutralize each other, and were not powerful or numerous enough to have much effect at that time. Gas warfare, however, made life in the trenches even more hellish, cost more lives, but hardly affected

the progress of either of the two sides. Technology, which was assumed to be able to achieve anything, had failed as the armies themselves had failed. As Germany moved even closer to military rule, as Russia edged towards the precipice of revolution, as Austria-Hungary's nationalities demanded more liberty, the French and British populations were tiring of war. Yet, since neither side would accept a peace without victory, victory had to be achieved. British efforts redoubled to bring the United States into the war to tip the scales, while Germany hoped that the long-awaited collapse of Russia would end the two-front war so that she could achieve the last big push in Flanders and France which would secure the victory she almost won before Paris in September 1914.

Germany had one last throw of the dice. As the power of Chancellor Bethmann Hollweg waned, his supremacy over the General Staff weakening with every passing month and with no sign of victory, Falkenhayn, Hindenburg and Ludendorff, supported widely by German public opinion, pressed for the resumption of unrestricted submarine warfare. The calculations of the *Kriegsmarine* that Britain could be brought to her knees within six months of the resumption prevailed. Since war could not be won in any other foreseeable way in early 1917, and since the peace overtures of 1916 had come to nothing, Germany took the gamble: to defeat Britain at once in the hope that America would not enter the war, and that even if she did, she could not bring her potential to bear upon Europe until 1918. By then, Germany hoped, it would be too late. After the submarines were unleashed on 1st February 1917, all eyes turned to the United States. Would Wilson act? And if he did, would American aid come in time to prevent German victory?

The chapter 'Total War' brings us to the point where Allied hopes turned in desperation to the United States, and her millions to fill the ranks of the men who had fallen at Verdun and the Somme . . .

The Battle of Jutland

The British view

With the arrival of spring 1916, the First World War was eighteen months old. On land a decision had eluded the opposing armies; they had settled into a war of attrition bleeding both sides white. At sea the two most powerful fleets the world had ever seen faced each other across the North Sea, each eager to engage the other, but neither able to bring about an encounter on terms favourable to itself.

The British Grand Fleet, under Admiral Sir John Jellicoe, was concentrated at Scapa Flow, in the Orkneys, whence, it was calculated, the northern exit from the North Sea could be closed to the enemy, while the German fleet could still be intercepted and brought to battle should it threaten the British coasts. The British ability to read German coded radio mes-

Signals before the battle. 31st May 1916: the greatest battle fleet the world had ever seen steams into the North Sea to meet its German rival

83

Overleaf: HMS Lion *leads cruisers* Warrior *and* Defence *into action (left) and battle-cruisers* Princess Royal, Tiger, *and* New Zealand *(right). Painted by W. Wyllie RA (Reproduced by permission of Earl Beatty)*

sages enabled them to obtain warning of any impending moves.

The German High Seas Fleet, numerically much inferior to its opponent, could contemplate battle with only a portion of the British Grand Fleet. From almost the beginning of the war its strategy had been aimed at forcing the British to divide their strength so that this might be brought about. Raids by the German battle-cruiser force, commanded by Rear-Admiral Hipper, on English east coast towns had been mounted. The failure of the Grand Fleet to intercept these had resulted in the Grand Fleet's battle-cruiser force, under Vice-Admiral Sir David Beatty, being based at Rosyth; and when Hipper again sortied in January 1915 he had been intercepted. In the battle of Dogger Bank which had followed, the German armoured cruiser *Blücher* had been sunk and the battle-cruiser *Seydlitz* had narrowly escaped destruction when a shell penetrated her after turret, starting a conflagration among the ammunition. Only flooding the magazine had saved her.

Further adventures by the High Seas Fleet had been forbidden by the Kaiser and the Germans had launched their first unrestricted U-boat campaign against Allied merchant shipping. For the rest of 1915 the High Seas Fleet had languished in port, chafing against its inaction.

But in January 1916, its command had been taken over by Admiral Reinhard Scheer who had at once set about reanimating it. Raids on the English coast were resumed. As before, the Grand Fleet, in spite of the warnings received through radio interception, had been unable to reach the scene from Scapa Flow in time to interfere. Jellicoe was forced to agree to his 5th Battle Squadron—the fast and powerful Queen Elizabeth-class ships—joining Beatty's Battle-cruiser Fleet at Rosyth.

When in May 1916, the U-boat campaign was called off at the threat of American intervention on the Allied side and the submarines recalled, Scheer had the conditions necessary for his ambition to bring about a fleet action on favourable terms by bringing the three arms of the fleet simultaneously into play. His surface forces were to sortie for a bombardment of Sunderland and lure the enemy to sea where his U-boats could ambush them, while his Zeppelin airships would scout far afield and so enable him to avoid any confrontation with a superior enemy concentration.

Plans were drawn up for the latter part of May; the actual date, to be decided at the last moment, would depend upon when the fleet was brought up to full strength by the return of the battle-cruiser *Seydlitz* from repairs caused by mine damage during a previous sortie, and upon suitable weather for the airships to reconnoitre

efficiently. Meanwhile the U-boats, sixteen in number, sailed on 17th May for their stations off Scapa, Cromarty, and the Firth of Forth. Their endurance made the 30th the latest possible date. The *Seydlitz* did not rejoin until the 28th, however, and then a period of hazy weather set in, unsuitable for air reconnaissance.

Against such a development, an alternative plan had been prepared. Hipper's battle-cruiser force was to go north from the Heligoland Bight and 'trail its shirt' off the Norwegian coast where it would be duly reported to the British. Beatty's battle-cruiser fleet from Rosyth would come racing eastwards to fall into the trap of the High Seas Fleet battle squadrons, waiting some forty miles to the southward of Hipper, before the Grand Fleet from Scapa could intervene.

The trap is set

Such a plan—assuming an unlikely credulity on the part of the British—was naïve, to say the least, even allowing for the fact that the British ability to read German wireless signals was not realized. Nevertheless, when the thick weather persisted throughout the 28th and 29th, it was decided to employ it. On the afternoon of 30th May, the brief signal went out to the High Seas Fleet assembled in the Schillig Roads—31GG2490, which signified 'Carry out Secret Instruction 2490 on 31st May'.

This was duly picked up by the Admiralty's monitoring stations and though its meaning was not known, it was clear from various indications that some major operation by the German fleet was impending. At once the organization for getting the Grand Fleet to sea swung into action; the main body under the commander-in-chief, with his flag in the *Iron Duke,* including the three battle-cruisers of the 3rd Battle-Cruiser Squadron, who had been detached there from Rosyth for gunnery practice, sailed from Scapa Flow; from the Cromarty Firth sailed the 2nd Battle Squadron, the 1st Cruiser Squadron, and a flotilla of destroyers. These two forces were to rendezvous the following morning (31st) in a position some ninety miles west of Norway's southerly point. When joined, they would comprise a force of no less than 24 dreadnought battleships, 3 battle-cruisers, 8 armoured cruisers, 12 light cruisers, and 51 destroyers. Beatty's Battle-Cruiser Fleet—6 battle-cruisers, the four 15-inch-gun, fast Queen Elizabeth-class battleships, 12 light cruisers, 28 destroyers, and a seaplane carrier—was to steer from the Firth of Forth directly to reach a position some 120 miles west of the Jutland Bank at 1400 on the 31st, which would place him some sixty-nine miles ahead of the Grand Fleet as it steered towards the Heligoland Bight. If Beatty had sighted

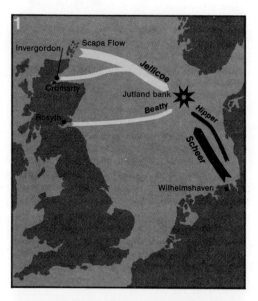

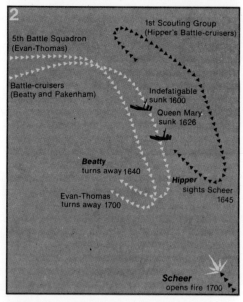

1 The titans weigh anchor and steam to battle stations on the Jutland Bank, 31st May 1916. 2 Battle-cruiser action, 1415-1800, 31st May. Lacking flash-tight magazines and betrayed by inadequate armour protection, Indefatigable *and* Queen Mary *exploded under a hail of fire from Hipper's ships. 3 First fleet action, 1815-1835. Scheer had manoeuvred into the worst possible situation for a fleet action. Only by ordering a simultaneous 'about turn' could he extricate himself from the trap so brilliantly sprung by Jellicoe. 4 Second fleet action, 1912-1926. The British battle fleet opened fire at 1912 but the engagement was broken off when Scheer executed a second 'about turn', at the same time launching a massed torpedo attack. Jellicoe promptly countered by turning his own battle line. 5 Loss of contact during the night of 31st May-1st June, 2100-0300. Scheer eluded Jellicoe and ran for home.*

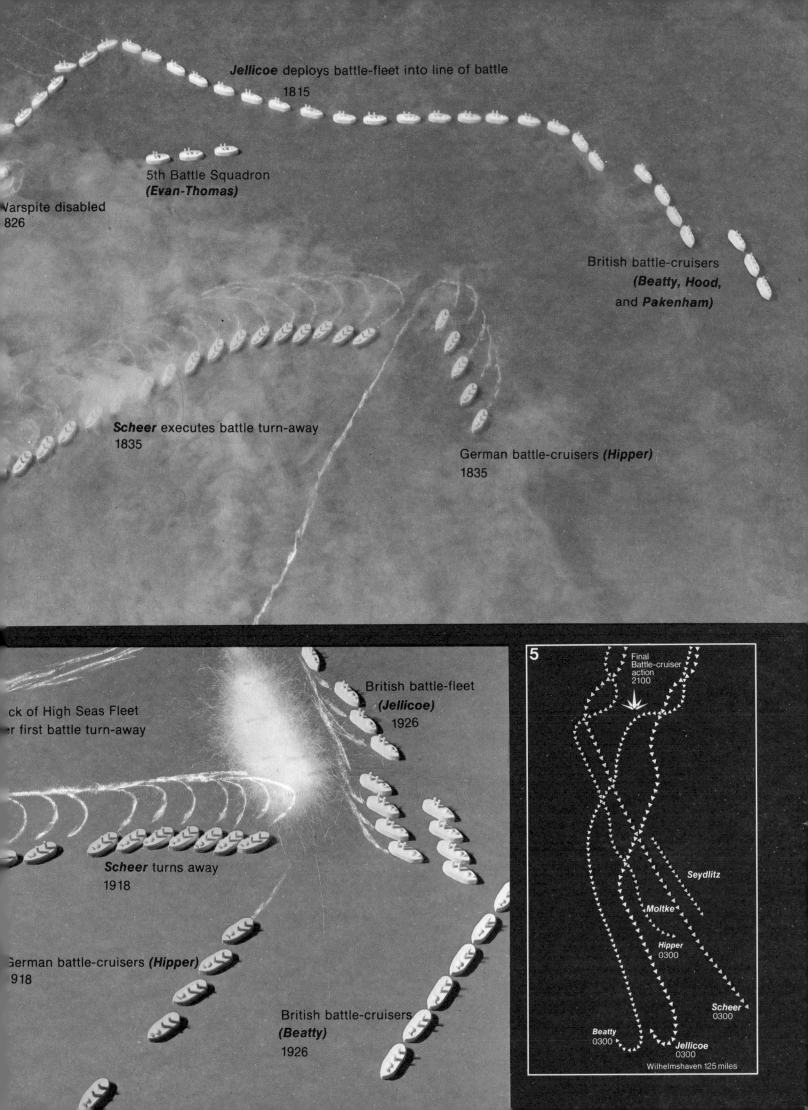

Jellicoe deploys battle-fleet into line of battle
1815

5th Battle Squadron
(Evan-Thomas)

Varspite disabled
826

Scheer executes battle turn-away
1835

British battle-cruisers
(Beatty, Hood, and Pakenham)

German battle-cruisers (Hipper)
1835

ck of High Seas Fleet
er first battle turn-away

British battle-fleet
(Jellicoe)
1926

Scheer turns away
1918

German battle-cruisers (Hipper)
918

British battle-cruisers
(Beatty)
1926

5

Final Battle-cruiser action
2100

Seydlitz

Moltke

Hipper
0300

Scheer
0300

Beatty
0300

Jellicoe
0300

Wilhelmshaven 125 miles

'Some Sea Officers, 1914-1918' painted by Sir Arthur S.Cope RA. Among them, left to right, are Beatty who led the battle-cruiser fleet at Jutland (left foreground), Sturdee (seated centre right), and Jellicoe, who was the commander-in-chief at Jutland (far right)

no enemy by that time, he was to turn north to meet Jellicoe.

Thus, long before the first moves of Scheer's plan to lure Beatty out had been made, the whole vast strength of the British fleet was at sea. The schemer was liable to have the tables turned on him. The first aim of Scheer's project had already been missed. His U-boats had failed to deliver any successful attacks on the British squadrons as they sortied; furthermore their reports of what they had seen added up only to various isolated squadrons at sea and gave no warning that the Grand Fleet was at sea in strength.

At 0100 on 31st May, therefore, the first ships of Hipper's force—five battle-cruisers of the 1st Scouting Group *(Lützow* (flagship), *Derfflinger, Seydlitz, Moltke, Von der Tann),* four light cruisers of the 2nd Scouting Group, and 33 destroyers led by another light cruiser—weighed anchor and steered north past Heligoland and through the swept channels, leaving the Horn Reef light vessel to the eastward of them. They were followed, fifty miles astern, by Scheer, his flag in the *Friedrich der Grosse,* leading 16 dreadnought battleships, 6 pre-dreadnoughts, and accompanied by 5 light cruisers of the 4th Scouting Group and 39 destroyers led by a light cruiser.

By 1400 Hipper was abreast the Jutland Bank off the Danish coast—his scouting light cruisers spread on an arc extending from ahead to either beam, some seven to ten miles from the battle-cruisers. It was a clear, calm, summer day with visibility extreme but likely to become hazy as the afternoon wore on. Unknown to Hipper and equally ignorant of his presence, Beatty was fifty miles to the north-westward, zig-zagging at 19 knots on a mean course of east and approaching the eastward limit set for his advance, with his light cruisers scouting ahead in pairs. The signal to turn north was made at 1415 and was obeyed by all except the light cruiser *Galatea*

which held on to investigate smoke on the eastern horizon. This came from a Danish merchantman and was simultaneously being investigated by the western-most of Hipper's light cruisers, the *Elbing.* The two warships thus came in sight of one another, reported, and fired the opening shots of the battle of Jutland.

The two battle-cruiser admirals turned at once towards the sound of the guns which soon brought them in sight of one another on opposite courses, when Hipper altered course to the southward to lead his opponents towards the advancing German battle squadrons. That these were at sea was still unknown to either Beatty or Jellicoe. The British radio monitoring stations had been led to believe that the High Seas Fleet was still in harbour, misled by an arrangement on the part of Scheer's staff which transferred the flagship's call-sign to a shore station so that the commander-in-chief would not be distracted by administrative matters.

The battle-cruisers open fire

The *Lion,* leading *Princess Royal, Queen Mary, Tiger, New Zealand* and *Indefatigable* (in that order), turned on a parallel course and at 1548 each side opened fire. Hipper was outnumbered, six ships to five. He would have been even more, perhaps disastrously, inferior, but for Beatty's impetuosity in racing at full speed into action without waiting for the 5th Battle Squadron, which was not only initially six miles farther from the enemy but, owing to signal confusion, failed to conform at once to Beatty's movements. By the time it did so, it was ten miles astern, and it was not until twenty-seven minutes after action had been joined that the 15-inch guns of the British battleships could open fire.

In the interval much had happened. Hipper's ships had quickly displayed a gunnery superiority over their opponents who were very slow to find the range. The *Lion,*

Princess Royal, and *Tiger* had all been heavily hit before a single German ship had suffered; though the *Seydlitz, Derfflinger,* and *Lützow* were then each hit hard, the advantage had continued to lie with Hipper's ships and at 1600 Beatty's rear ship, *Indefatigable,* had blown up and sunk as shells plunged through into her magazines. Almost simultaneously the *Lion* had been only saved from a similar fate by flooding the magazine of her mid-ship turret when it was penetrated by a shell from the *Lützow.*

But now, at last, the 5th Battle Squadron *(Barham, Valiant, Warspite, Malaya,* lying in that order) was able to get into action. Their gunnery was magnificent. The two rear ships of Hipper's line were quickly hit. Disaster must have overwhelmed him but for a defect of the British shells, some of which broke up on impact instead of penetrating the armour. Nevertheless, it seemed impossible Hipper could survive long enough for Scheer's battle-squadrons, still over the horizon, to come to his rescue. In spite of this the German battle-cruisers continued to shoot with deadly accuracy and at 1626 the *Queen Mary,* betrayed, like the *Indefatigable,* by her inadequate armour, blew up.

Meanwhile, a destroyer battle had been raging between the lines, the flotillas on each side moving out to attack with torpedoes and meeting to fight it out with guns. Of all the torpedoes fired, one only, from the British *Petard,* found a billet in the *Seydlitz,* but did not damage her enough to put her out of action. Two British destroyers were sunk.

The fast-moving battle had left the majority of Beatty's scouting cruisers behind, except for Commodore Goodenough's 2nd Light Cruiser Squadron which by 1633 had succeeded in getting two miles ahead of the *Lion.* At that moment to Goodenough's astonished gaze the top masts of a long line of battleships hove in sight.

The battle-cruiser Seydlitz, *one of the five ships in Hipper's 1st Scouting Group, on fire during the Battle of Jutland. Although she was heavily damaged both by the torpedo from the* Petard *and by shellfire, she was not put out of action*

In the radio rooms of the ships of the British fleet, the message, which all had almost despaired of ever hearing, was taken in: 'Have sighted enemy battle fleet, bearing SE. Enemy's course North.'

Hipper had been saved in the nick of time, and his task of luring Beatty brilliantly achieved. Goodenough's timely warning, however, enabled the latter to escape the trap. Before the enemy battle fleet came within range, Beatty reversed course to the northward. The 5th Battle Squadron held on for a while to cover the damaged battle-cruisers' retreat. By the time they turned back themselves they came under heavy fire from the German battle squadrons and *Malaya,* in particular, received damaging hits. In reply they did heavy damage to the *Lützow, Derfflinger,* and *Seydlitz,* as well as hitting the leading German battleships.

The situation had now been reversed, with Beatty drawing the enemy after him towards a superior force the latter knew nothing of—the Grand Fleet, pressing southwards at its best speed of 20 knots. Jellicoe's twenty-four battleships were in the compact cruising formation of six columns abeam of each other, with the fleet flagship leading the more easterly of the two centre columns. Before encountering the enemy they would have to be deployed into a single battle line to allow all ships to bring their guns to bear. If deployment was delayed too long, the consequences could be disastrous. To make a deployment by the right method, it was essential to know the bearing on which the approaching enemy would appear.

For various reasons—discrepancy between the calculated positions of the two portions of the fleet and communication failures—this was just what Jellicoe did not know. And, meanwhile, the two fleets were racing towards each other at a combined speed of nearly 40 knots. Even though Beatty's light cruisers had made

visual contact with Jellicoe's advanced screen of armoured cruisers at 1630, though the thunder of distant gun-fire had been audible for some time before the *Marlborough,* leading the starboard column of the Grand Fleet battleships, sighted gun-flashes through the gathering haze and funnel smoke ahead at 1750, and six minutes later Beatty's battle-cruisers were sighted from the *Iron Duke* racing across the line of Jellicoe's advance—and incidentally spreading a further pall of black smoke—it was not until nearly 1815 that at last, in the nick of time, the vital piece of information reached the commander-in-chief from the *Lion:* 'Enemy battle fleet bearing south-west.'

Jellicoe's vital decision
During the next minute or so, through the mind of Jellicoe as he stood gazing at the compass in its binnacle on the bridge of the *Iron Duke,* sped the many considerations on the accurate interpretation of which, at this moment of supreme crisis, the correct deployment and all chances of victory depended. The decision Jellicoe made—to deploy on his port wing column on a course south-east by east—has been damned and lauded by opposing critics in the controversy that was later to develop.

To the appalled Scheer, as out of the smoke and haze ahead of him, between him and retreat to his base, loomed an interminable line of dim grey shapes from which rippled the flash of heavy gunfire, and a storm of shell splashes began to fall round the leading ships of his line, there was no doubt. His 'T' had been crossed—the worst situation possible in a fleet action. Fortunately for him a counter to such a calamity, a simultaneous 'about turn' by every ship of the battle columns—a manoeuvre not lightly undertaken by a mass of the unwieldy battleships of the day—had been practised and perfected by the High Seas Fleet. He ordered it now,

and so, behind a smoke screen laid by his destroyers extricated himself from the trap so brilliantly sprung by Jellicoe.

His escape was only temporary, nevertheless. Between him and his base was a force whose full strength he had been unable as yet to determine, which he must either fight or somehow evade.

While the trap was thus being sprung on Scheer, some final spectacular successes had been achieved by the Germans. Of the 5th Battle Squadron, the *Warspite,* with her helm jammed, had charged towards Scheer's battle line and before she could be got under control again, had been severely damaged and forced out of action. Jellicoe's advanced screen of armoured cruisers had been caught at short range by Hipper's battle-cruisers and the leading German battleships as they emerged from the smoke haze. The *Defence* had been overwhelmed and blown up, the *Warrior* so heavily damaged that she staggered out of action to sink on her way back to harbour. Then the German battle-cruisers had encountered the three battle-cruisers attached to the Grand Fleet. In a brief gun duel at short range, the Germans had suffered many hits and further damage; but in reply had sunk the *Invincible.*

This was the last major success for the Germans, however. They had fought magnificently and, with the aid of superior ship design and ammunition, had had much the better of the exchanges, though the *Lützow* was by now fatally crippled, limping painfully off the scene, and only the stout construction and well-designed compartmentation of the other battle-cruisers was saving them from a similar state. But Scheer was now desperately on the defensive, though he had not yet realized that it was the whole Grand Fleet he had encountered. As soon as his initial retreat brought relief from the concentration of fire on his van, he reversed course once again in the hope of being able to cut

Above: Battle-cruiser Indefatigable *going into action at Jutland. Below: Battleship* Warspite *laid up in dry dock*

Above: Battleship Malaya *of the 5th Battle Squadron. Below: Battle-cruiser* Invincible. *Blew up like* Indefatigable

through astern of the enemy to gain a clear escape route to the Horn Reef lightship and safety behind his own minefields. Once again he ran up against the immense line of dreadnoughts of which all he could see in the poor visibility to the eastward was the flickering orange light of their broadsides. Once again he had hastily to retire or be annihilated.

While he was extricating himself he launched his much-tried battle-cruisers on a rearguard thrust and his destroyer flotillas to deliver a massed torpedo attack. The former miraculously survived a further hammering before being recalled. The latter launched a total of twenty-eight torpedoes at the British line. More than any other single factor they were to save the High Seas Fleet from disaster, robbing Jellicoe of the fruits of the strategic masterpiece he had brought about.

The counter to the massed torpedo attack by destroyers, which could be backed by long-range torpedo fire from retreating battleships, had been carefully studied. There were several alternatives; the only one sufficiently effective in Jellicoe's opinion, was a simultaneous turn away by his own battle line. This was promptly carried out – a turn of 45 degrees.

Contact lost

The two battle fleets were now on widely diverging courses and rapidly ran out of range and sight of one another. By the time the twenty-eight torpedoes had been avoided – not one scored a hit – and the British battle line turned back to regain contact, more than fifteen miles separated Jellicoe and Scheer. Sunset was barely half an hour away. Yet there was time in the long summer twilight ahead for the battle to be renewed on greatly advantageous terms for Jellicoe if he turned at once to an interception course. That he did not do so until too late for various reasons, not the least of which was the failure of his scouting forces to keep him informed of the enemy's position and movements, was to be the central feature of much criticism.

The van of the German battle fleet came, in fact, briefly into view from the nearest British battleship division at the moment that Jellicoe, who was not willing to accept the uncertain fortunes of a night action, ordered a turn away and the adoption of a compact night cruising disposition. The opportunity was let slip, never to return.

Nevertheless, at this stage, as night settled down over a calm sea, the outlook for Scheer was bleak, indeed. Between him and his base was an overwhelming enemy force. Unless he could get past it during the night, the battle must be resumed at daybreak and, with a long summer day ahead, it could only spell annihilation for him. He decided his only hope was to try

to bludgeon his way through, regardless of consequences. To his fleet he signalled the course for the Horn Reef Light at a speed of 16 knots, adding the instruction that this course was to be maintained at all costs.

Jellicoe, having formed his night disposition and ordered his flotillas (many of whom had not yet been in action) to the rear, was steering a course slightly converging with that of Scheer but at a knot faster. From Jellicoe's point of view, Scheer had the choice of two routes – to the entrance of the channels which began at the Horn Reef Light or southward into the German Bight before turning eastward round the mined areas. The extra knot would keep the Grand Fleet between Scheer and the latter. If he chose the former he must pass astern of Jellicoe's battle squadrons, where he would encounter the massed British flotillas which could be counted on to inflict severe losses and to keep Jellicoe informed.

In the event the British flotillas failed to do either of these things. The pre-dreadnought battleship *Pommern* and a light cruiser were their sole victims in a series of night encounters, and they passed no information of the position and course of the enemy. On the other hand Scheer's message to his fleet was intercepted by the Admiralty and was passed to Jellicoe, though a further message in which Scheer asked for airship reconnaissance of the Horn Reef area at dawn which would have clinched the matter, was withheld.

In the absence of certain knowledge of the enemy's movements, Jellicoe held on through the night. Scheer crossed astern of him and by daylight was safe, a development which seemed little short of miraculous to the German admiral.

The battle of Jutland was over. Controversy as to its outcome was to rage for decades. The bald facts, of which German publicity made the most in claiming a great victory, while the British Admiralty's communiqué did nothing to explain or qualify them, showed that a superior British force had lost three capital ships, three cruisers, and a number of destroyers against one battle-cruiser, a pre-dreadnought battleship, four cruisers, and some destroyers sunk on the German side.

Even to-day more than fifty years since the battle, it is not easy to strike a balance sheet of victory and defeat. British losses were largely the result of inferior armour protection in their battle-cruisers, which had been accepted in favour of mounting bigger guns, the advantage of which had been lost through faulty design of armour-piercing shells. Even so, one of the surviving German battle-cruisers only reached harbour in a sinking condition, another was a hideous shambles with 200 casualties, bearing witness to the pounding they had received even from defective shells.

The High Seas Fleet was no longer fit for battle on the morning of the 1st June 1916 and could only make for harbour and repairs, fortunately close at hand. The Grand Fleet was largely intact and ready to renew the fight. Jellicoe may be said, perhaps, to have lost the battle of Jutland. Scheer can hardly be judged to have won anything but an escape from annihilation.

So much for the immediate results of the encounter. They do not add up to a victory for either side. In the larger context of the war at sea as a whole, it is no easier to weigh the results. When Scheer led the High Seas Fleet out once again in August 1916 (except for *Seydlitz* and *Derfflinger,* still under repair), he narrowly escaped being caught in a second Jutland trap, with no safe base under his lee this time, in spite of Zeppelin reconnaissance aloft. Both Scheer and the Kaiser's general headquarters were finally convinced that the risks to be faced in attempting to bring about a sea fight were unacceptable. The High Seas Fleet, built at such cost to challenge Great Britain's seapower, was ordered back on to the defensive. The fatal decision was taken to revert to the unrestricted submarine warfare which was to bring America into the war.

It is true, of course, that the High Seas Fleet kept 'in being', forced the continued maintenance of the huge Grand Fleet, absorbing many thousands of trained seamen and a hundred destroyers which could have been more profitably employed combating the U-boats. On the other hand, that same High Seas Fleet, its ships lying idle in harbour, the morale of its crews sinking, degenerated into a centre of discontent and revolution. In August 1917 Scheer had to quell an open mutiny. A year later, when ordered to sea by its new commander, Hipper, it flared into revolt and led the disintegration of the Kaiser's Germany. This, too, can be accounted one of the consequences of Jutland—perhaps the most important when reviewing the war as a whole.

The German view

Jutland was the last of many naval battles fought by long lines of closely spaced big ships with heavy guns. Its tactical details are well-known, for each ship kept a log. Its results were inconclusive. It was the climax of the Anglo-German naval rivalry, with the scuttling of the German fleet at Scapa Flow three years later as the anticlimax.

This rivalry, which cost both nations dearly, was at least partly caused by the fact that the Germans did not fully realize the implications of seapower. In their difficult position in central Europe they needed a navy of some strength to balance the fleets of the Franco-Russian alliance. But from their inferior strategic position in the south-eastern corner of the North Sea they could neither protect their overseas trade nor attack the sea routes vital to Great Britain. When war broke out in 1914 the Royal Navy was not compelled to attack the German bases but could content itself on the whole with a distant blockade from Scapa Flow.

In the first two years of the war there were a number of operations and clashes in the North Sea which did not change the situation, since neither side wanted to give battle too far from their own bases. In 1916 this changed to some extent. Admiral Reinhard Scheer, the new commander-in-chief of the German High Seas Fleet, was more aggressive than his predecessors. On the Allied side, the Russians felt the blockade heavily and clamoured for the British to force the Baltic so that they might receive ammunition and raw materials which they needed desperately. An operation of that kind had no prospects of success, however, as long as the High Seas Fleet was intact. Therefore it was decided that stronger efforts should be made to bring it to battle. The Grand Fleet under Admiral Sir John Jellicoe had been considerably reinforced by new ships. In spring 1916 it was almost twice as strong as the German fleet.

Early in March, the German fleet made a sortie into the southern North Sea and came within sixty miles of Lowestoft. On 25th March British light forces operated south of Horn Reef, and aircraft from a seaplane-carrier tried to bombard airship sheds. Bad weather prevented contact of the heavy ships. On 25th April German battle-cruisers bombarded Lowestoft. Early in May the British repeated the attempt to attack airship sheds. Both fleets were at sea, but no contact was established.

For the second half of May, Admiral Scheer planned an operation with all his forces. The battle-cruisers were to bombard Sunderland, and twelve submarines were stationed off the British bases to attack the squadrons of the Grand Fleet when they put to sea. Scouting by airships was necessary for the German fleet to avoid being cut off by superior forces. When the time ran out for his submarines after two weeks at sea and the weather remained unfavourable, Scheer compromised on a sweep of his light forces through the Skagerrak backed up by the battle fleet. Shortly after midnight of 30th to 31st May 1916 the German scouting forces (5 battle-cruisers, 5 light cruisers, and 30 destroyers under Rear-Admiral Hipper) left Schillig Roads near Wilhelmshaven, soon followed by the battle fleet (16 new and 6 old battleships, 6 light cruisers, and 33 destroyers).

Above: German cruiser Blücher *sinking in battle of Dogger Bank, January 1915.* ***Below:*** Iron Duke, *Jellicoe's flagship*

Above: Beatty's flagship Lion *firing first shots in the battle.* ***Below:*** *Derfflinger, the battle-cruiser that sank* Invincible

Total War

The Grand Fleet at sea

At that time the Grand Fleet was already at sea, course set for the Skagerrak, too. The bombardment of Lowestoft had roused public opinion, the situation of the Russians had deteriorated, and Jellicoe now planned to set a trap for the German fleet. Light cruisers were to sweep through the Skagerrak deep into the Kattegat; in the meantime the main forces would take up position near Horn Reef to meet the Germans who were sure to come out in order to intercept the British cruisers operating in the Kattegat.

In the early afternoon of 31st May occurred the first of the incidents which greatly changed the course of the events. The British battle-cruiser fleet, under Vice-Admiral Sir David Beatty in *Lion*, changed course from east to north to rendezvous with the battle fleet under Admiral Jellicoe in *Iron Duke*. At 1430 *Lützow*, flying Admiral Hipper's flag, was only forty-five miles east of *Lion* steering a slightly converging course. Contact would have been made considerably later but for a small Danish steamer plodding along between the two forces. Two German destroyers and a British light cruiser were dispatched to examine her. Soon the first salvoes were fired; the first hit (a dud) was made by *Elbing* on *Galatea*.

Within minutes wireless messages informed the admirals of the situation. Signals went up, Hipper swung his force round, and Beatty soon followed suit. The crews were alerted by bugles sounding action stations, guns and powder rooms were manned, steam was raised in reserve boilers, and damage parties assembled deep down in the ships. The gunnery officers climbed to their elevated positions, received ready reports from turrets, range-finders, and fire-control-stations, and then reported their batteries ready for action to their captains. Now a hush of expectancy fell over the great ships while the distance decreased by nearly a mile a minute.

At first, sight was obscured by the smoke of the cruisers. Then these fell back on their battle-cruisers, and the huge shapes of the adversaries came into each other's sight, but only for the few men whose duty was to watch the enemy. Almost all the technical personnel and most of the sailors fought without seeing an enemy ship.

Hipper faced heavy odds, ten ships with heavier guns against his five. His plan was simple: to draw the enemy to Scheer's battle fleet, which was following at a distance of fifty miles. His smaller calibres (11- and 12-inch as against 12-, 13-, and 15-inch in the British ships) made it imperative for him to get comparatively close before opening fire. He offered battle on a north-westerly course, reversed course when Beatty tried to cut his force off, and with a few terse signals coolly manoeuvred his fine ships through the danger zone. At 1548 they were at the right distance (16,500 yards) and in perfect order. The *Lützow* opened fire.

Beatty's ships started answering quickly but they were not yet in formation to use all their guns. Because of delays in signalling, the four powerful and fast battleships of the Queen Elizabeth-class had fallen astern and were out of range. Conditions for a gunnery duel were perfect: visibility was good, especially to the west, and there was hardly any seaway.

First blood to the Germans

The first salvoes all appear to have fallen wide, perhaps because the range-takers were more interested in the details of their foes than in measuring the distance exactly. After three minutes the Germans obtained hits on *Lion, Princess Royal,* and *Tiger*. Because the first target in sight had been light cruisers, the gunnery officer of *Lützow* had given orders to load shells detonating on impact. For reasons of ballistics he did not change over to armour-piercing shells. *Lion* was hit twelve times and suffered heavy casualties, but minor injuries only, except for one shell which penetrated the roof of a turret, killed the gun crews, and ignited powder-bags. The turret-commander, Major Harvey of the Royal Marines, was fatally wounded but before he died he ordered the magazines to be flooded and thus saved the ship.

Now disaster struck the rear of the British line. Here *Indefatigable* and *Von der Tann* fought an even match. At 1604, *Indefatigable,* hit by two salvoes in quick succession, erupted in a violent explosion, turned over to port and disappeared in the waves. *Von der Tann* had fired fifty-two 11-inch shells in all. Twenty minutes later a similar fate overtook *Queen Mary* who had come under the concentrated fire of *Derfflinger* and *Seydlitz*. After vehement detonations she capsized and went down with her propellers still turning. *Tiger,* the next astern, barely avoided crashing into the wreck.

In spite of these losses the situation now eased for the British. The magnificent 5th Battle Squadron, ably handled by Rear-Admiral Evan-Thomas, came up and took the rear ships of the German line under fire. When one of the projectiles, weighing almost a ton, struck *Von der Tann* far aft, the whole ship vibrated like a gigantic tuning-fork. Hipper increased speed and distance and sent his destroyers to the attack. They were met by British destroyers, and in the ensuing mêlée *Nomad* and two Germans were sunk. At the same time 1630 the 2nd Light Cruiser Squadron under Commodore Goodenough sighted smoke to the south-east and, soon after, a seemingly endless column of heavy ships surrounded by light cruisers and destroyers.

Now the tables were turned. Under heavy fire Beatty reversed course and steered to the north to draw the High Seas Fleet to the British Battle Fleet. *Barham* and *Malaya* received several hits which did not, however, impair their speed, but, *Nestor,* attacking the German van with some other destroyers, was sunk. When her boatswain was rescued with other survivors he was mainly disgusted at the smallness and squalor of the coal-burning torpedo-boat which had picked him up.

All through these events the British Battle Fleet had been steadily drawing nearer, in cruising formation with its twenty-four battleships in six divisions, these in line abreast, screened by armoured and light cruisers and destroyers. The 3rd Battle-Cruiser Squadron, under Rear-Admiral Hood in *Invincible,* was twenty-five miles ahead and far to the east of its calculated position. Jellicoe, 'the only man who could lose the war in an afternoon', was now faced with the decision on which course to form his divisions into single line ahead. In all war games and exercises the rule had been 'towards Heligoland'. Yet the reports he received were incomplete and contradictory, it was impossible to get a clear picture of the situation. At the last moment, when Beatty's battle-cruisers came in sight, Jellicoe ordered his division to turn together to port to the north-east. In this way he gained a favourable position for crossing the enemy's T. He was unintentionally assisted by the 3rd Battle-Cruiser Squadron, which almost missed the Germans, but now closed in from the east and brought the German van between two fires. The light cruiser *Wiesbaden* soon lay dead in the water. For hours the battle raged around her, she was fired upon by many British ships, but did not sink until 0200 on 1st June. Only one survivor was picked up, two days later.

The delay in forming the line of battle put part of the screen and the 5th Battle Squadron in a difficult situation at what was later called 'Windy Corner'. Making room for Beatty's battle-cruisers to go to the van of the line, some armoured cruisers came into range of the German battleships. *Defence* blew up in view of both fleets; *Warrior* was saved a similar fate by the chance intervention of *Warspite*. The 5th Battle Squadron was forced to counter-march and came under the fire of several battleships. After a hit *Warspite*'s rudder jammed; she turned towards the German line, thus masking *Warrior,* who was able to creep away, but sank on the next morning. *Warspite* almost collided with *Valiant*

and made two full circles at high speed before her rudder was in working order again. Heavily damaged she was ordered home and reached Rosyth after evading the attack of a German submarine.

Visibility was now generally decreasing and greatly varying as a result of masses of funnel and artificial smoke. For the commanders-in-chief it was most difficult to gain a reliable picture of the actual situation from their own limited observations (radar was not yet invented) and the reports of their subordinates. For a few moments Scheer toyed with the idea of splitting his line to take Windy Corner under two fires. However, there was no battle signal for this promising but unusual procedure, his van was evidently hard pressed, and so he continued with his battleships in line ahead. With the loss of the destroyer *Shark* the 3rd Battle-Cruiser Squadron had inflicted heavy damage on the Germans and now took up station at the head of the British line followed by Beatty's battle-cruisers.

For more than half an hour the German ships could see no more than the flashes of the enemy guns. Then at 1830 visibility suddenly improved, *Lützow* and *Derfflinger* sighted *Invincible,* the leading ship, at a distance of 9,500 yards and sank her in a few minutes. There were only six survivors, among them the gunnery officer who, as he said, 'merely stepped from the foretop into the water'.

At that time Scheer ordered a battle turn reversing course to get his ships out of the overwhelming enemy fire. Beginning from the rear the heavy ships had to turn to starboard in quick succession until single line ahead was formed on the opposite course. Light cruiser squadrons and destroyer flotillas had to conform. This manoeuvre was all the more difficult because the fleet was now disposed almost in a semi-circle, but it was successful, supported by a destroyer attack on the centre of the British line. The fleets drew apart, and the fire slackened and then ceased altogether. A German destroyer was crippled and sank later, and the battleship *Marlborough* received a torpedo-hit which reduced her speed.

The German fleet now steamed to the west south-west, and the British fleet slowly hauled round to the south. With its higher speed it had a good chance of cutting off the Germans from their bases. Scheer sensed this even though contact had been lost completely. Therefore he ordered another battle turn to the old course with the express intention to deal the enemy a heavy blow, to surprise and confuse him, to bring the destroyers to the attack, to facilitate disengaging for the night, and, if possible, to rescue the crew of the *Wiesbaden*. The execution of this plan has been criticized but there is no doubt that Scheer succeeded in getting his fleet out of a difficult situation although his van suffered heavily.

The German thrust was directed against the British centre. The attacking ships soon came under heavy fire without being able to reply effectively because visibility was better to the west and favoured the British gunnery. Scheer saw his fleet rush into a wide arc of gun flashes and decided to support the destroyer attack by the battle-cruisers while the battle fleet executed its third battle turn. To the battle-cruisers he made the well-known signal, 'Ran' ('At them'), which meant charging regardless of consequences. *Lützow* could not take part because after twenty-three hits she was far down by the bow and could steam no more than 15 knots. So *Derfflinger* led that death ride. Her captain transmitted Scheer's signal to all battle stations and was answered by a thundering roar, gun crews shouting, stokers banging their shovels against bulkheads. The destroyers went in, fired torpedoes, and retreated, the battle-cruisers then turned after receiving numerous hits. Not a single torpedo reached a target, for Jellicoe turned away. Contact ceased again and a lull in the battle followed. Both fleets hauled round to the south until their courses converged. The Germans proceeded in inversed order and in several columns, the British in single line ahead, sixteen miles long.

At sunset (2020) the terribly mauled battle-cruisers again came under the fire of the leading British battleships, the old ships of the II Battle Squadron under that of the British battle-cruisers. The Germans were silhouetted against the western horizon, their opponents were hardly visible to them. As a British officer later wrote: 'I sighted an obsolete German battleship firing in a desultory way at apparently nothing.' All the German columns turned to the west; the British did not follow but took up night-cruising order, the battleships in divisions abreast, destroyer flotillas following in their wake, course south-east, speed 17 knots. Jellicoe intended to put himself between the Germans and their bases and to renew the battle at daylight. Scheer collected his units practically on the same course which took some time, and at 2300 headed south-east for Horn Reef, speed 16 knots. Because of the heavy odds against him, he wanted

to fight a renewed battle nearer to his bases. It was another whim of fate that, as a consequence, the German main body crashed through the British flotillas which were not looking for the enemy but were waiting for the day battle. In contrast the German destroyers searched in vain for the heavy ships of the enemy.

The night actions

During the short northern summer night there were numerous clashes. They started with a furious fight between light cruisers at short distance. *Dublin* and *Southampton* suffered heavy damage and casualties; the obsolete *Frauenlob* was hit by a torpedo and sank with most of her crew. Next the 4th Destroyer Flotilla, led by *Tipperary*, converged upon the German van, came under the fire of half a dozen battleships, and turned away in disorder firing torpedoes and leaving *Tipperary*, burning fiercely, behind. When the battleships turned to starboard to avoid the torpedoes, the light cruiser *Elbing* was rammed and remained stopped with flooded engine-rooms. The battleship *Nassau* tried to ram the destroyer *Spitfire*: they collided on nearly opposite courses, and the destroyer bounced off the side armour of her robust opponent leaving part of her bridge behind. With her forecastle a shambles, *Spitfire* succeeded in limping home.

Both sides resumed course and soon met again. In the intense fire *Broke,* and immediately afterwards *Contest,* rammed *Sparrowhawk,* which kept afloat to the morning. This time a torpedo crippled the light cruiser *Rostock.* Half an hour later, shortly after midnight, the unlucky 4th Flotilla encountered the same ships for the third time and lost *Fortune* and *Ardent.* Most of the other destroyers were damaged, it was no more a fighting unit.

A short time later a large ship approached the centre of the German line from port. It was the armoured cruiser *Black Prince.* She had probably been damaged when *Defence* blew up, and had tried to follow the battle fleet. Too late she turned away, and in minutes was a blazing pyre.

These clashes saved the 6th Battle Squadron from an encounter with German battleships. It lagged behind because torpedo damage prevented *Marlborough,* the flagship, from keeping up 17 knots. As it were the German van passed no more than three miles astern at around 0100. A little later it hit the rear of a line of thirteen destroyers belonging to four flotillas. *Turbulent* was sunk, others damaged, the Germans carried on. At early dawn, after a calm of an hour, they were sighted and attacked by the 12th Flotilla. The German ships succeeded in evading a great number of torpedoes but the old battleship *Pom-*

mern was hit and broke in two after several detonations.

The great battle was over. At 0300 the Germans were approaching Horn Reef, the British battle fleet, thirty miles to the south-west, reversed course, neither commander-in-chief was inclined to renew the fight. Jellicoe went north to look for German stragglers. However, *Lützow, Elbing,* and *Rostock* had already been scuttled after German destroyers had taken their crews off. Both fleets steered for their bases. The *Ostfriesland* struck a mine in a field laid a few hours earlier by *Abdiel* but reached port without assistance.

The battle changed neither the ratio of strength between the two fleets nor the strategic situation. The British blockade continued, and Russia remained cut off from the supplies she needed urgently. The tactical advantage was with the Germans: they had inflicted about double their own losses on a greatly superior opponent. The fleet was proud of this achievement, and Scheer was willing to go on baiting the British. On 19th August 1916 both fleets were again in the North Sea but missed each other by thirty miles. However, it was evident—and Scheer said so in his reports—that the war could not be decided by this strategy. The situation on the fronts deteriorated after Allied offensives, and lack of food was painfully felt at home. Therefore the German government declared unrestricted submarine warfare two weeks before the Russian revolution broke out. The submarines did great havoc to Allied shipping, but brought the United States into the war.

The losses in battle

	British	German
Battle-cruisers	3	1
Armoured cruisers	3	-
Old battleships	-	1
Light cruisers	-	4
Destroyers	8	5
	tons 112,000	tons 61,000
Killed	6,000	2,500

As to the High Seas Fleet it did not remain inactive in port as has been alleged. In April 1918 it made its last sweep to the latitude of Bergen/Shetlands. But its main duty was now to support the submarine war by protecting the minesweepers and by giving its best young officers and ratings to the submarine arm. Other reasons for the sudden break-up of this efficient fighting force in November 1918 were psychological mistakes, malnutrition, and subversion, aggravated by the hopeless political and military situation of Germany.

Verdun and the Somme

The year 1916 was the watershed of the First World War. Beyond it all rivers ran in changed directions. It was the year that saw German hopes of outright victory vanish, and the Allied prospects of winning the war with their existing tactics and resources—without the United States—disappear. It was the last year in which Russia would be a powerful military force, and by the end of it Great Britain would have assumed the principal burden on the Western Front. It was also the last year in which the 'Old World' of pre-1914 still had a chance of surviving by means of a negotiated, 'stalemate' peace; it would have been as good a year as any to have ended the war. Finally, 1916 was the year of heavy guns, and—with the exception of the cataclysm of 1918—the year that brought the highest casualty lists.

On land in 1916 there were two battles which more than any others came to symbolize the First World War for the post-war generation: Verdun and the Somme. Verdun was the occasion of Germany's only deviation—between 1915 and 1918—from her profitable strategy of standing on the defensive in the west and letting the Allies waste themselves against an almost impregnable line at unimaginable cost.

By the end of 1915 deadlock had been reached along a static front stretching from Switzerland to the Channel. The Germans had failed, at the Marne battle, to win the war by one sledge-hammer blow against their numerically superior enemies, while suffering three-quarters of a million casualties. In attempting to repulse them from her soil, France had lost 300,000 killed and another 600,000 wounded, captured, and missing. Great Britain's naval might had proved impotent to wrest the Dardanelles from Turkey. Isolated Russia staggered on from defeat to defeat, yet still the Central powers could not bring the war to a decision in the limitless spaces of the east.

But on neither side had these early losses and disillusions impaired the will to fight on. Civilian resolution matched military morale. The opposing troops of France and Germany were no longer the green enthusiasts of 1914, nor yet the battle-weary veterans of 1917-18; they represented the best the war was to produce. In the munitions industries of both sides, artillery programmes had also reached a peak. In Great Britain Kitchener's army of conscripts was about to replace the lost 'First Hundred Thousand'.

On 2nd December, 1915, Joffre, the 'victor of the Marne', was appointed supreme commander of French military forces throughout the world. A sixty-three year-old engineer with little experience of handling infantry, he was now incomparably the most powerful figure on the Allied side and his new ascendancy enabled him to concentrate everything on the Western Front. Four days later Joffre held an historic conference of the Allied commanders at his HQ in Chantilly. From it sprang plans for a co-ordinated offensive by all the allies the following summer. By then, for the first time, there would be an abundance of men, heavy guns, and ammunition. The principal component of this offensive would be a Franco-British 'push' astride the river Somme. Forty French and twenty-five British divisions would be involved. There were no strategic objectives behind this sector of the front; Joffre's principal reason for selecting it was his instinct that he could be most assured of full British participation if they went over the top arm in arm with the French— *'bras dessus bras dessous'*.

Sir Douglas Haig, who had also just taken over command of the British forces in France from General French, would have preferred to attack in Flanders (a preference which was to reassert itself with disastrous consequences a year later). However, after a meeting with Joffre on 29th December, he allowed himself to be won over to the Somme strategy. But on the other side of the lines, the chief of the German general staff, General Erich von Falkenhayn—a strange compound of ruthlessness and indecision—had his own plans. The Germans were to beat the Allies to the draw.

To bleed France white

Prospects would never again seem so bright for German arms as at the close of 1915. In mid-December Falkenhayn prepared a lengthy memorandum for the Kaiser in which he argued that the only way to achieve victory was to cripple the Allies' main instrument, the French army, by luring it into the defence of an indefensible position. Verdun, perched precariously at the tip of a long salient, about 130 air miles south-east of where Joffre intended to attack on the Somme and just 150 miles due east of Paris, fulfilled all of Falkenhayn's requirements.

Verdun's history as a fortified camp stretched back to Roman times, when Attila had found it worth burning. In the 17th century Louis XIV's great martial

Above: French soldier wearing gas mask mounts guard at an entrance to Fort Souville, Verdun. The fort, part of the main French defence line on the east bank of the Meuse, consistently defied capture.

engineer, Vauban, had made Verdun the most powerful fortress in his cordon protecting France; in the Franco-Prussian War of 1870 it had been the last of the great French strongholds to fall, surviving Sedan, Metz, and Strasbourg. After 1870 it had become the key bastion in the chain of fortresses guarding France's frontier with Germany. In 1914, Verdun had provided an unshakable pivot for the French line, and without it Joffre might not have been able to stand on the Marne and save Paris.

From his knowledge both of her history and character, Falkenhayn calculated that France would be forced to defend this semi-sacred citadel to the last man. By menacing Verdun with a modest outlay of only nine divisions, he expected to draw the main weight of the French army into the salient, where German heavy artillery would grind it to pieces from three sides.

In Falkenhayn's own words, France was thus to be 'bled white'. It was a conception totally novel to the history of war and one that, in its very imagery, was symptomatic of that Great War where, in their callousness, leaders could regard human lives as mere corpuscles.

The V Army, commanded by the Kaiser's heir, the Crown Prince, was appointed to conduct the victorious operation. Day and night the great cannon and their copious munition trains now began to flow toward the V Army from all other German fronts. Aided by the railways behind their front and the national genius for organization, preparations moved with astonishing speed and secrecy. By the beginning of February 1916 more than 1,200 guns were in position—for an assault frontage of barely eight miles. More than 500 were 'heavies', including 13 of the 420mm 'Big Bertha mortars', the 'secret weapon' of 1914 which had shattered the supposedly impregnable Belgian forts. Never before had such a concentration of artillery been seen.

Verdun lay less than ten miles up the tortuous Meuse from the German lines. Most of its 15,000 inhabitants had departed when the war reached its gates in 1914, and its streets were now filled with troops, but this was nothing new for a city which had long been a garrison town.

In notable contrast to the featureless open country of Flanders and the Somme, Verdun was surrounded by interlocking patterns of steep hills and ridges which provided immensely strong natural lines of defence. The key heights were studded with three concentric rings of mighty underground forts, totalling no less than twenty major and forty intermediary works.

Each was superbly sited so that its guns could dislodge any enemy infantry appearing on the superstructure of its neighbour. With concrete carapaces eight feet thick,

staunch enough to resist even the German 'Big Berthas', some of the major forts—such as Douaumont—were equipped with heavy artillery and machine-guns firing from retractable steel turrets. Outlying blockhouses linked by subterranean passages made them able to repel an attack from whatever direction it might come, and in their shell-proof cellars each could house as much as a battalion of infantry.

These forts lay between five and ten miles from Verdun itself. Between them and no man's land stretched a protective network of trenches, redoubts, and barbed wire such as was to be found throughout the whole length of the Western Front. Verdun deserved its reputation as the world's most powerful fortress. In theory.

In fact—despite, or perhaps because of, its reputation—by February 1916, Verdun's defences were in a lamentable state. The fate of the Belgian forts had persuaded Joffre to evacuate the infantry garrisons from the Verdun forts, and remove many of their guns. The troops themselves had become slack, lulled by many months spent in so quiet and 'safe' a sector, whose deceptive calm was deepened by the influence of one of the nastiest, rainiest, foggiest, and most enervating climates in France. The French soldier has never been renowned for his ardour for digging in, and the forward lines of trenches at Verdun compared poorly with the immensely deep earthworks the Germans had constructed at their key points on the Western Front. And, in contrast to the seventy-two battalions of elite storm troops, the Crown Prince held ready for the attack, the French trenches were manned by only thirty-four battalions, some of which were second-class units.

One outstanding French officer, Lieutenant Colonel Emile Driant, who commanded two battalions of *chasseurs* in the very tip of the salient, actually warned the French high command of the impending attack and the bad state of the Verdun defences. For this impertinence, his knuckles were severely rapped; the imperturbable Joffre paid little attention.

'Sauve qui peut!'

After a nine-day delay caused by bad weather (the first serious setback to German plans), the bombardment began at dawn on 21st February. For nine appalling hours it continued. Even on the shell-saturated Western Front nothing like it had ever been experienced. The poorly prepared French trenches were obliterated, many of their defenders buried alive. Among the units to bear the brunt of the shelling were Driant's *chasseurs*.

At 4 that afternoon the bombardment lifted and the first German assault troops

moved forward out of their concealed positions. This was, in fact, but a strong patrol action, testing like a dentist's probe for the weakest areas of the French front. In most places it held. The next morning, the brutal bombardment began again. It seemed impossible that any human being could have survived in that methodically worked-over soil. Yet some had, and, with a heroic tenacity that was to immortalize the French defence during the long months ahead, they continued to face the unseen enemy from what remained of their trenches.

On the afternoon of 22nd February the Germans' first main infantry wave went in. The defenders' front line buckled.

General Philippe Pétain in 1916. From warrior-hero he later turned defeatist

Driant was shot through the head while withdrawing the remnants of his *chasseurs*. Of these two battalions, 1,200 strong, a handful of officers and about 500 men, many of them wounded, were all that eventually straggled back to the rear. But the French resistance once again caused the German storm troops to be pulled back, to await a third softening-up bombardment the following morning.

On 23rd February, there were signs of mounting confusion and alarm at the various HQs before Verdun. Telephone lines were cut by the shelling; runners were not getting through; whole units were disappearing from the sight of their commanders. Order and counter-order were followed by the inevitable consequence. One by one the French batteries were falling silent, while others shelled their own positions, in the belief that these had already been abandoned to the enemy. 24th February was the day the dam burst. A fresh division, flung in piecemeal, broke under the bombardment, and the whole of the second line of the French defences fell within a matter of a few hours.

Total War

During that disastrous day, German gains equalled those of the first three days put together. By the evening it looked as if the war had again become one of movement —for the first time since the Marne.

Between the attackers and Verdun, however, there still lay the lines of the forts—above all, Douaumont, the strongest of them all, a solid bulwark of comfort behind the backs of the retreating *poilus*. Then, on 25th February, the Germans pulled off—almost in a fit of absent-mindedness—one of their greatest coups of the entire war. Acting on their own initiative, several small packets of the 24th Brandenburg Regiment, headed by a twenty-four-year-old lieutenant, Eugen Radtke (using infiltration tactics and armed with trench-clubs and pistols), worked their way into Douaumont without losing a man. To their astonishment, they discovered the world's most powerful fort to be virtually undefended.

In Germany church bells rang throughout the country to acclaim the capture of Douaumont. In France its surrender was rightly regarded as a national disaster of the first magnitude (later reckoned to have cost France the equivalent of 100,000 men). Through the streets of Verdun itself survivors of broken units ran shouting, *'Sauve qui peut!'*

At his headquarters in Chantilly even Joffre had at last become impressed by the urgency of events. To take over the imminently threatened sector, he dispatched Henri Philippe Pétain, France's outstanding expert in the art of the defensive. No general possessed the confidence of the *poilu* more than Pétain. Now—in tragic irony—this uniquely humanitarian leader was called upon to subject his men to what was becoming the most inhuman conflict of the whole war. Pétain's orders were to hold Verdun, 'whatever the cost'.

But the German attack was beginning to bog down. Losses had already been far heavier than Falkenhayn had anticipated, many of them inflicted by flanking fire from French guns across the Meuse. The German lines looped across the river to the north of Verdun, and, from the very first, the Crown Prince had urged that his V Army be allowed to attack along both banks simultaneously. But Falkenhayn—determined to keep his own outlay of infantry in the 'bleeding white' strategy down to the barest minimum—had refused, restricting operations to the right bank. Now, to clear the menace of the French artillery, Falkenhayn reluctantly agreed to extend the offensive across to the left bank, releasing for this purpose another army corps from his tightly hoarded reserves. The deadly escalation of Verdun was under way.

Mission of sacrifice

The lull before the next phase of the German offensive enabled Pétain to stabilize the front to an almost miraculous extent. He established a road artery to Verdun, later known as the Voie Sacrée, along which the whole lifeblood of France was to pour, to reinforce the threatened city; during the critical first week of March alone 190,000 men marched up it.

The Crown Prince now launched a new all-out attack along the left bank toward a small ridge called the Mort-Homme, which, with its sinister name, acquired from some long-forgotten tragedy of another age, was to be the centre of the most bitter, see-saw fighting for the better part of the next three months. On this one tiny sector a monotonous, deadly pattern was establishing that continued almost without let-up. It typified the whole battle of Verdun. After hours of saturating bombardment, the German assault troops would surge forward to carry what remained of the French front line. There were no longer any trenches; what the Germans occupied were for the most part clusters of shell holes, where isolated groups of men lived and slept and died defending their 'position' with grenade and pick helve.

'You have a mission of sacrifice,' ran the typical orders that one French colonel gave to his men. 'Here is a post of honour

where they want to attack. Every day you will have casualties . . . On the day they want to, they will massacre you to the last man, and it is your duty to fall.'

At Verdun most fell without ever having seen the enemy, under the murderous non-stop artillery bombardment, which came to characterize this battle perhaps more than any other. 'Verdun is terrible,' wrote French Sergeant-Major César Méléra, who was killed a fortnight before the armistice, 'because man is fighting against material, with the sensation of striking out at empty air . . .' Describing the effects of a bombardment, Paul Dubrulle, a thirty-four-year-old Jesuit serving as an infantry sergeant (also later killed), said: 'The most solid nerves cannot resist for long; the moment arrives where the blood mounts to the head; where fever burns the body and where the nerves, exhausted, become incapable of reacting . . . finally one abandons oneself to it, one has no longer even the strength to cover oneself with one's pack as protection against splinters, and one scarcely still has left the strength to pray to God.'

Despite the heroic sacrifices of Pétain's men, each day brought the sea of *Feldgrau* a few yards closer to Verdun. By the end of March, French losses totalled 89,000; but the attackers had also lost nearly 82,000 men. Even once they had taken the Mort-Homme, the Germans found themselves hamstrung by French guns on the Côte 304, another ridge still farther out on the flank. Like a surgeon treating galloping cancer, Falkenhayn's knife was enticed ever farther from the original point of application. More fresh German divisions were hurled into the battle—this time to seize Côte 304.

Not until May was the German 'clearing' operation on the left bank of the Meuse at last completed. The final push towards Verdun could begin. But the Crown Prince was now for calling off the offensive, and even Falkenhayn's enthusiasm was waning. The strategic significance of Verdun had long since passed out of sight; yet the battle had somehow achieved a demonic existence of its own, far beyond the control of generals of either nation. Honour had become involved to an extent which made disengagement impossible. On the French side, Pétain—affected (too deeply, according to Joffre) by the horrors he had witnessed—was promoted and replaced by two more ferocious figures: General Robert Nivelle and General Charles Mangin, nicknamed 'The Butcher'.

By now men had become almost conditioned to death at Verdun. 'One eats, one drinks beside the dead, one sleeps in the midst of the dying, one laughs and sings in the company of corpses,' wrote Georges Duhamel, the poet and dramatist,

who was serving as a French army doctor. The highly compressed area of the battle-field itself had become a reeking open cemetery where 'you found the dead embedded in the walls of the trenches; heads, legs and half-bodies, just as they had been shovelled out of the way by the picks and shovels of the working party'. Conditions were no longer much better for the attacking Germans; as one soldier wrote home in April under the French counter-bombardment: 'Many would rather endure starvation than make dangerous expeditions for food.'

On 26th May a 'very excited' Joffre visited Haig at his HQ and appealed to him to advance the date of the Somme offensive. When Haig spoke of 15th August, Joffre shouted that 'The French Army would cease to exist if we did nothing by then.' Haig finally agreed to help by attacking on 1st July instead. Although Haig entertained vague hopes of a breakthrough to be exploited by cavalry, neither he nor Rawlinson—whose 4th Army were to fight the battle—had yet arrived at any higher strategic purpose than that of relieving Verdun and 'to kill as many Germans as possible' (Rawlinson).

Meanwhile, at Verdun the beginning of a torrid June brought the deadliest phase in the three-and-a-half-month battle, with the Germans throwing in a weight of attack comparable to that of February—but this time concentrated along a front only three, instead of eight, miles wide. The fighting reached Vaux, the second of the great forts, where 600 men under Major Sylvain Eugène Raynal in an epic defence held up the main thrust of the German V Army for a whole week until thirst forced them to surrender.

The Suicide Club

Then, just as Vaux was falling, the first of the Allied summer offensives was unleashed. In the east, General Brusilov struck at the Austro-Hungarians with forty divisions, achieving a spectacular initial success. Falkenhayn was forced to transfer troops badly needed at Verdun to bolster up his sagging ally. Verdun was reprieved; although in fact it was not until 23rd June that the actual crisis was reached. On that day, using a deadly new gas called phosgene, the Crown Prince (reluctantly) attacked towards Fort Souville, astride the last ridge before Verdun. At one moment, machine-gun bullets were striking the city streets. Still the French held but there were ominous signs that morale was cracking. Just how much could a nation stand?

Two days later, however, the rumble of heavy British guns was heard in Verdun. Haig's five-day preliminary bombardment on the Somme had begun.

French troops attempt to take up position under fire in the Helby defile at Verdun

Because of her crippling losses at Verdun, the French contribution on the Somme had shrunk from forty to sixteen divisions, of which only five actually attacked on 1st July, compared with fourteen British divisions. Thus, for the first time, Great Britain was shouldering the main weight in a Western Front offensive. Of the British first-wave divisions, eleven were either Territorials or from Kitchener's 'New Armies'. Typical of the latter force was one battalion which had only three 'trained officers', including one who was stone deaf, another who suffered from a badly broken leg, and a sixty-three-year-old commanding officer who had retired before the Boer War. These new amateur units of 'civvies' had been trained to advance in rigid parade-ground formations that would have served well at Dettingen—straight lines two to three paces between each man, one hundred yards between each rank in the assault waves. In their rawness, their leaders did not trust them to attempt any of the more sophisticated tactics of infiltration such as the Germans and French had evolved at Verdun—despite a recommendation by Haig himself. French farmers were reluctant to allow their fields to be used for badly needed extra infantry training. But what 'K's' men

Total War

lacked in expertise, they more than made up for in zeal and courage.

The Somme meanders through a flat, wide, and marshy valley. In the areas where the battle was to be fought, there are few geographical features of any note, except the high ground running south-east from Thiepval to Guillemont. This lay in German hands, and was the principal tactical objective for Rawlinson's 4th Army. The British, therefore, would everywhere be fighting uphill; whereas opposite General Fayolle's 6th Army, the French faced more or less level ground. The Germans had superb observation points gazing down on the British lines, their excellence matched only by the depth of their fortifications.

In the nearly two years that they had sat on the Somme, they had excavated dugouts and vast dormitories out of the chalk

Haig: Architect of the 'Big Push'

as deep as forty feet below ground, comfortably safe from all but the heaviest British shell. Ironically, the British, by their policy of continual 'strafing' (in contrast to the prevalent German and French philosophy of 'live and let live'), had provoked the defenders to dig even deeper. When captured, the German dugouts astonished everybody by their depth and complexity. The German line on the Somme was, claims Churchill, 'undoubtedly , the strongest and most perfectly defended position in the world'.

British security surrounding the Somme offensive was by no means perfect. Among other indiscretions, the press reported a speech made by a member of the government, Arthur Henderson, requesting workers in a munitions factory not to

question why the Whitsun Bank Holiday was being suspended. In his diary for 10th June, Crown Prince Rupprecht, the German army group commander, wrote: '. . . This fact should speak volumes. It certainly does so speak, it contains the surest proof that there will be a great British offensive before long. . . .' Abundantly aware of just where the 'Big Push' was coming, for several weeks previously the German defenders had industriously practised rushing their machine-guns up from the dugouts. This had been perfected to a three-minute drill, which would give the Germans an ample margin on 'Z-day' between the lifting of the British barrage and the arrival of the attacking infantry.

For five days Rawlinson's artillery preparation blasted away without let-up (Haig would have preferred a short preliminary bombardment) – thereby dissipating what little element of surprise there still remained. By British standards of the day, it was a bombardment of unprecedented weight. Yet on their much wider front they could mount not nearly half as many heavy guns as the French; and they had nothing to compare with the French 240mm mortars and 400 'super-heavies' with which Foch (French northern army group commander) had equipped Fayolle. A depressing quantity of the British shells turned out to be dud; while defective American ammunition caused so many premature explosions that some of the 4.5 howitzer gun crews nicknamed themselves 'the Suicide Club'. The fire-plan also suffered from the same inflexibility which characterized the training of the new infantry. Through sheer weight of metal, large sections of the German front-line trenches were indeed obliterated, their skeleton outposts killed. But down below in the secure depths of the dugouts, the main body of the German defenders sat playing *Skat* while the shelling raged above.

The worst shortcoming of the five-day bombardment, however, was that it failed in its essential task of breaking up the barbed wire through which the British assault waves were to advance. Divisional commanders appear to have known this, but to have kept the knowledge to themselves. On the eve of the 'Big Push', Haig wrote in his diary with the misguided optimism that was to be found at almost every level prior to 1st July: 'The wire has never been so well cut, nor the Artillery preparation so thorough. I have seen personally all the Corps commanders and one and all are full of confidence. . . .'

At 0245 hours on 1st July a German listening post picked up a message from Rawlinson wishing his 4th Army 'Good Luck'. A little less than five hours later there was suddenly a strange silence as the British bombardment ended. Some-

where near a hundred thousand men left their trenches at this moment and moved forward at a steady walk. On their backs they carried their personal kit – including a spare pair of socks – water bottles, a day's rations, two gas masks, mess tins and field dressings, as well as rifle, bayonet, 220 rounds of ammunition, and an entrenching tool. Some also carried hand grenades or bombs for a trench mortar. The minimum load was 66lb; some men were laden with as much as 85 to 90lb. It was about to become a broiling hot day.

'. . . They got going without delay,' wrote the commanding officer of a battalion of the Royal Inniskilling Fusiliers;

'No fuss, no shouting, no running, everything solid and thorough – just like the men themselves. Here and there a boy would wave his hand to me as I shouted good luck to them through my megaphone. And all had a cheery face . . . Fancy advancing against heavy fire with a big roll of barbed wire on your shoulders! . . .'

Seen from the defenders' point of view, a German recorded that the moment the bombardment lifted:

'. . . Our men at once clambered up the steep shafts leading from the dug-outs to daylight and ran for the nearest shell craters. The machine-guns were pulled out of the dug-outs and hurriedly placed into position, their crews dragging the heavy ammunition boxes up the steps and out to the guns. A rough firing line was thus rapidly established. As soon as in position, a series of extended lines of British infantry were seen moving forward from the British trenches. The first line appeared to continue without end to right and left. It was quickly followed by a second line, then a third and fourth. They came on at a steady easy pace as if expecting to find nothing alive in our front trenches. . . .'

Reading from left to right along the line, the British forces involved in the principal offensive were the 8th, 10th, 3rd, 15th, and 13th Corps, while below them on the river Somme itself came the French 20th and 35th Corps. General Hunter-Weston's 8th Corps had the most difficult task of all – the terrain was particularly difficult – and, because of its inexperience, it was the corps about which Haig had entertained the most doubts. With the 31st Division holding its left flank, the Yorks and Lancs were encouraged to see ahead of them numerous gaps in the wire opened up by the shelling. But at the moment of reaching them, they were scythed down by devastating machine-gun fire from the weapons which the Germans had rushed up from their dug-outs. It was an experience that was to be repeated innumerable times that day. By early afternoon the 31st Division had lost 3,600 officers and men, of whom only eight were prisoners.

Next to it, the 29th Division, recently returned from Gallipoli, had the task of rushing the 'Hawthorn Redoubt' after an immense mine had been detonated under it. But the mine had been timed to go off ten minutes before zero hour; giving the German machine-gunners plenty of time to reoccupy the crater. Moving across no man's land the Royal Fusiliers could see ahead of them the bodies of their first waves festooning the uncut wire; all that came back from this one battalion was 120 men. The divisional commander, in a supreme understatement, noted that his men had been 'temporarily held up by some machine-guns', and pushed up another brigade; one battalion found itself so obstructed by the dead and the endless lines of wounded that it physically could not get forward. Attacking unsuccessfully but with fantastic courage at Beaumont-Hamel, the Newfoundlanders won their greatest battle honour: in a matter of minutes 710 men fell.

Also at Beaumont-Hamel, troops that had captured the Heidenkopf position were tragically shot down by the second wave, unaware that the German strong-point was already in British hands.

By nightfall, the 8th Corps alone had lost 14,000 officers and men without even broaching the main objective. It had taken only twenty-two prisoners. For the 10th, the 3rd, and part of 15th Corps the story of bloody failure was much the same:

'I get up from the ground and whistle,' recalled an officer commanding an Irish battalion in the second wave. 'The others rise. We move off with steady pace. I see rows upon rows of British soldiers lying dead, dying or wounded in no man's land. Here and there I see the hands thrown up and then a body flops on the ground. The bursting shells and smoke make visibility poor. We proceed. Again I look southward from a different angle and perceive heaped up masses of British corpses suspended on the German wire, while live men rush forward in orderly procession to swell the weight of numbers in the spider's web. . . .'

The Highland Light Infantry went into battle behind their pipers. Swiftly their leading companies invested the German trenches, but while they were still exulting at their success, hidden German machine-guns opened fire. Within little more than an hour of the beginning of the attack, half the HLI were killed or wounded, bringing the assault to a sudden halt.

Opposite Thiepval, the 36th (Ulster) Division came tantalizingly, tragically close to achieving success. Better trained than most of Rawlinson's units, the Inniskillings managed to advance a mile in the first hour of the attack, attaining the top of the ridge and capturing the Schwaben Redoubt, an important strongpoint in the

German first-line. But, following the experiences of 1915 when so many field officers had been killed off, it was Haig's orders that no battalion commanding officers or second-in-commands should go in with their men in the first wave. Thus there was no one senior enough to consolidate the Ulstermen's fine success. Communications with the rear were appalling. Runners sent back for fresh orders never returned. Precious time was thrown away, while the Germans recovered their balance. When finally a reserve brigade was sent up to reinforce the Inniskillings, it too had no senior officers with it; with the result it advanced too fast, running into its own artillery barrage, where it lost something like two-thirds of its soldiers. That evening, of the 10th Corps' 9,000 losses, over half came from the Ulster Division—a fact which was long to cause bitterness against the neighbouring English units. The division was left clinging precariously to the German front line.

On the 3rd Corps' front, the 8th Division was another unit to suffer appalling casualties in return for very little progress. It lost a shocking total of 1,927 officers and men killed; one of its battalions, the 2nd Middlesex, lost 22 officers and 601 men, another—the 8th Yorks and Lancs—21 and 576 respectively, out of an average of 27-30 officers and roughly 700 men to a battalion.

Over the whole British front, only Congreve's 13th Corps, next door to the French, registered any notable success that day. Attacking through Montauban, it captured the entire HQ of the German 62nd Regiment; making a total bag of 1,882 prisoners (compared with the 8th Corps' 22). At Montauban, the cellars were found to be filled with German dead; apparently killed by the French heavy mortars.

Fighting in hell

Indeed, for all the incredible fortitude of Kitchener's men, it was the French who won the laurels on 1st July. The terrain opposite them was admittedly much more favourable, the defences weaker; they had more and heavier guns, which had smashed up even some of the deepest enemy dugouts; their infantry moved with greater skill and flexibility; and they had the advantage of a certain degree of surprise. After the losses inflicted at Verdun, German intelligence could not believe that the French were capable of making a serious contribution on the Somme. To reinforce this belief, Foch cleverly delayed the French attack until several hours after the British.

By early afternoon, Fayolle's troops had taken 6,000 prisoners, destroyed the whole of the German 121st Division's artillery, and come close to making a breakthrough. Péronne itself was threatened. General

Balfourier, commanding the 'Iron' (20th) Corps which had saved Verdun in February, urged Congreve on his left to join him in continuing the advance. But Congreve would budge no farther. Above him, Rawlinson was bent more on consolidation than exploitation. Thus Balfourier, with his left flank hanging in the air, was unable to advance either. It was not until 10 o'clock that night that Rawlinson made any attempt to push reserves up to the areas of least resistance. What prospect there had been of capitalizing on any success gained during the 1st July was swiftly lost; the Germans were soon replacing the machine-guns destroyed that day.

When the casualties were counted, the British figures came to 60,000, of which the dead numbered 20,000. Most of the slaughter had been accomplished by perhaps a hundred German machine-gun teams. 1st July was one of the blackest days in British history. Even at Verdun, the total French casualty list for the worst month barely exceeded what Great Britain had lost on that one day. Fayolle lost fewer men than the defending Germans.

Haig had no idea of the full extent of the British losses until 3rd July and neither he nor Rawlinson quite knew why some efforts had succeeded and others failed. On the 3rd Haig ordered Rawlinson to attack again; this time rightly trying to follow up the good results achieved on his southern sector. But the guns were now short of ammunition, and the losses on 1st July greatly reduced the strength of the new blows. That night it rained, and the next day 'walking, let alone fighting, became hellish'.

On 14th July, Rawlinson—chastened by the terrible casualties his army had suffered—decided to try something new. He would attack by night. Describing it caustically as 'an attack organized for amateurs by amateurs', the French predicted disaster. Haig, equally dubious, caused the attack to be postponed twenty-four hours—a delay that diminished the chances of success. Nevertheless, throwing in six brigades which totalled some 22,000 men, Rawlinson after a short hurricane bombardment punched out a salient four miles wide and a thousand yards deep, breaching the Germans' second line—and thereby briefly restoring the element of surprise to the Western Front. A French liaison officer telephoned the sceptical Balfourier: *Ils ont osé. Ils ont réussi!'*

Once again, however, the fruits of victory were thrown away by poor communications and the painful slowness to react of the British command. As at Gallipoli, there was a horrifying absence of any sense of urgency. The cavalry were waiting in the wings, but too far back to be available to exploit any gains, and not until mid-after-

British go over the top in the Somme battle. Their dead bodies were to festoon the wire

mechanical toy but of very limited military value', the tank had been developed under the greatest secrecy and crews trained with similar security behind a vast secret enclosure near Thetford in Norfolk. Even the name 'tank' was intended to deceive the enemy. Its inventors begged the army not to employ the first machines, however, until they were technically more reliable; while even Asquith visiting the front on 6th September thought it: '. . . a mistake to put them into the battle of the Somme. They were built for the purpose of breaking an ordinary trench system with a normal artillery fire only, whereas on the Somme they will have to penetrate a terrific artillery barrage, and will have to operate in a broken country full of shell-craters . . .'

But Haig was determined. Historians will long continue to argue whether he was right or not; on Haig's side, the Cambrai raid the following year tends to prove that the surprise value of the tank had not entirely been thrown away, and undoubtedly, sooner or later, it would have had to be tried out under battle conditions.

On the day of the attack, only thirty-two of the original fifty tanks reached the assembly area in working order; twenty-four actually went into battle, and most of these broke down, became bogged, or were knocked out. At Flers the tank showed what it could do, and the infantry

noon that day was it decided to push up the already battle-weary 7th Infantry Division. Thus nine valuable hours were wasted, and darkness was falling when at last the British cavalry and infantry reserves attacked. By then the shaken Germans had rallied.

Deeply disappointed, Haig now settled for a long-protracted 'battle of attrition'. Writing to the government, he declared his intention 'to maintain a steady pressure on Somme battle . . . proceeding thus, I expect to be able to maintain the offensive well into the Autumn. . . .' All through August and into September the bloody slogging match continued. As seen by the Australian official history, Haig's new technique 'merely appeared to be that of applying a battering-ram ten or fifteen times against the same part of the enemy's battle-front with the intention of penetrating for a mile, or possibly two . . . the claim that it was economic is entirely unjustified'. By the end of the summer, one level-headed Australian officer was writing '. . . we have just come out of a place so terrible that . . . a raving lunatic could never imagine the horror the last thirteen days. . . .'

Meanwhile, however, Verdun had been finally and definitively relieved by the dreadful British sacrifices on the Somme. On 11th July, one last desperate effort was mounted against Verdun, and a handful of Germans momentarily reached a height whence they could actually gaze down on Verdun's citadel. It was the high-water mark of the battle, and – though not apparent at the time – was perhaps the turning point, the Gettysburg of the First World War. Rapidly the tide now receded at Verdun, with Falkenhayn ordering the German army to assume the defensive all along the Western Front.

At the end of August Falkenhayn was replaced by the formidable combination of Hindenburg and Ludendorff.

Visiting the Somme, Ludendorff criticized the inflexibility of the defence there; '. . . Without doubt they fought too dog-

gedly, clinging too resolutely to the mere holding of ground, with the result that the losses were heavy. . . . The Field Marshal and I could for the moment only ask that the front line should be held more lightly. . . .' It was a prelude to the strategic withdrawal to the 'Hindenburg Line' in the following spring.

'A pretty mechanical toy'

On the Somme, 15th September was to become a red-letter day in the history of warfare. Haig decided to throw into a third major attack the first fifty newly invented tanks. Rejected by Kitchener as 'a pretty

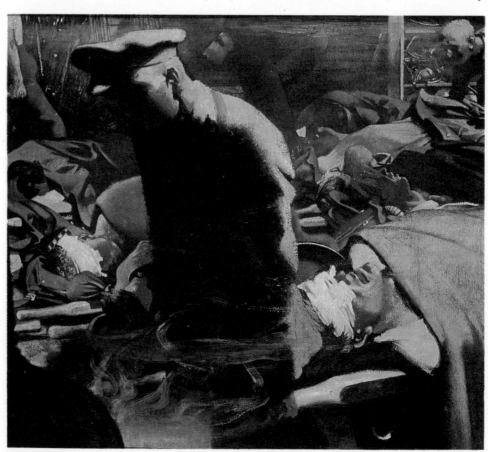

*Painters capture the meaning of these sacrificial battles. **Above:** 'Paths of Glory' by C.Nevinson. **Left:** 'Gassed and Wounded' by Eric Kennington*

advanced cheering down the main street of the village behind four solitary machines. But once again poor communications between front and rear gave the Germans a chance to reorganize before success could be exploited. By the evening of the 15th all the tanks were either scattered or destroyed. With them vanished the last of Haig's three opportunities on the Somme; Montauban on 1st July, Rawlinson's night attack on the 14th, and Flers on 15th September.

Now the equinoctial rains turned the battlefield into a slippery bog. But, pressed by Joffre, Haig stuck out his Celtic jaw and soldiered on, in the mystic belief that — somehow, somewhere — an exhausted foe might suddenly break. The British army was equally exhausted. Conditions became even more appalling. In November, a soldier wrote: '. . . Whoever it is we are relieving, they have already gone. The trench is empty . . . Corpses lie along the parados, rotting in the wet; every now and then a booted foot appears jutting over the trench. The mud makes it all but impassable, and now, sunk in it up to the knees, I have the momentary terror of never being able to pull myself out . . . This is the very limit of endurance. . . .'

In a last attack on 13th November, shattered Beaumont-Hamel was finally captured. Having won the bloodily disputed high ground, the British were now fighting their way down into the valley beyond — condemning themselves to spend a winter in flooded trenches. Nothing of any strategic value had been attained. The 'Big Push' was over.

At Verdun in the autumn, Nivelle and Mangin recaptured forts Douaumont and Vaux in a series of brilliant counter-strokes — plus much of the territory gained so painfully by the Crown Prince's men. By Christmas 1916 both battles were finished. After ten terrible months Verdun had been saved. But at what a cost! Half the houses in the city itself had been destroyed by the long-range German guns, and nine of its neighbouring villages had vanished off the face of the earth. When the human casualties came to be added up, the French admitted to having lost 377,231 men, of whom 162,308 were listed as dead or missing. German losses amounted to no less than 337,000. But, in fact, combined casualties may easily have totalled much more than 800,000.

What caused this imprecision about the slaughter at Verdun, as well as giving the battle its particularly atrocious character, was the fact that it all took place in so concentrated an area — little larger than the London parks. Many of the dead were never found, or are still being discovered to this day. One combatant recalled how 'the shells disinterred the bodies, then reinterred them, chopped them to pieces, played with them as a cat plays with a mouse'. Inside the great sombre *Ossuaire* at Verdun lie the bones of more than 100,000 unknown warriors.

On the Somme, the British had lost some 420,000 men; the French about 200,000 and the Germans probably about 450,000 — although a miasma of mendacity and error still surrounds the exact figures. On the battlefields of Verdun and the Somme, there also expired the last flickers of idealism; yet the war would go on.

The casualties of the two battles included among them the highest warlords on both sides. Falkenhayn had fallen; then Joffre, to be replaced (disastrously) by Nivelle, and Asquith by Lloyd George; a few months later Premier Briand's head would also topple. Because of the appalling extent to which Verdun had 'bled white' his own army, Falkenhayn's grim experiment had failed. Yet, in its longer-range effects, it contained an element of success. As Raymond Jubert, a young French ensign, wrote in prophetic despair before he was killed at Verdun: 'They will not be able to make us do it again another day; that would be to misconstrue the price of our effort. . . .' The excessive sacrifices of the French army at Verdun gerininated the seeds of the mutinies that were to sprout in the summer of 1917, thereby making it finally plain that the war could no longer be won without American troops.

In many ways Verdun and Somme were the First World War in microcosm, with all its heroism and futility, its glorious and unspeakable horrors. They were indecisive battles in an indecisive war. Of the two, Verdun undoubtedly had the greater historical significance. Years after the 1918 Armistice this Pyrrhic victory of the 20th century continued to haunt the French nation. From the role the forts at Verdun had played, France's military leaders (headed by Pétain) drew the wrong conclusions, and the Maginot Line — with all its disastrous strategic consequences in 1940 — was born.

Spiritually, perhaps, the damage was even greater. More than three-quarters of the whole French army passed through the hell of Verdun — almost an entire generation of Frenchmen. Nobody knew this better than Pétain who, years after the war, remarked that at Verdun 'the constant vision of death had penetrated him (the French soldier) with a resignation which bordered on fatalism'.

For a symbol of what Verdun did to France, one need hardly search beyond the tragic figure of Pétain, the warrior-hero of 1916, the resigned defeatist of 1940.

War in the Air

In the late summer of 1914 western Europe heard the familiar tramp and jingle of men and horses going to the wars. But this time there was a new sound, the hum and drone of a few aeroplanes overhead; a sound that would swell to a mighty roar before the war ended.

It was now eleven years since the Wright brothers had flown a power-driven biplane at Kitty Hawk in North Carolina and long before that event successful experiments had been made with balloons, gliders, man-lifting kites, and small dirigible airships. In its early days aviation was concerned with peaceful uses or sport, and even its first involvements in military affairs were strictly inoffensive. During the siege of Paris in 1870 balloons were used to carry messages and, occasionally, people in and out of the beleaguered city. Captive balloons had been used as high-altitude observation posts, notably by the Italians in the Eritrean War of 1887-88. Man-lifting kites were employed in the South African War, 1899-1902, for reconnaissance – in order to see, as General Sir Edward Swinton said, 'the other side of the hill'.

The first recorded use of aeroplanes in war was by the Italians in the war against Turkey in 1911, and on 23rd October the first wartime flight was carried out by Captain Piazza, who bore the high-sounding title of commander of the air fleet. On 1st November Lieutenant Gavotti made history by dropping four modified 2-kg Swedish hand grenades on a Turkish army camp. Soon afterwards the Turks protested that Italian aeroplanes had bombed a military hospital at Ain Zara. Independent inquiries failed to confirm the existence of a hospital in the camp, but it is possible that some tents were used as a casualty clearing station. The dropping of these diminutive bombs, and the Turkish protest, started a discussion in the press about the ethics of offensive air action, which has continued, more or less vehemently, ever since.

From sport to scouting

At about this time several countries began to form corps of military aviation. In 1911 the British made a start with the Air Battalion, Royal Engineers, which was superseded in July 1912 by the Royal Flying Corps (RFC). This was a joint service, intended to supply the needs of both the navy and the army, with a central flying school at Upavon, Wiltshire, staffed by a mixture of army and naval officers and

men. In July 1914 the Royal Navy decided to break away, and the naval wing of the RFC became the Royal Naval Air Service (RNAS). The army wing then reverted to being a corps of the army (RFC).

In Germany the army aviation corps was placed under the inspector-general of military transport, suggesting that it was regarded as a means of conveyance. The naval air service specialized in lighter-than-air craft, and at quite an early date it possessed several large Zeppelin and Schutte-Lanz airships. The range and lifting power of these ships, very great for those days, put them in a class by themselves. Their huge envelopes, however, were filled with hydrogen gas, which made them extremely vulnerable to any form of incendiary attack.

France formed military and naval units of aviation, but gave little thought as to the way in which they were to be used. Indeed Marshal Foch, who had commanded the *Ecole Supérieure de la Guerre,* had no faith in the military value of aviation. He is on record as saying: 'Aviation is good sport, but for the army it is useless.' The United States had an army air arm as early as 1907, but progress was incredibly slow. It was organized as the Aviation Division of the Signal Corps, and even by 1911 it possessed no more than two aeroplanes. Later the American navy set up a small air arm. Not much is known about early Russian military aviation – they were as secretive then as they are now – but little had apparently been done by the outbreak of the First World War.

Unlike most other countries, at the beginning of the First World War Great Britain had a perfectly clear, though very limited, idea of the role of military aviation. It was to be reconnaissance, pure and simple. The navy wanted aircraft to survey large areas of sea, and keep a watch on the enemy's main naval bases, so that they would know at any time the whereabouts of his main sea forces. The army hoped that aircraft would be able to fly over the enemy's rear areas, and provide a stream of up-to-date reports on the location of troops and depots, and the movements of traffic. Such reports would greatly help the intelligence staffs to assess the strength, dispositions, and intentions of the enemy.

For a long time it had been a military maxim that 'information must be fought for', and so long as war was confined to two dimensions this held good. Cavalry patrols

Top: The planes of the aces, Guynemer's Spad, a fast single-seat French design. Above: A Fokker Dr I as flown by von Richthofen taxis under horse-power on a German airfield. Left: Air to air combat 1917. The observer of a German Albatros engages British fighters

Left: French fighters from a camp in Artois beside one of their aircraft, a Nieuport. *Below: Bombing became a recognized technique of the aerial war. This Italian magazine illustration shows a surprise daylight raid on the Austrian port of Pola. In this raid the Italian pilots, led by an American, Wallis Fitch, succeeded in dropping sixty tons of bombs on Pola*

would seek to penetrate into enemy territory, make contact with his forces, and withdraw with their reports. Only such contacts, and the exchange of fire, could establish the presence and probable strength of the enemy's forces at any place.

Experience at the beginning of the First World War seemed to show that this maxim was no longer valid. The ocean of the air is all one, covering both land and sea, and aircraft could fly wherever they wished with no let or hindrance, save for some rather ineffective small-arms fire from the ground. Even when opposing aircraft met they had no means—short of ramming—of injuring each other. As these encounters

Right: French Nieuport giving chase to a German Brandenburg C. Both the French and the British encouraged their best pilots to go on lone hunting patrols.
Below: An observer with an air-cooled machine-gun in the tail of a German fighter. Air-cooled guns, using clips or drums of ammunition, became available quite early on. They were considerably lighter than earlier automatic weapons

became more frequent observers took to carrying fire-arms with them. Since a rifle was an uncommonly awkward thing to handle in a slip-stream of 70 mph or more, the most favoured weapons were revolvers and automatic pistols. But aircraft in motion are difficult targets for such weapons, and usually, after a harmless exchange of shots, aircraft would go on their way with a parting wave of the hand. Before long, however, army field guns were fitted with high-angle mountings, and anti-aircraft shell-fire (AA) became the chief menace to aircraft.

Many ideas were put forward from time to time for mounting machine-guns in aircraft. These fell into two groups: the rigid mounting which required the aircraft itself to be manoeuvred to bring the sights to bear on the target, and the movable gun which was under the control of the observer. The Maxim, Vickers, or Spandau type of gun, heavy, belt-fed, and originally water-cooled, did not lend itself to being fitted in aircraft except in a rigid mounting. But lighter types of automatic weapons, such as the air-cooled Lewis and Hotchkiss guns, using drums or clips of ammunition, were becoming available, and unit workshops in the field produced a great variety of experimental gun-mountings.

The ideal rigid mounting should provide a gun firing directly forward in the line of flight, thus enabling the pilot to point his aircraft straight at the enemy and enjoy the advantage of a 'no-deflection' shot. The difficulty was that if the gun was mounted in the fuselage, so as to be under the control of the pilot for the purpose of reloading, clearing stoppages, and so on, its line of fire was obstructed by the airscrew.

The Germans were the first to solve this problem by inventing an interrupter-gear, which prevented the gun from firing whenever an airscrew blade was in the line of fire. This device was fitted to the Fokker, a small fast monoplane, which thus became the first effective fighter. Its influence was immediately felt. During the winter of 1915-16 it shot down many Allied aircraft and, for the time being, the Germans gained a considerable measure of air supremacy over the Western Front. The old maxim again held good, and information had to be fought for.

The Allies possessed fast single-seater 'scouts', such as the Nieuport, the Morane parasol monoplane, the Martinsyde, and the Bristol Scout. These had been designed for longer-range reconnaissance work, relying on their speed to avoid interception and reduce the danger from AA fire. Various types of gun-mountings had been tried in these scouts, but none was satisfactory in the absence of an interrupter-gear.

The answer to the Fokker was the DH2, and later the FE8. These were single-seater

'pusher' scouts, with the engine behind the pilot and the normal fuselage replaced by tail-booms. They carried a Lewis gun firing forward in the line of flight, and the absence of an engine in front gave the pilot an uninterrupted view ahead. The DH2 came into service in the spring of 1916, and soon showed itself to be more manoeuvrable than the Fokker. Being a biplane, its short span and light wing-loading gave it a smaller turning-circle and it was more buoyant at high altitudes. These were great advantages in a 'dog-fight', when each aircraft manoeuvred to 'get on to the tail' of its adversary. Very soon the reign of the Fokker was over, and the Allied army co-operation aircraft were able to go about their business again in comparative safety, while the zone of air fighting was pushed eastwards beyond the German front line.

Air fighting became general over the whole of the Western Front, the fighters of each side trying to gain sufficient control of the air to permit their army co-operation aircraft to carry out their routine tasks of reconnaissance, the spotting and control of artillery fire, and some occasional bombing. Before long, however, Great Britain, France, and Germany began to evolve individual patterns of air warfare.

The British adopted a very formal and decentralized system. Each of the four armies on the Western Front had its own Brigade of the RFC, which included one or more fighter wings. It was British policy to work their army co-operation aircraft continuously from dawn to dusk, and it was therefore necessary for their fighters to patrol the sky over the front during the hours of daylight. This meant that although some fighters were always present, they were never very numerous. This lack of strength was largely offset by the almost incredibly aggressive spirit of the RFC fighter pilots. Neither the French nor the Germans adopted this system of continuous patrol. Both tended to restrict army co-operation work to short periods each day, and put up their main fighter strength to cover it.

It must be understood that the fighter, though strategically defensive, can carry out its task only by means of a sustained tactical offensive. The British pilots would immediately attack any enemy aircraft seen, even if they were outnumbered and in an unfavourable tactical situation. The French and the Germans were more cautious, or maybe more sensible. They seldom attacked except when in superior strength and from a favourable tactical position. They took every advantage of clouds, and the dazzle caused by looking towards the sun, to achieve tactical surprise, a factor of very great importance in air fighting.

During the latter part of 1916 the Germans had produced a new range of faster and more powerful fighters, such as the Pfalz, Albatros, Halberstadt, and Fokker Triplane, and the DH2 and FE8 were definitely outclassed. Their immediate replacements, the DH5, the Sopwith Pup, and the Sopwith 1½ Strutter, were not very successful. Though the Allies now had their own interrupter-gear, the Constantinesco, for fixed guns in tractor aircraft, the performance of these aircraft did not match that of their opponents.

The importance of technical superiority now became apparent. As the Allies gradually lost the air supremacy which they had enjoyed during the spring and summer of 1916, they were forced to realize that no amount of skill, courage, and training could fully compensate for inferior aircraft. A further cause of this decline was the rigidly decentralized organization of the RFC. During the height of the battle of the Somme in the autumn of 1916 the Allies had come perilously near to losing control of the air over the battle zone. The 4th Army, on whose front the battle was fought, had only one RFC brigade (the 4th) allotted to it. The other three brigades were allocated to the relatively disengaged Armies. All attempts by GHQ to induce them to lend fighters to the 4th Brigade were successfully resisted, because they were anxious lest they should lose their squadrons indefinitely, and perhaps in

German fighters attack a British DH4 flight

their turn find themselves short of fighters.

The Germans, operating a much less rigid system, were able to concentrate a high proportion of their air strength where it was most needed, over the battle front. General headquarters then decided to step up air activity, including bombing, on the disengaged army fronts, in the hope of inducing the Germans to disperse their concentrations of fighters opposite the 4th Army. This failed, because the Germans understood their business far too well to do any such thing. Eventually, the situation was largely restored by borrowing eight relatively unemployed fighter squadrons from the RNAS.

At various times fighters were used to escort long-distance photographic reconnaissance missions and bombing raids. This plan never proved very effective, because if the escorting fighters were attacked their only possible defence was to manoeuvre so as to bring their forward-firing guns to bear on the enemy. This brought about a dog-fight, and the aircraft which the fighters were supposed to be protecting were soon lost sight of, and left open to attack by a second wave of enemy fighters. Consequently escorts were largely discontinued in favour of a general fighter cover provided by offensive patrols. As early as 1916 rockets were used in air fighting, especially by French Nieuport

squadrons. They were carried on the interplane struts, and fired electrically. They were, however, difficult to aim and did not prove very successful.

By April 1917 the Allied air-power was at its lowest ebb, and the RFC suffered such heavy casualties that the month has been called 'Bloody April'. Later in the year things improved with the arrival in fair numbers of such excellent fighters as the Sopwith Camel, the SE5 and 5A, the improved Nieuport, and the very fast Spad. A small number of Bristol Fighters, a two seater fighter-bomber of outstanding worth, also became available. By the end of the year the Allies had overcome their technical inferiority, and the balance was restored.

Quite early in the war the German Zeppelins began night bombing raids on Great Britain. Interception in darkness, even of these huge and relatively slow ships, had proved very difficult. Observer posts were keen and alert enough, but communications were bad, and the division of responsibility between the Admiralty and the War Office caused confusion and delay. Also there were at that time no reliable means of conveying information to aircraft in the air. Public concern grew, but was alleviated when several Zeppelins were brought down in flames, as much by good luck as by good management. The Germans then

started raids by aeroplanes, at first by night and later, more boldly, by day. The climax came in July 1917, with raids by aeroplanes on London in daylight, and public indignation boiled over. It was realized that our air defences were badly organized and largely ineffective. This, and the contrast between the terribly overstretched RFC and the relatively unemployed RNAS, were the main causes of the unification of our air services in the Royal Air Force, following the Smuts report.

The year 1918 began with the British and French air forces enjoying a good measure of air supremacy. On the Western Front a ding-dong battle went on most of the time, with the Allied fighters, on the whole, just managing to keep the upper hand. By this time the differing national systems of conducting air warfare had become well established. The British maintained their system of continuous activity, covered by fighter patrols, but now in the fourth year of the war they had more and better fighters, and could maintain a stronger effort. A number of pilots, such as Andrew Beauchamp-Proctor, William Bishop, and 'Mick' Mannock attained large scores of enemy aircraft destroyed. In addition, especially able pilots were allowed to carry out lone 'hunting patrols', seeking out enemy aircraft and attempting to take them by surprise, and some of them were very successful at this stalking game. The best known of these were Albert Ball and J.B.McCudden.

The Germans maintained their centralized system, and once or twice a day put up their 'circuses'. These were large formations of fighters, led by their most experienced and successful pilots, such as Ernst Udet, Manfred von Richthofen ('The Red Baron'), and Hermann Goering.

The French system was not unlike that of the Germans, but their concentrations were not so large, and they also encouraged their best pilots to go on lone hunting patrols. The most famous of these pilots were Navarre, Fonck, and Guynemer.

The Americans came into the war too late to play a very significant part in air fighting, and their units were equipped with French or British aircraft. But quite a number of American pilots had voluntarily joined one or other of the Allied air forces, and had given very distinguished service in fighter squadrons. Their best known pilots were Rickenbacker and Vaughn.

These outstandingly successful fighter pilots became known as 'aces'. It was a term of French origin, but was used mainly by the press.

When large formations of fighters met, extensive dog-fights ensued, but casualties were usually fewer than might have been expected from the large numbers engaged. Dog-fighting involved a lot of difficult deflection shots and, even with the help of tracer bullets, many combats were inconclusive. It should be remembered that the amount of ammunition that could be carried in fighters was strictly limited. The DH2, for example, normally carried five double drums, a total of 490 rounds. This was sufficient for about 50 seconds' fire. The later twin-gun fighters, such as the Camel, the SE5A, and the Spad, carried on the average about 500 rounds per gun, also about 50 seconds' fire, though the volume of fire was doubled. Pilots, therefore, especially the inexperienced ones, soon ran out of ammunition in a dog-fight.

In addition to aerial combat, fighter pilots were frequently called upon to shoot down observation balloons, and carry out low 'ground-strafing' attacks against troops or transport. For the attack on balloons and airships incendiary bullets, known as Buckingham, were available. There was also an explosive type, called Pomeroy, but the legality of ammunition of this kind was doubtful, and it was feared that any pilot in possession of it, landing in enemy territory, might have to face trial with the possibility of severe punishment. Pomeroy was hardly used at all, and Buckingham only against balloons, whose occupants always had parachutes, or against

airships that were flying over the fighters' home territory.

When in March 1918 the German armies, reinforced by large numbers transferred from the Eastern Front after the collapse of Russia, broke through the defences of the 5th Army, all available Allied fighters were heavily engaged in ground-strafing attacks in order to stem the German advance. Though costly, these attacks were very successful, and were a major factor in restoring a very serious situation.

The German armies faltered and came to a stop. It was their last great effort, and a general retreat set in. The German air force began at last to decline; the morale of its pilots sank to a low ebb, as the prospect of total military defeat drew closer. In addition, some of its best fighter squadrons had been recalled from the front to defend the homeland against the bombing attacks, by day and by night, of the Independent Air Force. This was a small force of bombers – a development of the GHQ Bombing Wing – which was set up after the formation of the Royal Air Force in April 1918. It never had more than nine operational squadrons, out of a total of nearly 200 on the Western Front, but its attacks on centres of industry and communications in the Rhineland had caused much concern and, at times, consternation among the civic authorities. The German government was compelled to provide a fairly substantial fighter defence. There were many running fights between the day bombers of the Independent Force and the defending fighters. Equipped with the efficient Scarff-ring mounting for the observer's gun, the bombers' losses were not heavy, and they often gave as good as they got. Indeed, bad weather and unreliable engines hampered the bombers as much as did the German fighters. These experiences led, in the inter-war years, to a serious under-estimate of the effectiveness of fighter defences.

In Italy and the Near and Middle East, where the war could neither be lost nor won, all the belligerents – except Turkey, which had no other front – tended to employ their semi-obsolescent aircraft. The pattern of air fighting was much the same as on the Western Front, but at a lower intensity. In the Middle East, since German aircraft were few, and the Turks had not many effective fighters, the Allied fighters were mainly employed in ground-strafing.

The closing months of the war saw the Allies enjoying almost complete air supremacy in all the theatres of war. The Germans were short of aircraft, pilots, fuel, and transport. The war in the air was won.

In the First World War aerial warfare was superimposed on a war conducted in accordance with traditional two-dimensional strategy. It was the last war to be

fought in this way. This meant, however, that almost the whole of the air effort was engaged in the close support of land and sea operations, and the war ended without providing any convincing proof of the offensive power of aircraft as weapons in their own right. It also meant that there was but slight experience of what were to be two of the main tasks of air power in the Second World War – strategic air bombardment and the use of fighters in air defence.

This account would be incomplete without some description of the men who flew the fighters in those early days. The fighter pilots of the Royal Air Force were not untypical of those in all the air forces.

Almost all of them were very young – hardly any were over twenty-five years of age, and a large proportion were under twenty-one – and until the later stages of the war they were very inadequately trained. It was quite common for squadrons on active service to receive pilots with no more than a total of some thirty hours' flying experience, of which perhaps five or six hours might be of the operational type. Most of them had never fired a gun in the air, and had no idea of the tactics of air fighting. There were in those days no operational training units, and all such instruction had to be given by the more experienced pilots of hard-pressed squadrons at the battle front.

Once the first few dangerous weeks were over, the new pilots' chances of survival were greatly increased. The standard of training improved very much in the later stages of the war, especially in the Royal Air Force, where Colonel Smith-Barry's reforms did a great deal to reduce those tragic losses of young inexperienced pilots.

In those days there were no closed cockpits, no heating, no parachutes, and no self-sealing fuel tanks. Pilots on high-altitude patrols in winter were operating in Arctic conditions, and cases of frost-bite were not uncommon.

It was extraordinary how quickly these young men matured and found confidence, many of them leading their flights in the air with great distinction at the age of twenty.

Though constantly engaged in individual combat, and though none could fight harder, they fought cleanly. Untouched by wartime propaganda vilifying the enemy, they felt no personal hatred or bitterness towards their opponents. Indeed, it was always a highly traumatic experience to see an aircraft shot down in flames, and inspired the solemn thought 'There, but for the grace of God, go I'.

In the clear air, high above the mud and blood of the battlefields, a generous feeling of chivalry and fair play was shared by the vast majority of the fighter pilots of all nations involved in the war in the air.

Lawrence and the Arab Revolt

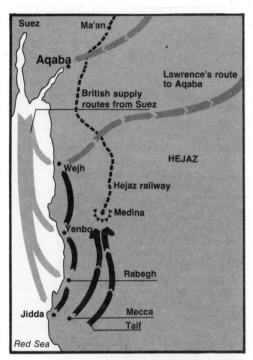

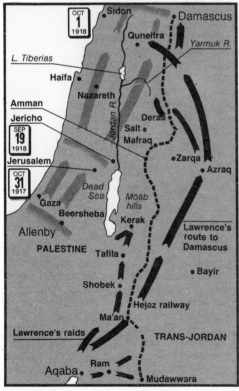

Top: *Mecca to Aqaba, June 1916–July 1917.*
Above: *Aqaba to Damascus, July 1917–October 1918. Damascus fell to Lawrence and Feisal on 1st October 1918*

Arabia, the land with which T.E.Lawrence will always be associated, is reputed to be a harsh and barren mistress, rewarding those who serve her with sickness of the body and distress of the mind. Lawrence's connection with the Arabs brought him at least as much pain as profit, and was in large measure responsible for his decision to retire at an early age from public life, once he judged that his work for the Arabs had been completed.

He is one of the most interesting personalities of his times, as well as one of the most controversial. He possessed the ability to achieve distinction in many fields, and yet, after flashing across the skies like a comet, he chose to become a recluse. Here again he was original, choosing neither the monastery nor the hermit's cave, but the anonymity of life in the ranks as a private soldier, first in the Royal Air Force, then the army, and then once more in the RAF. He believed himself immune from most human weaknesses, renouncing women, drink, and tobacco, but he worshipped speed. A few months after his final retirement from the RAF in 1935, he was riding his motorbike along a Dorset lane when he came upon two cyclists and in a vain attempt to avoid them, crashed and met his death.

A man so varied in accomplishment, so complex in character, so untrammelled by convention, inevitably invited hostile criticism. Richard Aldington, the poet and novelist, sought to destroy the Lawrence legend finally and for ever in his *Lawrence of Arabia* (1955), but he wrecked his case by confusing his facts. Others, too have belittled his contribution to Allenby's victory in Palestine, arguing that Lawrence was at most a gifted leader of guerrillas. Some believed that his desire for anonymity was inspired as much by a clever understanding of the media of publicity as by any genuine desire to withdraw from the hurly-burly of public life. But Lawrence was not an ordinary man. He did not fit, nor did he wish to fit, into the 'establishment'. If fame is a natural ambition, he achieved it, both in the world of action and in letters. If success is to be judged by the acquisition of wealth, he despised it; if it is to be determined by rank or status, he ignored it. The fact that throughout his life he enjoyed the friendship of such men as Churchill, Shaw, Liddell Hart, Wavell, E.M.Forster, and Trenchard is sufficient to demolish the charges brought against him by Aldington. These were not men

who admitted to their friendship the charlatan and the braggart.

The untidy subaltern

Thomas Edward Lawrence was born at Tremadoc in North Wales in 1888. He was the second son of Thomas Chapman, a rather eccentric Anglo-Irishman who later changed his name to Lawrence, and who subsequently inherited a baronetcy. T.E. Lawrence was born out of wedlock, a fact which undoubtedly affected him psychologically, but there is no evidence to suggest that he took the matter as seriously as Aldington has alleged. He discussed his illegitimacy quite openly with his more intimate friends. His father had sufficient private means to live comfortably, but not ostentatiously, and T.E.Lawrence gave early evidence of ability above the average. He learned to read at the age of four, and was learning Latin at six. He contributed towards the cost of his education by winning scholarships, first to Oxford High School, and then to the University. He was an omnivorous reader, with a particular interest in medieval and military history, and archaeology.

While reading history at Jesus College, Lawrence travelled in the Levant visiting Crusaders' castles, and subsequently took a first-class degree. Having been awarded a travelling scholarship, he joined D.G. Hogarth's expedition excavating Carchemish, and also worked with the archaeologist (Sir) Leonard Woolley. This brought him into contact with the Arabs, for whom he discovered he had a natural affinity, and he learned their language and as much as he could about their history and customs. On the outbreak of war in 1914, he tried to join the army, but was rejected at first, because he was below the minimum height of five feet five inches. It was several months before he was given a commission and employed in the intelligence branch of the general staff, where his knowledge of Arabic led to his posting to the 'Arab Bureau' at GHQ in Egypt. He was then a very junior and young-looking subaltern, whose untidiness in uniform and unconcern with the niceties of military protocol were not calculated to endear him to the more orthodox among his superiors.

The war against the Turks was going badly at the time. Their attack on the Suez Canal had been easily repulsed, but the ponderous British advance across Sinai had ground to a halt opposite Gaza. The failure at Gallipoli was fresh in men's

Total War

memories, and was soon to be followed by Townshend's surrender at Kut in Mesopotamia (now Iraq). In south-west Arabia the Turks had advanced to the gates of Aden, where they were to remain for the rest of the war. They may have been corrupt and incompetent, but they were not faring too badly against the might of the British empire. It was at this moment, 5th June 1916, that the Hashimite princes of the Hejaz chose to rise against their Turkish overlords. The Arab Revolt, or, as some would prefer it, the Arab Awakening, had begun.

As a military operation, it was no more likely to succeed than some of the more recent military undertakings of the Arabs, in which performance has fallen far short of promise. Mecca, Jidda, and Taif were quickly captured, but the Arabs failed to take Medina, the principal Turkish garrison. The revolt lost impetus, and in the meantime the Turks sent reinforcements down the Hejaz railway, which the Arabs failed to interdict. In October 1916 the British sent Mr (later Sir Ronald) Storrs, accompanied by Lawrence, to investigate the situation at first-hand, and to consult with the Amir Abdullah, second son of Sherif Hussein, ruler of the Hejaz, whose tribal levies had captured Taif the previous month.

After preliminary discussions with Abdullah, Lawrence was dispatched to visit his younger brother, the Amir Feisal, whose tribesmen had been repulsed at Medina, but who was lying up in the hills nearby. The two men established an almost immediate *rapport,* but it was clear to Lawrence that Feisal's ill-disciplined and badly-armed tribesmen were no match for the Turks in conventional positional warfare. Meanwhile, the Turks continued to reinforce Medina, and the unruly bedouin, disappointed in their hopes for loot, began to drift back to their tents in the desert.

Lawrence was completely untrained in military staff work, but he at once appreciated that the key to the strategic situation was the Hejaz railway. So long as this continued operating, the Turks would be able to build up sufficient strength to reconquer the Hejaz. Moreover, the Arabs, although natural guerrillas, lacked the discipline, and even the will, to fight a pitched battle against the Turks, however incompetent the Turkish leadership. Some other use must be made of their natural military qualities and their ability to operate for long periods in the desert, and this could best be done by abandoning the siege of Medina and carrying the campaign into the north, raiding the railway, the Turks' lifeline, and reducing the flow of reinforcements to a trickle. Lawrence was not the first military leader in history to understand the potentialities of guerrilla

warfare when operating against a conventionally-minded enemy, nor has he been the last, for Mao Tse-tung has been equally successful in China, and Giap in Vietnam. But he must at least be given the credit for appreciating how best the Arab Revolt could be harnessed to assist the Allied cause, and at the same time achieve the Arabs' aim, which was to win their independence from foreign rule.

In pursuit of his aim to tie down as many Turks as possible in the Hejaz, Lawrence launched a series of raids against the single-line, wood-burning railway linking Medina with Damascus. He sought not to destroy the railway, but to impede its working, and to compel the Turks to deploy an ever-increasing number of troops to guard it. Fakhri Pasha, the Turkish commander in Medina, lacked initiative, remaining static behind his defences, and clamouring for more and more reinforcements. As they trickled down to him, Lawrence moved steadily farther north, joining forces with the Trans-Jordan tribes, and carrying his raids against the railway nearer to the main British front in Palestine. On 6th July 1917, in company with the famous desert raider, Auda abu Tayi, and his Howeitat tribesmen, he captured Aqaba from the rear, having first overwhelmed a Turkish battalion moving down from Ma'an to reinforce Aqaba.

Feisal then moved his headquarters to Aqaba, which was nearer to the main front than Wejh on the Red Sea, and with Sherif Hussein's permission placed himself under the command of General Allenby, who had taken over command in Palestine. The mainly tribal contingents of Feisal were provided with a stiffening in the shape of armoured cars and light artillery; small detachments of British, French, and Indian troops were sent to Aqaba to support the Arabs; and above all, arms, ammunition, and gold were provided to keep the Arab tribesmen in the field. Allenby intended to employ the Arabs to protect his open flank east of the river Jordan, and to hinder Turkish attempts to reinforce their armies in Palestine. He also realized the political appeal of the Arab Revolt, and planned to harness it to his aim of destroying the Turkish armies, containing as they did large numbers of Arab officers and many thousands of Arab conscripts.

To Damascus

The British attack on the Gaza-Beersheba line was planned for early November 1917. The Arabs were asked to cut beforehand the Damascus-Haifa railway in the Yarmuk gorge, west of the junction of Deraa in Syria, in order to impede the flow of reinforcements to Palestine. The

raid involved an approach march from Aqaba of over 350 miles through the desert, but the final stretch was through cultivated country where the peasants gave the Turks warning. The operation was unsuccessful, and nearly a disaster, but the raiders managed to get away and destroyed sections of the railway north of Amman before retreating to Aqaba. Meanwhile, Allenby had successfully broken through the Turkish defences and was advancing on Jerusalem.

Lawrence was present when Allenby entered Jerusalem on 9th December 1917. He greatly admired Allenby, just as Allenby, at their first meeting, had immediately appreciated Lawrence's qualities. He was also unmoved by Lawrence's preference for wearing Arab dress, a practice that reduced many British regular officers to apoplectic fury. Allenby now required the Arabs to move north from Aqaba, through the hills east of the Jordan valley, and establish contact with the British near Jericho. Lawrence thereupon advanced through the mountains of Moab, fighting a fierce battle at Tafila in January 1918, a masterpiece in minor tactics which resulted in the annihilation of a Turkish battalion. However, a farther advance to Kerak and beyond was prevented by the bitterly cold weather which affected the Arabs' morale.

Allenby crossed the Jordan in the spring of 1918 and attempted to capture Salt on the Trans-Jordan plateau. This failed, as did the Arab attack on Ma'an, intended to coincide with the British attack, but large sections of the railway were permanently destroyed and the Turkish army in the Hejaz was effectively isolated. Lawrence had set off for the north to link up with the British, but this too had failed, and he established himself far out in the desert at the oasis of Azraq. There he waited for the main British offensive to begin.

The British attack was due to start on 19th September 1918. Allenby had asked that it should be preceded by a diversionary attack by the Arabs on the important railway junction of Deraa. This was carried out under Lawrence on 17th September with complete success. When, two days later, Allenby fell with massive strength on the Turkish army, its way of retreat through Deraa to Damascus was blocked. Moreover, Lawrence and Feisal, moving north, had raised the tribes south of Damascus. The Turks gave no quarter, nor did they receive any from the Arabs, as they struggled in hopeless confusion across the Jordan into Syria. Feisal entered Damascus in triumph, and for some weeks Lawrence was responsible for civil and military order in the city. On 31st October 1918 an armistice was concluded with Turkey.

It has sometimes been said of Lawrence's campaign in the desert that it was 'a sideshow within a sideshow'. This may be true if war consists of a counting of heads, or 'cipherin' ', as Robert E.Lee described it, but Wavell, in his semi-official history of the Palestine Campaign, certainly does not underrate the valuable contribution made by the Arabs under Lawrence's leadership to Allenby's victory. He makes it clear that a force of barely 3,000 Arabs tied down 50,000 Turks at a crucial moment, and compelled the Turkish high command to deploy some 150,000 troops 'spread over the rest of the region in a futile effort to stem the tide of the Arab Revolt'. As General Glubb has since written: 'To the student of war, the whole Arab campaign provides a remarkable illustration of the extraordinary results which can be achieved by mobile guerrilla tactics. For the Arabs detained tens of thousands of regular Turkish troops with a force barely capable of engaging a brigade of infantry in a pitched battle.'

Al Auruns

When Lawrence arrived in the Hejaz he was junior in rank and untrained in formal military matters. It is the measure of his strategic insight that he was able to perceive how best the Arab Revolt could be utilized to assist the British strategy in the Middle East, and his understanding of the characteristics of Arab tribesmen enabled him to employ them to the best advantage in the war against the Turks. Whatever may be said to the contrary, and there has recently been published a book by an Arab author which seeks to belittle the part played by Lawrence in the Arab Revolt, anyone with experience of the Arabs as soldiers will know that they would never have chosen such tactics of their own volition. They would have met the Turks head-on, and they would have been defeated.

The way in which Lawrence established his leadership over the Arabs is a fascinating study in itself. He proved to them time and again that he could out-match them in their own hardiness. No people live in a harsher environment than the bedouin tribesmen of Arabia. Lawrence lived in the same fashion as they did, enduring the same hardships, and demanding no favours. He rode his camels harder, and farther, and for longer periods, than his Arab companions were accustomed to do. He trained himself to be patient during the interminable, and often fruitless, discussions around the coffee hearth. He ate their food, and drank their water, and suffered in consequence from a succession of debilitating stomach ailments. He was never a fluent Arabic speaker, like Glubb for example, nor could he hope to pass himself off as an Arab, as Leachman did in Nejd; his piercing blue eyes, fair hair, and skin would soon have given him away. He could appreciate the Arabs' virtues without overlooking their weaknesses, as some Englishmen have done when subjected to the persuasive charm of the bedouin. No one who has lived with the bedouin can forget the attractive side of their characters, but very few men have possessed the ability to fix their bird-like minds on a stable course. Lawrence succeeded in doing this, and no amount of critical hindsight can detract from the part he played in maintaining the impetus of the Arab Revolt.

His work with the Arabs did not end with the conclusion of the armistice in 1918. He believed passionately that his own honour was committed to obtain for them the independence for which they had fought. He understood the force of Arab nationalism as did few others at that time. The Turks had hopelessly under-estimated the strength of the movement for Arab unity, just as the British and the French were to do in later years. The ramshackle Ottoman empire had no other solution for Arab nationalism than repression, but the Arabs' desire for unity is a burning faith, however distant its fulfilment may seem. Statesmen and politicians in London and Paris might scoff, but Lawrence was a visionary, and he understood the Arabs' longing. He gave himself body and soul to help them in their quest. This brought him into conflict with his own government after the war, since the aim of Great Britain and France was to substitute their influence for Turkey's in the Middle East.

Lawrence accompanied the Arab delegation to the Peace Conference at Versailles as an adviser, and found himself ensnarled in the tortuous negotiations conducted by Great Britain and France earlier in the war to carve up the former Turkish empire in Arabia into respective spheres of influence for themselves. It has been a dirty game, as power politics so often is, and Lawrence was soon to learn that pledges made in the stress of war are as likely to be overlooked as honoured after the peace. His practice of wearing Arab dress aroused hostile comment. It was far too unconventional for British tastes, but it was as good a way as any for Lawrence to demonstrate to the Arabs which side he was backing. Nonetheless, despite all his efforts, the outcome of the negotiations could have been predicted. The French received mandates in Syria and the Lebanon, and they at once ejected Feisal from his throne in Damascus. The British were given mandates in Iraq, and in Palestine and Trans-Jordan. Feisal was in due course to be given a throne in Iraq, and Abdullah in Trans-Jordan, but there had been left a legacy of bitterness which has soured our relations with the Arabs ever since.

Lawrence was far from fit at the time, either physically or mentally. His physical resistance had been lowered by his years in the desert. He had been scarred mentally by the vicious sexual assault he had suffered at the hands of the Turkish commandant in Deraa, where he had been captured while reconnoitring the town. He had managed to escape, his identity still not suspected, but not until after he had been subjected to appalling indignities and a merciless beating. Exhausted though he was, he fought his hardest for the Arabs at Versailles. After the peace treaty had been concluded, and there was nothing more he could do in an official capacity, he resigned from the army, and in letters and articles in the press sought to persuade the British government to honour its obligations and give the Arabs real, instead of sham, independence.

Adviser to Churchill

His vision of the Commonwealth was years ahead of his time, though he expressed himself in contemporary terms. 'This new Imperialism,' he wrote in *The Round Table* in 1920, 'involves an active side of imposing responsibility on the local peoples. . . . We can only teach them by forcing them to try, while we stand by to give advice. . . . We have to be prepared to see them doing things by methods quite unlike our own, and less well; but on principle it is better that they half do it than that we do it perfectly for them.' Much blood, treasure, and heart-ache would have been saved had the colonial powers understood the truth of this. The Middle East was in a turmoil, while Curzon's policy at the Foreign Office was out of tune with the times, old-fashioned imperialism that had had its day. The situation only improved when the Colonial Office assumed responsibility for the Middle East. Churchill was the minister, and he took Lawrence with him as adviser on Arab affairs to a conference convened in Cairo in 1921.

The outcome of the conference was regarded at the time as being entirely satisfactory, almost universally so among the British, and only to a lesser extent among the Arabs. In Churchill's words in *The Aftermath*, 'The Arabs and Colonel Lawrence were appeased by the enthronement of King Feisal at Baghdad; the British Army, which had been costing thirty millions a year, had been brought home; and complete tranquillity was preserved under the thrifty Trenchard'. Lawrence, writing in 1932 a second inscription in the copy of *The Seven Pillars of Wisdom* he had presented to Churchill, had this to say: 'And eleven years after we set our

T.E.Lawrence in RAF uniform. He was killed in 1935 riding his motorbike along a Dorset lane when, coming upon two cyclists, he crashed in a vain attempt to avoid them

strong meat for some people's tastes.

The newspapers tracked him down, and unwelcome publicity forced him to leave the RAF. He promptly re-enlisted in the Royal Tank Corps under the name of T.E.Shaw, which he later adopted by deed poll, but found himself more suited to the RAF than the army. He wangled himself back into the RAF in 1925, pulling every string he could in order to overcome bureaucratic resistance, and he served in India from 1927 to 1929. After India Lawrence was at first posted to the flying-boat station at Cattewater near Plymouth, before being sent to Calshot on the south coast, where he indulged his love of speed by working with high-speed air-sea rescue launches. He invented his own engine and spent hours tinkering with his motor-cycle to get more power out of it. All this time he was corresponding, as a leading aircrafts-man, with the great in the land, and on every imaginable kind of topic from cabbages to kings. He was a brilliant letter-writer, as the publication of *The Letters of T.E.Lawrence to his Friends* has shown. These friends came from all walks of life, and he devoted as much care to a letter to an old comrade from the ranks as he did to one addressed to Field-Marshal Allenby, or George Bernard Shaw.

It was an extraordinary situation, and it is certainly arguable whether a man so gifted is justified in shutting himself away from the world, and avoiding his responsibilities. 'No man is an island,' wrote Donne, but that is what Lawrence was determined to be. Perhaps he had nearly come to terms with himself by the time his service in the RAF ended early in 1935. He had had time to work the bitter-ness and disillusionment out of his system, and he could hardly have expected to insulate himself from the rapidly-growing menace of Nazism. Had he lived, it is almost certain that Churchill would have sought—even commanded—his services. The two men had high regard for each other. But it was not to be, for he was killed the same year in May. He was only forty-seven.

Nearly twenty years after his death, while I was serving with the Arab Legion in Jordan, I retraced many of his journeys and operations, and sought out those who had ridden with him across the desert with Damascus as their lodestar. They were growing few and far between, and most of those I met had reached the stage where memory fails. But in a bedouin tent I found one elderly sheikh who had ridden with Lawrence to Deraa, and I asked what he had thought of him. For a while he was silent, staring out from the tent into the distance, and then he turned to me and said quietly—'Of all the men I have ever met, *Al Auruns* was the greatest Prince.'

hands to making an honest settlement, all our work still stands: the countries having gone forward, our interests having been saved, and nobody killed, either on our side or the other. To have planned for eleven years is statesmanship.' Unhappily, Anglo-Arab relations, which seemed 'set fair' in 1932, were soon to be wrecked on the rocks of Palestine, and Lawrence was fortunate in being spared witnessing the collapse of all he had striven for.

He had been elected a Fellow of All Souls in 1919, and most of his spare time immediately after the war was devoted to the writing of his book, *The Seven Pillars of Wisdom*. His style is modelled on Doughty's in *Arabia Deserta*, and it is curiously stilted in places, but he manages to catch, and convey, the spirit of Arabia as no other book, apart from the Bible, has succeeded in doing. Whether or not posterity remembers Lawrence as a gifted strategist and brilliant guerrilla leader, his name will live in his epic literary account of the Arab Revolt. But although he wrote un-ashamedly for literary fame, he did not seek fame in other fields. In 1922 he en-listed in the ranks of the RAF, taking the name J.H.Ross, and sought his personal seclusion in the barrack-room. He described his experience in the ranks in *The Mint*, written in 1928, which was rather too

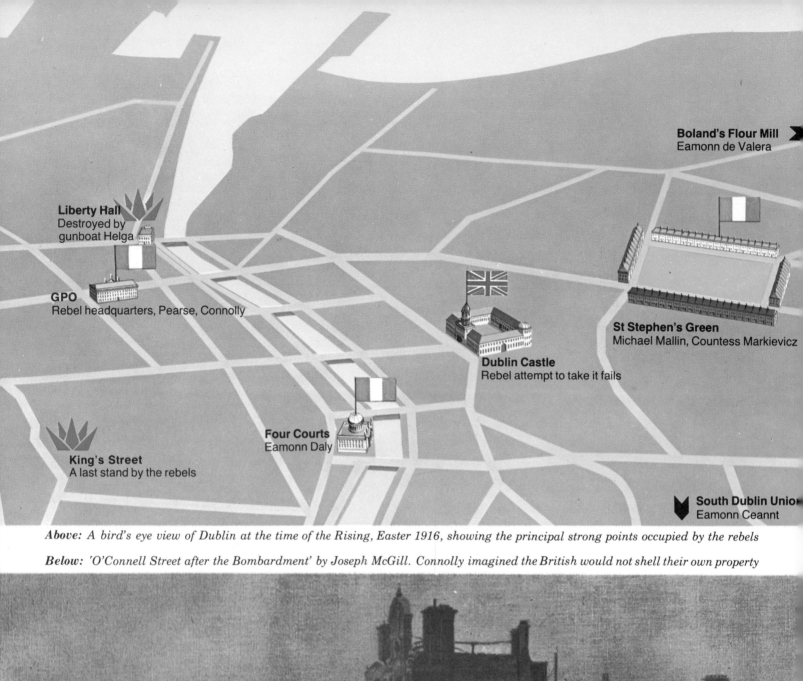

Liberty Hall
Destroyed by
gunboat Helga

GPO
Rebel headquarters, Pearse, Connolly

King's Street
A last stand by the rebels

Four Courts
Eamonn Daly

Dublin Castle
Rebel attempt to take it fails

Boland's Flour Mill
Eamonn de Valera

St Stephen's Green
Michael Mallin, Countess Markievicz

South Dublin Union
Eamonn Ceannt

Above: A bird's eye view of Dublin at the time of the Rising, Easter 1916, showing the principal strong points occupied by the rebels

Below: 'O'Connell Street after the Bombardment' by Joseph McGill. Connolly imagined the British would not shell their own property

The Easter Rising

The circumstances that led to the Irish rebellion of 1916 are of an intense complexity, historical, social, political, and perhaps above all psychological. Sean O'Faolain, that fine Irish writer, has written of his country: 'Most of our physical embodiments of the past are ruins, as most of our songs are songs of lament and defiance.' The Easter Rising was a complete failure, which left large parts of Dublin in ruins; yet without it Ireland might never have been free of English rule. The leaders, alive, had very few supporters even among the Irish patriots; dead, they became and have remained their country's heroes. It was a great historical paradox, and one that to this day the British have perhaps never really understood. Had they understood it, it is conceivable that the British might still have an empire, since the overthrow of British rule in Ireland became the model, the prototype, for the overthrow of imperial British might in Asia, in Africa, and elsewhere.

The historical complexity, from the British point of view, can be traced to a general misunderstanding of the Irish character and of Irish desires. The English were bewildered by the fact that most Irishmen, and all educated Irishmen, spoke English, and wrote it, as well as, and often better than, most Englishmen. They were further bewildered by the fact that a very large proportion of the Irish governing class was of English or Norman ancestry. In 1916, the English had not grasped the fact that for two centuries—since the brutal smashing of the old Irish governing class and the theft of their lands—it was precisely these people, Grattan, Tone, Parnell and so on, who had led the Irish in their longing to be free of alien rule. And the reason for this gross misunderstanding was that the English in England did not realize that the Irish way of life was in many ways—at least in terms of human relationships—culturally superior to the English way, less brutal, less materialistic, more spiritual, more dignified, with infinitely less snobbery and class distinction, directed more towards human happiness than to the acquisition of wealth or objects. Always technologically backward, the Irish were overwhelmed in the course of a thousand and more years by waves of conquerors. If those conquerors remained in Ireland, they became, as the English would and did say, seduced by the ease and pleasure of an Irish attitude that looks for charm, gaiety, and wit rather than for profit: they became 'more Irish than the Irish'.

And this the English, in England, dismissed as fecklessness. The fact that the Irish had different values from their own was regarded as funny—and the 'stage Irishman' was created in London. The fact that English might had always, eventually, crushed Irish rebellion was remembered; the fact that Irishmen had fought with immense distinction in all the major armies of Europe, and not least in that of Great Britain, was often forgotten. From the point of view of Whitehall at the turn of the century Paddy-and-his-pig was an essentially comical, child-like figure. He should know, in English terms, his proper station in life. Perhaps, at a pinch, the Anglo-Irish (an odious and meaningless term) might administer this province of Great Britain, but Paddy, never.

On the other hand, these people were politically troublesome and, furthermore, the English of the late Victorian age were a decent lot on the whole. During the Great Famine of 1846 the English liberals had let Ireland starve in the interests of their *laissez-faire* ideology—to have fed them would have interfered with the workings of the free market so far as corn chandlers were concerned—but later second thoughts prevailed. The Irish were to be given partial sovereignty over their own affairs, and a Home Rule Bill was passed. But then the First World War began. Home Rule was postponed until victory over the Germans should have been achieved. Paddy wouldn't mind, why should he? Paddy would join the British army, as he had always done and as scores of thousands of Irishmen did. Paddy wouldn't understand—and many, perhaps most, did not.

Mounting a revolution

But some Irishmen did understand. The most important of these were the members of the Irish Republican Brotherhood or IRB (which must not be confused with the Irish Republican Army, or IRA, a later creation). The IRB had been formed in 1858. It was a secret society which probably never numbered more than 2,000 including those Irishmen who belonged to it and who lived in England, America, or elsewhere. The majority of its members were what might be loosely called 'intellectuals' and in this, in their determination, and in their secrecy they bore a certain resemblance to their Russian contemporaries, Lenin's small Bolshevik Party. However, their aims were political rather than economic. They were patriots, dedicated to the ideal of national independence, and they were prepared to use all means—including force—to achieve this

Top: *Raging fires silhouette the Dublin skyline.* ***Centre:*** *British infantry fire on the Four Courts—a central rebel strongpoint.* ***Bottom:*** *After the Rising, rebels in a British gaol. The Irish suffered some thousand casualties in the Rising and hundreds were imprisoned*

Patrick Pearse, in barrister's robe and wig

Above: MacNeill — attempted to stop Rising
Below: Lord Wimborne — lord-lieutenant

Below: Countess Markievicz — a socialist

end. They provided, as it were, the general staff of the mass movement for Irish freedom from British rule, and their fortnightly publication, *Irish Freedom* (founded in 1910), advocated complete republican government for the whole of Ireland. It is significant that all the men who signed the proclamation of an Irish Republic on Easter Monday were members of the IRB.

When the First World War began, John Redmond, the leader of the Irish Nationalist Party and Parnell's heir, immediately proclaimed his acceptance of the postponement of Home Rule, both for himself and for his followers. These included the Irish Volunteers, perhaps then some 200,000 strong (of whom maybe a couple of thousand were trained and armed). This force had been created in November 1913 as a counter to the Ulster Volunteers, which were originally formed in order to fight against Home Rule. The Ulster Volunteers were also prepared to postpone a struggle that had recently seemed both inevitable and imminent, and from the North of Ireland as from the South scores of thousands of young men went off to fight, and only too often to die, in Flanders. As volunteers. Indeed, Redmond suggested to the government in London that they could remove all British troops from Ireland: his Volunteer force and the Ulster Volunteers were quite capable of seeing that there were no disturbances in Ireland throughout the period of the war.

The IRB had other ideas. At a meeting of their supreme council, as early as August 1914, the decision was taken — in secret of course — that there must be an Irish insurrection before the end of Britain's war with Germany. Until Easter Week 1916 the active members of the IRB were fully occupied in mounting this revolution.

They had at their disposal brains, a fairly considerable amount of money — mostly from Irish Americans — and little else. They had to act through the Irish patriotic organizations, over many of which they had obtained partial control, and if the rising were to be a military success they had to acquire arms, either from British arsenals, or from abroad, which meant in effect from Germany. The balance sheet was roughly as follows: apart from Ulstermen and certain landlords and industrialists, the people of Ireland wanted their freedom from British rule. However, the people were temporarily agreeable to the Home Rule solution, even though the postponed bill gave Ireland less than Dominion status in fiscal and other matters. Furthermore, the farming community, even more important in Ireland then than it is now, was doing very well out of the war. Thus the IRB could rely on very considerable emotional sympathy but little, if any, practical help

from the mass of the people. And since the Irish are in some measure a volatile race, there was no telling how they would react to a rising. Certainly the Roman Catholic Church would be against such a deed: and the parish priests were and are very powerful spokesmen in Ireland.

So far as fighting men went, any insurrection would seem doomed to certain defeat. Redmond's huge numbers of Volunteers were mostly unarmed, or were fighting for the British in France. However, some of those who remained in Ireland and were armed and trained could be relied upon. Their chief-of-staff was the historian Eoin MacNeill, and their commandant a schoolmaster in his early thirties named Patrick Pearse. Both of these men were members of the IRB, but as events will show they did not see eye to eye on tactics. The Volunteers were scattered throughout Ireland.

Resources of David and Goliath

The other para-military force was James Connolly's Irish Citizen Army. Connolly was a socialist who in 1896 had founded the Socialist Republican Party. He was a trained soldier. In 1908 James Larkin had created the Irish Transport and General Workers' Union. When that union organized a strike in 1913, and the strike was broken by strong-arm methods, Connolly decided that a workers' defensive force was needed and created his Citizen Army. It was led by himself and by an ex-British Army officer named Jack White. It has been said that this was the most efficient military force at the disposal of the Republicans. It was, however, very small. When it came to the actual fighting, it was only some 250 men who went out, as opposed to about 1,000 from the Volunteers.

Supporting these was the women's organization. Countess Markievicz — an Irishwoman, born a Gore-Booth, and of aristocratic ancestry — was one of the most prominent. She fought as an officer of the Citizen Army throughout the Easter Rising for she was not only a patriot but a socialist. There were also the so-called 'Fianna Boys', lads who enjoyed the manoeuvring before the Rising, as most boys would, and who also showed guts and resourcefulness when the real thing happened. They were messengers, runners, and so on.

Against them they had what was, on paper at least, a most formidable force.

To maintain their control over Ireland, the British relied primarily on the Royal Irish Constabulary, an armed police force, living largely in barracks, and some 10,000 strong. They were almost all Irishmen, knew their districts thoroughly, and were in 1916, with a very few exceptions, entirely loyal to the Crown. They were well trained, well equipped, only moderately unpopular (the Irish do not love police forces), and well informed. English HQ was Dublin Castle, and 'the Castle' relied on the RIC for its field intelligence.

In Dublin itself the police were not armed, though of course there were arms available. They numbered about 1,000 and were organized on the model of the London police. The Special Branch was concerned with politics. Through its investigations, and general infiltration of Irish republican politics, the Castle was supposed to know what the IRB was planning. The Special Branch did not seem, however, to have been particularly good at this job, nor to have infiltrated the IRB to any great extent. On the other hand the blame may rest with those in the Castle to whom they sent their reports. The evaluation of intelligence is infinitely more important than its accumulation.

And behind those 'occupation' forces there was a large British army in Ireland and what, in wartime and in Irish terms, were almost infinite reserves in Great Britain. If it were a mere question of manpower, the Irish had not a hope.

As for fire-arms, the David and Goliath ratio was even more vivid. Before the outbreak of the First World War the Ulster Volunteers had bought some 35,000 German rifles, the Irish Volunteers about 1,000. And of course the British army had everything, including artillery of all sorts. The Irish made an attempt to rectify this by getting rifles from Germany. Sir Roger Casement, an Irishman with a distinguished past, went to Germany from neutral America. He was to bring the weapons for the Easter Rising that the IRB had agreed on. His mission was a failure. British naval intelligence had broken some German cyphers. The British navy was thus able to intercept the German ship carrying the guns. Casement himself was immediately arrested when he came ashore from a U-boat near Tralee, in County Kerry, on Good Friday. Later the English tried him and hanged him as a traitor. The guns on which the Irish had been relying, even for this forlorn hope, had not arrived. Were they still to go on?

It is here that the different personalities and attitudes become important. We must pause to look at the men, English and Irish, involved; and also at the whole meaning of *Sinn Fein.*

Sinn Fein is usually translated as 'ourselves alone', and this is perhaps the best rendering in English of a complicated Irish concept. It means, first of all and above all, independence from British rule. But since Irish history was in those days so much bound up with contemporary Irish politics, it had a secondary meaning. For many centuries the Irish had been hoping for the help of England's enemies to get rid of the

English. The Spaniards and the French had let them down as the Germans were to do in 1916. This was not so much because Britain's enemies lacked the anxiety to defeat Britain in Ireland but because of geographical-military complications (tides, prevailing winds, and so on). Thus *Sinn Fein* also meant that the Irish must rely upon themselves alone in order to rid themselves of their British rulers. For the British, in the years to come, the 'Shinners' were to be the epitome of violent republicanism in Ireland. In fact the party, which only had its first annual convention as late as 1905, was essentially democratic. It had run a parliamentary candidate (who was defeated) in the Leitrim election of 1908. But as time went on it gained an increasing number of the extremists from Redmond's Nationalist Party. Arthur Griffith, its leader and also the editor of the *United Irishmen,* was never a fanatic. He believed in constitutional tactics – and was thus far less of an extremist than many of the IRB leaders – but, unlike Redmond's and Parnell's old party, he no longer trusted the alliance with the Liberal Party in Great Britain. Ourselves alone. To many young men it was a most attractive idea.

The British rulers were, on the whole, a shadowy lot. The Liberal government in London was inevitably devoting almost all its attention to the gigantic struggle on the Continent. Since Ireland appeared so placid in 1916, neither the best politicians nor by any means the best British soldiers were in the country. Augustine Birrell was Chief Secretary. Possessed, it was said, of extreme personal charm, he was a *belle lettrist* whose books, now forgotten, enjoyed in their time considerable esteem. He appears to have regarded his job in Dublin – which might be described as active head of the administration – as something of a sideline to his career as a *littérateur,* and spent a very large proportion of his time being charming in London. His principal Assistant Secretary, responsible for political affairs, was a civil servant experienced in colonial administration, Sir Matthew Nathan. He seems to have had little comprehension of the Irish temperament and to have been happiest behind his desk, dealing with routine paperwork. The general officer commanding the British army in Ireland was a Major-General Field. He, even more, seems to have had no idea of what was going on in Ireland at all. And finally there was Lord Wimborne, the lord-lieutenant and the King's representative, who presided over the British administration as a sort of constitutional monarch with all the powers, and most of the limitations, that that implies. However, he knew Ireland well. He had sponsored the land act of 1903,

which had pacified the Irish countrymen by further advantageous changes of the tenant-landlord relationship. He was popular with the Irish governing class, as was Birrell; but, unlike his Chief Secretary, he did not at all care for the situation that was developing.

The British intelligence services had, as we have seen, infiltrated the various Irish 'resistance' movements. The Volunteers, it must be assumed, had few secrets not known to Dublin Castle. And the Castle knew that a rising was planned to take place as soon as possible after the landing of Casement and his German guns. On 21st April 1916, Casement landed and was immediately arrested. Wimborne, who was to have gone to Belfast, cancelled his visit and on Sunday the 23rd, that is to say only a matter of hours before the Rising took place, demanded of Nathan that he immediately arrest 'between sixty and a hundred' of the Irish leaders. Had this been done successfully, it seems unlikely that any Rising would have taken place *at that time.* However, it was probably too late for a mere police action by that date. The men of the Citizen Army and the more militant Volunteers were under arms and ready to fight. As it was, Nathan persuaded his 'constitutional monarch' that there was no need for action. And Birrell was in London.

It would seem probable that Nathan's intelligence service had briefed him as to what was happening within the high command of the Volunteers after the news of Casement's arrest, that he knew Eoin MacNeill had decided that without the guns the Rising must be cancelled or at least postponed. What Nathan presumably did not know was that this decision finally split the Volunteers, and that the IRB was almost solidly behind Patrick Pearse and those other Irish patriots who were prepared to go ahead with the Rising even in these disadvantageous, indeed well-nigh suicidal, circumstances. All this sounds very neat and staff-officerish when put down on paper, but of course the reality was far more chaotic, involving a clash of multiple personalities, orders and counter-orders, and very considerable bitterness. Indeed MacNeill's decision to call off the Rising, and Pearse's to go ahead, was really the death-knell of the Volunteers and of the Nationalist Party whose armed force they were supposed to be. After the Rising, the political leadership of those hostile to British rule in Ireland passed to *Sinn Fein,* while those who fought in Easter week became the nucleus of the Irish Republican Army.

Certainly MacNeill's last-minute proclamation that the Rising be cancelled – he had boys bicycling all over the country, and even announced this supposed non-

Total War

happening in the Sunday papers—cannot possibly have been unknown to Nathan. He must have taken into account the fact that a few hot-heads were likely to ignore this order: he must also have known that the vast bulk of the Volunteers would breathe a sigh of relief and that the clergy —to whom the English have often attached an exaggerated political importance in Ireland owing to their ubiquity and their marked difference from the Anglican clergy in England—would support MacNeill and the mass of his supporters, content with the promise of eventual, diluted Home Rule. The handful of extremists could be dealt with—though not at all as easily as the English thought—by the overwhelming forces arraigned against them. No special precautions were taken, despite Lord Wimborne's fully justified fears. Indeed, on Easter Monday, the first day of the Rising, a great many British officers were at Fairyhouse Races.

The Easter Rising was suicidal. Patrick Pearse was well aware of this. Before ever it happened he said to his mother: 'The day is coming when I shall be shot, swept away, and my colleagues like me.' When his mother enquired about her other son, William, who was also an extreme nationalist, Pearse is reported to have replied: 'Willie? Shot like the others. We'll all be shot.' And James Connolly is said to have remarked: 'The chances against us are a thousand to one.' On the morning of the Rising, when asked by one of his men if there was any hope, he replied, cheerfully: 'None whatever!'

It was hard for the staff officers and colonial administrators of Dublin Castle, accustomed to weighing possibilities so far as their own actions were concerned, to realize that a group of men, perhaps 1,250 strong (the Citizen Army took no notice of MacNeill), was prepared to fight and die in such circumstances. But they should have been wiser in their age: Langemarck was recent, Verdun was going on, the Somme was about to happen. Seldom in history have men been so willing, indeed so eager, to throw away their lives for an ideal, almost any ideal, and the Irish ideal had long roots. The men went out and fought.

Easter week

The essence of the Irish plan was to seize certain key points in the city, and hold these for as long as possible, thus disrupting British control of the capital. It was then hoped that one of three things might happen: the country might rise in sympathy; the British might realize the ultimate impossibility of controlling Ireland and pull out; and last and faintest of hopes, the Germans might somehow come to the rescue of the rebels. Since the rebels had no artillery of any sort, their main

strong-points could only hold out provided that the British did not use their artillery. Connolly and the socialists hoped that the British would, for capitalist reasons, not bombard Dublin and thus destroy their own —or largely their own—property. This, too, was an illusion.

H-hour was 12 noon and since this was a Bank Holiday there were crowds in the streets who witnessed the small bodies of Volunteers and of the Citizen Army marching, armed, through the city to seize their various strongpoints. It went, on the whole, remarkably smoothly. Five major buildings or groups of buildings were seized north of the River Liffey, nine south of it, and some of the railway stations were occupied. Headquarters were established in the massive General Post Office in Sackville Street (now O'Connell Street) from which Irish flags were flown and where Patrick Pearse announced the creation of a provisional government of the new Irish Republic. With him in the Post Office were Connolly as military commander, Joseph Plunkett (a very sick man), The O'Rahilly, Tom Clark, Sean MacDermott, and other leaders. There, too, was a young man named Michael Collins. The rebels immediately set about preparing the Post Office against the attack which they expected almost at once. The four other principal strong-points seized were the South Dublin Union, a congeries of poor-houses and the like (commanded by Eamonn Ceannt); the Four Courts, the headquarters of the legal profession, where heavy law books were used as sandbags (Eamonn Daly); St Stephen's Green, where trenches were dug and barricades of motor-cars erected (Michael Mallin and Countess Markievicz); and Boland's Flour Mill, which covered the approach roads from Kingstown, now Dun Laoghaire, where any reinforcements from England would almost certainly disembark (Eamonn de Valera).

An attempt to seize Dublin Castle failed. An attempt to capture a large quantity of arms and ammunition from the arsenal in Phoenix Park known as the Magazine Fort was only partially successful and merely a few rifles seized. On the other hand, the rebels successfully cut telephone lines, and the Castle was for a time almost isolated. A further success was that a troop of Lancers which attempted to charge down Sackville Street was repulsed with casualties.

The British had been taken by surprise and were now almost completely in the dark. The Castle immediately ordered troops up from the Curragh and other camps outside Dublin and appealed to London for reinforcements. There, Lord French was commander-in-chief. He was an Irishman and an ardent Unionist. He immediately ordered that no less than four divisions be alerted for transfer to Ireland.

British policy was in fact thrown into reverse. Appeasement of the Irish was out; the rebels were to be crushed, rapidly, and massively. But if the British in Dublin were in the dark, so were the rebels. They had no wireless links either between the strong-points they had seized or with the outside world. Communication by runner became difficult and eventually impossible when the fighting reached its peak.

From a military point of view, Tuesday was comparatively calm. The British were closing in cautiously. Their strategy was to throw a cordon around that area of Dublin where the rebels' strong-points were, then cut that area in two, and finally mop up. They moved artillery and troops into Trinity College, a natural fortress which the rebels had failed to seize, though they had planned to do so. The reason was the small number of fighting men available. Looting began by the crowds. Martial law was declared. British reinforcements arrived at Kingstown. A mad British officer, a Captain Bowen-Colthurst, had three harmless journalists shot 'while trying to escape'—a phrase to become hideously familiar, and not only in Ireland. The atrocities had begun.

Dublin burns, Dubliners starve

By Wednesday morning the rebels were outnumbered twenty to one. The British now began to attack in earnest. Their first major action was to destroy Liberty Hall, the headquarters of the Labour Party and of the trade unions, by shellfire from the gunboat *Helga*. As it happened, the rebels had anticipated this, and the building was entirely empty. The British gunfire was inaccurate and many other buildings were hit and many civilians killed. The army also was using artillery: a 9-pounder gun was fired against a single sniper. Dublin began to burn, and the Dubliners to starve, for there was no food coming into the city. This was no longer a police action but full-scale war in which no attempt was made to spare the civilians. Meanwhile, British reinforcements marching in from Kingstown were ambushed by de Valera's men and suffered heavy casualties, but by dint of numbers forced their way through. St Stephen's Green had been cleared of rebels, who retreated into the Royal College of Surgeons, and established a strong-point there.

On Thursday the new British commander-in-chief arrived. Since Ireland was under martial law, he held full powers there. This was General Sir John Maxwell, a soldier of some distinction who had returned the month before from Egypt, where he had been commander-in-chief of the Anglo-Egyptian armies. Although he numbered the Countess Markievicz among his relations, he had no knowledge of the

Below: *Citizen Army parades outside Liberty Hall Dublin, centre of Connolly's Transport and General Workers Union and the Irish Labour Party*

Below: *Citizen Army parades outside Liberty Hall Dublin, centre of Connolly's Transport and General Workers Union and the Irish Labour Party*

current political mood in Ireland, and, indeed, as events were to prove, did more to undermine British rule in Ireland than all the rebels put together. He had been ordered by the British prime minister, Asquith, to put down the rebellion with all possible speed. And this he did regardless of political consequences.

The reinforcements from England were now in action. These were largely untrained men, and when they discovered that many of the men of the Irish Republican Army—as the rebels now and henceforth styled themselves—were not in uniform (how could they be?) they began shooting male civilians on sight.

On that day (Thursday) attacks were made on Boland's Mill, the men in the South Dublin Union were forced to give ground, and there was shelling of the General Post Office, which began to burn from the top down. Connolly was wounded twice. The first wound he hid from his men: the second was more serious, for one foot was shattered and he was in great pain. With the aid of morphia he carried on, directing the battle as best he could. The Dublin fires were now great conflagrations. With the streets full of small-arms fire and the water supplies often cut, these could not be dealt with. Still, no major rebel strong-point surrendered.

On Friday Connolly ordered the women who had fought so bravely to leave the General Post Office building, which was now cut off and burning. Later that day he and Pearse and the remaining rebels escaped from a building that was by now almost red-hot and about to collapse. They found temporary refuge nearby, while the British continued to shell the empty building. All knew that the end was near. A last battle was fought for King's Street, near the Four Courts. It took some 5,000 British soldiers, equipped with armoured cars and artillery, twenty-eight hours to advance about 150 yards against some 200 rebels. It was then that the troops of the South Staffordshire Regiment bayoneted and shot civilians hiding in cellars. And now all was over. On Saturday morning Pearse and Connolly surrendered unconditionally.

Like so much else about the Easter Rising, casualties are hard to estimate. It would seem that those of the British were about 500; those of the Irish, including civilians, about twice that figure. Material damage was estimated at about £2½ million. Large parts of Dublin lay in ruins.

When, on Sunday, the arrested rebels were marched across Dublin from one prison compound to another, they were at times jeered at and booed by the crowds, and particularly in the slum areas. The mass of public opinion had been against the rebels before the Rising and remained so until the reprisals began.

Left: The rebellious capital was not allowed to forget that British military might had crushed the Easter Rising. Tanks clatter past the saluting base during General French's peace parade, Dublin 1919

On the direct orders of the cabinet in London, reprisals were swift, secret, and brutal. The leaders were tried by court martial and shot: only when they were dead were their deaths announced. Among those thus killed were Willie Pearse, who was no leader and who, it was generally believed in Ireland, was killed because he had followed his famous brother; the invalid Plunkett; and, most disgusting of all to Irish minds, Connolly, who was dying and who had to be propped up in bed for the court martial in his hospital room. He was shot in a chair, since he could not stand. A wave of disgust crossed all Ireland. That wave did not subside when Asquith defended these measures in the Commons; nor when he realized that a mistake had been made, and sacked Maxwell.

When London at last understood that its methods were uniting all Ireland against Britain, there was yet another change of British policy. Many of the three thousand-odd men arrested after the Rising were released from British gaols. They returned to Ireland and began immediately to reorganize a new and more powerful IRA, now with the backing of the people. This was a gesture of appeasement by Lloyd George, the new prime minister, who called an Irish Convention intended to solve 'the Irish problem'. Since *Sinn Fein* boycotted the Convention, it was a complete failure. Again British policy was thrown into reverse, and the leaders of the new independence movement were arrested in the spring of 1918. Michael Collins, however, escaped arrest, though there was a price on his head, dead or alive, which eventually reached the sum of £10,000. He was to be the great guerrilla leader in the next round of the struggle. The Irish leaders, with much backing from the United States, both emotional and financial, set about creating a viable alternative government which could and did take over when the British should have at last seen that they could not win. *Sinn Fein* triumphed, and won most of the Irish seats in the 1918 election. The elected members, however, formed their own 'parliament', *Dail Eireann,* rather than sit in Westminster. Collins drew up a strategy of resistance, first passive, then obstructive, and finally active, which has since been pursued elsewhere against British imperialism, and indeed against the imperialisms of other nations. And in January of 1919 the first shots of the new rebellion were fired in County Tipperary.

The Easter Rising was a total failure. And yet it was a total success. After Easter week 1916 permanent English rule in Ireland became an impossibility. One tragedy was a triumph. Other tragedies were to follow. But the Irish achieved it, and alone.

The Brusilov Offensive

After its great retreat of autumn 1915 the Russian army, which had withdrawn in good order though with great losses, settled down on a new line. This ran from north to south for over 500 miles, from Riga on the Baltic through the Pinsk marshes to the Rumanian frontier. In the north it faced the Germans under Ludendorff, in the south the Austrians under Archduke Frederick. The line was divided into three fronts (army groups). The northernmost of these was the North-West Front, commanded by the same Kuropatkin who in the 1905 Russo-Japanese War had specialized in the tactic of the mis-timed retreat. The next sector was the West Front commanded by General Evert, who was also to manifest a dislike for offensive actions. Finally there was the South-West Front commanded by another master of timidity, General Ivanov.

Major-General Alekseyev who, as chief of staff to the commander-in-chief (Tsar Nicholas), was responsible for the Russian operations, was one of the better generals of the First World War—but his front commanders certainly were not. That men of their outlook held such responsible positions was, on the one hand, an indictment of the Russian political situation: with the Tsar, weak-willed in any case, out of touch at the front, the conduct of affairs at Petrograd (as St Petersburg was now called) was dependent more and more on the intrigues of the Tsarina and her favourites, and this circle tended to oppose the appointment of men of strong character and intellectual energy. On the other hand, there was another reason why so many Russian officers were unaggressive: the victory of 1812 over Napoleon had by now, aided by Tolstoy's dramatic and erroneous interpretation in *War and Peace,* entered the Russian tradition as a victory won by a great general called Kutuzov who had deliberately retreated in order to win the war. Thus there existed a concept—conscious and subconscious—of victory through retreat, which is why so many Russian generals seemed reluctant and over-anxious in attack.

During the winter of 1915-16 the Russian army was slowly restored to fighting condition. The deficiencies in 1915, the lack of rifles, of ammunition, of boots, and of properly-trained soldiers, would not be repeated in 1916. In early 1916 rifles were being produced at the rate of 10,000 per month; most front-line units had their full complement of field and machine-guns; ammunition, except perhaps for the heaviest guns, was being delivered fast

enough to build up stocks for a full summer campaign; the quiet winter months had given time for proper training of recruits—although the shortage of good experienced officers could not be remedied so easily. The Red Cross detachments organized by local civilians were doing much to maintain front-line morale, not least because they made it their business to provide for many of the physical and recreational needs which the war ministry had so obviously neglected.

The last battle of 1915 had been a minor Russian offensive in the south, aimed at helping the Serbian army, which had been driven into retreat when Bulgaria declared war. In the winter an inter-Allied military conference held at Chantilly in France laid plans for the 1916 summer campaign. Russia was to play a relatively small part in these plans, because of the heavy losses she had sustained in 1915: the main Allied offensive was to be on the Somme, and was to be preceded by a small diversionary attack made by the Russian army. However, the Germans disturbed this scheme by their massive attack on Verdun in February: not for the first time—nor the last—Russia was called upon to save her western allies by mounting a hastily-planned offensive to draw German divisions from the west to the east. In March and April a Russian army of the West Front, with artillery support whose intensity surprised the Germans, attacked through the mud of the spring thaw and overcame the German advanced lines. Ludendorff brought up reinforcements, for some reason the Russian GHQ withdrew its heavy artillery and aircraft from the sector, and the Russian soldiers were left almost defenceless in shallow marsh trenches, without gas masks. Unable to withstand the prolonged barrage of gas and high-explosive shells, and sustaining great losses, the Russians, still singing their hymns, were driven back to their start line in one day.

This disaster—the battle of Lake Naroch—was a relatively minor action, and the Russians were already planning bigger things, both to honour their pledge to the Allies (for the Somme operation was still scheduled) and to take pressure off the French, who were bearing heavy losses and in a desperate situation at Verdun. On 14th April the Tsar had presided at a meeting of the front commanders at GHQ. By this time the pessimistic Ivanov had been replaced by General Alexey Brusilov, who as an army commander had distinguished himself in the 1915 retreat even

General Alexey Brusilov. He later claimed that if his fantastically successful offensive had been properly exploited, Russia could have won the war for the Allies. Even if he had not won the war he probably prevented the Allies losing it

though he was a champion of an offensive strategy.

Brusilov risks his reputation

At the 14th April meeting the idea of attacking on the West (Evert's) Front was discussed. Both Evert and Kuropatkin declared that they preferred to stay on the defensive, alleging that there was not enough heavy artillery and shells to start an offensive. Brusilov disagreed, and recommended attacks on all fronts. This latter proposal was made in view of the superior rail communications on the German side of the line. By quickly shifting troops from a quiet sector the German command could easily reinforce that part of its line under threat: if the Russian attack came not at one point but at several this would be more difficult, especially as it would be hard to divine which of the attacks was intended to develop into the main thrust.

It was finally agreed that an offensive would be launched at the end of May, and that Brusilov's South-West Front would make the first move but that the main thrust would in fact start soon afterwards on Evert's West Front and be directed towards Wilno.

As he left this meeting Brusilov was told by a colleague that he had been unwise to risk his reputation by offering to launch an offensive. Unperturbed by this pessimism, he returned to his South-West Front to make the most of his six-week preparation time. He decided not to concentrate his forces but to ask each of the generals commanding his four armies to prepare an attack; with preparations being made at four places on his 200-mile sector of the line the enemy would be unable to anticipate where the main blow would fall. In previous actions, as Brusilov was well aware, both the place and the time of an attack had seemed to produce no surprise, so, in addition to avoiding troop concentrations, he took the precaution of dismissing newspaper correspondents. Also, since he suspected that the Tsarina was a careless talker, he avoided telling her the details of his plan.

The Austro-Hungarian line which Brusilov was preparing to break through was strongly fortified, consisting in most parts of three defensive belts one behind the other at intervals of one or two miles. Each belt had at least three lines of full-depth trenches, with fifty to sixty yards between each trench. There were well-built dugouts, machine-gun nests, sniper hideouts, and as many communication trenches as were needed. Before each belt there was a barbed wire barrier, consisting of about twenty rows of posts to which were attached swathes of barbed wire, some of which was very thick and some electrified or

mined. Brusilov's aircraft had made good photographs of these defences and the information was transferred to large-scale maps so that, as was shown later, the Russian officers had as good maps of the opposing line as had the Austrians. Moreover, although during the preparation period most of the soldiers were kept well behind the line, the officers spent much time in advanced positions studying the terrain over which they would fight. Meanwhile, with odd sighting shots the gunners were able to get the range of their prescribed targets, and shell stocks were building up. Trenches to serve as assembly and jumping-off points were dug near to the front-line Austrian trenches, in some places getting as close as one hundred or even seventy-five yards. Because this was to be a widely dispersed effort and not a conventional hammer-blow attack, no reserves were assembled.

While his four army commanders were each planning the details of their respective attacks, Brusilov was in touch – frequently acrimonious touch – with GHQ on the question of timing. On the one hand, Evert was declaring that his West Front attack, for which Brusilov's was only a preliminary diversion, needed more preparation time. On the other hand, to the urgent situation at Verdun was now added the rout of the Italian army by the Austrians at Trentino: unless Russia could do something to relieve the pressure Italy would be driven out of the war and the Central powers would be able to bring even greater strength against Verdun. In the end, 'Brusilov's Offensive', as it was later called (it was the only victory during the First World War named after a commander) was launched on 4th June.

The Archduke's birthday party

Three of Brusilov's four armies broke through at once, aided by thorough artillery preparation, surprise, and the alacrity with which the Czech elements of the Austro-Hungarian army offered themselves as grateful prisoners of war. Brusilov's main thrust was towards Lutsk and Kovel. The former was taken on the 8th: the Archduke Josef Ferdinand was forced by Russian shells to abandon his birthday party which he was celebrating there. With three deep and wide gaps in their line the Austrians were soon in full and fast retreat. However, the ever-reluctant Evert was still unwilling to start his own attack and on 9th June Brusilov learned that this attack would be postponed until the 18th. By this time Ludendorff was desperately trying to organize a counter-attack, and scraping together German units which he sent south to stiffen the demoralized Austrians. Fortunately for Austria, Brusilov's main thrust, confused by unclear instruc-

tions from GHQ, advanced in two directions at once, and thus lost the chance of capturing Kovel.

On 18th June Evert's promised attack towards Wilno did not materialize. Instead, that general made a minor, ill-prepared, and unsuccessful advance farther south at Baranowicze. By now it was clear that GHQ would do what Brusilov had always opposed: instead of attacking on the West Front it would send Evert's troops to Brusilov, believing that the latter with these reinforcements would be able to exploit his success fully.. As Brusilov expected, as soon as the Germans noticed these Russian troop movements they felt able to transfer their own troops southwards and, because they had better railways, got there first. In this way the German command was able to make the best possible use of its scanty resources. Despite a renewed push at the end of July, Brusilov made less and less headway as he found more and more German units opposing him. In general, the Brusilov Offensive came to an end about 10th August, by which time the Austrians had lost not only vast areas of territory but also 375,000 prisoners of war, not to speak of killed and wounded. But Russian casualties already exceeded half a million.

Brusilov later claimed that if his wildly successful offensive had been properly exploited, Russia could have won the war for the Allies. It does seem very possible that if Evert had carried out the main attack as planned (thus occupying those German troops which in fact were sent to help the Austrians) Brusilov would have been able to drive Austria out of the war – which almost certainly would have entailed the surrender of Germany before the end of 1916. In any case, Brusilov's Offensive achieved all the aims which it had been set, and more: Austrian troops in Italy had to abandon their victories and rush north to fight the Russians, and the Germans were forced to end the Verdun operation and transfer no less than thirty-five divisions from France to the Eastern Front. Even if Brusilov had not won the war, he probably stopped the Allies losing it.

Persuading Rumania

In mid-August, just as Brusilov's Offensive was slowing down, it was brought to a definite end by the decision of Rumania to abandon her neutrality and join the Allies, her first step in this direction being to sign a military alliance.

Right from the beginning of the war Allied diplomacy had been busy in Rumania. The Russian effort in this respect was two-pronged and, in view of the Tsar's habit of acting independently of his ministers, it is possible that neither prong knew what the other was doing.

The conventional weapon in this diplomatic campaign was the Russian ambassador in Bucharest, who enjoyed a certain influence in Rumanian political circles. But his talents were well matched by the Rumanian statesman Brătianu, who was long able to postpone a decision. Rumania at this time had well-balanced ties with both Russia and the Central powers, and public opinion was more or less equally

Below: Fund raising for Rumania. British poster depicts a serene King Ferdinand of Rumania warding off the sinister outline of the Kaiser in pickelhaube. *Rumania declared war on Austria on 27th August 1916*

split between those who favoured the Allies and those who supported Germany and Austria. It seems likely that most Rumanians were behind Brătianu in his efforts to delay a decision until the bandwagon of ultimate victory had moved unmistakably in one direction or another.

Russia's second agent in Bucharest was less correct than the ambassador, but may have been more effective in the long run. This was Rear-Admiral Veselkin, who from his miniature flagship *Rus* commanded the Danube Flotilla of the Russian Imperial Navy. This flotilla, directly controlled by GHQ, had been formed in 1914 by arming Danubian steamers and adding a few gunboats from the Black Sea Fleet. Its purpose had been to keep Serbia supplied, but after that nation was overrun it had little to do, apart from engaging in intrigues to push Rumania into war on Russia's side.

Veselkin was a witty, open-hearted, and eloquent officer, popular with his colleagues and, more important, a favourite of the Tsar. Whether he dabbled in genuine cloak-and-dagger activities is doubtful: the mysterious packages which he entrusted to transient Russians for strictly personal delivery to the Tsar contained not secret documents but merely Nicholas's favourite kind of Rumanian smoked sausage. But certainly he devoted all his spare time to the persuasion of the Rumanians. He had been entrusted with two million roubles' worth of jewellery which he distributed as 'gifts' to influential Rumanians and their wives. However, this was little compared to the wealth at the disposal of the German agents (who admittedly needed large sums to bribe railwaymen to turn a blind eye on the thinly-disguised war materials passing through on their way from Germany to Turkey). In mid-1916 it seemed that the pro-German party in Rumania was still strong enough to thwart Russian efforts.

In any case, some influential Russians believed that a neutral Rumania was more advantageous than an allied Rumania. Both the Russian naval and military attachés were sending mournful accounts of Rumania's unpreparedness for any serious war, and other Russian officials had the foresight to realize that an Allied Rumania would ask for help which Russia could not spare. However, a change of Russian foreign ministers was followed by what was virtually an ultimatum setting Rumania a time limit in which to make up her mind: the success of Brusilov's Offensive – then in progress – had encouraged this Russian move while at the same time providing an extra inducement for Rumania to choose the side of the Allies.

Rumania at war

Thus it came about that on 17th August Rumania signed the military alliance which had been pressed upon her, and then immediately began to disprove the belief – still current among the great powers fifty years later – that an ally is inevitably better than a neutral. The Allies had hoped that the more than half-a-million-strong Rumanian army would be sent south against Bulgaria, and then perhaps join up with their own forces at Salonika. However, Rumanian appetites in the direction of Bulgaria had already been satisfied by the Treaty of Bucharest of 1913 which had ended the Second Balkan War. On the other hand, Rumania still had desires (termed 'national aspirations') for Austrian Transylvania. So, on 27th August, to the consternation of friends and enemies alike, Rumania struck north.

Germany, which had been hoping that the Rumanian government would procrastinate just a little longer, was ill-placed to meet this new threat: help had already been sent to Austria to stop Brusilov, the western Allies were starting their Somme offensive at the same time as their forces at Salonika were becoming more active. So at first the Rumanian army carried all before it, capturing the capital of Transylvania in early September. However, by tight organization and by taking great risks in scraping together reinforcements from quiet sectors of other fronts, the German high command did just manage to master the situation. Falkenhayn attacked the Rumanians in Transylvania, while Mackensen went through Bulgaria and attacked the new enemy from the south, forcing the Rumanians to relinquish their Dobrudja territory. It now became evident that the Rumanian army was even worse trained and worse equipped than the pessimists had claimed, and in any case the easy-going Rumanian officers were ill-adapted to modern warfare. The Rumanians called for Russian help, and it was Russian troops which inflicted a temporary check on Mackensen in mid-September. Before the end of the month, despite Russian diversionary pressure farther north, the two German armies were threatening the heart of Rumania. In the south Mackensen drove his enemy over the Danube, while the Rumanian forces which had so cheerfully invaded Transylvania a month previously, were now in full retreat. On 23rd October Mackensen captured the key Black Sea port of Constanta, and in early December Bucharest fell. The Rumanian army was now finished for the time being: it occupied a small part of Rumanian territory around Jassy and was being reorganized by a French general in the hope of better days to come.

By this time two Russian armies were involved in Rumania, and it was not long before a quarter of the Russian army was devoted to this area. The Russian front had now, in effect, been extended to the Black Sea: no longer was there a safely neutral Russo-Rumanian frontier, so that for Petrograd at least the Rumanian alliance had proved to be of negative value. For Germany, once the immediate crisis was over, the entry of Rumania was a blessing: she now occupied the wheatlands and oilfields of that country and had better communications with her ally Turkey. Moreover, rightly or wrongly, the German high command had been anticipating the entry into the war of Holland and Denmark on the Allied side, and the rout of Rumania convinced it that these two countries were now unlikely to risk the same fate.

The Rumanian opportunists did the best they could to retrieve their country's fortunes: they declared peace in May 1918 but rejoined the Allies on the eve of their final victory.

Program for the Peace of the World

By *PRESIDENT WILSON* January 8, 1918

I. Open covenants of peace, openly arrived at, after which there shall be no private international understandings of any kind, but diplomacy shall proceed always frankly and in the public view.

II. Absolute freedom of navigation upon the seas, outside territorial waters, alike in peace and in war, except as the seas may be closed in whole or in part by international action for the enforcement of international covenants.

III. The removal, so far as possible, of all economic barriers and the establishment of an equality of trade conditions among all the nations consenting to the peace and associating themselves for its maintenance.

IV. Adequate guarantees given and taken that national armaments will reduce to the lowest point consistent with domestic safety.

V. Free, open-minded, and absolutely impartial adjustment of all colonial claims, based upon a strict observance of the principle that in determining all such questions of sovereignty the interests of the population concerned must have equal weight with the equitable claims of the government whose title is to be determined.

VI. The evacuation of all Russian territory and such a settlement of all questions affecting Russia as will secure the best and freest coöperation of the other nations of the world in obtaining for her an unhampered and unembarrassed opportunity for the independent determination of her own political development and national policy, and assure her of a sincere welcome into the society of free nations under institutions of her own choosing; and, more than a welcome, assistance also of every kind that she may need and may herself desire. The treatment accorded Russia by her sister nations in the months to come will be the acid test of their goodwill, of their comprehension of her needs as distinguished from their own interests, and of their intelligent and unselfish sympathy.

VII. Belgium, the whole world will agree, must be evacuated and restored, without any attempt to limit the sovereignty which she enjoys in common with all other free nations. No other single act will serve as this will serve to restore confidence among the nations in the law which they have themselves set and determined for the government of their relations with one another. Without this healing act the whole structure and validity of international law is forever impaired.

VIII. All French territory should be freed and the invaded portions restored, and the wrong done to France by Prussia in 1871 in the matter of Alsace-Lorraine, which has unsettled the peace of the world for nearly fifty years, should be righted, in order that peace may once more be made secure in the interest of all.

IX. A readjustment of the frontiers of Italy should be effected along clearly recognizable lines of nationality.

X. The people of Austria-Hungary, whose place among the nations we wish to see safeguarded and assured, should be accorded the freest opportunity of autonomous development.

XI. Rumania, Serbia and Montenegro should be evacuated; occupied territories restored; Serbia accorded free and secure access to the sea; and the relations of the several Balkan States to one another determined by friendly counsel along historically established lines of allegiance and nationality; and international guarantees of the political and economic independence and territorial integrity of the several Balkan States should be entered into.

XII. The Turkish portions of the present Ottoman Empire should be assured a secure sovereignty, but the other nationalities which are now under Turkish rule should be assured an undoubted security of life and an absolutely unmolested opportunity of autonomous development, and the Dardanelles should be permanently opened as a free passage to the ships and commerce of all nations under international guarantees.

XIII. An independent Polish State should be erected which should include the territories inhabited by indisputably Polish populations, which should be assured a free and secure access to the sea and whose political and economic independence and territorial integrity should be guaranteed by international covenant.

XIV. A general association of nations must be formed under specific covenants for the purpose of affording mutual guarantees of political independence and territorial integrity to great and small States alike.

Darf Belgien Englands Aufmarschgebiet werden?

War Weariness and Peace Overtures

Above: Kühlmann and his wife. He hoped to divide the Allies by negotiating separately with Great Britain. His unauthorized efforts only cemented British support for France and Italy. Far left: Sceptical German view of Wilson, May 1916. Wilson, a would-be peacemaker, strove to be 'neutral in thought and word'. But, this cartoon points out, Wilson's song of friendship to the German people is drowned by the organ of guns played by America — guns sold to the Allies. Left: Wilson's 'Fourteen Points' formulated the idealistic principles which Wilson had always felt should dominate peace negotiations. But the interest shown by the other powers in peace proposals was less idealistic. Below left: 'Must Belgium become open territory through which the English army can march on Germany?' German propaganda map showing how in ten days Great Britain could march through Belgium to attack the industrial heart of Germany. Belgium was the main stumbling block in peace negotiations. The Allies insisted that Germany evacuate Belgium: the Germans refused.

The First World War affected the lives of ordinary men and women to a far greater degree than any war between supposedly civilized powers had ever done before. In the autumn of 1914 the hopes of a quick victory for either side faded, and from that moment the war machine clamoured for more men and more resources, a clamour which continued for almost four years. Millions of men were drafted into the armed forces. More millions, and women also, were directed into work on munitions or other industries essential for war. In most countries, profits and wages were regulated, more or less ineffectively. Prices rose as the governments poured out paper money, and supplies ran short. The free market which had brought prosperity in normal times now broke down. There was rationing of essential goods, particularly of foodstuffs. Very often there was a sharp reduction of the pre-war standard of life, and even so the rations were not supplied in full. Quite apart from the countless dead on the battlefields, the war brought hardship and sometimes starvation to the living.

There was social discontent and political unrest. The surprising thing is how slowly and how late this was translated into war weariness. For much of the period, men were demanding instead that the war should be waged more fiercely and more completely. The demagogues who called for aerial reprisals or the internment of enemy aliens evoked more response than did the few enlightened men who sought a way out. Equally surprising, the rulers of most countries, though usually of a conservative cast, showed little anxiety that the war would shake the fabric of society. On the contrary, they believed that failure to achieve a decisive victory would open the door to revolution. In the last year of the war, the prospect of revolution came to haunt Europe in the shape of Bolshevism, but even this only spurred the governments of the various belligerents to more violent efforts.

In the first two years of the war, peace overtures came from Woodrow Wilson, President of the one great neutral power, and not from any of the countries at war. Wilson strove to be 'neutral in thought and deed'. He refused to judge between the combatants, though his private sympathies were on the Allied side. His sole aim was to bring the belligerent countries to the conference table, and he therefore shrank from propounding terms of peace himself. His overtures were rebuffed by both sides. The Allies and the Central powers remained equally confident of victory, though they did not know how to achieve it. Even the few who advocated compromise were fundamentally in disagreement. Compromise, it was agreed, meant an acceptance of the *status quo,* but each side had a different *status quo* in mind. On the Allied side, the *status quo* meant a return to the frontiers of 1914 with reparation for the devastated areas particularly in Belgium and northern France. For the Germans, the *status quo* meant the actual situation as established after their first victories: Germany would retain all she had conquered or at the very least be generously compensated for any territory from which she withdrew.

A question of territory

Thus there were few peace overtures during this earlier period, because any common ground was lacking. The Germans made some cautious soundings of Russia in the hope of detaching her from the Allied side. Even here they were trapped by their own victories after the campaign of 1915. They would not surrender all the Russian territory they had overrun, and the Tsar Nicholas II was equally determined to liberate the soil of Holy Russia. In the autumn of 1916 the reactionary Russian ministers at last took alarm. They began to fear that war weariness was really beginning in Russia and were ready to respond when the Germans made overtures through Stockholm. At exactly this moment the German high command insisted on a declaration in favour of Polish independence. General Erich Ludendorff, the real director of the German high command, imagined, wrongly, that thousands of Poles would then join the German army. The Poland he proposed to recognize was entirely drawn from Russia's share of the partition. The negotiations with Russia naturally broke down. The Germans lost their chance of ending the war on the Eastern Front.

The topic of peace was first publicly aired in December 1916, though there was no serious intention behind it of ending the war. The impulse came from the renewed demand in German governing circles for unrestricted submarine warfare. The Germans had tried this earlier in 1915 and had then given it up when faced by American protests. Also they did not possess at that time enough submarines to make their threat effective. Now Ludendorff insisted once more. The German attack on Verdun had failed to produce a French collapse. The German armies had been heavily

Total War

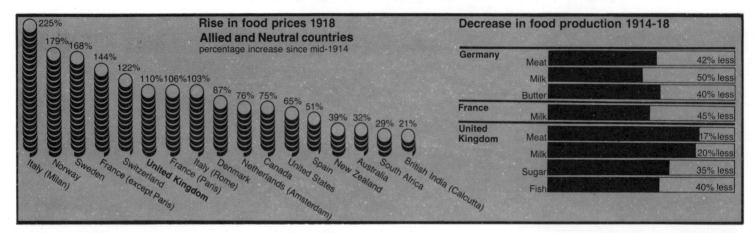

Rise in food prices 1918
Allied and Neutral countries
percentage increase since mid-1914

225% — Italy (Milan)
179% — Norway
168% — Sweden
144% — France (except Paris)
122% — Switzerland
110% — United Kingdom
106% — France (Paris)
103% — Italy (Rome)
87% — Denmark
76% — Netherlands (Amsterdam)
75% — Canada
65% — United States
51% — Spain
39% — New Zealand
32% — Australia
29% — South Africa
21% — British India (Calcutta)

Decrease in food production 1914-18

Germany		
Meat		42% less
Milk		50% less
Butter		40% less
France		
Milk		45% less
United Kingdom		
Meat		17% less
Milk		20% less
Sugar		35% less
Fish		40% less

strained by the prolonged engagements on the Somme, and Ludendorff did not believe that his armies could achieve a decisive victory in 1917. On the contrary he confessed that the Germans would have to stand on the defensive when he prepared a withdrawal to the Hindenburg Line. Ludendorff accepted, however, the claim of the German naval leaders that unrestricted submarine warfare would bring about the collapse of Great Britain. It might also provoke the United States into entering the war against Germany. Ludendorff did not care. He did not imagine that the Americans could develop any effective military strength, still less that this could be deployed on the European battlefield.

Bethmann's Peace Note

Theobald Bethmann Hollweg, the German chancellor, was less confident. He had seen the brave hopes of German generals and admirals dashed time and again. He was anxious to stave off unrestricted submarine warfare, but this could be done only if he offered a firm prospect of ending the war on Germany's terms. On 12th December 1916 Bethmann therefore issued a Peace Note. This merely announced Germany's willingness to negotiate. There was no indication of the terms Germany would propose. Privately Bethmann intended that they should be those of victory: control of Belgium and north-east France for Germany. Even so, he imagined that war weariness in the Allied countries would produce some sort of favourable response. There had in fact been some discussion behind the scenes in Great Britain whether victory was possible. The people had not been consulted and were still not disillusioned. David Lloyd George, who had just become British prime minister, rejected Bethmann's Peace Note out of hand and answered by demanding the complete defeat of Germany, or, as it was called, the 'Knock Out Blow'.

President Wilson, like Bethmann, wanted to avoid a breach between Germany and the USA. He, too, recognized that negotia-

tions for peace were the only way of achieving this. Despite the failure of Bethmann's Note, Wilson tried much the same tack. On 20th December he invited the contending powers to formulate their war aims: perhaps these 'would not prove irreconcilable'. The Germans failed to answer. They knew that their aims, if openly stated, would outrage Wilson and be the more likely to provoke him into war. The Allies, though offended at being put on the same moral level as the Germans, devised idealistic war aims which could not be denied Wilson's approval. The interchange had not much reality. Both sides were bidding for Wilson's favour, not trying to clear the way for negotiations. The Germans did not bid at all seriously. Even Bethmann had despaired of preventing the renewal of unrestricted submarine warfare and merely kept Wilson in play until the submarines were ready. The Allies picked out the more respectable bits of their aims, but there was a great deal more which they intended to demand and which they did not reveal to Wilson.

Obstacles to peace

These first manoeuvres brought out the obstacles to a negotiated peace then or thereafter. Governments had to display a confidence of future victory in order to keep up the spirits of their peoples. If any country stated the terms which it expected would follow its victory, the opposing side was indignant and spurred to new efforts. If, on the other hand, a country tried to be moderate, the enemy regarded this as a confession that it foresaw defeat. More than this, negotiations were not needed to demonstrate that Belgium was the insuperable obstacle to a negotiated peace. The Germans were in possession and would insist on remaining there more or less openly. They even perversely used their own invasion of Belgium as proof that her neutrality was no protection for the Ruhr. They argued that what they had done in 1914, the British and French would do next time. The British, on their side,

were equally adamant that Belgium must be evacuated and fully restored by the Germans. This was the ostensible reason why Great Britain had entered the war, and the British never wavered from it. The fumbling negotiations, far from making victory unnecessary, showed that nothing could be achieved without it.

Social unrest

Even so, the idea of a compromise peace, however impractical, had been aired for the first time, and this was not without effect on the warring peoples. The early months of 1917 brought the first open signs of war weariness, though rarely in the clear form of a demand to end the war. Living conditions were at their worst during the hard winter of 1916-17. Food, clothes, and fuel ran short. There were strikes everywhere in factories and coal mines. In Germany there was a mutiny among the bored sailors who never left harbour. But there was still a margin for concession. Wages were increased. The trade unions were brought into partnership with government departments and the armed forces. Rationing did something to ensure that the reduced supplies went round more fairly.

In two great countries, the social unrest had political results. In Austria-Hungary, the Emperor Karl, who had succeeded to the throne in November 1916, tried to conciliate the nationalities of his nondescript empire. In Russia, the Tsar, Nicholas II, abdicated and a republic was proclaimed, in the belief that this would provide a government more worthy of the national confidence. It is sometimes said that the first Russian revolution of 1917 was made by the army and was against the war. On the contrary, the army was never in better spirits or better equipped. The revolution came after bread riots in Petrograd and took the army by surprise. The generals and the politicians who most favoured the war at first welcomed the overthrow of the Tsar as a preliminary to waging the war more effectively. Nevertheless, the people of Russia were now given

Left: The cost of continuing the war was hunger and hardship. Food prices rose sharply, even in neutral countries, as trade routes were blocked, men taken from growing food to make or use munitions, and fertile land laid waste. Right: Prague housewives queue for food. Many countries introduced rationing systems — and even so the rations were often not supplied in full. In Germany, where shortages were greatest, civilian deaths exceeded by 760,000 the number which pre-war statistics indicated as probable

a voice, at least in theory, and this voice was soon raised for peace.

The Emperor Karl and the democratic politicians in Russia both recognized that their countries would be ruined unless peace was made in the near future. Both made overtures for peace though they used different ways of doing it. Emperor Karl's way was by secret negotiations, a last splutter of old-style diplomacy. His brother-in-law, Prince Sixte of Bourbon-Parma, approached President Raymond Poincaré of France with terms which he thought the French might accept. Poincaré did not object to them, and Prince Sixte then showed them to Karl as official French demands. The most solid point in them was that France should recover Alsace and Lorraine. To this, Karl on his side made no objection. The British and French governments were now highly excited. They imagined that they were in sight of a separate peace with Austria-Hungary which would deprive Germany of a valuable ally and perhaps even open a backdoor for the invasion of Germany.

In fact the whole affair was a muddle, as usually happens when amateurs dabble in diplomacy. Karl only meant to invite terms which he could show to his German ally. The British and French supposed that he was deserting his ally. There was a further difficulty. Great Britain and France were at war with Austria-Hungary only in theory. Their forces never clashed except for an occasional naval encounter in the Adriatic. Italy was the only Allied power seriously engaged against Austria-Hungary, and the Italian statesmen had no particular interest in securing Alsace and Lorraine for France. The Italians wanted South Tyrol and Trieste. In 1915 the Austrians had accepted war rather than surrender these territories, and their resolve was still unshaken.

However Lloyd George and Alexandre Ribot, the French premier, dangled peace with Austria-Hungary before the Italian foreign minister, Baron Sonnino, though

they did not reveal Emperor Karl's so-called peace offer. Sonnino was unmoved. No peace without victory was his policy as it was that of his allies, except that in his case it was victory over Austria-Hungary, not over Germany, that he wanted. The Austrian peace offer, never very seriously made, ran into the sands. Soon in any case the French decided that they would not welcome a peace which merely benefited Italy, while they went on fighting Germany. Only Lloyd George continued to pursue the dream of a separate peace with Austria-Hungary. General Smuts, for the British war cabinet, and Count Mensdorff, the Austrian diplomat, had long meetings in Switzerland. Their discussions always broke on the same point. Lloyd George wanted to be able to attack Germany through Austrian territory. The Austrians would only abandon their German ally after a general peace had been made. The Habsburg monarchy remained shackled to the war.

Socialist efforts

The Russian search for peace was more open and created more stir in the world. Russia was now theoretically a democracy, and the Provisional Government sought to satisfy the wishes of the Russian people. They abandoned the imperialist aims of tsardom which had been enshrined in the secret treaties and announced a programme of peace without annexations or indemnities. At the same time they remained loyal to their Western allies and desired a general peace, not merely Russia's withdrawal from the war. There were many in the West, particularly among the socialist parties, who desired the same thing. For the first time, public opinion in the West took the talk of peace seriously. Even in Germany there was a pull in the same direction. The moderate Russian socialists thought that peace without annexations or indemnities would prove irresistible, if socialists from all the warring countries combined to support it. They proposed a meeting of European socialists at Stock-

holm. The German socialists agreed to come. British and French socialists also wished to come, though their object was to show that Germany would not agree to the programme and thus to keep Russia in the war, not to secure a real peace. The French government refused to allow their socialists to go. The British government reluctantly gave their socialists permission to attend the Stockholm conference. However, the British seamen, who were furiously anti-German because of the U-boat warfare, refused to convey the socialist delegates. The Stockholm conference was never held.

With this, the hope for a general peace without annexations or indemnities was dead. However, its influence went on rumbling. In Germany, Matthias Erzberger, a leader of the Centre Party, began to doubt whether Germany would win the war. He put forward a peace resolution in the Reichstag, and the Social Democrats supported him. Bethmann also welcomed the peace resolution as a means of restraining the high command. Instead, the high command secured his dismissal. When the peace resolution was passed by the Reichstag, George Michaelis, the new chancellor, endorsed it 'as I understand it'. What he understood was that it would not count as annexation for Germany to keep her present conquests nor would it count as indemnities if she were paid to leave them. When later Germany made peace with Russia and Rumania, it turned out that the Centre and the Social Democrats understood the peace resolution in the same sense. The peace resolution of the Reichstag had no effect in Allied countries. In Germany it helped to stem war weariness. Many Germans believed that the Reichstag had proposed idealistic peace terms and that the Allies had rejected them.

There was another remarkable overture for peace in 1917. The pope — Benedict XV — wanted to save the old order in Europe. Especially he wanted to save the Habsburg monarchy, the last surviving Roman Catholic power. Also he felt the socialist competition for peace. On 12th August 1917 the

Total War

pope proposed peace to the warring powers in much the same vague terms as Woodrow Wilson had used earlier. The papal peace note envisaged a return to the *status quo* of 1914 and even mentioned the restoration of Belgian independence – not terms likely to please the Germans. The Western powers had promised Italy that they would not accept the help of the Vatican in peace negotiations. Arthur Balfour, the British foreign secretary, rashly asked for more precision in regard to Belgium. When France and Italy protested, he withdrew his enquiry. Nevertheless, the Vatican passed the enquiry on to the German government. The Germans, who meant to hang on to Belgium, gave an empty answer. The pope had failed to break the deadlock, like the socialists before him.

The German government was not wholly inactive. Richard von Kühlmann, who became secretary of state on 6th August, doubted whether Germany could win the war and was proud enough of his diplomatic skill to believe that he could end it. His aim was to divide the Allies by negotiating separately with one of them. There had already been some unofficial approaches from French politicians in the same direction. Joseph Caillaux, who had been prime minister before the war, gave repeated hints that he was ready for a separate peace with Germany, though it is uncertain whether he actually attempted to negotiate with German representatives in Rome, while Germany and Italy were still not at war with each other. Aristide Briand, another former prime minister, also fancied that he could make a separate peace and perhaps recover Alsace, or part of it, at the same time. None of this was more than empty talk by out-of-work politicians. The French people, after all their sacrifices, would not accept peace without regaining Alsace and Lorraine. The Germans would not surrender the two provinces unless they were defeated.

Kühlmann thought in any case that it was a waste of time to negotiate with any French politician. In his opinion, it was British resolve which kept the war going. If the British were satisfied, the war would come to an end. Kühlmann therefore approached the British government through the King of Spain. He hinted, quite without authority, that the Germans might withdraw from Belgium if the British made a separate peace. The British, far from wanting to desert their allies, were afraid that France and Italy, both in a shaky position, might desert them. The British answered Kühlmann that they were prepared to discuss peace terms only if their allies were included. Kühlmann announced that Germany would never surrender Alsace and Lorraine. Lloyd George in return pledged that Great Britain would fight by

the side of France until Alsace and Lorraine were recovered. The mere attempt to start discussions over peace terms thus, far from bringing understanding, drove the belligerents farther apart.

Pressure from below

The fumblings towards negotiation, which had always been pretty futile, now came to an end and were not seriously resumed until the end of the war. There was, however, considerable pressure from below for some sort of action. Indeed 1917 was the great year of war weariness and even of revolt against war. This went farthest in Russia. Once the Provisional Government had failed to secure a peace without annexations or indemnities, its hold over the Russian people crumbled. It sought permission from its Western allies to make a separate peace. This was refused, for fear of the effect it would have on public opinion in France and Italy. For in these countries war weariness reached the level of action and resistance to war. In both countries discipline was breaking down in the armies, and order was breaking down behind the lines. In France, after the military failures under General Robert Nivelle in April 1917, most of the army refused to obey orders for any new offensive. At one time fifty-four divisions were in a state of mutiny. The more rebellious soldiers talked of marching on Paris and overthrowing the government. In Italy there was less open mutiny, but soldiers deserted their units and went home, where the police dared not arrest them and often did not want to. Thus, by the summer of 1917, the French army was incapable of fighting, and the Italian army was at little more than half its paper strength. The spirit in the factories was little better. In Turin and Milan, the workers were already planning to take over the factories for themselves as they did after the war.

Yet this discontent did not last. The war weariness gradually faded away, and there was a revival of national enthusiasm, though on a more cautious scale. General Henri-Philippe Pétain, who took command of the French armies in May 1917, assured the French soldiers that they would not be flung into more futile offensives and declared his intention of waiting for the Americans. When there was a governmental crisis in November, President Poincaré recognised that he must decide between Caillaux, the man of compromise peace, and Clemenceau, the man of more ruthless war. He chose Clemenceau as premier. From this moment, France was committed to the bitter end. Clemenceau arrested a few so-called pacifist agitators and arraigned Caillaux before the high court for correspondence with the enemy. These gestures were hardly necessary.

There was still enough national enthusiasm to sustain Clemenceau, particularly with the Americans just over the horizon.

In Italy the national spirit was actually revived by a catastrophe – the great defeat of Caporetto. As the shattered Italian armies fell back behind the Piave, politicians of all parties rallied to the national cause. Disputes stopped in the factories. Soldiers went back to their units. The war actually became popular in Italy for the first time.

Russian overtures

The Russian army, it seemed, was beyond saving. It began to break up after an unsuccessful offensive in July. The Russian people had become indifferent to the war. There was no mass movement to stop the war, but still less was there any mass support behind the Provisional Government. There was merely indifference, and this indifference enabled the Bolsheviks to seize power in November. Peace was the most urgent point in the Bolshevik programme. Lenin, the Bolshevik leader, believed that the people of every warring country would immediately respond to an appeal for peace if it were made firmly enough. The imperialist governments, as he called them, would have to conform, or they would be swept away by their angry proletariats.

On 8th November 1917 Lenin read the decree on peace to the All-Russian Soviet. It proposed immediate negotiations for 'a just and democratic peace' – with no annexations, no indemnities, and self-determination for every people, however long they had been ruled by another. An armistice of three months should be at once concluded on every front, so that negotiations should proceed. Here was certainly an overture for peace, the most practical and urgent made throughout the war. The German government responded. They welcomed an armistice on the Eastern Front, though they were not moved by the idealistic phrases.

The Western powers were more embarrassed. They wanted the Russians to go on fighting, not to make an armistice. They did not believe that the Germans would ever make peace on Lenin's principles, nor did they intend to do so themselves. Lloyd George and Clemenceau were both symbols of war to the end. If they now compromised, they would be replaced by more sincere peacemakers – Caillaux in France, Lord Lansdowne in England. The old theme was repeated that the only way of saving society and beating off socialist revolution was to carry the war to a victorious resolution. On 29th November the Allied supreme council gave a sharp and final negative to Lenin's Decree on Peace. From this moment the Bolsheviks were denounced as treacherous and disloyal, and their withdrawal was blamed for the continuance of the war.

Below: Bitter Dutch socialist cartoon on the Stockholm conference. Mars: 'I must see to it that the light does not reach him.'
Below centre: The wounded—victims of Europe's determination to continue the war.
Bottom: Swiss cartoon of Lenin, who called for 'open dealings', an end to secret diplomacy, and peace

At the same time, anyone who proposed a compromise peace or even idealistic terms could be branded as a Bolshevik. This was a convenient arrangement, with rewarding results. War weariness became a symptom of Bolshevism. Most people disapproved of Bolshevism, which was supposed to maintain itself by Chinese methods of torture and to practise among other things the nationalization of women. Most people therefore did their best not to be war weary.

Peace at Brest Litovsk

Peace negotiations between Germany and Soviet Russia were duly held. The Germans interpreted no annexations in the peculiar form that they should keep what they possessed. They also interpreted self-determination to mean that the inhabitants of the Russian territories occupied by German armies did not wish to be put under Bolshevik rule. Trotsky, who led the Soviet delegation, resolved to appeal from the German rulers to the German people. On 10th February 1918 he announced to the astonished conference: 'No war—no peace' and departed. The German and Austrian workers were now supposed to come to the aid of their Russian comrades. So at first they did. There was a renewed outbreak of strikes in both countries. Once more the strikers were mollified by increased wages and more food, itself looted from the Russian land. The strikes died away. On 3rd March 1918 the Soviet government reluctantly concluded with Germany and her allies the Peace of Brest Litovsk. This peace was not based on the principles which Lenin had laid down. The confident hope that idealistic terms would automatically end the war was dispelled.

With this, overtures for peace virtually came to an end. Some vague chat drifted on between British and German spokesmen at The Hague and between British and Austrian in Switzerland. An American, George Heron, also talked interminably to well-meaning Austrian professors who had no influence on their government. In July 1918 Kühlmann said in the Reichstag that the war would ultimately have to be ended by negotiations. For this he was dismissed from office by order of the high command. No one in the Allied countries went even as far as Kühlmann, though Lord Milner and perhaps others had the bright idea of buying Germany out of western Europe by allowing her a free hand to dominate Russia. All such ideas were mere whimsy, another aspect of the anti-Bolshevism with which many Western statesmen were driving themselves demented.

War weariness, strangely enough, also declined. Food supplies improved in both Germany and Austria-Hungary, as the occupied Russian lands were more systematically looted. In many parts of Austria-Hungary there was a collapse of public order, or something near it. Deserters formed 'Green bands' and lived by terrorizing the countryside. These disturbances did not reach the industrial areas and had little effect on the Austro-Hungarian armies. In any case, with Russia out of the war, it did not much matter what happened in Austria-Hungary. Her armies in Italy could stand against the Italian forces which were in equally bad shape.

Both Germans and Allied peoples were shored up by the prospect of decisive victory. The Germans were inspired first by Ludendorff's offensives from March to July. During this period there was no war weariness in Germany—a clear indication that it sprang far more from boredom and discouragement than from hardship. During the same period the British and French people were actually stimulated by defeat. From the middle of July onwards they were inspired by victory. After 8th August the Allied armies rolled forwards. War weariness, though still there, was replaced by a confidence that the war would soon be over.

There were now peace overtures of a different kind. The earlier overtures had been political devices with which to embarrass the enemy or sometimes to placate a powerful neutral. At the end of September 1918 both Germany and Austria-Hungary made peace overtures with a genuine intention of ending the war. The two governments imagined that they were still free to choose: if the Allied terms were unsatisfactory, Germany and Austria-Hungary would go on with the war. This was an illusion. The two governments were making peace overtures only because they had lost the war. Moreover, as soon as the peace overtures became known, war weariness burst out. Later it was alleged that the German armies had been stabbed in the back. This was the reverse of the truth. Ludendorff confessed that the war was lost when he insisted on an immediate request for an armistice. Only then did political discontent blaze at home. Similarly, in Austria-Hungary the nationalities staked out their claim to independence only when the imperial government had begged for peace terms from President Wilson.

An ignorant, though rational, observer might assume that war weariness would provoke peace overtures. But, in the First World War, peace overtures, themselves usually a political manoeuvre, provoked war weariness, and when these overtures were rejected, enthusiasm for the war was revived. No doubt the people ought to have demanded an end to the war. In fact fiercer war was from first to last the popular cause.

I WANT YOU
FOR U.S. ARMY
NEAREST RECRUITING STATION

4 AMERICA: THE HOPE IN THE WEST

Introduction

If the First World War had a turning point, it was in the spring of 1917. Two great events took place almost simultaneously which seemed to augur well for both sides. In mid-March the Russian collapse, which the Allies had feared for so long, looked imminent when the Tsar was overthrown, inaugurating the Russian Revolution which could only strengthen German hopes. In April the United States abandoned its neutrality and declared war against Germany, which buoyed up Allied hopes. Neither event fulfilled the hopes and fears which preceded them. Although the revolt in Russia was serious indeed, Russia did not leave the war, and in the summer of 1917 Kerensky, the Russian leader after Tsar Nicholas II was forced to step down, launched a powerful offensive on the Eastern Front which threw the Germans back, if only temporarily. And the resumption of unrestricted submarine warfare did not bring America in at once. Woodrow Wilson still sought peace, and although diplomatic relations with Germany were broken on 3rd February, Wilson still hoped to bring about peace without American intervention. The Zimmermann Note, however, swung American public opinion toward intervention, when, thanks to a British leak of a German diplomatic letter which Britain had intercepted, it was felt that Mexico had been promised huge blocks of American territory in Texas, New Mexico and California by Germany if Mexico joined the war. The American West, until now rather indifferent to the neutrality-submarine issue, clamoured for action. Wilson's hand was forced and the US joined the Allies in April.

Uncle Sam joins the parade. America could bring little immediate help ... but she could bring hope

But would American aid prevent a German victory in the East and a German breakthrough in the West? American air forces were virtually non-existent in April of 1917. The American army was small and for the first year of intervention, ineffectual. But the American navy, strengthened by the Spanish-American War and the build-up of the American fleet under Theodore Roosevelt in the years after it, could be brought to bear immediately on the war in the Atlantic. The situation was exactly as the Germans had reckoned. Jellicoe, the British First Lord of the Admiralty, told Vice-Admiral W.S.Sims of the US navy in London that it would be impossible for Britain to continue for very long if the losses of merchant shipping continued. Prime Minister David Lloyd George gave Britain another six months.

Germany had miscalculated when she decided to risk American intervention. Six American destroyers arrived in Queenstown (now Cobh), Ireland, on 4th May, and by 5th June there were thirty-four American ships based there to convoy goods across the Atlantic. The more convoys, the fewer the losses to submarines. Meanwhile American men were conscripted in their hundreds of thousands. They could not play a role immediately, but if the combined US and Allied navies could keep Britain going until American soldiers arrived on the Western Front, the war could be won.

The Germans, on the other hand, hoped for a breakthrough in 1917. Morale was cracking in France. Her armies mutinied in the spring of 1917, and there was a real chance that France would be forced to make a separate peace to contain revolution at home. But the mutinies were quelled, despite continuing heavy losses on the Western Front. As 1917 progressed, German hopes were buoyed up by the Italian

collapse at Caporetto and the terrible losses sustained by the British at the Third Battle of Ypres. The Kerensky offensive in the East fizzled out, and by November the Bolsheviks had overthrown the Provisional Government in Russia, thereby inaugurating a civil war which almost certainly meant the withdrawal of Russia. As the Allies worked feverishly on a diplomatic front to keep Russia in the war, the effects of the long conflict were beginning to tell on the civilian populations of France, Britain and Germany. Rationing of certain items was introduced in Britain; shortages of almost every type were having their effect on the German war effort, now taken over completely by the military after the departure of Bethmann Hollweg from the Chancellory. The German gamble had failed. The nucleus of an American army was forming behind the lines in France and in the United States, and the American navy helped keep intact the convoys which kept Britain alive. The war of attrition had reached a new phase. Would Russia be brought to the peace table in time so that Germany could make one final, massive push that would bring her victory on the Western Front? And perhaps more fundamentally, could the nations which were at war maintain order and society at home and stave off the fate already suffered by Russia?

Despite all Allied efforts to the contrary, Russia, under Lenin and Trotsky, decided to make a separate peace with Germany in order to consolidate their position. By the spring of 1918, much of Russia was out of the control of the Bolsheviks. The Czech Legion hostile to Bolshevism controlled most of the Trans-Siberian Railway. British, French, Japanese and American troops began landing at Russian ports, ostensibly to keep Russia in the war, but actually to support

Total War

the anti-Bolshevik armies who were more anxious to oust Lenin than to force the Germans out of western Russia and the vast territories in the Ukraine and Baltic areas which Germany now occupied. The Treaty of Brest Litovsk removed Russia from the war and satisfied most of Germany's greatest war aims.

German-controlled states dominated the whole of Eastern Europe and huge chunks of Russian territory were separated from her. Russian leaders could then concentrate on winning their civil war, while Germany could now transfer most of her forces on the Eastern Front to make one final push against France and Britain before the force of the American army could be brought to bear. By early 1918, Britain had conquered most of the non-Turkish portions of the Ottoman Empire. Germany had long since effectively lost her colonies. The Allies had won the colonial conflict. The Germans had won the war in the East. Just as von Moltke, von Büllow and the great German military planner, von Schlieffen, had argued before the war, victory would come to Germany only by victory in the West.

As German U-boats were losing the battle on the seas, Erich Ludendorff started his big push in the West. The Michael offensive took German armies almost to the point that they had held in September 1914. The tank now began to play an ever more significant role for both sides, but the initial German offensive was stopped. Germany had pushed forward but had not broken through. By June American troops began to make their appearance near the Marne by throwing the Germans back at Château Thierry. The arrival of the Americans boosted flagging British and French spirits, and war weariness was thrown aside as it became clear that an Allied breakthrough, for so long a seemingly impossible goal, was now within reach. On one final throw, Ludendorff sent waves of Storm Troopers, his élite force, against the Allied lines. On the Black Day of the German Army, 8th August 1918, the Germans were thrown back, many of their best soldiers killed. The Allies pushed forward. German supplies and men were depleted. The blockade had taken its toll. German citizens were going hungry. Only the unfit, overaged or underaged were available to serve the crumbling Second Reich. With manpower weakened and the breakthrough a failure, Ludendorff and Hindenburg approached the Kaiser in September and told him that the war was lost. German salients were being overwhelmed by the Allies. Time was against the Kaiser.

Unless he made a peace of some kind, German positions in France and Belgium would be overrun and Germany herself invaded. By the end of September, as German soldiers fell back, regrouped, and fell back again, the Kaiser appointed Prince Max of Baden as his Chancellor to make the peace on Allied terms that Germany had shunned.

President Wilson had enunciated his plans for a peace with an Allied victory when he addressed Congress in January 1918. His speech, perhaps the most important of any statesman on either side during the war, enumerated the 14 Points upon which America felt a German surrender was acceptable. The 14 Points included a withdrawal of German troops from the territories they occupied in France, Belgium and Russia, an independent Poland with access to the Baltic Sea, a restoration of the disputed territory of Alsace-Lorraine to France and, above all, the principle of national self-determination for the peoples of Europe, particularly those of the Habsburg Empire. Wilson, like so many war-weary people in all countries, hoped that the First World War would be 'a war to end all wars'. Somehow the sacrifice of a generation of men could only be tolerable if, as a result of their sacrifice, peace could be established for all time. Thus, Wilson believed in the establishment of a League of Nations which could maintain the peace, freedom of the seas for all shipping, and a programme of general disarmament.

The Germans could not and did not object to these latter proposals. The loss of the war, which they now accepted as inevitable, would force them to abandon their own war aims and disgorge the territory they had occupied for most of the course of the war. By October the German government felt that the 14 Points were the best basis on which they could make a peace without suffering occupation or, even worse, partition. Germany, after all, was a young state not yet fifty years old. It was a federal state, and separatism, especially in the Catholic south of Germany, was still strong. If the war continued, there was a real possibility of the break-up of Germany into several parts which was a long-desired dream of the French. Germany accepted the 14 Points as a basis of surrender and a cessation of hostilities as the Allies continued to clear France and Belgium of German soldiers. The German Army was cracking. No time could be lost.

In the last weeks of the war Turkey and Bulgaria surrendered, and Austria-Hungary began to disintegrate. On 27th October Austria-Hungary sued for peace. Time was running out on the Second Reich. On 9th November, as armistice negotiations reached their terminal stage, revolution broke out in Berlin and other major German cities while the Kaiser was in the forward military headquarters just inside Belgium, at Spa. Hindenburg reluctantly urged the Kaiser to abdicate and flee to neutral Holland, which he did, as a German Republic was declared by the Social Democrats. Their rather conservative leader, Friedrich Ebert, was named provisional leader of the German nation, and the armistice was signed. The guns ceased to fire in Europe at 11 o'clock in the morning, 11th November 1918. As the shakily established German government formed its new constitution at Weimar, Wilson toured Europe and was ecstatically cheered in France, Italy and Britain, and then settled down in Paris with the other representatives of the victorious allies to make the peace that would end all wars . . .

If Wilson was most concerned in making a lasting peace, the other leaders of the Great Powers—Orlando, Clemenceau and Lloyd George—were even more anxious to secure and if possible widen the territorial gains they had already made. Britain, France and Belgium quickly agreed to partition the German and Turkish Empires outside Europe among them. But France hoped that if a partition of Germany were not possible, a long-term alliance between France and the Anglo-Americans was the only way she could make sure that another war of revenge would not break out within a generation. The United States was quickly moving towards isolationism, a fact which Wilson ignored, but even Wilson recognized that such an alliance would not be supported by the American people and placed his faith in a general guarantee of frontiers by the League of Nations. The blockade against Germany continued until the spring of 1919, and thousands starved or froze to death. A peace had to be made quickly. The fear that Bolshevism would spread throughout Europe was very real for the diplomats in Paris, and the overthrow of the Bavarian and Hungarian Soviet Republics did not allay their fears. Wilson and Lloyd George were able to contain the most venal of French demands, but the peace imposed upon Germany was far from the ideals of the 14 Points which Germany thought she would get. Disarmament was to begin with the defeated powers. The vanquished were presented with a *fait accompli*. Their choice was small: sign or be occupied. They signed. The Great War had ended.

U-Boats: The Fatal Decision

At long last, on 9th January 1917, Bethmann Hollweg, the German chancellor, at a conference at GHQ, Pless in Upper Silesia, signified his concurrence with the resolution in favour of unrestricted submarine warfare, that is he agreed to the torpedoing of enemy and neutral merchant and passenger ships without warning. His feelings were similar to those which had burdened him during the crisis of July 1914. For him the Pless decision was a leap in the dark, like the action of Austria-Hungary against Serbia in July 1914. On that occasion he realized that any attempt to overthrow Serbia might well lead to a European war. Now he was tormented by anxiety lest the reckless use of the U-boats result in war with the United States. And on both occasions his fears were justified.

In 1914 it was the growing consolidation of the Triple Entente, the increasing strength of Russia, and the critical situation in the Balkans which drove the German government to approve and guarantee the Austro-Hungarian attack on Serbia regardless of the risk of a European war. In 1917 the German government was impelled by the hopelessness of the land war to agree to unrestricted submarine warfare and thereby to run the risk of a conflict with the USA. In 1917, as in 1914, Bethmann Hollweg yielded to the military demands through a mixture of fatalism and a hope that the general situation might be changed by violent action. Bethmann Hollweg's two shattering decisions resembled each other in that each was based on a collapse of political leadership and an excessive regard for the military standpoint.

The arguments about U-boat warfare among the military and political leaders of the German empire had begun as far back as late 1914. The first impulse was given by the unsatisfactory progress of the naval war. At enormous cost a German battle fleet had been built up in sharp naval rivalry with Great Britain. On the outbreak of war, however, any large-scale naval enterprise was discouraged by the government, which needed to maintain the German fleet intact as a political instrument. It was not until 1916 that the naval commanders ventured to engage the Royal Navy, and the battle of Jutland finally showed that Germany had not enough naval power to defeat the great

Below: A U-boat puts out to sea, festooned with garlands, the tribute of the German people's faith in its destructive power. Almost all the press and the people believed, like the high command, that unrestricted submarine warfare could bring Great Britain to her knees

Left: German approval for the new development 'U-boats go forth'

British fleet in a battle on the high seas. The pretensions of the German naval leaders were badly injured because of the limited effectiveness of the fleet since 1914, and Germany was driven more and more to rely on submarine warfare against British seaborne commerce. The aim was to destroy the economic life and supply lines of Great Britain and thus force it to sue for peace. But this strategical switch was by no means due solely to the German navy's ambition to play some part in the war. It was forced on the naval leaders by the grim fact that in a few months Great Britain had won complete command of the world's seas and was trying to cut off Germany's overseas imports by a distant blockade. It seemed essential not to accept this gigantic British success meekly but to find some counterstroke in reply. In the first months of the war German U-boats had destroyed several large British warships by underwater torpedo attacks, and these brilliant successes led to an over-estimation of the U-boat weapon, which in fact was still comparatively undeveloped. The chief of the naval staff, Admiral von Pohl, pressed for a blockade of the British coasts as early as the beginning of November 1914. And a little later Admiral von Tirpitz, state secretary of the imperial navy office, gave an interview to Karl von Wiegand, a representative of the American press, in which he drew the world's attention to the possibility of a German blockade of Great Britain by submarines. Among the German people an impression grew that the U-boats were an infallible weapon in the war with Great Britain. The result was a violent public agitation concerning U-boats.

Commercial warfare by U-boat actually began as far back as February 1915 and was consistently carried on in various forms for two years, until January 1917. During this period the German government had time and again to justify the employment of a novel method of warfare in face of the vehement complaints of the European neutrals and, especially, of the United States. Yielding to such opposition, it set its face, until 9th January 1917, against the unrestricted use of the U-boat weapon demanded by the naval authorities. But at the same time, in internal debates, it repeatedly asserted that its negative attitude was not due to consideration for international law but was purely for military and political reasons. When, in January 1917, the ruthless exploitation of U-boat warfare was finally decided upon, Bethmann Hollweg expressly declared that he had never opposed it on principle, but had always been governed by the general situation and the respective strengths of U-boat weapons. In the various deliberations it was the Kaiser Wilhelm II alone

who expressed humanitarian scruples. For him the drowning of innocent passengers was 'a frightful thought'.

As the U-boat was a new weapon, there were in 1914 no international rules regarding its use in commercial warfare. The German government should have striven to obtain international recognition for the new weapon, for both the present and any future war. But instead, the Germans admitted the illegality of U-boat commerce war from the first by describing it as a reprisal measure against the illegal methods adopted by the British in their commercial blockade. For Great Britain, like Germany, had been forced by the advance of weapon technique to break the traditional international rules dealing with blockades. Because of the danger to its naval forces it could not carry on a close blockade of the German coasts—hitherto the only permissible method—but had to engage in a distant blockade directed at neutral as well as German ports. For this purpose the British declared the whole of the North Sea to be a war zone and prescribed for neutral shipping fixed navigational routes which could be supervised by British naval vessels. Moreover, Great Britain extended the regulations about war contraband and the confiscation of cargoes in neutral vessels. Liable to seizure were not only goods useful for the arming and supply of enemy forces, but all foodstuffs and raw materials intended for the Central powers. It was immaterial whether the cargoes were being carried direct to enemy ports or through neutral countries.

The new British contraband regulations initiated an economic and hunger blockade which was aimed at the enemy's civilian population. The German reprisal measure, commercial war by U-boat, was similarly directed against the civilian population. It might therefore be considered as merely a similar measure, by way of reprisal. But in fact there was one great difference. The British blockade was merely a confiscation of material goods, but the German submarine attacks endangered the lives of crews and passengers. When an underwater torpedo was fired without warning, it was impossible to take any steps to save the lives of those on board. And if the ship was attacked from the surface the crew and passengers taking to the lifeboats were exposed to the perils of wind and wave on the open seas, for the U-boat was in no position to pick them up and bring them to a place of safety.

The most difficult thing to justify was the effect of commercial war by U-boat on the neutrals, in whose case there was, of course, no question of reprisal. Instead, the German government demanded that the neutrals submit to submarine warfare as they had submitted to the British block-

ade of the North Sea. But there was only partial justification for this demand. True, neutral shipping used the prescribed routes through the English Channel and submitted to examination of cargoes in British ports. Nevertheless, the European neutrals, in spite of the British blockade, had delivered large food cargoes to Germany down to 1916. On the German side there was no desire to suppress neutral shipping by submarine warfare, but only to drive it out of certain sea areas. In the proclamation of 4th February 1915, which initiated submarine warfare, the waters

Bethmann Hollweg, who struggled in vain against the demands of the high command

around Great Britain and Ireland, including the whole of the English Channel, were declared a war zone. Every enemy merchant ship encountered in the war zone would be destroyed. Neutral ships were advised to avoid it, as attacks on enemy ships might, in the uncertainties of naval warfare, well affect neutral ships also. It was hoped that this warning might frighten neutral shipping off trade with Great Britain. Admiral von Pohl wanted to emphasize this warning by ordering all ships within the war zone to be sunk without distinction, a step which meant unrestricted submarine warfare. He actually wanted a few neutral ships to be sunk without warning at the outset of the U-boat operations so that there should be general uncertainty and neutral trade with Great Britain stopped as soon as possible. In subsequent deliberations the deterrent effect on neutral shipping was an important factor

At the beginning of 1915, and again at the beginning of 1916, such intimidation seemed especially necessary, for Germany at those times was far from possessing enough U-boats to carry on a successful economic war with Great Britain. In February 1915 there were only twenty-one U-boats available for watching the shipping lanes to Great Britain. As the voyage to the war zone, the return journey, and the

America: The Hope in the West

overhaul afterwards, took a considerable time, there were never more than three or four boats operating at any one time on the coasts of Great Britain. Obviously there were not enough of them to inflict any considerable damage to Great Britain's trade by direct action. Thus it was very important to keep neutral ships, and as many enemy ships as possible out of the war zone. But the Germans had no success. Even before the announced U-boat commerce war started on 18th February, very firmly worded notes of protest reached Berlin from the neutral maritime powers affected. Most serious of all, the American government held the German government strictly accountable for all measures that might involve the destruction of any merchant vessel belonging to the United States or for the death of any American subject. The war situation of the Central powers in February 1915 was much too strained to risk complications with powerful neutral states. The chancellor therefore persuaded the Kaiser to order the U-boats to spare neutral ships, especially those belonging to the United States or Italy. The U-boat commerce war began four days late, on 22nd February 1915, in this modified form. In March 1915, out of 5,000 vessels entering and leaving British ports only twenty-one were sunk. Neutral shipping soon resumed trade with Great Britain.

The Lusitania incident

In spite of precautions taken during the period of restricted submarine warfare, a grave incident occurred on 7th May 1915, when a German U-boat sank the British ocean liner *Lusitania* with an underwater torpedo attack. Among the drowned were 128 American citizens. The sinking of the *Lusitania* aroused intense indignation in the United States, and a sharp exchange of notes between the American and German governments ensued. President Wilson had no desire to precipitate an armed conflict with Germany by his *Lusitania* notes, but he feared that a continuation of the U-boat war would one day leave him no other choice. He tried repeatedly to persuade Great Britain to allow food imports into Germany through neutral countries. At the same time he took a firm stand against the contempt for humane principles shown in the kind of warfare used by the U-boats. The first *Lusitania* note of the American government on 15th May 1915 denied the legality in international law of any form of U-boat commerce war, inasmuch as in neither an underwater nor a surface attack could the safety of passengers and crew be guaranteed. In the third *Lusitania* note of 23rd July 1915 Wilson conceded that submarines were a novelty in naval warfare and that no provision could have been made for them in the international regula-

tions. At the same time it was admitted that the German submarine operations of the last two months had complied with the customs of war and had demonstrated the possibility of eliminating the chief causes of offence. This remarkable concession on the part of the Americans was based on the fact that since May 1915 the U-boats had been fitted with deck guns and, owing to the uncertainty of hitting the target with torpedoes, had carried on the commerce war in 'cruiser' style, according to the rules laid down for the taking of prizes. The U-boat came to the surface when attacking a ship and before sinking it allowed the persons on board to take to the boats. All enemy vessels were sunk without exception, but neutral ships were sunk only when they were carrying contraband.

Although this was the actual method of operation during the *Lusitania* crisis, the German naval authorities obstinately opposed any restriction being placed on submarine warfare and especially any attempt to confine U-boats to the rules of 'cruiser' warfare. They maintained that such methods were an intolerable danger to the submarine and its crew. They named as the chief dangers attempts of the merchant ships to ram the submarine, concealed guns on the ships, the use of a neutral flag by British ships, and attacks by enemy warships during the necessarily lengthy searches. The German government was not informed by the navy that in the period May-July 1915 eighty-six per cent of the merchant vessels that were sunk were dealt with according to the cruiser warfare rules, and that from February to July 1915 250 merchant ships carrying a neutral flag were examined and only on three occasions was any misuse of the flag dis-

covered. By its policy of secrecy the navy apparently wanted to avoid being permanently restricted to 'cruiser' warfare and losing for ever the chance of unrestricted submarine warfare. On 6th June 1915 the Kaiser ordered that all large passenger liners, whether enemy or neutral, must be spared. Nevertheless, on 19th August, the British liner, *Arabic*, was sunk without warning, two more American citizens losing their lives. The Kaiser then ordered that no passenger liner was to be sunk until it had been warned and the passengers and crew given a chance to escape. During the arguments about U-boat methods in the summer of 1915 Tirpitz, in order to put pressure on the Kaiser, twice offered his resignation. His offers were abruptly refused. Yet the Kaiser changed his chief of naval staff at the beginning of September. Vice-Admiral Bachmann, a Tirpitz adherent who had held the office since February 1915, was replaced by Admiral von Holtzendorff, who was more amenable to the political views of the chancellor. On 18th September 1915 Holtzendorff gave orders that the U-boat commerce war on the west coast of Great Britain and in the Channel should be carried out on the 'cruiser' system. The naval commanders were not ready for this step and brought the U-boat war around Great Britain to a standstill. Thus ended the first phase of the U-boat war. The *Arabic* case was settled on 6th October by German compliance. The German government did not defend the action of the U-boat commander, which infringed the order of 6th June. The *Lusitania* case remained unsettled. The German government refused to admit that the U-boat attack on the *Lusitania* was contrary to international law, for if it did so future

Arming at sea – a U-boat takes ammunition on board. From May 1915 U-boats were fitted with deck guns as well as with torpedoes, and surfaced before attacking an enemy ship

unrestricted submarine warfare would be impossible.

In 1915 several U-boats, large and small, were sent to the Austro-Hungarian naval base of Pola, and also to Constantinople. These carried on trade war in the Mediterranean and the Black Sea with great success, limiting their actions to the 'cruiser' rules. They restricted the flow of supplies to the Anglo-French forces in the Dardanelles and Salonika. But at the beginning of 1916 U-boat activities were severely handicapped by the progressive arming of the enemy's merchant vessels. The U-boat flotilla at Pola therefore asked the naval staff for permission to sink any armed merchant ship without warning. Holtzendorff granted the request, but with the proviso that passenger ships should continue to be exempt. At the same time he re-opened the trade war around Great Britain by issuing the same orders. A new phase in the submarine war was begun on 29th February 1916 and was termed 'intensified' U-boat war.

The high-ranking officers of the German navy looked on the new measures as a mere transitional phase. Since the beginning of the year the prospects for unrestricted submarine war had considerably improved, for General von Falkenhayn, chief of the army general staff, was now expressly demanding it. Since the autumn of 1914 the German armies, in co-operation with those of Austria-Hungary, Turkey, and Bulgaria, had created firm front lines on enemy territory; they had driven the Russians far back to the east, and by the occupation of Serbia had opened the way to Constantinople. Falkenhayn was at the peak of his military successes. In February 1916 he intended to deliver an all-out offensive on the Western Front, starting with a holding attack on Verdun. In the summer and autumn of 1915 he had firmly advised against the ruthless use of the U-boat weapon because he thought that a break with the United States might produce unfavourable reactions from the European neutrals and in particular might make Bulgarian assistance in the campaign against Serbia doubtful. In 1916, on the other hand, when the Balkan situation had been stabilized, such considerations were no longer valid. He believed that unrestricted submarine warfare directed against Great Britain would help his offensive on the Western Front. The U-boat action was timed to start in the middle of March. Almost the whole of the German press advocated ruthless use of the U-boats. The alliance between Falkenhayn and the navy on this point put Bethmann Hollweg in a very difficult position, and he spent the first weeks of the New Year in a very worried state. He feared that the adoption of un-restricted submarine warfare 'might result in condemnation by the whole civilized world and a sort of crusade against Germany'.

The Charleville conference

In the decisive conference with the Kaiser on 4th March 1916 at GHQ, Charleville, Falkenhayn declared that, in view of the dwindling resistance of the German allies and the German civil population, the war must be brought to an end before the year was out. The only means of achieving this was by unrestricted submarine warfare. On his part Bethmann Hollweg argued that Germany could stand another winter campaign. He would rather have a compromise peace than risk prolonging the war indefinitely by challenging America. In his opinion there were still insufficient U-boats. In the middle of March 1916 there were only fourteen large submarines capable of carrying on a commerce war in British waters.

On 4th March 1916 the Kaiser, unable to make up his mind, postponed his final decision until the beginning of April and then indefinitely. Nevertheless, with the agreement of the chancellor, a further tightening of the U-boat blockade was ordered on 13th March 1916. In the war zone both armed and unarmed merchant ships were to be destroyed without warning. Outside the war zone the previous orders remained in force. Tirpitz, who had not been called to the Charleville conference, reported sick to the Kaiser in protest and on 15th March he agreed to resign. One of Bethmann Hollweg's chief opponents had left the scene.

Whereas the instruction for the sinking of armed merchant ships was made public, the new order of 13th March was kept secret. Its effects, however, were viewed by the neutrals with growing alarm. Washington suspected that Germany had already started unrestricted submarine warfare. A new incident soon gave rise to another German-American crisis. On 24th March 1916 two Americans were injured when the cross-Channel passenger steamer, *Sussex,* was torpedoed without warning. In the erroneous belief that American citizens had lost their lives in the sinking President Wilson sent a note on 18th April threatening to break off diplomatic relations with Germany if it did not abandon its current methods of submarine warfare. Under pressure from this ultimatum the Kaiser gave orders, at Bethmann Hollweg's request, cancelling the tightened-up rules for submarine warfare in the combat zone around Great Britain. The rules of the 'cruiser' system were to be observed until further notice. The commanding officers on the naval front declared that such a procedure was un-

Cynical German cartoon protesting against the outcry over the drowning of passengers — a 'blind' American passenger on an 'unarmed' merchant ship

workable, because of the danger to the U-boats, and they brought the submarine war in British waters to a complete standstill. In the Mediterranean the U-boats continued the campaign according to the new rules.

At the end of April 1916, when the reply to the American note had to be drafted, Falkenhayn again tried to persuade the Kaiser to agree to unrestricted submarine warfare. He asserted that he would have to forego action against Verdun if the U-boat war was suspended. Bethmann Hollweg indignantly rejected such an alternative and after a bitter dispute he once again convinced the Kaiser. In a note dated 4th May 1916 the German government agreed to the demands of the American government and informed it that the German naval forces had been instructed to observe the canons of international law with regard to the stopping, searching, and destruction of merchant vessels. At the same time it expressed its expectation that the United States would now induce the British government to abandon as soon as possible such of its methods of waging naval war as were contrary to international law. The German government reserved its complete freedom to alter its decision if this were not done. Wilson at once protested against the German claim to make respect for the rights of American citizens on the high seas dependent on the behaviour of the British government. Responsibility in such matters was individual not joint, absolute not relative. The two opposing standpoints were thus definitely laid down. If Germany again intensified the submarine war, it was to be expected that the

'This is how your money can fight—turn it into U-boats.' An appeal for war loans. In the background is a sinking enemy ship

United States would promptly enter the war.

It was but a few months after the settlement of the *Sussex* case that the problem of unrestricted submarine warfare once again became acute. During the summer of 1916 the war situation was completely transformed. The Central powers, who had held the initiative for a whole year, were now forced into defensive battles lasting for months by the persistent offensive of the Russians in Volhynia and eastern Galicia and of the British and French on the Somme river, which could only be withstood by enormous efforts and casualties. Falkenhayn had to break off the battle for Verdun, which was bleeding not only France but also Germany to death. His prestige was shattered, and when Rumania entered the war against the Central powers on 27th August 1916 he was replaced by Hindenburg and Ludendorff. Hindenburg, who was the most popular of the German military leaders, became chief of the general staff. Bethmann Hollweg had worked for Hindenburg's appointment to this post during the critical summer months of 1916 because he thought that a moderate peace could be made acceptable to the German people, so misled by exaggerated hopes, only if it were covered by the name of Hindenburg. In other words, Bethmann Hollweg hoped to use the great authority of the field marshal in his efforts towards a peace of understanding. But Hindenburg's authority was fatal to Bethmann Hollweg's policy. Hindenburg and Ludendorff were advocates of unrestricted

submarine warfare. After they had been summoned to take up the highest posts in the army they pleaded for a temporary postponement of this war measure only with respect to the difficult military situation. For at the moment great danger threatened from Rumania, and sufficient troops had to be made available as security against the European neutrals, who might regard unrestricted submarine warfare as a challenge. By the end of December 1916 the Rumanian army was defeated and in the following months military deployments against European neutrals could be initiated.

Bethmann Hollweg had previously been able to stifle the arguments of Falkenhayn and the naval authorities in favour of unrestricted submarine warfare because the war situation in the spring of 1916 did not make such a risky measure absolutely essential. By the summer, however, the war was threatening to become one of attrition of man power and exhaustion of resources. Germany would not be strong enough in 1917 to undertake a large-scale offensive with the land forces available. A weapon that might well win the war was offered by the U-boats.

In these circumstances Bethmann Hollweg, in the latter part of 1916, tried to avoid the necessity of unrestricted submarine warfare by bringing about an early peace of compromise. President Wilson was working for the same end, because he wanted to keep America out of the war. On 12th December 1916 the Central powers made a peace offer to the Allies. On the 21st President Wilson invited the belligerents to state their war aims and announced his willingness to take part in the discussions. Hindenburg and Ludendorff had notified their concurrence with the peace offer of the Central powers, but as soon as the first negative reports began to arrive from the camp of the Allies they demanded, at the end of December 1916, speedy and energetic action at sea.

The prospects for unrestricted submarine warfare at the beginning of 1917 were much better than they had been a year before. Germany now had 105 U-boats, of which 46 large and 23 small vessels were available for the campaign in British waters. In view of the bad world harvests of 1916 unrestricted submarine warfare, if started before the chief overseas transport season began in early February, would foreseeably have a grave effect on Great Britain's grain supplies. Since 6th October 1916 the U-boats had carried on the commerce war in British waters on the 'cruiser' rules. Total sinkings were reckoned at 400,000 tons a month (in actual fact the figure was round about 325,000). By the removal of restrictions one expected an increase to 600,000 tons. The navy esti-

mated that such a figure, enhanced by the consideration that neutral shipping would be frightened away, would in five months reduce the trade with Great Britain by thirty-nine per cent. This would force Great Britain to sue for peace. About the results of an American intervention in the war there was wide difference of opinion. The army thought that any great increase in the supply of American war material to the Allies was impossible, nor did it expect the arrival in Europe of large numbers of American troops. The politicians, however, thought that the American entry would encourage the Allied nations to hold out, would put large financial resources at their disposal, and would bring many American volunteers to join the Allies in Europe.

On the question of U-boat warfare Hindenburg and Ludendorff found their views supported by the vast majority of the German people. The largest party in the Reichstag, the Centre Party, passed a resolution on 7th October 1916 saying that the decision of the chancellor regarding submarine warfare must be based on the views of the supreme army command. As the Conservatives and National Liberals were in any case outright champions of unrestricted submarine warfare, Bethmann Hollweg knew that if he refused to make use of the U-boat weapon in opposition to Hindenburg and Ludendorff he could no longer count on a majority in the Reichstag. The feeling of the people was summed up by Bethmann Hollweg in his memoirs: 'No nation will stand for not winning a war when it is convinced that it can win.' He himself, in spite of his constant resistance to unrestricted submarine warfare, seems at times to have wondered whether, after all, the use of this extreme weapon might not achieve a turn for the better.

For the moment Bethmann Hollweg left the problem unsolved. When on 9th January 1917 he went to Pless to discuss the ever more pressing problem, he found the naval staff and the supreme army command united against him and they had already won over the Kaiser to their side. Hindenburg and Ludendorff saw no possibility of bringing the war to a victorious end unless the U-boats were used without restrictions. They declared themselves ready to shoulder all responsibility for any results caused by this war measure. The chief of the naval staff guaranteed that he could force Great Britain to its knees before the next harvest. Once again Bethmann Hollweg produced all his objections, but after the failure of the Central powers' peace move all hopes for a peace of understanding seemed to have vanished. Bethmann Hollweg could no longer maintain his opposition to the demands of the military and he told the Kaiser that he could not recommend him to oppose the vote of his military advisers. He felt he must refrain from offering his resignation, so as not to expose the inner dissensions in the German leadership to all the world. Until the last moment, however, he continued to doubt the wisdom of the decision of 9th January 1917. When towards the end of the month the prospects for a successful outcome of Wilson's peace efforts seemed more favourable, he tried to secure a postponement of unrestricted submarine warfare, but the naval staff assured him that most of the U-boats had already been despatched.

The beginning of unrestricted submarine warfare on 1st February 1917 was at first countered by Wilson with the rupture of diplomatic relations, whereby he hoped to bring Germany to its senses. The political tension between the two countries was increased at the beginning of March by the publication of a German offer of alliance to Mexico (intercepted by the British intelligence service) should the United States enter the war because of the submarine war. The sinking of seven American merchant ships by U-boats by 21st March finally obliged Wilson to summon Congress, which on 4th and 6th April approved a declaration of war.

At first the figures of sinkings by the U-boats surpassed the forecasts and expectations of the German naval authorities, reaching its maximum in April 1917. But when in the course of the summer merchant ships sailing for Great Britain were assembled in convoys and protected by destroyers the number of successes dwindled. Nevertheless, unrestricted submarine warfare brought Great Britain difficulties which led the British government to begin to take an interest in political solutions. But on the whole the strong urge towards peace that was expected from the U-boat menace failed to materialize. Looking back, it is clear that the German military leaders and politicians regarded the unrestricted submarine warfare as a failure. For from March 1917 onwards the Central powers were relieved of a great burden by the Russian Revolution. Russia dropped out of the war in the winter of 1917-18, and negotiations for a general peace of understanding might have been possible had not the Allies been encouraged to hold on by the prospect of American armed assistance. But the principal effect of unrestricted submarine warfare was on America itself, for it caused the abandonment of America's policy of isolation and its entry into world politics.

'Shelling a merchantman' by H.R.Butler. This U-boat has warned the crew before firing, and they are escaping in lifeboats

Wilson and the Ordeal of Neutrality

The outbreak of war in Europe in August 1914 came, in its suddenness, to President Wilson like a bolt of lightning out of a clear sky. To be sure, Wilson had not been unaware of the possibility of a conflagration, for his confidential adviser and some-time agent, Colonel Edward M.House, writing from Berlin in May 1914, had warned that Europe was a powder keg about to explode. However, House's talks with German and British leaders had raised the tantalizing possibility of an Anglo-American-German entente under Wilson's auspices. No one in Washington (or in European capitals, for that matter) saw that the fuse was burning rapidly after the murder of the heir to the Austrian and Hungarian thrones and his young wife by a Serbian nationalist in Sarajevo on 28th June 1914. Moreover, when the great European powers went over the brink in late July and early August, Wilson was mired in controversy with Congress and in deep despair over the fatal illness of his wife. He could only wait in fascinated horror as Sir Edward Grey, the British foreign minister, wept as he told the American ambassador in London, Walter Page, about the British ultimatum to Germany, and King George exclaimed, 'My God, Mr Page, what else could we do?' One American well expressed what was surely Wilson's reaction when he wrote: 'The horror of it all kept me awake for weeks, nor has the awfulness of it all deserted me, but at first it seemed a horrid dream.'

But Armageddon *had* come. Wilson, as head of the greatest neutral power, whose interests would be vitally affected by belligerent measures, had perforce to work out his policies towards the warring powers.

Throughout the long months of American neutrality, from August 1914 to April 1917, Wilson, whatever his own pre-dispositions, had to work within limits imposed by American public opinion. That opinion was so divided in its preferences for various belligerents during the first months of the war that any policy for the United States other than a strict neutrality would have been inconceivable. Wilson remarked to the German ambassador, Count Johann von Bernstorff, that 'we definitely have to be neutral, since otherwise our mixed populations would wage war on each other'. More important still, in spite of the attachments of various national and ethnic minorities, and of all the efforts of British, French, and German propagandists in the United States, the predominant American public opinion was consistently neutral before 1917. But Americans, even though they clung doggedly to their traditional isolationism and refused to believe that their vital interests were sufficiently involved in the outcome of the war to justify voluntary intervention, were none the less jealous of their sovereignty and international prestige. In other words, they would tolerate only a certain amount of provocation, and no more. To an extraordinary degree Wilson understood and shared the attitudes of the majority of his fellow-countrymen. Both expediency and conviction dictated policies that were agreeable to the great majority of Americans.

Although Wilson had strong emotional attachments to the Allies, particularly Great Britain, he profoundly admired German contributions to modern civiliza-tion. As a sophisticated student of modern history, he well understood that the causes of the war were complex and never imputed exclusive responsibility to either side. He was able to detach emotions from decisions and policies and, self-consciously, to make decisions on the basis of what he considered to be the best interests of America and Europe.

Wilson exercised greater personal control over foreign policy than any other chief of state among the great powers of the world. Constitutionally, as President he was sovereign in the conduct of foreign relations, subject only to the Senate's veto on treaties. Weak Presidents have abdicated their responsibilities to strong secretaries of state or congressional leaders. But Wilson was a 'strong' President. He be-lieved that the people had invested their

Different views of Wilson's conduct.
Above: *The British view, from a* Punch *cartoon. 'Hail Columba! President Wilson (to American Eagle): "Gee! What a dove I've made of you!"'* ***Below left:*** *A German view. Big Chief Old Serpent letting out a war-cry. The Germans felt Wilson was threatening Berlin.*
Left: *President Wilson is seen here holding up a baseball at a World Series match, 1915. He 'played a part in the fate of nations incomparably more direct and personal than any other man'. Although he was an intellectual and an idealist, in this vital period Wilson understood and shared the attitudes of the majority of his fellow-countrymen*

sovereignty in foreign affairs in him. He not only refused to delegate this responsi-bility, but insisted upon conducting foreign relations himself. Because he used his full constitutional powers to execute policies that the great majority desired, Wilson not only held the conduct of foreign affairs in his own hands, but was irresistible while doing so. 'It seems no exaggeration,' Churchill later wrote, 'to pronounce that the action of the United States with its repercussions on the history of the world depended, during the awful period of Armageddon, upon the workings of this man's mind and spirit to the exclusion of almost every other factor; and that he played a part in the fate of nations incom-parably more direct and personal than any other man.'

Wilson's whole world came tumbling down in the first week of August 1914. Ellen Axson Wilson, his beloved wife since 1885, died on 6th August. Great Britain, which he loved, and Germany, which he admired, were already beginning to tear at each other's throats. Near hysteria reigned in Wall Street as a consequence of the disruption of international trade and exchange.

With his customary iron self-control, the President moved confidently and serenely to meet emergencies and establish American neutrality. The formalities were observed easily enough. Wilson proclaimed official neutrality on 4th August and, two weeks later, admonished his fellow-countrymen to be 'impartial in thought as well as in action'.

However, being neutral in the midst of a great war was easier said than done. For example, should the American government permit its citizens to sell vital raw materials and munitions to the Allies when British cruisers prevented the Germans from having access to such supplies? More difficult still, should the government permit American bankers to lend money, which the secretary of state, William Jennings Bryan, called the 'worst of all contrabands', to the belligerents?

Having decided upon a policy of strict neutrality, Wilson, helped by Bryan and the counsellor of the State Department, Robert Lansing, proceeded as systematically and as impartially as possible to be neutral in every circumstance. Hence he permitted the Allies to purchase as much contraband as they pleased, for to have denied them access to American markets and the benefits that flowed from dominant seapower would have been not only un-neutral, but tantamount to undeclared war. For the same reason he permitted American bankers to lend money both to the Allied and German governments.

Wilson followed the rush of the German army through Belgium into northern France and was obviously relieved when the French and British were able to establish a secure defensive line by early autumn. At this point, at any rate, Germany seemed to threaten neither America's vital interests nor her neutral rights. Wilson's main problem in late 1914 was defending American trading rights against British seapower, or, to put the matter more realistically, coming to terms with the British maritime system.

Acting as neutrals always have during wartime, Wilson wanted to keep the channels of commerce to all of Europe open as widely as possible to American ships and goods. Acting as dominant seapowers always have, the British set about to cut off the flow of life-giving supplies from the United States to Germany and Austria-Hungary. Consequently, dispatches about these matters passed frequently between Washington and London, not only during the first months of the war, but as late as

1916. There was much talk of 'freedom of the seas' on the one side and of legitimate belligerent rights on the other. Actually, what sounded like the rhetoric of developing crisis masked the fact that there was substantial goodwill and accommodation on both sides. For their part, the British instituted maritime measures that were not only largely legitimate, but also were based upon precedents established by the United States government itself during the American Civil War of 1861-65. For his part, Wilson, understanding these facts, rejected demands of highly partisan German Americans and American economic interests with a large stake in free trade with Germany for measures to break the British blockade or prevent the Anglo-American trade in contraband.

Having passed through troubles that might have burgeoned into serious Anglo-American crisis, Wilson, at the end of 1914, could view the general state of American relations with the belligerents with some equanimity. There seemed to be no chance of serious conflict with Germany: there were simply no points of contact between the two nations. By Wilson's reckoning, the war would end either in stalemate or, more likely, in an Allied victory. He told a reporter for the *New York Times*, in an off-the-record interview on 14th December 1914, that he hoped ardently for a peace of reconciliation based upon negotiation. But, Wilson added, he did not think that it would 'greatly hurt' the interests of the United States if the Allies won a decisive victory and dictated the settlement.

Between the cruiser and the submarine

The German decision, announced on 4th February 1915, to use an untried weapon, the submarine, in a war against merchant shipping in the English Channel and a broad zone around the British Isles, created an entirely new situation, fraught with peril for the United States. Actually, at this time, the German navy did not possess enough submarines to prosecute an effective campaign, even against Allied merchant ships. But the Germans had compounded the blunder of acting prematurely, largely in bluff, by adding that *neutral* ships might be torpedoed because of the Allied use of neutral flags. It was only the first of a series of blunders by the German admiralty and the high command that would drive the United States into the war.

President Wilson replied to Berlin on 10th February with a stern warning that the United States would hold the German government to a 'strict accountability' and probably go to war if German submarines indiscriminately and illegally attacked American vessels on the high seas.

As it turned out, the gravest German

blunder was to provide the British and French governments with a good excuse for doing what they had already planned to do—severely to tighten their blockade measures. Now they need fear no serious American reprisal. Invoking the ancient right of reprisal, the London and Paris authorities announced on 1st March that, in retaliation against the illegal and ruthless German submarine campaign, they would stop *all* commerce of whatever character to the Central powers, even commerce through neutral ports.

Wilson and Bryan worked hard to arrange an Anglo-American agreement that would provide some protection for American shipping against the cruisers and submarines. Their efforts foundered upon the shoals of the German refusal to give up the submarine campaign except at the price of virtual abandonment by the British of an effective blockade. Wilson was in fact now helpless; he could only acquiesce in the new Anglo-French blockade so long as the sword of the submarine hung over his head.

The President waited in uncertainty all through the early spring of 1915 to see what the Germans would do. There were several attacks against American ships that might have set off a crisis. However, the submarine issue was brought to a head suddenly and dramatically when *U20*, Kapitänleutnant Walther Schwieger, without warning torpedoed the pride of the Cunard Line, the unarmed *Lusitania,* in the Irish Sea on 7th May 1915, killing 128 American citizens among many others.

It was impossible for Wilson to temporize, so violent was the reaction in the United States. Yet what could he do? It was evident after the first shock that a majority of Americans wanted their President to be firm and yet avoid war if possible. This, actually, was Wilson's own intention. In three notes between May and early July, Wilson eloquently appealed to the imperial German government to abandon what was obviously a campaign of sheer terror against *unarmed Allied passenger ships*. In the last note he warned that he would probably break diplomatic relations if the Germans did not abandon that campaign. To each of Wilson's pleas, the German foreign office replied by truculently refusing to admit the illegality of the destruction of *Lusitania*. The impasse was broken by a second incident that came hard on the heels of the *Lusitania* affair—the torpedoing without warning of the White Star liner, *Arabic,* on 19th August (see the previous chapter). Only when they saw that Wilson was on the brink did the Germans yield and promise not to sink unarmed Allied passenger liners without warning. Indeed, Wilson's firmness, and the lack of enough submarines to prosecute

Below: An election truck decorated with Wilson's claim for the trust of his country. In 1916 a wave of neutralist feeling swept the USA and persuaded Wilson to stand as a 'peace' candidate

a decisive underseas campaign, paid even larger dividends in the form of guarantees that the German navy would sink American ships only after making full provision for the safety of human life, and that compensation would be made for all ships and cargoes captured or destroyed.

The subsequent German-American *détente* (encouraged by a temporary abandonment of the submarine campaign in general) set off demands in the United States, primarily by southern cotton producers in deep depression on account of the closing of their central European markets, for action against the total Allied blockade as firm as that taken against the German submarine campaign. Bryan had resigned in the middle of the *Lusitania* crisis, because he feared that Wilson's notes might lead the Germans to declare war against the United States. The new secretary of state, Robert Lansing, did prepare a formidable indictment of the British maritime measure, and Wilson permitted it to go to London on 5th November. But the President had no intention of enforcing the note's demands until German-American differences were clarified.

On the face of it, American relations with Great Britain and Germany had reached

a state of tolerable equilibrium by the end of 1915. The Germans had quietly abandoned their submarine campaign in the North Atlantic, hence there were no incidents in that area to exacerbate German-American relations. For their part, the British had gone to extraordinary (and successful) lengths to support American cotton prices and to come to terms with other American producers who had been hard hit by the Allied blockade. But Wilson and his two principal diplomatic advisers, Colonel House and Lansing, were not reassured as they contemplated potential dangers in the months immediately ahead. The Allies were beginning to arm not only passenger liners but ordinary merchantmen as well, and, apparently, were ordering these ships to attack submarines upon sight. Second, reports from Berlin made it unmistakably clear that there had been only a respite in the submarine campaign, and that the Germans were preparing to use the arming of Allied ships as an excuse for an all-out campaign. So far *ad hoc* solutions had sufficed to preserve the peace, but it now seemed that events might develop which would remove all options. For example, a really ruthless submarine campaign might drive the United States,

willy-nilly, into war, without any other purpose than sheer defence of national rights.

Wilson and House pondered long about the situation in the hope of gaining some initiative and of giving some purpose to American belligerency if it had to come. Sir Edward Grey had said only two months before that his government might be willing to consider a negotiated settlement if the United States would promise to join a post-war league of nations and guarantee to help maintain future peace. Seizing the seeming opportunity offered by Grey's suggestion, Wilson sent House to London in late December 1915 with instructions to work for Anglo-American agreement to co-operate in a drive for peace under Wilson's auspices. If that *démarche* should fail on account of German obduracy, Wilson said, the United States would probably enter the war on the Allied side.

While House was in London opening negotiations, Lansing and Wilson launched their own campaign to get the United States off the submarine hook. The secretary of state, on 18th January 1916, urged the Allies to disarm their merchantmen if the Germans would agree to warn such vessels and evacuate their crews before

sinking them. Lansing added that his government was contemplating treating armed merchantmen as warships, which would mean that they could not engage in commerce at American ports. The Germans, gleefully agreeing with the secretary of state, announced that submarines would sink all armed merchantmen without warning after 28th February.

Reaction in London to what was called Lansing's *modus vivendi* was so violent that it threatened to wreck House's negotiations. Wilson thereupon hastily withdrew the *modus vivendi*. This action in turn set off a panic in Congress that the United States would go to war to protect the right of citizens to travel on armed ships. Wilson beat back a congressional resolution warning Americans against travelling on armed ships, but he made it clear that only lightly-armed merchantmen would be permitted to use American ports, and, more important, that he did not intend to make a great issue with the German government over armed ships in any event.

There was considerable relief both on Capitol Hill and in Whitehall. In London, Sir Edward Grey and House initialled, on 22nd February 1916, what is known as the House-Grey Memorandum embodying Wilson's plan of mediation.

Colonel House returned to Washington on 5th March in high excitement to tell the President that the British and French were eager to move as rapidly as possible for peace under Wilson's aegis. While Wilson and House were in the midst of planning for the great venture, a German submarine torpedoed a French packet steamer, *Sussex,* in the English Channel on 24th March with heavy loss of life. Reports of ruthless attacks against unarmed merchantmen followed in rapid succession.

After much backing and filling, and mainly in order to pave the way for his mediation, Wilson sent an ultimatum to Berlin on 18th April warning that he would break relations with Germany if she did not agree hereafter to require her submarine commanders to observe the rules of visit and search before sinking all unarmed ships, whether passenger liners or merchantmen. The German admiralty lacked enough U-boats to justify the risk of war with the United States and European neutrals like Holland and Denmark. Consequently, the imperial chancellor, Theobald von Bethmann Hollweg, won the Kaiser's support for submission to Wilson's demand. However, while yielding the Germans reserved the 'right' to resume freedom of decision on the use of submarines if the American government failed to compel the Allies to respect international law in the conduct of their blockade.

The happy settlement of the *Sussex* crisis, coupled with intimations that the Germans were eager for peace talks, spurred Wilson to action to put the House-Grey Memorandum into operation. His first public move was to announce, in an address in Washington on 27th May, that the United States was prepared to abandon its traditional isolationism and join a post-war league of nations. Privately, through Colonel House, he exerted heavy pressure on Grey to put the memorandum's machinery into motion by signalling his government's readiness for Wilson's mediation. Grey responded evasively at first; but Wilson would not be diverted, and then Grey had to tell him frankly that neither the British nor the French governments would consent to peace talks at this time or in the foreseeable future.

Grey's refusal to execute the House-Grey Memorandum, a crushing blow to the President's hopes for an early peace in itself, combined with other developments to cause Wilson to effect what would turn out to be an almost radical change in his policies towards the European belligerents. First, the British government not only refused to relax its controls over American commerce, but, on the contrary, intensified its maritime and economic warfare in the spring and summer of 1916. In retrospect, the new British measures (including search and seizure of American mail on neutral ships and publication in the United States of a 'blacklist' of American firms still doing business with the Central powers) seem trivial when compared with policies in which the Washington administration had already acquiesced. However, Wilson and a majority of Americans resented the new measures as direct affronts to their national sovereignty. Second, the British army's severe repression of the Easter Rising in Dublin in April 1916 not only inflamed Irish Americans, but also caused a tremendous diminution in Great Britain's moral standing throughout the United States. Finally, the German-American *détente* following the *Sussex* crisis sent a wave of neutralism across the country, one so strong that it engulfed the Democratic national convention that re-nominated Wilson for the presidency.

These developments, of course, had their most important impact upon the man in the White House. They convinced him that the American people did not want to go to war over the alleged right of Americans to travel and work on belligerent ships. They forced Wilson to stand as the 'peace' candidate and to accuse his Republican opponent, Charles Evans Hughes, of wanting war. More important, they caused a very considerable hardening of Wilson's attitudes against the Allies, particularly the British. By the early autumn, Wilson believed that the Allies were fighting for victory and spoils, not for a just peace.

Wilson could do nothing, of course, while the presidential campaign was in progress. However, once the voters, on 7th November 1916, invested him with their sovereignty for another four years, Wilson was free to act. And action of some kind seemed to be imperative, for it was growing increasingly evident that both sides were preparing to use desperate measures to break the stalemate.

For the British, these would mean further intensification of economic warfare; for the Germans, it would mean revoking the *Sussex* pledge and launching a wholesale campaign against maritime commerce. The only way to peace and safety, Wilson concluded, was to bring the war to an end through his independent mediation.

Diverted briefly by domestic developments and Germany's own offer to negotiate, Wilson launched his peace bolt on 18th December 1916 by asking the belligerents to state the terms upon which they would be willing to end the fighting. The British and French were stunned and furious. But they were helpless to resist, so dependent had they become upon American credit and supplies for continuation of their war efforts. Then Lansing intervened. Committed emotionally to the Allied cause, he set out to sabotage the President's peace move by encouraging the British and French governments to state such terms as could be won only by a decisive military victory. The Germans, who very much wanted Wilson to force the Allies to the peace table but did not want him meddling once the conference had begun, returned an evasive reply.

Wilson was undisturbed. In mid-January 1917 he launched the second and decisive move in his campaign for peace—high-level, direct, and secret negotiations with the British and German governments to obtain their consent to his mediation. While waiting for their replies, the President went before the Senate on 22nd January to tell the world what kind of settlement he had in mind and the American people would support by membership in a league of nations. The peace to be made, Wilson said, had to be a peace of reconciliation, a 'peace without victory', for a victor's peace would leave 'a sting, a resentment, a bitter memory upon which terms of peace would rest, not permanently, but only as upon quicksand'.

For reasons that are still obscure, the new British cabinet headed by David Lloyd George sent word on 26th January to Wilson that it was prepared to accept the President's mediation. The Austro-Hungarians were desperately eager for peace. But on 31st January Wilson was informed of the German decision to adopt unrestricted submarine warfare. The stage was set for American participation.

America Declares War

It was Lloyd George who once remarked that Europe slithered into war in 1914, and this description, graphically accurate, applies equally well to the entrance of the United States into the World War in 1917. Prior to these separate if similar *dénouements*, neither the Europeans nor the Americans quite knew what they were doing. As previously stated, within weeks of the fateful date of the declaration of war on 6th April, President Woodrow Wilson was asking the belligerents for a peace without victory and hoping to achieve it through his efforts at mediation, while the United States remained outside the war as a neutral power. But then came a series of unexpected military, diplomatic, and political changes, none of them American in origin. Before long, Wilson, to use the description of Senator Henry Cabot Lodge, was 'in the grip of events'. On 6th April 1917 some of the election posters of November 1916 were still up on the billboards, and Americans could ponder the Democratic Party slogans which had helped re-elect the President: 'He Kept Us Out of War'; and 'War in the East, Peace in the West, Thank God for Wilson'. They were not, however, angry with Wilson, for they too had reacted to unforeseen events.

What were these events of early 1917 which moved the President and people? It is easy now to see that, given what had gone before, in January 1917 it would take only

a few more blows from the German government to make America abandon her neutrality. Given that government's almost complete lack of understanding of the sensitivities of the American government and people, the wonder is that neutrality lasted as long as it did, that German blunders did not come sooner. It is also curious that Wilson and the American people believed in January 1917 that they still possessed freedom of manoeuvre. The President early that month told his confidant Colonel House 'There will be no war'.

On 19th January 1917 the German government thoughtfully told Ambassador Johann von Bernstorff about the decision to resume unrestricted submarine warfare on 1st February but Bernstorff was to inform the American government, and duly did so, only on 31st January, at 4 pm. It was a crude beginning, this eight hours' notice. Bernstorff had done his best to prevent this stupidity, this tactic of loosing the submarines, which he knew would drive the Americans into war. It was not only the trans-Atlantic munitions trade, or the export of American food (harvests had been poor in 1916), that the Germans were seeking to prevent; they wanted to strangle British economic life by cutting off all imports. They did not have to use so thorough a submarine blockade, which would inevitably affront the Americans, Bernstorff thought. He had cabled his views,

Wild enthusiasm and waving flags on Broadway—America has entered the war

America: The Hope in the West

but the German leaders paid no attention.

Bernstorff meanwhile had lowered his stock with the American government and public, and with his own government (he deeply offended the Kaiser), by allowing a peccadillo to get into public print. On a vacation in the Adirondacks with a lady who often entertained him, he posed in a bathing suit for a photograph, with his arms intimately encircling two ladies similarly attired. At the very time when he needed whatever personal influence and dignity he could muster, this photograph found its way into the hands of the Russian ambassador who passed it to the newspapers. Americans snickered at the Bathing Beauty Scandal. Bernstorff was a generally competent diplomat to whom both the American and German governments should have listened. Instead this 'good German' found himself ignored on public matters and laughed at over private ones. 'I am not surprised,' he said upon the break of diplomatic relations when he received his passports. 'My government will not be surprised either. The people in Berlin knew what was bound to happen if they took the action they have taken. There was nothing else left for the United States to do.' In despair he told a press conference that he was through with politics.

After the formal break, two events followed which together pushed the country into war. The first was a clear-cut case of a German submarine sinking a passenger vessel with American citizens aboard. Wilson on 3rd February, when he informed Congress that he was breaking relations, had added that 'I refuse to believe that it is the intention of the German authorities to do in fact what they have warned us they will feel at liberty to do. . . . Only actual overt acts on their part can make me believe it even now'. For two weeks after resumption of unrestricted submarine warfare no incident occurred, no open violation of what Americans liked to believe was one of their principal neutral rights. There was no paralysis of shipping during the period, as American tonnage clearing United States ports dropped only from 1,019,396 in January to 847,786 in February. The day the fatal vessel, the 18,000-ton British liner *Laconia*, sailed from New York harbour, sixty-six ships of all nationalities were in the roadstead, loaded or loading for ports in the zone of war. Wilson spoke again to Congress on 26th February, reporting that 'The overt act which I have ventured to hope the German commanders would in fact avoid has not occurred'. That very moment, however, news of the sinking of the *Laconia* the day before was being flashed to Washington. It was whispered around the House chamber before the President finished his speech, and printed in the country's newspapers the next day.

Three Americans, including two women, had lost their lives. The deaths of the women were not pretty to contemplate: a torpedoing at night, a lifeboat half stove-in as it swung down over the careening hull, this fragile craft itself slowly sinking while it wallowed off into the darkness, Mrs Albert H. Hoy and her daughter Elizabeth standing waist deep in icy water throughout the long night.

This was interpreted as an open challenge, by the German government which authorized it, and by the American government and people who had brought themselves into a frame of mind to oppose it.

The Zimmermann telegram

The second precipitating event came almost immediately when American newspapers on 1st March published the Zimmermann telegram. The *Laconia* disaster had proved that the Germans held no regard for international law and human rights. The Zimmermann telegram showed that they were guilty not merely of legal and moral turpitude but were enemies of the United States, willing to endanger the nation's very existence. In the annals of international stupidity during the 20th century, or any other century, this famous telegram hardly has an equal. It was a German proposal of an alliance to the government of Mexico (an alliance which was possibly to include the Japanese government as well). The Mexicans were to attack the United States during the hostilities now deemed imminent, in exchange for which the Germans promised a return of the 'lost territories' of the Mexican War of 1846-48: Texas, New Mexico, Arizona. The genesis of the proposal is now quite clear. The Americans had been giving Mexico much trouble in the past few years, even to the extent of sending in a punitive military expedition in 1916 under command of General Pershing. The Mexican regime of General Venustiano ('Don Venus') Carranza began to take interest in Mexican-German co-operation, and Don Venus in November made a suggestion, going so far as to offer submarine bases. An assistant in the German foreign office, one Kemnitz, turned the proposal into a project for an alliance. It was so preposterous a project that the German foreign secretary, Zimmermann, should have forgotten it. Instead he picked it up as a great idea.

Zimmermann sent his telegram to Mexico by several means, one of which was through the American embassy in Berlin and thence from Washington to Mexico City by Western Union. Ambassador Gerard transmitted this German message, in its original German code, as part of an arrangement which Colonel House had made, with Wilson's permission, for cable transmission of German messages pertain-

ing to mediation. Ambassador Bernstorff had promised to use the arrangement only for peaceful purposes, but Zimmermann was not put off by that engagement.

The British government intercepted and decoded all three of Zimmermann's transmissions. Under the leadership of Admiral Sir William Reginald Hall, the Admiralty early in the war had set up a code and cipher-cracking operation, which triumphed with the deciphering of Zimmermann's idiotic telegram. Not wishing to show his knowledge of the German code,

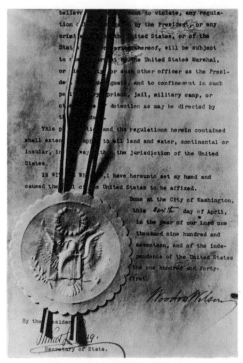

Above: The text of Wilson's declaration of war. Right: Bernstorff, the ladies' man— a diplomat discomfited by scandal

Hall at first was in a quandary about publishing, but ingenuity triumphed. One of his agents in Mexico City procured from the Mexican telegraph office a copy of the still-encoded telegram which Bernstorff had obtained from the American State Department and relayed from Washington. It contained certain small differences from the other intercepts, and upon publication the impression prevailed that someone had stolen or sold a decoded copy of the telegram, getting it from the German legation in Mexico City. The Germans reassured Hall that they were without suspicion by engaging in a lively inquiry with Eckhardt, the German minister in Mexico City, asking how many copies of the decode Eckhardt had made and who had handled them, using of course the same code which Hall had cracked. Hall found it amusing to read that Eckhardt tried to pass the blame off on to Bernstorff in Washington.

No denial

Even after the cat was out of the bag, the telegram published in every American newspaper, it was still possible for Zimmermann in Berlin to quiet the uproar, or at the very least to make the Americans disclose how they obtained the telegram, by baldly denying that he had sent it. President Wilson himself, the author in 1918 of 'open diplomacy', once in a confidential conversation with Colonel House said, admittedly for House's ears only (and, as it turned out, for House's diary), that a man was justified in lying for two purposes, to protect the honour of a lady and to preserve secrets of state. Had Zimmermann but known it, he could have cited the President in support of a diplomatic denial. Secretary Lansing in Washington was certain that Zimmermann would lie his way out, and was incredulous to learn that the German foreign secretary almost at once admitted authorship of the telegram in a burst of truthfulness which was as naïve as the composition which inspired it.

What could the American government do after the publication of the telegram on 1st March? If Wilson does not go to war now, Theodore Roosevelt wrote to Lodge, 'I shall skin him alive'. The Prussian Invasion Plot, as the newspapers labelled the telegram, was transparently clear. Newspapers in the hitherto isolationist Middle West acknowledged the end of neutrality. The Chicago *Tribune* warned its readers to realize now, 'without delay, that Germany recognizes us an enemy', and that the country no longer could hope to keep out of 'active participation in the present conflict'. The Cleveland *Plain Dealer* said there was 'neither virtue nor dignity' in refusing to fight now. The Oshkosh (Wisconsin) *Northwestern*, an authentic voice from the Middle West, said that the telegram had turned pacifists, critics, and carpers into patriots overnight. Zimmermann, as Mrs Tuchman has written, 'shot an arrow in the air and brought down neutrality like a dead duck'.

The rest was anticlimax. The first Russian Revolution of March 1917 forced the abdication of the Tsar and the proclamation of a republic, and removed an embarrassing despotism from the ranks of the Allies, making it easier to say that the Allies were Democracy fighting the Central powers who represented Autocracy. About the same time, U-boats sank four American ships. The presidential decision to arm merchant ships, taken in mid-March, constituting a sort of armed neutrality, had no discernible effect on German policy. The President called a special session of Congress. On the evening of 2nd April 1917, Wilson went before both Houses, duly assembled in the Capitol building in Washington, and as the lights gleamed in the crowded chamber he asked his countrymen for what they were ready to give him. Many Senators had brought small American flags to the House chamber where the President spoke; during the speech they clapped their hands and waved their flags in assent.

British postcard. For Great Britain, America's declaration promised men – and hope

"We are coming, brothers, coming, A hundred thousand strong!"

The New Military Balance

On 6th April 1917 the United States entered the First World War. At the beginning of June General John J. Pershing, the commander-in-chief of the American Expeditionary Force arrived in England for a four-day visit, and then went on to France to began organizing his command. His reception by the British and French was warm to the point of hysteria: the King welcomed him, the crowds cheered and threw roses. The illustrated magazine *The London Graphic* caught the mood and the style of the time by surrounding a photograph of Pershing and his officers with a tabernacle in classical style, in which a luscious symbolic figure of a woman held a laurel wreath over Pershing's head; the caption read: 'Now is the winter of our discontent made glorious summer by this sun of (New) York.' (In fact, Pershing had been born in Missouri.)

The hopes, the great expectations, that were aroused in the British and French peoples by American entry into the war were understandable. The spring and early summer of 1917 saw Allied fortunes at their lowest ebb. The year 1916 had ended with apparently nothing to show for colossal losses but small territorial gains on the Somme and the preservation of Verdun. The expulsion of the Germans from French soil seemed as difficult and as far off as ever. The very real and heavy damage done to German power by the Allied offensives in the late summer and autumn of 1916 was hidden from view.

The third year of the war now unfolded for the Allies a prospect of catastrophe. On 1st February 1917 the Germans began unrestricted submarine warfare. The results of the first three months fully justified German calculations that before the end of the year Great Britain would be unable to prosecute the war because of lack of shipping to transport food, raw materials, and troops: the tonnage sunk rose from 470,000 in February to 837,000 in April. Admiral Jellicoe, the British first sea lord, believed that unless an answer to the submarine could be found – and in his estimation, none was in sight – the war was certainly lost. In March revolution exploded in Tsarist Russia and the Tsar Nicholas II abdicated. Although the Russian army had never fulfilled the hopes of 1914 that it would prove an irresistible steam-roller, it had nevertheless heavily engaged Germany's Austrian ally and brought her to the point of exhaustion, and had also drawn German resources away

Left: US forces arrive in England

from the Western Front. In 1916 General Alexey Brusilov's Offensive had inflicted a smashing defeat in the east on the Central powers. Now Russia was paralysed by revolution, no man could say what help she would bring.

Finally, at the end of April and the beginning of May 1917, the French army, under a new commander-in-chief, General Robert Nivelle, was crushingly, appallingly, repulsed in a general offensive on the Western Front which Nivelle had promised would lead to a swift breakthrough and a rapid, and victorious, end to the war. In the aftermath of this shattering disappointment, all the accumulated war-weariness and exhaustion of the French nation exploded in widespread army mutinies and civil disorders. It was no wonder that the Allied leaders and peoples alike greeted the belligerency of the richest, most industrially powerful nation in the world, with all its unblooded manpower, with somewhat hysterical relief. America brought on to the Allied side a population of 93,400,000 and a steel production of 45,060,607 tons. The human resources went far to make up for the 180 million Russians now perhaps lost to the Allied cause. The industrial power was overwhelming; American steel production alone was nearly three times as great as that of Germany and Austria together. However, all this was only *potential*. How long would it be before American resources, human and industrial, were translated into vast, superbly-equipped armies on the Western Front able to crush down the exhausted and outmatched Germans? In view of the German submarine successes and the manifest unsteadiness of the French army and nation, would there even *be* a Western Front by the time the Americans had deployed their power?

Whatever its enormous long-term importance in 20th-century history, the American entry into the First World War in April 1917 in fact was in itself of far smaller strategic significance at the time than the cheering British and French crowds supposed. There was no progressive transformation of the war—no massive rescue operation. On the other hand, it is certain that without America, the Allies would have lost the war. The clue to this apparent paradox lies in the fact that American help *before* her entry into the war was more vital than many recognize; and American help *after* her entry rather less vital, at least for some fifteen months or so.

The German and Austrian war effort was

Top: Tank Corps recruiting poster. At first the Americans tried to equip military units before sending them to France.
Above: Appeal for the war loan

Left: British tank passes US skyscraper in
recruiting drive

entirely based on their own industries and
technological skill. By the spring of 1915,
after a temporary shortage of munitions,
Germany had converted her vast chemical
industry and her varied and highly modern
engineering industries to the production
of explosives, propellants, fuses, shells,
ammunition, and weapons. Her machine-
tool industry—the most modern and inventive in the world except for that of America
—had no difficulty in equipping new munitions plants.

Great Britain and France, in sharp contrast, found when they tackled the problem
of a massive expansion of war production
that their industrial resources were largely
out-of-date in equipment and techniques—
and that they even lacked completely a
whole range of the most modern kinds of
industries. Thus, Great Britain and
France before the war had been almost
entirely dependent on Germany for
chemical products, such as dyes, drugs, and
photographic processing materials. It was
plant that made dyes and drugs that could
also easily make explosives. Great Britain
had to create a chemical industry from
scratch, based on seized German patents.
While it was being built up, there was a
bottleneck at the very base of shell manufacture—the propellant and the explosive.

British manufacturing industry was still
largely mid-Victorian in its types of product, its methods of production, its skills
and techniques. Mass-production plant,
with lines of automatic or semi-automatic
machines, producing all kinds of precision
light-engineering work, was hardly known.
Before 1914 Great Britain was dependent
mostly on Germany, partly on America,
for almost all the sophisticated products of
the second phase of the industrial revolution—ball-bearings, magnetoes, sparking
plugs, cameras, optical goods.

Great Britain therefore lacked both the
general and the particular industries to
sustain a modern war. Nor could her
machine-tool industry equip the vast new
factories that had to be created. Machine-
tools were—and are—the basic industry of
modern technological growth; they are the
machines which make machines. The
British machine-tool industry was also
essentially mid-Victorian; it was small-
scale, it made a limited range of tools to
order by almost craft methods in small
workshops. For the 'modern' kind of
automatic or semi-automatic machine for
a production-line, it contented itself in
peacetime by acting as a distribution agent
for American and German imports.

France was in no better case. Thus,
American resources and know-how were,
from the end of 1914, absolutely essential
to the survival of the Allies. It was to
America—and to a lesser extent to Sweden
and Switzerland—that they looked to

supply the specialized sophisticated products that they had imported from Germany. It was on American industry that Great Britain especially depended for shells and other munitions during 1915 and 1916, while Great Britain was still painfully creating her chemical and munitions industries. Even in 1915 a third of all shells issued to the British army were made in North America. In 1916 the debut of the mass British armies in battle was only made possible by shells from America and Canada. As the history of the ministry of munitions expressed it: 'During the early part of 1915, in fact, overseas contractors assumed a place of utmost importance, since upon them the War Office was forced to depend for the bulk of the shell supplies required for the 1916 campaign.'

The Allies were just as dependent on America for their longer-term needs in constructing their own munitions industries. The essential basis of the whole vast programme of national munitions factories, on which Lloyd George's fame as minister of munitions hangs, was the American machine-tool and the American methods and organization it made possible. In 1916, when Great Britain's new war industries were at last getting into full production, *The Times* wrote: 'One of the new factories has grown up on a spot which last November was green fields. Now there are 25 acres covered with buildings packed with machinery. Most of the machines are of American make, and some are marvels of ingenuity.'

The extent of Allied dependence on American technology, and also of their purchases (at the cost of their accumulated overseas investments) is illustrated by the increase in production of certain American industries *before* America began her own war-production programme. Between 1914 and 1917, American exports of iron, steel, and their products to Europe rose four-fold; American explosives production grew ten times between 1913 and 1917. Bernard Baruch, chairman of the US war industries board, wrote: 'Cincinnati is the greatest machine tool manufacturing center in the world. In 1913 the total value of the annual product of the United States was about $50,000,000. During the war period preceding our entrance, our productive capacity was more than doubled, but the expansion took place largely in the output of small and medium-sized machines — machines for the production of shells, rifles, fuses etc.'

It is therefore beyond question that without access to American resources, Great Britain and France would have lacked the material to sustain the war while their own industries were being created, and could not have created the industries at all. This indeed was acknowledged by the

Above left: 'This destroyer is needed to sink Hun submarines' reads the sign on the right. The destroyer was built in seventeen days. Above right: The American commanders of the army and the navy, General Pershing (on the left) and Admiral Sims (on the right)

Above: The first American prisoners to fall into German hands. Below: Loading a troopship for France. As the soldiers, fresh recruits for slaughter, tramp across the dock, girls in Red Cross uniform give each a last gift from the American people and wish them good luck

America: The Hope in the West

British history of the ministry of munitions: 'Great Britain was practically dependent upon the United States of America for material for propellant manufacture, for a large proportion of her explosives material. She depended to a considerable extent upon the United States for shell steel and other steel . . . for machine tools.'

Thus America had proved a decisive influence on the course of the First World War long before her own entry into it.

However, by April 1917 the creation of the Allied—especially the British—war industries had been largely completed. Great Britain was now able to supply munitions freely to France and Italy. There was no longer so desperate or so large a need for American shells or machine-tools. The American declaration of war was therefore largely irrelevant and unimportant where Allied war production was concerned. Indeed, the flow of help was reversed once the American armies began to build up in France; it was France and Great Britain who largely equipped the American armies, as they were formed in France. The Americans made the capital mistake of deciding to produce their own designs of artillery pieces and aircraft, instead of adopting French or British designs for which many of their own factories were already producing ammunition or parts. The inevitable teething troubles of new designs were such that the American army received American guns just about in time to fire a salute in celebration of the armistice in November 1918. Not only this, but acute shortage of shipping space made it evidently more sensible to fill ships with men rather than guns, and then equip the men in Europe. So in the event the AEF was given French 75's for its field artillery, French 155-mm guns and howitzers for its medium artillery, and mostly British mortars. The British also supplied machine-guns, steel helmets, and even uniforms. The air component of the United States was equipped with French aircraft.

Obviously the prime fact about American *belligerency,* as opposed to mere industrial availability, was that United States armed forces would henceforth take part in the war. This indeed was the hope that inspired the civilian cheers, when the 1st Division, AEF, landed in France at the end of June 1917. These were the healthy men, from a nation twice as numerous as the British, or the French, who would take over the weight of the fighting from the tired, battle-shaken survivors of three terrible campaigns. Unfortunately, the American declaration of war was by no means followed by a breakneck expansion of the army and its swift deployment in France, such as the British had achieved in 1914-15. The 1st Division was not followed by the 2nd until September; by 31st October 1917

the AEF numbered only 6,064 officers and 80,969 men. Lloyd George has pointed out in his memoirs the poorness of the American performance compared with the British in creating an army: '. . . at the end of six months (after the outbreak of war) the British Expeditionary Force on the Western Front numbered 354,750. The First American Division was put into a quiet sector of the French front on 21st October 1917—nearly seven months after the severance of diplomatic relations with Germany. The tide of American forces in France . . . mounted only in dribbling fashion during these early months. By the end of October it was 87,000; by the end of November, 126,000; and at the beginning of 1918, 175,000. That was nine months after the entry of America into the war. At that stage in our own war effort we had already thrown 659,104 into the various war theatres.'

Thus the United States exerted no military effect at all on the critical year of 1917, when Russia subsided more and more from the war, when Pétain strove to quell the mutinies in the French army and keep it together until such time as the Americans should arrive in force, when the Italians suffered a catastrophic defeat at Caporetto, when the *only* Allied army still capable of an offensive—the British—slogged doggedly forward towards Passchendaele. And, the Germans hoped and expected, 1917 was to be the decisive and final year of the war. For it was their calculation that the American army, as a great force, would never arrive because the U-boats would have destroyed the shipping that might have carried it across the Atlantic; if in fact the war itself had not been ended by the U-boat blockade before the Americans were ready to cross. In 1917 the Americans provided hope, little else to the Allies.

The Americans are not to be entirely blamed for the extreme slowness of their military mobilization. The peacetime American army had been even smaller than the British, and far less prepared for modern war. Whereas the British had at least trained and prepared an expeditionary force of six divisions for a European campaign, and completed all the staff studies about organization and methods necessary for subsequent expansion, the Americans started absolutely from scratch in every way. For example, the size, organization, and ancillary services of the basic infantry division had to be worked out and decided upon, as well as of corps and armies. In peacetime the United States army had numbered 190,000 officers and men spread in small detachments across the face of America and her own overseas dependencies. The very size of America posed its own problems, for before troops

could go aboard the troopships, they had to be concentrated and accommodated near the eastern seaboard. This meant a vast programme of camp construction, on top of other programmes for training camps and training facilities. In France itself port facilities had to be enormously extended, and lines of communication built up from the ports allotted to the Americans to their designated sector in the right-centre of the Allied line, in the Argonne. This entailed major construction work to increase the carrying capacity of the rail links. Colossal supply depots had to be constructed and filled in France. The British had found that supporting an army in another country over twenty-two miles of sea involved enormous rearward services; America had to make war across 3,000 miles of sea. The major bottleneck however was shipping, both for troops and cargoes. The United States mercantile marine had nothing like enough ships available to move the American army across the Atlantic.

Finally, there was a fundamental difference of views between Pershing on the one hand and Haig and Pétain on the other about the employment of American troops. Haig and Pétain at the beginning of 1918 were keenly aware that their armies were seriously under strength and without hope of adequate national reinforcements. They wanted American infantry to fill out their own divisions; they wanted help quickly. Pershing on the other hand (and his government) was resolved to build up

Industry steps up production for America's participation in the war—war workers making steel helmets for doughboys

a completely independent, self-contained American army in France, with its own divisions, corps, and armies. He was not prepared to see Americans swallowed up in Allied formations; he was prepared to wait, for months if need be, until all the artillery and supply services, the higher headquarters and staffs, necessary for an independent force were organized, trained, and equipped. Thus it was that when on 21st March 1918, the Germans launched the first and greatest of a series of titanic offensives on the Western Front, there was only one American division actually in the overstretched and outnumbered Allied line and three divisions in training areas.

The rate of the American build-up in France had been crucial to the calculations of the German high command in deciding on great offensives in the west in the spring of 1918. By November, 1917, when the German decision was taken, unrestricted U-boat warfare had failed in its object of knocking Great Britain out of the war; it had been beaten by the convoy system. Therefore, the Germans had to reckon on the entry into battle, sooner or later, of a mass and entirely fresh American army: certain defeat for Germany and her allies. Therefore, the war must be decided before that mass army arrived. Ludendorff told his colleagues: 'Our general situation requires that we should strike at the earliest moment, if possible at the end of February or beginning of March, before the Americans can throw strong forces into the scale.' In other words, since Russia had finally been knocked out of the war by the Treaty of Brest-Litovsk, the bulk of German strength could be concentrated on France and Great Britain before they could be rescued by their second great ally.

The crisis on the Western Front lasted from 21st March to 18th July, as the German onslaughts fell successively on different parts on the Allied front. Twice the British faced real danger of being driven into the Channel; once there was an acute risk of the French and British being separated; three times the French front was temporarily smashed and the French capital exposed again to possible occupation. In this largest, most violent, and most decisive campaign of the war, the American army played little part. Some units took part in the defence of the Amiens sector after 28th March; the 1st Division carried out a spirited counter-attack at Cantigny, near Montdidier, on 28th May; in June the 2nd Division helped the French block the German drive across the Marne, and launched a successful counterattack which led to the recapture of Belleau Wood; units of the 3rd and 42nd Divisions fought defensively in the sector of Château-Thierry. These were very welcome, but hardly decisive contributions to a campaign against 192 German divisions.

What was far more important—indeed decisive—in terms of the issue of the war was the effect of the German offensive on the speed of the American build-up. A week after the Germans attacked on the Somme, on 28th March 1918, Pershing abandoned

his somewhat deliberate and pedantic attempt to create an independent American army before entering the conflict, and offered Pétain as a temporary expedient all the troops he had, to use as Pétain wished. So the individual American units saw action under French or British corps and army command, not American. This immediate gesture was one sign of the American realization that the French and British might not last long enough to be rescued; that there was a need for desperate haste in getting American troops over to France and into battle. At the same time, Pershing still remained anxious that his Allies should not rob him of his own independent army by the feeding of Americans into their own divisions. It was only after long arguments between the Allied and American governments and commands, that it was finally agreed, at the beginning of June, that shipping space should be saved by bringing over men—infantry mostly—instead of complete divisions with all their space-occupying equipment. 170,000 combat troops were to come in June and 140,000 in July out of some 250,000 men ready to be transported in each of the two months. New divisions would be formed and equipped in France. These shipments of men were made possible by the British mercantile marine, made available as part of the bargain by the British government by cutting down British imports.

Whereas in March 84,000 Americans had crossed the Atlantic, 118,500 crossed in April, 246,000 in May, 278,800 in June, and 306,703 in July—nearly half of them in British ships. These figures, far higher than the German command had thought possible, spelt defeat for Germany.

On 15th-17th July the last phase of the great German 1918 offensive petered out in failure. On 18th July the French launched a surprise attack, led by massed tanks, from the Forest of Villers-Cotterêts. The attacking troops included two American divisions, each with a strength of 27,000 men, three times as large as a French or German division. The French attack marked the turn of the campaign; from then to the end of the war the Germans were to fight on the defensive.

It was now—and at very long last—that the American military presence in the war proved decisive. The great battles of March to July 1918, which the Allies had won virtually without American help, had left the British, French, and German armies all exhausted, with scant reserves and little hope of reinforcement from the homeland. For the original combatants of the war nothing remained but to break up divisions—to see their armies gradually decrease. A German battalion now numbered on average 660 men. The German gamble on victory had failed: neither the

German army nor the German people (hungry, miserable, and despairing after years of blockade) had any further hopes to clutch at. In August, when the British offensive on the Somme (some American units took part), confirmed that the Allies now possessed the initiative, and confirmed also that the morale and discipline of the German army was beginning to disintegrate, there were nearly 1,500,000 Americans in France. The only German reservoir of fresh manpower lay in the 300,000 youths of the 1919 class called up in June. Whereas Allied leaders were planning for a campaign in 1919, whose principal weight was to be borne by a hundred American divisions, for Germany's leaders another year of battle was absolutely unthinkable.

Thus it was that even in the last months of the war, it was the American military *potential,* advertised by their limited offen-

Big guns under construction. But the army only received the new American guns just before the armistice in November 1918

sives at St Mihiel and in the Argonne, rather than the actual fighting achievements of American troops, that affected the outcome of the Great War in 1918. In point of fact, the brunt of the fighting from July to November 1918 was borne by the tired but still dogged British, who took 188,700 prisoners as against 196,000 taken by the French, Belgians, and Americans together.

The American role in the First World War was therefore decisive: decisive industrially between 1914 and 1917, decisive in terms of military potential from midsummer 1918 onwards. It illustrated two facts of enormous importance to the future balance of power in Europe: that Germany was militarily the equal of the British and French empires together; and that Great Britain, the 19th-century 'work-shop of the world', was no longer a first-rank industrial and technological power, no longer able to defend herself and her empire out of her own resources.

5 BACKS TO THE WALL

The French Army Cracks

By the start of 1917 the war on the Western Front had settled into a state of apparently endless stalemate. For over two years the opposing sides had faced each other across the hardly shifting no man's land of northern France, wearing themselves down in a series of costly and ineffective offensives – Artois, Champagne, Verdun, the Somme. In this prolonged struggle of attrition no nation had suffered more than France. Not only was the war being fought on French soil, with all that this meant in devastation and loss of coal, iron ore, and other industrial resources, but her troops had suffered relatively the highest casualties of any belligerent power, amounting to some two and a quarter million men. As January 1917 dawned, with no promise of decisive action – let alone victory – in sight, the strain on the nation was beginning to tell. Soldiers and civilians alike were becoming weary and disillusioned. The current mood was expressed by a French officer from general headquarters, Colonel Emile Herbillon. 'The year is opening in a grim atmosphere,' he wrote on the 2nd January 1917. 'Promises and hopes have been followed by too many disappointments.'

Joffre dismissed

All that the Allied war leaders could plan for 1917 was another great Franco-British offensive just as they had ordained for 1915 and 1916. The stage seemed set for a repetition of the great attrition battles of those years. But one significant change had just occurred. Sixty-four-year-old

General César Joffre, commander-in-chief of the French army and the main advocate of the attrition strategy, had been replaced. Bulky and imperturbable, 'Papa' Joffre had won enormous prestige as the victor of the Marne in 1914 and since then, at his Chantilly headquarters, had reigned supreme in Allied military affairs. But late in 1916 French deputies, resenting his autocratic powers, had attacked him – ostensibly for his mishandling of the recent Verdun and Somme campaigns and they had virtually forced Aristide Briand, the French prime minister, to dismiss him. With Joffre honorifically created a marshal of France and shunted into the post of the government's military adviser in Paris, General Robert Nivelle was appointed as his successor.

General Nivelle, a dapper, dynamic artilleryman aged sixty, had risen to rapid fame as an army commander at Verdun. 'We have the formula!' he had proclaimed on assuming command. His aggressive spirit and bounding self-confidence had so impressed Briand and his colleagues – now anxiously seeking a leader who would end the impasse on the Western Front – that he was promoted over the heads of France's most senior generals, Ferdinand Foch, Henri-Philippe Pétain, and Edouard de Curières de Castelnau. Nominated commander-in-chief of the armies of the north and north-east, Nivelle caused an immediate stir by brusquely re-shaping the Allied offensive plans for 1917. Now, as at Verdun, he was convinced he had the 'formula' for success, but on a much larger scale. Instead of Joffre's scheme for a combined Franco-British attack on a broad front to take place in February, he prescribed, as

the principal operation, a massive French assault on the thirty-mile Soissons-Rheims sector, flanking the river Aisne, to be launched in April. This was to be supported by British and French attacks designed to contain the German reserves. By this plan, reversing Joffre's aim to let the British take some of the weight off the tired French troops, Nivelle envisaged a spectacular French break-through that might even lead quickly to victory in the west.

Nivelle's formula

Almost a million men were to take part in the main assault – a force commanded by General Micheler, consisting of three armies, the 5th (General Mazel), the 6th (General Mangin), and the 10th (General Duchêne). In support would be 5,000 guns. After a preliminary bombardment the 5th and 6th Armies were to attack and break the German line, and the 10th Army would then advance in the centre to exploit the rupture. The conception ran counter to all current military thinking. It relied on swift, sudden, surprise attack, delivered with overwhelming force and calculated to destroy the main enemy force – as Nivelle emphasized – within forty-eight hours. Considering the formidable power of the defensive as developed by 1917, it was a bold plan by any standards. But seen in relation to the enemy's Soissons-Rheims line it was foolhardy. The terrain was difficult, comprising a series of plateaux and ridges rising 200 feet above the Aisne; and the entire sector, held by the Germans for two years, was honeycombed with elaborate fortifications and bristled with guns and automatic weapons. Yet, dubious as the scheme was, Nivelle obtained approval

for it, in both Paris and London, through sheer persuasiveness and his personal conviction that it would succeed.

From the first, fate seemed to be against Nivelle. In January unprecedented cold descended on the Western Front, hindering offensive preparations, intensifying the troops' hardships as they huddled in their frozen trenches, and depressing still further their already low morale. Then Nivelle's whole plan was jeopardized by a major German withdrawal. In February the Germans began retiring from the ninety-mile Arras-Noyon-Soissons sector (west of the Soissons-Rheims line) to the heavily defended Hindenburg Line. They were thus eliminating a dangerous salient, shortening their front, and breaking contact with the French over a large part of Nivelle's projected field of operations (though a secondary one). Meanwhile they increased the number of their divisions in the Soissons-Rheims line from nine to forty. These moves radically changed the strategic picture; and doubts now arose about the wisdom of Nivelle's scheme. In Paris members of Alexandre Ribot's new government, especially the war minister, Paul Painlevé, received the plan with marked uneasiness. So did some of Nivelle's own generals and, on the British side, commander-in-chief Sir Douglas Haig and his colleagues. But Nivelle, fervently backed by his *chef de cabinet* (chief of staff), the fiery Colonel d'Alenson, refused to modify his main assault plan.

Building false hopes
But as the massive build-up proceeded behind the Aisne's left bank in the continuing wintry weather of March, one element essential to French success—surprise—had already been lost. It was impossible to hide the preparations from the enemy. And among the French troops, faced with yet another offensive that they had no reason to think would end any differently from previous ones, enthusiasm was at rock-bottom. But here Nivelle scored a psychological triumph. By a concentrated morale-boosting drive he wrought a spectacular change in the army's mood. In anticipation of his promised break-through, apathy disappeared and discipline and bearing noticeably improved. At last, the troops believed, there was a goal worth fighting for: this attack would achieve results. There was striking evidence of the new spirit in letters from the front, as examined by army postal control. In contrast to their earlier gloomy, bitter tone, these now expressed hope and confidence.

Security about the coming offensive was almost non-existent. In the Paris bars and bistros it was discussed openly—and with extravagant optimism. But no such optimism was felt by the French war cabinet, or by an increasing number of Nivelle's officers, senior and junior. Many of these wrote to Painlevé at the war ministry, reporting their misgivings. And so apprehensive were Ribot and his colleagues that, on the 6th April, an emergency top-level council was held at Compiègne (to whose historic Palace Nivelle had just transferred his headquarters) to decide whether the attack should go ahead as planned or not. President Poincaré, ministers, and army chiefs, including Nivelle, assembled in the President's special railway coach at Compiègne station. In a tense discussion almost all present voiced doubts about the operation. Nivelle forcibly argued that it would succeed: he even promised that if his armies had not broken through within forty-eight hours he would call off the assault. Finally, realizing he had no support, he angrily offered his resignation. Amid the general dismay, Poincaré hastened to reassure Nivelle that he had the government's con-

Craonne, April 1917. A painting by François Flameng. It was here in atrocious weather conditions that Nivelle's ill-starred offensive predictably foundered

fidence, and full responsibility for proceeding with the offensive.

The bubble bursts
Nivelle had got his way; and in the sleet-filled dawn of Monday 16th April—a week after a preliminary British attack at Arras—the assault was launched. It turned out to be a disaster. Within a fortnight it had ground to a halt (though local operations continued), broken on the deadly Craonne plateau, the slopes of the Chemin des Dames and the heavily defended heights all along the front. Its failure was evident in the first hours: there were ghastly scenes as French troops struggled against uncut barbed wire and were mown down by withering automatic fire from undestroyed strong-points, and misdirected fire from the French 75s fell among panicking French Senegalese. Poor security, ineffective artillery preparation, and atrocious weather had—quite apart from the basic weakness of the whole conception—all combined to doom the operation from the start. Instead of the promised break-through, Nivelle's troops gained a few miles of ground at the price of almost 200,000 casualties. Their new-found euphoria collapsed like a pricked bubble. The reaction was catastrophic but in the circumstances predictable. In bitter frustration and resentment at their 'betrayal', the men of Nivelle's armies rebelled.

For some six weeks in the spring of 1917 much of the French army was in a state of mutiny. Elements of fifty-four divisions refused to obey orders, demonstrated, deserted, called for peace, brandished red flags, threatened or attempted to march on

French line-drawing 1917: 'The Grumble'. When Nivelle's offensive yielded only a few miles of ground at a cost of 200,000 casualties the grumble became a mutiny

Paris and overthrow the government. At the gravest moment, in early June, only two entirely dependable divisions stood between Soissons and the capital sixty-five miles away. The wonder is that the Germans did not take advantage of the situation to launch a counter-attack on the Soissons-Rheims front. Had they done so the course of the war must have been incalculably altered. But equally remarkable is the factor that prevented them from doing this — the maintenance of almost total secrecy which concealed news of the mutinies from the enemy and the French home front, to say nothing of the British high command and government. Such scant information as the Germans received through agents or escaped German prisoners they demonstrably discounted.

Dark episode
The official secrecy over the mutinies has never been relaxed. French military archives are virtually inaccessible and the official French war history *(Les Armées Françaises dans la Grande Guerre)* reveals little detail. Something of the story can be gleaned from contemporary diaries and memoirs; but the fullest and most reliable account comes from Marshal (then General) Philippe Pétain who, as commander-in-chief in succession to Nivelle, was called on to restore order in the demoralized armies. Pétain's record (which he entrusted to Major-General Sir Edward Spears, and which Spears published in his book, *Two Men Who Saved France,* Eyre and Spottiswoode, 1966) throws much light on this dark episode, even to the naming of individual units involved.

The main wave of mutinies lasted from 29th April to 10th June. They reached their height on 2nd June, with seventeen separate outbreaks. Of the 151 incidents recorded (some occurred after the 10th June)

110 were listed as 'grave', and altogether 110 units were affected, mostly in the camps and barracks of the Aisne region behind the Chemin des Dames sector. There were also disorders on over 100 troop trains and at 130 railway stations. The first outbreak took place east of Rheims, where an infantry regiment refused to parade on being ordered back to the line after only five days' rest. On the 4th May a number of infantrymen in the Chemin des Dames area suddenly deserted, and men of a colonial regiment circulated anti-war leaflets and noisily refused to fight. The tempo of revolt now quickened. On the 16th and 17th a Chasseur battalion and an infantry regiment rebelled. On the 19th another Chasseur unit demonstrated, and next day two entire infantry regiments refused to march. Violence had so far been absent; but on the 22nd and 27th, near Tardenois (in the Aisne region), there were two cases of officers being assaulted. On the 28th seven regiments and a Chasseur battalion from five different divisions mutinied. And as the month ended, disorder swept through eight divisions which had fought at Chemin des Dames or were about to move there.

Mutiny spreads
One mutiny was, in Pétain's words, 'conceived in cold blood'. This involved a crack infantry regiment which had fought gallantly at Verdun and since then been in almost constant action until February 1917. Told to stand by for the front, on 27th May it moved from rest quarters to billets near Soissons. On the 29th over 800 men paraded — in excellent order — to protest against making further useless and costly attacks. Rejecting the pleas and threats of their divisional and corps commanders, they recruited more followers with the aim of seizing trains, travelling to

Paris and putting their demands before the Chamber of Deputies. The officers, who had stood by helplessly, now managed to control the situation. At dawn next day the mutineers were ordered into lorries and driven, still demonstrating, to a quiet area and finally to Verdun. The sequel: courts-martial in which four men were sentenced to death, and the ceremonial stripping of the regiment's colours.

Early June brought more and worse outbreaks. On the 1st one regiment near Tardenois — again with a fine fighting record — was ordered to the front after a brief rest period. Chanting the *Internationale,* the men marched in angry protest to the local town hall. The brigade commander, who tried to stop them, was attacked and his insignia ripped off. The divisional commander intervened but was shouted down. Then the ringleaders freed prisoners from a detention camp and the troops ran wild, overturning lorries and smashing windows. By next evening a 2,000-strong mob was on the march, waving red flags and calling for peace and revolution. On the 3rd the regiment was moved to another camp and the agitation quickly subsided.

Their brief duration was often a feature of these outbursts — even the violent ones. On the 2nd a Chasseur battalion rioted in the same area, opened fire on the commanding officer's quarters and burned the huts of a unit that tried to restrain them. But by nightfall the mutiny had fizzled out and there was no repetition. Meanwhile trouble was rife on leave trains and at railway stations in the rear. Pétain cites two typical cases. At Château-Thierry, on 7th June, police battled with rebellious leave-men from Paris who finally had to be controlled by armed troops. Next day, in a clash at Esternay station, soldiers mobbed and assaulted railway officials who tried to shepherd them back to their trains.

Russian influence

The disorder had now passed its peak, subsiding almost suddenly, like a worked-out fever. From the 10th to the 30th June incidents averaged one a day; and by September had ceased altogether. The whole uprising was essentially a spontaneous protest by desperate and overtried troops rather than a concerted rebellion. Many men saw themselves as strikers, not mutineers. Heinous though this collective indiscipline of an army was in military terms, it should be remembered in mitigation that some mutinying units – among the French army's best – had fought with heroism in previous battles. And the mutinies had their moments of pathos, as when captured rebel formations marched back to face court-martial and the direst penalties with their uniform spruce and their boots shined. French troops already had a list of long-standing grievances over vast and seemingly needless losses, derisory pay, exiguous leave, harsh discipline, wretched welfare conditions. Coming on top of these, the Aisne *débâcle* was the crowning blow. 'The fighting troops were at the end of their tether,' wrote Pétain. A GHQ officer, Lieutenant Henry Bordeaux, reporting on the state of one rear division, observed 'a sort of moral nihilism'. 'It is an army without faith,' he added.

Yet the mutinies were at least encouraged by two external factors. One was the Russian Revolution, which shook the world in mid-March 1917. In France it inspired a wild revolutionary spirit among the two Russian brigades – Russia's small expe-

ditionary force – serving alongside the French. This mood infected many less steadfast *poilus* (French 'Tommies') in the nearby camps – the more so when the Russians, suffering crippling losses in the Aisne offensive, staged their own mutiny. Moved first to bases in the rear, they were then isolated in central France, where they were finally shelled into submission by other Russian troops. The frequent waving of red flags, chanting of the *Internationale,* and calls for revolution by the French mutineers testified to the influence the Russians had on them.

Defeatist campaign

The other factor was more sinister: subversive propaganda spread by civilian agitators in the rear. Active since the previous November (and even earlier) in conjunction with labour troubles in the war plants, it had intensified in the New Year. Military security produced strong evidence of a defeatist campaign being directed at the troops through anti-war tracts and newspaper articles, and illicit meetings and inflammatory speeches in the leave centres. Late in February Nivelle unavailingly requested the minister of the interior, Louis-Jean Malvy, to suppress the traffic and its chief instigators, whom he named. It was only Nivelle's forceful boosting of the troops' morale before the Aisne offensive that damped down the defeatist threat at this crucial moment. But when disorder swept the armies in May, the agitators renewed their assault. They haunted the Paris termini distributing anti-war leaflets to troops in transit; incited them to desert (there were desertion agencies near the stations, where men could obtain civilian clothes); used every means to push the disaffected *poilus* into revolt, including the clandestine dispatch to the army zone of extremist, left-wing news-sheets – like *Le Bonnet Rouge* and *La Tranchée Républicaine* – that defied the censor's ban.

But the anti-war campaign was also being waged against the home front. Playing on the war-weariness of French civilians – and these were almost as spiritless and disillusioned as the soldiers, especially after the hope-shattering fiasco of the Aisne offensive – the saboteurs were provoking labour unrest and infiltrating the war factories with their defeatist-pacifist propaganda. From mid-May – when militant *midinettes* (Parisian working-girls) paraded the Paris boulevards – onwards, demonstrations and strikes became frequent, until by the end of June there were over 170 stoppages in war plants in Paris and the provinces. Sympathizing troops joined in some marches. Occasionally violence erupted, incited by agitators. Beneath the capital's workaday surface there was unwonted tension. Never in the war had

Above: French soldier with wooden crosses sets out to mark graves during the offensive. Left: General Nivelle. It was hoped that his aggressive spirit would end the impasse on the Western Front

national morale been so uneasy. Through the June weeks Ribot's war cabinet met in an atmosphere of constant crisis. The corridors of the Chamber of Deputies buzzed with alarm and pessimism. And in two stormy secret sessions of the Chamber, left-wing members bitterly attacked the government and high command, questioned France's ability to continue fighting and canvassed the possibility of peace. 'The fever is spreading,' wrote President Poincaré. 'Must we await a new victory of the Marne to be healed?'

France's whole war-making capacity was undermined by a grave *malaise*. The superficial unity she had achieved in August 1914 – burying her acute political, social, and labour differences in face of the national emergency – was breaking down under the exhausting strain of nearly three years of war. But the particular defeatist-pacifist menace that now threatened her might have been minimized if, at the outset, the government had taken a different decision about national security.

Lukewarm reprisals

Instead of arresting, as intended, some 2,500 potential troublemakers – listed in the police dossier, *Carnet B,* which had been compiled for just this eventuality – the authorities had detained only the known spies, largely on the ground that action against left-wing labour leaders and other suspects might antagonize the workers and impede the call-up. This policy had paid ill. A mixed assortment of pacifists, internationalists, left-wing extremists, Marxists, and anarchists – each with their own pretexts for sabotaging France's war-effort—were left free to disseminate their propaganda. They ranged from Merrheim, the trade union chief, to sponsors of illicit news-sheets like Faure, Duval, and Almereyda, and a host of other undesirables, many of them aliens. And behind them were traitors such as the notorious Bolo Pasha, Lenoir and the police chief Leymarie, working directly for Germany. Under the complacent tolerance of Louis-Jean Malvy, minister of the interior, these men operated with almost total immunity. Their task was made easier by continued government reluctance to suppress them for fear of provoking labour disturbances. The treason trials of 1918, bringing Malvy and many lesser fry to justice, were to expose the full extent of the internal danger assailing France.

Pétain to the rescue

How far was the defeatist propaganda responsible for the mutinies? The answer seems to be that while it was not the root cause, it was a strong contributory element. This at least was the verdict of General Pétain, who succeeded Nivelle as commander-in-chief as the troubles were boiling up in mid-May. Nivelle had been dismissed amid a resounding command crisis. Sixty-one-year-old General Philippe Pétain, famous as the saviour of Verdun, was undoubtedly the right man to replace him. Aloof and reserved, he hid beneath his cold exterior an unsuspected warmth: he understood the troops and they trusted him. His method of handling the mutinies was a mixture of sternness and humanity. First he moved ruthlessly to stamp out disorder and punish the ringleaders. He stiffened the faltering authority of his officers. He took vigorous steps to curb the prevalent drunkenness—a potent factor in inflaming the revolts. And he vehemently attacked the 'contamination' from the rear. Furious at the government's failure to suppress the defeatist groups, he bombarded ministers with demands for action, warning them that if the agitation continued he could not answer for the army's recovery. But Pétain knew that much was wrong within the army itself. Thus he set about a whole range of welfare reforms.

Perhaps most effective of all were Pétain's contacts with the troops themselves. Almost daily in these weeks his white-pennanted car left GHQ, Compiègne, on a comprehensive tour of formations. In about a month he covered over ninety divisions. A tall, magisterial figure with his flowing moustache and frosty blue eyes, he addressed officers and men, exhorting, encouraging, explaining his plans for limited operations designed to avoid heavy losses. He talked with individual soldiers, listening sympathetically to complaints and suggestions. The visits were of inestimable value. At last the men felt that someone was caring for their interests, that they counted as human beings. By late summer the French army was well on the way to restoration. The price it had paid for mutiny was not, in the circumstances, high. While many convicted mutineers were sentenced to long terms, of the 412 men condemned to death between May and October, only 55 were executed.

Now the home front remained to be purged. As with Pétain and her army, France providentially possessed the right man for the task. Late in 1917 the elderly Georges Clemenceau emerged from the political wilderness to become prime minister. None of France's previous wartime premiers—René Viviani, Aristide Briand, Alexandre Ribot, and latterly Paul Painlevé—had been able to command a sustained, united war-effort. But Clemenceau was a leader of different calibre. A merciless enemy of all anti-patriotic elements, he feared no party or faction. Having denounced Malvy in the Senate in July, as prime minister he proceeded to liquidate the defeatist cliques, silence the pessimists and doubters, and renew France's bruised and battered fighting spirit. His one aim was victory. 'Home policy? I wage war! Foreign policy? I wage war!' he bluntly stated. 'All the time I wage war!' As 1917 ended, France seemed to have narrowly surmounted her gravest crisis.

Below: The commander-in-chief sympathizes with a soldier's complaint. Pétain handled the mutinies with sternness and humanity, but he knew much was wrong with the army. Bottom: Militant midinettes on the march. Even Parisian working girls were restive

In Flanders' Fields

The name 'Passchendaele' applies, strictly speaking, to the last phase of the 3rd Ypres campaign of July-November 1917. But it is far more usual to find it used as a damning synonym for prolonged battles of attrition in the Flanders mud during the First World War. Half a century later, people are still arguing passionately about whether the offensive should ever have been undertaken in the first place, why it was allowed to go on for so long, and what effect it had on the course of the war as a whole.

On 15th November 1916 General Joseph Joffre, the French commander-in-chief, assembled a conference of the Entente military representatives at Chantilly to determine Anglo-French strategy for the coming year. He and Sir Douglas Haig, the British commander-in-chief, agreed that the attrition battles of the Somme and Verdun in 1916 had left the German army on the Western Front near to breaking point. Joffre feared that the French army could undertake only one more major offensive, but he hoped this would be decisive. He proposed a concerted offensive on all fronts in the spring of 1917 with the British cast for the leading role in the west. In December, however, General Joffre was replaced by the most junior of the French army commanders, General Robert Nivelle, who had persuaded both the French prime minister Aristide Briand and the British prime minister David Lloyd George that he could achieve a complete break-through in under forty-eight hours—a feat which had eluded both sides since September 1914. In Nivelle's plan the French were to strike the major blow on the Aisne sector, while Haig launched diversionary attacks near Arras and took over part of the French line south of the Somme.

Nivelle fails

In February and March 1917 the effective German director of strategy, General Erich Ludendorff, forestalled Nivelle's planned offensive for the spring by withdrawing between fifteen and twenty-two miles on a front of about seventy miles to a strong defensive position known—after the nominal commander—as the Hindenburg Line. Nivelle was reluctant to adjust his aims and—oblivious of the need for surprise—made no secret of his highly ambitious plan. The French offensive began on April 16th in an atmosphere of political and military mistrust between the Allies and lasted until May 7th. It pene-

trated up to four miles on a sixteen mile front, but this limited success contrasted too sharply with Nivelle's personal promises. Frustrated by failure, the French armies began to disintegrate. Long-festering grievances came to a head in mutinies that broke out in May and June in nearly half the units in the French army. General Henri-Philippe Pétain, the hero of Verdun, who replaced Nivelle on 15th May, quickly restored order, but also dropped strong hints that the French would have to remain largely on the defensive for the rest of the year until they could be backed up by American divisions and more tanks and heavy artillery. Meanwhile, after prolonging the gruelling battle at Arras to shield the French during their offensive on the Aisne, the British had to take a fresh look at the projected Flanders offensive in the light of conditions very different from those that had applied when the Allies had planned their strategy earlier in the year.

On May 4th, the French and British civilian war leaders and their military advisers met at Paris to revise their strategy after Nivelle's failure and the Russian February Revolution. The military chiefs agreed unanimously that offensive operations must be continued on the Western Front. Allied attacks, they believed, had already exhausted a large proportion of Germany's reserves and she must be prevented from throwing her full weight against either Russia or Italy. But, in the words of the chief of the imperial general staff, Sir William Robertson: 'It is no longer a question of aiming at breaking through the enemy's front and aiming at distant objectives. It is now a question of wearing down and exhausting the enemy's resistance. . . . We are all of the opinion that our object can be obtained by relentlessly attacking with limited objectives, while making the fullest use of our artillery. By this means we hope to gain our ends and with the minimum loss possible.' Both the British and French governments gave their approval to these recommendations. Before the seriousness of the French army mutinies began to be revealed to him early in June, the British commander-in-chief, Sir Douglas Haig, was already contemplating a bold stroke in Flanders very different in spirit from the cautious policy outlined above. The British government had laid down in November 1916 that the clearing of German submarine bases from the Flanders coast was a strategic objective of the first importance.

Top left: Gough, the young 'thruster' put in charge of the opening offensive. Top right: Robertson, chief of the imperial general staff. 'It is now a question of wearing down and exhausting the enemy's resistance.' Above: Haig, Joffre, and Lloyd George. Haig and Joffre agreed in 1916 that the Germans on the Western Front were near breaking point. To this misjudgement Haig owed his confidence, and his disastrous persistence in Flanders. Left: 'Canadian gunners in Mud', a painting of Passchendaele by Bastier. 'Passchendaele' assumed the importance of historical myth —a myth of men smothered and helpless in mud, sacrificed for nothing

Backs to the Wall

Haig believed that such a break-through could be achieved from the Ypres salient, assisted by a supporting advance along the coast and an amphibious landing near Ostend. This aim rested on a very optimistic view of weakening German morale and reserves. It also assumed full French co-operation in supporting offensives, and this Pétain – who had just replaced Nivelle – promised on May 18th.

French support crumbles
But on 1st June the picture changed. General Debeney brought Haig a message from Pétain which mentioned euphemistically that 'the French army was in a bad state of discipline' and would not be able to fulfil the promise to attack in support of the opening of the British offensive at Ypres. A week later Pétain himself revealed in more detail the gravity of the situation but added that things were improving – as indeed they were. Thereafter, though hopes of really active French participation faded, Haig remained confident that the British army (assisted by six French divisions) could gain a major victory in Flanders. Lloyd George who, incidentally, knew even less about the breakdown of French discipline than Haig, grew increasingly sceptical about French co-operation. By 13th June he was harrying Robertson with a plan to remove twelve divisions from Haig's command 'to settle the war in Italy'. Robertson, a firm 'Westerner' who usually saw eye to eye with Haig, nevertheless cautioned him against 'large and costly attacks without full co-operation by the French'; and on 13th June he wrote: 'Don't argue that you can finish the war this year, or that the German is already beaten. Argue that your plan [the concentration of all available troops and material on the Western Front] is the best plan – as it is – that no other would be *safe* let alone decisive, and then leave them to reject your advice and mine. They dare not do that'.

Why in these unpropitious circumstances, with even the loyal Robertson urging caution, did Haig decide to launch the Ypres offensive? It had long been apparent to the British commander-in-chief that the French war effort was flagging, so that the collapse of morale after Nivelle's abortive offensive came as no surprise to him. Judging from his diary entries Haig's motives were mixed: he wished to shield and encourage the French, but was also eager to gain a great victory for the British army which had now, at last, become the predominant partner. What needs to be stressed, however, is that the senior French commanders had no enthusiasm for a major offensive in Flanders designed to clear the Channel coast. Pétain, in fact, was opposed to any major

offensive on the Western Front in 1917, and on 19th May he told Sir Henry Wilson – who had been attached to Nivelle's headquarters – that Haig's projected advance towards Ostend was certain to fail. General Ferdinand Foch, chief of the French general staff, was, if possible, even less encouraging and sarcastically referred to the campaign as 'a duck's march'.

Jellicoe's bombshell
The crucial incident, as far as the indecisive British war cabinet committee was concerned, occurred at a meeting on 19th June; namely 'Jellicoe's bombshell'. Not a single member of the committee, consisting of David Lloyd George, Andrew Bonar Law, Sir Alfred Milner, Lord Curzon, and General J.C.Smuts, favoured a major offensive on the Western Front in 1917, but the first sea lord shattered their assumption that time was on their side by declaring that German submarines were taking such a toll of merchant shipping that it would be impossible for Great Britain to continue the war into 1918. The Royal Navy would be in grave difficulty unless the Belgian coast could be cleared by the Army. Although this alarmist prediction suited Haig's own military views, it is very doubtful if he took Jellicoe's warning as seriously as is often supposed. As recently as 7th May Haig had described Jellicoe in a letter to his wife as 'an old woman', and after the meeting on 19th June he noted: 'No one present shared Jellicoe's view, and all seemed satisfied that the food reserves in Great Britain are adequate'. Even more revealingly General Charteris, Haig's chief of intelligence, recorded in his diary on 28th June: 'No one believed this [Jellicoe's] rather amazing view, but it had sufficient weight to make the Cabinet agree to our attack going on.'

The fundamental reason for Haig's determination to launch the Flanders offensive was, it seems clear, neither the necessity to shield the French nor to clear the Channel coast of enemy submarine bases. It was rather his conviction that the Germans were so near to collapse that six months of fighting at the present intensity on the Western Front could end the war that year. His confidence was increased by the auspicious beginning of operations on 7th June, when General Sir Herbert Plumer's 2nd Army – assisted by the explosion of nineteen enormous mines under the German front line – was brilliantly successful in carrying out a limited advance to seize the Messines Ridge and so straighten out the salient south of Ypres.

The interval of fifty-three days which then occurred between this successful preliminary advance and the opening of the main offensive on 31st July was to prove fatal.

Haig's plans were not finally approved until 25th July and then only after the desirability of reinforcing the Italian Front in preference to Flanders had been endlessly debated by the war cabinet. Haig certainly had grounds for the bitter remark that he would have liked such confidence and support as the prime minister had recently given to Nivelle. More important however, as Haig's most recent biographer, John Terraine, has pointed out, Haig had intended even in the preliminary planning stage that there would be a delay of some six weeks between Messines and the main attack. Moreover, as the same author has written, Haig made his 'gravest and most fatal error' in 1917 of entrusting the main role in the Flanders battle to the 5th Army commanded by General Sir Hubert Gough. It could be argued that Gough was the obvious choice for the bold strategy envisaged. He was, at forty-seven, the youngest army commander (whereas Plumer at sixty was by far the eldest); he was a cavalryman and a 'thruster' whereas Plumer – rather like Pétain – was noted for his cautious approach to planning and tactics, and his great concern to minimize casualties. Yet, quite apart from criticisms levelled at Gough and his staff for revising and mishandling Haig's plans, the transfer of command at such a time was bound to cause administrative complications and delays, particularly as the French contingent (General Anthoine's 1st Army) had to be fitted in on Gough's left between the 5th Army and Rawlinson's 4th Army on the coast.

Third Ypres opens
Like so many campaigns of the First World War, the actual operations of Third Ypres – which at last began on 31st July after a fortnight's preparatory bombardment and several postponements at the request of the army and corps commanders – soon ceased to bear much resemblance to the original plan. Essentially Haig had assumed that after eight days the 5th Army would have advanced fifteen miles and would have got control of the Ypres-Roulers-Thourout railway. Only when this was done would the 4th Army begin to attack along the coast, assisted by amphibious landings and, with Gough's support, would turn the German defences. Meanwhile the 2nd Army, after playing only a minor supporting role in the opening days, would advance to the north-east to secure the whole Passchendaele ridge.

This schedule proved to be far too optimistic. The campaign degenerated into a struggle for control of a plateau some sixty metres high. The operation fell into three distinct phases each containing three major actions. In the first phase Gough's 5th Army played the major role, and fought the

'The whole surface of the ground consisted of nothing but a series of overlapping shell-craters, half full of yellow, slimy water. . . . The original roads had almost ceased to exist and it was necessary to lay down corduroy tracks . . . These and the "duck board" walks were daily machine-gunned by low-flying aeroplanes. Every yard of ground had been carefully "registered" by the enemy's guns, and a peculiarly effective form of gas shell, containing "mustard gas", had been evolved . . .' (Brigadier General Baker Carr.) **Above:** 'Void', painted by Wellard. **Below:** 'Gassed. "In Arduis Fidelis"' by Gilbert Rogers

battles of Pilckem Ridge (31st July), Gheluvelt Plateau (10th August) and Langemarck (16th August). The British had deliberately thrown away the chance of a surprise attack and they were hampered by driving rain. But despite this the first day, unlike the opening of the Somme battle on 1st July 1916, was far from being a disaster. The main assault was made by fourteen British and two French divisions supported by over 2,000 guns and howitzers on a very wide front of nearly twenty miles. The troops in the centre and to the left managed to reach the third and farthest target lines, and the only real check was suffered on the right of 5th Army's frontage. Here, from the Gheluvelt Plateau, specially trained German divisions made a fierce counter-attack, while the strength of the enemy's counter-bombardment during the battle as a whole showed how little real damage the British army's 'softening-up process' had done. Yet even if GHQ's initial assessment of British casualties at 15,000 was too low, it still compared very favourably with nearly 60,000 on the first day of the Somme.

Unfortunately atrocious weather had already begun to hamper further advance. On the first day the weather had completely prevented the British from using their superior air force for artillery reconnaissance. Far worse, as Colonel Fuller noted at Tank Corps headquarters: 'By July 31st from the Polygone de Zonnebeke through St Julien and northwards past Langemarck the Steenbeck had become a wide moat of liquid mud.' The British were unlucky in that the weather broke on the very first day. But meteorological reports for the previous eighty years could have showed GHQ that Flanders was notoriously wet in August. Rapidly, the swamp expanded, greatly assisted by the bombardment which had effectively destroyed the already precarious drainage system. Tank Corps headquarters daily sent a 'swamp map' to GHQ until instructed not to send any more. It seems unlikely that Haig ever saw these maps, and neither he nor Gough at this stage grasped the full significance of the appalling ground conditions. As early as 4th August General Charteris noted: 'All my fears about the weather have been realised. It has killed this attack. Every day's delay tells against us. We lose, hour by hour, the advantage of attack. . . . Even if the weather were to clear now, it will take days for the ground to harden, if indeed it ever can before the winter frost. . . . I went up to the front line this morning. Every brook is swollen and the ground is a quagmire. . . .'

Although there were some fine days in August, the weather and the terrain dictated the course of operations: Gough's second and third attempts to press forward

Backs to the Wall

Overleaf: 'The Harvest of Battle' by C.R.W. Nevinson. Normally it took two men to carry a stretcher: by October it took sixteen. Mules and horses sank beneath the mud with their loads. A survivor wrote: '. . . we had often to drink shell-hole water, not knowing what would be at the bottom. Many a lot I helped to pull out of shell holes, where fellows were sinking and could not move'

(on 10th and 16th August) were thrown back by fierce counter-attacks. In his book *The Fifth Army,* Gough wrote that after 16th August he 'informed the Commander-in-Chief that tactical success was not possible, or would be too costly under such conditions, and advised that the attack should now be abandoned'. This advice was consistent with Lloyd George's prior condition that the attack should be discontinued if casualties were incommensurate with the amount of ground gained. In ignoring this condition and advice, Haig may still have been concerned to assist the French, but another explanation seems more likely. To call off the offensive at this

German prisoner captured in the successful battle of the Messines Ridge, an auspicious opening for Haig's campaign

stage would have entailed surrender to Lloyd George's nagging pressure to divert large forces to Italy. Haig and Robertson were fully agreed that such a move might result in losing the war on the Western Front.

Plumer plans carefully
At the end of August Haig transferred the main role in further operations from Gough to Plumer. This signified a return to a more cautious approach based on concentrating overwhelming artillery cover for each short infantry advance. Contrary to the caricature presented by his extreme critics, Haig did not favour remorseless tactical attrition once the initial attempt at a breakthrough had lost its impetus. Indeed he criticized Gough for ordering too many small attacks on isolated farmhouses and strong points since they were seldom effective and were too costly in lives and

ammunition. It was ironic that although September was to be generally dry, in sharp contrast to August, Plumer spent the first three weeks of it meticulously preparing the next short step forward. The main sector of the offensive was limited to 4,000 yards with four divisions packed into the front line. The depth of the advance was restricted to 1,500 yards when a halt would be made to hold off counter-attacks and to await the ponderous advance of the huge mass of artillery. Plumer, and his chief of staff General Sir Charles Harington, calculated that the Passchendaele-Staden ridge could be cleared by four such limited attacks.

Anzac advance
The first of the three battles of the second phase – that of the Menin Road Ridge on 20th September – resulted in a clear victory. This was essentially an artillery triumph. General Birdwood, who commanded the 1st Anzac Corps in the battle, recalled that it was quite the best artillery barrage the Australians had ever seen. 'Creeping forward exactly according to plan, the barrage won the ground, while the infantry followed behind and occupied all the important points with a minimum of resistance.' The attack began at 5.40 am, and by mid-day the final objectives had been reached. The Germans were unable to counter-attack before 3.15 pm and were successfully beaten off. In bright sunshine British aircraft were able to report nearly four hundred objectives to the artillery. Ludendorff recorded: 'Another terrible assault was made on our lines on September 20th. . . . The enemy's onslaught was successful, which proved the superiority of the attack over the defence. . . .'

Plumer's second offensive – at Polygon Wood on 26th September – closely resembled the Menin Road battle both in its careful preparation and encouraging results. It too was fought in good weather. Prince Rupprecht of Bavaria, commanding the German forces in Flanders, now began to worry about his defensive tactics and the scarcity of reserves. General Charteris, whose optimistic reports fed and fortified the convictions of his chief, noted that the situation at the end of September closely resembled that on the Somme the previous year. 'Now, as then, we had worn down the German resistance to very near breaking point; then as now the weather went against us. It is a race with time and a fight with the weather. One thing is certain, no other army but ours could fight on as we are fighting. D.H. is asking for the last ounce from it and getting a wonderful response.' Encouraged by Plumer's gains and Charteris's assessment of German exhaustion, Haig on 28th September revived the idea that the next advance should be

immediately exploited. 'I am of the opinion that the enemy is tottering, and that a good vigorous blow might lead to decisive results. If we could destroy, or interrupt for 48 hours, the railway at Roulers there would probably be a débâcle, because the enemy would then have to rely on only one railway line for the supply of his troops between Ghent and the sea. . . .'

Plumer's third attack, the battle of Broodseinde on 4th October, followed the same pattern as the previous two: it was a heartening tactical victory but showed no signs of yielding those 'decisive results' which Haig had mentioned to his army commanders. It also marked the zenith of the artillery's contribution to the Third Ypres campaign before casualties, loss of guns, and the sheer impossibility of movement reduced its effectiveness. The Germans suffered particularly heavy casualties in this battle because the British barrage fell on five divisions just as they themselves were forming up to attack. This battle at last afforded the 2nd Army a foothold on the Passchendaele ridge. But a decision now had to be quickly made as to whether to halt the advance, particularly as the amphibious operations against Ostend had by now been abandoned and with them any real hope of reaching the Channel coast that year.

The day after Broodseinde Haig conferred with his army commanders. Charteris noted: 'We are far enough on now to stop for the winter, and there is much to be said for that. Unless we get fine weather for all this month, there is now no chance of clearing the coast. If we could be sure that the Germans would attack us here, it would be far better to stand fast. But they would probably be now only too glad to remain quiet here and try elsewhere. . . . Most of those at the conference, though willing to go on, would welcome a stop.'

Passchendaele – a 'porridge of mud'
The final phase of the campaign from 4th October to 6th November was fought for the almost obliterated village of Passchendaele, and as John Terraine rightly stresses, it 'bore throughout the characteristics which have generally been associated with the whole of it'. After the respite in September rain fell almost unceasingly through October and, with the continuing barrage, destroyed the few remaining signs of roads and tracks. By this time the whole area had reverted to a 'porridge of mud': mules and horses were known to have sunk beneath it with their loads; guns could find no solid ground to fire from; and it took sixteen bearers instead of two to carry each stretcher case the 4,000 yards to the field dressing stations. These conditions characterized the battle of Poelcapelle (9th October), the two battles fought

*Above: Desolation after a battle—a strafed wood. **Left:** The dying huddled with the dead, after the battle of the Messines Ridge. **Below left:** A soldier struggles forward. 'Even if the rainfall had been below instead of above the average, the destruction of the drains would have sufficed. . . . The drenching rains simply helped the broken drains to convert a reclaimed marsh into an impassable quagmire' (Lloyd George). By September, Gough wrote, 'Men of the strongest physique could hardly move forward at all and became easy victims to the enemy's snipers. Stumbling forward as best they could, their rifles also soon became so caked and clogged with mud as to be useless.' **Below right:** Reserves waiting in the trenches to advance on the village of Veldhoek*

The terrible price of seven miles of mud

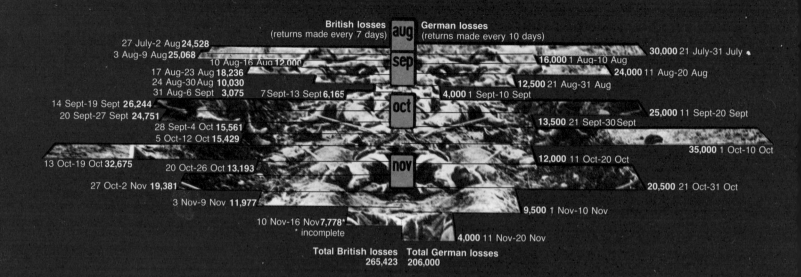

British losses (returns made every 7 days)	German losses (returns made every 10 days)
27 July-2 Aug **24,528**	**30,000** 21 July-31 July
3 Aug-9 Aug **25,068**	**16.000** 1 Aug-10 Aug
10 Aug-16 Aug **12,000**	**24,000** 11 Aug-20 Aug
17 Aug-23 Aug **18,236**	**12,500** 21 Aug-31 Aug
24 Aug-30 Aug **10,030**	**4,000** 1 Sept-10 Sept
31 Aug-6 Sept **3,075**	
7 Sept-13 Sept **6,165**	
14 Sept-19 Sept **26,244**	**25,000** 11 Sept-20 Sept
20 Sept-27 Sept **24,751**	**13,500** 21 Sept-30 Sept
28 Sept-4 Oct **15,561**	**35,000** 1 Oct-10 Oct
5 Oct-12 Oct **15,429**	
13 Oct-19 Oct **32,675**	**12,000** 11 Oct-20 Oct
20 Oct-26 Oct **13,193**	**20,500** 21 Oct-31 Oct
27 Oct-2 Nov **19,381**	
3 Nov-9 Nov **11,977**	**9,500** 1 Nov-10 Nov
10 Nov-16 Nov **7,778***	**4,000** 11 Nov-20 Nov
* incomplete	

Total British losses	Total German losses
265,423	206,000

Above: The struggle of attrition — casualty figures month by month for the British and German armies. Below: Haig's plan of campaign, showing the projected naval attack on the coast and the preliminary engagement at Messines Ridge. Haig did not realize that the customary rainfall in Flanders made an autumn campaign impracticable. Right: What the dead had won: the ground gained by the British between July and November — seven miles

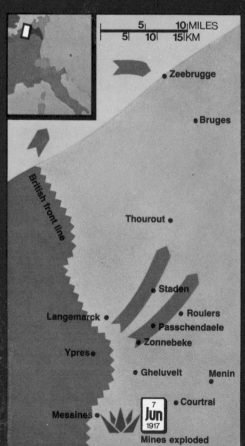

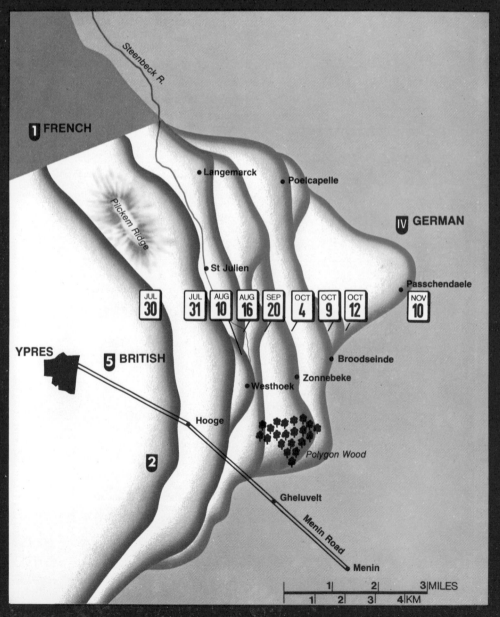

for Passchendaele (12th and 26th October) and the eventual capture of the village by the Canadians on 6th November. For the troops it was, in Terraine's succinct phrase 'a month of dire misery and absolute frustration'. The Germans, as the defenders, at least had less problems of movement, but conditions were not much better for them. Ludendorff did not exaggerate when he wrote: 'It was no longer life at all. It was mere unspeakable suffering.'

Had Haig decided to halt after Broodseinde it is unlikely that even the abominable conditions which characterized much of the fighting in August would have given the campaign its terrible reputation. Even Haig's warmest defenders have been obliged to look beyond the borders of Flanders in order to justify the Passchendaele battles. Thus Charteris wrote on 7th November: 'We have now got to where, with good weather, we should have been in early September, and with two months in front of us to carry on the operation and clear the coast. Now, from the purely local point of view, it is rather a barren victory, and if the home people decide on a defensive next year, it will be almost lives and labour thrown away.' The campaign had pushed out the Ypres salient to a maximum depth of seven miles and ended without capturing the whole Passchendaele-Staden ridge—which had been the first objective. Had Jellicoe's prediction—that Great Britain's ability to continue the war depended on the army clearing the Belgian coast—been well-founded the war would have been lost. Nor did the German IV Army voluntarily retire, as after the Somme campaign, to give the attackers the illusion of victory. Instead the Allies were obliged to defend the Ypres salient through yet another winter while the Germans were reinforced from the Eastern Front. The campaign had failed to realize Haig's hope of inflicting a decisive defeat on the German army.

Defending the disaster
There is a deep-rooted belief that Haig continued to fight at Passchendaele 'to save the French'. Haig's diaries contain several references in the summer to the need to 'encourage the French to keep fighting', and to give the Germans no opportunity to exploit their weakness. That the Germans were not actually planning to attack the French is no reflection on Haig's sincerity, though it was a surprising misjudgement by so experienced a staff officer. For the later phases however, Haig's own diaries reveal that his assessment of French capabilities changed. Thus on 1st September he noted: 'The result of our pressure at Ypres is shown by the slackening of German efforts on the Chemin des Dames, and the comparatively

weak resistance which they have made to the French attack at Verdun. The French army has consequently had the quiet time desired by General Pétain in which to recover from the Nivelle offensive.' Moreover after Pétain had proved reluctant to attack in support of the British in September, Haig wrote to Robertson (on 8th October): 'Though the French cannot be expected to admit it officially, we know that the state of their armies and of the reserve manpower behind the armies is such that neither the French government nor the military authorities will venture to call on their troops for any further great and sustained offensive effort, at any rate before it becomes evident that the enemy's strength has been definitely and finally broken. Though they are staunch in defence and will carry out useful local offensives against limited objectives, the French armies would not respond to a call for more than that, and the authorities are well aware of it.'

Ten years after the campaign Haig asserted that Pétain had repeatedly urged him to attack 'on account of the awful state of the French troops'. But Haig meticulously recorded meetings with all important soldiers and statesmen and there is no suggestion that in his four meetings with Pétain *during the campaign* such a request was even hinted at. Pétain denied the postwar rumour, while Haig never mentioned this crucial piece of intelligence to the British government. Possibly Haig was confusing French requests during the Arras operations in April and May with later events in Flanders.

Counting the cost
It does not seem likely that by prolonging the Flanders offensive Haig gave indirect help to the Allies on other fronts. The Passchendaele phase prevented neither the final collapse of the Russian armies during the autumn of 1917 nor the rout of the Italians at Caporetto towards the end of October. Indeed Ludendorff was actually able to detach several divisions from the Western Front during the British offensive. There is plentiful evidence, including the war memoirs of Prince Rupprecht and Ludendorff, to support Haig's conviction that the Flanders attrition was having a serious effect on the IV Army's morale. But the Allies also suffered severely. Indeed, since the Germans were for the most part defending, and for much of the campaign adopted economical tactics of defence in depth from dispersed strong points, it would not be surprising if the attackers' morale was the more severely strained of the two. Moreover, Haig and his staff (though not Robertson) seem to have underrated the tonic effect on morale of Germany's tremendous victory over Russia

The wounded in a bleak and sodden world. ***Above:*** *Stretcher-bearers carry a wounded man through mud which reaches their knees.* ***Below:*** *Wounded German carried on a stretcher by South African Scots*

Below: *Canadian and German 'walking wounded' on their way to a dressing station. They are resting on the devastated ground just outside Passchendaele*

The town of Ypres, its houses ruined and deserted, pitted by huge water-filled shell craters

which became ever more certain as the Flanders fighting dragged on inconclusively. Victory in the east gave the Germans vastly increased numbers – forty divisions were transferred to the Western Front from Russia and Rumania between 1st November and the middle of March and more followed later. And it gave them renewed hope – for a decisive blow in the spring of 1918.

Confusion and controversy over casualty statistics spring not only from gaps in the reliable first-hand sources against which differing estimates can be checked, but also from the different methods used by the belligerents in reckoning their losses. The British total of 245,000 killed and wounded given by the *British Official History* has been widely accepted as approximately correct, though in August 1918 the general staff gave the war cabinet an estimated total of just over 265,000, and Sir Basil Liddell Hart puts it as high as 300,000. The higher of the two German estimates (in their *Official History*) for their IV Army between 1st July and mid-November – covering a much wider front than the Ypres sector – is 202,000 including missing. The *German Medical History*, however, puts the total as low as 175,000. Even if the *British Official History* is accurate for British losses, and the higher German total is on the low side, it would still be impossible to argue that in the gruesome computation of casualties the third battle of Ypres had resulted in a clear gain for the British and French.

Haig misjudges Germany

Although at the time the gradual effects of attrition on enemy numbers and morale was regarded by GHQ as a valid reason for prolonging the battle, Haig himself appears to have been motivated chiefly by his persistent belief that Germany was near to total collapse. The baneful influence of General Charteris in sustaining this illusion has been widely recognized. 'In retrospect,' as one careful historian has written, 'we can say with certainty that General Charteris's estimates of enemy strength and morale were almost criminally optimistic, and that Haig was badly misled in basing his plans upon them.' Well-founded though this criticism is, it would be unjust to make the chief of intelligence a scapegoat for the commander-in-chief. Haig's extremely powerful and self-confident personality could be a source of a weakness as well as of strength: once his mind was made up on a subject he was not easily swayed. In his book *At G.H.Q.*, Charteris, without seeking to denigrate his former commander, cites more than one instance of Haig going well beyond his (already over-optimistic) intelligence reports and predictions. Haig's published papers, while they show clearly the size of the problems he faced also show that he just did not have the critical intelligence needed to judge objectively the enemy's capacity to go on fighting.

Civil-military relations, and Allied cooperation were strikingly defective during the campaign. Lloyd George and the war cabinet committee had little faith in Haig or his plan yet they neither felt able to replace him nor gave him their full support. In turn the commander-in-chief had no confidence in the prime minister and consequently appears to have withheld information about the French mutinies lest it should provide justification for weakening the Western Front. The French war minister and later prime minister, Paul Painlevé, gave Lloyd George stronger assurance than was proper that the French armies could and would give full support to Haig's offensive, and the commander-in-chief

Pétain, similarly made promises which he was reluctant to fulfil. Robertson was perhaps in the least enviable position, for in trying to restrain Lloyd George in his obsession with the Italian front and at the same time caution Haig against attempting too much in Flanders, he earned the former's hostility and the latter's suspicion. Haig did nothing to prevent his removal from office early in 1918.

Tragic waste

In legend, the battles of the Third Ypres campaign appear as nothing but ill-prepared bloodbaths. But they were more than this. Where conditions permitted they were carefully planned and skilfully executed. In particular Plumer's set-piece advances in June and September, and Pétain's operations on the Verdun sector, showed what could be achieved if objectives were strictly limited and superior artillery cover could be concentrated. Yet the Ypres salient was particularly unsuitable for an attempted break-through because of the precarious drainage system, the climate, and the terrain. Indeed, the faint possibility of a break-through to the Channel coast probably depended not only on the complete success of Gough's opening offensive, but also on the simultaneous launching of amphibious operations. Although the latter were carefully planned, the obstacles remained so formidable that it was probably a wise decision to cancel the operation when the land advance failed to make good progress.

The 1914-18 War still retains much of its terrible reputation because, on reflection, so much waste and suffering seem to have been exacted for no sufficient cause. Three years of indecisive slaughter, and the frailty of human judgements combined to produce the tragedy of the Third Ypres campaign in which the heroic endeavour of the troops appeared to yield only negligible results. No one, however, can be certain that the lives lost in Flanders were sacrificed in vain. Also, in changed circumstances – and because he had grown wiser from experience – Haig showed in 1918 that he could fight a more mobile and less costly campaign, culminating in the final victory which he had falsely anticipated in 1916 and 1917. 'Passchendaele', however, transcended the historical reality of an inconclusive campaign and became a potent historical myth. As such its influence reached far beyond 1918. Statesmen and soldiers are activated by such historical myths as well as by present realities. In 1939-45 Churchill and many of his generals had the memory of Passchendaele vividly before them: never again, they were resolved, should British troops be subjected to such a battle of attrition for anything short of national survival.

The Struggle for the Sea-lanes

Whereas in 1915-16 the German naval and military 'Hawks' had been subdued by the political 'Doves' over the prosecution of unrestricted U-boat warfare, at the beginning of 1917 the renewed tussle in Berlin ended in success for the 'Hawks'. They guaranteed victory within six months—despite the likelihood of the USA entering the war on the Allied side. Accordingly orders were issued to resume unrestricted warfare on 1st February; and three days later President Wilson broke off diplomatic relations. Meanwhile, on 16th January, the German foreign minister had sent via Washington to the ambassador in Mexico City the message still known as the 'Zimmermann Telegram'. It promised to Mexico that in return for alliance with Germany the 'former lost territory' of the southern states of the USA would be restored to her. This astonishing *gaucherie* was intercepted and deciphered in London, and was passed to the American ambassador, Walter Page, at a carefully chosen moment. The indignation it aroused in America made active intervention certain, and on 6th April the USA declared war on Germany.

In actual fact, the claims put forward by the German 'Hawks' were by no means as fantastic as they may now appear, and for the first four months it seemed quite likely that they would be fulfilled. In 1916 the U-boat fleet had more than doubled (from 54 to 133) and only twenty-two had been sunk. Allied and neutral shipping losses rocketed from 386,000 tons in January 1917 to the colossal total of 881,000 tons in April—a figure which, if maintained for a few more months, would have brought a German victory. The chief burden of countering the U-boat campaign naturally fell on the British navy, and as the many and varied antidotes adopted had failed to prove effective the dispute over whether convoy should be introduced grew hotter. The Admiralty, supported by a good deal of Merchant Navy opinion, considered that the disadvantages, such as lengthened 'turn-round' of ships, outweighed the possible advantages. But the Ministry of Shipping was confident that such arguments, which were in fact supported by wholly misleading Admiralty statistics regarding the relation between losses and safe arrivals of ships, were false. Lloyd George, the prime minister, took the same view. At the end of April he forced the Admiralty to try convoy, and the recommendations of the Atlantic Convoy Committee, which was set up in May and produced a comprehen-

sive scheme early in the following month, were at once adopted. Admiral W.S.Sims, commander of the US Naval Forces in Europe, was also a strong supporter of convoy, and with the help of the American destroyers, which soon began to operate from Queenstown (now Cobh) in southern Ireland, the experiment proved wholly successful. Not only did shipping losses decline sharply after April, but sinkings of U-boats increased from twenty in the first half of the year to forty-three in the second half. However, the confrontation between Lloyd George and the Admiralty caused a considerable loss of confidence in the Board on the part of the political leaders. In July therefore Lloyd George appointed Sir Eric Geddes first lord in place of Sir Edward Carson, who had consistently supported the sea lords' views on the convoy issue; and in December Geddes abruptly dismissed Admiral Sir John Jellicoe, the first sea lord.

A barrage of mines

Though the introduction of convoy was without doubt the most important factor in surmounting the crisis, it would be misleading to ascribe it entirely to that measure. The conflict between minelayer and minesweeper was now at its height, and in the autumn the British at last had available an efficient mine—copied from the Germans. The Straits of Dover were the crucial area, since unless both the long-range High Seas Fleet U-boats working from the German North Sea bases and the smaller boats based on Zeebrugge and Ostend could pass through the English Channel they would be forced to take the much longer route round the north of Scotland to reach their operational areas in the western approaches to the British Isles. In consequence the British concentrated a great effort on creating an impenetrable barrage of mines and nets, with surface vessels patrolling constantly overhead, in the Dover Straits. Though these measures gradually took effect, in 1917 U-boats made no less than 250 successful transits through the English Channel, mostly at night and on the surface. Not until the end of the year, by which time the barrage had been provided with night illumination, did it become really

German sailors take aim for mines—the U-boats' most dangerous enemy. They accounted for forty-eight known losses throughout the war

The U-boat campaign

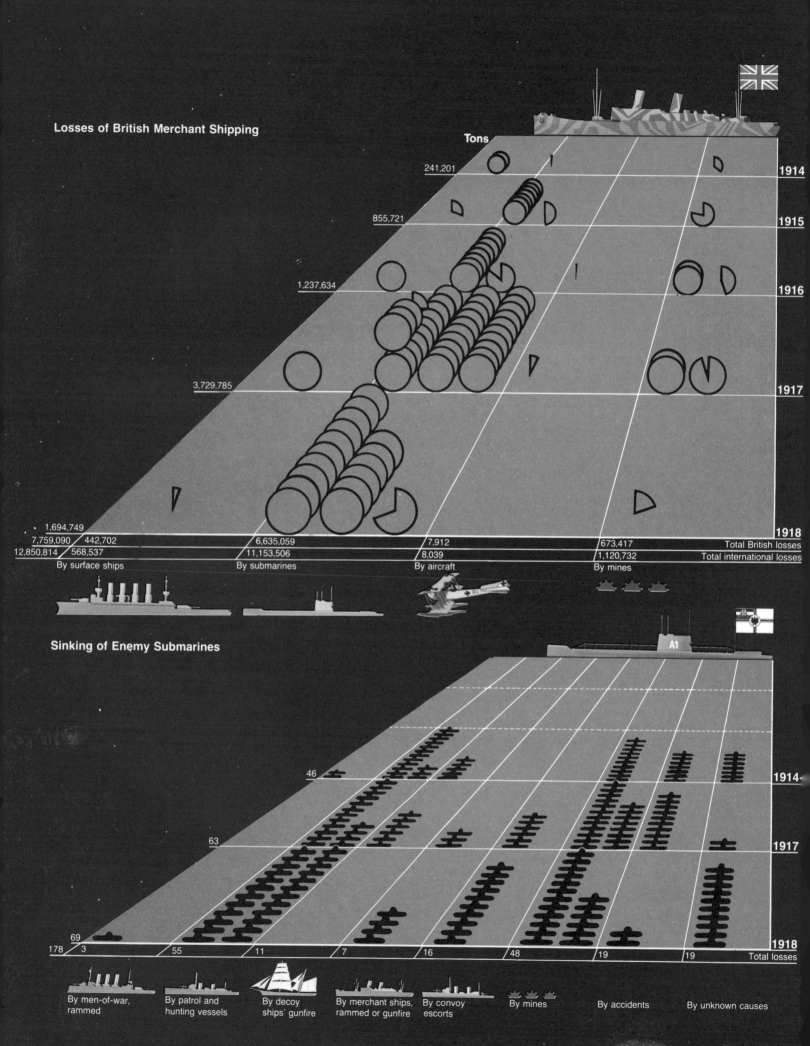

Losses of British Merchant Shipping

Tons

241,201				1914
855,721				1915
1,237,634				1916
3,729,785				1917
1,694,749				1918

	By surface ships	By submarines	By aircraft	By mines	
Total British losses	7,759,090	442,702	6,635,059	7,912	673,417
Total international losses	12,850,814	568,537	11,153,506	8,039	1,120,732

Sinking of Enemy Submarines

46		1914
63		1917
69		1918

	By men-of-war, rammed	By patrol and hunting vessels	By decoy ships' gunfire	By merchant ships, rammed or gunfire	By convoy escorts	By mines	By accidents	By unknown causes
Total losses	178 / 3	55	11	7	16	48	19	19

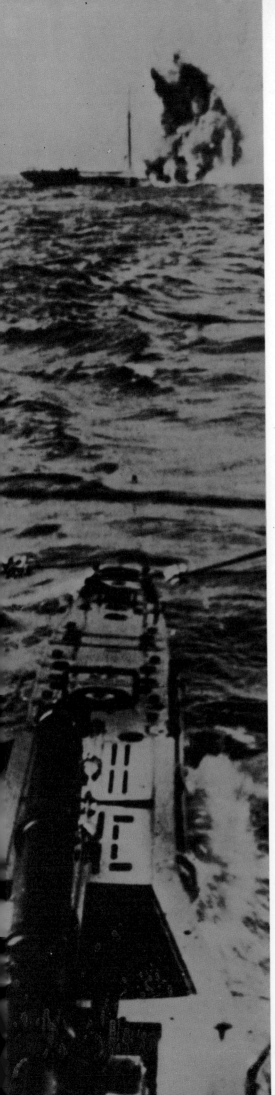

Left: A victim of the German blockade—a steamer torpedoed by a U-boat. In April 1917 the U-boats sunk 881,000 tons of Allied shipping. If this success had continued a few months longer, Germany might have won the war. Far left: Balance sheet of the German blockade by U-boat: figures for the losses in Allied merchant shipping (above) and the losses in German submarines (below), 1914-18

dangerous for U-boats to attempt the short passage. Nor was minelaying confined to the narrow waters of the Channel. The British discovered, from deciphered messages, the routes used by the U-boats to pass in and out of the Heligoland Bight, and hundreds of mines were laid to catch them at the beginning or end of their patrols. The Germans did not, of course, take the strengthening of the Dover Barrage and the obstruction of the U-boat routes lying down. Their minesweeping service struggled hard to keep the channels to and from the North Sea bases clear, while their surface ships several times attacked the vessels patrolling the Dover minefields. But although the British patrols sometimes suffered quite heavy losses, the Germans could not reverse the current trend, which showed all too plainly that the passage of the Straits was becoming unacceptably hazardous.

Of all the many anti-submarine measures adopted in 1917 the mine, with twenty U-boats sunk, was by far the most successful U-boat killer. Surface ship or submarine patrols sank sixteen enemies, convoy escorts and Q-ships (decoys) each sank six, and about a dozen were lost through accidents of one sort or another. Yet although the total sinkings in 1917 (sixty-three) were nearly three times greater than in the previous year, new construction more than kept pace with losses. At the end of the year the U-boat fleet of 142 was actually greater by nine than it had been twelve months earlier; and many of the new boats were of improved types. Plainly, then, the battle was as yet far from won by the Allies.

Blocking the blockaders

To turn back to the German scene, the entry of the USA into the war enabled the Allied naval-economic blockade to be tightened to a stranglehold. German merchant ships which had long sheltered in American ports were seized; and—more important still—there was no longer any question of American firms trying to send contraband goods to Germany, or of American merchant ships running the British blockade to reach Scandinavia or Dutch ports with such cargoes. Almost overnight on 6th April 1917 Allied control of seaborne traffic became worldwide and complete. To make matters worse for Germany the 1917 harvest was again bad, largely because of the lack of imported fertilizers; and civilian food rations were cut to a level at which it was no longer possible to remain in good health. Furthermore, there was now an acute shortage of many metals, and in consequence the equipment of the armed forces began to suffer. The renowned discipline of the German people had not yet weakened seriously, but by the end of 1917

it was becoming plain that unless the shortages of every kind, and sheer hunger, were alleviated in the fairly near future a collapse was likely on the home front.

By the beginning of 1918 some 5,000 mines had been laid in the Dover Barrage, but U-boat transits none the less continued—in March there were twenty-nine. The British were especially anxious to put the Flanders U-boat bases out of action—if the army could not capture them. Indeed the terribly costly prolongation of the 3rd battle of Ypres into the autumn of 1917 must be ascribed partly to Admiralty pressure to capture Ostend and Zeebrugge. When that offensive had plainly failed the earlier idea of a blocking operation was resurrected, and after several false starts it was carried out on the night of 22nd-23rd April. Although at the time the British believed that Zeebrugge had been effectively blocked, it is now clear that this was not so. Despite the great gallantry with which the attack was carried out (no less than eleven Victoria Crosses were awarded to participants) by early May the U-boats could work their way round the blockships. And the attack on Ostend, though repeated on 10th May, was a total failure on both occasions.

Germany feels the pinch

With the U-boats forced increasingly to use the long route round the north of Scotland the possibility of laying a gigantic minefield between the Orkneys and the Norwegian coast was raised. As the distance was some 250 miles, and the depth of water was in places far greater than the Straits of Dover, this was an undertaking of a very different order from the blocking of the twenty-mile-wide Straits. In July 1917 a new American mine was ready for mass production, and the decision was taken to go ahead. The US Navy carried out the lion's share of the laying, often in very bad weather. By the end of the war 56,000 American and 13,000 British mines had been laid in this Northern Barrage. Unfortunately, many of the American mines exploded prematurely, and there was always a gap at the eastern end in Norwegian territorial waters—which the U-boats were not slow to exploit. Though this barrage probably did make U-boat passages to their operational areas slower and more dangerous, the results achieved (three U-boats possibly sunk and another three damaged) were hardly commensurate with the effort involved.

The Mediterranean had until 1918 been a happy hunting ground for U-boats, which had sunk merchant ships with almost complete impunity. The Austrian submarine fleet totalled twenty-seven boats, most of them ex-German, and they were reinforced by German boats sent out periodically

Backs to the Wall

Below: Survivors from the Jacob Jones, *painted by Beal. It was impracticable for submarines to pick up survivors at sea. The underwater menace often spelt death to passengers and crew, who in earlier naval warfare had been warned to get into lifeboats, and then were picked up by the attacking vessel*

through the Straits of Gibraltar to work from Cattaro (now Kotor) or Pola. Hence arose the attempt to construct yet another barrage – across the Straits of Otranto – to block the routes to and from the Adriatic bases. Once again mines, nets, and surface and air patrols were all used; but with very little success. It was without doubt the introduction of convoy which defeated the Mediterranean U-boats. Of the ten sunk in those waters in 1918 at least half can be attributed to convoy escorts. One of the most interesting of these successes was the capture of Karl Dönitz from UB.68 on 4th October 1918, since he was to command Germany's U-boat fleet in the Second World War.

In July 1918 the Germans made a last desperate attempt to pass U-boats down-Channel to attack the troopships which were bringing an ever increasing flood of American soldiers to the Western Front. Of the six boats sent out only three returned home, and two of them were severely damaged. The last west-bound transit took place in August, and at the end of that month the Germans accepted that only the long northern route remained open to them. Meanwhile, a mine barrage had been laid off the east coast of England, where U-boats had previously achieved considerable successes; and more mines were laid in the Heligoland Bight. It was at this time that the British laid the first magnetic mines, off the Flanders bases, which were now virtually useless to the Germans. Also in August a heavy attack was made on the morale of the U-boat crews by publishing the names of 150 officers, most of them captains of boats, known to have been killed or captured. Recent analysis of this list shows how well-informed were the Admiralty's anti-submarine and intelligence departments.

Submarine death toll

On 25th October Admiral Reinhard Scheer, commander of the High Seas Fleet, recalled all U-boats from the sea routes with a view to their taking part in a final sortie by his fleet. There were twenty-three at sea at the time. Nine days later all possibility of carrying out that desperate plan was eliminated by widespread mutinies among Scheer's major warships; but the U-boat crews remained loyal to the end. A condition of the armistice terms signed at Compiègne on 11th November was that all surviving U-boats should be surrendered.

There is no doubt at all that in 1918

Allied anti-submarine forces inflicted a heavy defeat on the U-boats. Though seventy new ones had been built, sixty-nine were sunk, and total strength declined from 142 to 134. The convoy escorts and surface ship patrols between them accounted for thirty-four enemies; but mines, with eighteen U-boats destroyed, again proved very effective. Air escorts and patrols sank few, if any, enemies; but they played an increasingly important part by reporting U-boats' positions and forcing them to remain submerged. Of all the varied weapons in the armoury of the Allied anti-submarine forces the mine was, taking the war as a whole, much the most effective, with forty-eight successes to its credit. The depth charge with thirty came second, the torpedo with twenty third, and the ram with nineteen fourth. But the sinkings achieved by the U-boats totalled the immense figure of 11,153,506 tons out of total losses by all nations from all causes of 12,850,814 tons. The British Merchant Navy was by far the heaviest sufferer, and the 7,759,090 tons lost was no less than thirty-seven per cent of its pre-war total tonnage. The loss of 178 U-boats was perhaps a small price to pay for the amount of shipping destroyed.

As to the Allied blockade of the Central powers, by August 1918 the civilian ration in Germany was reduced below 2,000 calories daily, resistance to disease had been much lowered by malnutrition, and the death rate was rising very sharply. Perhaps the best indication of the effect of the blockade on the German people is the fact that during the four years 1915-18 civilian deaths exceeded by 760,000 the number which pre-war statistics indicated as probable. Though the German armies were as thoroughly defeated on land as their U-boats were at sea, and the so-called 'stab in the back' by the civil population's collapse is a fiction of German militaristic imagination, it is nonetheless true that the blockade inflicted great suffering on the German and Austrian people. In Great Britain and France, though rationing of food was made increasingly stringent after 1916, there was no comparable degree of suffering; nor did the war industries of the Allied nations suffer difficulties such as the shortage of raw materials caused in Germany. Thus there is a good deal of truth in the saying that the Allied victory of 1918 was achieved through 'the triumph of unarmed forces', as well as by the successes of the fighting services on land, at sea, and in the air.

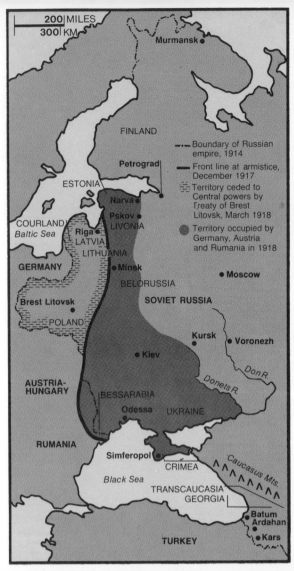

Far left: The humiliation of Russia by the Central powers. By the terms of a 'dictated' peace Russia lost Poland, Courland, Riga, and parts of Lithuania and Bessarabia. Then the Germans and Austrians moved in to occupy the Ukraine. Above: Germans and Russians sign the ceasefire in December 1917. Left: Skoropadsky, Hetman of the Ukraine, talks to the Kaiser. Germany signed a separate peace treaty with the Ukraine—but Skoropadsky had not the power to fulfil his promise to supply Germany with badly needed food. Below: Captured Cossack guerrilla leaders being interrogated by German officers in Tiflis

The Treaty of Brest Litovsk

No more than eight months separated the victorious peace settlement imposed on Russia by Kaiser Wilhelm's Germany at Brest Litovsk from Germany's capitulation at Compiègne. For eight months her rulers could dream that at last a decisive turning point had been reached in the war and that the most far-ranging aspirations would now be fulfilled—plans for establishing a ruling position for Germany throughout the world. The great power on Germany's eastern border, Russia, had been abased and compelled to sign a separate peace and her vast territory, seized by revolution and debilitated by civil war, appeared to be an easy prey.

The Peace of Brest Litovsk had wider implications than its effect on German-Russian relations. On 3rd March when Sokolnikov signed the treaty as Soviet representative it seemed that more had happened than the mere winning of the first round in the war; most contemporaries thought the balance had definitely shifted

in favour of Germany and the Central powers. It looked as if willingness to risk a fight on two fronts had paid off. It seemed to have justified those military circles that favoured expansion and adventure.

The fanfares of triumph in Berlin and Vienna inevitably caused serious alarm among the Allies. Wheat from the Ukraine would make the sea blockade of the Central powers impotent, and there was reason to fear the transfer of huge contingents from the German and Austro-Hungarian armies to the French and Italian theatres before the American Expeditionary Force could arrive. In some Allied countries voices were again raised, suggesting that it would be better to reach a compromise than face a long drawn out war. The spokesmen for the national liberation movements among the suppressed peoples of Austria-Hungary were worried, and with reason.

The road from the ceasefire signed in December 1917 to the Treaty of Brest Litovsk was neither short nor easy. Each

Above: A professional revolutionary on his way to talk peace with a Prussian general—Trotsky sets off for Brest Litovsk. The Germans knew that Russia could not stop their armies; but Trotsky looked for a revolution in Germany that would cripple her military might

side needed time to analyse the actions of the other in order to clarify its expectations of what peace might bring. The Central powers, and in particular their economies, were on the verge of complete exhaustion. Ludendorff admits in his memoirs that he was waiting for a 'miracle', for a revolution in Russia to eliminate from the war an enemy whose endless territory had been swallowing up division after division. The problem of making peace on the Eastern Front was a double-edged one. As good a balance as possible had to be struck between the expansionist ambitions of some circles, particularly military ones, and more realistic intentions to bite off only as much as the Central powers could chew. Russia's withdrawal from the war had helped to spark off a highly unwelcome surge of discontent and revolutionary unrest in Austria-Hungary and Germany, which would be fanned by the conclusion of a palpably annexationist treaty.

Among the foremost exponents of a relatively realistic line were Richard von Kühlmann, first secretary in the German foreign office, and the Austrian foreign minister, Count Czernin. It would be wrong of course to imagine that there was any idyllic measure of agreement between Berlin and Vienna about the approach to peace with Russia. Early in December Czernin threatened to sign a separate treaty if necessary, regardless of Berlin's policy. This he hoped would eliminate the influence of extremist circles in Germany whose exaggerated demands were likely to prevent any peace settlement with Russia —a settlement which the Danubian monarchy needed even more urgently than its ally. Czernin seems to have realized that the insatiability of the German imperialists outran their real capabilities. This does not mean, however, that he was prepared to abandon all plans of annexation; he agreed with Kühlmann that Poland, Lithuania, Courland, and the greater part of Livonia should stay in the hands of the Central powers.

In Petrograd, similarly, the views of the Soviet government about the peace problem were slowly changing. The Bolsheviks had gone into the revolution with the slogan of 'peace without annexations or indemnities', a policy of dissociation from both sides in the war and rejection of the aims of both great power alliances. Refusing to fight on, the Soviet government 'declared war on war'. It nevertheless made intensive efforts to avoid being identified in its peace offers with either side in the battle and proposed terms to all the contestants. Even after signing a ceasefire with the Central powers—who in view of their military, economic, and domestic political plight were in no position to reject any proposals out of hand—

the revolutionary government in Petrograd continued to urge the Allies to join in the negotiations. It was reluctant to embark on a separate peace and its spokesmen went so far as to get the German negotiators to undertake that there would be no transfers of troops from the Russian to the Western Front. Indeed, even after the Brest negotiations had been broken off in February 1918 and the German offensive had started, the Bolsheviks appealed for help to the Allied missions in Russia.

Revolutionary hopes

Not even the Bolshevik Party was untouched by disagreements about the whole complex of issues involved in making peace with the Central powers. One wing of the party, and similarly one wing of the coalition partners in the government and in the Central Executive Committee of Soviets, was sharply opposed to the conclusion of the Brest Litovsk Treaty. Bukharin, as leader of the Left Communists, declared that the first proletarian state in the world must not sign an agreement which would betray the revolutionary movement in the other countries and repress the rising wave of revolutionary action. Similar arguments were used by the Left Socialist Revolutionaries, who were anti-German and pro-Allied in their sympathies. Without a close familiarity with the political theories then prevailing in Soviet Russia it is hard to understand how these ideas of a 'revolutionary war' could have been used in protest against the Brest negotiations—especially since the Russian army had virtually disintegrated.

It must be admitted that there were many illusions and unrealistic, though revolutionarily optimistic, assessments of the situation on the Soviet side. One illusion was that the curtain was about to go up on a pan-European, if not worldwide, revolution arising from the extraordinary intensification of political, class, and social antagonisms and conflicts brought about by the war. Even before the victorious October Revolution in Russia, Lenin had formulated his theory of the 'prologue', the theory that the Russian events would be a spark setting fire to a revolutionary conflagration throughout the main industrial countries of Europe—all of which were involved in the war—and above all in Germany. The spate of demonstrations and manifestations that followed the opening of negotiations in Brest Litovsk, both in Germany and still more in Austria-Hungary, seemed to bear out this expectation, and this was bound to influence decision-making quarters in Soviet Russia.

The first few weeks of negotiation, in December 1917 and January 1918, gave no indication of the slightest approximation of views between the two sides. On the

contrary it became ever more clear that the real dictator at the conference was not Kühlmann, the titular head of the German delegation, but the brutal Prussian general Max Hoffmann, a spokesman of the most extreme imperialist and militarist circles in Germany. His *extempore* outbursts, culminating in the famous moment when he banged the table with his fist and demanded that the remaining Baltic territories should be evacuated by the Russians and taken under German 'protection', caused a crisis in the negotiations.

From January 1918 the Soviet peace delegation was headed by Trotsky, who shared Lenin's view that from a purely military standpoint Soviet Russia had no chance at all in a conflict with the Central powers. He agreed that a treaty must be signed as soon as Germany presented an ultimatum, and before leaving for Brest he assured Lenin that he had no intention of putting over a doctrine of 'revolutionary war'. But at the same time Trotsky considered that the radical mood of the population had made the home front of the Central powers so unstable that their armies would be incapable of launching an effective anti-Soviet offensive. It was therefore his policy to postpone the conclusion of an agreement until it might appear plain that the Central powers were not only determined, but actually able, to start large-scale military operations against Russia. When the German ultimatum was delivered, then, he declared the standpoint of the Soviet government to be 'neither peace nor war'; with that, the Soviet delegation went back to Petrograd.

The subsequent course of events fully bore out Lenin's attitude, which had previously failed to win majority support. The German and Austrian armies of intervention advanced without meeting serious obstacles, and the assumption that there would be a revolutionary upheaval inside Germany proved false. Soviet historians have recently considered the question of the magnitude of the opposition put up by improvised Red Army units and some at least now take the view that the much-vaunted victories of Narva and Pskov were isolated phenomena compared with the general abandonment of positions by the army. At the Seventh Congress of the Bolshevik Party Lenin ruefully described the capture by the enemy of railway stations which no one attempted to defend. 'Yes, we shall live to see worldwide revolution,' he remarked. 'But so far it is only a pretty fairy-tale, a most attractive fairy-tale.' Not that Lenin had ceased to believe in the forthcoming world revolution, but he recognized that revolution in Europe was not probable at that moment.

During the night of 23rd-24th February 1918 the Central Executive Committee of the Congress of Soviets ended a lively debate by voting 116 to 84 in approval of the earlier decision of the Bolshevik Party's Central Committee to accept the German peace ultimatum. A telegram in these terms was immediately despatched to the German headquarters, where meanwhile fresh and still stiffer conditions had been drafted. For Trotsky's previous reply had caused consternation among the German politicians. At the meeting of the Imperial Council called to seek a way out of the unexpected situation ('Are we to go running after the Russians, pen in hand?' Kühlmann had exclaimed) the state secretary had proposed taking note of Trotsky's declaration and awaiting further developments. Kühlmann felt obliged to take account of domestic reaction and to avoid needless exacerbation of the anti-war mood of the masses by any aggressive prolongation of the war. But as usual in such moments of decision, it was the intransigent, expansionist, and annexationist views of the general staff that won the day, demanding the formal signature of a treaty incorporating further annexations. The same quarters were even playing with the idea of continuing the war, overthrowing the Bolsheviks, and setting up a new 'national' government of supporters of the monarchy to guarantee pro-German policies for the future—for the whole German offensive had virtually become a technical problem of organization rather than one of military strategy. German military circles were well aware that the Soviet government was 'inwardly hostile' to them.

After making a declaration that he was signing the document not as a negotiated peace treaty but as a *Diktat* under the pressure of *force majeure,* the Soviet representative put his name to the list of demands presented by the Central powers and by Germany in particular. The hostilities between the Central powers and Soviet Russia were formally at an end. For the temporary victors, the booty was enormous. Russia gave up so-called Congress Poland, Lithuania, Courland, Riga, and part of Belorussia pending a decision by the Central powers about the fate of these lands; in the Caucasus Kars, Ardahan, and Batum fell to Turkey; some million square kilometres with a pre-war population of forty-six million was ceded. Reparations totalling three thousand million roubles in gold were imposed on Russia.

The Treaty of Brest Litovsk had an immediate effect, of course, on the course of the war elsewhere. So far events had not been dominated by revolution, but by the war itself, whose general course determined the pattern and outcome of happenings that seemed to be only marginally connected with it. It is not surprising, then, that so many voices were raised immediately after the signing of the treaty, especially in the Allied countries, accusing the Soviet government of being a lackey to Germany. The dictated settlement was quoted as evidence that Lenin and his Bolsheviks, far from being a defeated party obliged by circumstances to swallow humiliating peace terms, were in fact the instrument and partner of Germany and of its general staff in their fight for world domination. Even in Soviet Russia itself, indeed, not everyone saw the force of Lenin's argument that Russia had to sign the Treaty of Brest Litovsk because she had at this point to give way before superior force since she lacked the military strength to defend herself.

Bread at bayonet point

It soon became apparent, however, that the Brest Litovsk Treaty involved deep and insuperable contradictions which made co-operation between the parties impossible. The contrast in attitudes toward the peace, toward its short-term and long-term aims alike, condemned the agreement to failure before the signatures were even dry. Representatives of two social systems, one imperial and nationalist, the other proletarian and internationalist, based their attitudes on doctrines which promised ultimate results on an international scale. Germany, the undoubted leader of the Central powers, had a rapacious and undisguised desire to become the leader of Europe and so lay the foundations of world domination. The Soviet government, on the other hand, sought to be a beacon for pan-European, if not worldwide, revolutionary upheavals. Both aims were at the time unrealistic. Germany failed to foresee all kinds of developments latent in the situation of the moment, Russia paid no attention to anything except that its partner in the newly signed peace treaty would not be its partner for long. A relationship founded on such a basis was practically doomed to be short-lived and could not even furnish a practicable *modus vivendi* for forces which, however antagonistic to each other, continued to recognize to some extent a certain appreciation of the realities of power and the basic purposes of the other side. So the Treaty of Brest Litovsk could not outlast the First World War.

It was the Central powers, and especially Germany, who were the first to realize (and that very speedily) that the optimism they had invested in the treaty, loudly proclaimed on the home front as the *Brotfrieden* or Bread Peace, was built upon sand. The only hopes that were fulfilled were those associated with the freeing of part of their troops. By June 1918 there were over 200 divisions on the Western Front and only 40 on the Eastern. This transfer made possible the Germans' spring offensive, which the Allies required the utmost effort to withstand; for the Allies victory and peace now seemed distant indeed, a prospect for 1919 at the earliest.

The German hope that failed most completely was that of turning Russia, particularly the Ukraine, into an economic hinterland for the supply of food and raw materials to the Central powers, so that the catastrophic effects of the Allied blockade would be removed. Germany made a secret agreement with the Viennese government about economic policy in the eastern areas previously belonging to Russia. Since December a special office had also been set up under the former state secretary Helfferich not only to do the preparatory work, particularly on the economic and financial side, for the impending peace treaty, but in the long run to lay the ground for the complete domination of Russia's food and raw material supplies, by German industry. The meeting of 16th May 1918 held between leaders of German economic and industrial life, showed that the permanent influence of Germany in Russia was to rest, above all, on the bayonets of the German army and the assistance of the entire military machine. But Germany's ruling circles had overestimated her strength and they mistook a temporary pattern of power for a valid foundation of long-term policy. The idea of basing economic exploitation on a military apparatus proved quite ineffective even during the course of 1918; the classic instance of this was the experience that befell the Austro-Hungarian occupying forces in the Ukraine.

The Ukrainian Central Council led by Hetman Skoropadsky had induced the Central powers without any difficulty to sign a separate peace recognizing its independent status, and the Brest Litovsk Treaty incorporated a commitment on the part of the Soviet government to come to terms with the Central Council too. But who was there to make peace with? The German politicians were well aware that they were treating with a fictitious government fully justifying Trotsky's sarcastic remark that the only territory the Central Council ruled over was the suite its delegates occupied in the Brest Litovsk hotel. In fact on the day before the signature of the separate peace with the Ukraine the entire Central Council had to flee from Kiev. The treaty was nevertheless signed, such was the beguiling effect of the delegates' 'personal guarantee' to deliver 'at least one million bushels of grain' to the Central powers.

Military requisitioning of grain in the countryside took too many soldiers and was ineffective anyway, while for normal trade relations there were not the most elementary economic conditions. The occupying power was unable to carry out any commercial acquisition of grain because its own militarized industry was incapable of furnishing capital or consumer goods in exchange, and had too few roubles for ordinary purchases in the villages.

Between the German and Austrian purchasing organizations there arose with increasing frequency not merely rivalry but mutual deception and fraud. In Kiev the German representatives were forever complaining that their Austrian colleagues were unfairly outbidding them, in violation of their agreement. The Austrians, moreover, exploited the more favourable communications between their own country and the Ukraine in order to seize the lion's share of the grain purchases, such as they were. In mid-May 1918 the German military inspectors reported that a mere 4,000 tons of grain had been exported to Germany to date, whereas Austria had procured 25,000 tons from the Ukraine. In all, the German and Austro-Hungarian conquerors were only able to squeeze out of the Ukraine about a fifth of the expected quantities of foodstuffs and agricultural products. In absolute terms the procurements were pretty sizeable, but they looked small in comparison with the conquerors' requirements and, indeed, with the hopes invested in the conquest of the Ukraine's 'black earth' belt. German officers and diplomats based on Kiev came gradually to the conclusion that the Central Council's authority was 'not to be taken seriously', for it showed itself incapable of organizing even the foundations of a viable economy. Ironically enough, one of the major problems of implementing the *Brotfrieden* in the Ukraine was rail transport. Although the Central powers had acquired among other things the whole hard-coal minefield of the Donets, they had to import 80,000 tons of coal month by month from Germany to keep transport going.

Hopes of economic profit from Soviet Russian deliveries likewise fell far short of expectations. The commercial attaché in Moscow, Lista, found that the Soviet government was putting a number of obstacles in the way of trade with Germany. In the summer of 1918 a practical barter operation was started up, but it remained small in scope and had no serious effect on Germany's food and raw material shortages. Nor did the forced surrender of part of Russia's gold reserve demanded by the Protocol of 27th August 1918, which supplemented the Brest Litovsk Treaty with provisions concerning reparation for German property nationalized or confiscated in Soviet Russia.

German political plans for Russia's future also underwent an interesting development after the Brest Litovsk Treaty, under the influence of extreme annexationist views, especially those represented by the military clique around General Ludendorff. To be fair, these views were not shared by some of the more sober civilian politicians like Kühlmann who (it has been said), when it came to argument over eastern policy, 'must always have felt doomed to defeat in any dispute with Ludendorff'.

Foretaste of Nazism

In recent years the attention of historians has been drawn not only to the nature of German aims at the beginning of the First World War, but also to a detailed examination of German objectives in the east after the signing of the Brest Litovsk Treaty. The subject is all the more important because of the number of similarities, in scope and strategy, between the annexationist aims of that period and those of Nazi Germany formulated a quarter of a century later at the zenith of the *Wehrmacht*'s successes. In both periods we find the same limitless and overweening rapacity, together with the crudest contempt for the basic rules of international life: the respect for treaties and for the rights of other countries. The appetite of the German high command ranged from Finland and the Baltic to Murmansk, from the Ukraine and the Crimea to the Caucasus, Georgia, and Baku. These ideas were fully supported by the still decisive influence of the court in the First World War; Wilhelm II was delighted by the *élan* of his generals. Objections raised against such flagrant violation of the recently concluded peace settlement were imperiously dismissed as 'fear politics', on the grounds that 'peace with Russia can only last as long as they are afraid of us'. In the spring of 1918, pursuing this strategy of fear, German troops crossed the arbitrarily fixed frontiers and entered the central Russian districts of Voronezh and Kursk, lending aid in money and arms to the Cossack leader Krasnov on the Don. Ludendorff even toyed with the idea of setting up a 'South-Eastern League', covering the whole area between the Don and the Caucasus, under German surveillance.

The policies of Ludendorff and the high command in the Crimea, after the peninsula had been occupied in the summer of 1918 by German troops from the Ukraine, were the very prototype of Nazi ambitions to establish a German enclave there. The original plan was to assign a certain influence on the Crimea to Germany's ally Turkey, as her Pan-Ottoman enthusiasts, remembering the former glories of the Ottoman empire, wished; but this plan soon collapsed. Instead, the Kaiser's headquarters started to think about a 'State of Crimea and Tauris', perhaps in federation with the Ukraine; under this plan the Crimea, of course, was to be settled mainly by German colonists from the Caucasus, the Volga basin, Bessarabia, and so on. Germany would be given sole use of the port of Simferopol and exercise a dominating economic influence over this whole artificial entity. The purpose of this fantastic plan was evidently to guard the Ukraine from the rear and ensure its obedience to German orders. This is clear, for example, from Ludendorff's argument that it was in the interests of the *Reich* 'that there should exist on the Black Sea a state under chiefly German influence to serve as a buttress to our significant economic interests in the East'.

These wide-ranging militarist plans for the east were of course quite out of proportion to Germany's military means at the time and merely put further strains upon them as the situation developed. They were in the strictest sense 'boundless', as leading officials of the *Wilhelmstrasse* described them. In order to 'secure' existing territorial gains and hopes of further spheres of influence, these plans always required involvement in more and more distant regions. In the case of the Caucasus they even led to a conflict of interests within the camp, between Germany and Turkey. For in addition to her immediate territorial gains under the Brest Litovsk settlement Turkey was already trying, exactly in German style, to enlarge her own sphere of influence at Russian expense to the north of the Caucasus, where she proposed to set up a chain of vassal buffer-states. Berlin, however, did not intend to make way for these ambitions. For Germany regarded Transcaucasia as a bridge for further penetration into Central Asia; she wanted to 'use an opportunity which occurs perhaps once in many centuries'. Ludendorff was personally disposed at the beginning to leave the Turks a free hand in the Caucasus. But he soon swung round to the opposite policy, in its extreme form as usual, and proposed sending 'small forces' into Transcaucasia. These he described as mere 'training units' for a future Georgian army, yet in the same breath he defined their role as similar to that of the German expeditionary force in Finland – a force which took on a decisive role in the civil war there.

In June 1918 Ludendorff explained Germany's expansionist aims in the Caucasus quite pragmatically. He stressed the importance of securing rich mineral deposits and supplies for Germany's war economy. He hoped it would be possible to form a native army to fight side by side with Germany against Russia and to create another 'Caucasian Bloc', possibly in alliance with the above-mentioned 'South-Eastern League' and with various Cossack

Below: The arrival of the first delivery of Russian gold to Berlin. Reparations totalling three thousand million roubles in gold were imposed on Russia, but neither this nor the requisition of wheat from the rich lands of the Ukraine made any real difference to the war economies of Austria-Hungary and Germany

and other states to the south-east of Russia. The German militarists gave willing support, especially in arms, to the most dubious local and tribal leaders who now converged on Berlin with offers of collaboration (a 'Kalmuk Prince' amongst them); they were to accept German protection after their artificial states had been set up with the help of German bayonets. This fully accorded with Wilhelm's idea of breaking up the Russian state into four tsardoms—the Ukraine, Transcaucasia and the whole South-East, Great Russia (Muscovy), and Siberia. Such a programme of course, if ever attempted, would mean further protracted warfare with Russia.

The real loser—Germany

The real victor to emerge from the Peace of Brest Litovsk was not Germany, who had dictated its brutal conditions, but Soviet Russia, who had accepted them with all the humiliation they involved. Lenin's tactics of prevarication and temporary retreat brought their expected reward. They gave Soviet Russia the necessary time for consolidation at a critical stage. The economic gain the Central powers had anticipated from a separate peace remained, despite the best efforts of the occupying powers to purchase or requisition goods, far below the expected levels. The 35,000 wagons of corn and other foodstuffs and raw materials sent out of the occupied area, mainly the Ukraine, in the course of six months'

exploitation were not enough to make any appreciable difference to the war economies of Germany and Austria-Hungary.

The treaty also spelt defeat for the Central powers in another and equally sensitive field. Multitudes of prisoners returned to Germany and Austria-Hungary after experiencing the revolution in Russia; they returned with very different scales of values and concepts than those they had had when they put on uniform in 1914. They were glad to be back home, of course —but not to get back into uniform and resume fighting. They became a source of infection in the army and doubtless accelerated its collapse as the Russian revolution itself and the dissemination of the politics and ideology, especially peace propaganda, that went with it undoubtedly did. The Austro-Hungarian army, like the state it served, broke up into its national components. In November 1918 German regiments started to set up military councils which took part in the revolutionary movements on German soil.

In November, too, the Soviet government denounced the Treaty of Brest Litovsk and Germany undertook to cancel it by signing peace terms at Compiègne. The time when she could enforce the conditions of a dictated peace had passed. The Soviet government no longer had to fear the possibility of German intervention. And official Berlin could no longer hope to maintain its hold in Russia with bayonets; it could not even maintain relations with

the Soviet government when, under the impact of revolution at home, the very German soil was shaking under its feet.

The surprise and anxiety caused in the Allied countries by the signature of a separate peace in 1918 had a kind of epilogue in the fears aroused among some of the new post-war states of central Europe at the thought of a possible German-Soviet *rapprochement.* But these fears were groundless at the time when they occurred. The Brest Litovsk Treaty had left too sour a taste behind it to serve as a suitable psychological model for future policy. Besides, external circumstances had changed too much. When the November revolution broke out in Germany it seemed as if the moment which the Bolsheviks had prophesied, the moment of pan-European revolution, was finally approaching. Only gradually was it seen with sufficient clarity that none of the revolutionary outbursts in the rest of Europe had been powerful enough to overturn the existing structure of society. No link in Europe's social chain had been as weak as Tsarist Russia. The German-Soviet treaty later signed at Rapallo, some aspects of which were anticipated as early as 1920, was in no way a continuation of the Brest Litovsk pattern; it was not a *Diktat* but a treaty between equal partners. It implied a new approach to international problems and it signalled the creation of a new and more permanent constellation of forces.

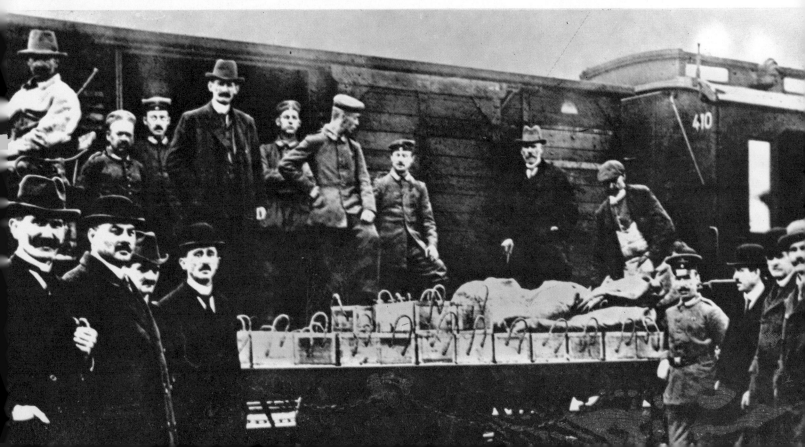

Germany's Last Throw

By the end of 1917, Europe was on the verge of bankruptcy—but a bankruptcy far more vitiating than one declared in some centre of commercial law, for it was of blood and spirit, of manhood and human hopes. Three and a half years of war had bled the nations white. France alone had provided the burying-ground for two million men: in the Ypres Salient and at Loos in 1915, at Verdun and on the Somme in 1916, and as a result of the Nivelle and Passchendaele Offensives of 1917.

Grim despondency was the mood which dominated the peoples of the warring nations—not yet plunged into defeatism, but unable to perceive the means of victory. All Europe—indeed the whole world—was hypnotized by that appalling spectacle known as the Western Front.

To its embittered inhabitants, the Front was known as 'The Sausage Machine'; for it was fed with live men, churned out corpses, but remained firmly screwed in place. This was its keynote—frustration and deadlock; it was a massive block to the progress of humanity, robbing it of happiness, ending so many lives in futile and inconsequential agony. From the Belgian coast near Nieuport down in a straggling curve to Beurnevisin on the Swiss border, the trench lines and the strips of shattered earth between and behind them, lay smeared across the land like the trail of a gigantic snail.

Along it, all day and every day, Death was present—and at night the working parties went out to court it. From dusk until just before dawn they were out, hacking at the earth to carve connecting trenches between isolated posts or even between shell-holes which could be used by machine-gunners, driving iron screw-pickets or wooden stakes into the ground to support lines of hastily-draped wire, lying close to enemy trenches all night in order to overhear their conversation; perhaps leaping into them, and after a few minutes' nightmarish activity with bomb and bayonet, dragging back to their own lines some whimpering, blood-smeared prisoner for the sake of a few morsels of incoherent military intelligence.

Draped on the wire belts were the bodies of the men killed during those white, nerve-racked, back-breaking nights. Some were killed by rifle-bullets as they crawled over the ground carrying coils of wire, some caught by scything machine-gun fire as they stood to fix the wire, some bombed by prowling patrols as they worked, hearing above their own exertions only the last few footfalls of the oncoming enemy, or the soft thud of the grenade as it landed at their feet. The entire trench system from the Channel to the Swiss frontier was dug, fortified, and held by pain and death.

At any hour of the day or night, death or mutilation could come from the guns. In winter, the shells would burst on the ice-hard ground with devastating violence, slivers of steel sighing or screaming as they sped through the frost-laden air to clatter on the ground, or to thud dully into animate or inanimate obstruction. Each type of gun had its own noise, each type of shell its own evil. German 77-mm field artillery spat 'whiz-bangs' which arrived with the noise of giant fire-crackers; 5·9s threw out their shells with vicious barks, the shells whining and growling over the valleys and ridges before ending their lives with vicious, ill-tempered crashes. Heavy guns pounded the back areas with shells that roared overhead like express trains and smashed to earth with tremendous and awful effect: and every now and then *Minenwerfer*—huge trench-mortars—would cough their black burdens into the air, to wobble uncertainly in terrifying parabolas.

The infantry hated the artillery. They hated its wantonness, its random, murderous power: above all their defencelessness against it. It was like a primitive god, uncertain, inconsistent, and unjust.

As 1917 died, a battle was fought in a sector of the British front known as the Flesquières Salient which typified the bitterness and the fury, the bravery and the squalor, the resolution and the waste of all the trench fighting which had taken place along the Western Front since it had first been formed. From just before dawn on 30th December until the early afternoon of 31st December the men of the British 63rd Division fought to hold a derisory hillock called Welsh Ridge, under attack from two and a half divisions of the German II Army. For thirty hours, the sector was a cauldron of fire, of bursting shell and erupting bomb, of drifting smoke and creeping gas, of savage bayonet attack and counter-thrust, laced throughout with the dry rattle of machine-gun fire.

And at the end, less than a mile of trench had changed hands. One thousand four hundred and twenty British soldiers and nearly two thousand Germans had died, and four thousand men of both sides were wounded or missing; and ironically, those who had been driven back found themselves in far better and stronger positions

Left: An echo of 1914. The speed of the German advance brought war once more to the open field. Right: German tank man

than those which they had originally occupied, while the victors were so exposed to hostile fire and counter-attack that they quickly abandoned their gains.

There was little other fighting along the Western Front on that last day of 1917 — sporadic sniping, routine shelling, a few lengths of trench blown in by mortar fire. It is probable that the average daily 'wastage' of some two thousand men of all nationalities due to action or sickness caused by the conditions in which they lived, was maintained.

As light began to fail, the armies stood to. Flares and starshell rose into the sky with the evanescence and sinister loveliness of tropical plants; the crater-studded, moon-like waste vibrated spasmodically to the percussion of desultory shell-fire and explosion. More men were killed, more were wounded, more died. As midnight approached there were sounds of music and singing along the German and Austrian trenches, and there was a little mild celebration among the British.

Just south of the Ypres Salient a battalion of the Royal Sussex Regiment were in the line, and a group of junior officers drank healths together, and stared out across the snowy miles at the lines of casual flares, rising, floating, dropping. One of them was Edmund Blunden, the poet, who wrote of the scene: 'The writing on the night was as the earliest scribbling of children, meaningless; they answered none of the questions with which the watcher's eyes were painfully wide. Midnight; suc-

cessions of coloured lights from one point, of white ones from another, bullying salutes of guns in brief bombardment, crackling of machine-guns small on the tingling air; but the sole answer to unspoken but importunate questions was the line of lights in the same relation to Flanders as at midnight a year before. All agreed that 1917 had been a sad offender. All observed that 1918 did not look promising at its birth.'

Yet, in fact, 1918 was to bring the end of the conflict, and despite the atmosphere of horror and waste which mere mention of the year 1917 evokes in European memories, two events had occurred during the twelve previous months which would dangle the golden prize of victory first before the eyes of the Central powers, then of the Allies.

In March 1917 had begun the Russian Revolution. It did not immediately release German and Austrian divisions from the Eastern Front — indeed the Russian General Brusilov was to launch yet another offensive there — but it was obvious to the German rulers that by early 1918 they should be able to concentrate their strength in the west. In order to expedite the Russian collapse, the German government even allowed the passage of Lenin across the country ('in a sealed carriage, like some dangerous bacillus' as Churchill was to describe the episode), for they knew that if they were to grasp their chance of victory, they must do it quickly. Germany's chance was *now,* for in April 1917 had

German artillerymen haul field guns into position during the opening of what Ludendorff hoped would be Germany's final offensive. This was to knock out the Western Allies before American troops could arrive in force

occurred another event which might well serve to snatch victory from her; America had entered the war, and her vast potential of men and materials would undoubtedly tip the scales against the Central powers if given time to do so. So it became a race — *against* time for Germany, *for* time for Great Britain and France.

Race against time

To nobody was the reality of this situation more clear than to the first quartermastergeneral of the German forces, Erich Ludendorff. Since August 1916, this large, rather stout, typically Teutonic soldier had been virtual dictator of Germany, for there was no doubt that although his great friend and admirer Hindenburg held the higher rank — chief of the general staff of the field army — Ludendorff's was the guiding brain and personality.

Ludendorff had realized for some time that between the end of the British 1917 offensive and the summer of 1918, Germany must win the war; otherwise the arrival of the American armies would tip the balance against the Central powers and all their hopes and ambitions would be tumbled in the dust.

The decision must be forced in the west

and on 11th November 1917, he had presided at a conference held at Mons to decide how it could be brought about. Present at the conference were the chiefs of staff of the groups of armies nominally commanded by the Crown Prince and Prince Rupprecht of Bavaria, but it is noteworthy that neither of these two exalted personages were invited, and neither were the Kaiser himself nor Hindenburg — even though both of them were in the neighbourhood. The subject of discussion was deemed of too great an importance for any but strictly professional soldiers.

The main, broad issue first to be decided was whether to launch an attack westwards against the British-held sector of the front, or southwards against the French. The disadvantage of the first was that if the British retreated, they would do so across old battlefields and the desolation and waste intentionally created by the Germans when they retreated to the Siegfried Line (known to the Allies as the Hindenburg Line). This would undoubtedly hamper the attackers, and the British were likely to prove difficult enough to dislodge from the first line of trenches, without giving them the advantage of successive lines to protect them as they fell back.

On the other hand, the French to the south had almost unlimited space into which they could retreat, thus bulging out the trench line until even Ludendorff's reinforcement from the Russian front would not provide sufficient numbers to hold the line of advance — especially with ever-lengthening lines of communication. A successful onslaught on Verdun might dislodge the eastern hinge of the French army — with enormous effects on French morale and probably on Franco-American co-operation (for the newly-arriving Americans were stationed in that area) — but as Ludendorff presciently remarked, the British might not feel themselves compelled to send assistance to the French so far away from their own areas of interest, and he would then be faced with mounting another large-scale offensive in Flanders.

He eventually summed up the conclusions of the conference in the following words: 'The situation in Russia . . . will, as far as can be seen, make it possible to deliver a blow on the Western Front in the New Year. The strength of the two sides will be approximately equal. About thirty-five divisions and one thousand heavy guns can be made available for *one* offensive: a second great simultaneous offensive, say as a diversion, will not be possible.

'Our general situation requires that we should strike at the earliest moment, if possible at the end of February or beginning of March, before the Americans can throw strong forces into the scale.

'We must beat the British.

'The operations must be based on these conditions.'

There were to be many more conferences, many more planning sessions before final directions could be issued, but eventually on 21st January, 1918, Ludendorff gave his final decisions with regard to the direction and scope of his great offensive.

Ludendorff's plans

He would greatly have liked to attack the Allied line along its northernmost fifty miles — from just south of Armentières up to the coast — in converging attacks on each side of the Ypres Salient which would meet near Hazebrouck and cut the vital north-south railway which fed the Allied armies, then turn north and drive the British into the sea. Two schemes, code-named St George 1 and St George 2, were drawn up on these lines but reluctantly Ludendorff came to the conclusion that they would be too dependent upon the weather. He had no desire to engulf his armies in virtually the same mud as that which had absorbed the force of the British attacks in 1917.

South of this area, the British held the thirty-five-mile front covering Béthune and Arras along the Vimy Ridge in great strength, and although his staff produced plans Valkyrie and Mars to push them off it, Ludendorff was well aware of the tenacity of British infantry when well dug in.

However, from Arras down past St Quentin to la Fère was a stretch of line held by the British 3rd Army in the north (down to Flesquières) and their 5th Army (down to la Fère) which seemed to promise very well indeed. Not only was it likely to be thinly manned in view of the fact that the British had only just taken over the most southern stretch from the French (thus extending existing forces) but opposite it was his own immensely strong and capaciously excavated Hindenburg Line — surely the best place in which to concentrate his force and launch his attack. Accordingly, his staff produced an overall plan under the code-name St Michael, which was then sub-divided into three sections, numbered downwards from the north.

The left flank of the St Michael 3 attack lay therefore on the banks of the Oise where it flowed through la Fère. As that river flowed on across the lines, it could conveniently continue as the left flank of the attack in that area, and then four miles on behind the British lines lay the Crozat Canal — which again would act as a line upon which his southern attack group could rest and guard its flank, while the remainder of the XVIIIth Army (the main force chosen for the opening of the offensive, under General von Hutier) broke the

British front on each side of St Quentin and flooded forward until it reached the concave line of the Somme between Ham and Péronne. This would be the flank of the whole offensive, and Hutier's duty would be to see that no counter-attacks broke through to upset the balance of the attack to the north, to be borne by General von der Marwitz's II Army (St Michael 2) and General von Below's XVII Army (St Michael 1). These two armies would drive forwards until they reached, respectively, Albert and Bapaume, and on that line they would swing north and obtain a decision.

As Ludendorff knew only too well the vanity of man's proposals and the myriad accidents which can overset them, he also had plans drawn up for offensives along all the rest of the front from la Fère south and east as far as the Verdun Salient, naming them with an odd mixture of classical and religious fervour, Archangel, Achilles, Roland, Hector, Castor, and Pollux.

But the main emphasis was to be on Michael — with perhaps some assistance from Mars to the north and Archangel to the south.

The offensive opens

As early as the beginning of February, British Intelligence had garnered sufficient information for the staffs to be able to make a fairly accurate assessment of Ludendorff's plans; not that there was much they could do to protect the most immediately threatened area around St Quentin and la Fère, for there was hardly enough labour available to make good the front-line trenches just taken over from the French (who, after the Nivelle Offensive, had been so occupied with their own internal troubles that they had been content — so far as battle was concerned — merely to observe the gigantic conflicts in the Ypres Salient and do little else even to strengthen their own defences).

General Sir Hubert Gough, commanding the twelve infantry and three cavalry divisions of the British 5th Army, had thus been able only to strengthen the forward zone as far as its occupiers could manage in night working parties, the main battle zone immediately behind (varying in depth up to four thousand yards depending on the lie of the land) so far as fatigue parties from the units 'resting' could manage, and the rear zone only insofar as his labour force (consisting mostly of Chinese coolies) could construct roads along which material could be brought for the more urgent work farther forward.

Given time, Gough's men would undoubtedly have constructed defences comparable to those along Vimy Ridge, but no amount of labour — nothing short of a fairy wand — could have prepared the neces-

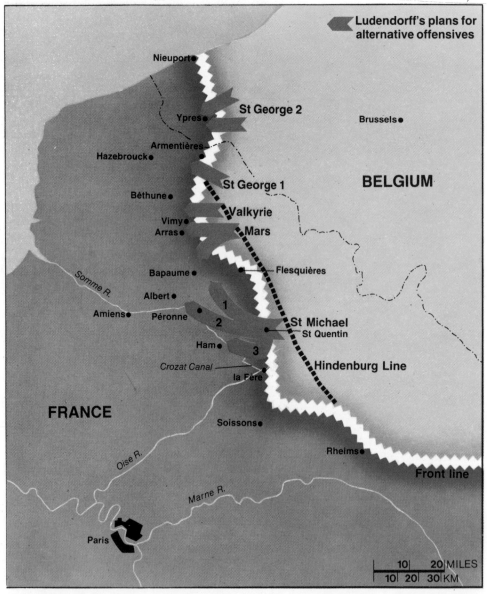

Ludendorff's plans for alternative offensives

St George 2

Brussels●

Nieuport●

Ypres●

Armentières●

Hazebrouck●

BELGIUM

St George 1

Béthune●

Valkyrie

Vimy●

Arras●

Mars

Bapaume●

Flesquières

Albert●

Somme R.

1

Amiens●

Péronne●

2

St Michael

St Quentin

Ham●

3

Crozat Canal

Hindenburg Line

la Fère

FRANCE

Soissons●

Oise R.

Rheims●

Front line

Marne R.

Paris●

10   20 MILES
10 20 30 KM

The alternative plans Ludendorff considered for the blow which was to defeat the Allies

sary defences in a few weeks. But the men of the 5th Army did what they could, and awaited the onslaught with that mixture of resignation and bitterness which by now typified the front-line soldier's attitude to the war, to his commanders, and to his probable fate.

Just before five o'clock on the morning of Thursday 21st March, 1918, began the most concentrated artillery barrage the world had known. Nearly 6,000 German guns opened fire almost simultaneously along the forty-mile stretch between the Sensée river and the Oise, and when 2,500 British guns answered, the additional noise was hardly noticed even by the men who fired them.

Tons of steel and high explosive fell with shattering force upon the 5th Army forward and battle zones, and as the men crouched

deafened and dazed in their trenches or staggered drunkenly towards control points, the ground rocked and heaved under them and the air filled with the taint of lethal and lachrymatory gas.

In the battle zone gun positions, battery and brigade headquarters, telephone exchanges, and road junctions collapsed or split apart under the weight and volume of fire, ammunition dumps blew up in towering mushrooms of flame and destruction, laboriously-laid signal wires were ripped apart and cannon were pounded into unrecognizable lumps of metal. For forty miles the eastern horizon was a line of leaping red flame, with dulled reflection beneath a sheet of fog which covered the southernmost of the British positions near the Oise.

For four and a half hours this barrage of

fire continued, sweeping back and forth across the forward and battle zones, obliterating the trenches, blasting the control organizations and tearing up what flimsy obstructions the British troops had been able to lay down. And at 9.40 am the German infantry rose to their feet and stormed forward.

The main assault troops moved fast as they had been recently trained to do, generally with rifles slung—relying for effect upon the ample supplies of stick-bombs they all carried, and upon the effect of the light machine-guns and flame-throwers which accompanied each section. Where aided by the fog, they passed quickly through the forward positions, evading the known strong-points and redoubts, leaping across the trenches, racing ahead to reach the remains of communications centres and artillery batteries in the battle zone. Behind them the second and third waves mopped up—sometimes by merely directing dazed and bleeding prisoners to the rear, sometimes completing the havoc of the guns with bayonet and rifle butt. Then they followed the first wave on into the battle zone.

Their fortunes varied inversely with their distance from the Oise, where the fog was thickest. Along the banks of the river where the fog had originated and was slowest to disperse, German infantry were right through the battle zone by early afternoon; but around St Quentin and to the north the British were able to hold on, though at a terrible price; of eight British battalions in one part of the front line only fifty men survived to reach the battle zone, and no indication of the fate of two whole battalions of the King's Royal Rifle Corps was found until months later, when the few survivors were discovered in a German prison-camp, recovering from their wounds.

Farther north still, towards the Flesquières Salient, the British infantry were proving the value of Ludendorff's forecast of their tenacity. Here the fog had not been so thick and had dispersed by 10.30 am; and the British were also fighting in trenches which had been their own responsibility for some time. The result was that by the end of the day, in the far north all positions had been held, down as far as St Quentin the battle zone had been entered but not penetrated by the Germans, and only in the extreme south had it been overrun. Here, by evening, the line was back to the Crozat Canal, and Hutier's southern flank had done all it had been asked.

That night, the Kaiser presented the Iron Cross with Golden Rays to Hindenburg (the last occasion had been to Blücher in 1814), Ludendorff and General von Kuhl (chief of staff to Rupprecht of Bavaria) coolly and dispassionately studied their maps, while on the field of battle, streams

British defenders watch the advancing Germans appear through the mist. Fog aided the German attackers. Near the banks of the Oise they broke right through the battle zone on the first day of the offensive. But where the fog dispersed the British clung on grimly—for both sides knew that if the Germans did not win the war in the spring of 1918, they would lose it

of British soldiers made their way surreptitiously back towards their own lines from positions in which they had been isolated, while the German attackers rested after their vast labours and prepared themselves for ordeals still to come.

During the days which followed, the pattern of the opening hours of the offensive was repeated, with the British positions in the north holding fast but those in the south being forced back as Hutier's advance pressed relentlessly forward against ever-weakening obstruction. By the evening of the second day, the British in the south had been flung back over the Somme almost as far up as Péronne, and positions north towards Flesquières had perforce been abandoned in order to keep some form and shape of a defensive line. It was as though a door was being forced open, hinged on Flesquières and with its outer edge

swinging ominously back towards Amiens.

But this movement, of course, opened a gap in the wrong direction so far as Ludendorff was concerned. He had no wish—or perhaps more important, no plans—for a break-out to the south-west, despite the fact that it could lead towards Paris. His plans were for a break-out to the north and, with this in mind, he tried to shift the weight of his attack to the Michael 1 section, along the Cambrai-Bapaume road, in order to smash the door off its hinge. Gradually, between the Salient and the Sensée Canal, the weight of this attack forced the defences to yield until a bulge formed anchored on the Arras defences in the north and the Flesquières Salient in the south, and it seemed as though these two positions were iron spikes driven into the ground, each anchoring the end of a flexible and slightly elastic cable; but it seemed that

the Michael 1 offensive could not break it.

All through Saturday 23rd March, the pressures everywhere continued and under it the defences in the south crumbled, the 5th Army slowly but surely disintegrated. Reeling with weakness and fatigue, the troops fought on until they were killed, or retreated until they dropped unconscious—and inevitably contact with the forces holding to the north was lost. At 7 am the following day the six battalion commanders of the Royal Naval Division holding the tip of the Flesquières Salient, having apparently lost contact with higher command and concluding—as they watched the gaps on either flank widen—that their position was fast becoming untenable, decided that in order to avoid annihilation, they must withdraw. The Salient was evacuated and the iron spike wrenched from the ground.

The Great Retreat had begun.

6 THE DEFEAT OF THE CENTRAL POWERS

The Collapse of Germany's Allies

Throughout the First World War most military leaders in London and Paris assumed that the prime task of the British and French armies was to defeat the Germans on the Western Front. Victory, they believed, would come only after a long war of attrition, in which the German army would be bled to death by endless attacks across the shell-scarred fields of France and Flanders. To these 'Westerners' the struggle against Germany's allies—Austria-Hungary, Turkey, and Bulgaria—was at best a tiresome sideshow and at times a dangerous distraction, ravenously consuming both men and munitions. Yet, from the first, the Western strategy had its critics on either side of the Channel. 'Why', they asked in effect, 'pit thousands of men against heavily fortified positions in a theatre of operations selected by the Germans themselves for their main effort? If there is deadlock between the huge armies on the Western Front, then surely a decision should be sought elsewhere, by striking at Germany's vulnerable partners so as to isolate the principal enemy and turn the natural fortress of central Europe from the rear?' This policy was broached in the first winter of war; and yet it was not until September 1918 that the Allies managed, almost as an afterthought, to put it into practice effectively.

Not all the delay stemmed from the obduracy of the Westerners. The differing importance of Germany's partners to the various Allied governments led to confusion, and even suspicion, in their counsels. To the Italians, for example, the war remained a last chapter in the *Risorgimento*, with the Austrians no less an

Left: Hungarian War Loan appeal

enemy than in the days of Cavour and Garibaldi; and the nationalists in Rome regarded Turkey and Bulgaria as insignificant adversaries, less of a danger to Italy's aspirations than her nominal ally, Serbia (who also aspired to win influence in Dalmatia). The French, too, could not neglect the Austrian threat in northern Italy, for there was always a possibility of a Napoleonic campaign in reverse, with a joint Austro-German army sweeping across Lombardy and making for Lyons and the heart of France (a strategic project which was actually proposed by the Austrian chief-of-staff to the German high command in 1916). Although the French had clearly defined ambitions in Syria, they had in general little interest in Turkish affairs, but there was far greater concern in Paris than in London for the 'Army of the Orient', that supremely cosmopolitan force which, under French command, had been gathered at Salonika to succour the Serbs and keep the Bulgarians out of Greece.

The British, by contrast, became increasingly convinced as the war continued that Turkey was second only to Germany among their enemies. Each successive Turkish affront rankled: the sanctuary afforded to the *Goeben* and *Breslau* in 1914; the gullies of Gallipoli, silent with the humiliation of vain endeavour; and the ominous lists of prisoners from Mesopotamia dying in Turkish camps. On the other hand, in London, Austria-Hungary and Bulgaria seemed of little account. There was a tendency to leave the Habsburg empire to the Italians, for it was assumed—at least until Caporetto—that fifty-two divisions and 5,000 guns concentrated on so small a front as the Isonzo would, sooner or later, crack the Austrian defences. And, although the London press

made much of Bulgarian atrocities in Macedonia, a Gladstonian-Liberal sympathy with the Bulgarians lingered on at Westminster, where the war was notoriously slow to shatter the enchantment of lost illusions. The prospects of entering Sofia in triumph held little appeal compared with the glory of liberating Jerusalem or of humbling the Turk in his capital on the Bosphorus.

The changes in the British attitude are clearly illustrated by the evolution of Lloyd George's ideas on general strategy. Even before becoming prime minister in December 1916, Lloyd George had convinced himself that the surest method of defeating Germany was by 'knocking away the props' afforded by her allies. But his priorities for destruction varied with the fluctuations of the war: thus in December 1914 he wanted an inter-Allied force from the Balkans to advance up the Danube; by January 1917 he had come to favour a joint offensive in northern Italy, with supporting attacks on the Bulgarian positions in Macedonia; but six months later he emerged as a latter-day Crusader, seeking Jerusalem as a Christmas gift for the British people, and triumphs in Turkey continued to fire his imagination until the final collapse of 1918. He maintained that, if the Turks were forced by defeat in Palestine to make a separate peace, the Allies could insist on occupying Constantinople and its hinterland and thus roll up the map of German-dominated Europe from its south-eastern tip. Few military advisers agreed with him; but Lloyd George was not to be inhibited by the disapprobation of brass-hat pundits.

The instrument chosen by Lloyd George in June 1917 to fulfil his wishes in Palestine was General Sir Edmund Allenby, who

had gained a striking success for British arms at Arras that spring, but had subsequently fallen out of favour with Haig. Allenby was a soldier of personality, a physical and moral giant. His predecessor as commander of the army in Egypt, Sir Archibald Murray, had lost nearly six thousand men in the last assault on the olives and cactus-hedges of Gaza; and Allenby, weary of the wastage on the Western Front, was determined to avoid all such costly attacks on the heavily fortified positions along the Palestinian coastal plain. He had the cavalryman's instinctive liking for a war of movement. At the end of October 1917 he struck at Beersheba, in the Judaean hills, twenty miles east of Gaza, breaking through the Turkish lines and swinging round so as to take Gaza from the sand-dunes on the flank of its defences. A rapid pursuit carried the advance fifty miles up the coast to the port of Jaffa. With rain falling night after night, so that the army was forced to rely on mules and donkeys for transport along the mud-caked tracks, Allenby himself pressed forward from Beersheba north-

westwards to Jerusalem. On 9th December the city, which had been in Muslim hands for over 600 years, fell; and the victory was hailed in London as the most impressive conquest yet achieved by British troops in the war. Yet the Turkish army, bolstered by a leavening of German officers and specialist units, was still far from beaten. Heavy rain prevented any further British advance. In February 1918 Jericho was taken; but Allenby, who was forced to send sixty battalions back to France after the German spring offensive, had to mark time all that summer, improvising an army of British, Australian, New Zealand, and Indian divisions which, supplemented by Lawrence's 'Arab Legion', would be capable of striking a decisive blow in the autumn.

Across the Mediterranean, the Allies in Salonika were also preparing to go over to the offensive. Maurice Sarrail, the politically ambitious general who had presided like a proconsul over the 'Army of the Orient' since its inception in October 1915, was recalled by Clemenceau in December 1917. His post was offered to General

Franchet d'Esperey, an 'Easterner' by conviction and a soldier who knew from his enterprising travels before the war the Balkans and central Europe better than any other high-ranking Frenchman. But Franchet d'Esperey was reluctant to relinquish his command on the Oise and the Aisne at this crucial hour in what he regarded as a personal duel with Hindenburg. It was accordingly General Guillaumat whom Clemenceau sent to Salonika, with the hard task of reconciling the British, Serbian, Greek, and Italian commanders, long estranged from the French by Sarrail's slights and pinpricks. He restored some of the confidence of this much despised army, but before launching an offensive he was summoned back to a Paris menaced by the Germans on the Marne; and Franchet d'Esperey, whose Army Group had sustained a reverse on the Chemin des Dames, was peremptorily sent east as Guillaumat's successor.

Although totally different in appearance and physique, Franchet d'Esperey had much in common with Allenby: the same liking for independence in command, the

Austrian POWs after Vittorio Veneto

same sudden eclipse on the Western Front, the same broad strategic sweep of the mind, the same conviction that, after years of entrenchment, the hour of the cavalry was at hand and that fast-moving squadrons could turn tactical success into final triumph. Like Allenby, he combined a volcanic temper with the personal magnetism which lifts the spirit of a downcast army; and, again like Allenby, his determination to achieve victory was hardened by the tragic loss in battle of an only son. When he landed at Salonika on 17th June 1918 he bluntly told the group of officers assembled to greet him, 'I expect from you savage vigour'. His British subordinates, struggling with the unfamiliar penta-syllabic surname, promptly dubbed their new commander 'Desperate Frankie'. It was an apt nickname; for, within nineteen days of arriving in Macedonia, his energy and drive had produced plans for an offensive to smash the Bulgarians and carry the war back to the Danube, nearly three hundred miles to the north.

The proposed Balkan offensive was discussed at a meeting of the supreme war council at Versailles on 3rd July, which was attended by the French and British prime ministers and their principal military advisers. The plan came under attack not only from the die-hard Westerners, who disliked any enterprise which might draw troops away from France, but from Lloyd George as well, primarily because he feared that it would divert men and material from Allenby in Palestine. A sub-committee of inter-Allied military representatives studied the project in detail and, on 3rd August, gave it their support, provided that it did not interfere with operations on the Western Front or require extensive re-routing of shipping in the Mediterranean. The British government was, however, still reluctant to give its consent, while the chief of the imperial general staff, Sir Henry Wilson, remained positively hostile to any operations in the Balkans. A curious situation thus developed: General Milne, the commander of the British Salonika Army, was confident of success and informed Lloyd George that 'an offensive here at the psychological moment may have more than local effect';

and he therefore made preparations for an attack which London was reluctant to authorize. In great secrecy but, in this instance, with cautious British backing, Allenby too was putting the final touches to plans which bore some resemblance to those contemplated in Macedonia.

Franchet d'Esperey wished to attack on 15th September and Allenby on 18th September. Not until 4th September did Lloyd George, overruling General Wilson's objections, finally give his approval to the Balkan offensive. He came firmly down on the side of the Easterners after a visit to London by General Guillaumat who, drawing on his own experience of the Macedonian Front, was able to assure the prime minister that a resolute attack would sap the war-weary Bulgarians' will to resist. Characteristically, once Lloyd George had decided to give his backing to Franchet d'Esperey, he reverted to his earlier argument for a comprehensive knocking aside of all the 'props'; and he insisted that every effort should be made to induce General

The Defeat of the Central Powers

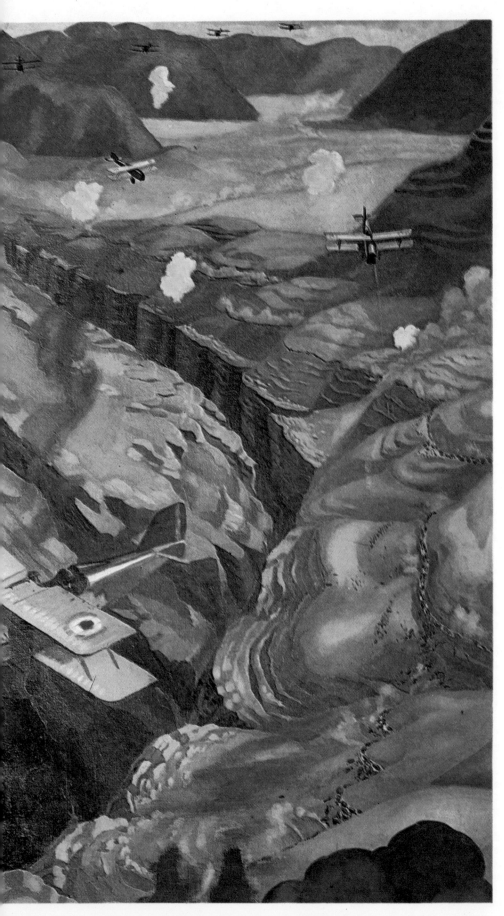

Left: 'The Destruction of the Turkish Transport' by Sydney W. Carline. British aircraft strafing a Turkish column in Palestine. The British also used the new air arm to penetrate Bulgarian valleys, and strike at enemy columns in rocky ravines.
Right: Italian painting of Vittorio Veneto.
Far right above: Allenby, architect of British victory in Palestine. *Far right below:* General Franchet d'Esperey

Diaz, the Italian commander-in-chief, to take the offensive against the Austrians along the river Piave. Marshal Foch, watching his armies in France roll the Germans slowly northwards, was also eager for a simultaneous Italian attack, but Diaz refused to move until he had some clear evidence that Austria-Hungary was on the verge of disintegration. As recently as the middle of June the Austrians had crossed the Piave in force and, although they had been repulsed with heavy casualties, the Italians were taking no risks. They could not afford a second Caporetto.

The cancer of defeat

The bonds binding Germany's partners to the government in Berlin were under considerable strain even before the joint Allied offensives. The sentiment for peace was probably most widespread in Bulgaria, as Guillaumat and Milne had perceived. Such industry as the country possessed was harnessed by German managers to the German war machine. A few businessmen in the towns made fat profits from German contracts, but for hundreds of workers there was nothing but hard work and low wages. With agriculture hit by the absence of able-bodied peasants, there was a threat of starvation. Moreover, the casualties suffered by the small kingdom in the combined campaigns of the bitter Balkan Wars and the two-year struggle in Macedonia had eliminated a higher proportion of the active population than in either Germany or France. The Bulgarians had made enormous sacrifices without gaining a single tangible reward; and, with the example of their fellow-Slavs in Mother Russia to look to, it was hardly surprising that many of the younger generation were thinking in terms of revolution.

Turkish disaffection took a different form. The Germanophile leaders, Enver and Talat, were still in power in Constantinople but, since the collapse of Russia, they had been solely interested in acquiring territory in Armenia and the Caucasus. Reinforcements — often only raw recruits — were sent to the Tigris to meet the danger from General Marshall's Mesopotamian Army, toiling northwards from Baghdad with the thermometers registering 110°F. for days on end; but few Turkish levies (and even less equipment) found their way to Palestine. There the commander was General Liman von Sanders, the greatest German expert on Turkish affairs, whose flair for organization had saved Gallipoli in 1915. However von Sanders could do little with an army which was short of food and plagued with typhus and malaria. Morale had declined considerably during the winter and spring; and in June 1918 Liman gloomily reported to Berlin that his effective strength was less than the

number of deserters who had slipped away in the previous three months. There was no threat of revolution in the Ottoman empire; but a mood of apathy and surrender pervaded almost every unit on the Palestine Front. More and more Liman was forced to rely on his German 'Asia Corps'; for, of the beys, only General Mustafa Kemal was still willing to offer spirited resistance.

The oldest of Germany's allies, Austria-Hungary, was no less tired of war than Bulgaria and no more able than Turkey to prevent desertion in large numbers among the reluctant conscripts, especially those from Czech, Slovak, or South Slav districts. The Emperor Karl (who came to the throne on Franz Josef's death in November 1916) did not conceal his desire for peace and there was a movement to break all bonds with Germany even among the more intransigent Hungarians. Everyone dreaded another winter of privation. But it is easy to exaggerate the demoralization in the Dual Monarchy. The Italians were wise to treat their adversaries along the Piave with respect; for, although the 'Imperial and Royal Army' was short of supplies, short of food, and deployed for internal security as well as for external war, the hard core of professional soldiery was steeled by two centuries of tradition and discipline. In the old battle zone at the head of the Adriatic the Army still offered strong resistance: it was among the scattered units who were in the Albanian mountains, or struggling back from the Ukraine, or policing the Serbian lands, that the cancer of defeat consumed the will to fight. And it was in this very area of south-eastern Europe that the Allies struck their first blow.

Early on 14th September five hundred guns began to pour shells on the Bulgarian positions along eighty miles of mountain and ravine in Macedonia; and on the following morning Serbian, French, and Senegalese infantry stormed the heights of a broken formless ridge known as the Dobropolje, more than 7,000 feet above sea-level. It was a dramatic start to Franchet d'Esperey's offensive; and it took both the Bulgarians and their German advisers completely by surprise, for no one anticipated an attack across such grim terrain. At first the Bulgarians resisted fanatically and the French were forced to use flamethrowers against their emplacements, but after three days of fierce fighting several Bulgarian regiments were on the verge of mutiny, and the Serbs were able to thrust an arrow-head fifteen miles into the enemy position, threatening the supply depot in the small town of Gradsko and the vital artery of the Vardar valley.

On 18th September, fifty miles to the east, the British and Greeks launched their assault on the hump of hills above Lake Doiran, where concrete casements and concrete machine-gun nests protected the frontier of the Bulgarian homeland. Twice in 1917 the British had sought to win these three miles of scrub and rock, looming over lake and trenches like some miniature Gibraltar. Now they tried once more to scale 'Pip Ridge' and the 'Grand Couronné', while a Cretan division moved round the lake to cut communications. But, though the South Wales Borderers reached the last defences, courage and enterprise could not carry the Grand Couronné. And yet, after two days' fighting, a strange silence settled on the ridges and ravines. Cautiously the British and Greeks advanced. They found the emplacements abandoned. On German orders, the Bulgarians had pulled back into the Balkan mountains rather than risk being cut off by Franchet d'Esperey's columns from the west.

There followed nine days of hectic pursuit. The French and the Serbs advanced up the Vardar valley, covering twenty-five miles in a day, with no regular rations, 'in rags and bare-footed', reported one French general. A French colonial cavalry brigade of Spahis from Morocco, led by General Jouinot-Gambetta (a hard-riding and hard-swearing nephew of the radical statesman of the 1870's), swung left from the line of advance and, by crossing some of the worst country in the Balkans, succeeded in seizing the key town of Skoplje on 28th September, while the main body of Serbs and French were still thirty miles to the south. At the same time, the British began to penetrate the valleys of Bulgaria, with the RAF obliterating the enemy columns, caught on impossible roads through the rocky ravines. The cascade of bombs turned the retreat into a rout; although barely noticed at the time, it was the first real victory of air power. With riots in four Bulgarian towns and local soviets striking Leninist attitudes, the Bulgarian high command asked for an armistice. Peace delegates waited on Franchet d'Esperey at Salonika; and on 30th September Germany's least powerful ally withdrew from the war. The British entered Sofia and a battalion of the Devonshire Regiment reached the Danube at Ruse.

The Salonika Armistice terms included the occupation of strategic points in Bulgaria and the use of Bulgarian railways. It was thus possible to isolate Turkey and march overland on Constantinople from the west and from the north. Accordingly, while Franchet d'Esperey continued to pursue German and Austro-Hungarian units through Serbia, General Milne was ordered from London to concentrate the bulk of the British Salonika army against

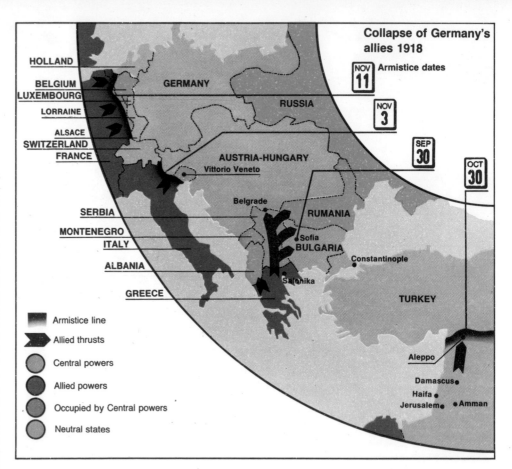

Turkey 'with a view to helping her surrender', as Lloyd George wrote. Yet it may
be doubted if these dispositions were
necessary, for the Turks had already been
defeated in Palestine and were on the
verge of collapse in Mesopotamia as well.

Allenby opened his offensive in Palestine on 18th September, the same day as
Milne. Elaborate deception had convinced
Liman von Sanders that the main British
attack would come from the east, beyond
Jordan. But the blow fell on the coastal
plain of Megiddo, where the cavalry broke
through to the hills under a fierce artillery
bombardment. As in Macedonia, heavy
bombing threw the Turkish rear into confusion and Liman himself narrowly
avoided capture in a daring cavalry raid
on his headquarters at Nazareth. With
Lawrence's Arabs helping in the east, the
Turks and the German 'Asia Corps' were
thrown back towards Damascus and
Aleppo. An impressive roll of captured
cities graced the war communiqués—
Haifa and Acre on 23rd September, Amman on 25th September, Damascus itself
on 2nd October. The French, far more
interested in Syria than in Palestine, took
a hand in the operation on 7th October,
when their naval forces seized Beirut; but
the victory was Allenby's, and it was his
divisions which pursued the Turks relentlessly northwards to Aleppo.

With General Marshall pressing along
the Tigris towards Mosul (whence he, too,
could have advanced on Aleppo), realization of defeat slowly penetrated the
palaces of Constantinople. At last on 13th
October Sultan Mahmud VI plucked up
the courage to dismiss Enver and Talat,
and on the following day the new grand
vizier, Izzet, sought an armistice. The
Turks, however, made contact, not with
Allenby, but with the commander-in-
chief of the British Mediterranean Fleet,
Admiral Calthorpe. It was, accordingly, at
Moudros—the island base in the Aegean
established by the British before the
Dardanelles expedition—that the Turkish
armistice was duly signed on 30th October.
All fighting in the Middle East officially
ceased on the following day; and on 12th
November an Allied naval squadron sailed
up the Dardanelles, past the rusting wrecks
on the Gallipoli beaches, to anchor below
the Golden Horn in Constantinople.

While Turkey was seeking peace, the war
against Austria-Hungary was entering its
final phase. But one Allied commander, at
least, was in no mood for peace. With the
towns of Serbia falling into his hands
throughout October, Franchet d'Esperey
was confidently preparing to march on
Berlin by way of Belgrade, Budapest,
Vienna, and Dresden. Spurred forward by
Napoleonic notions of grandeur, he reported
on 19th October that French guns had been

heard on the Danube for the first time in
109 years. Belgrade was liberated on 1st
November and with one Serbian army following the French into southern Hungary
and a second one marching on Sarajevo,
the wheel of war had come full circle.

Yet the final blow against the Habsburgs came, not from the French and the
Serbs, but from the enemy they had despised since Metternich's day; for the
Italians, fearing that peace might break
out before they had avenged Caporetto,
went over to the offensive at last on 24th
October. With British and French support,
they launched a furious attack on the
Piave, which cost them 25,000 men in sixty
hours of grim fighting. On 30th October
the Austrian line caved in, and squadrons
of cavalry and armoured cars took the
Austrian headquarters at Vittorio Veneto
(the name subsequently given to the whole
battle). Already the Austrians were suing
for peace and fighting ceased on 3rd November. In ten days the Italians had no less
than half a million dispirited prisoners.

A last tragi-comedy was played out on
7th November in Belgrade. The newly-
independent Hungarian government did
not consider itself bound by the Italian
armistice, which was signed by representatives of the old order. The Hungarian Liberal, Count Mihaly Károlyi,
accordingly travelled to Belgrade, confident that he would obtain generous treatment for his country from the spokesman
of republican France. Károlyi asked that
Hungary might be occupied by the French,
British, Italians, and Americans and not
by the east European peoples or by 'colonial
troops'. But Franchet d'Esperey brusquely
turned aside his requests. By the Belgrade
Armistice more than half of the old Hungarian kingdom was occupied by Allied
soldiery, including Serbs, Rumanians, and

Czechs. The revenge of the 'subject nationalities' was complete—but it was not without significance for the future that they
owed their newly found status to the
favours dispensed by a French general.

The successes gained by the Allied
armies from Salonika and Cairo and Baghdad were soon eclipsed in the public eye
by the humbling of Germany; and only
Italy among the great powers regarded a
victory against one of Germany's allies
as the crowning glory of the war. With
the coming of peace, private disputes
hardened into an open controversy which
was sharpened by the publication of
military and political memoirs: some
writers insisted that final victory had come
when it did only because German might
was vanquished on the fields of France
and Flanders; others argued that the
rapidity with which Germany's collapse
followed the fall of her partners fully
vindicated Lloyd George's policy of 'knocking away the props'. In the bitterness of
this debate, the achievement of the soldiers
and airmen in the distant theatres of war
was sometimes misrepresented or deni-
grated. All too frequently people forgot that
Germany's allies were no less the declared
enemies of Great Britain and France than
the government in Berlin; and it was
hardly possible for their military potential
to be ignored, especially when they were
already in occupation of so much Allied
territory. The great merit of the offensives
of Allenby and Franchet d'Esperey was
that they formed part of a general strategy
for enveloping Germany, while disposing
of her partners with a limited use of manpower and resources. Militarily they are
of particular interest, for they combined
the tactical employment of both the oldest
and newest instruments in a war of movement, cavalry and aircraft.

Ludendorff's Defeat

Ludendorff was making a bid for final victory. At the end of 1917 he had decided that he must knock the French and, above all, the British out of the war before the promised American reinforcements could arrive and turn the tide once and for all in the Allies' favour. On 21st March 1918 the greatest bombardment the world had ever seen started up on the Western Front. In heavy fog the German assault troops stormed through the British strongpoints from St Quentin to la Fère, and in the following days they pushed the British back over the old hard-fought battleground of the Somme. Ludendorff's plan, St Michael, envisaged a complete breakthrough down from Arras through the Flesquières Salient to St Quentin and la Fère. On 24th March, while the Germans pushed through to north and south, the British started to withdraw from the Flesquières Salient, the last point they held south of Arras on the old front line. But Arras, contrary to German plans, stayed firm as the British front line retreated. It was as though a door hinging on Arras was swinging open.

As a result of the mutual respect which existed between the British and French commanders-in-chief, Sir Douglas Haig and General Philippe Pétain, French divisions had been hastily flung into the gap left as the door opened, and after a conference held at Doullens, on 26th March, the Allied armies had an overall commander-in-chief in the person of General Ferdinand Foch. It was to prove a happy choice, and in the existing circumstances the British could only gain from this apparent surrender of their independence; reserves could only flow towards them – at least until this vast emergency was over.

By 29th March reserves were coming up from the south to fill the gaping holes in the British line – which now ran from Arras down through Albert, Villers Bretonneux, and Cantigny – and it was also evident that the steam was going out of the German attack. Many factors contributed to this – inevitable casualties, accumulated fatigue in the surviving assault troops, the ever-lengthening lines of communication, and the foreseen difficulties of moving men and supplies forward across the enormous confusion of the old Somme battlefields.

But there was another reason, illustrated by an entry in the diary of a German officer, Rudolf Binding: 'Today the advance of our infantry suddenly stopped near Albert. Nobody could understand why. Our airmen had reported no enemy between Albert and Amiens . . . our way seemed entirely clear. I jumped into a car to investigate.

'As soon as I got near the town I began to see curious sights. Strange figures which looked very little like soldiers . . . were making their way back out of the town. There were men driving cows before them in a line: others who carried a hen under one arm and a box of notepaper under the other. Men carrying a bottle of wine under their arm and another one open in their hand. Men who had torn a silk drawing-room curtain from its rod . . . more men with writing paper and notebooks. Evidently they had found it desirable to sack a stationer's shop. Men dressed up in comic disguise. Men with top hats on their heads. Men staggering.'

Ludendorff's dream vanishes

Three and a half years of grim austerity had led to this. As the front of the German advance crept out of the battle area into the line of villages which had until a few days before been inhabited by civilians – grown rich on commerce with the British troops – it seemed to the Germans that they had stumbled into Aladdin's cave. All were affected, officers and men, rich and poor alike, for the wealth of Prussia had been unable to buy during the last years the booty which now lay around them for plunder. Binding himself writes, almost with hysteria, of 'smearing our boots with lovely English boot-polish . . .'

And together with this understandable but uncontrollable lust for trivial comforts and luxuries which had been for so long denied them, drunkenness now joined to check the German armies. Fear and battle had dried the moisture from the soldiers' bodies quicker than the desert sun – and after a week living on scummy water from the bottom of shell-holes foul with cordite and decomposition, the troops found themselves in deserted villages whose houses still held wine-stocked cellars. To those few who could remember, the scenes stirred memories of the great sweep to the Marne in 1914.

And so the March offensive petered out. In all, it won from the Allies some 1,200 square miles of territory, vast quantities of stores, over 90,000 prisoners, and 1,000 guns; it had also presented the victors with nearly fifty extra miles of front to hold, none of which could possibly be as strongly fortified, as defensible, or even as comfortable as the Hindenburg Line from which it had started.

With the halting of St Michael (and also the failure of a brief attack aimed at smashing away the door-hinge at Arras)

Above: French prisoners captured in the opening stages of the German offensive.
Left: Canadian Highlanders on the march painted by Eric Kennington

The Defeat of the Central Powers

Ludendorff realized that his dream of a break-through in the southern half of the British front was fast vanishing — but there were still other schemes produced by his staffs, notably the St George attacks, which had attracted him when they had first been presented to him in December. These plans proposed attacking the Allied line along its northernmost fifty miles — from south of Armentières to the coast — in offensives on each side of the Ypres Salient, which would meet near Hazebrouck and then turn north and drive the British into the sea. Ludendorff had originally rejected them because of the uncertainty of the weather — he had no desire to engulf his armies in the Flanders mud as the British had done in 1917.

March 1918, however, had proved an exceptionally dry month and the ground was likely to be firm — so as many men as could be spared from the coalescing fronts between Albert and Cantigny were withdrawn, the German artillery train hurriedly transferred north, and the plans examined for converging attacks on the Ypres Salient.

However, it soon became evident that insufficient numerical strength was available for so grand a project, and only the southern half of the blow could be launched. Even this was limited to a twelve- instead of a thirty-mile front, and at the suggestion of one of Ludendorff's more sardonic staff officers the code-name was changed from St George to Georgette.

While the German general staff busied itself with the organization of this second act of their offensive, the Allies — severely shaken but thankfully aware of the passing of their most immediate peril — held a series of rapid and salutary post-mortems, which resulted firstly in the dismissal of the unfortunate Sir Hubert Gough, and secondly in the further strengthening of General Foch's position. The agreement reached at Doullens was superseded by the following announcement: 'General Foch is charged by the British, French, and American governments with the co-ordination of the action of the Allied armies on the Western Front. To this end all powers necessary to secure effective realization are conferred on him. The British, French, and American governments for this purpose entrust to General Foch the strategic direction of military operations.'

There were certain reservations with regard to tactical direction in the final passages of the agreement, but the Allies were at last obtaining for themselves the immense advantage of a single supreme commander — which the Central powers had enjoyed for many months. Another most hopeful factor was the presence of two American generals at the conference, Generals Pershing and Bliss.

It was tacitly admitted that in the circumstances the sooner American troops were in action the better; and that General Pershing's natural desire for the American army to fight solely as a national army under his own command might in days of such emergency be modified to allow separate American divisions to be fed piecemeal into the front wherever the Allied requirements were greatest.

According to legend, General Pershing made a high-flown speech ending 'I come to tell you that the American people will esteem it a great honour that our troops should take part in the present battle. . . . There is at the moment no other question than that of fighting. Infantry, artillery, aeroplanes, tanks, all that we have is yours. Dispose of us as you wish. . . . The American people will be proud to take part in the greatest and finest battle in history.'

Apart from the fact that no American aeroplanes, artillery, or tanks had as yet arrived in Europe (in the event, none arrived before the Armistice), a study of Pershing's character reveals that it is most unlikely that he would ever indulge in such verbal histrionics. It is far more likely that whatever he said approximated far more closely to General Bliss's remark.

He had said: 'We've come over here to get ourselves killed; if you want to use us, what are you waiting for?'

Despite its mordant note, few speeches have ever afforded greater relief. Munitions for the front were ready and to hand, but only America could replace the lost legions – and within a week American engineers were working on the defence lines and taking part in repelling German attacks on British positions.

It was, of course, problems of manpower which most deeply worried Sir Douglas Haig, the British commander-in-chief during the days immediately following the last spasms of the St Michael offensive – and the condition of some of the divisions which had been involved in it. Five of these divisions he removed from the line and replaced by rested divisions from the northern sector – transferring the battered remnants of the 9th, 19th, 25th, 34th, and 40th Divisions to a quiet section between the Ypres-Comines Canal and la Bassée; as neighbours on their right flank, they should have had the 1st and 2nd Portuguese Divisions, but as it happened, shortly after the arrival of the British divisions from the south, the 1st Portuguese left the line and as no replacements seemed to be forthcoming the 2nd Portuguese thinned themselves out to occupy the spaces left vacant by their compatriots.

On 7th and 8th April, Armentières to the north and the area around Lens to the south were deluged in mustard gas, and at 3 am on the 9th the opening of Georgette

was signalled by an intense bombardment from Ludendorff's 'battering train', followed shortly after 8 am by a violent onslaught by the infantry of nine full-strength German divisions. The main weight of the attack fell upon the Portuguese sector, and pausing only long enough to remove their boots, the troops fled to the rear, several of them assisting their passage by commandeering the bicycles of the British 11th Cyclist Battalion who had been rushed up to hold the gap.

The remainder of the morning was a wild confusion of attack and counter-attack, as every available British unit was hastily flung into the breach, but by evening the Germans had stormed forward for six miles as far as the banks of the River Lawe, behind which the Highlanders of the 51st Division waited in grim anticipation of the next morning's battle.

As it happened, the main weight of the next day's attack was directed by Ludendorff farther to the north than the Highlanders' positions. In the first onslaught, only half of Georgette had been delivered (against the northern flank of the British 1st Army, commanded by Sir Henry Horne) and now it was time for the southern flank of Sir Herbert Plumer's 2nd Army to take the brunt of the attack. As the Ypres Salient was a part of the 2nd Army's responsibility, both the men and their beloved commander were well used to the horrors and vicissitudes of battle.

All day long the battle raged (again the attackers were aided at first by thick fog in the Lys valley) but unlike the previous day – and unlike the previous weeks of the March offensive – the British line remained unbroken as it went slowly back; it was yielding ground quite methodically, and just as methodically exacting an enormous price in German blood for every inch it gave. Armentières and Erquinhem, Messines and Ploegsteert, all fell into German hands that day – to the dismay and astonishment of many armchair strategists weaned on the belief that to lose ground was to lose the battle – but already Plumer sensed his command of the situation was secure, and this was confirmed on 12th April when Sir Douglas Haig extended his sector southwards so that the whole British defence would be directed by one man.

Plumer's sector thus resembled a gigantic reversed S from the right bank of the Coverbeek stream north of Ypres, right around the Ypres Salient through Poelcapelle to the Passchendaele Ridge of fearful memory; back across the Wytschaete Ridge, and around in the first twelve miles of the bottom curve of the S as far as Merville. It was a line won at dreadful cost during three and a half years of slaughter and agony, and every yard of the northern sector in the Salient

itself had been the site of deeds recorded in some British regimental history – and with a refreshing realism Plumer decided to withdraw from it in order to shorten his line and accumulate reserves for the defence of Béthune and Hazebrouck.

As a result, when Ludendorff again shifted his attack north to probe for a weak spot, his opening bombardment fell on empty trenches, and to attack the new British line his infantry had to advance down the open face of the deserted ridge, while their support artillery tried to heave its way over two miles of churned mud.

Georgette bogged down. A week after that first storming success against the Portuguese, the battle of the Lys began to show the same signs of stagnation as those which had heralded the halting of the St Michael offensive. Although the attacking troops still made progress – and Baillieul fell into their hands a smoking ruin on 15th April – they were tired, their supplies were arriving late and were inadequate, while all the time the defences against which they battered, grew stronger. The defensive crust, in fact, had been given time to harden, and Ludendorff's chance of a break-through was vanishing. On 16th April, violent but unsuccessful German attacks were launched to the south against the left flank of Sir Henry Horne's army, but on 19th April a lull descended on the entire front.

French divisions now came up to take over the line from Méteren to Wytschaete, and the five British divisions most severely mauled on the Lys – including the 19th and 25th which had been brought up from Flesquières after their battering during St Michael – were transferred south to a quiet section of the French front along the Chemin-des-Dames, where it was confidently believed that they would enjoy ample facilities for rest and recovery.

The British hold fast

During the whole of the recent crises, the new Allied commander-in-chief General Foch had been indomitably and sometimes infuriatingly optimistic whatever happened. His invariable reaction to every piece of news, however alarming, had been 'Bon!' until on one occasion Haig's patience had worn thin and he slapped the table and retorted 'Ce n'est pas bon du tout!' – but nonetheless Foch's attitude of supreme confidence and energy played some considerable part in the battle.

But Ludendorff, on the other side of the line, had been growing increasingly depressed. Despite the gains in territory, booty, and prisoners – vast in comparison with those of any Allied offensive on the Western Front – he had nevertheless failed to attain the type of sweeping victory which had attended his efforts on the

Eastern Front, and which he knew would be necessary if the Central Powers were to win the war. However loudly the German press might proclaim his genius as a military commander and however striking the gains might look on the maps and in the balance sheets of the stores depots, the cold fact remained that a large number of his finest soldiers had been killed and those that were left had to hold fifty more miles of line than when St Michael began.

He had, he began to feel, been mistaken in attacking the British section of the front, however sound his reasoning had appeared when the decisions were made, and on 17th April he instructed his staff to prepare plans for yet another large-scale offensive, this time against the French, in the area adjacent to the southern edge of the now moribund St Quentin attack. It was here that the original line of the Western Front had curved around from roughly north-south to west-east, before beginning its sixty-mile straight run to Verdun.

There were still two battles to be fought against the British, however, the last spasms of Georgette and St Michael. On 24th April thirteen German tanks led an attack which finally succeeded in taking Villers Bretonneux though the town only remained in German hands a matter of hours, a combined British and Australian attack retaking it during the following night. And on 25th April a violent German attack captured Mont Kemmel from the French troops who had just taken it over from the exhausted British.

But again, gaps torn in the Allied lines were not exploited. Plumer poured his accumulated reserves like cement into the line, the line hardened and set, and nothing Ludendorff could do could break it; in any case, his attentive and slightly bulbous gaze was now fixed on the scene of his next offensive which, abjuring both religion and the classics and placing his trust in history, he had now christened 'Blücher'. Perhaps he hoped for an Iron Cross with Golden Rays for himself.

When the men of the British divisions transferred south for a well-earned period of rest and recuperation first arrived in the delightful Champagne country, blossoming now in the warm spring sunshine, the contrasts from the drab mists and mud of the Flanders plain had been to them a blissful revelation. The verdant countryside was broken by hills among which nestled charming villages untouched by war, and if the trenches were shallow and insanitary to a degree which only French troops could have tolerated, they were nevertheless so screened in foliage as to resemble more the brambled hideouts of childhood games than the fortifications

of more adult pursuits. Not that this mattered, for this was a cushy front.

At first.

But after a week the men began to wonder, for in addition to glorious weather May brought an increasing feeling of tension coupled with an almost imperceptible daily increase in the amount of German shell-fire. And if the troops felt uneasy, the battalion commanders were soon horrified to discover the manner in which their men were disposed along so shallow a defensive line.

Unfortunately, there was nothing which could be done about this, for these British divisions were now in the command area of the French 6th Army, under the command of General Duchesne, whose choleric disposition was such that he fiercely resented criticism even from superior officers of his own nationality. When suggestions for changes in disposition came from subordinates, and when the subordinates were British—and those moreover who had recently and disgracefully retired in front of German attacks—then they met with flat rejection, worded in the most insulting terms. When the British staff remonstrated further, he dismissed them with a basilisk stare and breathed a curt *'J'ai dit!'*

All troops in Duchesne's sector, British and French alike, were thus herded compactly up into front lines of dubious protective value, and when, despite Duchesne's repeated announcements that no German attack was imminent, the opening bombardment of Blücher fell upon them at 1 am on the morning of 27th May, it trod them into the ground with an obliterative effect even greater than the opening barrage of St Michael. At 3.40 am German Storm Troops began to move forward behind the wall of their own bursting shells, through scenes of carnage and destruction beyond the imagination of Hieronymus Bosch.

By mid-day they were across the Aisne —Duchesne had delayed blowing the bridges until too late—and by evening German spearheads had reached the Vesle on both sides of Fismes. The following morning they crossed the river and surged onwards towards the Marne, at the same time broadening the base of their advance to threaten the rail centre of Soissons—thus advancing twelve miles in one day, a feat long considered impossible upon the Western Front.

An attack launched in conditions which applied in France between 1914 and 1918 has been aptly compared to the overturning of a bucket of water on a flat surface. Unless action is taken with extraordinary rapidity and decision in the first vital seconds, attempts to dam or channel the floods are of no avail, and

there is nothing to do but wait until the waters lose their impetus and reach the limit of their dispersion.

This happened with Blücher. Day after day the German tide flooded southwards, until on 30th May troops of General von Böhn's VII Army reached the Marne, with Paris lying fifty miles away straight up the corridor between the Marne and the Ourcq. But however entrancing this view may have been to the Kaiser and the Crown Prince (both following their armies some fifty miles to the rear), to Ludendorff and his staff two ominous facts were emerging which thoroughly dampened their spirits. Firstly, the map now showed a huge bulge depressingly similar to those lately and abortively formed by their own efforts to the north; and secondly, their troops were now passing through the Champagne country and the reports coming back from the front indicated that all ranks were appreciating the contents of French cellars far more than the need to press forward; and *Feldpolizei* dispatched to restore order far too often succumbed to temptation themselves.

Thus Blücher, too, lost impetus and died—and one of the most significant facts about the halting of the tide occurred on 1st June at Château-Thierry, when for the first time a German attack was met and firmly repulsed by American troops. It had taken rather longer than had been expected for General Pershing to augment his promises made at Doullens, but now the 2nd American Division was in action and American troops were to take part in all the battles still to come.

The Black Day of the German army

It was now that the essential book-keeping behind warfare began to reveal the true state of affairs. There was no denial of the fact that, so far as possession of real estate in France was concerned, Germany had made vast gains during the past few weeks, to the direct loss of the Allies—but the cost had been excessive. Ludendorff's strength in divisions on paper was little less than it had been at the beginning of St Michael, but the average battalion strengths had been reduced by this time from 807 to 692—despite the arrival of 23,000 recruits of the 1899 class, and some 60,000 men withdrawn from rail, transport, and other supply services. Moreover, the quality of the battalions was distinctly lower than at the beginning of the year, for the simple reason that Ludendorff had creamed off the best men to form his Storm Troop units; these had inevitably suffered the highest casualties, as they had both led every attack and then been flung in to hold any gaps.

Now, therefore, his best men were gone and in their place were the unfit, the very

1 German supply wagons choke a road on the Somme. The difficulties of moving war-weary troops and their supplies forward across the old battlefields sapped the impetus of the German offensive. 2 French troops take cover as one of their tanks is hit. 3 Artist's impression of German tank attack on Villers Bretonneux. 4 Men of a New Zealand division support British tanks during the counter-offensive. In the background, captured German guns

The Defeat of the Central Powers

Top: Bespectacled German soldier surrenders during the counter-offensive. With his best men dead, Ludendorff replaced them with the unfit, the very young, and the middle-aged. Above: Men of a Lancashire regiment pose excitedly in German headgear

young and the middle-aged, and that irreducible proportion of men in every army which normally manages to occupy the safest and most lucrative positions, and who are therefore most aggrieved when circumstance forcibly exchanges their comfort for danger. This undesirable faction had already been responsible for some ugly incidents; desertion had increased, troops had failed to return from leave, and many of those who did return as far as the railheads behind the lines, now joined up with others as sullen and mutinous as themselves to roam the back areas, defying the *Feldpolizei,* raiding stores and generally spreading confusion.

On the Allied side, however, once American troops joined the line, the manpower problem was solved. Not only did Pershing's command form an apparently inexhaustible supply of young, fit, eager —and, most important of all—inexperienced and therefore confident soldiers, but their very presence in such visible abundance spread optimism through the Allied armies, who, despite the vast bulges on the maps, regained during the early summer of 1918 that feeling of certain victory which had been missing since the days of Verdun and the Somme.

There were to be two more attempts by Ludendorff to break out of the net in which his armies seemed to be caught—one at Noyon, between the St Michael and Blücher bulges, and the second on the eastern flank of the Chemin-des-Dames bulge—a double-pronged attack aimed at isolating Rheims; but the Allies were now in growing strength and well able to absorb and counter Ludendorff's everweakening blows.

On the morning of 18th July, after a violent cloudburst, the first stage of the Allied counter-attack opened under command of General Mangin on the western flank of the Chemin-des-Dames bulge, aimed at cutting the German supply route down to Château-Thierry. Three hundred and forty-six Renault tanks took part in the opening phase, and although these broke down within a matter of hours, they gave essential aid during the first break-through—and the menace of the flank attack was enough to bring Ludendorff hurrying back from a conference in the north.

The following day, American divisions attacked in the south of the bulge, and Ludendorff—acutely conscious of the exposed position of his troops at the bottom of the sack—authorized, and indeed organized, a retreat; that he was still a competent soldier is shown by the fact that despite another Allied flank attack, this time from the east, he managed to wedge open the jaws of the trap west of Soissons and west of Rheims, until by 4th August most of his men were back behind the line of the Aisne and the Vesle, and the sack formed by Blücher had vanished.

But on 8th August, British, Canadian, and Australian divisions, supported by almost the whole of the British Tank Corps—604 tanks in all—struck at Ludendorff's line in front of Amiens, in an attack stretching from the Ancre in the north, down across the Somme and past Villers Bretonneux to the Luce. The blow had been elaborately and most efficiently prepared and was, almost ironically, aided on this occasion by nature who provided the Allies with fog—almost the first time an Allied attack had been so favoured.

All the way along the attack front, the first thrusts were successful and the tanks proved an immense success in supporting the infantry, who whenever a machine-gun post gave trouble lay down and waited for one of the mastodon shapes of their armoured protection to lumber forward and crush the opposition. By that evening, fifteen miles of the German front had been stove in and British Whippet tanks and infantry, with their Dominion comrades, were seven miles in advance of their startline.

Ludendorff was shocked when, on the following day, he appraised the results of the fighting on 8th August—but not so much by the loss of territory, of material, or even of men; the Allies had lost far more in all these categories every day for over a week during the March offensive, but they had not lost the war. It was an entirely different loss which spelled out to him the presage of doom. It was the loss of spirit.

According to the reports on his desk, six German divisions had collapsed that day in scenes unprecedented in German military legend. Companies had surrendered to single tanks, platoons to single infantrymen, and on one occasion retreating troops had hurled abuse at a division going forward resolutely to buttress the sagging line, accusing them of blacklegging and 'toadying to the Junkers'.

'8th August was the Black Day of the German army . . .' he wrote afterwards, and history has justified the comment.

On 8th August began the Allied advance to the Rhine.

From then on, the front was never quiet. Whatever shortcomings may have in the past blemished Foch's planning, in the summer of 1918 his doctrine of the continual offensive brought success—so long as attacks were switched as soon as the defensive crust in front hardened.

On 11th August the battle of Amiens was called off after an advance of ten miles, but two days before, the French army under General Debeney had attacked and taken Montdidier, while the following day General Humbert's French 3rd Army —one stage farther south—advanced towards Noyon and liberated Lassigny in fighting which lasted until the 16th. And on the 18th, Mangin's army struck on Humbert's right, and took the Aisne heights on the 20th.

Each attack was broken off as soon as it lost its initial impetus, by which time another attack had been launched near enough to the previous one to profit from its success—and again continued only until resistance stiffened to such a point that further attacks would be unprofitable.

So it was to continue. On 21st August the British 3rd Army, under General Sir Julian Byng, attacked north of Albert (an

Below: Ludendorff's desperate gamble. He had decided it was imperative to knock the French and above all the British out of the war, before the promised American reinforcements could arrive and turn the tide, once and for all, in the Allies' favour

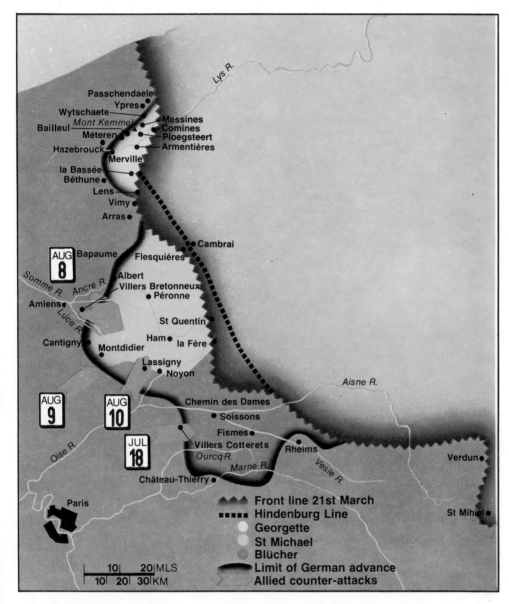

Front line 21st March
Hindenburg Line
Georgette
St Michael
Blücher
Limit of German advance
Allied counter-attacks

10 | 20 MLS
10 | 20 | 30 KM

attack buttressed by 200 tanks salvaged from the battle of Amiens), and the following day Rawlinson's 4th Army struck a few miles to the south, between Albert and the Somme. By that evening the front was back running along the edge of the old Somme battlefields across which the flower of British manhood had gone to its death two years before, and twenty-four hours later both Byng's and Rawlinson's troops were three miles farther forward!

23rd August was thus an even blacker day for the German army than had been 8th August and there was to be no respite for them until an armistice was signed. Throughout the remaining days of August and the opening week of September, the Allies beat a continual tattoo on the German line, and by 9th September almost the entire territorial gains of the Ludendorff spring offensive had been lost, a hundred thousand German soldiers had

entered Allied prison-camps, many more had been killed or wounded, and—most ominously of all—had deserted.

Two days later the American attack on the St Mihiel Salient opened and within two days this perpetual thorn in French flesh had vanished, 14,500 German prisoners and 443 German guns lay behind American lines, and Pershing was regrouping his forces for a vast offensive northwards through the Argonne.

But there was still one slender hope in Ludendorff's mind—that the concrete fastnesses of the Hindenburg Line might give him some respite; he thus watched the opening moves of the attack on it with great anxiety. It began with a fifty-six-hour bombardment, launched on a five-division front by British, American, and Australian divisions. Again, fog aided the attackers, allowing the British to cross the St Quentin Canal almost unseen, then to

turn and lever away the defensive positions on each flank as these came under frontal attack. With admirable organization, reserve divisions came up through the gaps created, leap-frogged through the remnants of the assault divisions and drove even deeper into the complex of trenches and dug-outs, wire belts and tunnels which all Germany had confidently expected to withstand any onslaught.

All day long German troops had fought from the defences of their famous line with much of the skill and ardour which had distinguished them in the past—their defeat was due mainly to fog, to the offensive spirit of the Americans and the Australians, and the spirit of victory which animated the British; and possibly to German luck, which had changed.

For although no one realized it then, that afternoon Germany had lost the war.

Under the accumulating strain, Ludendorff's nerve had cracked, and at four o'clock that afternoon he had suffered a minor stroke while staying—appropriately—at the Hôtel Britannique, in Spa. He had gone there to attend another of the eternal conferences to which he was of late always being summoned, in order to convince politicians from home that his plans for victory were developing well.

That evening, pale and shaken, he visited his superior and constant ally Hindenburg in the suite below his own, and admitted that he could see no way out of the impasse into which Germany had been manoeuvred; and sadly, Hindenburg—as ever—agreed with his chief subordinate. An armistice must be asked for, and the staff must immediately commence drawing up movement orders for a planned withdrawal of the army, together with as much of the heavy materials of war as could be moved, back to the western frontier of Germany. There they would present to the world a spectacle of an unbeaten force still capable of defending their honour and the fatherland.

That two men in such high position in the world could be so divorced from reality that they could believe their position was such that the Allies would agree to this, merely exemplifies the lack of political common sense which permeated the entire military conduct of the war, on both sides. In the event, the Allied powers exacted a surrender as unconditional as the one they were to exact twenty-seven years later, though the actual terms agreed to were less demonstrative of Allied victory.

The conditions of the Versailles Treaty may well have been harsh and ungenerous, but German memories might not have been so short if their own country had been subjected to some of the physical damage which had been inflicted upon France, and affected future French attitudes to war.

The Road to Armistice

Germany's unlimited submarine warfare had in fact been a military as well as a political gamble. In the short run, the military gamble seemed to come off, for the results of the first four months were far above expectations. It was only later in 1917 that Allied counter-measures made the number of German submarine successes decline sharply.

Politically, however, submarine warfare was one unmitigated failure from the outset. It brought the USA into war, and with its entry, the defeat of Germany. American participation in the war infused the war-weary Western nations with new hopes, while it discouraged correspondingly the Central powers who were no less sick of the war, in particular the Slav nationalities in Austria-Hungary. Their hearts had never been in a war which had started as a 'punitive action' against an independent Slav nation – Serbia.

By the spring of 1917 the situation in the Dual Monarchy had become so desperate for the ruling German and Hungarian groups that the new Emperor Karl took to heart a deeply pessimistic memorandum by his chief minister, Count Czernin, on the urgent necessity to make peace very soon, and passed it on to Matthias Erzberger, a leading member of the German Catholic Centre Party. Erzberger was deeply impressed. In Germany disillusionment about submarine warfare, and political unrest under the stress of the war reached a new intensity in the summer of 1917. Even the SPD (the Social Democratic Party), smarting under the sharp attacks by the USPD (the Independent Social Democratic Party), their left-wing breakaway, was becoming restive and threatened for the first time to vote against the war credits. It was in this situation that Erzberger and the SPD took the parliamentary initiative to relieve somehow the domestic pressure by attacking Chancellor Bethmann Hollweg. Philipp Scheidemann and Friedrich Ebert, the two outstanding leaders of the loyal Socialists, criticized both the over-optimistic assessment of submarine warfare and the chancellor's refusal to come out for a peace of moderation, and demanded political reform in Prussia. On 4th and 6th July Erzberger joined the fray in the central committee of the Reichstag. Erzberger declared the submarine warfare a failure and suggested that the Reichstag should pass a resolution declaring itself in favour of a peace without annexations.

The result was shattering, and Erzberger initiated one of the most extraordinarily muddled political affairs in Germany, the so-called crisis of July 1917. In it aspects of foreign and domestic policy were inextricably mixed – submarine warfare, war aims, war credits, reform of the franchise in Prussia and of the political structure in the Reich, the fear of the Majority Socialists that they would be out-manoeuvred by the left-wing USPD. The main results of the crisis were a vote of the Prussian ministry for equal franchise in Prussia (11th July), Bethmann Hollweg's fall (12th July), the Peace Resolution of the Reichstag (19th July), and the uncertain beginnings of parliamentary government in the Reich.

Since early 1917 Bethmann Hollweg had been in favour of reforming the Prussian franchise in order to appease the working class and to strengthen the majority leaders of the SPD against the USPD. His success in carrying a reluctant Prussian ministry with him on 11th July was, however, only a Pyrrhic victory for it incensed the high command against him even more. Ludendorff and Hindenburg hurried to Berlin and threatened to resign, if equal franchise and the Peace Resolution, as drafted by an informal committee of the three new majority parties (Centre, Progressive Party, and Majority Socialists), were accepted. The Kaiser, on the other hand, did not want to come to a decision without consulting the Crown Prince, whose views were consistently reactionary and Pan-German. The Crown Prince took the unusual step of consulting the leaders of the political parties. To his surprise, he found that all of them, except the Progressives, were against the chancellor: the Conservatives and National Liberals thought he made too many concessions to the Left and was too weak in pursuing vigorous war aims; the Centre Party and the SPD felt he had become a liability because of his ambiguity over war aims and because it was in any case he who had led Germany into war.

The Crown Prince presented his father triumphantly with the result of his soundings. In a hectic atmosphere of confusion the Kaiser dismissed the chancellor, before Ludendorff and Hindenburg had time to storm in and confront their sovereign with their resignation. When they arrived, the Kaiser merely told the surprised generals: 'He is gone.' Thus Bethmann Hollweg was felled by a strange alliance. That he had incurred the enmity of the conservative and military element could not astonish anybody. But the Centre Party and the SPD turned against him at the very moment when he had adopted their programme of domestic reform

Two faces of Peace. **Above:** *Gloom in Berlin – its streets full of demobilized men.* **Left:** *Jubilation in London at the signing of the Treaty of Versailles*

The Defeat of the Central Powers

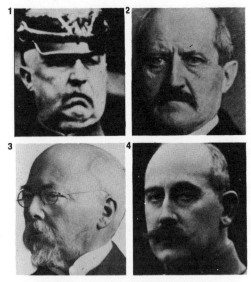

Above: *The men in the middle while Imperial Germany crumbled. 1. Ludendorff, who rose from Quartermaster General to virtual military dictator. 2. Michaelis, the civilian front-man. 3. Hertling, his conservative successor. 4. Prince Max of Baden, last Imperial chancellor*

and relatively moderate war aims. On the other hand, if Bethmann Hollweg had gained the support of a Centre-Left coalition in the Reichstag and had fought for his new moderate line, defying the will of his sovereign, it would have amounted to revolution by German standards.

Some German historians recently make out Bethmann Hollweg's fall as the beginning of parliamentary democracy in Germany. But it was a very curious beginning, for the 'victory' of parliament had been achieved in a most haphazard and unexpected way, over a chancellor who was about to collaborate with the new majority. Bethmann Hollweg's fall solved nothing. The parliamentary parties were unable even to nominate any successor, let alone one who would suit them. Out of continuing malaise and confusion emerged the new chancellor, Georg Michaelis, a non-political non-entity, who only ushered in the dictatorship, barely veiled, of Ludendorff and the army high command. On 19th July the Reichstag did vote the Peace Resolution, after it had been modified and accepted by Ludendorff and Michaelis. But even the Peace Resolution, if looked at in the light of the general concept of German war aims in the First World War, was far from being a straightforward and honest declaration of the intention to return to the *status quo.* Whatever propaganda value it may have had was destroyed by the new Chancellor's notorious rider that he accepted it, 'as I understand it', and by the violent reaction of the Right against the 'weaklings' in Parliament.

The immediate effects on the constitution of Bethmann Hollweg's fall were negligible. The committee of the majority parties, which had drafted the Peace Resolution, did keep together during sessions of the Reichstag. But their tortuous debates on reforms only demonstrated painfully their utter inability to reach any positive conclusions at all, except for the pious wish for some modification of the constitution which would create the impression that a peaceful parliament had come to power. Far from being revolutionaries, they wanted neither the republic nor genuine democracy, nor a peace on the basis of the *status quo,* so long as Germany was powerful. In the days following the signing of the Treaty of Brest Litovsk coupled with the apparently successful German offensive in the west, even the outwardly moderate appearance of the new majority faded away. The Treaty of Brest Litovsk was carried in the Reichstag by a huge majority. Only the USPD voted against it; the Majority Socialists meekly abstained.

The only perceptible result of the whole crisis of July 1917 in political terms was the appointment of one Prussian minister, two secretaries and two under-secretaries of state in the central government of the Reich, who were representatives of the political parties in favour of domestic reforms. Even these modest gains, however, were more than offset by the fact that most of the freshly appointed party politicians stood on the conservative wing of their respective parties, and by Ludendorff's unproclaimed yet effective dictatorship. If parliamentary government started in Germany in July 1917, it did so only in outward appearance; more than ever before parliament served as a fig leaf for a regime which remained autocratic and undemocratic.

Fear of the Socialists

The progress of the Russian Revolution and its repercussions on Germany made that delicate and artificial structure less and less tenable. The influence of radical groups on the left, in particular of the USPD and, to a lesser extent, of the Spartacists (the followers of the Socialist Karl Liebknecht), increased amongst Berlin workers and sailors of the fleet, whereas the Pan-German element rallied in the *'Vaterlandspartei'* (Fatherland's Party), a combination of various right-wing organisations. Under the leadership of Tirpitz, the proto-Fascist element in Germany thus found its first powerful organizational form.

While war went on without hope of peace, the increasing polarization of political forces in Germany weakened the empire from within. The extreme Right was dissatisfied with the formal concessions to the moderate Left, and mistrusted them as a halfway-house to revolution and Socialism. The extreme Left rightly feared that small political changes were only made in order to forestall genuine reform and to patch up the regime, which remained intrinsically undemocratic.

In autumn 1917 these tensions came into the open for the first time when they brought about the downfall of Michaelis. For all his political inexperience, the new chancellor was intelligent and open-minded enough to realize that Germany would never be able to conclude peace on the basis of German war aims. This is why he demanded, at a crown council on 11th September, that Germany give up claims on Belgium in order to facilitate peace. His act of political independence and relative shrewdness did not endear him to the generals or the Kaiser, who dropped him at the first opportunity.

During the days of the Peace Resolution there had been an agitation among sailors of the German battle fleet in favour of a peace without annexations, which they found most strongly championed by the USPD. There were arrests and courts-martial among the sailors; five were

Illustration from British propaganda leaflet dropped over the German lines: a jovial German prisoner savouring one of the delights of captivity

German plenipotentiaries, displaying white flags, arrive in the French lines to hear Allied armistice conditions. The surrender was later concluded in Foch's railway coach

sentenced to death, two of them actually executed. When he was attacked in the Reichstag by leaders of the USPD on 9th October, the chancellor created the impression that he wanted the USPD banned. The majority parties, no friends of the USPD, baulked, because they feared the chancellor would turn next against them. In a turbulent session of the Reichstag the parties clearly expressed their lack of confidence in the chancellor. The high command did nothing to keep Michaelis, and the Kaiser did not want to antagonize the parties who once again had to vote the war credits. Less than three weeks later, Michaelis was dismissed.

His successor was Count Hertling, seventy-three years old and half-blind. He had been one of the leaders of the Centre Party in the Reichstag before the war, and Bavarian prime minister since 1912. Although he was a party politician, he had not been nominated by the majority parties, nor was he their representative. Hertling, a staunch Conservative throughout his political life, was willing enough to appease the majority parties by agreeing to their political demands, especially the reform of the franchise in Prussia, but he definitely felt himself to be the servant of the crown, not dependent on parliament. The reform of the Prussian franchise made, indeed, no progress under Hertling. As for German war aims, the high command succeeded in committing the new chancellor to their programme. The Germans decided to pin down the Austrians, with whom they were at that time conferring, to staying in the war until all the German war aims had been accomplished. The conference with the Austrians took place on 6th November.

One day later the Bolsheviks seized power from the Provisional Government in Russia.

From now on the domestic situation in Germany became hopeless. While internal polarization continued, the parliamentary façade disguising Ludendorff's dictatorship had been strengthened a little by appointing Payer, a south German Progressive, vice-chancellor under Hertling. The south German, non-Prussian element apparently was destined to save the Reich from its impending catastrophe. But following developments showed that the ostentatious prominence of south German Liberals and Catholics at the top of the government did not alter the policy of the Reich. When President Wilson announced his Fourteen Points for peace, January 1918, Hertling rejected them out of hand, whenever they affected Germany. During the great strike of the metal workers in Berlin, which spread to other German cities in the last days of the same month, the government did not budge an inch to meet the political demands of the striking workers. In spring 1918 even the pretence had gone that parliament ruled Gemany, when Erzberger, during the debate on the Treaty of Brest Litovsk, declared it perfectly compatible with the demands of the Peace Resolution, following in fact the guidance of Ludendorff.

Thus, the German Reich drifted unreformed into its next political crisis in the autumn of 1918. Now Germany was even more exhausted, her people even more embittered than in summer 1917. The last illusions about submarine warfare, the miracle in the east and German offensives in the west were definitely gone. The Allied counter-offensives of July and August 1918 had, at last, destroyed even Ludendorff's hopes of winning the war.

In autumn 1918 the end of the war came,

where it had started—in the Balkans. At the end of September the Allied Army of the Orient smashed the Macedonian front and Bulgaria sued for peace. Turkey was tottering, Austria-Hungary was on the brink of political decomposition. It was only a matter of weeks before Turkey and the Dual Monarchy would leave the war. However firm the German front might keep in the west, Allied troops would be able to invade Germany from the south and south-east within a few months.

On 28th September, when Ludendorff learned of Bulgaria's collapse, it was not difficult for him to foresee the chain of future events. It was only now that he admitted military defeat.

Yet, typically, Ludendorff, the military dictator at the end of his tether, blamed chiefly the forces of the Left for the coming débâcle. On 1st October he explained to his closest collaborators in the army high command, why it had become necessary to have a parliamentary government. He had asked the Kaiser, 'to include also those circles in the government to whom we owe chiefly our present situation. . . . Let them now make that peace, which has to be made. Let them now bear the consequences of what they have done to us'. The famous 'stab-in-the-back' legend was invented as a face-saving device by Ludendorff even before Germany laid down her arms.

In a desperate effort to save what could be saved Ludendorff ordered parliamentary government into existence in Germany and coupled it with the demand for an immediate armistice, before the German Western Front broke as well. Hertling, honest Conservative to the last minute, refused to become chancellor of a parliamentary government and resigned. After a few days of hurried search, the last imperial chancellor was found. Again, he was not chosen by the now 'victorious' parliamentary forces. He was not even a party politician or a member of any parliament, but the member of a south German dynasty, Prince Max von Baden, who had a reputation for liberal leanings. There was a certain historic logic and justice in this choice: Baden and her Grand Duke had been Bismarck's most important agent and ally in 1870-71 when he was founding the Second Empire. Now, in its dying days, a member of the same dynasty was called to save the Reich and the monarchy. Prince Max was half successful. It was beyond his power to keep the monarchy, because the Kaiser stubbornly clung to his throne, when hardly any one, even in Germany, wanted him there any more. But he managed to preserve the Reich and its social order by a most liberal interpretation of the Constitution and by ingeniously handing over power on 9th November to another south

'Work ceased in shops and offices, as news of
the armistice spread . . . Omnibuses were
seized, and people in strange garments
caroused on the open upper deck. A bonfire
heaped against the plinth of Nelson's column
in Trafalgar Square has left its mark to this
day. Total strangers copulated in doorways
and on the pavements. They were asserting
the triumph of life over death. The celebrations ran on with increasing wildness for
three days, when the police finally intervened
and restored order.' A.J.P.Taylor: *English
History, 1914–1945* (OUP)

Above: *After the armistice, German troops
enter Berlin, accompanied by cheering
children.* **Left:** *French soldier's reunion
with his wife and child.* **Below:** *Armistice
celebrations in Paris.* **Right:** *London goes
wild. Buses became carnival-floats as
Londoners celebrated the end of war*

The Road to Armistice

German, Friedrich Ebert, the conservative SPD leader from Heidelberg.

On 3rd October Prince Max was appointed chancellor. Payer remained vice-chancellor, while several members of the Reichstag joined the cabinet, among them Scheidemann for the SPD and Erzberger for the Centre Party. The political changes were institutionalized on 26th October, when the Reichstag voted an amendment to the constitution, which made the chancellor dependent on the confidence of parliament. Parliamentary government had been formally introduced for the first time in the Reich. Germany, by a simple vote in parliament, had become a *'Volksstaat'*, although for the time being the monarchy remained.

Yet political progress had not been spontaneous. It had only been effected with one eye to threatening unrest from inside and another to certain military defeat from outside. Wilson had made it clear in his note of 23rd October that he did not want to conclude a negotiated peace with the old autocratic regime in Germany. The constitutional changes of 26th October were the German response. With disturbing flexibility Germany had suddenly donned parliamentary democracy in the hope of some tactical advantage; less than fifteen years later she was to divest herself of this alien political structure, the adoption of which, after all, had not apparently brought the advantages Germany had hoped for.

Once Ludendorff had made up his mind that the war was lost, he was in a hurry. He got his way without serious trouble on the domestic front by hastily installing the Prince Max-Scheidemann-Erzberger government on 3rd October. But it was more difficult to convince the political leadership of the urgent need for an armistice. Their reluctance was understandable, because the majority parties did not want the responsibility for having surrendered. It was only after hard pleading on the part of Ludendorff and a special session of leading members of the Reichstag on 2nd October to whom an officer of the general staff explained the catastrophic military situation, that the political leadership gave in once more to the pressure of the generals. On 3rd October 1918 the new government under Prince Max officially asked for an armistice.

'November criminals'

Even in the hour of defeat Germany tried to make the best of a bad situation. The note asking for an armistice also indicated Germany's willingness to conclude peace on the basis of Wilson's Fourteen Points, and it was addressed not to the Allies, Great Britain and France, but to the United States. Wilson's Fourteen Points,

The Defeat of the Central Powers

scorned only nine months ago, now became the saving plank for the Reich. The choice of the American President as addressee of the German note was a very clever move, because it appealed to his ambition to bring peace to the world.

Meanwhile, fighting went on, submarine warfare as well as the battles on land. The German armies, retreating under pressure on the Western Front, practised the policy of 'scorched earth'—systematic destruction —on French and Belgian soil. At Wilson's demand Germany made an end to submarine warfare, but protested that she had done nothing contrary to international law on her Western Front. At the last minute, the armistice demanded by Germany seemed to be in danger. In his third note to Germany of 23rd October, Wilson had pointed out that the only form of armistice acceptable to the United States and the Allied powers was one which would make it impossible for Germany to renew hostilities. Now Ludendorff brusquely reversed his position again. He suddenly found that Germany's military position turned out not to be so gloomy as he had first thought, and it would be better for Germany to perish than conclude peace on dishonourable terms. Ludendorff spoke for a certain segment of Germany's political leaders, who toyed with the idea of a last-minute *levée en masse* for the defence of the Fatherland to the last ditch. Even Walter Rathenau joined the chorus in demand for an end worthy of *Götterdämmerung*. A phrase went round, which Goebbels was to take up one generation later in a similar situation: 'Better an end in terror than terror without end!'

This time it was the civilian government that resisted the temptation of a heroic demagogic gesture. Collective suicide was not practical policy for a nation of sixty-five million people, as one minister put it. Ludendorff was relieved of his post on 26th October and thus happily escaped the formal responsibility for concluding the armistice. He fled abroad incognito to hibernate in neutral Sweden, in wait for better times, in which he could stage his comeback. Ludendorff's successor was yet another south German, General Groener. Hindenburg remained as formal head of the German army.

Whatever doubts may have lingered in German minds about the necessity of laying down arms, they were definitely destroyed by events inside and outside Germany. On 27th October Emperor Karl of Austria-Hungary threw up the sponge and announced to the German Kaiser his intention to sue for peace. Austria-Hungary fell apart, and so did her army. On 3rd November Austria signed an armistice which put her roads and railways at the disposal of the Allies. Germany lay practically open to invasion through Bohemia and Tyrol into Silesia, Saxony, and Bavaria. To wage war on foreign soil was one thing, to have the destructions of modern warfare on sacred German soil was another.

This explains why the spontaneous, quasi-revolutionary movement of soldiers and workers to end the war started at the periphery of the Reich, in Bavaria and Saxony. It became even more urgent for the ruling groups to avoid a crushing defeat in the west and to effect an orderly retreat into the Reich. This alone could prevent a genuine social revolution.

But some kind of revolution was already in the offing when on 29th and 30th October sailors of the battle fleet refused to join in a last naval battle. From then on there existed in Germany two competing movements for ending the war quickly, an official one from above and a popular one from below. The official one sought an early armistice in the hope of preserving the political and social *status quo*. It was supported by approximately the same kind of alliance that had supported the war: the army high command, the bureaucracy, industrialists, and the majority of the Reichstag. The popular one hoped, by ending war through revolutionary pressure, for the establishment of democracy and—very vaguely—of some kind of socialism. Although the movement from above had started earlier, on 28th September, Wilson's delaying tactics resulted in the movement from below overtaking the official one. The revolutionary upsurge reached Berlin and its culminating point on 9th November, the armistice was concluded near Compiègne only two days later.

The victory of the German revolution was more apparent than real. Even the democratic wing of the parliamentary establishment was not rewarded for its self-effacing loyalty to the Reich. After Erzberger had played Ludendorff's game and signed the armistice on 11th November 1918, he and his friends were denounced 'November criminals' by the extreme Right. Erzberger himself was murdered in 1921, less than twelve years before the Weimar Republic was strangled by the same political forces who had dreamed first of Germany's bid to become a world power and then to stage national suicide when they saw they had miserably failed.

The Treaty of Versailles

The Germans surrendered to the Allies on 11th November 1918. Seven months later they signed the Treaty of Versailles, accepting new frontiers and stern penalties. During those seven months the victorious powers debated, both openly and secretly, every aspect of the future of Germany. Was it to be split up into small, separate states? Was it to be crippled economically? Was it to be deprived of territory? Was it to lose its empire in Africa and the Pacific? Was it to be prevented from ever having a powerful army, navy, or air force again? These were some of the questions on which every public figure, and most private people, held strong opinions, and argued over during the seven months between the military cease-fire and the signature of the treaty.

Yet the peace conference did not decide all of these issues. Many had been determined beforehand. During the war itself each side had worried continuously over the post-war settlement. Every nation had its dreams, its hopes, its secret agreements, and its publicly proclaimed aspirations. France was pledged to take back the provinces of Alsace and Lorraine which Germany had annexed in 1870. Great Britain was determined to absorb as much of the German colonial empire as possible. As early as 1915 Italy had been promised Austrian, Turkish, and German territory in return for entering the war on the side of the Allies. Serbia was promised parts of Bosnia and Albania; Russia was promised Constantinople; the Jews were promised a 'National Home' in Palestine; the Arabs were promised independence from the Turks; and the Poles were offered the restoration of an independent Poland.

Woodrow Wilson, the President of the United States, had, in January 1918, offered *all* subject peoples the right of 'self-determination'. This gave an impetus to many ambitious nationalists, to Czechs and Slovaks, to Serbs, Slovenes, and Croats, to Ukrainians, to the Baltic peoples, to the Rumanians inside Austria, to the Armenians inside Turkey, indeed, to a hundred groups, however small, who saw in 'self-determination' a chance, however slim, of statehood. Even the young Vietnamese Communist, Ho Chi-Minh, asked the Paris Peace Conference to liberate his people from the 'curse' of French imperial rule. But most of the small nationalities, like Ho Chi-Minh's, were doomed to be disappointed. Wilson's idealism shone like a beacon to the dispossessed; but to the French and the British, with their large empires and many subject peoples, and

with their own hopes of territorial gain, 'self-determination' was a theme to be dampened down wherever it conflicted with their own ambitions.

The 'war for human liberty'

Wilson believed that the war was the 'final war for human liberty'. He therefore wished to infuse the peace treaties with his own concept of liberty. For him, the central issue was that of national dignity: the right of people to be independent, with secure frontiers and unavaricious neighbours. When he spoke to Congress in February 1918 Wilson made it clear that, in his and the American view: 'Peoples are not to be handed about from one sovereignty to another by an international conference or an understanding between rivals and antagonists. National aspirations must be respected; peoples may now be dominated and governed only by their own consent. "Self-determination" is not a mere phrase. It is an imperative principle of action, which statesmen will henceforth ignore at their peril.'

Great Britain and France had little faith in self-determination. As a vague, idealistic liberal concept, they approved it in their public utterances, but during the heat of battle they had to consider other pressures besides liberal sentiment. At various moments in the war the Allied position was precarious. New allies had to be found. But neutrals do not easily agree to join in a war which they see to be one of terrible carnage, both on land and sea, involving the suspension of peaceful trade and industry, hardships in daily life, and, above all, the ever-present risk of defeat, occupation, humiliation, and national ruin.

The pledges made during the war had thus one dominating purpose, to persuade the uncommitted and the uncertain that it was in their full interest to support the Allied cause. Once that support had been forthcoming, the Allies could hardly go back on their promises. Where they did so, as in the case of Italy, they created a sense of grievance which had widespread repercussions. Italy had been promised, by Great Britain, France, and Russia, a share in any partitions of Turkish or German territory in Africa and the Near East. She was promised also the Austrian provinces of the Trentino, the South Tyrol, Gorizia,

Right: 'We Germans in foreign lands protest against the seizure of our property' —protest in Berlin against the treaty. Germany had to agree to the sale of German property in Allied countries

The Defeat of the Central Powers

and Istria, the Dalmatian coast and control over Albania. But most of these promises were unfulfilled. Albania became fully independent. The Dalmatian coast vent to Yugoslavia. Great Britain and France kept all Germany's African colonies for themselves, and gained all the benefits of the Turkish collapse. At the peace conference all Italy's protestations were in vain. Although she emerged from the peace treaties with her territory enlarged, she had become an unsatisfied nation, anxious to see a further revision of the treaty frontiers. Within a few years Mussolini was exploiting this sense of deprivation. He demanded the fulfilment of what Italy had been promised. But immediately the peace conference ended the world sought only to be done with alarms and crises, wars and arguments. At Paris, from January to June 1919, any claim could be made with impunity, for the six months of the conference was essentially a period when every nation pressed for as much as it dared to claim, and urged its claims with passion. But once the treaties were signed, any call for revision was made to seem an incitement to aggression, and the word 'revisionist' quickly became synonymous with 'troublemaker', even when the power demanding revision was a former ally.

In one case the war-time pledges could be easily ignored. For in 1917 the Russian Bolsheviks renounced the secret treaties and declared that they would not accept any of the territorial gains promised to Russia. As a result, the Anglo-French promise of Constantinople to the Tsar could lapse. But even so, the strategic waterway from the Black Sea to the Mediterranean was not to return easily into Turkish hands. From 1918 to 1924 the 'Zone of the Straits' was occupied by an Allied force, and for six years a British High Commissioner was the effective ruler of the former Turkish capital. Only the military successes of Kemal Ataturk made it possible for Turkey to retain Anatolia intact, and, although deprived of all her Arabian, Syrian, and Mesopotamian territory, to survive as a robust national state.

The spoils of war

The secret treaties were not the only complications confronting the peace-makers when they reached Paris. Territory had changed hands at every stage of the war, and it proved difficult to dislodge claimants who were already in possession of what they claimed. During the conference Woodrow Wilson criticized the Australian Prime Minister, William Hughes, for insisting that Australia should keep control of German New Guinea, which Australian troops had occupied as early as 1914, within a month of the outbreak of war. Did Hughes really intend, questioned Wilson, to flout the opinion of the civilized world by annexing territory? Would she let it be said that she took part of the German empire as the spoils of war? Was Australia proposing to make a profit out of Germany's defeat, to impose her rule on aborigines, to take over valuable mineral rights, to extend her sovereignty as far north as the equator? To all of which Hughes replied acidly: 'That's about it, Mr President.'

The Australians were not alone in insisting upon the maxim of 'what we have, we hold'. Japan pressed vigorously for control over the Chinese port of Tsingtao, a German possession which the Japanese had occupied in 1914, after a month's hard fighting. To the chagrin of the Japanese, the peace-makers forced them to return Tsingtao to China. As a result, the Japanese, like the Italians, felt cheated of a 'fruit' of victory, and looked for a chance to redress the balance. The Japanese invasion of China in 1937, like the Italian invasion of Albania in 1939, was in part a legacy of the frustrations of the peace conference. Other victor nations were less frustrated. No one dislodged the New Zealanders from German Samoa, the South Africans from German South West Africa, the British from German East Africa, or the Australians from New Guinea. Even the Japanese were allowed to retain control of most of Germany's vast Pacific island empire, which included over two thousand islands and covered three million square miles. Great Britain and France partitioned the German territories of Togoland and the Cameroons between them; the Italian occupation of the former Turkish Dodecanese Islands was made more secure; Cyprus, occupied by Great Britain under nominal Turkish suzerainty for forty years, was transformed into a permanent British possession. The areas of Turkey conquered in October 1918 remained firmly under the controlling hands of their conquerors – the British in Palestine, Transjordan, and Iraq, the French in Syria and Alexandretta, the Arabs in the Yemen and the Hejaz.

Such were the many territorial gains which were made during the course of the war. Most were criticized at the peace conference, particularly by Woodrow Wilson. But all survived the peace-making, and became a part of the new world order. Some even survived the Second World War; South Africa still rules German South West Africa; Australia still controls German New Guinea; New Zealand still occupies Samoa. Japanese control over Germany's Pacific Islands north of the equator passed, in 1945, not back to Germany, but on to the United States, the third imperial power to come into possession of the islands and atolls which stretch in a broad band out from the coast of China across three thousand miles of ocean.

The new map of Europe

When the victor powers met in Paris they had to consider more than the promises which each ally had made, and the existence of new possessions which particular Allies had every intention of making permanent. They had also to take into account the people who, even before the war was ended, had proclaimed themselves independent. There were many such people, each determined to keep the territory which they claimed as the basis of permanent national frontiers. Thus the Czechs and Slovaks had declared their complete severance from Austria-Hungary before the Austro-Hungarian surrender; and they were insisting upon a new state which would include the historic frontiers of Bohemia, thereby placing over two million German-speaking people within their proposed territory. The South Slavs had also declared themselves an independent state, ruling over territory in which were to be found Hungarian, Italian, and Austrian minorities. These frontiers were of course still open to negotiation and change. But the Allies had for most of the war given support to all enemies of Austria-Hungary. In April 1915 they promised the future Serb state a part of the Adriatic coast and the Austro-Hungarian provinces of Bosnia and Dalmatia. They might strive to create 'ideal' frontiers, excluding minorities and satisfying conflicting claims and promises, but since the same territories were often occupied by different nationalities this was no easy matter, even from the point of view of abstract national geography.

As a result the frontiers in existence before the conference met tended to become the permanent ones. The pre-conference frontiers had been established by the subject peoples of Germany, Austria-Hungary, and Turkey. As the conference was made up of those who had fought these three empires in the war, the likelihood was that the pre-conference frontiers would, in the main, be allowed to survive – as indeed they were. When the Paris Peace Conference met a new map of Europe had already come into existence, drawn by new nations upon the ruins of the German, Austrian, and Turkish empires. The victor nations did not redraw the old map of Europe; instead, they fussed and argued over the new one. The conference obtained many marginal modifications; but the map which they saw in January was in most respects the same one which they were to agree upon in June.

Woodrow Wilson obtained some verbal changes in the war-time decisions. Instead of Germany's colonies being described as integral parts of the empires which conquered them, they were given the name of 'Mandates'. The new owners were then

The World after Versailles

Below: Europe before 1914, dominated by Germany, Austria-Hungary, and Tsarist Russia. **Right:** Europe after the peace treaties. From the Austro-Hungarian empire have come three new states, Austria, Hungary, and Czechoslovakia. The Austrian-ruled South Slavs have joined the old kingdoms of Montenegro and Serbia in the new state of Yugoslavia. Italy and Rumania have gained large chunks of Austro-Hungarian territory. Poland has been re-formed from Russian, Austrian, and German territory. Amongst other changes, France has regained Alsace-Lorraine, and Greece has gained Bulgaria's Aegean coastline.

Bottom left: The break-up of the Turkish empire. Turkey kept only her northern, Turkish, territory. In Arabia the Hejaz and Yemen (and later Saudi-Arabia) became independent Arab kingdoms. **Bottom right:** What happened to Germany's colonies

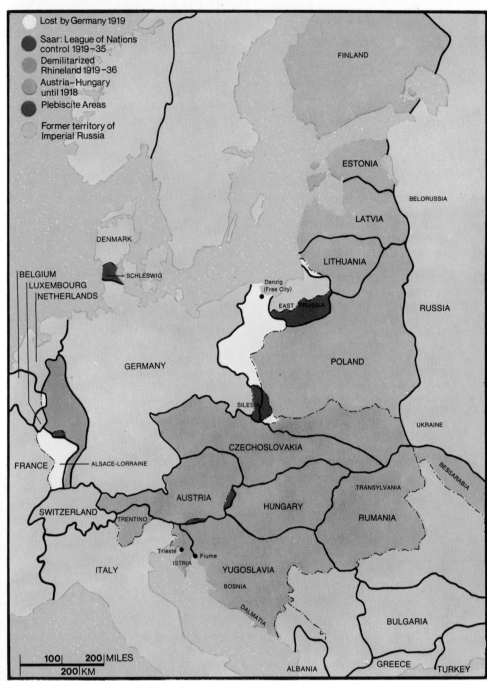

Lost by Germany 1919
Saar: League of Nations control 1919–35
Demilitarized Rhineland 1919–36
Austria–Hungary until 1918
Plebiscite Areas
Former territory of Imperial Russia

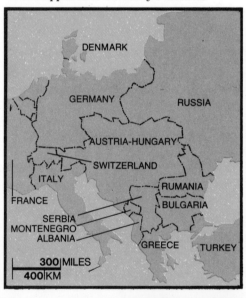

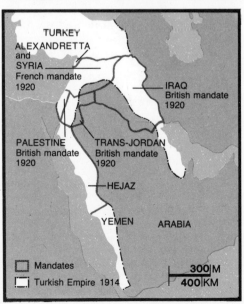

Mandates
Turkish Empire 1914

Loss of German overseas possessions

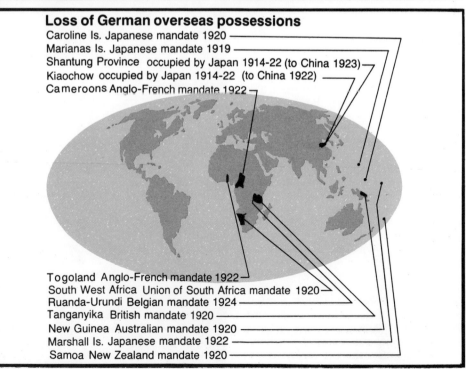

Caroline Is. Japanese mandate 1920
Marianas Is. Japanese mandate 1919
Shantung Province occupied by Japan 1914-22 (to China 1923)
Kiaochow occupied by Japan 1914-22 (to China 1922)
Cameroons Anglo-French mandate 1922

Togoland Anglo-French mandate 1922
South West Africa Union of South Africa mandate 1920
Ruanda-Urundi Belgian mandate 1924
Tanganyika British mandate 1920
New Guinea Australian mandate 1920
Marshall Is. Japanese mandate 1922
Samoa New Zealand mandate 1920

in theory responsible to the League of
Nations, a world organization designed
by Wilson to secure permanent peace and
the just settlement of all international
disputes, and which was transformed in
1945 into the United Nations. But the
'Mandates' remained securely under the
powers who obtained them. The new
League of Nations was also to safeguard
the rights of minorities: and, this being
so, minorities were allowed to remain in
Poland, Czechoslovakia, Rumania, and
Yugoslavia. Yet when persecution and discrimination began, the League was power-
less to intervene.

Conditions of armistice

The main barrier to a well-balanced treaty
was built before the peace conference.
When Germany, Austria, Bulgaria, and
Turkey each surrendered, they did so by
signing armistice agreements with the
Allies. These agreements contained sets
of conditions, on the acceptance of which
the Allies agreed to stop the fighting. The
armistice conditions were severe, and had
to be carried out immediately. As a result
of this, long before the Paris Peace Conference began, they had irrevocably altered
the map, and the mood of Europe. Much of
what politicians later denounced and historians criticized in the peace treaties was
in fact created by the armistices.

The atmosphere at the time of the draft-
ing of the armistice agreements was an
atmosphere of war: the guns still roared,
the fighting was still savage, the outcome
was still uncertain. The terms were therefore harsh. It was necessary for the Allies
to ensure that the armistice agreements
were not tricks, brief halts engineered to
obtain the breathing space necessary for
recuperation and renewed fighting. Each
armistice agreement was intended to make
absolutely certain that the fighting capacity of the enemy was utterly broken. This
they did. As a result, when the Paris Peace
Conference opened, Germany, Austria, Bulgaria, and Turkey had already been treated
with a severity which was both inten-
tional, effective, and by its nature largely
irrevocable.

The first armistice to be signed was with
Bulgaria, on 29th September 1918. The
Bulgarians were desperate for peace: their
armies in Greece and Serbia were in retreat, while a large corps of Bulgarian
mutineers was marching on Sofia, the
capital. They therefore agreed to evacuate
all Serbian and Greek territory which their
troops still occupied, and which they had
hitherto claimed for themselves. A month
later, on 30th October, the Turks, two-
thirds of whose Palestinian army had been
taken prisoner, the remnant of which was
in retreat, signed their armistice. They
were obliged to accept the use of their

FABRIQUE DE PRODUITS CHIMIQUES
R. GUICHARD
47 48 49 50 RUE DUBOURDIEU BORDEAUX

Below: 'The Surrender of the German
High Seas Fleet' — part of the armistice
agreement. *Above:* Advertisement for a
bleach, typical of French feelings. Clemenceau uses it to wash out the Kaiser's crimes

*American signatures to the Treaty of
Versailles (the American representatives
signed it but Congress refused to ratify
it). Wilson's utopian idealism left its
mark on the final form of the treaty*

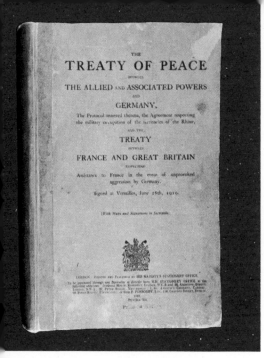

The transcript of the treaty sold in
Great Britain. The British negotiators,
in particular Lloyd George, had tried
to temper the French demand for revenge
and a crippled Germany—but in vain

British press poster after Versailles.
The press had been a powerful agitator of
patriotic emotion during the war. Its
power to whip up hatred was less welcome
to the men trying to create a fair peace

The stamp of a new nation—Czechoslovakia,
which had declared its independence
from the Habsburg empire during
the last months of the war, and to
whom the treaty gave generous frontiers

Left: Versailles, 28th June 1919. Painting by Sir William Orpen. German delegates (with their backs to the artist) Johannes Bell (seated) and Hermann Müller (standing) sign the treaty under the eyes of (seated, from left to right) Henry White, Lansing, Wilson, Clemenceau, Lloyd George, Bonar Law, Balfour, and Milner. **Right:** *Whitehall: a crowd waits for news of the treaty*

capital, Constantinople, as an Allied naval base; to surrender the Black Sea port of Batum and the oilfields of Baku, both of which they were occupying; and to surrender all garrisons in Arabia, the Yemen, Syria, Mesopotamia, and Cilicia. The surrender of these garrisons was to be followed by immediate French and British occupation; the obvious prelude to political control.

On 3rd November the Austrians, beaten back on the Italian front, signed an armistice which was similarly decisive. Italian troops were allowed to occupy the territory which they claimed, and the Allies obtained the right to move at will along every line of communication throughout the Austro-Hungarian empire. The new nations had already proclaimed themselves. The Allied presence provided them with a firm guarantee that they would survive. They were thus two months old before the peace conference met.

'Reparation for damage done'

But it was towards Germany that the armistice was most severe. The total collapse of Bulgaria, Turkey, and Austria was taken for granted once the Allied military advances had begun. But Germany was believed to be stronger and more resilient than her allies. On 12th September, speaking at Manchester, Lloyd George, the British prime minister, insisted that 'Prussian military power must not only be beaten, but Germany herself must know that'. With the Allied armies reinforced by fresh, enthusiastic troops from the United States, and the German trench fortifications in Flanders broken, such a double aim seemed feasible. But a month later Sir Douglas Haig, the commander-in-chief of the British forces in France, sounded a warning note. On 19th October he returned to London from France to tell the war cabinet that all was not well. The American army, he claimed, 'is disorganized, ill-equipped, and ill-trained. . . . It has suffered severely through ignorance of modern war'. As for the French army, it seemed 'greatly worn out'. The British army, he concluded, 'is not sufficiently fresh or strong to force a decision by itself' and the war would go on, in Haig's view, well into 1919. All this pointed to the need for a severe armistice, which would deprive the Germans of any opportunity of hitting back once they had agreed to surrender. The war cabinet felt that if the armistice terms were comprehensive, they would serve as 'pledges for the fulfilment of our peace terms'.

On 11th November the fourth and last armistice of the war was signed. Germany accepted total defeat. Lloyd George's conditions were fulfilled: all military power was broken, and the German people were presented with a document both comprehensive and severe. Of the thirty-four clauses, the following give a picture of how much Germany had to agree to, not to make peace, but merely to bring an end to war.

Immediate evacuation of the invaded countries — Belgium, France, Luxembourg, *as well as Alsace-Lorraine*.

Surrender in good condition by the German Armies of the following equipment—
    5,000 guns
    25,000 machine guns
    3,000 trench mortars
    1,700 aeroplanes
5,000 locomotives and 150,000 wagons, in good working order, with all necessary spare parts and fittings, shall be delivered to the Associated Powers. . . . 5,000 motor lorries are also to be delivered in good condition.

To surrender . . . all submarines at present in existence . . . and
    6 battle-cruisers
    10 battleships
    8 light cruisers
    50 destroyers of the most
        modern types

Evacuation by the German Armies of the districts on the left bank of the Rhine. These districts . . . shall be administered . . . under the control of the Allied and United States Armies of Occupation.

By signing this armistice, Germany abandoned all hopes of territorial gain; even of retaining Alsace-Lorraine. She also agreed to accept a four-word financial condition: 'Reparation for damage done.' The interpretation of what was meant by these four words proved a major point of argument during the treaty negotiations, and poisoned the international atmosphere for twenty years, giving Adolf Hitler a powerful lever against the western democracies. The four words that the Germans, at the moment of defeat, accepted without discussion, provoked the most bitter discussion of the inter-war years.

The idea of 'reparation for damage done' was not a new one. Germany had imposed such reparations on France in 1870, even though the fighting took place on French soil. Nor was there any doubt that the 'damage done' by Germany in France and Belgium was severe. Some small damage was done by Allied aeroplanes dropping bombs on Germany, but this was offset by the many more German air-raids, particularly on London, and by the German naval bombardment of undefended seaside towns on the east coast of Great Britain. The amount of damage done by Germany was immense, and little of it was made necessary by the dictates of war. In German-occupied France nearly 300,000 houses were completely destroyed. Six thousand factories were stripped of their machinery, which was sent to Germany. The textile mills of Lille and Sedan were smashed. Nearly 2,000 breweries were destroyed. In the coal mines around Roubaix and Tourcoing 112 mineshafts were blown in, and over 1,000 miles of underground galleries flooded or blocked. During their retreat, the Germans burned and looted on a massive scale, destroying over 1,000 miles of railway line, blowing up 1,000 bridges, looting thousands of houses, and stripping churches. During the four years of occupation the Germans took away half a million cows, half a million sheep, and over 300,000 horses and donkeys. These were the acts of vandals. And in the military sphere too it was France and Belgium, not Germany, that suffered most. After the war the French had to pull up over 300,000,000 metres of barbed wire, and fill in over 250,000,000 cubic metres of trenches. Much agricultural land was rendered useless because so many shells had fallen on it; some remained dangerous for many years because of unexploded shells and the leakage of poison gas from unused canisters.

The British were equally determined to secure reparation. The Germans had torpedoed five hospital ships during the war; an action which inflamed the public and created an atmosphere in which the demand for high reparations flourished. The German U-boats had taken a cruel toll of merchant shipping. They had sunk thousands of unarmed ships mostly without warning. The British lost nearly 8,000,000 tons of commercial shipping; and many of the crews had been left to drown. Among the Allied nations, France, Italy, and the United States lost between them 2,000,000 tons of shipping; among neutrals Norway lost over 1,000,000 tons, Denmark, Holland, and Sweden over 200,000 tons each. No nation had been spared the deliberate terror of submarine war. The Allies had not, of course, sat idly by to watch these losses. The blockade of Germany was rigorously enforced, and as a result as many as 500,000 German civilians probably died of starvation. But in the moment of victory these victims of war's all-pervading cruelty did not seem to compensate for what the Allies had suffered. Nations use victory to settle the debt which they feel is owed to them; the other side of the account is ignored. The demand for reparations combined the physical damage that had been done with the psychological need to have tangible evidences in the form of gold, that the 'enemy' would make amends. Rudyard Kipling, who had lost a son in the fighting, expressed this feeling in a bitter poem (he wrote it in 1917 when the reparations issue was being discussed in public):

These were our children who died for our lands: they were dear in our sight.
We have only the memory left of their home-treasured sayings and laughter.
The price of our loss shall be paid to our hands, not another's hereafter.
Neither the Alien nor Priest shall decide on it. That is our right.
But who shall return us the children?

That flesh we had nursed from the first in all clearness was given
To corruption unveiled and assailed by the malice of heaven
By the heart-shaking jests of Decay where it lolled on the wires—
To be blanched or gay-painted by fumes— to be cindered by fires—
To be senselessly tossed and retossed in stale mutilation
From crater to crater. For this we shall take expiation.
But who shall return us the children?

'Squeeze the German lemon'

During the British general election held before the treaty negotiations began, the public cried out for heavy reparations. Almost every responsible politician tried to soften the public mood. But one, Sir Auckland Geddes, told an eager audience in London that 'we would squeeze the German lemon till the pips squeaked' and even Lloyd George, tired out by the strains of electioneering, told a large meeting at Bristol that the Germans 'must pay to the uttermost farthing, and we shall search their pockets for it'. These were not his true views. He had begun, from the day the war ended, to adopt a moderate stance. He feared most of all that if Germany were humiliated too much by the treaty it would go Bolshevik, and not a single clause would be fulfilled, nor a penny of reparations paid.

In secret Lloyd George pressed his colleagues to adopt a certain leniency towards Germany, to send food to the starving millions in Germany and Austria, to think in terms of a peace free from vindictive clauses. But the public did not approve of such liberal sentiments. As Winston Churchill, who was then minister of munitions, recorded: 'The Prime Minister and his principal colleagues were astonished and to some extent overborne by the passions they encountered in the constituencies. The brave people whom nothing had daunted had suffered too much. Their unpent feelings were lashed by the popular press into fury. The crippled and mutilated soldiers darkened the streets. The returned prisoners told the hard tale of bonds and privation. Every cottage had its empty chair. Hatred of the beaten foe, thirst for his just punishment, rushed up from the heart of deeply injured millions. All who had done the least in the conflict were as

might be expected the foremost in detailing the penalties of the vanquished. . . . In my own constituency of Dundee, respectable, orthodox, life-long Liberals demanded the sternest punishment for the broken enemy. All over the country the most bitter were the women, of whom seven millions were for the first time to vote. In this uprush and turmoil state policy and national dignity were speedily engulfed.'

Like Lloyd George, Churchill urged a moderate treaty. He too feared that harsh terms would force Germany into the Bolshevik embrace. But when Lloyd George reached Paris in January 1919, he found the French determined to obtain maximum reparations, and the sternest possible treaty.

At the peace conference Lloyd George was handicapped by the moods and utterances of the general election: the anti-German moods, continuing fierce, meant that in any moderation he urged he had to keep one eye on his own public opinion, which, when it felt that he was exercising undue leniency, could, and did, protest; while the bravado of the election speeches, vivid in French minds, meant that when Clemenceau, the French prime minister, urged severity he could always refer to Lloyd George's public statements as support for his own contentions. Although Lloyd George tried, throughout the negotiations, to control the evolution of the treaty, he began from a position of weakness from which he was unable fully to recover, and which obstructed many of his efforts to obtain a viable peace.

At Paris Lloyd George was the leading advocate of moderation. He sought to act as if he were above national antagonisms. He tried to be the arbiter of conflicting passions. But the House of Commons would not let him forget in what tone the election had been fought. When it became clear the reparations were being calculated on the basis of what Germany 'could' pay, rather than on what she 'ought' to pay, 370 Coalition Conservatives sent a petulant telegram, reminding him of what they and the electorate expected, and ending: 'Although we have the utmost confidence in your intention to fulfil your pledges to the country, may we, as we have to meet innumerable inquiries from our constituents, have your renewed assurance that you have in no way departed from your original intention?'

Within a week of receiving this challenge Lloyd George returned to London, and on 16th April 1919 rebuked the House of Commons for its impatience. He reminded MPs that he was having to settle the fate of five continents in Paris; that ten new states had to be brought into existence; that territorial, military, and economic questions had all to be decided upon, and that 'you are not going to solve these problems by telegram'. He reminded them that, even if mistakes were made, the League of Nations, which was being set up as part of the treaties, would be able to make the necessary adjustments later. He made it clear to his critics that if they insisted upon terms which the League were ultimately to judge unduly severe, those terms would be modified. For an hour Lloyd George cajoled, threatened, appealed to, and won over his listeners: '. . . and when enormous issues are dependent upon it, you require calm deliberation. I ask for it for the rest of the journey. The journey is not at an end. It is full of perils, perils for this country, perils for all lands, perils for the people throughout the world. I beg, at any rate, that the men who are doing their best should be left in peace to do it, or that other men should be sent there. . . .

'We want a stern peace, because the occasion demands it. But its severity must be designed, not to gratify vengeance, but to vindicate justice. . . .

'[It is the duty of] statesmen in every land, of the Parliaments upon whose will those statesmen depend, of those who guide and direct the public opinion which is the making of all—not to soil this triumph of right by indulging in the angry passions of the moment, but to consecrate the sacrifice of millions to the permanent redemption of the human race from the scourge and agony of war.'

Lloyd George as moderator

Lloyd George returned to Paris. But although he appeared to have convinced the House of Commons that leniency was needed, he was unable to convince the French. They made some concessions, abandoning their hopes for the creation of a separate Rhineland State, and for a Polish annexation of Danzig, but in general French desires were met. The treaty as finally published had a vindictive tone about it.

In a memorandum which Lloyd George wrote while at the peace conference, he declared that his concern was to create a peace for all time, not for a mere thirty years. A short peace might be possible if punitive measures were taken against Germany. But unless the Germans were placated, they would go Bolshevik, and Russian Bolshevism would then have the advantage, according to Lloyd George, 'of the organizing gift of the most successful organizers of national resources in the world'. The initial shock of war would pass, and then, wrote Lloyd George: 'The maintenance of peace will depend upon there being no causes of exasperation constantly stirring up either the spirit of patriotism, of justice, or of fairplay to achieve redress. . . . Our Peace ought to be dictated by men who act in the spirit of judges sitting in a cause which does not personally engage their emotion or interests, and not in a spirit of a savage vendetta, which is not satisfied without mutilation and the infliction of pain and humiliation.'

This was utopian. Yet Lloyd George was convinced that he was right. He went on to criticize all clauses which might prove 'a constant source of irritation', and suggested that the sooner reparations disappeared the better. He deprecated putting Germany under alien rule, fearing that by doing so 'we shall strew Europe with Alsace-Lorraines'. He emphasized that the Germans were 'proud, intelligent, with great traditions', but that those under whose rule they would be placed by the treaty were 'races whom they regard as their inferiors, and some of whom, undoubtedly for the time being, merit that designation'. These arguments fell upon

The German delegation to Versailles. They had been forced to accept not only humiliating losses, but blame for causing the war

The Defeat of the Central Powers

stony ground: the French could not understand Lloyd George's sudden conversion to what they could only describe as imbecilic pro-Germanism. Clemenceau replied icily to Lloyd George's memorandum that 'if the British are so anxious to appease Germany they should look . . . overseas . . . and make colonial, naval, or commercial concessions'. Lloyd George was particularly angered by Clemenceau's remark that the British were 'a maritime people who have not known invasion', and countered angrily that 'what France really cares for is that the Danzig Germans should be handed over to the Poles'.

These bitter exchanges were symptomatic of a growing rift in Anglo-French relations. For Clemenceau, the treaty was perhaps the best chance that France would have of designing effective protection against a Germany that was already almost twice as populous as France, and must therefore be shown by deliberate, harsh action that it would not pay to think of revenge. For Lloyd George, the treaty was an opportunity to arbitrate for Europe without rancour, and to create a continent whose future problems could be adjusted without malice. Great Britain, by supporting the League of Nations, would be willing to help in the process of adjustment. Clearly it was the treaty that would first need to be altered: Lloyd George did not fear that. For him the treaty was not a sacred instrument but a pliable one. It was obvious from his comments while it was being drafted that he would not be content to see it become the fixed rule of the new Europe.

At Paris Lloyd George opposed strenuously, but in vain, the transfer to Poland of areas predominantly German. His protest was a forceful one, yet it was not forceful enough to break the French desire for the reduction of German territory.

'I am strongly averse,' Lloyd George wrote, 'to transferring more Germans from German rule to the rule of some other nation than can possibly be helped. I cannot conceive any greater cause of future war than that the German people, who have certainly proved themselves one of the most vigorous and powerful nations in the world, should be surrounded by a number of small states, many of them consisting of people who have never previously set up a stable government for themselves, but each of them containing large masses of Germans clamouring for reunion with their native land. . . . [These proposals] must, in my judgement, lead sooner or later to a new war in Eastern Europe.'

The Treaty of Versailles was not as vindictive as France had hoped; nor was it as moderate as Lloyd George desired. It was certainly not as utopian as Woodrow Wilson envisaged. A study of its clauses reveals great concern for detail, an often

punitive attitude, and very little account taken of the personal hardships and political discontent which the clauses might arouse. Thus Austria and Germany were forbidden, by Article 80, to unite, a future possibility which the British foreign secretary, A.J.Balfour, had regarded as a sensible solution which might soften the blow of defeat. Article 100 took away from Germany the entirely German city of Danzig, turning it into an isolated 'Free City' within the 'customs frontiers' of Poland, and depriving all its citizens of German nationality. Under Article 118 Germany renounced all her 'rights, titles and privileges . . . whatever their origin' outside Europe. This meant that even purely commercial concessions, freely negotiated before 1914, were lost. All Germany's colonies were taken from her, together with 'all movable and immovable property in such territories'; even the property of the German school at Shanghai was given to the French and Chinese governments. All pre-war German trading agreements were declared null and void, and the patient, innocent, costly efforts of German businessmen in China, Siam, Liberia, Egypt, and Morocco were entirely undone. Article 153 laid down that 'All property and possessions in Egypt of the German empire and the German states pass to the Egyptian government without payment'; and Article 156 transferred to Japan all German state submarine cables in China 'with all rights, privileges, and properties attaching thereto'.

The military clauses were as one would expect. The size of the German army was limited to 100,000 men. Germany was forbidden to import any arms or munitions. Compulsory military training was abolished. Universities and sporting clubs were forbidden to 'occupy themselves with any military matters'. They were specifically forbidden to instruct or exercise their members 'in the profession or use of arms'. All fortresses in the Rhineland were to be dismantled. At sea, Germany was restricted to six battleships, six light cruisers, twelve destroyers, and twelve torpedo boats. She was allowed not a single submarine. Her naval personnel were limited to 15,000 men. All warships under construction were to be broken up.

One clause was a dead letter from the moment it was signed. Under Article 227 the Allies announced the trial of the Kaiser 'for a supreme offence against international morality and the sanctity of treaties'. He was to be tried by five judges, an American, an Englishman, a Frenchman, an Italian, and a Japanese. It was their duty 'to fix the punishment which it considers should be imposed'. Despite the British public's keenness to 'hang the Kaiser', Lloyd George felt that such a solution was a

mistake. When, therefore, the French began to demand the return of the Kaiser from Holland, Great Britain refused to give France any support. The Kaiser remained safely in exile, cultivating his garden.

'War guilt'

The most controversial clause in the Treaty of Versailles was Article 231, the notorious 'War Guilt' clause against which successive German governments argued in vain, and which even many British politicians thought too extreme. The Article read: 'The Allied and Associated Governments affirm and Germany accepts the responsibility of Germany and her allies for causing all the loss and damage to which the Allied and Associated Governments and their nationals have been subjected as a consequence of the war imposed upon them by the aggression of Germany and her allies.'

How had this clause come into being? What made the Allies so anxious to get Germany to accept responsibility for 'all the loss and damage'? Why was 'the aggression of Germany' referred to so bluntly?

The War Guilt clause originated before the end of the war. The Supreme War Council, meeting under the leadership of Clemenceau and Lloyd George at Versailles on 4th November 1918, had drafted a note to President Wilson, explaining to him the need for reparations from Germany. The note began: 'They (the Allied governments) understand that compensation will be made by Germany for all damage caused to the civilian population of the Allies by the invasion by Germany of Allied territory. . . .'

As Germany had never denied invading Belgium, Luxembourg, or France, this clause was a fair one: a statement of acknowledged fact. But someone at the meeting pointed out that as the clause stood, while Germany would have to pay for damage done from the Channel to the Vosges, there was nothing in this wording to enable any economic compensation to go to the non-continental allies, the USA, India, Australia, Canada, or even Great Britain, and that certainly the Dominions, who had played such a large part, not only in providing men but also materials, would resent their exclusion from money payments. The clause would therefore need redrafting. The new draft cut out 'the invasion by Germany of Allied territory' and replaced it by 'the aggression of Germany'. Aggression was a word that could cover a much wider sphere: it could be claimed that every aspect of war costs was involved. But it was also a condemnatory word. Invasion had been admitted; aggression had not. The justification in German eyes for the invasion was self-defence; aggression was a word pregnant with moral dis-

Below: Germany's air fleet reduced to firewood—wooden propellers being sawn up after the planes were destroyed as the Treaty demanded

approval, allowing of no subtle interpretation; spelling, all too clearly, guilt.

Lloyd George's personal assistant recalled in 1931: 'I remember very distinctly discussing with L.G. the interpretation to be put upon the question of "restoration" or "reparations". His view was—"We must make it clear that we cannot charge Germany with the costs of the war. . . . She could not possibly pay it. But she must pay ample compensation for damage and that compensation must be equitably distributed among the Allies and not given entirely to France and Belgium. Devastated areas is only one item in war loss. Great Britain has probably spent more money on the war and incurred greater indirect losses in, for instance, shipping and trade, than France. She must have her fair share of the compensation."

'He then instructed me to prepare a form of words. . . . I did so. . . . I remember thinking, after the draft had been taken by L.G., that it did not cover adequately the point that compensation was due to all the Allies. . . . I therefore revised it to read "damage to the civilian population of the allies by the aggression of Germany by land, air and sea".'

Thus was written the clause which most aggravated Anglo-German relations between the wars, made the task of appeasement with Germany so difficult, and made the Germans feel that, whatever concessions Great Britain made, whatever gestures of friendship she volunteered, in reality her policy was dictated by an explicit belief in German guilt.

The reparations clauses were the most often criticized part of the treaty. Yet the total demand of £24,000,000,000 was whittled away at a series of international conferences, until finally, at Lausanne in 1932, reparations were brought to an end. Great Britain was paying off her war debts to the United States until the end of the 1960's; Germany stopped paying for the war over forty years ago.

The new frontiers

The treaty's most lasting clauses were those which created new frontiers. They were also the most defensible. Many were established, not by Allied insistence, but as a result of plebiscites, in which the inhabitants were asked where they wanted to go. The plebiscites in East Prussia resulted in the province remaining entirely German. In two border areas of Austria the inhabitants voted to remain Austrian. The people of the Saar, after fifteen years of League of Nations supervision, voted to return to Germany, and were reincorporated into Hitler's Reich—this, his first territorial acquisition, was a positive gain made possible only because of the treaty which he was always denouncing. In Silesia the plebiscite results were indecisive, and this rich industrial region was therefore divided between Germany and Poland. The Danes of Schleswig voted to leave Germany: the sole plebiscite to go wholly against the German interest.

The lands which Germany lost outright were Alsace-Lorraine, a German war gain of 1871, and territory in the east which went to Poland. Germany had helped destroy Polish independence at the end of the 18th century, and had annexed Polish territory during the three partitions: now that territory was returned to the recreated Polish state, and with it a corridor which gave Poland an outlet on the Baltic Sea. The Germans later made a great fuss about this corridor. But its inhabitants were mostly Poles, and Poland, after over a hundred years of subjugation, was entitled to a measure of security.

The greatest frontier changes arose from the disintegration, in the last weeks of the war, of the Austro-Hungarian empire. Czechoslovakia had proclaimed itself an independent state; the treaties gave it a generous frontier. Yugoslavia did likewise, fulfilling the Slav dream of a new South Slav kingdom; and the Allies were again generous, though not allowing the port of Fiume to go to the new state. The Poles obtained territory from both Germany and Austria, and the Allies, eager to see Poland as a bastion between Bolshevik Russia and the west, encouraged an eastern frontier drawn very much at Russia's expense. Yet even here, Lloyd George was reluctant to see Poland push too far east or west, and

The Defeat of the Central Powers

PEACE AND FUTURE CANNON FODDER

1940 CLASS

PEACE TREATY

The Tiger: "Curious! I seem to hear a child weeping!"

Prophetic cartoon—Clemenceau leaving the conference, which had met to ensure peace, hears one of the children it had doomed to become a soldier in 1940 weeping at his fate

British control, four independent states—Iraq, Transjordan, Saudi Arabia, and the Yemen. A fifth state, the Jewish national home in Palestine, remained under British rule for nearly thirty years, but was then partitioned between Arabs and Jews. The Armenians, too, were given a state of their own: but when the Turks destroyed it in 1922 the Allies did nothing to intervene. Over a million Armenians were murdered by the Turks during the war; but the Allies made no efforts to protect them after the war. Soviet Russia provided a haven for some, in the Soviet Republic of Armenia. Others fled to Europe as refugees, stateless, without a national patron.

Out of the collapse and Bolshevization of Russia emerged four new independent states—Finland, Latvia, Lithuania, and Estonia. The Caucasian states also declared their independence; and the Allies encouraged Georgia to maintain its sovereignty. But when Stalin sent Soviet troops into the land of his birth, the Allies accepted the fall of Georgian independence.

The German problem

Of the four empires shaken by the war only the German empire survived; it had lost one eastern province and restored Alsace-Lorraine to France, but its sovereignty was secure. As the Kaiser had abdicated before the end of the war, Germany became a republic; but alone of the defeated nations it preserved its territorial unity. The treaty restrictions were irksome, but made no serious inroads on national sovereignty, and, if anything, provided a powerful stimulus to German nationalism. The Treaty of Versailles may have created Hitler; it also preserved as a state the country in which he was to make his mark.

Neither the defeat of Germany nor the Treaty of Versailles solved the German problem. Germany was still the country with the largest population in Europe. The day after the treaty was signed Austen Chamberlain, the chancellor of the exchequer, wrote to his sister: 'So Peace is signed at last . . . Will the world have rest? . . .

'Even the old Germany would not, I think, rashly challenge a new war in the West, but the chaos on their Eastern frontier, and their hatred and contempt for the Poles, must be a dangerous temptation. . . .'

If the First World War was fought to prevent Germany from creating hegemony in Europe it failed. Germany was weakened, but not so weakened that it could not rise within a generation to threaten the balance of world power once again. The Empires of old Europe had been swept away. The provisions of the victorious peacemakers failed to fill the vacuum—millions had died in vain.

it was left to Polish military action, not any Allied treaty, to secure parts of the Ukraine, Belorussia, and Lithuania for the new Poland. To Rumania the Allies allotted the primarily Rumanian districts of Austria-Hungary, principally Transsylvania. Bulgaria, an 'enemy' power, lost her outlet on the Aegean Sea, which went to Greece; but her full independence, secured from Turkey not ten years before the war began, was not tampered with. Austria lost only one basically Austrian province, the South Tyrol, which went to Italy. The nation with the most convincing grievance was Hungary; large communities of Hungarians found themselves inside Czechoslovakia, Rumania, and Yugoslavia.

But once again, Hungarian independence was secured, and although Hungary extended her frontiers when in alliance with Hitler, she returned to her 1919 borders in 1945; and they survive to this day.

What was the balance sheet of the peace treaties? Out of the collapse of the Austro-Hungarian empire emerged three independent states—Czechoslovakia, Hungary, and Austria; and three states gained from the old empire territory filled mostly with their fellow-countrymen—Poland, Yugoslavia, and Rumania. Two states, Austria and Hungary, felt deprived of territory; the other four were well satisfied.

Out of the collapse of the Ottoman empire emerged, after a brief period of

Balance Sheet of the First World War

Below: Civilian casualties directly or
indirectly caused by the war. *Right:*
Military casualties. *Far right:* Comparison
of casualties per day with previous wars

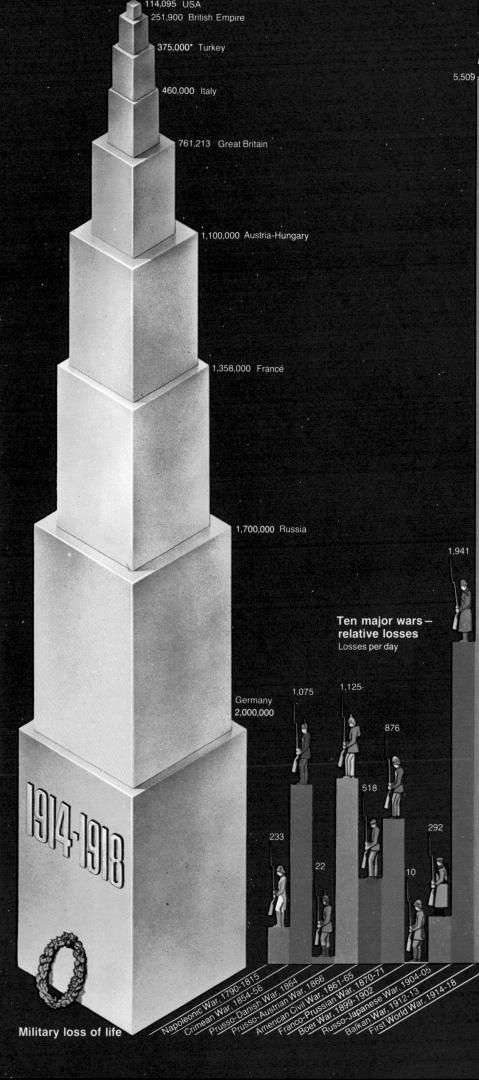

114,095 USA
251,900 British Empire

375,000* Turkey

460,000 Italy

761,213 Great Britain

1,100,000 Austria-Hungary

1,358,000 France

1,700,000 Russia

Germany
2,000,000

1914-1918

Military loss of life

CIVILIAN LOSSES

Deaths at sea
and in air raids
100,000*

Belgium 30,000

Rumania 800,000
Germany 812,296
Serbia and Austria 1,000,000

Russia 2,000,000*

Deaths due to famine,
disease and starvation
except where otherwise stated

Massacre of Armenians,
Syrians, Jews and Greeks 4,000,000

Deaths from Spanish influenza 6,000,000*

* at least

Civilian loss of life

Ten major wars —
relative losses
Losses per day

5,509

1,941

1,125

1,075

876

518

292

233

22

10

Napoleonic War, 1790-1815
Crimean War, 1854-56
Prusso-Danish War, 1864
Prusso-Austrian War, 1866
American Civil War, 1861-65
Franco-Prussian War, 1870-71
Boer War, 1899-1902
Russo-Japanese War, 1904-05
Balkan War, 1912-13
First World War, 1914-18

WORLD WAR 11

WORLD WAR II

Introduction

Most people who lived through the Second World War see it in rather simplistic terms. Hitler, Mussolini and Tojo started the war; they attacked the democracies; we gave them better than we got; and Germany, Italy and Japan got exactly what they deserved. Thirty years after the war ended one can afford to take a less emotional look at the greatest war in all history and examine its causes, course and results with a more critical eye. In history there are few genuine villains and even fewer genuine heroes. Interest in the war has increased in recent years, especially among those to whom it is only a distant memory and to those who were born after the war was already part of history. Interest is growing too among historians, for only now are documents being made available which cast new light on the once seemingly simple story of the good guys defeating the bad guys.

It can no longer be argued that Hitler, and Hitler alone, caused the war in Europe, any more than it can be argued that an unprovoked Japan started the war in the Pacific. Both Germany and Japan were provoked by the Western powers. The Germany of the Weimar Republic was a creation of the First World War. Born of defeat and humiliation, it reluctantly commanded the support of its people as long as the economy of Germany maintained its equilibrium. At least twice during the early Weimar years the régime was almost toppled, and was propped up only with the help of those who were yearning for the return of the Kaiser and the stability of Wilhelmine Germany.

By 1933 the Weimar Republic was wholly discredited, blamed both for the Treaty of Versailles, which shackled German ambitions in Europe, and for the Great Depression, neither of which it could have done much to avoid. When Hitler threw off the constitutional bonds of the Weimar régime, he did so with the consent of most people in Germany. Hitler promised jobs and an end to the humiliating terms of Versailles. And Hitler provided jobs, less than five per cent of which had anything to do with arms manufacture or the build-up towards war. He also eradicated civil liberties and most political rights, and soon after his takeover began his active harassment of the Jews, most of whom began to leave Germany in great numbers. All this was viewed with a certain equanimity by the Western powers, Great Britain and France, and with a certain disinterest on the part of the United States. Britain and France did not begin to stir until Hitler's troops re-occupied the Rhineland in March 1936, which was supposed to remain demilitarized according to the terms of the Treaty of Versailles. At this stage France alone had the capability of moving into the Rhineland and if she had done so, Hitler would have withdrawn rather than face a confrontation. But France, without Britain's support, lacked the will. From this moment on Hitler knew that the Western democracies could be pushed. While the newly constructed Luftwaffe and Condor Legion practised against the Spanish in their civil war at the invitation of General Franco, Hitler planned to rewrite the Treaty by force and threats.

As Britain rearmed, at a faster rate than Germany, producing planes such as the Hurricane and Spitfire, France's will to resist German threats crumbled during the years of the Popular Front. Only France believed in upholding the letter of the Treaty, and with her will shaken, Britain had no interest in supporting certain clauses in the Treaty which she no longer believed were just, or those which she had never really supported at all. It was the French in 1919 who insisted that a union or *Anschluss* between Austria and Germany be forbidden. When Hitler marched the Wehrmacht into Austria in March 1938, Britain and France complained but did nothing. The annexation of the Sudetenland of Czechoslovakia was another matter. But Hitler argued that the people there were German-speaking and wanted union with Germany, which was true. Neville Chamberlain, the Prime Minister, had no intention of going to war for the Sudetenland, and the Munich Conference of September 1938 sealed the fate of the Sudeten Germans and Czechoslovakia itself. Britain was unready for war and needed more time to rearm. Although it is now known that if Britain and France had resisted and if Germany had been forced to invade, the German General Staff would have overthrown Hitler, for they knew that in 1938 Germany was equally unready for an all-out conflict. When Czechoslovakian integrity was abandoned, the Western powers relinquished all claim they might have had on influence in Eastern Europe for all time. From 1938 onwards it would be Russia and Germany who would decide the fate of Eastern Europe.

The occupation of the rump of Czechoslovakia in March 1939 was a decisive moment for the West. Now it could no longer be argued that Germany only wanted to bring Germans in Central Europe 'heim ins Reich'. Millions of Slavs were unwillingly wedded to Germany, and Hitler's long-term goal of a German empire in the east was clear. The will of Britain stiffened after the Prague spring of 1939, and with it the resolve of France, who was pledged to defend most of the states of Eastern Europe. Britain allied with Poland, and when Hitler began to ask for German Danzig, then under the League of Nations authority as a free city, Britain began to talk to the nation that she feared as much as Germany, the Soviet Union. Stalin saw at once that Britain's tentative steps towards a Russian alliance were not sincere, and soon began covert negotiations with her bitter ideological enemy, the Third Reich.

The Molotov-Ribbentrop Pact shocked the world and made the partition of Poland possible. It did not necessarily mean that the Second World War was inevitable. Although Britain and France reluctantly declared war against Germany in September 1939 they did not wage it in defence of Poland. Neither did they wage it after Poland fell. The legacy of appeasement which itself was the legacy of the First World War still hung like a pall over the West. That war seemed to have accomplished nothing, and with so many millions of lives lost, it seemed insane to repeat the error. It was this disillusionment and horror of war which blinded the West to the threat Hitler posed. But as long as he confined his activities to Eastern Europe, the West was more or less content to let him have his way. Only when he turned his attentions to Norway and Denmark, and subsequently to the Low Countries and France, did the war begin in earnest.

Even in May 1940 there were still those in Britain who favoured a policy of accommodation with the New Order. The appointment of Churchill rather than Lord Halifax as the replacement for Chamberlain as Prime Minister put an end to any thought of appeasement. Come what may, Britain, if necessary alone, would continue the war despite Hitler's pleas for peace after the fall of France—which would have guaranteed the British Empire against German aggression and, with Russia still at peace with Germany, ended the war. But the appeasement factor was still present in America and in Britain's policy towards Hitler's ally, Imperial Japan.

As the United States withdrew from overseas commitments after the First World War, she sought to contain Japanese ambitions in the Far East through a policy of mutual limitation of arms and the neutralization of the Pacific. As Germany turned to Hitler partly out of the despair of the Great Depression, Japan turned towards consolidation of her position in Northeast Asia when her greatest market and supplier of raw materials, the United States, sank into the slump. Although Britain and America waxed eloquently about the Japanese takeover of Manchuria in 1931, neither did anything concrete about it. The same was true when Japan expanded into Inner Mongolia, bombed Shanghai and finally, in 1937, invaded China proper. Short of active intervention there was little that either nation could accomplish. Britain was more concerned with rearmament and the containment of Germany. She could not take on Germany and Japan at the same time and hope to win without the support of the United States. Despite Roosevelt's warnings, the United States remained steadfastly isolationist throughout the 1930's. In the election of 1940 both Roosevelt and his Republican opponent, Wendell Willkie, promised not to involve American boys in any foreign wars even after the fall of France. As Japan took over the China coast and moved into French Indo-China, the United States made provisional and thoroughly inconclusive war plans with Britain, Australia and the Dutch, but only took some economic sanctions against Japan. When the Japanese effectively overran what is now South Vietnam in July 1941 the Americans took their most decisive action so far when Japanese assets in the United States were frozen. Britain and the Dutch did the same.

The United States took a bellicose stance against Japan with the full knowledge that this could easily lead to war. True, if Japan attacked Malaya and the Dutch East Indies, which had the natural resources which she required, such as rubber, tin and especially petroleum, without touching the American-owned Philippines, the United States would have been in an awkward position. But, quite deliberately, the Japanese military command, now in charge of the Japanese government when Hideki Tojo became the Premier in October 1941, chose to try to knock out the American Pacific Fleet with one staggering blow. This could not fail to involve America in the war, and of course, the United States declared war against Japan immediately after Pearl Harbour was attacked.

But the United States might have fought in the Pacific alone had it not been for Germany's declaration of war against the United States on 10th December. Hitler did Roosevelt a real favour when he honoured his alliance with Japan. For public opinion in America was all for avenging Pearl Harbour. It did not necessarily follow that isolationist America would support the war in Europe as well. But the decision was taken by Germany. Thus only in December 1941 could it be said that the Second World War actually began. Until that time several not wholly related wars had been going on: Japan was fighting China, Russia fought Finland, Germany fought Poland, and Britain and (after June 1941) Russia were fighting Germany and Italy. The reluctance born of British appeasement in Eastern Europe and Asia, and American isolationism generally, had allowed Germany and Japan to advance as far as they did. Either power could have been stopped far earlier and defeated far more quickly if the West had not tried to bury its head in the sand when war clouds began to loom in the 1930's. As a result, Western Europe lost the world hegemony which it had held for a century or more. Now the banner was passed to the United States and the Soviet Union.

The Second World War was effectively won by those two powers, since it was primarily Russia which defeated Germany and America which defeated Japan. The British impact on the Axis was peripheral after 1941, apart from the significant role the British Navy played in the Atlantic and the Mediterranean. Although the British 8th Army was chiefly responsible for the defeat of the Afrika Korps in the North African desert, and despite the fact that the British cleared Burma of the Japanese before the war came to an end, she could not hope to reap the benefits of the war, won by Russia and America. Without any doubt, Germany would have been defeated by Russia whether or not the Allies invaded Western Europe. Likewise, and to an even greater extent, the United States would have defeated Japan without British and certainly without Russian assistance, since the Soviet Union chose to declare war against Japan only after Hiroshima had been levelled by the atomic bomb.

There are many lessons to be learned from the Second World War, but perhaps the most important is this: the horrors of cities destroyed, mass murder and genocide, atomic warfare, concentration camps, death marches, starvation, occupation and human degradation of an unparalleled nature, all these could have been avoided. In order to avoid the disappointments and tragedy of the First World War, the Western powers tried to ignore what was happening in Europe and Asia until it was almost too late. By trying to pretend that aggression was not really aggression, that events in far-off countries about which they 'knew nothing' did not concern them, by callously ignoring racism and human suffering, the western democracies themselves were forced to suffer. It can only be hoped that this lesson, lost on the generation who did not want to repeat the First World War, is not lost on the generation which does not want to repeat the tragedy and horror of the Second World War.

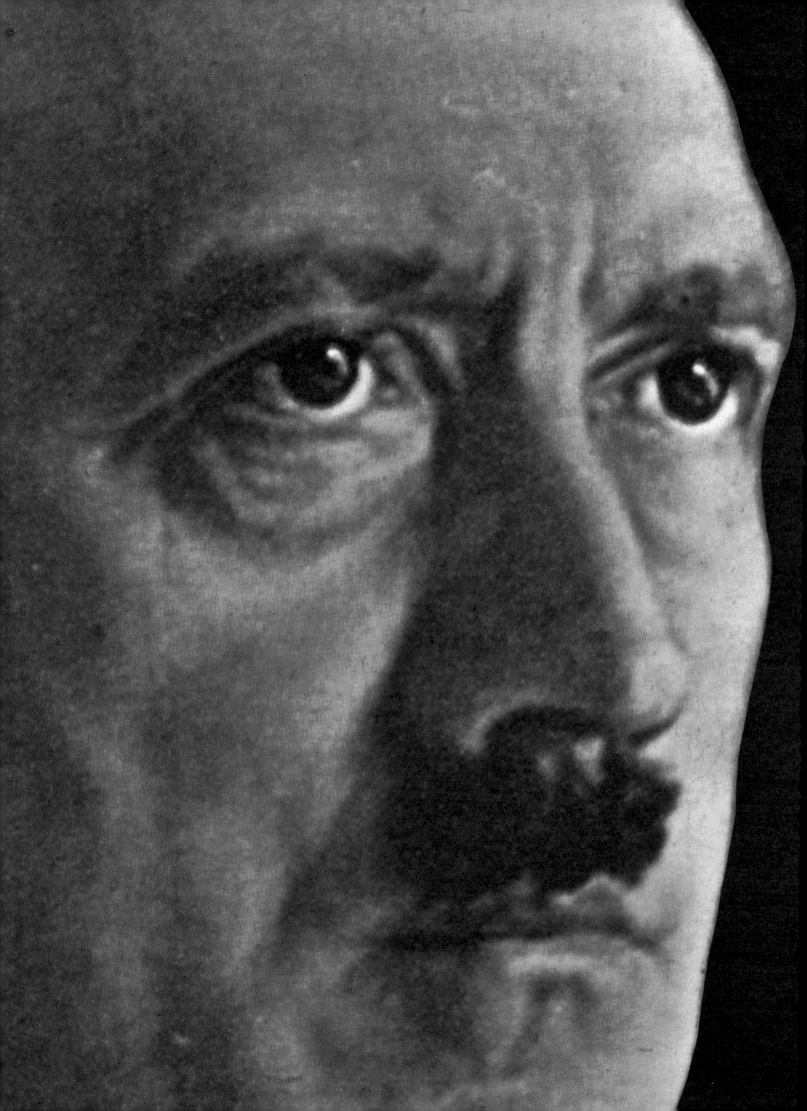

1 THE FRAGILE PEACE

Hitler's Germany

Nazi Germany's attempt to win absolute power within Europe was the mainspring of the Second World War. It was, however, on a grander scale, the continuation of that process by which the National Socialists had won power in Germany itself.

Hitler took office on 30th January 1933 not as dictator of Germany but as head of a coalition government in which the Nazis held only three out of eleven ministerial posts. The paradox of his career up to this point had been the combination of a movement built on a revolutionary appeal with the insistence that he meant to come to power by legal means. But once he had got his foot inside the door, Hitler had no intention at all of being bound by the rules of the conventional political game. He very soon showed that it was the façade of legality, not the revolutionary character of the Nazi movement, which was the sham.

The first step was the decree suspending all guarantees of individual liberty on the excuse that the Reichstag Fire on 27th February 1933 was in fact the sign for a Communist rising. Göring, placed in control of the Prussian police, enrolled 40,000 of the Nazis' strong-arm bands, the SA and the SS, as police auxiliaries. This gave them a legal immunity which they used to the full to arrest and beat up political opponents and Jews. The election on 5th March failed to produce the majority the Nazis had hoped for, but by eliminating the Communist deputies (most of whom were already in concentration camps) and pressuring the other parties, they obtained a clear vote for the so-called Enabling Law (23rd March 1933) which set aside the constitution and for four years empowered the

chancellor, Hitler, to enact laws without parliamentary approval.

In the next few months the Nazis proceeded to carry out a political 'take-over' of Germany for which they coined the phrase *Gleichschaltung,* 'co-ordination'. Their political partners were not asked for their agreement but were ignored and elbowed out of the way. Theirs and all other political parties, as well as the trade unions, were abolished.

This was the Nazi revolution, and it was compounded of three elements. The first was the use the Nazis made of the legal authority to command the resources of the state and its administrative machine. This guaranteed to the Nazis control of the police, the neutrality of the armed forces, and the power, which they exercised without scruple, to dismiss any official suspected of opposition or even lukewarmness towards the new regime. The second was terrorism—not the breakdown of law and order, but something more shocking, its deliberate withdrawal. A free hand was given to the Nazi Stormtroopers to seize persons or property and do what they liked with them. The effect of this terrorism extended far beyond the numbers of those who actually suffered death, injury, or loss of property: it created an atmosphere of menace, a pervasive fear of violence which inhibited any thought of opposition. The compulsive power of terrorism was matched by the attractive power of propaganda drummed out by radio, press, and cinema, proclaiming a national rebirth of Germany. This was the third element. Propaganda produced on this scale and directed with the consummate skill of Goebbels was

something new in politics, and it had a great impact on a people which had suffered for fifteen years from a deep sense of national humiliation. Most important of all was the impression of success which Goebbels' propaganda created: the Nazi band-wagon was on the move and anyone eager for power, position, and jobs (in a nation with six million unemployed) rushed to jump on it.

In every move they made, the Nazis showed the advantage enjoyed by a political movement which refused to be bound by any rules, which did not try to avoid but did everything it could to exploit surprise and shock, and instead of repudiating violence in the streets employed the threat of it to break down opposition. The result was that the stability of a society already weakened by the successive experiences of defeat, inflation, economic depression, and mass unemployment was profoundly shaken. But the Nazis' methods, if they repelled many, also attracted many, especially among the younger generation, who felt a great sense of liberation at the promise of action after years of frustration. 1933 produced a feeling that the future held great possibilities.

The question Hitler had to answer in the summer of 1933 was how far he was prepared to let the revolutionary process continue before calling a halt. Was it to extend to the economic as well as the political institutions of the country? There had been a strong element of anti-capitalism in the Nazis' radicalism and there was now a demand to give expression to this in drastic economic reforms. What Hitler saw, however, was that radical economic experi-

Left: Arresting Communists, Berlin, 1933. The Nazis won popularity as bulwark against Bolshevism. **Right:** Hitler and group of admirers

ments would destroy any chance of co-operation from industry and business to end the depression, bring down the unemployment figures, and start rearming Germany. In July he told a meeting of Nazi provincial governors: 'The revolution is not a permanent state of affairs and it must not be allowed to develop into such a state . . . The ideas of the programme do not oblige us to act like fools and upset everything . . . Many more revolutions have been successful at the outset than have, when once successful, been arrested and brought to a standstill at the right moment.' By the end of the summer Hitler had made it quite clear that he chose close working relations with big business in preference to the Nazi enthusiasts who talked about 'the corporate development of the national economy' and who were now disowned or pushed into obscure positions.

Hitler's own wish, however, to halt the revolution, at least for the time being, encountered opposition in the Nazi movement, particularly in the brown shirt SA. The SA was a genuine mass movement with strong radical and anti-capitalist leanings, and attracted to it all those dissatisfied elements in the Party who felt they had been left out in the cold and who wanted no end to the revolution until they too had been provided for. And the SA did not lack a leader. Its chief of staff, Ernst Röhm, was the most independent of the Nazi leaders, a man who, having started Hitler on his career in politics in Munich, was not at all afraid to speak his mind.

This quarrel over the so-called 'Second Revolution' was the dominant issue in German politics between the summer of 1933 and the summer of 1934, and threatened to split the Nazi movement. In particular, Röhm and the SA leadership, which contained many who had been through the rough school of the Freikorps and were contemptuous of the conservatism of the German officer corps, were incensed at not being allowed to take over and remodel the German army on revolutionary lines.

Hitler, as his subsequent behaviour showed, was as distrustful of the generals and contemptuous of their conservatism as Röhm, but in 1933 and 1934 he needed their support if he was to rebuild Germany's military strength and, more immediately, if he was to secure the succession to Hindenburg as head of state as well as head of the government. On their side, the generals were determined to resist any attempt by Röhm to incorporate the SA in the army and take it over.

The crisis reached its climax at the end of June 1934 when Hitler suddenly ordered the liquidation of the SA leadership on the pretext that they were planning a putsch. The purge, however, extended far beyond the SA. Amongst those summarily shot besides Röhm – all without any pretence of a trial – were General von Schleicher, Hitler's predecessor as chancellor, and Gregor Strasser, once Hitler's rival for the leadership of the Nazi Party. Hitler had not merely connived at murder, but ordered it to be carried out.

The generals, however, were satisfied to see the threat from the SA removed and when President Hindenburg died on 2nd August, there was no delay in announcing Hitler's succession as head of state, with the new title of Führer (leader) and Reich chancellor. The same day the officers and men of the German army took the oath to their new commander-in-chief, swearing allegiance not to the constitution or to the Fatherland, but to Hitler personally.

June 1934 was a major crisis, a crisis of the regime and the acid test of Hitler's leadership. In the weeks preceding the purge (for example, during his visit to Mussolini at Venice) Hitler gave every impression of being anxious and unsure of himself. This was the characteristic period of hesitation and weighing the odds which so often preceded one of his big decisions: equally characteristically, when the decision was made, it startled everyone by its boldness and brutality. Hitler repudiated the so-called 'Second Revolution' but he

did so in such a radical way as to give no comfort at all to those who wanted to see the rule of law restored and a return to the conservative traditions of the German state.

Nazification

In contrast to the tumultuous days of 1932 and 1933 and the crisis atmosphere of the summer of 1934, the next three and a half years, 1934 through 1937, saw political peace in Germany: no more elections, no more purges. This left the Nazis free to get on with the 're-modelling' of German society. Like other totalitarian creeds, Nazism was unwilling to leave any part of German life unorganized or to allow any group or individual to contract out. German men and women were to be as accountable for their thoughts and feelings as for their actions, and no claim of individual conscience was to be allowed to withstand the demands of the Party and the state.

Practice, of course, as in every form of society, totalitarian as well as democratic, was never so consistent as theory. In the first place, it is necessary to distinguish between the lengths to which the Nazis went in enforcing their style of government in the 1930's, during peace time, and in the 1940's, under war-time conditions. It is to the later period, for example, that the extermination camps, slave labour, and 'the final solution' of the so-called Jewish problem belong. There were concentration camps in Germany from the beginning of the Nazi period, but the total number of prisoners at the beginning of the war was roughly 25,000 compared with ten times that number a few years later.

Up to the outbreak of war, Germany was still open to visitors and foreign correspondents in a way in which the Soviet Union has never been, and the Nazis showed themselves surprisingly sensitive to hostile comment from abroad, for example in their dealings with the Churches. This was an issue on which Hitler several times intervened personally to curb the zeal of those in the Party who wished to push

*Left: Burning of 'degenerate' books by Nazi students, 1933. **Right:** Cartoon showing purified German poetry rising from the flames*

their hostility to the Churches to the limit. Accordingly, Nazi practice towards the Churches was confused and inconsistent, marked by fundamental hostility in outlook and much petty local persecution (such as the expulsion of monks and nuns, the closing of churches, the imprisonment of pastors and priests) but still stopping short of the sweeping measures which some of the Party leaders would have liked.

Even setting aside considerations of expediency, it proved more difficult to translate totalitarian control into practice than is always recognized. It took time for Himmler and Heydrich to create the SS which was eventually to prove the most effective instrument for Hitler's purposes. One important reason for this was the clash of rival authorities which was characteristic of Nazi Germany from the very beginning. Its organization was anything but monolithic. After the summer of 1934 Hitler's authority at the top was uncontested, but right up to the top there was a fierce struggle for power. Hitler himself not only possessed no gift for administration; he was instinctively distrustful of creating settled administrative procedures which would limit his own arbitrary power of decision. Difficulties were to be met by emergency action, by creating special agencies, a method which led almost invariably to overlapping and conflict of authority, between ministries, between Party and state, between different Party organizations. Each minister and Party boss fought for his own hand, a situation which strengthened Hitler's own position — since each sought the Führer's favour against his rivals — but reduced the efficiency of operation and control.

Nonetheless, when all this is said, there is no doubt that between 1933 and 1939 the Nazis went a long way towards remoulding German life, not just German politics, on a totalitarian pattern. The key lay with the younger generation. In a speech on 6th November 1933, Hitler declared: 'When an opponent says, "I will not come over to your side", I calmly say, "Your child belongs to us already . . . you will pass on. Your descendants, however, now stand in the new camp. In a short time they will know nothing else but this new community."'

To make sure, a start was at once made on the nazification of the schools and universities. All teachers, from kindergarten to university, were compelled to join the National Socialist Teachers' League and to teach what they were told to. German universities, once famous for their scientific research, now became the homes of racist science. Outside the schools, independent youth organizations (including those of the Churches) were banned and all German boys and girls from the age of six were required to join the Hitler Youth. At eighteen boys were conscripted into labour service and the army, girls into farm and household service. Throughout these impressionable years they were subjected to continued indoctrination in the Nazi faith

To make Nazi propaganda doubly effective and allow no independent voice to be heard, Goebbels was made minister of culture as well as propaganda. This gave him control over all the arts, literature, and the cinema, as well as the press. Nothing could be published without the consent of the Propaganda Ministry.

'Jews not wanted here'
A particular object for attack was anybody or anything Jewish. The Jew, according to Nazi teaching, was the source of all corruption and Germany must be purged of this racial poison, if not yet by physical extermination then by the complete exclusion of all Jews from German life. Jews (defined as anyone with a single Jewish grandparent) were excluded from all official posts (with loss of pension rights), from the professions, including teaching, medicine, and the law, from sport, and the arts. Holiday resorts, restaurants, and hotels were decorated with notices, 'Jews not wanted here', and any Nazi hooligan

could beat up, evict, or rob a Jew with impunity. In 1935 the Nuremberg Laws prohibited marriage or any form of sexual intercourse between Jews and German nationals. Those who sought to escape abroad were only allowed to go after they had been deprived of their assets and property. Finally, after a young Polish Jew, driven off balance by the persecution of his people, had assassinated the German legation secretary in Paris, Ernst vom Rath, a deliberately organized attack (represented as a 'spontaneous' outburst of German anger) was made on Jewish synagogues and businesses throughout the country on the night of 9th-10th November 1938. The perpetrators of the attack went scot-free, while the Jews were fined a billion and a quarter marks and saw the insurance payments to which they were entitled confiscated by the state. This so-called 'Crystal Night' was followed by the forced sale of Jewish businesses and property, their eviction from their houses, wholesale arrests, and conscription for forced labour.

No Jew had any hope of protection by the courts. But it was unlikely that any German had more ground for hope if he became suspected of independent views or got involved in a dispute with state or Party officials. Not content with the *Gleichschaltung* of the judiciary and the ordinary courts, the Nazis set up special courts to try offences against the state, a category which could be enlarged at will. The orders and actions of the Gestapo (*Geheime Staatspolizei*, Secret State Police) were in any case not subject to the law. 'Protective custody' was the term cynically employed for those arbitrarily arrested and sent to concentration camps. One of the significant dates in the history of Nazi Germany was 17th June 1936 when Himmler was able to merge control of the two empires which he had built up, the police and the SS. So was created what German historians call 'the illegal executive', an agency with which the Führer, Hitler, responsible to no one but himself, could brush aside any

The Fragile Peace

limitation at all on his power to act outside or contrary to the law.

Terrorism and the secret police, like propaganda and censorship, were essential parts of the totalitarian society the Nazis were seeking to create. And they produced their familiar accompaniments of informers, persecution, and corruption. For those Germans who did not fall into line but stood out against the pressures to conform (and for all Jews) these were years marked by constant fear, often imprisonment and' brutal treatment, sometimes death. But these people formed a minority and a small one at that. What counted with the majority was the Nazis' success. In a country which had suffered more severely from the Depression than any other in Europe, the Nazis could claim credit for cutting unemployment from six million to less than a million in four years, for raising national production more than one hundred per cent between 1932 and 1937, and for doubling the national income. This reconciled the millions of Germans who had lost, or feared to lose, their jobs to a regime which might have taken away some of their rights but had given them back security.

In addition to security, the Nazis had given the German people back their pride in Germany as a great power. By the plebiscite of January 1935, Germany recovered the Saar. Two months later (March 1935) Hitler repudiated the military restrictions of the Treaty of Versailles, restored conscription, and announced that the German army would be raised to a peace-time strength of over half a million men. A year later (March 1936) German troops reoccupied the demilitarized Rhineland. The deeply felt national humiliation of the defeat and the 'Diktat' of Versailles had been removed, and there is no reason to doubt that the result of the plebiscite which followed (99 per cent voting and 98.8 of these voting in favour) represented overwhelming gratitude and approval for Hitler's restoration of Germany's status as the leading power of Central Europe.

Finally, it must be said that in abolishing the multiplicity of political parties, which had produced only a series of weak coalitions, and replacing them by a single strong government proclaiming national unity in contrast to sectional interests, the Nazis successfully appealed to the most deeply rooted political tradition in Germany, that of authoritarian government.

Right: Poster urging return of Saar— worker heaves open gates of Saar to Nazi Germany. It was Hitler's last stop before resorting to force to reverse the Treaty of Versailles. Opposite: Nazis march past in snowstorm at political meeting near Saarbrücken on 7th March 1935, the day the Saar plebiscite returned the Saar to Germany

Once his power was established, Hitler showed little interest in the details of domestic administration, except when he had to intervene to settle a dispute. His attention was turned more and more to foreign policy and rearmament. The conquest of political power, even the remoulding of German society, were only stages on the way to his ultimate aim, the recreation of German national power, the reversal of the defeat of 1918.

It suited the Nazis in the early years of

their regime when Germany was still unprepared, to conceal this. Hitler never spoke without protesting his love of peace and reproaching the victorious powers of 1918 with the promises they had broken, particularly the promise to disarm. This, however, was the diplomatic equivalent of the tactics of 'legality' which he had practised in Germany before coming to power and was no more reliable a guide than 'legality' to his real aims in foreign policy.

By 1936 there was a change. The re-

Zŭ Deŭtſchland

occupation of the Rhineland (March 1936) was a gamble: Hitler later called it the most nerve-wracking forty-eight hours of his life. But it was a gamble that came off and strengthened his belief that, if he played his cards with skill, limiting the issue at stake in each case, the Western powers would always draw back rather than risk a general war. From the summer of 1936 the political balance in Europe moved sharply in Germany's favour. The outbreak of the Spanish Civil War gave Hitler the opportunity to proclaim with redoubled effect Germany's role as the bulwark of Europe against Bolshevism. Italy, quarrelling with the Western powers over Abyssinia, was drawn into the Berlin-Rome Axis. France, divided by the Popular Front and by the Spanish Civil War, no longer had the will to maintain the system of alliances built up to contain Germany. Great Britain was reluctant to face the possibility of another war. The smaller countries began to gravitate to the new centre of power in Berlin and it was of German power that Hitler now began increasingly to speak.

There is no doubt from the evidence now available that accounts of German rearmament before the war were exaggerated. The programme took longer to produce results than was supposed and even in 1939 had not given Germany the military superiority commonly assumed. Most surprising of all is the fact that nothing like the full capacity of the German economy was devoted to war production before 1942. But the type of war for which Germany was preparing was very different from that which she had lost in 1914-18: it was a *Blitzkrieg,* a series of short campaigns in which surprise and an overwhelming initial blow would settle the issue before the victim had time to mobilize his resources or other powers to intervene. This is the sort of war the German army fought in all its campaigns from 1939 to 1941, and it demanded a quite different pattern of rearmament, not long-term rearmament in depth, involving the whole of the economy, but concentration on a short-term superiority and the weapons which would give a quick victory. How nearly the plan worked can be seen from the history of 1939-41 when Germany's 'limited' rearmament pro-

gramme produced an army capable of overrunning the greater part of Europe and very nearly defeating the Russians as well as the French.

It has often been said that Hitler was an opportunist in foreign policy. This is perfectly true, so far as tactics were concerned: he did not proceed by any timetable or 'blueprint of aggression', but kept his options open until the very last moment. Hitler, however, was able to take advantage of the opportunities offered by the mistakes of others because he alone among the European leaders of the 1930's knew what he wanted to achieve: the others only knew what they wanted to avoid.

Hitler set out the Nazi programme in *Mein Kampf*: not simply the restoration of Germany's 1914 frontiers but the conquest of living space *(Lebensraum)* in Eastern Europe from which the existing populations would be cleared by force and a Germanic empire established on a foundation of slave labour. These views have been treated as the fantasy of an unbalanced mind. But they cannot for that reason be dismissed. For not only did Hitler consistently repeat them in private talk for twenty years, but during the war he put them into practice in the most literal way, with the aid of Himmler and the SS, first in Poland, then in Russia.

The 'Blitzkrieg' victories

What Hitler did not know was how he was going to achieve his objective, the order in which he would proceed, what opposition he would encounter. But from late 1937 onwards he was prepared to enlarge the risks he was ready to take. As part of the process he asserted stronger control over the two institutions which had been allowed to escape nazification, the army and the foreign office. Early in 1938 he seized an opportunity to get rid of Blomberg and Fritsch, the minister of war and commander-in-chief of the army, suppressed the office of war minister altogether, and took over the high command of the armed forces (the OKW) as his own personal staff. Schacht, who had protested at the economic risks of the Nazis' rearmament programme, had already been allowed to go, leaving Göring to dominate the economic field, with a clear brief to pre-

pare for war, and Neurath, whom Hindenburg had made foreign minister to safeguard the foreign service against Nazi influence, was replaced by Ribbentrop who for years had been pushing a radical Nazi policy in open rivalry with the more cautious official line of the foreign office.

The annexation of Austria which followed (March 1938) was an improvisation, but an improvisation which fitted in perfectly with Hitler's long-term programme and illustrates the relationship between this and the tactics of opportunism. Throughout the rest of 1938 and 1939, it was Hitler who forced the pace in foreign affairs, both externally by the demands he made on Czechoslovakia and Poland and internally by his determination to take risks which still, in 1938, alarmed the army leaders and led to the resignation of the army's chief-of-staff, General Beck. Neither in 1938 nor in 1939 did Hitler deliberately plan to start a general European war: in August 1939 he was convinced that the masterpiece of Nazi diplomacy, the Nazi-Soviet Pact, would remove any danger of Western intervention and either break the Poles' determination to resist or leave them isolated. But when his bluff failed, he steeled himself to gamble on the chances of a Blitzkrieg victory over Poland before the British and French could bring their forces to bear. The gamble came off and came off again, with the stakes increased, in Norway, the Low Countries, and France in 1940, against Yugoslavia, and almost against Russia the next year. By then the stakes had been raised to the point where failure meant the long-term, two-front war which Hitler had sworn to avoid, and for which Germany was ill-prepared.

The particular war which broke out in September 1939 was not inevitable—what event in history is? But it was no accident either. Nazism glorified force and conflict, and if one thing seemed certain in the later 1930's it was that this movement which had fastened its hold on Germany must, from the necessities of its own nature, seek to expand by force or the threat of force. Once Nazism—a philosophy of dynamism or nothing—came to a standstill and admitted limits to its expansion, it would lose its rationale and its appeal. The only question was whether the other powers would allow this expansion to take place without resistance or would oppose it. The Nazis themselves had always assumed that at some point they would meet opposition and had prepared to overcome it by force of arms. For this reason, while it is right to point to the differences between Nazi Germany up to September 1939 and after the outbreak of war, it is important to see the continuity between the two periods as well. What followed was a logical, if not inevitable, consequence of what went before.

233

The Brink of War

The international conference at Munich on 29th September 1938 had a practical task: to 'solve' the problem of the three million German-speakers in Czechoslovakia and so to prevent a European war. Apparently it succeeded in this task. The Czechoslovak territory inhabited by the three million Germans was transferred to Germany; the Germans were satisfied; there was no war. The controversy which has raged over the conference from before it met until the present day sprang more from what it symbolized than from what it actually did. Those who welcomed the Munich conference and its outcome represented it as a victory for reason and conciliation in international affairs – appeasement as it was called at the time, 'jaw, not war', as Winston Churchill said of a later occasion. The opponents of Munich saw in it an abdication by the two democratic powers, France and Great Britain; a surrender to fear; or a sinister conspiracy to prepare for a Nazi war of conquest against Soviet Russia. Munich was all these things.

The problem of the German-speakers in Czechoslovakia was real. They had been a privileged people in the old Habsburg monarchy. They were a tolerated minority in Czechoslovakia. They were discontented and grew more so with the resurgence of national pride in Germany. No doubt Hitler encouraged their discontent, but he did not create it. Those in the West who called out, 'Stand by the Czechs', never explained what they would do with the Czechoslovak Germans. Partition seemed the obvious solution. In fact, as later events proved, Bohemia was the one area in Europe where partition would not work. Czechs and Germans were so intermingled that one or other had to dominate. Once Czech prestige was shattered, a German protectorate inevitably followed six months later, to the ruin of the Munich settlement. The Czechs themselves recognized that there was no room in Bohemia for both nationalities. When independent Czechoslovakia was restored at the end of the war, the Germans were expelled – a solution which is likely to prove final.

The timing of the Czech crisis was not determined by the Czechoslovak Germans or by Hitler. It was determined by the British government, and especially by Neville Chamberlain, the British Prime Minister. He wanted to restore tranquillity in Europe and believed that this could be done only if German grievances were met. Moreover they must be met willingly. Concessions must be offered to Germany, not extracted under threat of war. Until 1938 Hitler had been destroying one bit of the 1919 settlement after another, to the accompaniment of protests from the Western powers. This time Chamberlain meant to get in ahead of him. Hitler was to be satisfied almost before he had time to formulate grievances.

Fear not reason

Chamberlain set himself two tasks. First, the French must be induced not to support their ally, Czechoslovakia. Second, the Czech government must be persuaded or compelled to yield to the German demands. He succeeded in both tasks, but not in the way that he intended. He had meant to use the argument of morality: that German grievances were justified and therefore must be redressed. Instead, as the months passed, he came to rely on practical arguments of force and fear. The French were driven to admit, with a reluctance which grew ever weaker, that they were unable to support Czechoslovakia. The Czechs were threatened with the horrors of war unless they gave way. When Chamberlain flew to Munich on his first visit to Hitler, it was not as the emissary of even-handed justice. He came in a desperate effort to avert a war which the Western powers dreaded. Thereafter fear, not reason, was his main argument, and the principal moral which the British drew from Munich was not that conciliation had triumphed, but that they must push on faster with rearmament.

At the Munich conference there was certainly an abdication by the Western powers. France especially had been the dominant power in Eastern Europe since the end of the First World War. Germany was disarmed; Soviet Russia was boycotted; all the new states of Eastern Europe were France's allies. She regarded these alliances as a source of strength. As soon as her allies made demands on her, she turned against them. France had been bled white in the first war, and Frenchmen were determined not to repeat the experience. They believed that they were secure behind their fortified frontier, the Maginot Line. Hence they did not care what happened beyond it. As to the British, they

Left: A poster distributed throughout Czechoslovakia in 1938: 'We will all become soldiers if necessary.' Czech morale remained high during the war of nerves conducted by Hitler.
Right: Britain's Prime Minister Neville Chamberlain arriving at Heston Airport, London, promising 'Peace in our time'

The Fragile Peace

had always insisted that their interests stopped at the Rhine. Austen Chamberlain had said that no British grenadier would ever die for Danzig—or for anywhere else in Eastern Europe. The British recognized that German predominance would take the place of French. But this did not trouble them. Eastern Europe and the Balkans were no great prize economically. If they absorbed German energies and ambitions, it was all the more likely that Germany would leave Western Europe and the British Empire alone.

Fear of war was also a dominant motive at the Munich conference, but for the Western powers it was war that was feared rather than defeat. The French had confidence in their army, the British in their navy. But while they did not expect the Germans to defeat them, they doubted whether they could defeat Germany—except at a terrible price. There was no way in which the Western powers could give limited aid to the Czechs, as they might have done to the Spanish Republic. The facts of geography stood in the way. It was war on the largest scale or nothing. In those days, everyone believed that aerial bombardment would reduce the cities of Europe to ruin within a few weeks. European civilization would come to an end. This was the peril which Chamberlain sought to avert.

The Czechs themselves shared this fear of war. President Beneš believed that Hitler was bluffing and would give way if faced with a firm united opposition. When Hitler did not give way, even Beneš in the last resort preferred surrender to war. The Czechs, Beneš held, were a small people, who must preserve their lives for a better future. Their country had been occupied before and they had survived. They would survive again. In a sense, his arguments were justified by events. The Czechs were abandoned by the Western powers. Their country fell under German tyranny for six years. But only one or perhaps two hundred thousand of them lost their lives. Prague, their capital was the only great city of Central Europe to remain undamaged in the Second World War, and Czechoslovakia re-emerged with unbroken spirit, at the end. In contrast, Poland was guaranteed by the Western powers, who went to war for her sake. As a result, six million Poles were killed. Warsaw was reduced to a heap of ruins, and Poland, though restored, lost much of her territory and of her independence.

Was Munich a conspiracy?
Did more lie behind? Was the Munich conference not merely a surrender, an abandonment, or even a betrayal of Czechoslovakia? Was it also part of a deliberate attempt to promote a German hegemony

and to clear the way for a German attack on Soviet Russia? This is a view strongly held by Soviet and other Communist-inclined historians. The Munich conference was certainly an assertion that Europe could settle its own affairs. Only the purely European powers—France, Germany, Great Britain, and Italy—were represented. The two world powers, Soviet Russia and the United States, were absent. The United States had persistently refused to be involved in European conflicts ever since the end of the First World War. It is likely, too, that the Western powers welcomed the absence of any American representative. If one had attended the conference, he would have preached morality to others without being prepared to act on it himself. Great Britain and France looked forward to a time when there might be a great war and they would need American aid. Even with this in mind, they preferred not to be exposed to American reproaches before the time came for action.

Soviet Russia was a different matter. The Western powers never counted on Soviet aid. They did not believe, and quite rightly, that even if Soviet Russia entered a war against Germany she would be fighting either for democracy as they understood it or for the sanctity of treaties. After all, the settlement of 1919 had been made quite as much against Soviet Russia as against Germany, and the Russians would aim to take Germany's place in Eastern Europe, not to defend the independence of the small states. As well, the Western powers doubted whether Soviet Russia intended to fight Germany seriously or whether she was capable of doing so. They distrusted Soviet Russia quite as much as she distrusted them. Each side suspected the other of pushing it into the front line. Moreover, this was the period of Stalin's great purges. Nearly all the marshals and generals of the Red Army had been murdered or imprisoned. Under such circumstances, it was hard to believe that Soviet Russia could conduct a successful offensive. Geography stood in Russia's way even more than in theirs. Soviet Russia could not strike at Germany without crossing the territory of either Poland or Rumania. Both countries refused to allow the passage of Soviet troops—the Poles more rigorously than the Rumanians. The Western powers were supposed to be defending the rights of small nations and could hardly begin their campaign by trampling on the rights of Poland and Rumania.

On paper, the Soviet government had a position of impregnable righteousness. According to the Czech-Soviet treaty of 1935, Soviet Russia was committed to supporting Czechoslovakia only if France did so first. The Soviet rulers surmised correctly that France would not honour

her word. Therefore they were quite safe in declaring that they would honour theirs. Soviet leaders went further. They often hinted that they would be prepared to aid Czechoslovakia even if France did not act. But they would do this only if President Beneš and the Czechoslovak government asked them to do so. Here again the Soviet government was quite safe. The Czechoslovak government was predominantly right-wing, and President Beneš, though less on the Right, was determined not to fight with Soviet Russia as sole ally. This, he thought, would invite the fate of Republican Spain, and he was not far wrong. Hence we cannot tell what the Soviet government really intended to do. They could promise great things in the secure confidence that they would never be called on to fulfil their promises. Similarly, we do not know whether the Soviet government made any serious preparations for war. Most Western observers reported at the time that the Red Army had taken no measures of mobilization. Nowadays the Soviet spokesmen claim that the Red Army had mobilized thirty divisions. This, even if true, was a derisory force to use against Germany, and suggests that the Soviet government were intending only to seize some Polish territory. But as the Soviet government refuses to release evidence, all statements about its policy are guesswork.

We may dismiss one guess the other way round. Soviet writers then and later alleged that the Western powers aimed to switch German aggression eastwards, against Soviet Russia. Many Soviet writers even allege that the Western powers dreamed of joining in this aggression themselves. There is virtually no foundation for their theory. The Communists imagined that everyone in the capitalist world was afraid of them and therefore wanted to destroy 'the workers' state'. In fact, Communism had lost its appeal. Soviet Russia was the best propaganda against Communism—it offered tyranny, starvation, inefficiency. No one in Western Europe feared Soviet Russia any more. Indeed, sensible English people regretted that Soviet Russia was so weak. In the end, German aggression was indeed switched. But it was switched from east to west by the Nazi-Soviet pact. It was not switched from west to east by the conference at Munich.

The Danzig question
The Munich conference was supposed to inaugurate a new era in international relations. The 'slave treaty' of Versailles, as the Germans called it, was dead. A negotiated settlement had taken its place. Greater Germany had at last come into existence, and Hitler himself professed to be satisfied. He declared: 'I have no more

territorial demands to make in Europe.' Nor was this mere pretence. Hitler formulated no plans for aggressive action during the winter of 1938-39. His generals were told to be ready 'to smash the remainder of the Czech state if it adopted an anti-German policy.' But this was no more than a precaution against the counter-offensive which Hitler half-expected from the Western powers. German expenditure on armaments was considerably reduced after Munich and remained at this lower level until the outbreak of war in September 1939 — clear indication that Hitler was not expecting a great war.

There was still one German grievance left over from Versailles which Hitler intended to remove. Danzig, though entirely German in population, was still a Free City, and the Polish Corridor still separated East Prussia from the rest of Germany. But Hitler did not anticipate conflict over these issues. Poland and Germany were on good terms, and Poland had been Germany's faithful jackal during the Czech crisis. Settlement seemed easy. With the creation of Gdynia, Poland was no longer dependent on Danzig as her only outlet to the world. Danzig could remain a free port for Poland and yet return to the Reich, as its inhabitants wanted. It should also be easy to arrange for German extra-territorial roads and railways across the Corridor. Friendship between Poland and Germany would then be secure, and the two could join in conquering the Ukraine from Soviet Russia.

Hitler did not understand Poland's policy of independence. Colonel Beck, the arrogant foreign minister of Poland, was determined to balance between Germany and Soviet Russia. He would not commit himself to either. He would certainly not enlist Soviet aid against Germany. Equally, he would not co-operate with Germany against Soviet Russia. Hitler wanted to get Danzig out of the way as the only stumbling block between Germany and Poland. For exactly this reason, Beck kept it in the way. Moreover, Beck had learned a lesson from the Czechoslovak affair. He believed that any negotiations or offers of compromise were a slippery slope to ruin. In his view a firm 'no' at the outset was the only safe course. He knew, too, that the Western powers sympathized with Germany over Danzig and would urge concession if they were consulted. He therefore did not consult them. Great Britain and France were assured that Polish relations with Germany were unclouded, while Beck was simultaneously showing a blank and uncomprehending face to Hitler's proposals for compromise.

The limits of appeasement

The Western powers had given up Poland for lost. As Halifax, the British foreign secretary, said: 'Poland can only presumably fall more and more into the German sphere.' British and French statesmen assumed that Soviet Russia and Germany were irreconcilable. Russia would remain as a vague menace on Germany's eastern frontier, and, if Hitler were determined to go somewhere, it were better that he went east. The two Western countries were determined never to be involved again in 'an Eastern quarrel'. The British particularly were anxious to dodge out of the guarantee they had given to Czechoslovakia. Nor had they much faith in their French ally. France, once the advocate of resistance to Germany, now set the pace in appeasement. In December, Ribbentrop came to Paris. He and Bonnet signed a pact of friendship, in which France washed her hands of Eastern Europe — or so it seemed.

The British did not like this. Their idea was to restrain France, not the other way round. Now they needed some other associate who would help to warn Hitler off Western Europe. In January 1939 Chamberlain and Halifax journeyed to Rome. Once more they urged Mussolini to play the moderating part which he had done at Munich. Mussolini was frightened. He knew that Italy was in no state for war and, more wisely than others, recognized that Great Britain might go to war if Hitler pressed too hard. From this moment he importuned Hitler for a firm written alliance — seemingly a move towards Germany. But in Mussolini's eyes, the essential clause of this alliance, finally concluded in May 1939, was that the two powers agreed not to start a general war before 1942 or 1943, and many things could happen before then.

The early months of 1939 saw everyone in a state of undefined apprehension. The British, alarmed by the deficiencies shown during the Czech crisis, were pushing on with their rearmament, a good deal faster indeed than the Germans were. Hitler snapped at every increase in British arms expenditure and complained that they were incompatible with the trust in his word which Chamberlain had professed at Munich. In his crude way, Hitler imagined that he would shake the British 'warmongers', from Churchill to Eden, if he denounced them. Instead he pushed up their reputation and began to shake Chamberlain's. London ran over with rumours of new German aggressions.

Then one came, though not at all as Hitler intended. Czecho-Slovakia, hyphenated since Munich, broke up. This was not altogether Hitler's doing. The Slovaks had always been discontented and could no longer be restrained when Czech prestige was shattered. They demanded first autonomy and then independence. The Czechs prepared to act against them. The Hungarians prepared to move in on the other side. Hitler could allow neither course. He recognized the independence of Slovakia. Hácha, President of the Czech rump, appealed to Hitler for guidance. He came to Berlin and transformed Bohemia into a German protectorate. On 15th March 1939 German troops occupied Bohemia, and Hitler spent the night in Prague.

Nothing was changed except for the unfortunate Czechs, who received all the blessings of German rule — the secret police, persecution of Jews, and the loss of freedom. The British government rejoiced to be freed from 'the somewhat embarrassing commitment of a guarantee'. But British public opinion was in an uproar. Hitler was supposed to have gone back on his word. He was on the march to the domination of Europe. Neville Chamberlain, much against his will, had to speak words of protest and even of resistance. Secretly, Chamberlain, Halifax, and the rest wanted to settle with Hitler. They believed that war would achieve nothing except the ruin of Europe. But they needed to be stronger if they were to bargain at all and so became the prisoners of public opinion. As for the British people, this was the moment when most of them decided that the only thing to do with Hitler was to 'stop' him.

The British government were in a panic. They thought, quite wrongly, that Hitler was about to overrun the Balkans and Turkey. Any day the Middle East would be in danger. At precisely this moment, Tilea, the Rumanian minister, turned up with the news that German troops were about to enter Rumania. This was a totally false

1938 Czech Communist poster

The Fragile Peace

alarm. The British statesmen believed it. Helter-skelter, they tried to organize a peace front for joint resistance. The French agreed to join. The Russians agreed on condition all the others did. The Poles refused. They were still determined not to take sides. Negotiations over Danzig were becoming tenser as Beck kept up his negatives. But Hitler remained hopeful. As late as 25th March he issued a directive: 'The Führer *does not* wish to solve the Danzig question by force.'

Then came another alarm. There were reports, again unfounded, of German troop movements against Poland. These reports were fed to a British newspaper correspondent by German generals. Why? So that the British would resist Hitler? Or so that they would make the Poles give way? No one knows. At any rate, the correspondent was invited to attend the British cabinet. Chamberlain, convinced, wrote out with his own hand the offer of a British guarantee to Poland. Beck was conversing with the British ambassador when the message from London was brought in. He accepted the guarantee 'between two flicks of the ash from his cigarette'. It seemed to him to be a perfect solution. The British guarantee strengthened his hand against Germany. At the same time, it enabled him to refuse any co-operation with Soviet Russia. The British were entangled in 'an Eastern European quarrel' and yet could not appeal

Above: SA recruits in Memel following the city's return to Germany. Memel's population was predominantly German in origin and many were willing to fight for the Führer. Right: A new mood of resolution was seen in Great Britain after Hitler's move into Prague

to Russia for aid. Poland would remain the dominant power in Eastern Europe, calling the tune on all sides.

When the British government came to their senses, they did not like what they had done. By giving to Poland an unconditional guarantee, they had committed themselves over Danzig, a cause for which they did not care at all or on which they even agreed with Hitler. Colonel Beck visited London a few days later. The British then tried to modify their guarantee. Beck would not yield. With continued arrogance, he merely offered to make the guarantee mutual. He assured the British that they were in more danger from Hitler than he was. He said not a word of the deadlock over Danzig, and the British were taken in by his self-confidence. They even feared that, unless they stuck by Beck, he would take Poland into the German camp. Besides, British public opinion would not forgive them if they again ran away. Beck departed from London with the assurance that the guarantee would soon be turned into a formal alliance. Actually, this was delayed until 25th August, on the eve of war.

The British guarantee to Poland provoked Hitler instead of restraining him. He was still convinced that his opponents would give way—'they are little worms. I saw them at Munich'—and so raised his bid. On 3rd April he told his generals to be ready for war with Poland in September, though he added an assurance that he would go to war only if Poland were isolated. On 28th April he denounced the Non-Aggression Pact with Poland of 1934 and the Anglo-German Naval Agreement of 1935. He still declared that he wanted agreement over Danzig and looked forward to friendship with the British later, when they too had given way over Danzig. Then, having stated his terms, Hitler withdrew into silence. There were no official exchanges between Germany and Great Britain until the middle of August, and none at all with Poland until the day war broke out.

Alliance without risks?

This was a nerve-racking situation. Hitler had made no precise demands. He had merely stated his dissatisfaction and left others to remedy it. In 1938 the British knew how to do this, or so they thought: concessions from Czechoslovakia would do the trick. Now this road was barred, and Colonel Beck had made it clear that there would be no concessions from Poland. The British government threatened that they would not support him. No good. Beck had their guarantee and knew that they dared not go back on it. The British government had to make the gestures of preparing to resist Hitler, whether they intended to or not. A Ministry of Supply was solemnly

instituted, though Chamberlain had earlier dismissed it as a measure of war. It was in fact instituted only in theory and did not operate before war broke out. Compulsory military service was introduced—again an empty gesture. The young conscripts would not make any significant contribution to the British Army until 1942.

The greatest gesture hung over the British government like a hideous black cloud—the proposal for an alliance with Soviet Russia. It would seem to have obvious advantages—a great power enlisted on the side of collective security, aiding Poland, and distracting Germany with an eastern front. The British Opposition clamoured for a Soviet alliance. So did the French, who, having been committed to the Polish guarantee without being consulted, now wanted someone else to fulfil their guarantee for them. But there were grave disadvantages also. The Poles would not make an alliance with Soviet Russia, and Beck insisted that he would reject Soviet assistance even if offered. Some members of the British government believed that Soviet Russia, bled by Stalin's purges, was too weak to fight. Others believed that she would not be a reliable ally. All were shocked at the idea of associating with Bolsheviks and regarded the prospect of Soviet victory, however remote, as even worse than that of a German one. Yet there was no escape. British public opinion wanted the Soviet alliance as the best means of deterring Hitler from war or of winning a war if it came. The French were determined to go forward. The British government therefore timidly set out on the quest for an alliance without risks, much as a man trying to go swimming without getting wet.

The basis of the British proposal, feebly dangled before the Soviet government time after time, was that Soviet Russia should provide aid 'if requested' or 'if desired'. Soviet aid was to be turned on and off like a tap. The Poles were to be allowed to turn the tap. Later the Baltic states were to be allowed to turn the tap. The British were to be allowed to turn the tap. But the Soviets were not to be allowed to turn the tap themselves. They were to stand by patiently, active or inactive according to the will of others. This was not an attractive proposition for the Russians. No one knows the original intentions of Stalin and his associates. Perhaps they hoped for a solid alliance with the Western powers. Perhaps they planned a deal with Hitler all along. Perhaps they intended to play with both sides and see what happened. Speculation is not rewarding and is made less so when the Soviet rulers are denounced for following the path of self-preservation like everyone else. The Bolsheviks lose either way: they are condemned as criminal monsters at one

May 27, 1939

PICTURE POST

AFS LONDON

AN OFFICER OF THE AUXILIARY FIRE SERVICES PREPARES FOR THE WORST

(See inside)

HULTON'S NATIONAL WEEKLY

In this issue:

BRITAIN PREPARES

3D

MAY 27, 1939   Vol. 3. No. 8

moment and expected to follow a more idealistic course than others at the next.

According to such evidence as exists, the Soviet government was anxious to conclude a firm alliance, and the British, when not evasive, were spinning things out. Each British subterfuge received a prompt Soviet answer. Then the British would take ten days or a fortnight devising another one. By the middle of May, negotiations had reached deadlock. The Russians would look at nothing except a straight defensive alliance. The British inserted the fatal 'if desired' into every draft. When this was rejected, they were ready to break off. Hitler had remained quiet, and perhaps there would be no trouble after all. The French were not so complacent. Failing all else, they would make a simple Franco-Soviet alliance without caring what happened to Poland. To prevent this, the British went reluctantly forward. This time they appeared to offer a pact of mutual security. But there were still problems. The Russians feared that Hitler would attack other countries before attacking them, and a glance at the map suggests that he could do nothing else. The Russians therefore demanded that 'indirect aggression', that is attack on some neighbouring country, should be regarded as attack upon themselves. They even demanded that

peaceful surrender to Hitler by some small country should be treated as indirect aggression on themselves.

The British refused these Soviet proposals. They had made the cause of small countries their own. Besides, they suspected Soviet Russia as an imperialist power, with plans much like Hitler's. In that case, they should not have been seeking a Soviet alliance at all. Finally Molotov, now commissar for foreign affairs, suggested a way out. They should postpone the search for a political agreement and should hold military talks to consider how the alliance could work if it were ever made. The British jumped at this as an excuse for further delay. The French hoped to get military co-operation with Soviet Russia after all. The British and French governments appointed military delegations which departed on a slow boat for Leningrad. By the time they arrived all chance of a united front against Hitler had disappeared.

During the negotiations, both Russians and British had received offers from unofficial German sources. The Russians had indicated their willingness to renew trade relations with Germany. The British had gone further. Chamberlain's agents, though perhaps not Chamberlain himself, had displayed British anxiety to satisfy Hitler

Above: Local police remove customs barrier following Germany's annexation of Danzig, 1st September 1939—the day Poland was invaded. The Free City of Danzig had been under Polish economic domination

over Danzig, if only this could be done in a respectable peaceful way. Once Danzig was settled, Great Britain would forget her guarantee to Poland. She would give Germany a loan of one thousand million pounds. Happy relations would be restored.

By the beginning of August, Hitler knew that negotiations between Soviet Russia and the Western powers were stuck. He knew also that the British government would pay almost any price to avoid a war. He thought that the time had come for him to pull off his great stroke. The British people, he believed, were hoping for a Soviet alliance. If he could show that this hope was vain, the British would back down. He was right, or very nearly, about the British government. He failed to allow for the fact that the British people might have a will of their own. It was a very foolish proposition to suppose that Great Britain and France, without Soviet Russia, could do anything to aid Poland or indeed to deter Hitler in any way. But it was a proposition to which most British people were committed.

The Nazi-Soviet Pact

The Russian view

The Soviet-German Treaty was signed on 23rd August 1939, but to this day the strong feelings it aroused have not calmed down: discussions and intense arguments still go on about the nature of this treaty, about the circumstances in which it was made, and about its consequences.

After the Munich agreement had been signed on 30th September 1938, political events in Europe developed along two different lines. On the one hand, the aggressive behaviour of Germany was intensified. On 15th March 1939 German forces occupied Bohemia-Moravia. A week later Germany seized the Lithuanian port of Klaipeda, and the next day Hitler imposed a shackling economic agreement upon Rumania. On 21st March the German government demanded that Poland hand over Danzig, and shortly afterwards repudiated their pact of non-aggression with Poland. In April Germany's ally Italy grabbed Albania. Thus, the appetite of the Nazis was growing, aggressive deeds were being committed one after another, and the danger of war in Europe was becoming more and more evident.

On the other hand, Great Britain and France continued to follow their policy of appeasing the aggressor, which had culminated in the Munich agreement with Hitler and Mussolini. However, Germany's aggressions, and the increasing alarm caused in Europe by the fascist aggressors, obliged the British and French governments to take certain measures during the first half of 1939. Great Britain announced on 31st March that she guaranteed the independence of Poland, and this was

Below: Molotov signs the non-aggression pact with Nazi Germany on 23rd August 1939, while von Ribbentrop and Stalin look on

followed by guarantees to Greece and Rumania on 13th April and to Turkey on 12th May. France endorsed these British guarantees. At the same time, Great Britain and France agreed to begin negotiations with the Soviet Union for joint resistance to Hitler's aggression.

On 18th March the Soviet government handed a special note to Schulenburg, the German ambassador in Moscow, stating that it did not recognize the inclusion of Czechoslovakia in the German Reich. On the same day the USSR proposed that a conference of the states concerned be convened to discuss the situation caused by the German threat to Rumania. The British government said it considered such a conference to be premature, and in mid-April proposed that the USSR guarantee Poland and Rumania against possible German aggression.

Later, Great Britain repeated her proposal, with the aim of binding the USSR to go immediately to the aid of Poland and Rumania if Hitler should decide to attack these countries, and also in case Hitler were to turn westward. But the British government did not want to give similar guarantees against possible German attacks on Latvia, Estonia, or Finland, although from the point of view of the USSR attacks on the Baltic countries would represent no less danger than attacks on Rumania or Poland.

The calculation made by the leaders of British and French foreign policy became clear. They wished to make sure of Soviet aid in the event of attacks by Germany on those countries in which Great Britain and France were interested, but they had no intention of undertaking similar obligations towards the USSR.

The USSR put forward counter-proposals for the formation of a powerful coalition capable of resisting any aggression by Germany. For three weeks the British government left these Soviet proposals unanswered. It then tabled its own plan, which again provided only for Soviet guarantees to Poland and Rumania.

In June the Soviet government invited Halifax, the British foreign secretary, to come to Moscow; but he was unable to find the time for this visit. On 23rd July the Soviet government proposed that negotiations begin in Moscow between military representatives of the three powers, so as to agree on possible joint military action against the aggressor. Again, however, London and Paris did not hasten to answer. Nineteen days elapsed between this proposal by the Soviet government and the arrival in Moscow of the British and French missions.

The talks began in Moscow on 12th August. The Soviet delegation was headed by the people's commissar for defence,

Marshal K.E. Voroshilov, and included the commissar for the navy, the chief of General Staff of the Red Army, and his deputy, who commanded the Soviet air force. The British and French missions were headed by men of only secondary rank, without the necessary authority.

The course taken by the talks further showed that the Anglo-French side did not wish to discuss definite military plans, the conditions for allowing Soviet troops to traverse Polish and Rumanian territory, the number of divisions to be committed, and so on. The talks arrived at an impasse when Poland announced that she would not agree to allow Soviet troops to cross her territory.

Anglo-French plan

About the same time, reports appeared in the press about talks going on between Great Britain and Germany. Though the details did not become known until much later, the USSR was obviously threatened by the possibility of another Munich.

It was in this situation that the German government offered the Soviet Union a pact of non-aggression. Actually, the Germans had begun sounding the USSR about the possibility of an agreement as early as the beginning of 1939. At that time the Soviet government had left these German approaches unanswered and entered into talks with Great Britain and France. When, however, in mid-August, it became more and more obvious that no agreement could be reached with Great Britain and France, the Soviet government consented to the visit by Ribbentrop to Moscow which had been proposed by the Germans.

The Anglo-French plan was to direct Germany's appetite towards the East and involve Hitler in conflict with the Soviet Union. The USSR was faced with the immediate danger of finding herself facing Hitler on her own. Munich and the subsequent negotiations provided clear proof of the unwillingness of the British and French governments to form an anti-Hitler alliance. And in these same months Soviet-Japanese relations became strained. Japanese troops invaded the territory of the Mongolian People's Republic in the area of the River Khalkhin Gol. The Soviet Union, acting in accordance with the mutual aid treaty of 1936, sent forces to help the MPR. At the very moment when fruitless negotiations were going on with the British and French in Moscow, the Red Army was engaged in battle with substantial Japanese forces.

In these circumstances the USSR was confronted with the prospect of a war on two fronts, without any allies. To ensure the country's security, the Soviet government accepted the German proposals. On 22nd August 1939 Ribbentrop arrived in

Moscow, and on the 23rd the Soviet-German Treaty of non-aggression was signed.

In signing this treaty the Soviet Union followed one of the principles of its foreign policy, namely, to make use of the contradictions between the capitalist countries. It was not easy for the Soviet Union to sign this treaty. There had to be taken into account, in the first place, the effect on public opinion of an agreement made between the land of socialism and fascist Germany, against whose policy the USSR had fought for many years. The problem was further complicated because the general public did not know about all the vagaries of the Anglo-Franco-Soviet negotiations.

In the second place, it was clear to everyone, including the USSR, that the treaty meant only a temporary postponement, that sooner or later Hitler would proceed to carry out his programme of struggle against Communism and the USSR.

The treaty with Germany was a step which the USSR was forced to take in the difficult situation that had come about in the summer of 1939. The Soviet government did not deceive itself regarding Hitler's aims. It understood that the treaty would not bring the USSR lasting peace but only a more or less lengthy breathing-space. When it signed the treaty with Germany the Soviet government undertook the task of using the time thus gained to carry through the political and military measures needed in order to ensure the country's security and strengthen its capacity for defence.

THE PACT

'The Government of the German Reich and the Government of the Union of Soviet Socialist Republics, desirous of strengthening the cause of peace between Germany and the USSR, and proceeding from the fundamental provisions of the Neutrality Agreement concluded in April 1926 between Germany and the USSR, have reached the following agreement:

'Article I. Both High Contracting Parties obligate themselves to desist from any act of violence, any aggressive action, and any attack on each other, either individually or jointly with other powers.

'Article II. Should one of the High Contracting Parties become the object of belligerent action by a third power, the other High Contracting Party shall in no manner lend its support to this third party.

'Article III. The Governments of the two High Contracting Parties shall in the future maintain continual contact with one another for the purpose of consultation in order to exchange information on problems affecting their common interests.

'Article IV. Neither of the two High Contracting Parties shall participate in

Left: Soviet cartoon, 1936, sees Western capitalists as Hitler's guardian angels. Criticism stopped abruptly with signing of Nazi-Soviet Pact. *Right:* Japanese soldiers captured by Russians in Mongolia. Committed to aid Mongolia, Russia wanted to avoid war in the West

any grouping of powers whatsoever that is directly or indirectly aimed at the other party.

'Article V. Should disputes or conflicts arise between the High Contracting Parties over problems of one kind or another, both parties shall settle these disputes or conflicts exclusively through friendly exchange of opinion, or, if necessary, through the establishment of arbitration commissions.

'Article VI. The present treaty is concluded for a period of ten years, with the proviso that, in so far as one of the High Contracting Parties does not denounce it one year prior to the expiration of this period, the validity of this treaty shall automatically be extended for another five years.

'Article VII. The present treaty shall be ratified within the shortest possible time. The ratification shall be exchanged in Berlin. The agreement shall enter into force as soon as it is signed.'

'Secret Additional Protocol

'On the occasion of the signature of the Nonaggression Pact between the German Reich and the Union of Soviet Socialist Republics the undersigned plenipotentiaries of each of the two parties discussed in strictly confidential conversations the question of the boundary of their respective spheres of influence in Eastern Europe. These conversations led to the following conclusions:

'1. In the event of a territorial and political rearrangement in the areas belonging to the Baltic States (Finland, Estonia, Latvia, Lithuania), the northern boundary of Lithuania shall represent the boundary of the spheres of influence of Germany and the USSR . . .

'2. In the event of a territorial and political rearrangement of the areas belonging to the Polish state the spheres of influence of Germany and the USSR shall be bounded approximately by the line of the rivers Narew, Vistula, and San.

'The question of whether the interests of both parties make desirable the maintenance of an independent Polish state and how such a state should be bounded can only be definitely determined in the course of further political developments. . . .'

The division of Poland

'Further political developments' were provided by the Germans themselves when they invaded Poland. Four weeks later, on 28th September, Germany and the USSR carried their co-operation a step further with a treaty dividing Poland:

'The government of the German Reich and the government of the USSR consider it as exclusively their task, after the collapse of the former Polish state, to re-establish peace and order in these territories and to assure to the peoples living there a peaceful life in keeping with their national character. To this end, they have agreed upon the following:

'The government of the German Reich

and the government of the USSR determine . . . the boundary of their respective national interests in the territory of the former Polish state . . .

'. . . *the territory of the Lithuanian state falls into the sphere of influence of the USSR, while, on the other hand, the province of Lublin and parts of the province of Warsaw fall to the sphere of influence of Germany . . .*

'*Both parties will tolerate in their territories no Polish agitation which affects the territories of the other party. They will suppress in their territories all beginnings of such agitation and inform each other concerning suitable measures.*'

The American view

Any Soviet historian dealing with the history of the events leading to the outbreak of the Second World War and the subsequent Soviet involvement in it starts with four great difficulties.

Firstly, despite a quite substantial degree of de-Stalinization among Soviet military historians, who now feel free to discuss Stalin's errors as a military commander, Soviet diplomatic historians are unable to admit that Stalin's and Molotov's conduct of foreign policy could in any way have been influenced by misjudgment or misinformation. Secondly, although the British, Italian, American, German, and even the Hungarian diplomatic archives have been published *in extenso,* we still have no idea what the various Soviet ambassadors were reporting, or the instructions that were going out from Moscow to them. Thirdly, despite the implications heavily underlined by Soviet historians that the British government would have preferred to find a way of avoiding war with Germany, the fact remains that Great Britain chose to fight Hitler in 1939 and the Soviet Union chose to make an agreement with him that made it possible for him to conquer all Europe between the Channel and the Soviet frontier the following summer. Fourthly, whatever else the Soviet government did during the years 1939-41, it did not 'carry through the political and military measures needed in order to secure the country's security and strengthen its capacity for defence', or at least not with any great energy, efficiency, or enthusiasm. The Soviet government dismissed the warnings that reached them, even from their own intelligence sources such as Richard Sorge in Tokyo, of imminent German attack. The German forces that attacked in June 1941 achieved complete tactical surprise; they found no fortifications to oppose them, and they virtually obliterated the Soviet armies in the west. Only the innate heroism of the Soviet people saved the Soviet Union from conquest by those with

whom a non-aggression pact had been signed two years earlier.

The inadequacies of the Soviet interpretation of the period January to August 1939 are evident, for example, on the subject of the development of British policy against Hitler. In January 1939, *before* the German invasion of Prague, the British authorities had already both expressed their anxieties lest Hitler seek new adventures in the Ukraine, and asked for concerted staff action with the French to face a possible German attack westwards. They had also begun to mend their fences with the Soviet Union, in the face of much Soviet suspicion. The British answer to the occupation of Prague and the reports of an economic ultimatum to Rumania was an immediate approach to the Soviet Union. The Soviet proposal of 18th March was in answer to this. The British proposals that the Soviet Union guarantee Rumania and Poland were, after all, only that the Soviets should follow the British example. The reason why Great Britain was reluctant to give guarantees to the Baltic states and Finland was that these states flatly refused to ask for them, and Great Britain did not wish to drive them into Germany's arms. The Baltic states also turned down the Soviet offer of a non-aggression pact preferring to conclude one with Germany. Great Britain had constantly to labour, as her published documents make clear, with the absolute refusal of the states between Germany and the Soviet Union to commit themselves in any way to contacts with the Soviet Union.

Nor does the Soviet view account for the evidence on German-Soviet relations. The German approach to the Soviet Union in January is not reflected in the German diplomatic documents (unless this is a reference to Hitler's talk at a New Year's reception with the Soviet diplomatic representative). At the end of January 1939, when Ribbentrop recalled the German trade mission to Moscow in his eagerness to obtain an agreement with Poland, German-Soviet relations were at a very low ebb. They continued that way until the reopening of contacts ostensibly *from* the Soviet side in April. (We have, of course, no way of knowing whether the Soviet representative was acting on his own, or even if the German report, prompted by the wish for better German-Soviet relations, misrepresented this initiative as coming from the Soviet side. Soviet historians who deal with this episode at all simply dismiss the German record as a forgery.) The real signal was, however, the replacement as commissar of foreign affairs of Litvinov, a Jew, by Molotov on 3rd May, an event which struck Hitler as so important that the German ambassador in Moscow was

immediately recalled to report. He advised an approach to Molotov beginning with economic affairs, and it was Molotov's remark that good economic relations were impossible unless political relations improved which encouraged the Germans to proceed. The truth is that through Sorge in Tokyo and their agents in Germany, the Soviet authorities knew that Hitler was preparing to attack the West if he could not frighten them off—and he expected the signing of the Nazi-Soviet Pact to do this. Yet no serious evidence has been produced which would show that British policy was directed to attempting to procure a German attack on the Soviet Union. If the Soviet leadership believed this to be the aim of British policy, they would appear to have been influenced by a major misjudgment.

The real defence of Soviet policy in 1939 is that the British were casting them in a role which if it succeeded in restraining Hitler would redound to the credit of Great Britain, whereas if it failed, the Soviet Union would have to bear the burden of fighting on land. Great Britain had no forces available for a major land offensive in Europe and the French saw no point in abandoning their fortifications. The Soviets thus had every reason for rejecting the early British proposals. The later ones, however, gave them everything they had originally asked for. It is the difficulties that Molotov made in the negotiations in June and July which make British historians suspect that Molotov was holding the option of an agreement with Germany open all the time and that the decision to conclude the agreement with Germany was not the last minute affair it is so often represented as being by Soviet historians. It is clear that despite their intelligence in the West, the Soviet military had no idea actually how weak Great Britain and France were. Otherwise the revelations made by Admiral Drax, and General Doumenc, heads of the British and French missions, would not have struck them with such suspicion.

British policy in this period is a record of misordered priorities and misunderstood information. Great Britain was much weaker than even her leaders believed; and they were attempting to create a deterrent bloc in Eastern Europe without properly considering who was to provide the real element of deterrence behind that bloc. British intelligence, partly from ideological conviction, possibly from awareness of the Soviet-German exchanges (the Americans knew of them through the German embassy in Moscow) was dominated by suspicion of the Soviet Union. Yet in the end Great Britain was not deterred by the Nazi-Soviet Pact and went to war against the Nazi menace in September 1939.

The Storm Breaks

The war crisis of 1939 began on 21st August, with the announcement that Ribbentrop, German foreign minister, had been invited to Moscow by the Soviet government. Though the Nazi-Soviet Pact was not formally concluded until 23rd August, it was obvious that Ribbentrop would not go to Moscow unless agreement had already been reached in principle. Hence it was certain that the negotiations for an alliance between France, Great Britain, and Soviet Russia had broken down. This is what Hitler wished to establish. Soviet neutrality in itself was not enough for him. What he needed was public news of this neutrality so that he could shake the nerves of the British and French governments. Stalin, the Soviet dictator, exacted his price in return. Though he, too, like Hitler, probably expected British and French resolution to collapse, he wanted to keep the Germans far from the Soviet frontier if war occurred after all. Hence the Nazi-Soviet Pact drew a barrier in Eastern Europe which the Germans were not to cross.

The pact was neither an alliance nor a partition agreement. The Soviet government merely promised to stay neutral which is what the Poles had always asked them to do, and in addition they set a limit to German expansion. However, the immediate effect was certainly discouraging for the Western powers. Until the last moment they had gone on dreaming either that Hitler would be frightened by the Soviet bogeyman or that Soviet Russia would do their fighting for them. Now they had to decide for themselves, and Hitler was convinced that they would run away. On 22nd August he delivered to his generals a wild oration: 'Close your hearts to pity. Act brutally.' He boasted: 'I have got Poland where I wanted her,' and added cheerfully: 'The probability is great that the West will not intervene.' Hitler was play-acting in order to impress the German generals. He guessed that some of them would leak to the British, and sure enough some did. Almost at once the British embassy received an exaggerated version of Hitler's speech and was correspondingly alarmed.

On 23rd August Hitler went a step further. He moved forward the attack on Poland, fixed for 1st September, to 4.40 a.m. on 26th August. This, too, was play-acting. The German preparations could not be complete before 1st September. Attack on Poland before then was possible only if she had already surrendered. Thus Hitler counted confidently on the collapse of the Western powers.

The French almost came up to his expectations. Georges Bonnet, the foreign minister, had always wanted to desert the Poles. He accepted the German case over Danzig. He had no faith in the Polish army. On 23rd August Daladier, the Premier, summoned the Committee of National Defence at Bonnet's request. Bonnet asked: should they push Poland into a compromise and postpone the war until they were stronger? Gamelin, the French commander-in-chief, would not admit the weakness of his army. He asserted that the Poles could hold out until the spring. By then, France would be 'impregnable'. There was no suggestion that France could aid Poland in any way. Nor did the French attempt to discuss the situation with the British. There were no Anglo-French meetings of ministers such as had marked the Czech crisis. Ideally, the French would have liked the British to force surrender on them. But they would not take the lead in abdication themselves. There was a choice between abandoning Poland and fighting a great war in which France would carry most of the burden. The French refused to choose. They sat helplessly by throughout the week when others decided the fate of Europe and of France.

British obstinacy

The British government were apparently more resolute. On 22nd August they issued a statement that the coming Nazi-Soviet Pact 'would in no way affect their obligation to Poland'. There was nothing else to do. The British ministers were proud and obstinate. They were not going to have the Opposition crowing that their policy was in ruins. Besides, they feared to be swept away in a storm of public opinion if they showed weakness. Conservative backbenchers had disliked the negotiations with Soviet Russia. But many of them had fought in the First World War. They could not imagine that Great Britain was unable to impose her will on Germany if she determined to do so. As for the Opposition, they had championed the Soviet alliance. Now they were resolved to show that, unlike Stalin, they stuck to their principles.

In secret, the British ministers wanted to

Right: In contrast to the scenes of August 1914, Britain and France went to war in September 1939 with a sense of weary foreboding, although their resolution to fight for Poland had not collapsed as Hitler had expected; appeasement had run its course. This newsvendor in London's Trafalgar Square tells his own story

The Fragile Peace

give way. Chamberlain told Kennedy, the American ambassador: 'The futility of it all is frightful; we cannot save the Poles; we can only carry on a war of revenge that will mean the destruction of all Europe.' Chamberlain said he could not put pressure on Poland himself. Would President Roosevelt do it for him? Roosevelt refused. The only hope was to warn Hitler, or rather to plead with him. On 23rd August Nevile Henderson flew to Berchtesgaden. He delivered a warning that Great Britain would stand by Poland. But he also asserted that Hitler could get Danzig peacefully, and he spread out the delights of an Anglo-German alliance. Hitler appeared to be unimpressed. He stormed and ranted. When Henderson left, Hitler slapped his thigh and exclaimed: 'Chamberlain will not survive that conversation. His government will fall tonight.' Back in Berlin, Henderson told Lipski, the Polish ambassador, that the only chance was for Poland to start negotiations immediately. Lipski took no notice.

On 24th August the British Parliament met. It unanimously applauded what it supposed to be the government's firm stand. Hitler began to doubt whether the British government had yet reached the point of surrender. He flew to Berlin and held a conference with Ribbentrop and his leading generals. He asked: should they stick to 26th August as the date for the attack on Poland? He decided that he would make a further attempt to detach the Western powers from their alliance with Poland. This took the form of a 'last offer' which Hitler made to Henderson soon after midday on 25th August. He declared that the problems of Danzig and the Corridor must be 'solved'—though he did not say how. Once this was done, he would guarantee the British Empire, accept an agreed limitation of armaments, and renew his assurance that Germany's western frontier was fixed for ever. Henderson was impressed as usual and thought that Hitler spoke 'with apparent sincerity'. Henderson promised to take Hitler's offer to London the next morning. Hitler approved. What was he up to? By the time Henderson left Berlin the German attack on Poland would presumably have begun. Did Hitler think that the British would abandon the Polish alliance on sight of his offer? Had he forgotten his own time-table? Or was advancing the date of attack to 26th August a bluff all along?

The last seems the most probable explanation. All afternoon on 25th August Hitler raged round the Chancellery. At 3 p.m. he ordered the attack to proceed. Three hours later Attolico, the Italian ambassador, brought the news that Italy could not enter the war unless she received vast quantities of raw materials

Henderson (second from left), escorted by German officials, arrives to see Hitler on night of 30th-31st August. He had come to ask for time to start talks—but time had run out

which Germany was in no position to supply. Immediately afterwards Ribbentrop reported that the Anglo-Polish treaty had been formally signed in London. Hitler pulled back. He summoned Keitel, the chief-of-staff, and said: 'Stop everything at once. I need time for negotiations.' The attack on Poland was called off at the last moment.

The British government seemed to have committed themselves for good when they signed the alliance with Poland, particularly as it included a guarantee of Danzig. Their real attitude was quite different: they were still eager to sell out. The Foreign Office drafted terms for an offer to Hitler which stated that Danzig should have 'the right to determine its political allegiance', and Halifax, the foreign secretary, told the Polish ambassador that the Polish government would make a great mistake if they ruled out 'peaceful modifications of the status of Danzig'. Hitler and the British government thus agreed how negotiations should end—with a Polish surrender. The problem was how to get negotiations started. The two sides circled round each other like wrestlers before a clinch. The British offered to arrange direct negotiations between Germany and Poland if Hitler promised to behave peacefully. Hitler answered that there would be no war if he got his way over Danzig.

Göring, who did not want war, now

called in an unofficial intermediary, a Swedish businessman called Dahlerus. Dahlerus flew to London on 25th August and back to Berlin on 26th August; to London and back on 27th August; and the same again on 30th August. In Berlin he saw Göring and sometimes Hitler. In London he saw Chamberlain and Halifax. Each side got the impression that the other was weakening. Both wanted another Munich, but on favourable terms, and neither side knew how to push the Poles over the brink.

On 28th August Henderson delivered the British reply to Hitler's last offer. The British government urged that there should be direct negotiations between Germany and Poland. If these reached agreement, the way would be open for 'a wider and more complete agreement between Germany and Great Britain'. Hitler had repeatedly declared that, as his offers to Poland had been rejected in the spring, he would never negotiate directly with the Poles again. On the other hand, Henderson made no objection when Hitler said that negotiations must involve a Polish surrender over Danzig and the Corridor. Thus Hitler thought he would succeed either way. If the Poles yielded, he would get Danzig and the Corridor. If they refused, the British government would repudiate them. He decided to accept direct negotiations, but to do it in such a way that Germany would still seem to be dictating to both Great Britain and Poland.

On 29th August Hitler saw Henderson again and delivered his answer. He agreed to direct negotiations, but a Polish representative, with full powers, must arrive in Berlin within the next twenty-four hours. Henderson objected that this was an ultimatum. Hitler and Ribbentrop answered, with typical German pedantry, that the word 'ultimatum' nowhere appeared in the German note. Ultimatum or not, Henderson was eager to accept it. Hitler's offer, he telegraphed to London, was 'the sole chance of preventing war'. Henderson urged acceptance on everybody—on his own government, on the French, on the Poles. He hurried round to Lipski and urged immediate acceptance. Lipski was unmoved and did not even report Hitler's offer to Warsaw. The French were as resolute in the opposite direction. Bonnet telegraphed to Beck that he should go to Berlin at once.

Decision rested with the British government. Here was the proposal they had always wanted: direct negotiations between Germany and Poland. Hitler had agreed. Now they could not deliver the Poles. Chamberlain told Kennedy that he was 'more worried about getting the Poles to be reasonable than the Germans'. And with reason. Beck replied firmly: 'If invited to Berlin of course he would not go, as he had no intention of being treated like President Hácha.' (President Emil Hácha of Czechoslovakia had, five months before on 15th March, been forced by Hitler, Göring, and Ribbentrop to sign away his country's independence.) The British government had to make a temporizing reply, which Henderson delivered only twenty-five minutes after midnight on 30th August, that is after the German 'ultimatum' had run out. The British welcomed Hitler's proposal, but they asked him to wait a bit—they could not produce a Polish representative at such short notice.

Hitler meanwhile had prepared terms which he would present to the Poles. They were for him moderate: immediate return of Danzig and a plebiscite in the Corridor. Henderson thought that these terms were 'not unreasonable'. Back at the British embassy, he summoned Lipski and urged him to seek an interview with Ribbentrop at once. Lipski refused and went back to bed. The next morning Göring sent Dahlerus to Henderson with the German terms in writing. Henderson again summoned Lipski, and when he refused to come, sent Dahlerus round to him. Lipski was still obstinate. He declared that 'German morale was weakening and that the present regime would soon crack'. Dahlerus reported his failure to London and added that the German terms were 'extremely

reasonable'. The British agreed. Henderson telegraphed to London that 'on German offer war should be completely unjustifiable', and Halifax telegraphed to Warsaw: 'I do not see why Polish government should feel difficulty about authorising Polish Ambassador to accept a document from the German government.'

Hitler's manoeuvre was succeeding. A breach was opening between Poland and her Western allies. But Hitler was trapped by his own time-table. He had repeatedly declared to his generals that he would either produce a Polish surrender by 1st September or go to war. He dared not face their contempt if he confessed failure. Besides, military action could not be improvised at a moment's notice. If the attack planned for 1st September were called off, it would have to be postponed for many weeks or even months. All the British messages had been intercepted, and Hitler knew how anxious the British government were to surrender. He had to gamble that they would surrender even if war against Poland had started. In this tight situation he had no choice if he were to maintain his prestige. Maybe too, he liked gambling. As he told Göring: 'I always call *va banque*. It is the only call I know.' At 12.40 p.m. on 31st August he ordered that the attack on Poland should proceed.

At 1 p.m. Lipski asked to see Ribbentrop. He was asked whether he was coming as a plenipotentiary. He replied: 'No, as ambassador.' This was enough for Hitler. The Poles were still obstinate. At 4 p.m. Hitler confirmed the order for war. At 6.30 p.m. Lipski at last saw Ribbentrop. Lipski said that the Poles were 'favourably considering' the idea of direct negotiations. Ribbentrop again asked whether he was a plenipotentiary. Lipski again said no. Ribbentrop did not communicate the German terms. If he had tried to do so, Lipski would have refused to receive them. The Poles had kept their nerve unbroken to the last moment. At 4.45 a.m. on 1st September the German forces attacked Poland without warning or pretext. At 6 a.m. German aeroplanes bombed Warsaw.

Trapped into war

The ally of Great Britain and France had been wantonly attacked. It only remained for them to declare war on the aggressor. They did nothing of the kind. The two governments merely 'warned' Hitler that they might have to go to war unless he desisted. Meanwhile they hoped that Mussolini would save them as he had done during the Czech crisis, and he duly did his best. He proposed a European conference to survey all causes of conflict, with the condition that Danzig should return to Germany at once. Hitler replied that he would answer on 3rd September.

The British and French governments were therefore desperate to postpone any action until that day. But they, too, were trapped—by the indignation of British opinion. The French remained supine. The British were in an uproar. At the very least, German troops must be withdrawn from Poland before the proposal for a conference was accepted. Mussolini knew that this was hopeless and dropped his proposal. The British and French governments went on hoping for a conference which was already dead.

On the evening of 2nd September Chamberlain addressed the House of Commons. MP's expected to hear that war had been declared. Instead Chamberlain said that, if the German government would agree to withdraw their troops from Poland (not actually to withdraw them), the British government would forget everything that had happened, and diplomacy could start again. Chamberlain sat down in dead silence. Greenwood, rising to speak for Labour, was greeted with a shout from Amery: 'Speak for England, Arthur.' Afterwards Greenwood warned Chamberlain that there would be no holding the House if war were not declared. The cabinet met late at night and resolved that an ultimatum should be sent to Germany at once. Halifax, who regretted this decision, put off the ultimatum until the next morning.

The British ultimatum was delivered in Berlin at 9 a.m. on 3rd September. The German government made no reply, and the ultimatum expired at 11 a.m. The French trailed after their ally and declared war at 5 p.m. The Second World War had begun. It is possible that Hitler intended to conquer Europe at some time. It is also possible, though less likely, that the British government intended at some time to resist him. Neither of these intentions caused the actual outbreak of war. Then Hitler merely wanted Danzig and the Corridor, and the British government wanted to give them to him. These plans were wrecked first by Polish obstinacy and then by the indignation of Conservative backbenchers. The very men who had applauded Munich now insisted on war.

There was much talk later about a crusade against fascism. In fact most countries were pushed into war. The Poles had no choice. The French were dragged along by the British. Russians and Americans, mighty boasters both, waited supinely until Hitler chose to attack them. Only the British people and their dominions went to war of their own free will. They were not concerned about fascism. They did not even save Poland. They went to war out of national pride and for the sake of national honour. Ultimately they brought Hitler down, and this was something to be proud of.

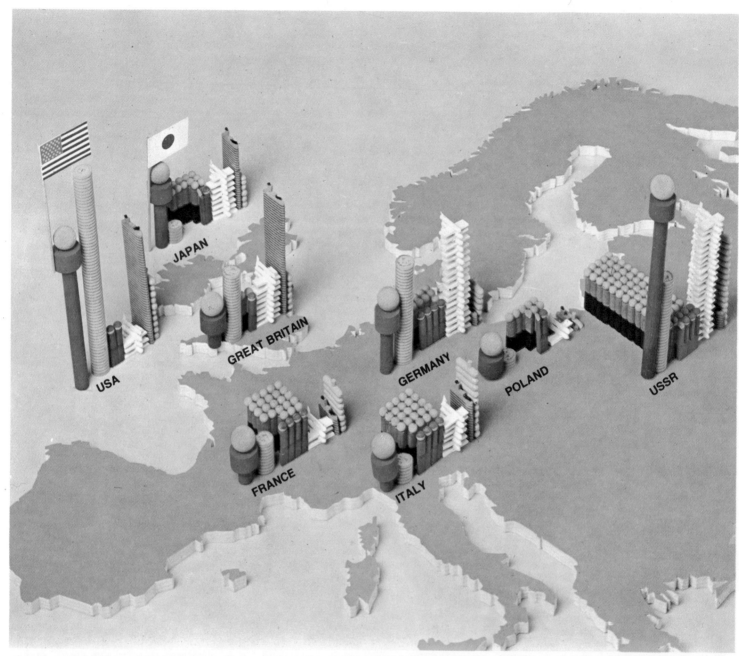

*Relative strength of all major belligerents in Second World War. The number increased after the first blows: Italy entered in 1940
and Russia, Japan, and the USA the following year. Russia's apparent dominance was offset by the obsolescence of her land forces*

		Great Britain	France	USSR	USA	Poland	Germany	Italy	Japan
	Population (thousands)*	47,692	41,600	167,300	129,825	34,662	68,424	43,779	70,590
	National income ($m)*	23,550	10,296	31,410	67,600	3,189	33,347	6,895	5,700
	Reserves (millions)	0.4	4.6	12.0†	**	1.5	2.2	4.8	2.4†
	Peacetime armies (millions)	0.22	0.8	1.7†	0.19	0.29	0.8	0.8	0.32†
	Aircraft (first line)	2,075	600	5,000†	800	390	4,500†	1,500††	1,980
	Destroyers	184	28	28	181	4	17	60	113
	Submarines	58	70	150	99	5	56	100	53

*1938   **not available   †approximate   ††1940

The Military Balance

Germany, from a population a little under sixty-five millions, lost in the First World War just under two millions killed. Despite their support for Hitler and their enthusiasm for the successful outcome of his early military adventures, the German people dreaded another war no less than those of other nations. The generals and admirals, while willing to contemplate war to redress what they saw as the iniquities of the Versailles Treaty, knew in 1939 the work of rearmament and expansion to be far from complete. Yet events were to show the Germans better equipped psychologically, technically, and materially to fight again

than the other nations of the world who watched the re-appearance of German power with fascinated alarm and growing—if supine—horror.

The Versailles Treaty limited the German army to 100,000 and forbade Germany tanks, heavy artillery, aircraft, gas, submarines, and a general staff. General Hans von Seeckt, head of the Reichswehr from 1920 to 1926, rigorously selected officers and men, re-established discipline and professionalism, and sought to combine the old Prussian tradition with a more modern and flexible spirit. Against the day of expansion, officers and men were prepared for

German pilots before their Henschel Hs 123s strap on parachutes, 1937. These aircraft were to give tactical support to the army in the early months of the war

higher rank and secret arrangements enabled the training of personnel and development of the forbidden weapons to be carried out abroad.

When expansion came Seeckt would have preferred an élite striking force of some 2-300,000 backed by a national militia—de Gaulle advocated something similar for France. Hitler, however, demanded a modernized version of the old mass Imperial Army. In October 1934 he announced the expansion of the Reichswehr to 300,000, then in March 1935 denounced the Versailles Treaty, proclaimed conscription, and set the strength of the army at 600,000 and thirty-six divisions. By 1939 it had reached a peace-time strength of 730,000 with 1,100,000 in the reserves.

An increase in strength by eighteen times in seven years was far greater than anything contemplated by Seeckt, and only a minority of the officers and experts needed could be found in the Reichswehr. Every possible source was tapped for the rest—police, Party organizations, former officers of the Imperial Army, and, of course, mass intake and training of the young. The Nazi philosophy lent itself to rigorous training and discipline, and a combination of extreme standardization in training and equipment, on the one hand, with encouragement of initiative and flexibility in action, on the other, was remarkably successful in the rapid production of highly effective forces.

Although he failed to appreciate the full potential of the tank, Seeckt had believed in the traditional Prussian strategy of dynamic mobility. Heinz Guderian, a young infantry captain appointed in 1922 to the motor transport staff, became the leading German proponent of armoured warfare. As chief of staff to the director of motorized troops in 1931, pressing for armoured divisions, he met the same sort of opposition that had appeared in other armies, but Hitler, when he came to power, took up the idea. 'That's what I need,' he exclaimed when he first saw Guderian's armour, 'that's what I want to have!'

An experimental armoured division took part in the summer exercises of 1935, and that autumn the first three armoured divisions were formed. Next year they were

Top left: Battle simulation in the Nuremberg stadium, 1938. Amid smoke effects, infantry and Panzer II tanks cavort for a capacity crowd. **Top right:** *Refuelling Stuka dive-bombers, January 1939. The dreaded gull-winged Ju 87 was to win easy victories in Poland and France in the absence of adequate fighter opposition.* **Left:** *Battleship* Bismarck, *1940. Her fifteen-inch guns, massive armour, and high power made her the pride of Hitler's navy and the strongest battleship of the day*

formed into an armoured corps, while three light divisions—a throwback to earlier doctrine—and four motorized divisions were formed. Massed armour appeared in the manoeuvres of 1937 and again in 1938. In March 1937, under Guderian, one armoured and one SS motorized division entered Vienna, having driven 420 miles in forty-eight hours. The Panzers of the Second World War had appeared.

When the army mobilized in September 1939 there were six armoured, four light (later converted to armoured), four motorized, and eighty-four infantry divisions. There was, however, a shortage of the later types of tanks—even in May 1940 only some 600 of the new Panzerkampfwagen (armoured fighting vehicle) III and IV had reached the armoured divisions, which had over 300 modern Czech tanks and about 1,500 of the older, lightly armoured and armed, Pzkw I and II. The superiority of the forceful, energetic Panzer groups lay in their organization into self-contained divisions and corps, and in their insistence on using these forces massed for a breakthrough in depth.

At the head of the army, generals such as Brauchitsch, Halder, Rundstedt and Bock were orthodox, able, and more forceful, though little younger, than their French opponents. It was at the next level that the architects of victory were to be found: Guderian, 51, commanding XIX Panzer Corps, Manstein, 52, who devised the plan that routed the French, and Rommel, 46, a divisional commander in France.

Limited under the Versailles Treaty to warships of 10,000 tons, Germany had built three 'pocket battleships'. Planned as commerce raiders, more powerful than any cruiser and faster than most battleships, these caused anxiety in Great Britain. The new German submarine force that began to appear under Admiral Dönitz caused less, for it was believed that the new sound-echo system Asdic (later Sonar) would deal with submarine attack. By September 1939 two new 31,000-ton fast battle-cruisers, the *Gneisenau* and *Scharnhorst,* had been completed, and, in addition to the pocket battleships, there were one new heavy cruiser, five light cruisers, seventeen destroyers, and fifty-six submarines.

Grand-Admiral Raeder had counted on a much stronger navy for war against Great Britain, for under his Plan Z four 42,000-ton battleships were being built or projected, besides an aircraft-carrier, two more heavy cruisers, and a large ocean-going submarine force. Now all work on surface ships was stopped, except on the battleships *Bismarck* and *Tirpitz* and the cruisers *Blücher* and *Prinz Eugen,* and transferred to submarines.

It was, however, fear of German air-power, rather than of Panzers and U-boats,

that kept the statesmen and peoples of Europe awake at night. Forbidden military aircraft were being built. Germany had become very air-minded. Flying and gliding clubs flourished. Aircraft factories were established abroad. The Reichswehr secretly trained military pilots in Russia and Italy. The state airline Lufthansa held men and operating resources that could be transferred to the Luftwaffe when it was formed. In December 1933, four months before its existence was announced, Göring had assembled 1,888 aircraft for it, 584 of them operational types.

By September 1939 the first-line strength of the Luftwaffe was between 4,000 and 4,700 aircraft: some 700 Me 109 fighters, 1,100 Ju 88 and He 111 day-bombers, 350 Ju 87 (Stuka) dive-bombers—all new and successful types—400 Me 110 two-seater fighters—an unsuccessful new type—and 550 transport aircraft. The remainder were army and naval co-operation aircraft and a few older fighters and bombers.

Despite the cold-blooded destruction of Guernica by the Condor Legion in the Spanish Civil War, the Luftwaffe was not primarily an anti-city or strategic bombing force. It was planned for army support, and paid little attention to the development of a long-range heavy bomber, concentrating instead on medium day-bombers and dive-bombers. These latter, although very vulnerable to fighters, could be highly effective in support of the Panzers.

Maginot Line and Maginot-mind
Although for France, victory had in 1918 avenged the defeat of 1870, the nation's confidence in itself and in the army had been deeply eroded by the frightful years of the more recent war—the shattering miscalculations of 1914, the repeated failures in the offensives from 1915 to 1917, and, etched in memory, Verdun in 1916. A

Left: Life on the Maginot Line, the French fortification system built in the 1930's along the eastern frontier. The fortresses proved practically useless: Germany's fast-moving armour bypassed them in the 1940 invasion. 1 Troops in an underground gallery. They were quartered in air-conditioned compartments and typical forts had underground recreation areas and railways. 2 Food for the garrison. 3 Artillery casemate, gun, and crew. Soldier in foreground is fusing shells.
Right: British weaponry. 1 British Vickers Mark 6 light tanks on manoeuvres, October 1939. These obsolescent tanks operated in France and the desert in a scouting role. 2 Practice scramble. RAF pilots race for their Spitfires, May 1939. 3 Aircraft-carrier, HMS Ark Royal. Completed in 1938, she was sunk by a German submarine in 1941

△1

△2 ▽3

population of under forty million had lost 1,385,000 men killed, and large areas had been occupied or devastated. The price of victory was remembered with bitterness that turned to cynical despair when, after what France saw as the undue leniency of Versailles and the culpable failure to enforce reparations, Germany rearmed and threatened war.

In the years between the wars, the mass army was retained, but its effectiveness was sapped by financial stringency, by successive reductions in the length of military service, and by distrust of its usefulness to do anything but bring about another bloodbath. The doctrine of offensive à outrance was abandoned for one of slow, heavily prepared infantry advance, and the Maginot Line was built. The generals of 1918 stayed on, in the words of de Gaulle, 'growing old at their posts, wedded to errors that had once constituted their glory'.

Alsace and Lorraine, lost in 1870 and now returned, lay vulnerable to a German war of revenge. Along the Rhine the Alsatian frontier is easily defensible, but the Lorraine frontier, running westwards from the Rhine to the southernmost point of Belgium, is much less so. André Maginot, renowned for his gallant war record and subsequent work as minister of pensions, forced through financial provision for the line that bears his name, sited primarily to guard the Lorraine frontier, with an extension along the Rhine.

To the obvious criticism that the line did nothing to guard against a repetition of the German advance through Belgium of 1914, the French General Staff gave several answers. Germany was the potential enemy, not Belgium. The ground was low lying and unsuitable for Maginot-type fortifications and the Lille industrial complex too close to the frontier to be protected. In the north a field force would advance to the rescue of Belgium, while further south the Ardennes were impracticable to large armies. Much of this, though certainly not the last point, was sound enough, but the Maginot Line soon began to absorb far too much of the material resources and moral commitment of the nation, diverting them from the developing concept of mobile, armoured warfare.

The French generals, indeed, paid lip service to the tank, and, as war drew near, large numbers were provided for the army. But neither Pétain, nor Weygand, who followed him as the head of the army in 1931, nor Gamelin, who followed Weygand in 1935, would accept the idea of self-contained armoured divisions concentrated for breakthrough in depth. Infantry, they insisted, was the dominant arm. The tank should support it.

In September 1939, after mobilization, some sixty infantry divisions, two cavalry divisions, two light armoured divisions (divisions légères mécanisées, DLM) and two heavier armoured brigades faced the Germans in north-eastern France. Nine infantry divisions faced the Italians in the south-east. There were, in addition, fortress units on both fronts and training units and new units forming in reserve. In the colonies there were about ten infantry divisions and some cavalry brigades. By May 1940 one more DLM would be formed and the armoured brigades would be expanded to armoured divisions (divisions cuirassées), while a third armoured brigade would be forming. This was, however, from a total of some 2,250 reasonably modern tanks, roughly equivalent to the German and Czech tanks, and 440 First World War Renault FTs, completely obsolete and out of place on a 1940 battlefield.

Gamelin, 67, aide to Joffre in 1914, imperturbable, colourless, complacent, held the supreme command, and his pale orthodoxy set the tone for lower commanders. 'We need tanks, of course,' he had written to Reynaud, '. . . but you cannot hope to achieve a real breakthrough with tanks. . . . As to the air, it will not play the part you expect. . . . It'll be a flash in the pan.'

The French navy was relatively more formidable than in 1914. As well as five reconstructed older battleships, there were seven modern 10,000-ton cruisers, ten slightly smaller ones, sixty flotilla leaders and destroyers, seventy submarines and an aircraft-carrier as well as two fine new 26,500-ton battle-cruisers, the Dunkerque and Strasbourg. Four 35,000-ton battleships and two aircraft-carriers were building or about to be laid down.

The air force, an independent service, had stagnated both in doctrine and material. The vital factors of aircraft performance and industrial capacity had been neglected and continued to be even after rearmament had started in the other services. In September 1939 the first-line strength of the French air force was some 600 fighters, 170 bombers and 360 reconnaissance aircraft. Of these 520 were modern fighters but outclassed by the Me 109; most of the remainder were obsolete. The warning system was rudimentary. By May 1940 improvements would have been made, but France would still be fatally weak in the air.

Great Britain — weak on land

Great Britain, traditionally a sea power, was confirmed in her distrust of continental commitment by the experiences of her armies on the Western Front. There and elsewhere on land she had lost 700,000 dead. Yet in the First World War the Royal Navy had not come up to expectations. The stranglehold of blockade, though effective in the long run, had been far too slow to rescue France and Russia, let alone Belgium, from invasion. German submarines had brought Great Britain close to defeat. Perhaps independent air-power, to which Lloyd George and Smuts had looked hopefully in 1917 when all attempts to break the German line in France seemed doomed to failure, might offer something better than the two older modes of warfare.

The vulnerability of Great Britain to sea blockade, however, continued to demand adequate naval strength, and imperial commitments seemed to require conventional land forces. Painting a lurid picture of cities under air attack, proponents of air-power raised ethical problems, and also, by making defence appear hopeless, strengthened the hands of the appeasers who would condone aggression at any price. Under these influences British strategic policy developed much as might be expected. In another war Great Britain would fight at sea and in the air, it was decided, rather than commit an army to the continent, but, until well into the 'thirties, most of the limited funds available for defence went to the two older services and was spent by them on traditional arms.

Great Britain had led the way with the tank in the First World War, and for a while continued to hold her lead in its postwar development. Liddell Hart and Fuller developed the concept of the armoured breakthrough, and their writings were avidly studied in Germany and Russia. An experimental mechanized force was set up rather half-heartedly in 1927, but a tide of reaction was setting in. The British Army, small in size, long-serviced, based on a fully-developed industry, was singularly well-adapted to the armoured concept, but Great Britain, having given birth to the idea, now turned away from it to the compromise of restricted armoured support for an infantry army and to nostalgic horse-worship. Tank design faltered, and production failed to get into its stride when rearmament began.

At almost the last moment, in the spring of 1939, Great Britain woke to the reality that France dared not face Germany without British assistance in the defence of her land frontier. In quick succession the doubling of the Territorial Army and the imposition of conscription were announced in a belated attempt to provide an army adequate to the need, but shortage of weapons and outmoded leadership went near to stultifying the effort.

Thus in the autumn of 1939 Great Britain was able to send to France only four regular infantry divisions with fifty cavalry light tanks. By May 1940 one more regular and five more divisions from the Territorial Army had arrived, and tank strength had grown to a two-battalion infantry tank brigade (100 tanks) and two cavalry light tank brigades (200 tanks). One—largely regular—armoured division was about to cross for final training in France. Three other Territorial Army divisions, for whom there were only rifles and no artillery, had spent the winter building airfields in France. The equivalent of one division had fought in Norway. Other divisions were arming and training in Great Britain.

In contrast the Royal Navy was a major world force. Under the Washington Treaty the navies of Great Britain, the USA, and Japan had been set at the ratio of 5:5:3 for battleships and aircraft-carriers. British battleships were on the whole rather older than those of the other two powers, and her carriers, like theirs, a mixed collection. Denounced by Japan, the Washington Treaty ended in 1935, and now nine new British battleships of 35,000 tons or over and six excellent new carriers were building or projected, as well as cruisers and smaller ships, but only the carrier *Ark Royal* had joined the fleet, which in September 1939 comprised: twelve battleships, three battle-cruisers, seven aircraft-carriers, sixty-four cruisers, 184 destroyers, and fifty-eight submarines.

Naval aviation remained a weakness owing mainly to the poor performance of carrier-borne aircraft. Reliance was placed on the gun against air attack and on the Asdic against submarines. In general, the navy was surface-ship minded, regarding the air and submarines as ancillaries, but in spirit and confidence nothing was lacking.

When in July 1934 Mr Churchill had warned Parliament that Germany possessed a rapidly expanding secret air force, the Royal Air Force at home amounted to 488 first-line bombers and fighters in forty-two squadrons, with nine squadrons for naval and army co-operation, and twenty-four overseas. The programme then announced to raise forty-one new squadrons in five years soon gave way to new and more ambitious programmes, each overtaken by its successor before completion. As radio location (later Radar) was developed and the high-performance eight-gun fighter appeared, fighters began to get priority over bombers. The four-engine heavy strategic bombers under development would not be ready for several years.

By September 1939 first-line strength had reached a total of 2,075 aircraft, of which 415 were overseas and 1,660 at home, which included 530 bombers, 608 fighters and 516 reconnaissance and co-operation. 500 fighters were modern, Hurricanes and some Spitfires, but the bombers, intended for day-bombing, were highly vulnerable to fighters. An advance air striking force was to leave for France, so as to bring bombers closer to German industrial targets.

Poland – an easy victim

Cut off from Great Britain and France on the eastern frontier of Germany, Poland after mobilization had an army of thirty-nine infantry divisions and eleven horsed cavalry brigades, but only one tank and two motorized brigades totalling together 225 modern and 88 obsolescent tanks in addition to armoured cars and reconnaissance vehicles. First-line air-strength, mostly obsolescent, amounted to 150 fighters, 120 reconnaissance bombers, 36 medium bombers and 84 army co-operation aircraft. In the navy there were four destroyers, five submarines, and some light craft. Including frontier defence the whole amounted to a peace strength of 370,000 with 2,800,000 in reserves.

Failing a land offensive in the West against Germany, for which as we have seen the French army was neither trained nor organized, or strategic air bombardment, for which at the time Great Britain was neither technically capable nor ethically prepared, help for Poland could only come from Russia. By signing the non-aggression pact with Germany on 23rd August 1939 Russia declared that no help would be given. For the present Poland was on her own against Hitler.

Force of a vanished era: Polish cavalry, 1939. During the German invasion of Poland a cavalry unit charged Panzers

2 GERMANY'S TRIUMPH

Blitzkrieg on Poland

The Polish Campaign opened in the early morning of 1st September 1939, when German forces crossed the Polish frontier shortly before 0600, preceded by air attacks which had begun an hour earlier. It was of great significance in the history of warfare because it was the first exposition of the theory, originated in Great Britain in the 1920's, of fast-moving mechanized warfare by armoured forces and aircraft in combination.

Britain's early protagonists of the theory depicted its action in terms of the play of 'lightning'. From now on, aptly if ironically, that simile came into world-wide currency under the German title of Blitzkrieg (lightning war).

Poland, with its far-stretching frontiers —3,500 miles in extent—was well fitted, all too well fitted, for the practice and demonstration of the Blitzkrieg theory. The stretch of 1,250 miles adjoining German territory had recently been extended to 1,750 miles by the occupation of Czecho-Slovakia. This also meant that Poland's southern flank had become exposed to invasion—even more than the northern flank, facing East Prussia, already was.

The Polish plain offered flat and fairly easy going for a mobile invader, though not so easy as France would offer because of the scarcity of good roads in the country, the deep sand often met off the roads, and the frequency of lakes and forests in some

The Panzer Mk IV. Cutting edge of the Panzer Divisions and the forefront of tank design in the period of Germany's early victories. The commander's black uniform with the soft beret changed after Poland

areas. But the time chosen for the invasion—when the terrain was dry and hard-surfaced—minimized these drawbacks.

In view of the geographical and strategical conditions, it would have been wiser if the Polish army had assembled farther back, behind the Vistula and the San. That, however, would have meant abandoning some of the most important industrial areas. The Silesian coalfields lay close to the frontier, and most of the main industrial area, although farther back, lay west of these river-lines.

The economic argument for delaying the enemy's advance was reinforced by national pride and military over-confidence, as well as an unrealistic idea of what Poland's allies in the West could do to relieve the pressure. A third of the Polish forces were concentrated in or near the 'Corridor', where they were exposed to a double envelopment from East Prussia and the west combined. This indulgence of national pride—in opposing Germany's re-entry into the piece of her pre-1918 territory for which she had been agitating —seriously reduced the forces available to cover the areas more vital to Poland's defence. Nearly another third of Poland's forces lay in reserve north of the central axis, between Łódź and Warsaw, under the Commander-in-Chief of the Polish Army, Marshal Smigly-Rydz.

The Poles' forward concentration in general forfeited their chance of fighting a series of delaying actions, since their foot marching army was unable to get back to man rear positions before they were overrun by the invader's mechanized columns. Lack of mobility was more fatal than incomplete mobilization.

On the other side the forty German infantry divisions used in the invasion counted for much less than their fourteen mechanized or partially mechanized divisions. These included six armoured divisions, four light divisions (motorized infantry with two armoured units), and four motorized divisions. Their deep and rapid thrusts decided the issue, in combination with the attacks of the Luftwaffe—which smashed the Polish railway system, besides knocking out most of the Polish air force before it was able to come into action.

The Luftwaffe operated in a very dispersed way, instead of in large formations, but it thereby spread a creeping paralysis over the widest possible area. Another weighty factor was the German radio bombardment, disguised as Polish transmissions, which did much to increase the confusion and demoralization of the Polish rear. All these factors were given a multiplied effect by the way that Polish over-confidence in the power of their men to defeat machines led, on the rebound, to disillusionment and disintegration.

In the north, the invasion was carried out by Bock's Army Group, which comprised the III Army (under Küchler) and the IV Army (under Kluge). The former thrust southward from its flanking position in East Prussia, while the latter pushed eastward across the Polish Corridor to join it in enveloping the Poles' right flank.

The principal role was given to Rundstedt's Army Group in the south. This was nearly twice as strong in infantry, and more in armour. It comprised the VIII Army (under Blaskowitz), the X (under Reichenau), and the XIV (under List). Blaskowitz, on the left wing, was to push towards

the great manufacturing centre of Lódź, and help to isolate the Polish forces in the Poznań salient, while covering Reichenau's flank. On the right wing, List was to push for Kraków and simultaneously turn the Poles' Carpathian flank, using Kleist's armoured corps to drive through the mountain passes. The decisive stroke was delivered by Reichenau, in the centre, who had the largest part of the armoured forces.

By 3rd September—the date Great Britain and France declared war—Kluge's advance had cut the Corridor and reached the lower Vistula, while Küchler's pressure from East Prussia towards the Narew was developing. More important, Reichenau's armoured forces had penetrated to the Warta, and forced the crossings there. Meanwhile List's army was converging from both flanks on Kraków, forcing the Poles in that sector to abandon the city and fall back to the Nida and the Dunajec.

On the following day Reichenau's leading forces had reached and crossed the Pilica, fifty miles east of the frontier. By 6th September his left wing was well in rear of Lódź, and his right wing had driven into Kielce. The other German armies had all gone far towards fulfilling their part in the vast enveloping operation planned by Halder, the Chief of the Army General Staff, under the direction of Brauchitsch, Commander-in-Chief of the Army. The Polish armies had begun to split up into unco-ordinated fractions, some of which were in retreat while others were delivering disjointed attacks on the enemy columns nearest to them.

Exploiting a gap, one of Reichenau's armoured corps drove through to the edge of Warsaw on 8th September—having covered 140 miles in the week. The next day the light divisions on his right wing reached the Vistula farther south, between Warsaw and Sandomierz, and turned north.

Near the Carpathians, List's mobile forces had swept across the Dunajec, and a series of other rivers in turn, to the San

Left: 1 Russian tanks move into Poland. 2 Motorized German infantry advances. The leading car carries insignia plundered from a Polish frontier post. **Right: 1** *Sarcastic German comment on Paderewski playing while Warsaw burns. The famous pianist and former Prime Minister was invited to succeed Moscicki as President of Poland after the latter fled to Rumania. He declined because of ill health. 2 Cavalry—the pride of the Polish army but hopelessly obsolete. 3 The campaign, showing subsequent Russo-German boundary. 4 'Luftwaffe' by the Polish artist B.W.Linke portrays horror felt by those who experienced the Blitzkrieg. 5 Hitler on a visit to the Polish front stands before the bust of Pilsudski*

Germany's Triumph

on either flank of the famous fortress of Przemyśl. In the north Guderian's armoured corps (which was in Küchler's army) had driven across the Narew and was attacking the line of the Bug, in rear of Warsaw. Thus a second and wider pincer-movement developed outside the inner pincers that were closing on the Polish forces in the bend of the Vistula near Warsaw.

This stage of the invasion had seen an important variation of plan on the Germans' side. Their view of the situation was momentarily obscured by the extraordinary state of confusion on the Poles' side, where columns appeared to be moving in many different directions, raising clouds of dust that obscured aerial observation. Under these circumstances the German High Command thought that the bulk of the Polish forces in the north had already escaped across the Vistula. On that assumption it gave orders that Reichenau's army was to cross the Vistula between Warsaw and Sandomierz, with the aim of intercepting the Poles' anticipated withdrawal into south-eastern Poland. But Rundstedt demurred, being convinced that the bulk of the Polish forces were still west of the Vistula. After some argument his view prevailed, and Reichenau's army was wheeled north to establish a blocking position along the Bzura west of Warsaw.

As a result the largest remaining part of the Polish forces was trapped before it could withdraw over the Vistula. To the advantage which the Germans had gained by their strategic penetration along the line of least resistance was now added the advantage of tactical defence. To complete the victory it had merely to hold its ground – in face of the hurried assaults of an army which was fighting in reverse, cut off from its bases, with its supplies running short, and increasingly pressed from the flank and behind by the converging eastward advance of Blaskowitz's and Kluge's armies. Although the Poles fought fiercely, with a bravery that greatly impressed their opponents, only a small proportion ultimately managed to break out, by night, and join troops of the Warsaw garrison.

On 10th September the Polish commander-in-chief, Marshal Smigly-Rydz, ordered a general retreat into the south-east of Poland and put General Sosnkowski in charge there, in the hope of developing a defensive position for prolonged resistance on a comparatively narrow front. By now the Germans were already penetrating deeply into the country beyond the Vistula, while they had also outflanked the line of the Bug in the north, and that of the San in the south. On the northern flank Guderian, with his armoured corps, swept southward to Brest Litovsk, while on the southern flank Kleist's armoured corps

reached Lwów on 12th September. These mechanized spearheads were running short of fuel, after their deep drives, but the Polish command system was so badly disjointed that it was unable to take advantage of the Germans' diminishing pace, and increasing tiredness.

Guerrilla resistance

Then on 17th September the forces of Soviet Russia advanced, and invaded Poland from the east, at a moment when there were scarcely any Polish troops left to oppose them. On the following day the Polish government and the Commander-in-Chief of the Army left Polish soil and took shelter in Rumania. Even after that, the garrison of Warsaw held out for a further ten days, under heavy bombardment both from the ground and the air. Indeed, the last large fraction of the Polish army fought on until 5th October before it surrendered, and many fragments continued resistance in a guerrilla manner throughout the winter.

The Russian forces met the Germans on a line mid-way through Poland, running south from East Prussia past Brest Litovsk, to the Carpathians. The fresh partition of Poland that followed was short-lived. It did not cement their temporary partnership but increased the friction that arose once the two countries were in close contact along a common frontier.

Meantime the French had merely made a small dent in Germany's western front. It looked, and was, a feeble effort to relieve the pressure on their ally. In view of the weakness of the German forces and defences it was natural to feel that they could have done more. But deeper analysis tends to correct the obvious conclusion suggested by the comparative figures of the opposing forces.

Although the French northern frontier was 500 miles long, in attempting an offensive the French were confined to the narrow ninety-mile sector from the Rhine to the Moselle – unless they violated the neutrality of Belgium and Luxembourg. The Germans, however, were able to concentrate the best part of their available forces on this narrow sector, and they sowed the approaches to their Siegfried Line with a thick belt of minefields, thus imposing delay on the attackers.

The conscript mass

Worse still, the French were unable to start their offensive until about 17th September – except for some preliminary probing attacks. By that date, Poland was so obviously collapsing that they had a good excuse for countermanding it. Their incapacity to strike earlier arose from their mobilization system, which was inherently out of date. It was the fatal product of their

reliance on a conscript army – which could not come effectively into action until the mass of 'trained reserves' had been called up from their civil jobs, and the formations

Marshal Smigly-Rydz, C-in-C of the Polish Army. He was quite unable to defend his country against the German Blitzkrieg

had been made ready to operate. But the delay was increased by the French command's persistent belief in old tactical ideas – particularly the view that any offensive must be prepared by a massive artillery bombardment on the lines of the First World War. They still regarded heavy artillery as the essential 'tin-opener' in dealing with any defended position. But the bulk of their heavy artillery had to be brought out of storage, and could not be available until the last stage of mobilization. That condition governed their preparations to deliver an offensive.

For several years past one of France's political leaders, Paul Reynaud, had constantly argued that these conceptions were out of date, and had urged the necessity of creating a swift-moving mechanized force of professional soldiers ready for instant action – instead of relying on the old and slow-mobilizing conscript mass. But he had been a voice crying in the wilderness. French statesmen, like most French soldiers, placed their trust in conscription, and numbers.

The military issue in 1939 can be summed up in two sentences. In the East a hopelessly out-of-date army was quickly disintegrated by a small tank force, in combination with a superior air force, which put into practice a novel technique. At the same time, in the West, a slow-motion army could not develop any effective pressure before it was too late.

The Invasion of Norway

German airborne invasion

German seaborne invasion

German land invasion

Allied withdrawal

Airfield

10th-13th April: British sink ten German destroyers

Narvik
Harstad

Lofoten Islands

8th June

8th April: British lay minefield

31st May

8th June: Scharnhorst sinks Glorious

Bodo

2nd -3rd May

8th April: Hipper sinks Glowworm

Namsos

Steinkjer

SWEDEN

30th April -1st May

Trondheim

Andalsnes

Dombas

NORWAY

Lillehammer

Bergen

Fornebu   **Oslo**

Stavanger
Sola

Jøsenfjord
16th February: Altmark boarded

Kristiansand

Aalborg
Copenhagen

DENMARK

| 40 | 80 | 120 | MLS |
| 60 | 100 | 160 | KM |

Left: The campaign: by evening on 9th April all Norway's main cities, ports, and airfields were in German hands. The first Allied landings were not until 14th April. They proved ineffective

Neither Norway nor Denmark, avowedly pacifist and neutral, had done anything to provoke German aggression. Yet the plan for the invasion and occupation of the two Scandinavian states, innocuously code-named *Weserübung* or 'Exercise Weser', was dictated by the need to prevent possible British encroachment on Scandinavia and the Baltic, to safeguard vital iron-ore supplies from Sweden which passed through Narvik when the Gulf of Bothnia was frozen, and in order to provide the navy with bases from where submarines and surface raiders might be able to elude the British naval cordon and then break out onto the high seas.

The Commander-in-Chief of the Navy, Grand Admiral Erich Raeder, had impressed Hitler with the importance of obtaining naval bases in Norway, and the value of airfields in both countries had not been lost on the Luftwaffe. But Hitler did not show any real enthusiasm for the Norwegian operation until after 16th February when it became clear that Great Britain no longer intended to respect Norway's neutrality. As soon as the Allies began to organize an expeditionary force to aid the Finns in their struggle against the Soviet Union, German invasion plans took on a new urgency for it was realized that while crossing Norway and Sweden on their way to Finland the Allies could easily sever Germany's supply of Swedish iron-ore. On 12th March the Russo-Finnish war ended and General Jodl gloomily noted in his diary 'Conclusion of peace between Finland and Russia deprives England, but us too, of any political basis to occupy Norway.' But Hitler and Ribbentrop were at no loss for a pretext to invade. On 9th April 1940 Denmark was occupied and Norway invaded ostensibly to protect them from Anglo-French occupation. The two countries had been conferred with the 'protection of the Reich'.

Early the previous day, eight British destroyers entered Norwegian waters south of the Lofoten Islands and laid mines in the Leads on the approaches to the Arctic iron-ore port of Narvik. Four hundred miles to the south, two others marked a dummy minefield off Molde. A few hours later the British destroyer *Glowworm*, a hundred miles west of Trondheim, sighted German destroyers, and, giving chase in heavy seas and poor visibility, met the heavy cruiser

Hipper. Damaged and hopelessly outmatched, the *Glowworm* rammed the *Hipper,* then dropped astern burning and sinking. Still further south that morning, near the southern tip of Norway, villagers heard a dull explosion at sea. Later fishing boats brought in German soldiers from the transport *Rio de Janeiro,* who told them that they had been torpedoed on their way to Bergen to protect the Norwegians against the British.

In Oslo a distracted cabinet met. Norwegian sympathies lay with the Allies and against Hitler, but, hopelessly exposed to overwhelming German land and air strength, Norway longed to stay neutral. When on 16th February Captain Vian in the destroyer *Cossack* had defied Norwegian protests and boarded the German supply ship *Altmark* in Jøsenfjord to rescue three hundred captured British merchant seamen, from ships sunk by the *Graf Spee* and bound for German prison camps, German propaganda had raged against the British 'crime'. How would Hitler take this new violation of Norwegian neutrality?

Since the 3rd April reports had been coming in of ships and troops concentrating in north German ports, and more warnings came on the 8th. At 3 a.m. on the 9th the Norwegian cabinet ordered mobilization, but only 'silent' mobilization by post instead of by proclamation. By then the Norwegian coastal defences, manned only at one-third strength, were in contact with warships of unknown nationality entering the country's main ports.

The first ships of the German invasion, unescorted merchant ships carrying follow-up troops and equipment, had in fact sailed from Germany on the 3rd. On the morning of the 7th the fast battle-cruisers *Gneisenau* and *Scharnhorst* left the Schillig Roads escorting the *Hipper* and fourteen destroyers with mountain troops on board to seize Narvik and Trondheim. Other warships followed later with troops for the more southerly Norwegian ports and for Copenhagen.

Norway fights on

Invaded by land and sea, Denmark surrendered early on the 9th, but Norway decided to fight on. Narvik, Trondheim, Bergen, and Kristiansand fell quickly, but, two-thirds of the way up Oslofjord, the heavy guns and torpedoes of the old fort, Oscarsborg, set ablaze and sank the new German heavy cruiser *Blücher,* and turned back the German seaborne invasion of the capital. Aircraft carrying parachutists to seize Fornebu, the Oslo airport, met low

Germany's Triumph

cloud and were recalled, but ten Me 110 fighters, their petrol exhausted, were forced to land at Fornebu, and were followed by a squadron of Junkers 52s carrying infantry, which had failed to obey the recall. Oslo, the vital key-point of the German plan, fell that afternoon, and the ships came up the fjord next day. Stavanger with the main west coast airfield, Sola, fell early on the 9th to German parachutists and air-transported troops respectively. Thus by the evening all the main cities, ports, and airfields of Norway were in German hands.

For the next few days the Germans built up strength in Oslo, and the Norwegians mobilized as best they could in the hope of containing the Germans in the cities. Then on the 14th the Germans struck out, first to the south-east and west, then on the 15th north and north-west for Trondheim and Bergen. By the 20th they were close to Lillehammer and Rena, 120 miles from Trondheim, at the entrance to the Gudbrandsdal and Østerdal valleys.

Having failed to intercept the Germans at sea on the 9th, or, under air attack, to follow them into the Norwegian ports, the British Home Fleet had turned north to Narvik. There, on the 10th, Captain Warburton-Lee had led five British destroyers up the fjord to attack ten larger German destroyers, sinking two for the loss of two of his vessels. On the 13th the British destroyers returned accompanied by the battleship *Warspite,* and finished off the German ships, isolating the Germans in Narvik.

Although the British, foreseeing some German reaction to the mining, had held a small land force ready in Scottish ports for Norway, the speed and daring of the German landings threw their plans into confusion. The first Allied troops landed at Harstad, forty miles from Narvik, on 14th April. Weaker detachments also landed at Namsos in central Norway on the same day and troops who landed at Åndalsnes on the 17th, moved south to join the Norwegians at Lillehammer. British plans to enter Trondheimfjord, land near the small airfield at Vaernes, and re-capture Trondheim were, in the face of dominant German air power, finally abandoned on the 19th.

A mishandled campaign

On the 21st the Germans attacked in strength up the Gudbrandsdal and Østerdal, driving back the Norwegians and British, and, eight days later, linking up with elements pushing south from Trondheim. By then the British had decided to withdraw from central Norway. The last soldier re-embarked from Åndalsnes under heavy air attack early on the 1st May, and from Namsos on the 2nd. Deserted by their allies, the Norwegians in central Norway capitulated on the 3rd.

Deep snow in the north had held up operations around Narvik, and it was not until the 28th May that a British, Norwegian, and French force together with a brigade of Poles recaptured the port, while the British delayed the German relief force coming north from Trondheim. By then disastrous events in France had forced Churchill to order withdrawal from north Norway. The last convoys left Harstad on the 8th June, and the Norwegians, who had fought a gallant campaign in the mountains, capitulated.

The *Gneisenau* and *Scharnhorst* had returned to Germany after the April landings. Early in June they came north again undetected by the British, and on the 8th June met the aircraft carrier *Glorious* and two escorting destroyers off Harstad, sinking all three with heavy loss of life. However, a last torpedo from the destroyer *Acasta* struck the *Scharnhorst* and seriously damaged her, forcing both ships to return to Trondheim and so saving the troop convoys. Off Trondheim the British submarine *Clyde* torpedoed and damaged the *Gneisenau*.

The Norwegian campaign was for the Allies, and especially for the British, muddled both in concept and execution. As first lord of the Admiralty, Churchill had since September 1939 pressed for action against the winter iron-ore trade through Narvik, but Chamberlain and Halifax had wisely restrained him. The German invasion, almost simultaneous with the British mining of the Leads, revealed the extent of Churchill's misjudgment of the strategic position. Yet there were moments when Hitler was on the point of losing his nerve, first over Narvik, then over Trondheim. Had the British acted then with comparable skill and daring they might have inflicted serious reverses on the Germans. That the fall of France would, in the end, almost certainly have forced the British to evacuate Norway, is little excuse for the mishandling of the campaign.

Right: As dusk gathers over the Norwegian fjords, a German anti-aircraft unit keeps watch over this outpost in the north, a new bastion in Hitler's Fortress Europe. The date: 15th June 1940, six days after the Norwegian capitulation. Churchill eloquently expressed this new Allied defeat when he said: 'For many generations Norway, with its homely, rugged population engaged in trade, shipping, fishing, and agriculture, had stood outside the turmoil of world politics. . . . A tiny army and a population with no desires except to live peaceably in their own mountainous and semi-Arctic country now fell victims to the new German aggression'

Victory in the West

At the end of the Polish campaign, on 27th September 1939, Hitler ordered his generals to prepare for an offensive in the West that same autumn. At that moment the German army was quite unready. Its armoured and motorized divisions needed re-equipping and the line divisions needed officer reinforcements and further training.

Hitler insisted, against his generals' advice, that the offensive should be launched on 12th November. The army command produced a plan of attack on 19th October code-named *Fall Gelb* or 'Plan Yellow'. It was a half-hearted scheme, so conservative and uninspiring that it might well have been thought up by a British or French general staff of the inter-war years, with objectives far less ambitious even than those of the Schlieffen Plan of 1914. Its main effort was directed through Belgium towards the Ghent—Bruges area, with the object of covering the Ruhr against any Allied attack, and providing air and sea bases nearer Great Britain. There was no thought of striking a decisive blow against the Allied forces.

Hitler's natural ingenuity now came into play. He had already ordered that aircraft and tanks were to be used on a broad front for the offensive, the latter operating in open country and in massed formations to achieve surprise. Now he introduced the idea of parachutists and gliders to facilitate the crossing of the Meuse north of Liège; and he was also thinking of an attack on the Meuse south of Liège, followed through with an advance in the direction of Rheims and Amiens. Thus by 29th October the army's objective was 'to destroy the Allied forces in the sector north of the Somme and to break through to the Channel coast.'

The weight of the offensive still lay in north Belgium, with the German Army Group B under General von Bock. Hitler, however, produced a 'new idea' which required the utilization of the east—west gap in the Belgian Ardennes (along a line from Arlon through Tintigny to Florenville), which was guarded only by neutral Luxembourg, to reach the French frontier town of Sedan on the upper Meuse.

The commander of the German Army Group A on the southern sector, facing the Ardennes, was General von Rundstedt. He and his brilliant chief-of-staff, General von Manstein, saw the weaknesses and hesitations in the army's directives for 'Plan Yellow', which did not provide for the rapid and complete destruction of all the enemy's forces. They proposed that Army Group A should be made strong enough to cross the Meuse south of Namur and roll round south of the Allied armies (which were expected to have moved up into Belgium) and then sweep through in the direction of Arras and Boulogne. The commander-in-chief, Field-Marshal von Brauchitsch, was not interested in these proposals, and so Hitler did not hear of them; neither Rundstedt nor Manstein were aware of Hitler's simultaneous 'new idea.'

'Plan Yellow' compromised

Bad weather early in November compelled Hitler to agree to a series of postponements, and gave the generals time to elaborate his ideas. The task of leading Hitler's proposed thrust through the Ardennes to Sedan, was entrusted to XIX Panzer Corps under the command of Germany's chief exponent of tank warfare, General Heinz Guderian. This thrust would open up the possibility of expanding the offensive on the heights beyond Sedan; but Brauchitsch still turned a deaf ear to Manstein's plea for the strengthening of Army Group A to enable it to drive through the lower Somme.

By the end of December, Hitler and Brauchitsch had still not decided where the main weight of the offensive was to fall. Rundstedt and Manstein, however, were continuing their private campaign on behalf of Army Group A in the south, with detailed plans for a crossing of the Meuse from Dinant, in Belgium, southwards—the main effort being directed initially at Sedan.

The prospect of a period of bright weather brought the German forces into readiness for the launching of the offensive in the middle of January. The Luftwaffe had now persuaded Hitler to concentrate the landing of parachutists and airborne troops in Holland, where they feared the British might obtain air bases for the bombing of the Ruhr.

The weather again changed for the worse. Furthermore the German command had been made uneasy by the forced land-

Left: German anti-tank gunners cover a road during the attack on Northern France. Mobile and hard-hitting German anti-tank guns could not deal with the heaviest Allied armour, but the French frittered their advantage away in penny-packets.
Right: Hitler breaks into a jig of joy on hearing the French offer of an armistice

Invasion of the West
10th-20th May 1940

NETHERLANDS

Amsterdam

The Hague
German airborne
landings
Rotterdam

Bock
Army group B

Maas R.

Boulogne
Ostend
Calais
Dunkirk
Ypres
BELGIUM
Louvain
Brussels
Fort Eben-Emael
Antwerp
Albert Canal
Namur
Liège
Ardennes

Rundstedt
Army group A

Arras
Cambrai
Sedan

Leeb
Army group C

Amiens
Abbeville
Approximate Allied
front, 20th May

LUXEMBOURG

Paris

German starting line,
10th May
Siegfried Line
Maginot Line

20   40   60 MLS
20 40 60 80 KM

Basle

18th-26th May

Ostend
Gravelines Dunkirk
Calais
BELGIUM
Ypres
Boulogne
fell 25th May
Aa R.
Lille
Montreuil
St Pol
Arras
Noyelles
Abbeville
Péronne
Amiens
Somme R.

█▶ German attacks
◁ Allied counter-attack
---- Canals

10   20   30 MLS
10 20 30 KM

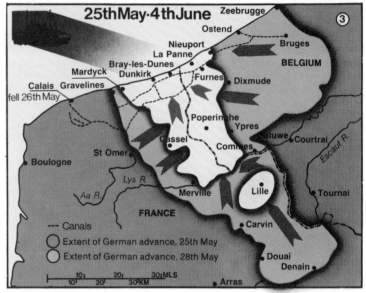

25th May-4th June

Zeebrugge
Ostend
Nieuport   Bruges
La Panne
Bray-les-Dunes   BELGIUM
Mardyck Dunkirk Furnes Dixmude
Calais Gravelines
fell 26th May
Poperinghe Ypres
Cassel   Comines Houluwe Courtrai
St Omer
Boulogne
Escaut R.
Lys R.
Aa R. Lille Tournai
Merville
FRANCE   Carvin
Douai
Denain
Arras

---- Canals
◯ Extent of German advance, 25th May
◯ Extent of German advance, 28th May

10   20   30 MLS
10 20 30 KM

ing in Belgium of two senior German air force officers carrying documents describing aspects of 'Plan Yellow'. It was now postponed indefinitely. Although the German officers partially destroyed the documents, enough information filtered back to French Intelligence to convince the Allied High Command that, as in 1914, the main German blow was going to come through the north of Belgium.

Manstein had meanwhile crystallized his ideas in a memorandum which Rundstedt sent to Brauchitsch on 12th January but the commander-in-chief, sensitive of his authority, refused to forward it to Hitler. However, two sets of map exercises in February made General Halder, Brauchitsch's chief-of-staff, realize that Army Group A needed reinforcement in any case. In the next few days Hitler's staff officers brought Manstein's plan to his attention and in it he saw his own un-schooled ideas set out with professional clarity and detail. Brauchitsch also had by now come round to shifting the offensive's centre of gravity away from Bock's Army Group B in the north to Rundstedt's Army Group A in the south. There was agreement all round.

Brauchitsch and Halder now put these general proposals into precise form. Manstein's contribution had been his insistence on the use of Army Group A to swing round south of the Allied armies in Belgium and trap them there. Hitler's contribution had been the exploitation of the Ardennes gap and the choice of Sedan for the crucial crossing of the Meuse, and the use of special air operations to secure vital objectives. The perfected plan, in masterly working detail, was Brauchitsch's and Halder's contribution; and to effect the Meuse crossings between Dinant and Sedan they now capped the operation with a spearhead of seven out of the Wehrmacht's ten Panzer divisions. From its original twenty-two divisions, Rundstedt's Army Group A had escalated to $45\frac{1}{3}$ divisions; while von Bock's Army Group B had dwindled from 43 to $29\frac{1}{3}$ divisions. On 24th February the new directive was ready, under the appropriate name of *Sichelschnitt* – or 'the sweep of a scythe'.

Patchy morale

Now at last the generals were ready. But because the invasion of Denmark and Norway had acquired priority, the attack in the west was postponed into May.

When *Sichelschnitt* came into action at dawn on 10th May the skill and balance of the German planning in themselves ensured a measure of success. The generals' obstinate delaying tactics in the face of Hitler's impatience in the autumn had been justified: the winter had been spent in perfecting their plans, and in training their troops for the precise and demanding requirements of the Blitzkrieg, which had tightened morale and whipped up considerable enthusiasm.

The picture was very different on the Allied side. After the first few weeks of war, all pretence of offensive action on land had been given up. French and British troops were subjected to a hard and unending winter, waiting for an enemy who never came, despite the many alarms during which they stood to in wet or icy weather, while Hitler and his generals, oblivious of the good they were doing their own cause, battled over their dates for the offensive. In the French army, and particularly in those units in the Sedan sector where the main weight of the German attack was due to descend, morale was extremely patchy.

The French High Command, in charge of Allied land operations, thought only of defence. But the Maginot Line, to which their faith was pinned, guarded nothing more than Alsace and Lorraine in the east. It ended opposite the south-eastern corner of neutral Belgium, and French and British troops spent much of the winter navvying, in a poorly co-ordinated attempt to extend the French frontier fortifications, north-westwards to the Channel. Even this measure held contradictions, since General Gamelin, the French commander-in-chief, had decided to rush the Allied forces for-

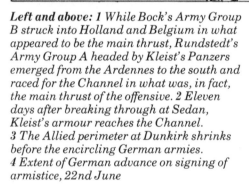

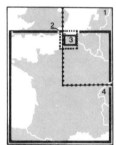

Left and above: 1 While Bock's Army Group B struck into Holland and Belgium in what appeared to be the main thrust, Rundstedt's Army Group A headed by Kleist's Panzers emerged from the Ardennes to the south and raced for the Channel in what was, in fact, the main thrust of the offensive. 2 Eleven days after breaking through at Sedan, Kleist's armour reaches the Channel. 3 The Allied perimeter at Dunkirk shrinks before the encircling German armies. 4 Extent of German advance on signing of armistice, 22nd June

ward into central and northern Belgium as soon as the German offensive started.

The French army was powerful on paper; it had more tanks than the Germans, and some that were better, but it had no conception of massing them for a breakthrough in the way the Germans had already tried out in Poland. The French tank strength was instead spread out thinly and ineffectually, ready, like a lot of small corks, to plug holes in the line. The few really mobile armoured units were earmarked for the Allied defensive line in Belgium.

The British contribution in France amounted to nine divisions, and in its smallness became the butt of German propaganda broadcasts. A modest support air force was also sent to France, but the valuable Spitfire fighter, which had suffered from production delays, was held back for the defence of Great Britain.

It was in the air that the Allies were at their greatest disadvantage. French aircraft production had been doubly hit by strikes and nationalization, and the French air force was largely filled out with obsolete machines. Gamelin, to whom it was theoretically subordinate, had little use for aircraft in battle, and the air crews' efforts were to be fruitlessly dissipated.

The German air force, under the vainglorious leadership of Göring and the energetic administration of his secretary of

state, Milch, had been built up into a fearsome weapon, tested and hardened in the earlier Spanish Civil War and the Polish campaign, and supplied with an extra gloss of terror by German propaganda. It was designed and trained, too, for a single clear-cut purpose—to be an integral part of the German offensive machine. Its fleets of medium bombers were ready to wreak havoc behind the enemy's lines while its dreaded dive-bombers—the Stukas or Junkers 87s—gave direct support to the advancing tanks and infantry.

The Breakthrough

Germany's intended victims in the West had expected terror from the air, and it arrived at dawn on Friday, 10th May. Troop-carrying gliders descended silently beside the crossings of the lower Meuse in south-eastern Holland, and landed on the very roof of the key Belgian fort of Eben-Emael near by; paratroops rained down from the sky round Rotterdam and The Hague; air transport planes unloaded fresh troops onto the half-captured airfield at Waalhaven; and formation after formation of bombers blasted railway junctions and air bases in north-eastern France.

The paratroops and gliders, though not numerous, served to focus the Allied attention on this northern sector, and the cream of the French army and the whole of Lord

1 Field-Marshal Walther von Brauchitsch. Initially he showed no interest in the winning stroke. 2 General von Rundstedt. He saw the weaknesses of 'Plan Yellow'. 3 General Ewald von Kleist. His Panzers led the dashing southerly thrust. 4 General Erich von Manstein. He insisted Army Group A swing south of the Allies.

Gort's British Expeditionary Force, under the overall command of the French general, Billotte, went racing forward into Belgium to meet and hold what they considered to be the main German thrust. Not only that, for the French 7th Army, under its dashing general, Giraud, was sent headlong up through Belgium into southern Holland. Giraud took with him the most valuable mobile reserves of the French army and he was protected, through some curious decision, by the main weight of the French fighter force—although he was moving up on the flank furthest from the main German effort.

When Hitler heard that Gamelin had sent forward the bulk of his forces into the Belgian trap to counter the secondary effort of the German Army Group B, he 'could have wept for joy'.

Army Group A, providing the principal thrust, had started its advance through Luxembourg into the wooded hills of the Belgian Ardennes at the same time, but it was virtually ignored by the French command. It had become an axiom of the French defence planning that armoured forces could not negotiate the restricted roads of the Ardennes in any appreciable strength, and air reconnaissance reports of a build-up on this sector were treated as irrelevant.

German organization, however, was equal to the challenge of the Ardennes. The spearhead of its two armoured corps, which had been put under the command of General von Kleist, crossed Luxembourg and moved forward steadily along parallel forest roads, meeting almost no opposition from the Belgians, and only startled French cavalry groups on reconnaissance, emerging on their horses as if from another age of warfare. The worst problems confronting the Germans in their approach were the vehicle jams occurring on the inadequate roads of the Ardennes. Stretching back fifty miles east of the Rhine, the advancing columns were protected by a massive and constant umbrella of fighters, for a few well-placed bombs on these roads would have impeded the onslaught of the armour for mile upon mile; but the eyes of the Allies were focused on the attack they had expected, in the north.

Guderian's XIX Panzer Corps, making for the Meuse at Sedan, formed the southern wing of Kleist's armoured group. They were through the Ardennes and into France by 1200 on 12th May, Whit Sunday, and in the afternoon I and X Panzer Divisions reached the Meuse on either side of Sedan. During the evening the French troops, fearing a German outflanking movement, evacuated the town; and there was a general withdrawal from the east bank of the Meuse all the way northward to Dinant in Belgium, in the face of the advancing German armour.

While in the south the Germans were already drawing up along the Meuse, the Allies were still advancing through central Belgium to their planned holding positions on the line of the little River Dyle. The advance guard, consisting of France's fine armoured Cavalry Corps under General Prioux, was managing to cover the Dyle line against the first German tank attacks on 12th May, while behind it the French 1st Army, under General Blanchard, moved forward, albeit too slowly, to positions which proved to be virtually unprepared.

An all-out tank battle between Prioux's Cavalry Corps and the German XVI Panzer Corps developed on 13th May and lasted into 14th May. The French tanks fought tenaciously and enabled 1st Army to reach its position; but German training, leadership, and mobility had their effect, and the Germans' ancillary weapon, the Stuka dive-bomber, against which the French had

no defence, was hurled in at crucial stages of the battle. The Cavalry Corps withdrew and its units were dispersed by Billotte along 1st Army's front; the courageous Prioux saw one of the few modern instruments the French possessed broken up into useless fragments.

On 1st Army's right flank, the French 9th Army under General Corap had also moved forward into Belgium, to take up their positions on the Meuse southwards from Namur. In the north they were therefore opposed to the German XV Panzer Corps, under Hoth and approaching Dinant, further south in French territory, to Reinhardt's XLI Panzer Corps, the right wing of Kleist's armoured group which was attacking the Meuse bends at Monthermé. Reinhardt's troops were successfully pinned down at Monthermé for three days by the French 102nd Fortress Division. On the north side of Dinant, however, the Germans were able to establish bridgeheads across the Meuse on the 13th and 14th of May, as much through French carelessness in defending the west bank as through the energy and courage of the German VII Panzer Division's young and unknown general, Erwin Rommel.

But it was in the south, at Sedan, that the decisive battle was being fought. So blind had the French command been to any serious threat through the Ardennes that the skilled and massive thrust by the three armoured divisions of Guderian's XIX Panzer Corps against the Meuse at Sedan, was opposed only by two divisions of flabby, reluctant reservists, who made up the left wing of Huntziger's 2nd French Army. Unfortunately for the French, Sedan also happened to be right on the hinge between two armies, Huntziger's 2nd and Corap's 9th—a situation which greatly increased the difficulties of command for the French. Furthermore their concrete emplacements on the left bank of the Meuse, which should have enabled them to direct a withering fire on any Germans attempting to cross the river were far from complete, as the sharp eyes of a German photographic interpreter had noticed. Many of the French guns, massed on the Marfée Heights opposite Sedan, had not been properly dug in.

Guderian breaks through

Encouraged by his successful advance on Sedan, Guderian agreed with his superior, Kleist, on the evening of 12th May that he would attack at once, even though one of his three Panzer divisions had not yet emerged from the forest. Guderian was promised maximum air support, in particular from the dive-bombers of Richthofen's VIII Flying Corps, and the attempt to cross the Meuse was ordered for 1600 next day, 13th May. The French comman-

ders, however, were estimating that the Germans would need several more days to bring up artillery and infantry for a crossing of the river, and they were summoning up their reserves with little urgency.

The German dive-bombing attacks on the French positions on the left bank, which started in the morning of 13th May and continued with ever increasing force, reached their climax in the half-hour before the German assault and met with only the slightest opposition in the air. On the ground, the French gunners, who should have found the Stukas easy targets, cowered in their shallow trenches beneath this appalling new method of attack; the howling, diving aircraft, and the screaming bombs seemingly aimed at each individual Frenchman. The material damage the bombers did was not important, but by 1600 they had demoralized these civilian soldiers and garrison troops, trained during the past tedious winter to little more than concrete-mixing.

It was the assault troops of the German I Panzer Division, attacking immediately downstream from Sedan against the base of the vulnerable Iges peninsula, that made the first usable bridgehead in the afternoon of 13th May. On their left, above Sedan, X Panzer Division only managed to establish a small foothold across the river with difficulty; and on their right, at Donchery, II Panzer Division would not be assembled in sufficient strength until the following day.

By nightfall on 13th May I Panzer Division troops had fought their way up the Meuse's southern escarpment, through the French main and secondary defence lines, to the dominating height of Marfée Wood. The division now held a bridgehead on the south bank three miles wide and four to six miles deep. During the night they were busy throwing a pontoon bridge across the river and pushing their tanks forward into the bridgehead.

Everything the French tried to do on 14th May to neutralize this dangerous pocket opposite Sedan was too slow and too late. A dawn counter-attack by two light tank battalions and an infantry regiment—there had been no thought of a counter-attack the previous evening—eventually got partly under way at 0700, in time for the French 7th Tank Battalion to be caught on the flank by a newly arrived wave of German tanks, and the counter-attack quickly petered out. And in the afternoon, when there was still an opportunity to drive a powerful wedge into the exposed eastern flank of the German I Panzer Division, before X Panzer Division had broken out of its own small bridgehead, the French threw away their 3rd Armoured Division, full of spirit and eager to attack, with delayed orders and slow refuelling arrangements. When the division could still have attacked with some effect, the order was suddenly countermanded and its precious armour was utterly and finally dispersed by the new local corps commander, who strung it out in a series of weak defensive positions.

On 14th May the Allies despatched all available tactical bombers, the greater part of them British, to attempt the destruction of I Panzer Division's pontoon bridge. They pressed home their attack heroically in obsolete planes, but never concentrated in sufficient numbers to overwhelm the excellent anti-aircraft defences. Their losses were disastrous, and the bridge remained intact. This was the day that broke Allied offensive air-power in the Battle of France.

To Guderian, the Channel coast far away to the west was now his clear objective. Early in the afternoon of 14th May, though X Panzer Division was still struggling up from the Meuse to the east of Marfée Wood, he swung I and II Panzer Divisions

sharply westwards, their wheeling southern flank only tenuously protected by the Waffen-SS Infantry Regiment Grossdeutschland against any French counter-attack. This was a risk Guderian rightly took, for the French wasted the whole of 15th May in preparing and then abandoning a counter-attack by the dispersed 3rd Armoured Division; and by then the German XIV Motorized Corps had crossed the Meuse as a much-needed reinforcement.

Having dealt a crippling blow to Huntziger's 2nd Army, Guderian's tanks were now pushing westward into the territory of Corap's 9th Army. But already, to the north, behind the Belgian Meuse, this army was in complete disarray.

As in the south, the French, faced with Rommel's small bridgeheads to the north of Dinant, had muffed all arrangements for a counter-attack, and Rommel's VII Panzer Division had been able to complete a bridge by dawn on 14th May and to start sending its tanks across. On this day, too,

the German dive-bombing effort, which had lacerated French nerves opposite Sedan the previous day, was concentrated on 9th Army, and its formation headquarters, its lines of communication, and its artillery. Its supply lines were, moreover, disrupted by incessant bombing and machine-gun fire from low-flying fighters.

By nightfall on 14th May, Rommel's tanks were four miles west of the Meuse, and their companion formation, V Panzer Division, was crossing the river. Corap himself was extremely dejected, and during the night informed Billotte, his army group commander, that his units were withdrawing everywhere. But there was confusion over where the new line was to be; communications were seriously disturbed; and in the darkness, with memories

Tanks of General Erwin Rommel's VII Panzer Division pause during the lunge across France. Rommel's inspired use of armour prompted Hitler to appoint him Afrika Korps commander in February 1941

of the day's bombing and the threat of German tanks already in their rear, 9th Army's withdrawal became a disorderly retreat.

The dash to the sea

A French armoured counter-attack, which could still have restored the situation on the 13th and 14th of May proved to be a repetition of the missed opportunities opposite Sedan. When, after many delays, the French 1st Armoured Division, coming from Charleroi, was refuelling at dawn on 15th May, halfway between Philippeville and the Meuse, with 9th Army retreating rapidly to its rear, it was caught and fiercely attacked on two sides near Flavion by strong elements of VII Panzer Division on its southern flank and of V Panzer Division to the north. After a bitter fight, the French had only seventeen tanks left.

In the meantime, the main body of VII Panzer Division had by-passed the battle on the south: at noon Rommel was in Philippeville, and at the end of 15th May he was well on his way towards the French frontier.

By the end of 15th May Giraud, brought over to replace Corap at the head of 9th Army, found nothing to command, just an open gate for the enemy, sixty-two miles wide. Even the French 41st Corps, on 9th Army's right wing, which had been holding the Meuse line resolutely on the Monthermé and Mézières reaches, was caught out by Corap's withdrawal order. Their attempt at a fighting retreat was rapidly demolished by the unleashed forces of Reinhardt's XLI Panzer Corps, and by the end of the day Reinhardt's tanks were in Montcornet, thirty-seven miles west of the Meuse, and only eleven miles from 9th Army's HQ at Vervins. This alarming news was the first positive indication Gamelin had received in the rarefied fastness of his HQ of the disasters which were overtaking his armies.

On the boundary between the French 9th Army and 2nd Army, west of Sedan, units from both armies had been offering poorly organized though occasionally stiff resistance to Guderian's westward-plunging armour. But, coincidental with Corap's withdrawal order to 9th Army, Huntziger's 2nd Army units, unable to hold their own, had fatally pulled back southwards and eastwards—thus increasing the width of the gap rent in the French defences. Tearing through the hole opening in front of him, Guderian's II Panzer Division was also well on its way to Montcornet by the evening of 15th May.

Although that day it seemed to the German corps and divisional commanders that the road to the west lay open to them, matters looked less assured to the German higher command. Hard fighting during 14th

May at Stonne, on Guderian's left flank as he wheeled westward, had revived old fears of a massive French counter-attack from the south. The Germans were not yet aware that, out of the strong French armoured reserve, 1st and 3rd Armoured Divisions had already frittered away their strength, and 2nd Armoured Division, while deploying, had been cut in two by Guderian's sudden advance towards Signy-l'Abbaye. Nor did they know that on the evening of 15th May Gamelin was admitting to Daladier, minister of national defence, that he had no reserves left, and that this was the end of the French army.

To the German generals who had not themselves come face to face with the wilting enemy, the French collapse and the brilliant success of their own daring operational plan were hard to believe; all had bitter memories of the French army's powers of resistance in the First World War. Hitler particularly, who had realized better than most that France, with its weak leadership and divided political loyalties, was no longer a formidable military power, was extremely nervous.

So it was that Kleist, commanding this spectacular armoured force, and anxious to keep personal control of its advance, called a halt on the evening of 15th May to permit the infantry to catch up and consolidate before the tanks moved on. Guderian was furious at this denial of the new principles of armoured warfare, and managed to gain a twenty-four-hour extension. But on the morning of 17th May he was still pushing forward, and Kleist descended on him in a towering rage, insisting that he halt. Guderian offered his resignation. A compromise was reached, and Guderian, reinstated, was allowed to continue a 'reconnaissance in force'— an arrangement which he was to interpret very liberally.

Summoned by Paul Reynaud, the French Prime Minister, Churchill arrived in Paris on 16th May amid an atmosphere bordering on panic. It was his first visit since becoming Prime Minister the day the German Blitzkrieg had begun. To some extent he managed to restore French government morale by promising to send to France additional RAF fighter squadrons; much against the wishes of Air Chief Marshal Dowding of Fighter Command. But, not for the last time in the war, it was to be a case of 'too little, too late'.

The following day the French attempted one more offensive action, towards Montcornet with a hastily agglomerated 4th Armoured Division under Colonel de Gaulle. But unsupported to its rear and unprotected in the air, it was soon repulsed by the incessant Stuka attacks and by German tanks of XIX Panzer Corps infiltrating behind it.

Now began the German dash to the sea. On 16th May Rommel was through the French frontier defences south of Maubeuge and had advanced another fifty miles, reaching Avesnes in the night; by the evening Reinhardt's XLI Panzer Corps was on the river Oise beyond Vervins; and south of Vervins, Guderian's XIX Panzer Corps had reached the river Serre. On the morning of 17th May French resistance on the upper Oise collapsed, and the road seemed clear, either to Paris, or to the Channel coast in the rear of the Allied armies in Belgium. The French command still had no idea what the objective of *Sichelschnitt* was to be.

On 18th May the Germans were again driving furiously westwards, their advance always many miles and several townships ahead of the fumbling French orders. Billotte, withdrawing the Allied forces south-westwards out of central Belgium, started to establish a line facing south, roughly along the Belgian frontier, attempting to contain the quickly forming Panzer corridor on its north side, while the main French command set up a defensive line along the Somme on the corridor's southern flank, defending Paris, which of course was not Hitler's immediate goal.

On 20th May the German I Panzer Division captured Amiens, while II Panzer Division reached Abbeville in the evening and the Channel coast at dusk after an advance of over sixty miles that day. The Allied forces were cut in two. Reinhardt's corps was heading for St Omer, and Rommel, to the north, had reached the area of Arras. After a brief delay, while the German command took breath, the order was given for Guderian's divisions to swing northward up the coast to Boulogne and Calais, in order to complete the envelopment of the Allied armies in Belgium.

The German armour was now far ahead of even the motorized infantry, and their southern flank was very vulnerable. The French command was aware of the enemy's present weakness and knew that a counterattack undertaken simultaneously from the south and the north, cutting through the middle of the corridor, might entirely sever the cream of the German armour. But the Allies no longer had the ability to coordinate such an action. Gamelin's replacement as commander-in-chief by Weygand on the evening of 19th May contributed nothing except two days' delay in ordering a pincer movement. By then, Allied communications were as confused as their troop movements, and a limited British tank attack southwards from Arras on 21st May with French support on its flank, was carried out with no corresponding French attack from the south. The British achieved a fine local success and made a strong impression upon Rommel; but then, seeing no French follow-up, withdrew and proceeded to concentrate their plans on the evacuation of the British Expeditionary Force across the Channel.

The northern armies now suffered from the additional disarray caused by the death of their commander, Billotte, in a motor accident, and tension between the Allies in Belgium quickly came to a head. Gort had become disillusioned by the weakness and incompetence of the French command and by the poor resistance of its troops; the French felt that the British were thinking of nothing except saving their own skins across the Channel; and the Belgians, their country almost entirely overrun, were considering surrender. It was in this atmosphere that the retreat to Dunkirk and the evacuation to England took place.

Once the German thrust had reached the Channel and isolated the élite of the Allied armies in the north, the outcome of the campaign had been virtually decided. After Dunkirk it became largely a matter of marching for the Germans, now wheeling southwards to face the French forces which had dug themselves in on the line of the Somme and the Aisne—the so-called 'Weygand Line'. Fighting with often greater tenacity than they had shown on the Meuse, though against hopeless odds, the French resisted the first German onslaught on 5th June. But the 'Weygand Line' was a line in little more than name, and once the Germans had broken through it—Hoth's armour to Rouen, Kleist's to Burgundy, and Guderian's to the Swiss frontier—there was nothing to stop them. On 14th June Paris fell, undefended. The French armies holding the redundant fortifications of the Maginot Line were taken in the rear, Italy administered her infamous 'stab in the back', and on 22nd June France was forced to agree to a humiliating armistice—signed in the same railway carriage where Foch accompanied, among others, by Weygand had accepted the German surrender in 1918.

The brilliantly improvised German operational plan for the attack in the west had succeeded beyond all dreams. France had been utterly defeated in six weeks. But Great Britain, strangely, was not yet seeking terms. The plan had made no further provision; and while the Germans gorged themselves on their triumph and the delights of Paris, the RAF was spending the unexpected respite in bracing itself for the defence of Britain—in which it was to rob Germany of final victory.

Right: France 'in extremis'. Two German soldiers watch Rouen burn after attack from the turret of a knocked-out Renault FT 17, a relic of the First World War

Deliverance at Dunkirk

'Dunkirk,' A.J.P.Taylor has written, 'was a great deliverance and a great disaster.' Yet it might simply have been a great disaster.

The German Blitzkrieg offensive in the West had whirled into the Low Countries on 10th May 1940 with its customary surprise, violence, ruthlessness, and treachery. As a counter-measure three days later 1st, 7th, and 9th French Armies together with the nine divisions of the British Expeditionary Force under Field-Marshal Lord Gort raced to join the Belgian army in defensive positions running along the River Dyle from Antwerp to Namur and south along the Meuse to Sedan. It was a trap. While General von Bock's Army Group B struck into Holland and Belgium in what seemed the primary German thrust, General von Rundstedt's Army Group A, its formidable armour to the fore, emerged from the Ardennes between Dinant and Montmédy in what was in fact the main German assault, and advanced against a front lacking permanent fortifications and manned by only two divisions of professional troops. On 14th May the avalanche broke. Preceded by waves of Stukas, General von Kleist's Panzer Group, comprising the armoured corps of Guderian and Reinhardt, forced a crossing of the Meuse at Mézières, Monthermé, and Sedan. Cutting a swath through the weak and ill-prepared 9th and 2nd Armies the mass of armour, unopposed by any French reserves, plunged towards the Channel threatening to isolate the British, Belgian and French armies in the north. On 21st May Kleist's Panzer Group reached the mouth of the Somme at Abbeville, captured Boulogne, enveloped Calais, and advanced within twelve miles of Dunkirk.

Thus between a formidable wedge of seven armoured divisions and Bock's advancing Army Group B lay the Belgian army, ten divisions of the French 1st Army, and the bulk of the BEF. They were trapped and Kleist was poised to hammer them against the anvil of the advancing VI and XVIII Armies which had just crossed the River Schelde after breaching the Dyle line. For the dazed Allied forces annihilation seemed inevitable. The final phase of the great encirclement battle appeared to be at hand. But suddenly, on 24th May, the bounding armour stopped dead in its tracks. For the reeling Allied armies disaster was about to be mitigated.

On Hitler's orders Kleist's Panzers were halted west and south of Dunkirk on a line from Lens, through Béthune, Aire, St Omer to Gravelines. It was the first of the German High Command's major mistakes in the Second World War. It reprieved the Allies and made possible the 'miracle' of Dunkirk.

The only hope the Allies had of extricating themselves from encircling German forces was for the armies in Belgium to disengage from VI Army attacking them there, turn south-west and fight their way through the German armoured wedge and link up with French forces pushing northwards from the Somme. But by 25th May Lord Gort realized that with the forces at his disposal such a break-out, with Belgian resistance crumbling fast and no evidence of a French attack northwards, stood little chance of success.

The British, French, and Belgian armies were by now confined to a triangle of territory with its base along the Channel coast from Gravelines to Terneuzen and its apex at Valenciennes. There could be no escape but by sea. On 27th May the British government, which on 19th May had insisted Gort attack southwards to Amiens, informed the Commander-in-Chief of the BEF that his sole task was 'to evacuate the maximum force possible'. It was a measure he had foreseen and for which contingency plans had been prepared.

Seven days earlier in the deep galleries below Dover Castle Vice-Admiral Bertram Ramsay had inaugurated a discussion on 'emergency evacuation across the Channel of a very large force'. In the following days the Admiralty began to amass shipping for a possible evacuation of the BEF and Allied forces from France. The desperate venture code-named 'Operation Dynamo' was in large part to be facilitated by the interruption of the German Panzer onslaught.

What was the reason for this apparently inexplicable order to arrest the progress of the armour on the threshold of what could have been one of the worst disasters in military history? Who was responsible for it? The generals led by Halder, the Chief of the Army General Staff and Rundstedt, commander of Army group A, have since put the blame exclusively on Hitler. The peremptory order, although emanating from the Führer in his capacity as Supreme Commander of the Armed Forces did, however, enjoy the support of both Rundstedt and Göring.

The Führer visited the former's headquarters at Charleville on the morning of 24th May where he listened to a report of the fighting and heard the intentions of Army Group Command. Rundstedt suggested that the infantry should attack to the east of Arras, where on 21st May the British had shown they were still capable of vigorous action, while Kleist's armour, which he knew had suffered serious losses, stood on a line west and south of Dunkirk in order to pounce on the Allied forces withdrawing before Army Group B. Hitler expressed com-

*Above: British soldier replies to German aircraft strafing him on Dunkirk's beaches. Though the British troops were dangerously exposed, the sand partially muffled the blasts of the German bombs. **Left:** Relics of a defeated army. German soldiers examine the debris of the BEF's hasty exit strewn along Dunkirk's promenade. The British Army lost most of its heavy equipment, tanks and artillery in the evacuation. All the soldiers could carry back were their rifles*

plete agreement with the Army Group commander and underlined the need to husband the armour for the coming operations south of the Somme. Hitler and Rundstedt were thus in agreement in their judgement of the situation.

Göring makes an offer

But the Führer had other reasons for issuing the apparently inexplicable order to restrain the armour. He recalled how in 1914 the low-lying Flanders plains between Bruges, Nieuport, and Dixmude had flooded and bogged down the German northern flank. The low-lying terrain to the west and south of Dunkirk was similarly intersected by thousands of waterways and was, Hitler believed, clearly unsuited for large-scale armoured operations. In view of Hitler's concern for Kleist's armour, Göring's characteristically flamboyant offer to the Führer on 23rd May was received enthusiastically.

From his mobile HQ in the Eifel mountains the Commander-in-Chief of the Luftwaffe telephoned Hitler to propose that 'his' air fleets which, after all, were 'to settle the fate of the German nation for the next thousand years' should destroy the British Army in northern France. After this had been accomplished Göring claimed the German army would only have to 'occupy the territory'. He further urged acceptance of his proposal by remarking that the final destruction of the enemy should be left to the 'National Socialist' Luftwaffe as Hitler would lose prestige to the army generals if they were permitted to deliver the coup de grâce.

It is clear that Hitler's plan, prompted by Göring and Rundstedt, was to let the Luftwaffe and Army Group B, which with very little armour was slowly driving back the Belgians and British south-west to the Channel, eliminate the troops in the Dunkirk pocket. It would, of course, be essential to halt Kleist's armour for fear of hampering Luftwaffe operations in the area. But neither the Luftwaffe nor Bock's Army Group were to prove capable of achieving their objectives.

Hitler, however, had yet further reason to impose his own military leadership on the army for on 24th May a crisis of leadership had occurred. From 2000 on that day Field-Marshal von Brauchitsch, the Commander-in-Chief of the Army who was determined to see that Army Group B fought the last act of the encirclement battle, decided that Rundstedt should surrender tactical control of Kluge's IV Army and that together with all mobile units it should pass under the command of Army Group B. Whether Brauchitsch preferred to make the transfer rather than restore harmony between the two Army Groups and confront the organizational problems that their conjunction

would pose or whether he was dissatisfied with the less dynamic Rundstedt is not clear. Knowledge of the transfer may have led Rundstedt to propose measures he knew the Führer would support when they met at Charleville, but what is clear, however, is that neither Hitler nor OKW, which had replaced the War Ministry and become Hitler's personal staff, knew anything about this Army High Command (OKH) transfer order. Hitler was highly indignant that Brauchitsch and Halder had reorganized command responsibilities without informing him. He promptly cancelled the order.

Thus in halting the armour Hitler sanctioned Rundstedt's proposal besides demonstrating that on the battlefield his position as Supreme Commander of the Wehrmacht was no mere formality. But Halder was not prepared to accept the Führer's order and on the same night issued a wireless message to both Army Groups stating that the continuation of the attack up to Dunkirk on the one hand and Ostend on the other was permissible. In an act unprecedented in German military history Rundstedt decided not to pass on the communication from his superiors to IV Army. Supported by Hitler, and assuming his observations on the morning of the 24th represented his own opinions, he could afford to hold a different view of the situation from that of OKH. In his opinion Army Group B would sooner or later subdue resistance in Flanders and it therefore appeared wiser to preserve the armoured forces for later use.

Although Hitler may have genuinely taken political objectives into consideration when he restrained the armour it is patently obvious that he did not intend to spare Great Britain a bitter humiliation and thereby facilitate a peace settlement by such action. Both the Luftwaffe and the German army had clear and definite instructions to destroy the entrapped enemy in Flanders and this was made unmistakably apparent in Führer Directive No. 13, signed by Hitler on the evening of 24th May 1940. Halder has since claimed that Hitler expressed his determination to fight the decisive battle in northern France rather than on Flemish soil for political reasons. The Führer, Halder maintains, explained that his plans to create a National Socialist region out of the territory inhabited by the 'German-descended' Flemish would be compromised if war was permitted to ravage the region. Therefore although Hitler was partially responsible for the decision to halt the armour he has undoubtedly been unjustly credited with the sole responsibility for the fatal error.

The perimeter shrinks

'Operation Dynamo' was based on the assumption that three ports would be avail-

able but the fall of Boulogne, followed on 26th May by the collapse of British resistance in Calais left only Dunkirk. Yet the defence of Calais termed by Guderian 'heroic, worthy of the highest praise' gave Lord Gort time in which to elaborate his plan for evacuation. The Allies' predicament grew steadily worse. On 25th May the Belgians expended their last reserves and their front broke. On the following day Hitler rescinded the halt order in view of Bock's slow advance in Belgium and the movement of transports off the coast, authorizing the resumption of Rundstedt's advance by 'armoured groups and infantry divisions in the direction of Dunkirk'. However, for technical reasons sixteen hours were to pass before the armoured units were ready to move forward and assail the town. By 28th May the Allies had organized a tighter perimeter defence around Dunkirk stretching from Nieuport along the canals through Fumes and Bergues to Gravelines. Repeatedly assaulted by German tanks and without the support of the Belgian army which had capitulated the same day, the perimeter shrank. South-west of Lille, however, the Germans encountered spirited resistance from the French 1st Army which detained seven of their divisions from 29th May to 1st June thus preventing their participation in the assault on the Dunkirk pocket. The exhausted and bewildered Allies often fragmented into separate battalions or separate companies retreated steadily along congested roads into the perimeter and by midnight on the 29th the greater part of the BEF and nearly half of the French 1st Army lay behind the canal line, by which time the naval measures for evacuation had begun to demonstrate their effectiveness.

At 1857 on 26th May the Admiralty launched Operation Dynamo. Besides an inspiring example of gallantry and self-sacrifice it was to display what Hitler had always held to be one of Great Britain's greatest strengths—the genius for improvisation.

The first day of the evacuation, 27th May, proved disappointing. Only 7,669 troops were brought out by a motley assortment of destroyers, passenger ferry steamers, paddle steamers, self-propelled barges, and Dutch *schuiten* which Vice-Admiral Ramsay had collected. But after the loss of Boulogne and Calais only Dunkirk with its adjacent beaches remained in Allied hands. For the intrepid rescuers, entering the harbour, when not impossible, was a hazardous task. Not only had they to contend with fire from shore batteries and ferocious air attack but they had to negotiate the many wrecks that lay between them and the blazing town.

It became clear that the hungry, exhausted troops would have to be embarked from the sandy beaches on either side of the

An orderly line of British troops wading out to a rescue steamer. The evacuation by larger boats was mostly well-ordered, though there was some panic in the rush to smaller vessels

Deliverance at Dunkirk

town, but as yet Ramsay had few small craft capable of embarking men in shallow water. He signalled urgently for more. The next day, 28th May, utilizing the beaches together with the surviving but precarious East Mole of the harbour 17,804 men were embarked for Britain. The losses in craft on that day, however, were very heavy. Ships that left the congested mole unscathed were frequently damaged or sunk by bombing as they steamed down the narrow offshore channel unable to manœuvre adequately for wrecks, debris, and corpses.

Despite the fact that 47,310 men were snatched from Dunkirk and its neighbouring beaches the following day, as soon as the wind had blown aside the pall of smoke obscuring the harbour and roadstead, the Luftwaffe wreaked fearful havoc with a concentrated bombardment of the mole, sinking three destroyers and twenty-one other vessels.

On 30th May smoother seas, smoke, and low cloud ceiling enabled the rescuers to remove 13,823 men to safety. Although a number of small craft had arrived off Dunkirk on 29th May they were only the vanguard of a volunteer armada of some 400 yachts, lifeboats, dockyard launches, river tugs, cockle boats, pleasure craft, French and Belgian fishing boats, oyster dredgers, and Thames barges which, with small craft called into service by the Royal Navy, ferried 100,000 men from the beaches to the deeper draught vessels from the following day. Moved by the desperate plight of the Allies, the seafaring population of south and south-eastern England had set out in a spontaneous movement for the beaches of Dunkirk where in innumerable acts of heroism they fulfilled a crucial role in the evacuation.

On 31st May despite intense bombing and shelling, 68,014 troops were removed to

safety but on the following day a furious artillery bombardment and strafing of the whole length of the beaches together with resolute dive-bombing of shipping out at sea and in the harbour effectively halted daylight operations.

The climax of the evacuation had taken place on 31st May and 1st June when over 132,000 men were landed in England. At dawn on 2nd June only 4,000 men of the BEF remained in the perimeter, shielded by 100,000 French troops. On the nights of 2nd and 3rd June they were evacuated along with 60,000 of the Frenchmen. Dunkirk was still defended stubbornly by the remainder who resisted until the morning of 4th June. When the town fell 40,000 French troops who had fought tenaciously to cover the evacuation of their Allied comrades marched into captivity.

'Let us remember,' wrote Churchill, 'that but for the endurance of the Dunkirk rearguard the re-creation of an army in Britain for home defence and final victory would have been gravely prejudiced.'

The British with French and Belgian assistance had evacuated 338,226 troops, of whom 139,097 were French, from a small battered port and exposed beaches right under the noses of the Germans. They had extracted every possible advantage from the valuable respite accorded them when the armour was halted, consolidating defensive positions in the west, east, and on the Channel front. Moreover they had fought tenaciously, upholding traditions that had so impressed the Germans in the First World War.

The primary German error was to regard the Dunkirk pocket as a subordinate front. In fact its strategic importance was not recognized until too late largely because it was not clear until almost the last moment how many Allied troops were actually in the pocket.

Moreover, for the nine days of Operation Dynamo, the Luftwaffe, due to adverse weather conditions only succeeded in seriously interfering with it for two-and-a-half days—on 27th May, the afternoon of

29th May, and on 1st June. The Luftwaffe's mission, readily shouldered by the vain, ambitious Göring proved too much for it. If Rundstedt had made a mistake, Göring fatally miscalculated. His aircraft had failed to prevent the Allied evacuation because the necessary conditions for success —good weather, advanced airfields, training in pin-point bombing—were all lacking. Bombers and dive-bombers for the first time suffered heavy losses at the hands of British Spitfires and Hurricanes now operating from their relatively near home bases.

For Germany's military leadership Dunkirk was the first great turning point in the Second World War, for it was during the campaign that Hitler first forced OKH to accept his own military views, by short-circuiting it at a critical juncture of the fighting and transferring a decision of far-reaching importance to a subordinate command whose views happened to coincide with his own. OKH, the actual military instrument of leadership, was in future to be undermined, overruled, and with terrible consequences for the German people, finally abolished altogether.

The grim realities

At Dunkirk instead of winning a battle of annihilation the German army had to content itself with an ordinary victory. Great Britain on the other hand could console itself with the knowledge that almost its entire expeditionary force had been saved. 'In the midst of our defeat,' Churchill later wrote, 'glory came to the Island people, united and unconquerable . . . there was a white glow, overpowering, sublime, which ran through our Island from end to end . . . and the tale of the Dunkirk beaches will shine in whatever records are preserved of our affairs.'

If the British people felt they had won a great victory the grim realities belied their euphoria. The BEF, no longer in any condition to defend the country had suffered 68,111 killed, wounded, and taken prisoner. It had been compelled to abandon 2,472 guns, 90,000 rifles, 63,879 vehicles, 20,548 motorcycles and well over 500,000 tons of stores and ammunition. Of the 243 ships sunk at Dunkirk, out of 860 engaged, six were British destroyers. A further nineteen British destroyers were damaged. In addition the RAF had lost 474 aircraft.

Dunkirk had been a catastrophe alleviated, not by a miracle, but by German miscalculation and Allied tenacity and improvisation. Yet the elation of victory pervaded Britain. A supreme effort had cheated Hitler of his prey and a little self-congratulation seemed appropriate. The British had been the first to confound the German military juggernaut and after Dunkirk they resolved with a wholehearted determination to defeat it.

Italy: The Achilles Heel

Italy in June 1940 was in no condition to fight a major war. The Italian army simply did not possess the kind of equipment which had made possible the German successes in the West. Anti-aircraft guns were virtually non-existent, only half the motor vehicles required by the army could be supplied, and there was only fuel enough for seven to eight months. In the event of general mobilization, the troops could not even have been properly clothed. The navy and air force were only slightly better off, and underlying everything was the weakness of the Italian war economy. Italy was desperately short of such strategic raw materials as copper, nickel, aluminium, and rubber, and these shortages were accentuated when, after the declaration of war, the Royal Navy closed both the Suez Canal and the Straits of Gibraltar to Italian shipping.

Mussolini was well aware of these unpleasant facts, but in his view the war was as good as won already, and it was imperative to enter the conflict before it was too late.

But, unfortunately for the Duce, things did not quite go according to plan. After the conclusion of the Battle of France—in which the Italian forces failed to penetrate more than a few miles into French territory—Great Britain gave little evidence for the widespread view that she was finished, and failed to come to terms with Germany in spite of Hitler's apparently sincere appeal. The Germans began to prepare seriously for an invasion of the British Isles, and Mussolini offered Italian troops to participate in the landings. When Hitler somewhat disdainfully rejected this offer, Mussolini was left to obtain his military glory elsewhere. This prospect was by no means uncongenial to him, for even before Italy's entry into the war, he had repeatedly spoken of the need to wage what he called a 'parallel war': a war alongside Germany and against the same opponents, but in different theatres and for specifically Italian objectives. He now had the chance to put this conception into practice.

Africa was the obvious arena for the 'parallel war'. The Italians had some fourteen divisions (215,000 men) in Libya, excluding air force personnel, and the fall of France meant that they were now free to concentrate all their strength against the British in Egypt without having to bother about the French in Tunisia. Some twelve hundred miles to the south-east, in Italian East Africa, there were two divisions and twenty-nine colonial brigades, totalling 255,000 men exclusive of naval and air force units. This was a large force, strategically concentrated on the flank of the main British supply route to Egypt via the Red Sea. It was Mussolini's ambition to break out of the Mediterranean 'prison' in which the British had confined him: a concerted Italian attack from Libya and East Africa in the direction of Egypt and the Sudan would serve this purpose, and seriously embarrass the British.

But things were not so easy as that. In spite of repeated prodding from Rome, the Italian commander in Libya, Marshal Rodolfo Graziani, argued that his forces were in no state to take on the British without large-scale reinforcements, and it was not until 13th September 1940 that his army finally lumbered across the Egyptian frontier, only to come to a prolonged halt some four days and sixty-odd miles later.

A paper tiger

It should be emphasized at this point that it was not the 'parallel war' strategy as such which was at fault, but Italy's capacity to carry it out unaided. Some of Hitler's military advisers, particularly in the navy, saw the advantages of concentrating upon Great Britain's power position in the Middle East if the proposed invasion of the home islands failed to take place, or even as an alternative strategy altogether. They were well aware, however, that the Italians could accomplish little or nothing on their own, and it was as a result of this awareness that proposals were put forward in the autumn of 1940 to send German armoured units to North Africa. But for prestige and other reasons Mussolini would have none of it. 'If they set foot among us,' he told the Armed Forces Chief of Staff, Marshal Pietro Badoglio, 'we will never get rid of them.'

If, in view of Italy's weakness, Mussolini was rash to turn down the offer of German assistance in North Africa, he was mad to contemplate expanding his commitments still further by engaging in military operations on the continent of Europe. Yet, in the summer of 1940, we find him planning more or less simultaneous invasions of Switzerland, Yugoslavia, and Greece. All were the object of long-standing Italian ambitions. The desire to attack them at this stage can be explained partly by the desire to stake out a claim in time for the peace conference, and partly to guard against the threat of a German hegemony over areas which Italy considered vital to her security. However, Mussolini was com-

Top: Poster after the election of March 1934 'Year XII of the fascist era'. The approved list of fascist candidates were overwhelmingly voted in. *Above:* Mussolini watches with delight the collapse of the League of Nations after the invasion of Ethiopia. *Left:* 'Il Duce'

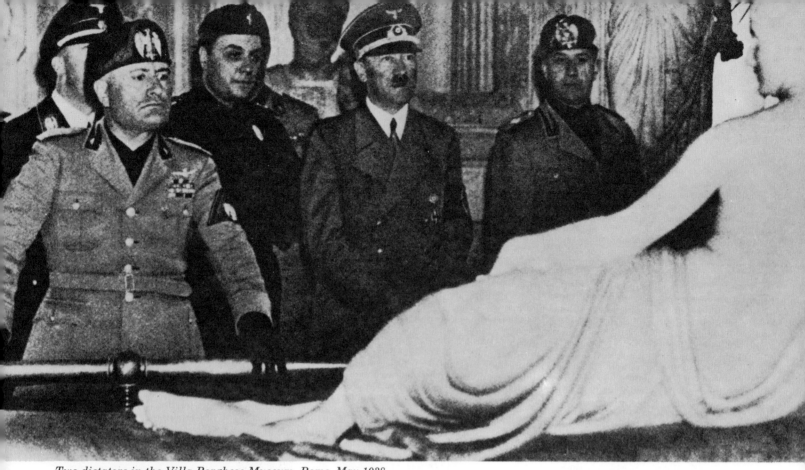

Two dictators in the Villa Borghese Museum, Rome, May 1938

pelled to drop the plan for the invasion of Switzerland because the troops for it were also needed to invade Yugoslavia, and he was compelled to drop the plan for the invasion of Yugoslavia because of opposition from his military advisers. Hitler was also anxious for stability in the Balkans on account of Germany's vital oil supplies from Rumania and because he wished to preserve — at least temporarily — his alliance with Russia. He had tried to veto the invasion of Yugoslavia, and would undoubtedly have tried to veto the invasion of Greece had he taken rumours of the invasion seriously; but he did not.

Italy invaded Greece on 28th October 1940 from Italian-occupied Albania. 'I shall send in my resignation as an Italian if anyone objects to our fighting the Greeks', Mussolini told his son-in-law and foreign minister, Count Ciano, a fortnight before the invasion, thereby indicating his belief that the operation would be a walk-over. Although this belief was shared by many others, and not least by Ciano and the Italian civil and military authorities in Albania, the Greeks soon expelled the invading forces and pressed on into Albanian territory. At one point, early in December, Mussolini was faced with the humiliating prospect of having to ask for an armistice through Hitler but, fortunately for him, the Italian forces managed to hold their ground. Shortly before, a daring raid by torpedo bombers of the Royal Navy had disabled a large portion of the Italian battle fleet in Taranto harbour (11th-12th November) and shortly afterwards (9th December), O'Connor launched the British counter-offensive in the Western Desert which was to drive Graziani not only out of Egypt, but out of Cyrenaica as well.

This series of disasters had far-reaching effects. There was a thorough shake-up in the Italian High Command, which included the dismissal of the Chief of Staff of the Armed Forces, Marshal Badoglio, and the Chief-of-Staff of the Navy, Admiral Domenico Cavagnari, as well as that of certain lesser lights. But the situation might well not have been saved had not Hitler responded favourably to his fellow-dictator's belated calls for help. At the end of 1940 and the beginning of 1941, Hitler decided first to support the Italians in Albania with a German attack on Greece from Bulgaria; second, to send units of the German air force to Sicily to help the Italians attack the British Mediterranean Fleet; third, to despatch German forces, including armoured units, to North Africa to prevent the loss of Tripolitania, and fourth, to increase German economic assistance to Italy. These decisions may have saved the Fascist regime from early extinction, but they also sounded the death-knell of Italy's autonomous 'parallel war'. From the beginning of 1941 onwards, Nazi Germany exercised ever greater control over the activities of her weaker partner, much to the latter's annoyance.

On the face of it, things went extremely well for the Axis during the first six months of 1941. Thanks largely to General Rommel and the Afrika Korps, the British were driven out of Libya, except for Tobruk, by the beginning of April. Greece was overcome in the same month, although the Italian forces were not able to do much more than hold the line in Albania. Moreover, an additional Blitzkrieg campaign was added to the list when, at the end of March, Yugoslavia finally spurned Axis offers of an alliance. Hitler resolved to 'smash Yugoslavia' and, after a brief campaign in which Italian forces also participated, the Yugoslavs were forced to

sign an armistice on 17th April 1941.

Only in East Africa, where Germany was unable to come to the aid of Italy, was the Axis defeated. Attacking from Kenya, the Sudan, and from across the Gulf of Aden, British forces occupied Italian Somaliland and Eritrea, recaptured British Somaliland, and thrust deep into Ethiopia. Addis Ababa fell on 6th April, and the Duke of Aosta himself was compelled to surrender at Amba Alagi on 16th May. Two sizeable concentrations of Italian troops remained in Ethiopia — one, under General Gazzera, in the south-west, and the other, under General Nasi, in the north-west — but both were eventually forced to surrender, the former in July and the latter in November. The empire which Mussolini had defied the League of Nations to create in 1935 was no more.

But Axis successes elsewhere were not nearly so impressive as they seemed at first sight. The German plans for an invasion of the British Isles had long since been abandoned, and the British power position in the Middle East remained intact, in spite of the Rashid Ali revolt in Iraq in April. It was true that the Axis intended to exploit Arab nationalism against the British, and the German army had worked out an elaborate timetable which involved simultaneous offensives against Egypt along the North African coast and, via Turkey, down through Syria and Palestine at the turn of the year 1941-42. But all this was to follow upon what was confidently expected to be the early defeat of the Soviet Union, an eventuality which never materialized. On the grounds that the Italians could not afford to stay out of the decisive struggle against Bolshevism, Mussolini initially contributed three divisions to the German invasion of Russia in June 1941. These troops would have been much better employed in North Africa, a theatre which, as a result of the Russian campaign, was inevitably down-graded in Hitler's eyes, with serious consequences for Italy.

The resultant withdrawal to the Balkans of the bulk of the German air force units which Hitler had sent to Sicily at the end of 1940 greatly reduced the pressure upon Malta, the British island base which lay athwart the main supply route from Italy to North Africa. In the autumn of 1941, as a result, Italian convoy losses increased to an intolerable degree. So, on 2nd December, Hitler issued a directive appointing Field-Marshal Albert Kesselring as Commander-in-Chief South, in charge of an entire air corps and with the threefold mission of protecting the supply route between Italy and North Africa, co-operating with the Italo-German ground forces in North Africa, and stopping enemy traffic through the Mediterranean. Kesselring's appointment, which was regarded with mixed feelings by the Italians, marked a further stage in the subordination of Italy to Germany.

Not long after Kesselring's arrival in Italy, the Second World War was transformed into a truly global conflict by the Japanese attack on Pearl Harbour and British and Dutch possessions in the Far East. Mussolini, together with Hitler, gratuitously linked his fate with that of the Land of the Rising Sun by declaring war upon the USA on 11th December 1941. Initially American intervention did not provide much relief for the British position in the Mediterranean and the Middle East, whereas Japanese intervention seemed to offer alluring prospects to the Axis powers. 'The Japanese admirals have informed us that they intend to proceed towards India,' Ciano noted in his diary on 7th March 1942. 'The Axis must move towards them in the Persian Gulf.'

Before this could happen, however, the Italo-German base in North Africa had to be made secure. The key to this was supply, and the key to supply was the elimination of Malta. Kesselring had set himself the task of 'neutralizing' the island from the air, but the Italians had come to the conclusion that nothing less than its seizure would suffice. In this they were surely right, for whatever the short-term success of an aerial assault, it could not be maintained indefinitely, particularly when it depended almost entirely upon German aircraft which were always liable to recall to the Russian front. As early as October 1941, the Armed Forces Chief of Staff, General Ugo Cavallero (who replaced Badoglio in December 1940), had instructed the army to plan the invasion of Malta. By the beginning of 1942, the other services were involved and the Germans were

also drawn in. At a meeting between Hitler and Mussolini at the end of April, it was decided to recapture Tobruk and advance as far as the Egyptian frontier by the middle of June, and then to take Malta before any further advance in North Africa.

Unfortunately for the Italians, however, they were dependent upon German help for the success of the Malta invasion, and it soon became clear that Hitler was not very enthusiastic about the operation. In a meeting with his military advisers on 21st May, he argued that the Italians were really incapable of carrying out such a complex manoeuvre and that, in any case, their security was so bad that the British would soon know as much about the plans as their own commanders. In these circumstances, it was not surprising that, after the Italo-German forces had captured Tobruk on 21st June and Rommel, confident in the belief that he could be in Cairo by the end of the month, had pressed for the restrictions upon his advance to be lifted, Hitler urged Mussolini to let him have his way. 'Destiny has offered us a chance which will never occur twice in the same theatre of war,' he wrote. 'The goddess of battles visits warriors only once. He who does not grasp her at such a moment never reaches her again.' But the Duce did not need such lyrical prose to persuade him. He was as mesmerized by the prospect of conquering Egypt as Hitler or Rommel and, in spite of the reasoned objections of Cavallero and Kesselring, he gladly gave the German field commander his head. The Malta invasion was postponed—indefinitely as it turned out—and the Duce even went to North Africa to preside personally over the fall of Egypt.

But Egypt did not fall. Auchinleck held Rommel's offensive and the initiative passed to the British with the second Battle of El Alamein in October. The following month, the Anglo-American landings in French North Africa (Operation Torch) put the Italo-German forces in a vice, and when they were finally expelled from Tunisia in May 1943, the way was clear for a direct assault upon *Festung Europa* ('Fortress Europe') itself—by way of Italy.

Was Italy a liability?

Later in the war Adolf Hitler pondered upon the effects of his partnership with Italy. 'When I pass judgement, objectively and without emotion, on events,' he wrote, 'I must admit that my unshakeable friendship for Italy and the Duce may well be held to be an error on my part. It is in fact quite obvious that our Italian alliance has been of more service to our enemies than to ourselves. Italian intervention has conferred benefits which are modest in the extreme in comparison with the numerous difficulties to which it has given

rise. If, in spite of all our efforts, we fail to win this war, the Italian alliance will have contributed to our defeat.'

Italy's presence at Germany's side, he claimed, prevented him from mobilizing the Muslim peoples in his support, 'for the Italians in these parts of the world are more bitterly hated, of course, than either the British or the French.' On a more purely military level, the Italian defeats in Greece 'compelled us, contrary to all our plans, to intervene in the Balkans, and that in its turn led to a catastrophic delay in the launching of our attack on Russia. We were compelled to expend some of our best divisions there. And as a net result we were then forced to occupy vast territories in which, but for this stupid show, the presence of any of our troops would have been quite unnecessary . . . Ah! if only the Italians had remained aloof from this war!'

When reflections such as these are placed alongside the actual record of Italian performance during the Second World War, it is easy to see the basis for the belief that Italy was Germany's Achilles heel. But is this belief justified? After all, it was not the Italian alliance which prevented Hitler from exploiting Arab nationalism, but his preoccupation with Barbarossa (the offensive against Russia). And even if that operation could have been launched a few weeks earlier but for the German campaigns in Greece and Yugoslavia (which is very doubtful), would it have made all that much difference to the final outcome? As for the German troops allegedly tied down in the Balkans, these amounted to seven divisions in June 1941 compared with the 153 massed for Barbarossa. It is hard to see how they would have had much effect upon the balance of forces on the Eastern Front.

It was not so much Hitler's support for Mussolini which contributed to his losing the Second World War, as his failure to give him adequate support by according the Mediterranean a higher priority in his overall strategy, as, for example, his naval advisers constantly urged. The Middle East was of great strategic importance to the British Empire, and a small increase in German resources devoted to the area could have resulted in proportionately large rewards. As it was, the main burden of Axis operations in the Mediterranean fell upon the Italians, who were totally incapable of shouldering it. The brilliant tactical successes of a commander like Rommel could obscure the harsh realities for a while, but by the end of 1942 they were plainly there for all to see, and Mussolini had cause to reflect upon the words of his fellow-Italian, Niccolò Machiavelli: 'Everyone may begin a war at his pleasure, but cannot so finish it.'

The Battle of Britain

Of all the innumerable battles fought during the last 2,500 years, no more than fifteen have been generally regarded as decisive. A decisive battle has been defined as one in which 'a contrary event would have essentially varied the drama of the world in all its subsequent stages'. By this reckoning, the Battle of Britain was certainly decisive.

To find another decisive battle fought so close to British homes we have to go back to the defeat of the Armada in 1588, when Drake's well-handled little ships, with some assistance from the weather, destroyed a vast array of Spanish warships. But a closer parallel is with the Battle of Trafalgar.

In 1805 Napoleon controlled the whole of Europe west of the Russian frontier, with the exception of Great Britain and some parts of the Iberian peninsula. He understood very well that if he could destroy British sea power he could invade and conquer that stubborn island kingdom, and the whole of Western Europe would fall under his sway. But at Trafalgar his own sea power was destroyed by Nelson's fleet, and with it disappeared his hopes of subduing Great Britain. The narrow waters of the Channel were an insuperable barrier to his invading armies. Thwarted in the west, he turned against Russia, and his Grande Armée was all but destroyed amid the ice and snow during the terrible retreat from Moscow in the winter of 1812.

In August 1940 Hitler had mastered all Western Europe, apart from Great Britain, Spain, and Portugal. Although most of the men of the British Expeditionary Force had been brought home—the miracle of Dunkirk—they had lost almost all their weapons and equipment. This disaster had left Great Britain without any effective land forces, for in the whole country it

Left: The much vaunted Me 110 which proved a failure in the battle. Below: The 'Battle of Britain' by Paul Nash, an artist during both wars

was scarcely possible to put into the field one division, fully armed and equipped.

Things had changed since the days of Napoleon. This time the Royal Navy could not save Great Britain, for its ships could not operate in the southern North Sea and the Channel against concentrated German air and submarine attacks. And many of its warships were absent, fully employed in guarding the convoys that brought in the vital supplies of food and raw materials.

The Germans knew that if they could destroy the Royal Air Force, they could invade and conquer Great Britain, and all military resistance in Western Europe would end. Hitler had every reason to feel confident of success. The German air force (Luftwaffe) had destroyed the Polish, Dutch, Belgian, and French air forces. Its Commander-in-chief, Reichsmarschall Hermann Göring, had no doubt that his powerful air fleets would make short work of the much smaller RAF.

In 1805 and again in 1940, Great Britain stood alone against a large continental army, flushed with success, and on both occasions, by a brilliant and decisive victory, she saved herself from invasion and Western Europe from complete military subjection.

But there the similarity ends. Trafalgar was fought and won in a day, but the Battle of Britain, the first decisive battle in the air, was a long drawn out battle of attrition. The daylight battle began in early August, and continued through a long fine autumn until the middle of October. After the day battle had died down, the struggle was carried on by night, through the winter of 1940-41. It ended only when Hitler, despairing of conquering Great Britain, turned, as Napoleon had done before him, against Russia. And, like Napoleon, Hitler was to see his great armies all but annihilated battling against the illimitable spaces and the bitter winter climate of Russia.

Looking back, the people of Great Britain may wonder why the battle had to be fought in their skies, over their heads, and why it was their towns and cities that were bombed and devastated by fire. The answer to this is to be found in the sequence of events between the two world wars.

After the Armistice in November 1918 the greatly expanded armed forces of the Allies were hastily and clumsily demobilized. Improvised war organizations were dismantled, and the watchwords of the British government were economy and retrenchment. The war had been won, there was no visible threat to Allied security, and Great Britain and France were swept by a wave of anti-war feeling, largely induced by the terrible casualties and intolerable conditions of trench warfare.

In 1925 the League of Nations had set

up a Preparatory Commission to explore the ground for a general disarmament conference. Progress in this field is never rapid, and for many years the commission was involved in interminable difficulties and arguments. Eventually a Disarmament Conference was convened in Geneva in 1932, at which proposals for outlawing air bombardment and drastically limiting the loaded weight of military aircraft were discussed. Hoping for success in these negotiations, the British government declined to authorize the design and construction of any effective bomber aircraft. In addition, it had introduced in 1924 what became known as the 'Ten-year Rule', which postulated that there would be no major war for ten years. Unfortunately each successive year was deemed to be the starting point of this tranquil epoch, and so the period always remained at ten years.

The Disarmament Conference finally broke up in May 1934 without achieving any result whatsoever. But meanwhile Hitler had come to power in Germany, and was clearly bent on a massive programme of rearmament. In 1933 the British government at last permitted the issue of Air Staff requirements for a high-performance multi-gun fighter, which in due course produced the Hurricane and Spitfire. It is often asserted that these two aircraft, and especially the Spitfire, were forced on a reluctant Air Ministry by a far-sighted aircraft industry and its capable designers. There is not a word of truth in this. Both aircraft were designed, ordered, and built to Air Ministry specifications.

Even after the collapse of the Disarmament Conference in 1934 the British government was reluctant to rearm. Alone

The aces. 1 Squadron Leader 'Sailor' Malan. He was the third highest RAF scorer with thirty-five enemy aircraft shot down. The RAF's top scorers were M.T.St John Pattle with forty-one kills, and Johnny Johnson (thirty-eight). 2 Squadron Leader Stanford Tuck. Between May 1940 and January 1942 he shot down twenty-nine German aircraft making him the eighth highest RAF scorer for the war. In 1942 he was shot down over France and captured. 3 Major Adolf Galland, top German scorer in the Battle of Britain with fifty-seven kills. Although he was grounded for three years he shot down 103 aircraft in the West and was the Luftwaffe's fourth highest scorer in that theatre. Top German scorer in the West, Captain Hans-Joachim Marseille, shot down 158 aircraft. 4 Lieutenant Colonel Werner Mölders. In the Battle of Britain he scored fifty-five kills. He was shot down and killed in 1941. 5 and 6 Spitfires seen from the nose gun position of Heinkel 111 bombers

5 △ 6 ▽

Beat
'FIREBOMB
FRITZ'

BRITAIN
SHALL NOT
BURN

BRITAIN'S FIRE GUARD IS BRITAIN'S DEFENCE

among nations the British seem to think that if they rearm it will bring about an arms race. The result of this curious delusion is that they usually start when the other competitors are half-way round the course. The bomber force was therefore given a very low priority, but development of the fighters was allowed to proceed, though without any undue haste.

In 1935 two British ministers, Mr Anthony Eden and Sir John Simon, visited Germany. They reported that Hitler's rearmament in the air had proceeded much farther and faster than the British government had believed possible. This was because the Germans had made a secret agreement to train the Soviet air force, an agreement enabling them to keep in being a sizeable corps of expert pilots and technicians. The government was alarmed, and ordered quantity production of the Hurricanes and Spitfires before the prototype had even flown – the so-called 'ordering off the drawing-board'.

Lord Trenchard, chief of the Air Staff from 1919 to 1928, had always believed that in air defence the bomber was as important as the fighter. He maintained that the air war should be fought in the skies over the enemy's territory, and he therefore advocated a bomber force powerful enough to take the offensive, and attack an enemy's vital centres from the outset. He argued that this would rob an enemy of the initiative and throw his air force on to the defensive.

Eventually Trenchard's views were accepted by the British government, and in the air defence of Great Britain two-thirds of the squadrons were to be bombers and one-third fighters. But because it was thought that the bombers were offensive while the fighters were defensive in character, it was judged that the building up of fighter strength would not be liable to trigger off an arms race. The seventeen authorized fighter squadrons were in existence by 1930, but at that date no more than twelve of the thirty-five authorized bomber squadrons had been formed, most of them

1 German air reconnaissance photograph of oil installations at Purfleet on the Thames after the heavy air raid on London on 7th September 1940. 2 Poster issued by Ministry of Home Security calling for national solidarity against incendiary attacks. The first heavy incendiary attack was on 15th October 1940. To meet the new threat, the minister of home security, Herbert Morrison, organized a compulsory fire-watching service and consolidated local fire brigades into a single National Fire Service. 3 German fighter pilots relaxing but ready to 'scramble'. 4 Remains of a German bomber brought down in an English farmyard

KEEP THEM BOTH FLYING!

SPEED IS *Vital!*

equipped with small short-range day bombers. In 1935 the alarm caused by German rearmament in the air occasioned a further shift of emphasis in favour of the fighters. A system of radio-location, later called radar, which would provide invaluable early warning and make it possible to track incoming raids, was pioneered by Robert Watson-Watt, and given all possible encouragement.

The Munich crisis of 1938, when for a time war seemed unavoidable, brought home to the British government, though not to the British people, their appalling military weakness and almost total unreadiness for war. France, which was in no better shape, and Great Britain had to make the best bargain they could with Hitler. The British government now realized that war was likely in the near future, with no possibility of building up a bomber force that could carry the war into the enemy's skies. The opening phase of the war was therefore bound to be defensive, to gain the time needed to modernize and build up the armed forces. The Air Ministry had to switch all remaining priorities to the expansion and equipment of Fighter Command, at the expense of the development of the bomber force. It was also necessary to build, with great urgency, a chain of radar stations to provide early warning and controlled interception of incoming enemy raids. The most that could be hoped for was to foil any attempt at invasion, and survive the opening defensive phase in good enough shape to begin to build an offensive capacity. For it must be remembered that even the most successful defensive action cannot win a war; it can stave off defeat and buy time to create the right conditions for an offensive, but no more.

At the outbreak of war in September 1939 the odds against the RAF, in terms of modern aircraft, were about four to one. Although money had been poured out like water during the years since the Munich crisis, it had been too late to redress the balance. It was only time—as much

1 Battle of Britain poster emphasizes importance of fighter aircraft for national survival. 2 Member of the Women's Voluntary Service carrying some of the aluminium pots and pans given in response to Lord Beaverbrook's appeal. The WVS drove mobile canteens, cared for the bombed-out, staffed rest centres and clothing depots, and helped with evacuation. 3 London street after an air raid in September 1940. 4 Ack-ack girls practise air raid drill. Women from the Auxiliary Territorial Service worked in anti-aircraft units and performed non-combatant duties, like plotting and ranging enemy aircraft, releasing men for active service

Germany's Triumph

time as possible—would be able to do that.

Hitler's assault on the West began on 10th May 1940, and within two months Belgium, Holland, and France were defeated and prostrate, with Denmark and Norway already occupied by German troops and air forces. During these two months the RAF operated at maximum intensity, in a vain effort to stave off disaster, and later to give protective cover to the evacuation from the continent. Losses were very heavy, and in some ways these operations put just as great a strain upon Fighter Command as did the Battle of Britain.

At the beginning of July Great Britain stood alone, with no more than a narrow strip of sea separating her from the victorious armed forces of Hitler's Germany. The strategy and assumptions with which the Allies had begun the war lay in ruins all around them. Had the Germans been able to follow up their success by an immediate invasion across the Channel they might have succeeded, for Fighter Command was exhausted, and Great Britain's land forces were so disarmed and disorganized that effective resistance would scarcely have been possible. But fortunately the Germans were also in need of a breathing space. They needed time to regroup their armies, collect barges and stores, re-deploy their air forces on new airfields in captured territories, build up stocks of bombs, ammunition, fuel, and spare parts, and to give their aircrews a much needed rest.

It is sometimes forgotten that the object of the RAF in the Battle of Britain was not simply to defeat the German air attacks, but the destruction of Hitler's plan, code-named 'Sea Lion', for the invasion and conquest of Great Britain. This was to involve not only Fighter Command, but the whole of Bomber Command too.

The battle began on 8th August 1940. Rising production of fighter aircraft and intensive training of pilots had by this time reduced the odds against the RAF to about three to one. On the very day that Hitler launched his assault against the West, a new Ministry of Aircraft Production was set up, with Lord Beaverbrook at its head. He was especially charged with doing everything possible to increase the production of fighter aircraft and all of the equipment needed for air defence. He was a man of boundless energy, whose administrative methods were ruthless, improvised, and fluid rather than methodical or orderly. He spared no effort to make the people of Great Britain realize the vital importance of fighter production. Householders were asked to give every aluminium saucepan they could spare, and many did so in the belief that in the twinkling of an eye their household utensils would be turned into Hurricanes and Spitfires.

In sober fact there were only three ways in which the planned production of fighters could be accelerated during the next three months. Firstly, by convincing the aircraft industry and the trade unions of the vital need to increase production; secondly, by concentrating every available priority on air defence; and thirdly, by reducing the production of spare parts and using the capacity thus released to build aircraft instead. Beaverbrook used all three methods. The first two had only a marginal effect, and the third produced the most obvious result, though largely at the expense of serviceability in the field. It compelled squadrons to 'cannibalize'; that is, to rob unserviceable aircraft of spare parts to keep the others going. Though Beaverbrook assumed office too late to achieve much genuine increase in production until the day battle was over, it was generally believed that he had done so. In addition, his iconoclastic activities and dramatic personality had a salutary moral effect, both on the RAF and the British public.

The German plan for the invasion of Great Britain required the destruction of the RAF, followed by the transport across the Channel of some 200,000 German troops and their impedimenta, conveyed in the huge barges used commercially on the Rhine and other great European rivers and canals. It was the task of Fighter Command to avoid destruction and to win the air battle, and that of Bomber Command to destroy the barges and dumps of war material collecting in the Channel ports.

At the beginning of the battle, Fighter Command consisted of fifty-four regular and auxiliary squadrons, of which twenty-seven were equipped with Hurricanes, nineteen with Spitfires, six with Blenheim night-fighters, and two with Defiants, a two-seater fighter which proved unsatisfactory in operations. Thus there was a total of forty-six effective day fighter squadrons, giving a front-line strength of about 820 aircraft. Against this, the Germans had deployed a total of some 2,600 aircraft, of which about 1,000 were day fighters, and the remainder bombers of various kinds.

The German fighters were the single-engined Messerschmitt 109, and the twin-engined Messerschmitt 110. The performance of the Me 109 was slightly better than that of the Hurricane, but not as good as the Spitfire. The Me 110 was regarded by the Luftwaffe as a destroyer rather than a fighter. It combined long range and a powerful armament, but was relatively unmanoeuvrable, and no match for the British interceptor fighters.

The 1,200 long-range bombers were mainly Dornier 17s and Heinkel 111s, both good fast aircraft, but with inadequate defensive armament. The normal bomb load of the Dornier was 2,205 lb, and that of the Heinkel about 3,000 lb, with provision in the latter for a maximum of 5,512 lb for short ranges. They flew in well-drilled formations, with the Me 110s as close escort, and the Me 109s providing high cover.

Göring was confident that he could achieve his aim by smashing the fighter defences around London, and then extending his assault northwards and westwards until all effective resistance ceased.

Fighter Command

Fighter Command, however, had immense confidence in its aircrews, its aircraft, and its well-developed system of ground-controlled interception. Its aircrews were as well-trained as any in the world, and second to none in courage and determination. They had inherited the great traditions of the gallant fighter pilots of the Royal Flying Corps in the First World War, and their morale was very high. They knew very well how much depended on their efforts, and they were obviously defending their homeland from a monstrous assault. Moreover, they had their parachutes and friendly territory beneath them. The Hurricanes and Spitfires were reliable and had an excellent performance. With their eight machine-guns they were superior in armament to any other fighter in the world. And there had been time to build the chain of radar stations, and accustom the pilots and operations rooms staffs to the new techniques of interception. Finally, a simplified and very effective system of battle tactics had been worked out.

Fighter Command was ready—but only just ready—for battle.

Air Marshal Sir Hugh Dowding, the Commander-in-Chief of Fighter Command, was a shrewd and very experienced commander. He was generally held in more respect than affection, for he had a sharp tongue and a gruff and somewhat ungracious manner, which had earned him the nickname of 'Stuffy'. But those who knew him well realized that this manner concealed a humane and rather shy personality.

Dowding understood very well the magnitude and importance of his task. He also realized that the battle would be one of attrition and that, while the most vigorous and resolute tactical offensive against the Luftwaffe was essential, he would have to husband his resources. He had to guard against exhausting his pilots and ground crews by asking too much of them. Except for short spells in an emergency, he must keep his operations at a level that could be maintained for a long period.

The command, group, and sector operations rooms, placed underground, each had

a large map in the form of a table. All incoming raids were plotted by radar, and counters were immediately placed on the map, indicating position, altitude, direction of flight, and approximate strength. Large numbers of officers and airwomen of the Women's Auxiliary Air Force were employed in the operations rooms on these duties, and in intelligence and codes and cyphers. The controller, in a gallery, could see all the information on the map at a glance, and issue orders to the appropriate squadrons. Once airborne, they could be given a course which would bring about an interception. Controllers had to be cool and experienced, to avoid being deceived by feints and to ensure that the main attacks were intercepted with maximum force. While delegating much to the group commanders, the command operations room retained general over-all control of the battle.

The first phase opened with a very intense attack on British shipping in the Channel. This was, however, a probing attack, involving but slight penetration of the defences. A few days later, on 12th August, orders were given for the full-scale offensive. On 15th August the pattern changed, and a widespread attack by 1,800 German aircraft was carried out against all sorts of objectives. That evening Göring gave orders that all further attacks were to be directed solely against the RAF—its bases and communications, and especially against the main strength of Fighter Command deployed in a ring of airfields around London.

This second phase was, from the British point of view, the most dangerous of the whole battle. Concentrated attacks severely damaged airfields at North Weald, Hornchurch, and Debden, and Biggin Hill was so wrecked as to be temporarily out of action. All the fighter airfields suffered varying degrees of damage. The defence of these airfields was vital, and so intense were the operations that the pilots and airmen were near to exhaustion. The worst hit squadrons were sent north to quieter sectors to recuperate, but all too soon the 'rested' squadrons would have to return to the south-east. The situation was becoming desperate, and had the Germans persisted in their policy for another fortnight the

Seen from behind the undercarriage of a British Hawker Hurricane, an RAF pilot adjusts his parachute before going into action. Hanging from the face mask are the oxygen line and the lead for the pilot's radio-telephone, which fed information from the chain of radar stations and plotting-rooms, and rapidly vectored the eight-gun Hurricanes and Spitfires on to the incoming enemy bomber streams

Germany's Triumph

result might well have been disastrous for Fighter Command.

Soon, however, affairs were to take a new turn. On the night of 23rd August the Germans bombed London, and the Prime Minister ordered a retaliatory attack on factories in Berlin. The night was almost too short for such an operation, but Bomber Command successfully carried it out. Hitler reacted promptly. He ordered that German air attacks should in future be directed against British industrial cities and towns, with London as the primary objective. Göring had told him that the air battle was all but won, and that the RAF was at its last gasp. Hitler believed that these new attacks would shatter British morale and pave the way for his invasion.

Invasion imminent

In fact, this change of emphasis in the third phase relieved the pressure on Fighter Command. Damaged runways and other airfield facilities were repaired, broken communications were quickly made good, and the Command's fighting capacity rapidly restored. On 7th September the Germans launched a tremendous attack, involving almost their whole strength. Wave after wave of bombers, escorted by hordes of fighters, crossed the coast. Many great fires were caused, especially in the London docks. Guided by the flames, the bombers continued the attacks through the hours of darkness. The damage and loss of life were grievous, but the British people were undaunted, and the over-all effect was far less catastrophic than the attack on the fighter airfields. An attempt to follow up these attacks on 8th September was repulsed with heavy losses.

There could be no doubt, however, that Operation Sea Lion was imminent, and on 7th September the British government issued a warning that invasion was probable during the next few days. That night the whole strength of Bomber Command was concentrated against the barges and military dumps in the Channel ports. The weather was good, and these attacks were highly successful. Night after night the bombers pounded the invasion ports. On 11th September Hitler postponed the date of Sea Lion to 24th September. But on the night of 13th September an especially successful bombing attack did enormous damage, sinking no less than eighty huge barges in the port of Ostend alone.

Göring remained optimistic. He assured Hitler that 'given four or five more days of good weather, the results would be decisive'. But another tremendous air assault on 15th September, which raged from dawn to dusk, suffered a severe defeat at the hands of Fighter Command. This day is generally regarded as the climax of the Battle of Britain.

On 17th September Hitler resolved to postpone Operation Sea Lion indefinitely. He realized, more clearly than did Göring, that the Luftwaffe had failed to defeat Fighter Command, and that he could no longer maintain his vast concentrations of barges, troops, and military stores in the Channel ports in the face of Bomber Command's devastating attacks. He gave orders for the remaining barges and stores to be dispersed, and the troops moved away from the danger areas around the ports.

Air reconnaissance soon confirmed that these German concentrations were melting away, and it was clear that the danger of immediate invasion was over. The supply of trained pilots had proved to be just sufficient, while the production of fighter aircraft just managed to cope with the wastage.

The German air force had failed utterly to achieve its aim of breaking Fighter Command, and had suffered severe losses in the attempt. It was not easy to assess these losses accurately. No doubt, at the time, the German losses were exaggerated, but this is inevitable in large-scale fighting in the air. But whatever the actual losses were, they were enough to call a halt to Göring's air attacks, while Bomber Command had destroyed a great part of the shipping and war material on which the invasion depended.

On 13th October Hitler postponed Operation Sea Lion until the spring of 1941, but in reality the plan was dead.

The Blitz continues

As the battle by day slowly died away, the fourth phase began and the German bombers were switched to night operations. There had been a fair number of night attacks during the day battle period, but these were not very heavy and were usually follow-up attacks of targets bombed during the preceding day.

The problems confronting aircraft operating in darkness were at that time largely unsolved. The bomber's problems were those of navigation by night, often in poor weather conditions over a blacked-out countryside, of target identification, and bomb-aiming. For the fighter there were the problems of finding the bomber in the dark, and making an effective attack on it.

The German bomber crews were not well trained or experienced in night operations. Hence they used a radio beam technique, called 'Knickebein' (crooked leg), which enabled a pilot to navigate by radio signals. The system had the disadvantage of being vulnerable to radio counter-measures. It could be interfered with by jamming, but the most successful method was to bend or deflect the beam.

By day the fighters could be vectored on to incoming enemy formations located by radar, and interception made relatively easy. By night, against a swarm of individual bombers, such methods failed. A means of interception had to be carried in the fighter itself. This was the AI (aircraft interception), which was at first fitted to the Blenheim, a fast bomber aircraft converted, in default of anything better, to a night-fighter. After many initial set-backs and failures, it was found possible to vector a night-fighter close enough to a bomber to pick it up on its AI, and a sighting made. But progress was slow. The Blenheim was not fast enough or well enough armed to be very successful.

Later in the period a new night-fighter, the Beaufighter, appeared. This was an adaptation of a sea-reconnaissance aircraft, the Beaufort. With improved AI, and armed with four 20-mm cannon and four machine-guns, it proved a most useful night-fighter. But it was not available in sufficient numbers until the night-blitz was almost over.

Considerable success was in fact achieved by the night air defences, but not enough to provide a deterrent.

The attacks on British towns and cities killed and wounded many civilians, and caused serious, if temporary, losses of industrial output. Indeed these losses, due not so much to the actual destruction of factories as to the disruption of gas, electricity, and water supplies, communications, and above all to absenteeism caused by the destruction of workers' dwellings, gave the British a somewhat exaggerated idea of the effectiveness of such operations.

For centuries, except for a few civil wars long ago, the British people had been used to the idea that battles were fought on the high seas, or far away in other countries and were exclusively the business of the armed forces. The First World War disturbed, but did not destroy, these beliefs.

The direct attack from the air on their homes and places of work shocked and angered the British people, but they were not dismayed. A new spirit of neighbourly friendship and concern developed. Little had been known, in the absence of actual experience, of the behaviour of a civilized population under air attack, and on the whole the courage and endurance of the British people exceeded most official expectations.

With the coming of the shorter summer nights the night bombing attacks died down, and when in June 1941 Hitler began the invasion of Russia, his bombers were moved to the Eastern Front.

The Battle of Britain had been fought and won. But it was not the beginning of the end of the war, but the end of the beginning.

The Battle of the Atlantic

The Second World War was only a few hours old when the British passenger liner *Athenia* was sunk in the Atlantic without warning by a torpedo from the German submarine U30. The loss of the liner, carrying a number of children, sent a wave of indignation through the country and persuaded the Admiralty to institute a convoy system for the protection of Allied merchant shipping.

The two main convoy systems were the east-west transatlantic convoys to and from North America and the north-south convoys to and from the South Atlantic, the Mediterranean, and West Africa. Although the very act of concentrating shipping into compact bodies in this way gave them a measure of immunity from attack by making them harder for an enemy to locate, warship escort was obviously essential. However, Admiralty policy had been to organize shipping into convoy only if the enemy resorted to unrestricted submarine warfare, believing that Hitler's navy would abide by the conditions for submarine warfare laid down by the Hague Convention, and no steps had been taken to acquire ships suitable for anti-submarine escort. The anti-submarine force available in September 1939 consisted of 150 destroyers (including those required to operate with the Fleet), six coastal patrol vessels, and twenty-four sloops.

With this number it was only usually possible to give convoys an escort of two ships. Fortunately the Germans entered the war possessing only forty-eight operational submarines, though a programme for rapid expansion was put in hand at the end of 1939. For the first eight months of the war, therefore, the scale of attack was small, almost ceased during the Norwegian campaign when the U-boats were recalled to take part in it, and was concentrated almost entirely on ships sailing independently.

U-boat commanders who did attack convoys, using the conventional method of approaching and firing submerged, came up against the combination in the escorts of the 'asdic' which could detect and locate them and the depth charge which, if accurately placed, could sink them. Asdic, details of which had been kept secret, was a device with which the range and bearing of an object under water could be determined, by transmitting a narrow sound beam of very high frequency and measuring the time taken for an echo from it to return.

Near the end of the Norwegian campaign in May 1940 the U-boats reverted to attacks on merchant shipping and, when the fall of France gave them bases from which the Atlantic trade routes could be easily reached, the Battle of the Atlantic began. The sinking of eleven German submarines in the first six months of the war by destroyers had induced a respect for the asdic among U-boat commanders. They therefore concentrated on unescorted ships whenever possible. These consisted not only of independently routed ships, of which there was still a large number, but also ships which had, for one reason or another, 'straggled' from their convoys, and ships from outward-bound Atlantic convoys which had been dispersed when the escorts left them to meet homeward-bound convoys. This took place at first some 200 miles west of Ireland, and extended a further 200 miles by the autumn of 1940, the limit imposed by the fuel endurance of the escorting destroyers.

Beyond this no anti-submarine protection for our merchant shipping could be given. Coupled with the desperate shortage of destroyers as a result of the number sunk or damaged in the Dunkirk operations and the need for others to be deployed on anti-invasion duties, this provided the U-boats with what their commanders were to call the first 'Happy Time'. In the period July to October 1940, 144 unescorted ships were sent to the bottom. Such convoys as were located were so meagerly escorted that they could be attacked with near impunity. From them seventy-three more ships were sunk. Only two U-boats were destroyed in reply by convoy escorts. The majority of the U-boats' attacks were made by night, operating on the surface where they enjoyed high speed and manoeuvrability. The U-boats' night attacks not only confirmed that their low silhouette made them virtually invisible against the dark background of the sea from the bridge of a ship high above them; they also discovered a fatal flaw in the asdic. Its performance against a surfaced submarine was almost negligible. Until the development of an effective ship-borne radar at the end of 1941, the advantage in a night-encounter, even with a destroyer, lay with the U-boat.

It was at this time, too, that another main feature of the tactics of the U-boats was first developed, the deployment of a number

Top: Commander F.J.Walker, the most successful U-boat killer of the war.
Centre: Otto Kretschmer, the top-scoring U-boat commander. He was taken prisoner when his U99 was destroyed in March 1941. Bottom: Günther Prien, another U-boat ace. In 1939 his U47 penetrated Scapa Flow and sank HMS Royal Oak. U47 was lost in March 1941 with all hands

Germany's Triumph

of them on a patrol line across the convoy route and their concentration into a 'wolf-pack' as soon as the convoy was located. It was immediately spectacularly successful.

The slow, homeward-bound convoy SC7 of thirty-four ships, which left Nova Scotia on 5th October 1940 with the solitary escort of a slow, lightly-armed sloop, had plugged through heavy seas to 500 miles west of Ireland by the 16th. There it was met by two more escorts—another sloop and one of the new Flower-class corvettes.

There, too, it was located by a lone U-boat which signalled its position, course, and speed to headquarters before attacking in the moonlight that night and sinking two ships. The escorts, engaged in picking up survivors and hunting vainly for the attacker, left the convoy to steam on without even their meagre support until the following evening when two of them were able to rejoin in time to suffer attack by another solitary U-boat. It achieved only a single torpedo hit which damaged but did not sink a freighter. Another sloop and a corvette now joined the escort, the corvette being directed to stand by the crippled ship.

There were thus two sloops and a corvette with the convoy when darkness fell on the evening of the 18th.

Just over the horizon ahead six U-boats of a patrol line, alerted by the sighting report, had been concentrating. Among them were two top-scoring 'aces', Joachim Schepke of U100 and Otto Kretschmer of U99. During the night that followed fourteen ships were sunk, seven of them by U99. The distracted escorts, unable to locate the attackers, could do nothing but pick up the crews of the sunken ships. By the morning the dwindling convoy had virtually disintegrated. Including three stragglers, which suffered the usual fate of such ships, twenty had been sunk and two more damaged out of the thirty-four which had set out. The remainder made their way individually to port, saved from further attack by the discovery of a fresh convoy for the wolves, the fast HX79 following two days behind SC7.

There the same scenes of destruction, the same failure by the escorts, either to defend their charges or exact any retribution, re-enacted themselves, twelve ships being sunk and two more damaged out of a convoy of forty-nine.

Another small pack attack mounted against a convoy in December 1940 sank eleven ships and the escorting armed merchant cruiser. Such shocking losses led to a searching enquiry to seek a solution.

One of the shortcomings in the defence was the lack of fast escort destroyers which had been held back in the anti-invasion forces. They were now released for trade protection duties. Strengthening of the convoy escorts in this way paid an encouraging dividend, three U-boats being destroyed by them in November 1940, the first success for five months. There were still too few destroyers to do more than add a leavening to the inexperienced and ill-equipped corvettes, however.

The prime antidote to the wolf-pack tactics—air escort—was in fact available but denied to the navy by priority decisions. The only long-range aircraft available to Coastal Command for support of the convoys were a few Sunderland flying-boats. Twin-engined planes of the Command came to join them when the onset of winter released them from anti-invasion reconnaissance duties.

In conjunction with much foul weather, these factors caused something of a lull in the battle during the winter of 1940-41, following the holocaust of October. But while escort numbers were slowly growing, so were those of the U-boat fleet which numbered under thirty in 1940. None was lost between November 1940 and March 1941 and meanwhile the numbers were growing. An ominous feature of this period, also, was the first appearance of U-boats on

the convoy route between Britain and Freetown, Sierra Leone, the assembly port for the large and vital trade with the Orient which, until the entry of Italy into the war, had passed through the Mediterranean and the Suez Canal. The spring of 1941 therefore saw a large upsurge of activity.

Although the Battle of the Atlantic refers primarily to the long struggle waged between the German U-boats and convoy escorts for control of the vital Atlantic life-lines, other forms of attack were also developed, each calling for specialized efforts to counter them.

First in point of time came the commerce-raiding cruise of the pocket-battleship *Admiral Graf Spee*. Her interception by a group of three British cruisers off the River Plate in December 1939, and her subsequent scuttling outside Montevideo harbour had all the elements of high drama. Her depredations had only amounted to nine ships sunk in three months, however. Her sister ship *Deutschland,* operating in the North Atlantic, accounted for only two merchantmen in two months before returning to Germany.

In October 1940 the Germans once again

Above: From a U-boat's conning-tower, German officers scan the horizon for the telltale smoke signals of a convoy. Left: Crew of a torpedoed merchant ship being picked up by an escort vessel. Right: On the bridge of an escorting destroyer on convoy duty in the Atlantic. As convoy escort improved the U-boats moved to new hunting grounds

loosed a major warship on the Atlantic trade routes. This was the pocket-battleship *Admiral Scheer*. Almost her first encounter was with a convoy of thirty-seven ships, escorted only by the armed merchant cruiser *Jervis Bay* which steamed out against her in gallant defiance. By the time the *Jervis Bay* had been sunk, the convoy had been able to scatter to such an extent that the *Scheer* was only able to catch and sink five of the merchantmen. The pocket-battleship went on to make a five-months' cruise in the South Atlantic and Indian Ocean during which she sank sixteen ships before returning to Germany.

A greater menace were the battlecruisers *Scharnhorst* and *Gneisenau* which broke out into the Atlantic on the 7th February 1941. They sank twenty-two independently steaming ships before the two ships re-

turned safely to Brest on 22nd March.

The last and potentially the most serious attempt to use major warships against Allied convoys was the famous foray of the giant battleship *Bismarck* in company with the cruiser *Prinz Eugen* in May 1941. Intercepted by the battleships *Hood* and *Prince of Wales*, the *Bismarck* sank the *Hood*; but, damaged by the *Prince of Wales*, and by a torpedo attack by aircraft from the carrier *Victorious*, she was forced to make for Brest for repairs, only to be again torpedoed and crippled by aircraft from the *Ark Royal*, and finally overwhelmed by the massed power of the Home Fleet. The *Prinz Eugen* escaped to Brest having accomplished nothing.

Alarming as these various forays by surface warships were, the sum of their achievements were small compared to those

of the U-boat fleet whose head, Admiral Karl Dönitz, never ceased to press for priority to be given to the one arm which he rightly believed could bring victory to Germany. That he was never listened to or given a free hand is perhaps the principal cause of his ultimate failure.

The other main threat to Atlantic convoys was that of long-range Focke-Wulf Condors, adaptations of civil aircraft. Operating from Bordeaux from August 1940, they caused serious shipping losses, some convoys having U-boats homed on to them while others were attacked by groups of Condors directed on to them by shadowing U-boats.

Steps to combat the new menace were taken. Surface escorts were reinforced as much as possible, long-range fighter escorts were provided from bases in Northern Ire-

land and anti-aircraft guns, manned by army crews, were mounted in merchantmen. On other ships a catapult was mounted from which a Hurricane fighter could be launched, the pilot baling out or 'ditching' his aircraft on completion of his mission. Deterred from bombing by these measures, the Condors reverted to their original task, reconnoitring the north-south convoy routes to and from Gibraltar and Sierra Leone.

U-boat war—measure and counter-measure

Meanwhile, on the transatlantic convoy routes, the battle had been a straight fight between the U-boats and the surface escorts supported by the slowly increasing but still scanty reconnaissance aircraft of Coastal Command. The majority of these were of medium endurance and their chief effect was to push the area of operations westwards, beyond their range. It was thus in an area south of Iceland that the first major encounters of the spring of 1941 took place.

During the winter lull, the steps taken to improve the quantity and quality of the convoy escorts under the control of the newly-established Western Approaches Command at Liverpool had borne fruit. Dönitz's 'aces' found much tougher opposition when they attacked an outward convoy in the first days of March. Sinking two freighters and damaging two more, they lost one of their own number and two others were forced to withdraw damaged. Continuing to shadow the convoy, Günther Prien's U47, in which he had achieved a hero's reputation by penetrating Scapa Flow in October 1939 to sink the battleship *Royal Oak*, was caught and sunk with all hands.

A week later the wolf-pack was directed on to a homeward convoy in the same area. Five ships were sunk in a single night; but before dawn two more U-boat 'aces' had been eliminated. Schepke had gone down with U100; Otto Kretschmer and the crew of U99 were prisoners in the escort commander's ship.

During this month it cost the Germans five U-boats to sink nineteen ships in convoy. They were shifted farther west again so as to catch the convoys before they joined their anti-submarine escorts. The result was the massacre of a slow convoy intercepted south-east of Greenland before its anti-submarine escort had joined. In reply the Admiralty based groups and aircraft in Iceland which could give escort as far as longitude 35° west (roughly 1,200 miles west of Ireland).

The ocean wastes to the south and south-east of Cape Farewell, Greenland, now became the U-boats' chosen field. At the end of May an unescorted convoy south of Greenland lost nine ships. On the other hand when the wolf-packs tried their luck

in June with a convoy which had picked up its escort, they lost two of their number in sinking five merchantmen. The total number of ships sunk by U-boats was steadily rising—from forty-two in April to sixty-one in June. But only twenty per cent of these were in convoy where escorts destroyed five U-boats in reply.

The lesson was plain to see and in July 1941 the Admiralty at last had the resources to benefit from it. Besides the over-age 'four-stacker' destroyers, acquired from the USA under Lend-Lease, and the large number of Flower-class corvettes coming from British shipyards, other corvettes built in Canada were being manned by the Royal Canadian Navy as well as seven of the 'four-stackers'. A Newfoundland Escort Force was formed in May, based at St John's, Newfoundland, which gave escort—weak at first but slowly growing—over the western portion of the convoy route. Thus end-to-end escort was now effective over the east-west trade route.

Frustrated in their search for easy prey on the transatlantic route, Dönitz sent U-boats south to the Freetown area. A rich harvest was reaped for a while, no less than eighty-one unescorted ships being sunk. Then end-to-end escort was extended to this route also. There were no soft spots now left. The U-boats would have to face the escorts to reach their prey.

For a while they concentrated in the Western and South-Western Approaches against the Freetown and Gibraltar convoys where it was hoped that in co-operation with the Condor aircraft the earlier successes might be repeated. But this brought the encounters inside the range of Coastal Command's long and medium range aircraft and into an area in which it was possible to give the convoys a large escort. The German move proved a failure and once again Dönitz sought a weak spot on the far side of the Atlantic where the escort groups provided by the Royal Canadian Navy were weak in numbers and experience. In September he found it when a slow, homeward-bound convoy was beset by a group of seventeen U-boats and in two days lost sixteen ships before an escort group from Iceland came to the rescue.

No way of strengthening the defence of the western portion of the convoy route was open to the Admiralty at this time. Dönitz prepared to take advantage of the fact; the disasters of a year earlier might have been repeated. But at this moment Hitler stepped in with an order for the entire force of operational U-boats to be transferred to the Mediterranean, where the fate of Rommel's Afrika Korps was being put in jeopardy by British domination of his sea supply routes, and to the approaches to the Straits of Gibraltar.

Although this greatly eased the situa-

tion on the transatlantic route at a critical moment, it brought the Gibraltar convoys once again under concentrated attacks. A combination of air and U-boat attack inflicted heavy losses on two of them. Two of the factors which were eventually to decide the Battle of the Atlantic in favour of the Allies were now, however, introduced.

A victory for the escorts

An escort group permanently organized and intensively trained under its own regular leader, such as had already been deployed on the transatlantic route, was allocated to the Gibraltar run. Its leader, Commander F.J.Walker, RN, was to become the most successful U-boat killer of the war. At the same time the first escort aircraft carrier, *HMS Audacity*, was also put into service.

A combination of these two factors inflicted the heaviest defeat so far suffered by the U-boats, when a wolf-pack supported by Condor aircraft concentrated on a homeward bound Gibraltar convoy in December 1941. Four U-boats were sunk, two Condors were destroyed, another two damaged. Two of the convoy, an escort and the *Audacity* herself were sunk.

In spite of the calamitous loss of the only British escort carrier as yet in existence, both sides saw this encounter as a notable victory for the escorts. The use of the long-range aircraft was abandoned, the Condor squadron being dispersed to other functions. The swing of the pendulum was clearly moving towards Allied superiority. Escorts were increasing in numerical strength and efficiency.

Up to this time, since the beginning of the war, shipping losses had exceeded replacements by nearly 7,000,000 tons, the great majority of the casualties being ships which for one reason or another were not sailing in convoy. These figures meant that the Allies had been slowly but steadily losing the battle along the trade routes. Now, however, with nearly all but the fastest ships absorbed into the convoy system and with the convoy defences being at last perfected, it could be expected with some confidence that the trend would be halted or reversed.

Then, on 7th December 1941, the whole situation was changed. Following the Japanese attack on Pearl Harbour, Hitler declared war on the United States. Immediately the stream of merchant shipping passing along the eastern seaboard of the United States, which had been immune to attack since the American declaration of a Security Zone covering those waters, became exposed to attack. A new 'Happy Time' for the U-boat commanders began, marked by a veritable holocaust of Allied merchant ships.

America, the Arsenal of Democracy

When war broke out in 1939 an overwhelming majority of the American people favoured neutrality for the United States. This was the natural outcome of almost two decades of isolationist sentiment. President Harding's call for a 'return to normalcy' in the 1920's first enshrined the doctrine. His successors continued it. When war broke out in Spain in 1936, President Franklin Roosevelt declared: 'We shun political commitments which might entangle us in foreign wars. . . . We seek to isolate ourselves completely from war.' In March 1937 a Gallup poll showed that ninety-four per cent of the American people wished the United States to keep out of all foreign wars. By 1939, this had risen to ninety-nine per cent. If Great Britain and France looked to the United States for assistance against Germany, therefore, the American mood was not auspicious.

On 3rd September 1939 President Roosevelt broadcast to the American people: 'This nation will remain a neutral nation, but I cannot ask that every American remain neutral in thought as well. . . .' Roosevelt's words provide a clue to his private thoughts. When war came to Europe, Roosevelt had two main aims for the United States: he wished to keep America out of the war, and he wished to prevent further Nazi aggression. These two aims were to prove mutually exclusive. Privately, Roosevelt favoured the cause of Great Britain, France, and the democracies, but neutrality was already built into American statutes. The Neutrality Act of 1937 prohibited the export of arms and munitions to all belligerent powers. Apart from this, powerful members of the Congress were determined that the United States should have no part in the European war.

Yet as Hitler's armies marched through Poland in September 1939, crushing all resistance in a matter of weeks, Roosevelt was faced with an uncomfortable truth. The American arms embargo favoured the Nazis—efficiently prepared and already geared for war. The United States was denying the unprepared democracies the arms and munitions they desperately needed to face Hitler's war machine.

Roosevelt acted quickly. In a message to Congress on 21st September he called for a repeal of the arms embargo. At the end of a fierce debate in Congress, the Neutrality Act of 1939 was passed on 4th November. This act repealed the arms embargo and allowed the belligerents to buy munitions and supplies from the United States provided they paid cash and provided they transported all such supplies in non-American ships. This 'cash and carry' policy undoubtedly favoured Great Britain and France, who had command of the seas. Their interests were further served by another American proclamation which excluded submarines from American territorial waters while allowing armed merchant vessels to use the same waters.

Despite the new 'cash and carry' policy, however, there were severe limitations on the amount of munitions and supplies Great Britain and France could hope for from the United States. The American economy was not adapted to war production. During the New Deal era the nation's resources had been devoted to peaceful, domestic programmes. In 1939, as in 1914, the United States was unprepared for war. Moreover, although the conflagration in Europe was now uppermost in Roosevelt's mind, the United States faced dangers in the Far East, where Japan's mounting ambitions showed clearly that the United States could not afford to distribute all its available munitions and supplies to the European democracies, however desperate their need.

By spring, 1940, however, President Roosevelt was faced with the disagreeable —and dangerous—possibility that Hitler might indeed become master of Europe. April brought the invasion of Norway and Denmark. May saw the fall of Belgium and the Netherlands. When Italy declared war on France, President Roosevelt cast aside all pretence of impartiality, saying: 'The hand that held the dagger has struck it in the back of its neighbour.'

In his annual budget message of January 1940 President Roosevelt requested $1,800 million for national defence. In May he requested additional expenditure of more than $1,000 million. Both requests were granted. Roosevelt could now turn more hopefully to Winston Churchill's urgent requests for arms and supplies. In June the United States War Department sold to Great Britain more than $43 million worth of arms, munitions, and aircraft. These were valuable, though most were drawn from outdated stocks and supplies. For Great Britain, the most urgent need was for warships, to help fight the submarine menace and retain mastery of the seas.

In May 1940 Churchill made a direct request to Roosevelt for fifty old American destroyers to help repair British losses

Two currents in American feeling, 1940. **Above:** *Comment on reluctance to face reality of Nazi threat—an attitude fast losing ground.* **Below:** *Preparing for war—Boeing works, Seattle, building Flying Fortresses*

Germany's Triumph

and protect the merchant fleets. American law prohibited the sale or loan of American warships, yet to deny or even to delay this assistance might mean defeat for both Great Britain and France. The German armies were already penetrating deep into France. When France fell, the Battle of Britain began and the Battle of the Atlantic continued with renewed ferocity.

Roosevelt was acutely anxious to help Great Britain in her plight, but he could not move too far ahead of American public opinion. Powerful members of the Senate were watching his movements and the direction of his policies. Many members of Congress had vivid memories of America's part in the First World War, and were bitterly opposed to any American participation in another European war. Moreover, 1940 was a presidential election year, and Roosevelt had to decide whether he should relinquish office or stand again for election. He had already served two four-year terms, and tradition and convention decreed that he should not seek a third term. But this was a time of crisis, and Roosevelt was convinced that it was his duty to serve if the nation wished him to. He declared his availability and meanwhile continued to give his unremitting attention to events in Europe.

As the Battle of Britain developed, Churchill bombarded Roosevelt with requests for help. Roosevelt knew that his critics would seize on any action calculated to involve the United States in war with Germany. Churchill's request for fifty destroyers was thus a delicate affair. By a shrewd political stroke, Roosevelt arranged to 'trade' the destroyers for ninety-nine year leases on a number of British bases in the American hemisphere, from Newfoundland to the Caribbean. Roosevelt could thus claim that the deal not only

provided for American security but was an excellent bargain for the price of fifty outdated destroyers.

American public opinion applauded the President's action, even though members of Congress grumbled at this use of executive power without the consent of Congress. For Winston Churchill, the occasion marked a new phase in Anglo-American co-operation. In the best Churchillian style he observed:

'These two great organizations of the English-speaking democracies, the British Empire and the United States, will have to be somewhat mixed up together in some of their affairs for mutual and general advantage. For my part . . . I do not view the process with any misgivings. No one can stop it. Like the Mississippi, it just keeps rolling along. Let it roll. Let it roll on full flood, inexorable, irresistible, to broader land and better days.'

In the November 1940 elections, Roosevelt defeated the Republican candidate Wendell Willkie. He could now claim another four-year mandate for his conduct of affairs. Churchill had already told Roosevelt in a long, secret memorandum that Great Britain's financial resources were rapidly running out and that she could no longer afford to pay for munitions on the 'cash and carry' basis. With his re-election confirmed, Roosevelt now devised a bold and imaginative policy to assist Great Britain. This policy was a 'Lend-Lease' programme, whereby the President was empowered to sell, transfer, exchange, lease, or lend war supplies to any nation whose defence was deemed by the President to be 'vital to the defence of the United States'. Roosevelt prepared the ground in a dramatic speech on 30th December 1940, calling for 'all out aid' to Great Britain and her allies. The United States, Roosevelt declared, must become the 'arsenal of democracy'.

The Lend-Lease Bill was introduced into Congress in January 1941. A prolonged and bitter debate followed. Isolationist senators such as Senator Burton K. Wheeler of Montana suspected a covert plan to bring the United States into the war. Others resented these new additions to the President's executive powers. But the President was assisted by his fresh mandate, and the favourable public reaction to his broadcast 'fireside chats' in which he brought home to the people the full extent of the Nazi menace. In March 1941 the Lend-Lease Bill became law. From now on the United States could indeed become the arsenal of democracy.

Such was the intention, though practical problems remained. An initial appropriation of $7,000 million was granted by Congress, but the American economy was not yet geared to war production. Nevertheless the capacity was there, if government and

industry combined to plan; and fortunately the experience of the New Deal, together with the planning expertise it bequeathed, helped to ease the transition.

Again, Roosevelt demonstrated his knack of picking the right men for the right job, for in Henry L. Stimson as secretary for war, Cordell Hull as secretary of state, and General George C. Marshall as Chief of the Army General Staff, he had advisers fully alive both to the urgency of the hour and also to the requirements of American policy. These men knew that in modern warfare, military strategy must be firmly linked to the world of science and technology. To take one example, air power

Left: US Army poster, produced after the United States entered the war, extols her new tanks. Below: Reporters watch one of 50 US destroyers the Allies were given in exchange for bases before lend-lease opened the way to all-out US aid

Joker from pack of war-time cards depicts Hitler being burned by the flame from the torch of Liberty

must be given a central role in all strategic thinking and planning, and not merely a peripheral role as hitherto. American logistical planning followed these determinants. Between 1940 and the end of 1944, the production of military aircraft rose from 23,000 per annum to 96,000. Military advisers also took note of the vital part played by Panzer divisions in the German victories. Accordingly, tank production was increased from 4,000 in 1940-41 to almost 30,000 in 1943.

Innovation and invention went hand in hand with greater efficiency in production. The assembly lines of the vast Detroit automobile factories were re-tooled and given over to the mass production of planes, armoured vehicles, and the engines of war. New methods of ship construction were devised and exploited, until American yards could claim to be launching a warship every day. The combination of American engineering and technology with boundless resources of coal, iron, and steel soon tipped the economic balance of power, even though Hitler's military successes in Europe and North Africa still made the outcome of the war uncertain.

Meanwhile, as Great Britain faced Hitler alone in Western Europe, Churchill took pains to further the Anglo-American alliance. British military secrets were passed to United States political and military experts in London, and joint consultation at the level of strategic planning became one of the less publicized aspects of Churchill's

direction of the war. In August 1941 Roosevelt and Churchill held secret meetings aboard the US cruiser *Augusta* off Newfoundland. From these meetings the two leaders issued the Atlantic Charter, a declaration of common aims and purposes. Among them were opposition to all forms of territorial aggrandizement, support for the right of all peoples to choose their own form of government, freedom from want and fear, freedom of the seas, and the disarmament of aggressor nations until a permanent peace-keeping organization was securely established.

By now, the United States was firmly on the side of the Allies, though Hitler was prudently avoiding a direct confrontation with the United States. Events moved a step nearer war with Germany when a U-boat attacked the *USS Greer* and brought American naval strength into direct conflict with German naval vessels. From then on, American warships had the President's orders to 'shoot first'.

On 7th December, when Japan perpetrated its 'day of infamy' by its attack on the American fleet at Pearl Harbour, the remaining vestiges of isolationist sentiment in the United States vanished. America now had a common cause with the democracies against the Axis powers. On 8th December, with only one dissenting voice in Congress, the United States declared war on Japan. Three days later Germany and Italy declared war on the United States, and the President and Congress recognized a state of war with these nations. The 'arsenal of democracy' now brought its army, its navy, and its air force to the task of defeating the Axis powers. The final result of the war was no longer in doubt.

America's economy is geared to war
American industry turned to full-scale wartime production. New plants were constructed in a matter of days. Six million women were added to the labour force as selective service took labour away from factory and farm. Older men returned to work and the unemployed were quickly drawn into the national effort. Between 1940 and 1943 the total labour force increased by eight million, from forty-seven to fifty-five million. The working week was increased from forty to forty-eight hours. By 1942, more fighter planes were being produced in one month than had been produced in the whole of 1939. Between Pearl Harbour and the end of the war the United States produced more than 295,000 aeroplanes. Germany's production was less than a third of this, a fact which made it certain that Germany would lose the mastery of the skies.

Not all of American expertise was given to the production and development of conventional weapons. As early as the autumn

of 1939, when Albert Einstein warned President Roosevelt that Germany was seeking to develop an atom bomb, federal funds were channelled into an atomic energy programme. Research and development proceeded with the utmost secrecy at Oak Ridge, Tennessee, and Los Alamos, New Mexico. In December 1942 physicists produced a controlled chain reaction in an atomic pile at the University of Chicago. Following this, federal funds of more than $2,000 million were poured into the development of an atomic bomb, although the first successful test did not take place until after the defeat of Germany in 1945.

By the autumn of 1943 Churchill, Roosevelt, and Stalin realized that the defeat of Germany was only a matter of time. The 'Big Three' discussed plans for a post-war settlement in conferences at Tehran and later at Yalta. Roosevelt and Churchill developed a close personal friendship in Anglo-American discussions at Casablanca and at Washington in 1943. Two further meetings at Cairo that same year cemented their friendship. Their common language, and the fact that both Roosevelt and Churchill found Stalin a somewhat impenetrable figure, inevitably brought the two English-speaking allies into closer counsel. Churchill, needless to say, was entirely happy at this development, even though the American President had doubts about Great Britain's apparent aim of preserving her Empire after the war.

In the field, military commanders did not always see eye to eye on strategy or tactics. When General Dwight D. Eisenhower was made Supreme Commander for the invasion of Western Europe, his commander in the field, General Montgomery, was a loyal but not an altogether uncritical colleague. Nevertheless, combined operations worked remarkably smoothly on land, sea, and in the air.

The final victory over Germany owed something to a common language, but much more to a common set of ideals. If Franklin Roosevelt had not declared the United States the 'arsenal of democracy' in December 1940; if he had not used his presidential power to hurry the Lend-Lease Bill through Congress, we may doubt — as Churchill doubted — that Great Britain could have survived her 'darkest hour'. It would be easy for Europeans to underestimate the skill and determination required by Roosevelt to bring the United States into the war on the side of the Allies. It is worth recalling that on the eve of the presidential election of 1940 Roosevelt's opponent wrung from him a categorical promise to the American people that: 'Your boys are not going to be sent into any foreign wars.' Fortunately for Great Britain, fortunately for Europe, President Roosevelt did not keep this promise.

The Desert War

In the months before the outbreak of war the importance of the Middle East in British grand strategical planning gradually increased. As early as spring 1939 the British and French staffs decided that in the event of war Italy rather than Germany would offer the best prospects for Allied offensive action in the early years. The Italian colony of Libya was sandwiched between the French in Tunisia and the British in Egypt, while Italian East Africa would be a wasting asset cut off from home. At the same time British and French forces in Palestine, Iraq, and Syria were well placed to support Turkey.

The fall of France in June 1940 obliterated these happy prospects. At once the balance of naval and military power swung in Italy's favour—indeed it was only the certainty that France was already beaten that induced Mussolini, the Italian dictator, to declare war. Now it was the British whose position in the Middle East was precarious. Against some 500,000 Italian troops, the Commander-in-Chief Middle East Land Forces, General Sir Archibald Wavell, could muster only some 60,000 to defend a theatre of war 1,700 miles by 2,000 miles, a theatre which encompassed nine countries from Iraq to Somaliland.

The importance of the Middle East to the British no longer lay in the Suez Canal route to the East, because the neutralization of the French fleet left the Royal Navy alone too weak to command the whole Mediterranean sea-route from Gibraltar to Egypt. The importance lay in the oil of the Persian Gulf. Its loss would throw Great Britain into dependence on dollar oil from the Americas, while on the other hand its possession by the Axis powers would solve their chronic fuel problems.

The most direct and serious threat to the oil was posed by the Italian army in Libya, some 300,000 men; and the most suitable place to parry the threat was Egypt. From a naval standpoint, the Egyptian port of Alexandria was the base for British sea-power in the eastern Mediterranean, while the Suez Canal was its emergency exit. From a military point of view Egypt

simultaneously blocked the invasion routes up the Nile into the Sudan, eastwards to the Persian Gulf, and northwards into Syria towards Turkey. Retention of Egypt would also hold enemy heavy bombers out of effective range of the Gulf oilfields. Lastly Egypt offered many advantages as a main theatre base—good ports and communications, abundant water and labour.

Thus the whole North African campaign from 1940 to 1943 arose from the need to defend the Persian Gulf oilfields from Egypt—and Egypt from the Western Desert. The area of desert where the battles of 1940-42 were fought stretches nearly 400 miles from El Alamein in the east to Derna in the west. The only road follows the coast. The railway from the Nile Delta ended at Mersa Matruh until extended by the army. The one dominating physical feature is a 500-ft escarpment facing north to the coastal plain, and descending from the limestone plateau where the armies manoeuvred. The desert is a featureless waste of gravel and scrub, dotted with ancient cisterns and tombs of sheiks. Armies therefore moved almost with the freedom of fleets, navigating by compass and the stars. However all supplies and water had to be imported. Long columns of trucks from horizon to horizon sustained the fighting troops, while dumps and water pipelines were the jugular veins exposed to enemy armour. The Desert Campaign constituted a unique episode in the history of warfare—war in its purest form, unencumbered by civilians and habitations except along the coast, or by natural obstacles other than the escarpment.

Wavell appointed Major-General R.N. O'Connor to command Western Desert Force. O'Connor, a small, immensely alert and alive man, had a reputation for high intelligence and unorthodoxy. He soon won and always retained the complete confidence of his officers and men. Immediately Italy entered the war on 11th June 1940, raids and ambushes on Italian territory established British moral superiority. However, Wavell's great weakness forced him to stand everywhere on the defensive for the time being, and so Western Desert Force was withdrawn to Mersa Matruh to await the expected Italian invasion of Egypt. This materialized only on 15th September after Mussolini had repeatedly prodded his reluctant commander, Marshal Rodolpho Graziani. Graziani halted after advancing some sixty miles and proceeded to organize his army in a series of defended camps stretching some fifteen miles inland from the coast at Sidi Barrani.

Left: Supply and defence for the Afrika Korps: Junkers 52 transports and Me 110 fighters on a Luftwaffe base in the desert. Right: The Campaign generals. Top: Graziani, the Italian commander. Centre: An immaculately attired Wavell (right), talks to his Western Desert Force Commander O'Connor, January 1941. Bottom: Auchinleck (right), with New Zealand General Bernard Freyberg

Italians surrendering at Bardia. Their strength of numbers was not enough to counter superior British leadership and equipment. O'Connor's 36,000-strong force had already taken 38,000 prisoners in its December offensive, and then in January took another 40,000 in Bardia. The Italians often showed immense individual heroism, but consistently failed where large-scale organization was demanded

It was his intention to march on the Nile Delta once he had built up supplies, metalled the coast road, and laid water pipelines. O'Connor on his part had prepared a model defensive battle at Matruh for Graziani's reception, to culminate with a counter-stroke by all the British armour. But Graziani never came. Instead the British prepared their own offensive.

Although Great Britain herself was threatened by invasion, and her home defence forces were terrifyingly weak, the Prime Minister, Winston Churchill, took the great risk of shipping 150 tanks to the Middle East. For it was the Middle East that was now the only place where there was contact between British and enemy ground forces, and attacking the Italians offered the best hope of a resounding victory to set against the catastrophes of the year. This belief was shared by the c-in-c, General Wavell, whose selected victim was the Duke of Aosta and his garrison of Italian East Africa, cut off from aid and reinforcements from Italy. However, before Wavell could open a campaign so far from Egypt, the threat from Graziani had to be neutralized. He therefore ordered O'Connor to plan a spoiling attack to last five days, after which O'Connor's infantry division would be wanted for Eritrea. O'Connor instead aimed at a decisive victory.

There were two groups of Italian fortified camps, separated by a gap in the centre, the Tummars and Nibeiwa near the coast, and the Rabia and Sofafi camps further inland, garrisoned by three divisions with tanks in support. Well to the rear and widely separated were another six divisions. No one could foretell how the army of Fascist Italy would fight. Although Italian tanks were known to be poor, their artillery outnumbered the British by two to one.

O'Connor's own forces numbered 36,000 men, organized in two divisions, 4th Indian (infantry) and 7th Armoured, together with a mixed group called Selby Force after its brigadier. 4th Indian Division, together with fifty-seven heavily armoured 'I' (infantry co-operation) tanks, was to assault, while 7th Armoured, with its cruiser-tanks, was to protect the British flank and then exploit and pursue. Western Desert Force was thoroughly well-trained, with a high proportion of professional soldiers. O'Connor's plan was bold and unorthodox. The assault force penetrated through the gap in the centre of the Italian camps and assaulted from the west, the Italian rear. At the same time British artillery, without waiting to register, opened heavy surprise fire from the east to demoralize and confuse the Italians. The British force had thus to assemble within the enemy's defence zone and make an approach march through his defences. The risks paid splendidly. On the first day of the offensive (9th December 1940), the Italians were taken completely by surprise, and although they fought stoutly, their camps fell one by one, Nibeiwa first, then the Tummars, while the British armour cut the coast road between Sidi Barrani and Buq Buq. The remaining camps were abandoned and the armour pursued the routed enemy towards the Libyan frontier.

In two days' fighting O'Connor had ended the threat to Egypt, smashed two Italian corps, taken 38,000 prisoners (including four generals), 73 tanks, and 37 guns at the cost of only 624 killed, wounded and missing. It was exactly the kind of victory the British at home needed in the grim winter of the Blitz. It also fulfilled Wavell's purpose and enabled him to withdraw the Indian division for use in Eritrea.

This was one of the decisive moments of the whole North African campaign. Wavell's strategic intention in the desert was defensive; O'Connor was expected now to halt, although not specifically ordered to do so. However, O'Connor pressed on with the forces remaining to him. By 16th December he had closely invested the fortress of Bardia, just inside Libya. His continued success induced Wavell to send him the understrength 6th Australian Division in place of the Indians. Thus the strategy of the campaign changed from the defensive to the offensive, and the consequences were to be far-reaching.

On 3rd January 1941 13th Corps (as Western Desert Force had been renamed) attacked Bardia and captured it in one day. The bag included 40,000 prisoners, 13 medium and 115 light tanks, 400 guns, and 706 trucks (a windfall for O'Connor). The British armour pressed on to cut off Tobruk, the next port and fortress along the coast. Like Bardia, Tobruk fell in a single day, on 22nd January 1941. This time the bag comprised 25,000 prisoners, 208 guns, 23 medium tanks, and 200 trucks.

In front of O'Connor now was the bulge of Cyrenaica, the Jabal Akhdar, a fertile region of hills colonized by Italian settlers, and beyond it the city of Benghazi. The remnants of Italian X Army were seeking to escape into Tripolitania along the coast road, which wound round the Jabal Akhdar to the Gulf of Syrte. Although O'Connor's force was now almost worn out mechanically, he flung it along appalling and unreconnoitred desert tracks south of the Jabal to try to reach the coast road ahead of the Italians and bar their retreat. On 5th February 1941 his trap closed with half an hour to spare. For two days the Italians strove desperately to break through, but

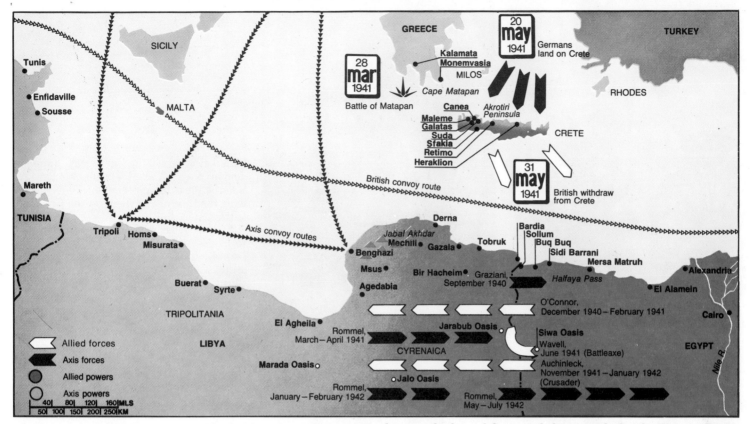

The war in the Mediterranean and North Africa from 1940 to 1942, showing the loss of Crete and the struggle for the Western Desert. O'Connor's devastating successes against the Italians were not followed through because of the need to help Greece. Rommel had his chance. After a year-long duel, during which he was thrown back by Auchinleck's offensive, Rommel finally broke through into Egypt

failed. In this Battle of Beda Fomm O'Connor achieved that rare military phenomenon, a complete victory, for the X Army had been utterly destroyed. In ten weeks O'Connor had taken 130,000 prisoners, 400 tanks, and 1,290 guns.

It seemed to O'Connor that Tripolitania, now almost defenceless, might also fall to a swift advance, and the whole of Italian North Africa be cleared. Thus a campaign that had begun with the defence of Egypt was now pointing towards the destruction of Italian power, first in Africa, later perhaps at home. However, the British government decided that instead of striking at Tripoli, the bulk of O'Connor's veterans should be made available to aid the Greeks against an expected German invasion. O'Connor went on sick leave and 13th Corps was broken up. The British never recovered the professionalism and cohesion of this matured formation.

There is little question that the decision not to drive on to Tripoli at the beginning of February 1941 was one of the most unfortunate of the war. The aid to the Greeks achieved nothing in the event, while on 12th February Lieutenant-General Erwin Rommel arrived in Tripoli with an advance party of German troops. O'Connor's victories, by being halted in mid-career, had only served to draw the Germans into North Africa, a vastly more potent danger to Egypt than the Italians could ever have been.

The Germans in North Africa

The danger became swiftly manifest. On 31st March 1941, long before either Wavell or the German High Command itself believed he could be ready, Rommel attacked the British round El Agheila. The bewildering speed and agility of Rommel's advance

brought about the collapse of the green formations that had replaced O'Connor's veterans. O'Connor himself, sent up to advise his successor Neame, was captured along with Neame. The whole of Cyrenaica was lost except for Tobruk which was cut off and besieged, and Rommel only halted, just over the Egyptian frontier, because he had outrun his supplies.

Henceforth the duel with Rommel in the Western Desert was more and more to fascinate the British, especially the Prime Minister, Winston Churchill. The Western Desert was the only place where the British Empire could fight Germany on land. It was now therefore less of a case of defending Egypt than of winning a great victory over Rommel's Panzer Group Africa; of, in fact, attempting again in very different circumstances to carry out O'Connor's intention of completely clearing North Africa.

British prospects were not good. The British Army had begun to prepare for modern tank warfare at least five years later than the Germans, and lacked German operational experience. The British Empire forces had been hastily and recently expanded. British military doctrine and staff methods did not equal those of Germany. These weaknesses were compounded again and again when half-raw divisions had to be committed to battle in haste because of the hunger at home for victories, or at least offensive action. British equipment, too, bore the signs of late and hasty rearmament. The British cruiser-tanks were highly unreliable mechanically, while the four-gallon petrol can wasted untold quantities of fuel because of its flimsiness. These British qualitative inferiorities in skill and equipment were never understood or ac-

cepted by the Prime Minister, who repeatedly urged his commanders-in-chief in the Middle East to attack before they felt ready. The consequences of such attacks were demonstrated in June 1941, when an offensive (Battleaxe) was heavily defeated. It was Battleaxe that finally doomed Wavell, already in disfavour.

His successor was General Sir Claude Auchinleck, of the Indian Army, a big man with a strong but warm personality. He too was immediately pressed for an offensive, but remained adamant that 1st November was the earliest that the green reinforcements and untried equipment now pouring into Egypt could be shaped into an army fit to meet Germans in battle. In the event, the offensive, code-named Crusader, was launched on 18th November, and its course was to bear out all Auchinleck's misgivings. Except in dogged courage, 8th Army (as the desert forces had now become) showed itself generally inferior in operational skill at every level to XV and XXI Panzer Divisions (the Afrika Korps), and 90th Light Division (trucked infantry). German tanks proved themselves superior mechanically and German tank recovery services were also better organized.

According to the British plan, the infantry divisions of 13th Corps would make an attack on the fixed Axis defences round the Halfaya Pass (leading up the escarpment from the coastal plain), while the armour of 30th Corps would swing wide through the desert, fight and beat the German armour, and relieve Tobruk. 8th Army fielded in an augmented 7th Armoured Division 453 gun-armed tanks against fewer than 200 German tanks in XV and XXI Panzer Divisions, and some 130 Italian. The British plan soon fell apart into sprawling actions all over eastern Cyrenaica, with

both sides mixed up in a way unprecedented in war. A sheik's tomb, Sidi Rezegh, was the focus for repeated encounters, and gave the alternative name to the Crusader battles.

At first it seemed that the British had won the armoured battle. Then news seeped back of appalling losses and stalled attacks. It was a proof of the superiority of German tactics and of British inexperience. While the British tried to charge home, cavalry-style, the Germans fought defensively, drawing the British on to their anti-tank guns, especially the deadly 88-mm guns adapted from an anti-aircraft role.

The 8th Army commander, Lieutenant-General Sir Alan Cunningham, who had never commanded such masses of armour or troops in battle before (what British soldier had?), was near a breakdown. He believed that the offensive had failed, and that unless the army fell back into Egypt, it would be destroyed and the Nile Delta endangered. Auchinleck relieved him and ordered the offensive to go on. In Cunningham's place, Auchinleck temporarily appointed Major-General Neil Ritchie, his Deputy Chief of the General Staff in Cairo, a burly, phlegmatic man who loyally carried out Auchinleck's order to grip Rommel and wear him down.

Rommel's reserves of tanks were smaller than the British and he was denied supplies from Italy. Gradually the stubborn British dominated the battlefield. Tobruk was relieved. The Germans slowly fell back to El Agheila (5th-6th January 1942). Despite its rawness 8th Army had taken 36,000 prisoners and reduced the German tank strength to thirty. Crusader was the first British victory over the Germans in the Second World War.

It now proved no more possible for Auchinleck to push swiftly on into Tripolitania than for Wavell a year earlier. Whereas Greece had competed with the desert for resources in 1941, it was now to the Far East, under heavy Japanese attack, that Auchinleck lost two divisions and much equipment. Once again Rommel took advantage of the British pause in front of the Agheila position. On 21st January 1942 he emerged from his defences to give one of his most brilliant displays of op-

Above left: Worthless medals used by the Italians as rewards to local population in North Africa. Above: German airmen resting in the desert. Left: British troops captured by Germans in North Africa. The conditions of desert fighting far from the parade ground and the supply depot bred a spirit of improvisation in uniforms and equipment. The British wear a mixture of battle-dress and tropical kit, and the armoured-car mounts a collection of infantry weapons

portunism and agility – 1st Armoured Division in the forward area, fresh from England, was routed. In the ensuing confusion Ritchie incorrectly read the situation and proved indecisive and slow to act; only round Gazala, on the Cyrenaican coast was the situation stabilized.

Auchinleck was now advised that there was lack of confidence in Ritchie among 8th Army commanders, and that he was not up to the job of commanding an army. Auchinleck nevertheless confirmed Ritchie's hitherto temporary appointment instead of asking for a more experienced and senior general from Great Britain; a decision partly owing to Auchinleck's lack of personal ruthlessness and partly to his belief that it would be bad for public opinion to sack another general so soon.

In spring 1942 both sides were preparing for major offensives. There were sharp contrasts. For Hitler the Mediterranean and North Africa were sideshows compared with Russia and deserved only minimal German support of Italy. Rommel's command therefore still numbered only two under-strength Panzer divisions (the Afrika Korps) and 90th Light Division plus one Italian armoured division and five infantry. This force, now designated Panzer Army Africa, and Rommel himself were supposed to be under Italian supreme command. Owing to British naval action and Italian incompetence, Panzer Army Africa was always short of supplies, reinforcements, and fuel. Thus for Rommel the only hope of keeping the North African campaign alive lay in bluff and risk. He brilliantly succeeded, not only in the field but through his own personality. The British – and again particularly the Prime Minister – had by 1942 become really obsessed with the duel in the desert. On the British side therefore North Africa was no sideshow. Sustained by an immense base in Egypt, it was the focus for the greatest single military effort of the British Empire – a miniature war economy. The ration strength of Middle East Command rose to over half a million men.

For both sides Malta was the key to the campaign. It served as a base for British interruption of Rommel's seaborne supplies and the Axis High Commands therefore decided that Malta must be taken before Rommel could hope to attack the Nile Delta itself. From the British point of view Malta itself could only survive if supplies were run in by sea. This required air cover; and this in turn required airfields in Cyrenaica further west than Gazala. Air cover was the more urgent in spring 1942 because of the collapse of British naval power in the Mediterranean. Here was the immediate spur to British offensive action.

However, Auchinleck was now the more cautious about 8th Army's chances because of the experiences of the winter battle. Like Haig in 1916 he knew he had less of an army than a collection of divisions untrained (to a greater or lesser extent) for the field. Nor was 8th Army a 'British' army. Its infantry formations were largely imperial – at one time or another, Australian, New Zealand, South African, and Indian – and the dominion divisional commanders had the right of appeal to their own governments if they thought dominion interests imperilled by British orders. In addition there were Greek, Polish, and Free French contingents. The 8th Army commanders and the c-in-c's Middle East were in fact Allied commanders, with all the difficulties therein traditionally involved.

It was Auchinleck's belief that inferiority of weapons and skill must be compensated for by numbers and careful preparation. The consequent long delay displeased the Prime Minister, who eventually ordered Auchinleck to attack in June 1942.

Rommel attacks

Instead Rommel attacked first, on 26th May. He fielded 561 tanks, of which only the 280 German mediums really counted, against some 850 tanks with 8th Army, of which the 167 American Grants, with a 75-mm gun, outshot all German tanks except 19 Mark III Specials. Unfortunately the Grant's gun was mounted in the hull and had only a limited traverse. Rommel's anti-tank guns were greatly superior to the British: 50-, 76-, and 88-mm as against 2-pounders.

Ritchie's defensive dispositions were faulty. His infantry were placed in static field defences ('boxes') inside minefields, a European-style defence system stretching from Gazala to Bir Hacheim but ending in an open desert flank. Behind lay the British armour, dispersed in brigades and much too far forward. Rommel, sweeping south of Bir Hacheim in a great column of tanks, trucks, and guns in a swing aimed at cutting the coast road behind the British, at first trampled through the British brigades one by one, taking them by surprise. Then British numbers and the powerful Grants began to tell. Rommel's offensive stalled in confused and bitter struggles and the problem of supply became acute. Rommel averted defeat by one of his most imaginative improvisations. He breached the centre of Ritchie's line of minefields from the east, or British rear, opening up direct communications with his base and covering his bridgehead with anti-tank guns.

Against this bridgehead through the British centre Ritchie belatedly launched ill-coordinated attacks which foundered miserably. Rommel then took the lynchpin of the whole Gazala Line, Bir Hacheim, garrisoned by the Free French, on 11th June. The Gazala Line thus demolished, Rommel swept again towards Tobruk. Ritchie had drawn on the large British reserves of tanks, so that 8th Army could still field 250 cruisers and 80 heavy 'I' tanks against some 160 German and 70 Italian tanks. However the precarious skill and cohesion of the British armoured divisions were disintegrating. In a great tank battle on 11th and 12th June 8th Army lost 200 cruisers and 60 'I' tanks. The virtual destruction of the British armour exposed 8th Army to disaster.

The defences of Tobruk were derelict, for the last siege had proved so costly and difficult to maintain that Middle East Command had decided it should never again be held in isolation. This decision had been communicated to London in the winter. Now, however, the Prime Minister signalled that he expected it to be held as in 1941. Following a series of equivocal signals between Auchinleck, London, and Ritchie, the Prime Minister was satisfied and Tobruk was allowed to be 'temporarily' invested, with 1st South African Division as the main part of the garrison.

Rommel first lunged after the main body of 8th Army as it retreated precipitately ('the Gazala Gallop') towards Egypt, and then pounced back on Tobruk. Its hastily improvised and feeble defence collapsed in a single day, on 21st June 1942, yielding 30,000 prisoners and much booty. Rommel, now a field-marshal, took the road for Egypt. It was the climax of his career. However, the Axis supreme commands in the Mediterranean had earlier agreed that Rommel should halt on the Egyptian frontier to allow Malta to be taken, so that adequate seaborne supplies could be assured for the final offensive against the Nile Delta. Nevertheless, because the British seemed so totally routed, Rommel persuaded his superiors to allow him to gamble on thrusting his way into the Delta before the British could recover.

On 23rd June Rommel crossed into Egypt, and by 25th June was in front of the old Mersa Matruh defences of 1940. Here Ritchie hoped to make a last stand with survivors of the Gazala defeat and new formations sent up by Auchinleck. Since 26th May 8th Army had lost 80,000 men, mostly in prisoners – a mark of the extent of the victory of the ruthless German professionals against superior numbers of British imperial troops.

Egypt and the entire British position in the Middle East were now exposed to catastrophe. On 25th June Auchinleck flew up from Cairo to take over personal command of 8th Army from Ritchie. He took command of a battered, retreating army. With Rommel still attacking, to give his forces time to reform, he planned withdrawal – to a place called El Alamein.

The Balkan Campaign

Throughout the first twelve months of the Second World War neither the British nor the Germans wished to disturb the peace of South-Eastern Europe. In London the War Office, notoriously unsympathetic to Balkan ventures, feared that extension of the conflict would pose taxing problems of aid and supply; and in Berlin it was felt that the Reich could gain far more from peaceful exploitation of the region's economic resources than by a war of conquest. Hitler was particularly concerned to safeguard the oilfields of Rumania from destruction by invaders or by bombing from bases in other Balkan states; and early in October 1940 he secured from a pliant Rumanian government the right to station German troops in the country so as to preserve its 'neutrality' and 'independence' from an increasingly menacing attitude by the Soviet Union to the north.

This assertion of German primacy in Eastern Europe irritated Hitler's Axis partner Mussolini. Fascist diplomacy habitually regarded the Balkans as an area designed by nature for the greater glory of Italian arms; and in the spring of 1939 Mussolini had made this clear to an unimpressed Europe by annexing Albania (which was already economically dependent on Rome) to the Italian crown. The Duce would have liked to have followed up this paper triumph by invading Yugoslavia; his foreign minister, Count Ciano, preferred a march on Athens; but Hitler, with a sounder sense of general strategy, persistently vetoed either project, and the Italians watched sulkily as Ger-

man units carried the swastika flag eastwards until on 8th October 1940 they reached the Rumanian Black Sea coast.

It was at this point that Mussolini decided to act. For once he would take a military decision without consulting the Germans. On 15th October preparations were hurriedly begun for a campaign against Greece from the Italian bases in southern Albania. Hitler, belatedly realizing that the Italians were about to bring war to the Balkans, hastened southwards in a last effort to hold his partner back. It was too late. He was greeted at Florence station on the morning of 28th October by an exultant Mussolini boasting that 'victorious Italian troops crossed the Graeco-Albanian frontier at dawn today'. The Führer did not offer his congratulations at the news.

The Albanian expedition was a disaster. Near the coast the invaders advanced some twenty-five miles in three days to the Kalamas river, but they were soon repulsed and farther west they ran into early difficulties. The Italian armoured divisions moved slowly through the valleys of Epirus towards the plains. Greek mountain regiments, holding heights above the columns, waited until they had reached the bleak Pindus gorges and fell on them from the rear. An Alpini division was wiped out. Within eleven days the Greeks had taken 5,000 prisoners and forced the invaders to pull back towards the frontier. The German military attaché sent gloomy reports to Berlin: rain and snow made the front an impassable morass; and there seemed no

Left: Hitler bails out his Italian ally. The Germans cross into Yugoslavia on the first stage of their Balkan conquest. **Below left:** *An Italian 'Alpini' colonel and his Greek captors.* **Below right:** *Italian prisoners march to a brief captivity*

ΟΙ ΗΡΩΙΔΕΣ ΤΟΥ 1940

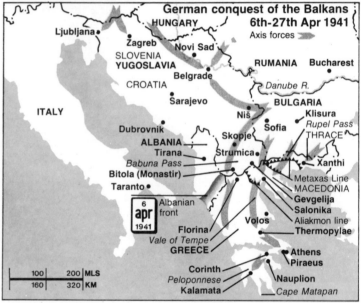

Left: Greek poster shows 'the heroines of 1940'. Peasant women head for the mountains with guns and ammunition to fight the Italians.
Right: Maps show the failure of the Italians and the sweeping success of the Germans in their campaigns against the Greeks, 1940—41

hope of transporting fresh divisions to prevent a rout. On 21st November Koritsa, the third largest town in Albania, fell to General Papagos's army. Before the wintry conditions halted all operations the Greeks had penetrated to a distance of thirty miles along the whole front. They inflicted 30,000 casualties and accumulated an impressive list of prizes—the town of Pogradec, upon Lake Ohrid; the fortress of Argyrokastron; and the naval base of Santi Quaranta, which sycophantic Italians had re-named 'Porto Edda' in honour of Mussolini's daughter, the Countess Ciano. The Duce thus suffered military defeat and political humiliation at the hands of the Greeks. Nor was this all. On 11th November three Italian battleships and a cruiser were put out of action in a raid on Taranto by torpedo-bombers from *HMS Illustrious*. Italian morale rapidly sank to a low ebb.

Hitler was furious with his ally, especially as the British began to establish bases in Crete and other Greek islands which brought the vital supply route from Rumania within range of the RAF. It was clear that the Italians would have to be rescued by German arms. As early as 12th November Hitler signed an order instruct-ing the High Command to prepare a Balkan campaign. Mussolini continued to ask that the Greeks should receive 'a first correction' from the Italians, although he accepted a proposal for the despatch of a German military mission to the front.

The Germans themselves had no intention of striking prematurely. Hitler was willing to wait until the spring, first making certain that the other states of South-Eastern Europe would render diplomatic support to the Axis. He was already sure of the Rumanians and he began to put pressure on the Bulgars. On 8th February an agreement was duly signed in Sofia permitting the German XII Army to concentrate in southern Bulgaria, along the Greek frontier. There remained only Yugoslavia; and throughout the winter months the Germans alternated threats and blandishments to draw the Yugoslav government into the Axis camp.

Yugoslavia and the 'New Order'

Yugoslavia was more directly concerned with the outcome of the Italo-Greek campaign than any other Balkan state. For twenty years the Yugoslavs had enjoyed special treaty rights in the Greek port of Salonika; they had no wish to see the city in the hands of their old rivals, the Italians. Hitler hoped to tempt the Yugoslavs by a promise to cede Salonika once Greece had fallen. But Prince Paul, the Regent of Yugoslavia, and his ministers were in a difficult position. They were unpopular with almost every section of opinion in the country, for they had tried to please too many conflicting groups. They knew that the sympathies of the Serbs, the largest of the nationalities in the kingdom, were with their old allies in Greece and collusion with Germany might precipitate an internal revolt. The Regent himself favoured the British cause, but he was a realist. He was certain that Germany could overrun Yugoslavia within a fortnight of the start of any campaign and he was bitterly conscious of Yugoslavia's isolation. When the American minister tried to strengthen his resolve, he replied with justice: 'You big nations are hard. You talk of our honour but you are far away.' He therefore chose a policy of strict neutrality.

This, however, was not enough for Hitler. By now the General Staff was planning not only Operation Marita against Greece, but Operation Barbarossa against Russia. It

German Dornier 17 bombers flying over Athens. The occupation of the Greek capital on 27th April 1941 was the culmination of Germany's three-week Balkan campaign. Athens fell with no resistance after the precipitate withdrawal of the Allied troops to Crete and Egypt

would be dangerous to leave an uncommitted Yugoslavia on the German flank during these forthcoming campaigns. Gradually Hitler increased pressure on the Yugoslavs to join the Tripartite Pact between Italy, Germany, and Japan, the charter of co-operation in the 'New Order' to which the Hungarians, the Rumanians, and the Bulgars had already adhered. Reluctantly Prince Paul authorized his Prime Minister and foreign minister to travel to Vienna and there, on 25th March, they duly signed the pact. At last Hitler was ready to rescue Mussolini from his Greek entanglement. Operation Marita was fixed for early April.

The Italians, for their part, were still making desperate efforts to administer that 'first correction' to the Greeks. They assembled no less than twenty-eight divisions, twice as many as their opponents. For the final Italian offensive, on 9th March, Mussolini even crossed to Albania in person; but though the Duce struck splendidly martial attitudes, his mere presence failed somehow to ensure success. Although under severe strain, the Greeks held their positions; and from 7th March onwards small groups of British and Common-

wealth troops began to arrive at the Piraeus and Volos so as to meet the threat from the German army in Bulgaria. At the same time the Royal Navy prevented any movement of the Italian fleet towards the Aegean and on 28th March gained a striking victory against two Italian squadrons off Cape Matapan. Mussolini's prestige remained low: there was even a music-hall song in Great Britain mocking his failure to 'put it over the Greeks'.

Yugoslavia finds her soul
Yet, as the snow-line began to recede along the mountains, both sides waited for the Balkan Front to erupt. The Germans were confident of an easy victory; but on 27th March their self-assurance was shaken by unexpected news from Belgrade—a revolt, headed by General Bora Mirković of the Yugoslav air force, had overthrown the government. The streets of the capital filled with cheering crowds ostentatiously supporting the British and Greeks. It was, as the *New York Times* wrote next day, 'a lightning flash illuminating a dark background'; and in London Churchill rejoiced that Yugoslavia had 'found her soul'.

Hitler regarded the Belgrade coup as both a personal affront and a military threat. That same day he issued a crisp directive: 'The Führer is determined, without waiting for possible loyalty declarations of the new government, to make all preparations to destroy Yugoslavia militarily and as a national unit.' Assistance would be sought from Italy, Hungary, and Bulgaria and every attempt made to turn the various nationalities of Yugoslavia against the dominant Serbs. No ultimatum would be issued; war would come with a massive aerial chastisement of the impudent city of Belgrade. The attack would coincide with the opening of Operation Marita against Greece; Operation Barbarossa would be delayed until order was restored in the Balkans.

Had Hitler waited he would have found the new government, which was headed by General Dušan Simović, far less hostile to the Axis than either he or the people of Belgrade supposed. Simović would do nothing to provoke the Germans; and secret talks between Yugoslav representatives and senior British and Greek commanders produced no real accord. If the Germans attacked, the Yugoslavs asked for fifteen

Germany's Triumph

British divisions to be rushed to Salonika. But most of the troops which could be spared from the Desert War in Africa were already in Greece: two Australian divisions, a New Zealand division, a Polish brigade and an armoured brigade from Great Britain. This army, which numbered no more than 58,000 men, was required to strengthen the Greek lines, for the winter campaign in Albania had sadly depleted General Papagos's reserves. It was hard to see how these limited reinforcements could afford succour to the Yugoslavs as well as the Greeks. There was never much hope that the British and their Balkan allies could stem the German tide.

Operation Marita: a triumph of planning

Operation Marita proved a triumph of staff-planning. The campaign duly began with the bombardment of Belgrade by squadrons of Stukas soon after dawn on 6th April. German raiders continued to dive on the city for more than two days until its centre was reduced to rubble and 17,000 of its citizens lay dead. At precisely the same moment as the first bombs fell on Belgrade, Field Marshal List's XII Army crossed the Bulgaro-Yugoslav frontier in Macedonia, thus opening the operations on land. This German gambit was unexpected, for the Yugoslavs were guarding their northern frontiers more closely than those in the south. But List's move had a double advantage: it struck deeply into Yugoslavia while, at the same time, providing for a southward thrust down the Vardar valley towards the vital Greek port of Salonika. List's deployment of troops virtually won the Balkan campaign for Germany within fifty hours of the first shots being fired.

Yugoslav resistance lasted for only twelve days. Some units fought bravely, especially to the east of Niš where two divisions which had no anti-tank guns at all sought to delay three armoured brigades of General von Kleist's XIV Corps. There was, however, little will to fight for Yugoslavia among the Croatian regiments, and the German-speaking minority carried out numerous acts of sabotage in the north. The first territorial losses came in the south: Skopje fell to List on 7th April and Niš to Kleist on 8th April. The German II Army in the north did not begin its main advance until 10th April but it encountered far less opposition and covered the seventy miles from the frontier-crossing at Gyékényes to the Croatian capital of Zagreb in under twelve hours. A 'Croatian State' was proclaimed under Axis patronage.

With Yugoslavia disintegrating, the Italians and Hungarians moved in for the kill and Bulgarian infantry divisions followed the German armour across the Macedonian frontier. On 11th April Italian troops cautiously approached the Slovene capital of Ljubljana, only to find it already under German control. The Hungarians reached Novi Sad on the Danube but their preparations lacked German efficiency and one Hungarian armoured unit ran out of petrol thirty miles south of the frontier. The military successes of the campaign were exclusively German and were gained at a cost of only 151 men killed in action. It was a German column which received the surrender of Belgrade on 12th April and it was German staff-officers who negotiated an armistice with a Yugoslav general on 17th April. That same day an Italian regimental band marched triumphantly into Dubrovnik — Mussolini's army, though magnificently warlike in time of peace, at heart owed less to the tradition of Caesar than to Verdi.

The vanguard of the German XII Army moved on to Greece in three columns: one made for Štip, crossed the Vardar river on 7th April and headed over the Babuna Pass towards Bitola (Monastir) and the mountains running from southern Albania into north-western Greece; a second column moved from Strumica on to Gevgelija and the main railway to Salonika; while a third column crossed the Rupel Pass and headed for Salonika from the north-east. By 0800 hrs on 8th April the first German tanks were rumbling into the Greek port, which had served as a base for the Allies for three years in the First World War. The German advance effectively cut all links between Yugoslavia and Greece. It also ensured that the Greek divisions which were manning the defences of Thrace, the so-called 'Metaxas Line', were isolated just as the garrisons of the French Maginot Line had been in the campaign on the Western Front a year before.

The commander of the British forces in Macedonia, General Sir Henry Maitland Wilson, had never liked the Greek plan to hold the Metaxas Line. He favoured a defensive position along the loop of the River Aliakmon, from the solid bastion of the Albanian mountains to the natural ramparts north of Olympus. When List's army struck at Greece, Wilson's troops were north-west of this line, guarding the broad corridor from Bitola to Kenali and Florina, the scene of fierce battles in the First World War. This time, however, the weight of German armour was too strong for the defenders. List's tanks thrust Wilson back to the Aliakmon on 12th April. Two days later the Germans began to turn his left flank, breaking through in the wild mountains around Klisura and heading south-westwards towards the Pindus gorges so as to cut off the Greek army on the Albanian front. Ironically it was in the Metsovon Pass, where the Greeks had destroyed an Alpini division only five months previously, that crack SS troops finally broke Greek resistance in the west. With his line of retreat cut the local commander, General George Tsolakoglou, opened negotiations with List's advance troops and on 20th April all Greek forces in Albania, Epirus, and Macedonia capitulated to the Germans. A general Graeco-German armistice was concluded on the following day but Mussolini insisted on a separate act of surrender to the Italians on 23rd April.

Meanwhile Wilson's forward troops sought to delay the German advance on Athens so as to enable the evacuation of the main British and Commonwealth army and those Greeks and Yugoslavs who wished to continue the fight. Australian and New Zealand units held the vital passes around Olympus and through the Vale of Tempe for three days before falling back on 20th April to the historic pass at Thermopylae, where British forces were already in defensive positions. List massed six divisions against the Thermopylae Line which became untenable on 24th April. It was impossible to use the port facilities of the Piraeus, for the town was devastated on the night of 6th April when an ammunition ship received a direct hit in an air-raid. Commonwealth troops made for the inhospitable open beaches of the Peloponnese, at Nauplion, Kalamata and Monemvasia. But on 26th April the Germans struck again: parachute troops seized the town and isthmus of Corinth so as to cut the British retreat. A series of moonless nights aided the last stage of the evacuation and by 1st May nearly 50,000 Allied troops had been got away to Crete and Egypt. But it had proved a costly expedition; many thousands had passed into captivity.

Swastika on the Acropolis

By mid-day on 27th April the Germans were in Athens and the swastika flag shaming the heights of the Acropolis. Although in the mountains of both Greece and Yugoslavia men were preparing to resist the occupation forces, there was no doubt that the Germans had gained a striking victory, of which the spoils were undeservedly shared by their Italian ally. Yet in retrospect it could be argued that the Balkan campaigns were a disastrous diversion of effort for the Axis armies. In order to deal with the Yugoslavs and Greeks the German High Command had postponed Operation Barbarossa from 15th May to 22nd June. It is anyone's guess what would have happened in the autumn of 1941 if the Red Army had been forced to hold the approaches to Moscow for another five weeks before the Russian winter came to its rescue. Inevitably the imponderable remains unacknowledged.

Barbarossa

On 22nd June 1941 Nazi Germany attacked the Soviet Union. The eastern horizon had hardly begun to lighten when thousands of German guns opened fire across the Soviet border. Without warning German aircraft attacked airfields of the Soviet air force situated near the border, and German assault groups opened the way for the main forces of the Wehrmacht.

Hitler and his generals had not the slightest doubt that Germany would rapidly vanquish the Soviet state. They had carried out prolonged preparation, secretly concentrating on the Soviet frontiers a huge army, three million strong, which had experienced no defeat during two years of war and which had confirmed on the battlefields of Europe its doctrine of Blitzkrieg. They had worked out in detail a war-plan (Barbarossa) according to which the main forces of the Red Army were to be wiped out in a single gigantic operation, and Soviet territory right up to the Volga occupied by the autumn of 1941.

When the invasion began the Soviet forces guarding the 2,000-kilometre frontier were not ready. On 22nd June the Red Army in the western border districts of the Soviet Union were being deployed, and the only forces that faced the German tanks and infantry as they crossed the border were frontier guards and a small part of the covering force which had succeeded in getting to the frontier in response to the alarm. The principal forces guarding the western frontier were scattered over a large area up to 280 miles from the front. Despite all the indications that war with Germany was approaching neither the Soviet people nor the Red Army were expecting the German attack when it came. In the summer of 1941 everyone hoped that war might be avoided for a little longer.

Apart from the complete surprise of their attack the Germans had great superiority of forces in the areas where the main blows were struck.

The German armies broke through deep into Soviet territory, trying to surround and destroy concentrations of Soviet forces and prevent a retirement by the effective forces of the Red Army towards the east, behind the Dnieper and Dvina.

At 0715, Marshal Timoshenko, people's commissar for defence, ordered retaliation. Air attacks were to destroy German planes on the ground, and land forces were to throw back the German army to the frontier, without, however, crossing it. But the order was impossible to fulfil. Deep penetration by German tank units, supported by aircraft, frequently resulted in the enemy appearing in the rear of Soviet troops, who were then surrounded.

The German armies were divided into Army Groups North, Centre, and South under the command of Field Marshals Leeb, Bock, and Rundstedt. Facing them were the Soviet troops of the north-western, western, and south-western fronts under Generals Kuznetsov, Pavlov, and Kirponos.

The situation became especially critical on the western front, in Belorussia. German Army Group Centre surrounded the principal forces of 3rd and 10th Armies of the western front near Białystok, broke through to Minsk with II and III Panzer Groups commanded by Generals Guderian and Hoth, captured Minsk (after it had first been largely destroyed by bombing), and then began to move towards the Dnieper. By the beginning of July there were wide gaps in the line of the western front, through which the German tank columns poured farther and farther eastwards. Meanwhile Army Group North invading from East Prussia had penetrated about 450 kilometres into the Baltic region by 10th July, and Army Group South was moving its main forces towards Kiev.

At Hitler's headquarters, the *Wolfs-schanze* (wolf's lair), set in strong bunkers of reinforced concrete amid the forests of East Prussia, near Rastenburg, a triumphant atmosphere reigned. In a report to Hitler on 3rd July, General Halder, Chief of Army General Staff, concluded: 'The main forces of the Russian army in front of the Dnieper and Dvina rivers have been largely destroyed . . . it will be no exaggeration if I say that the campaign against Russia has succeeded in a single fortnight' — a view with which Hitler entirely agreed. There were even plans for the withdrawal of troops to concentrate on the conquest of Great Britain and the Near East.

Hitler's war on the Soviet Union had not finished, however; it had only just begun. The Soviet government and the Supreme Command of the Armed Forces carried out far-reaching mobilization of the country's resources for the fight against the invaders. On 30th June the State Defence Committee (GKO) was set up, with Stalin at its head. The GKO concentrated all power in its hands. The national economy

Right: German troops move into the Ukraine

was reorganized and wholly geared to the production of war materials. Civilian factories were turned over to the production of weapons and equipment and more than 1,500 factories, with their entire plant and personnel, were moved bodily to eastern areas away from the western part of the country, where they were in danger of falling into enemy hands. This was a very large-scale operation, unprecedented in its complexity. All through the summer and autumn of 1941 trains ran in endless streams along all the main railway lines, carrying machine-tools and other factory machinery. On these same trains, some in carriages and some in open trucks, travelled the engineers and workers of these factories with their families and belongings. It was as though entire towns had been plucked up and were moving in a great migration to new lands. Having arrived at their new locations in the Urals, in Siberia, or in Central Asia, the war factories began production without delay. Often the workers and engineers got down to work on sites under the open sky, in rain and foul weather. In the opposite direction, towards the front, flowed another stream, carrying troops, tanks, guns, ammunition.

The Supreme Command of the Red Army did much to form fresh reserves. In the course of the summer of 1941 more than 324 divisions were sent to the front. It is interesting to note that, before the invasion, the German command estimated that the Soviet Union was capable of mobilizing a maximum of 140 divisions in the event of war.

In July 1941 the whole front was split into three strategic sectors: north-western, western, and south-western. Several fronts (army groups) came under the authority of each sector. Of decisive importance was the western sector commanded by Marshal Timoshenko, the Smolensk-Moscow axis. There, between 10th July and 10th September, the greatest battle of the summer and autumn of 1941 took place—the battle for Smolensk.

At the start of the battle the Germans outnumbered the Soviet forces on the western sector in men by 1.6 to 1, in guns by 1.8 to 1, in tanks by 1.5 to 1, in aircraft by 4 to 1. The Soviet reserves which had just arrived from the interior of the country

Top: German motorized infantry streams eastwards at the opening of Barbarossa. By the evening of 22nd June the forward units of the German armies had penetrated far into Soviet territory. Centre: Germans shell a Russian village. Bottom: Soviet supply train carrying guns to the front. Right: Two sequences from the German attack on Zhitomir—the artillery in action, and its effects

could not be fully deployed. The gigantic battle at first went in the enemy's favour. Between 10th and 20th July II, IX, and IV German Armies and their II and III Panzer Groups strove, along a 500-kilometre front, to break the forces of the western front into isolated sections, to surround 19th, 20th, and 16th Armies protecting Smolensk, and to seize the city which had long since been marked down by the invaders as the 'key to Moscow'.

The Germans, using powerful tank groups which they concentrated on narrow sectors of the front, and with massive air support, achieved a number of deep breakthroughs in the areas of Polotsk, Vitebsk, and Mogilev. Hoth's III Panzer Group succeeded in breaking through in the Yartsevo area and cutting the chief line of communication of the western front, the motor road between Minsk and Moscow. Farther south, Guderian's II Panzer Group penetrated the outskirts of Smolensk. On the right flank of the western front the Germans forced the Soviet troops to fall back on Velikiye Luki and Nevel, while on the left flank they captured Yelnya, establishing a salient extending far to the east. The German command began to consider this as the jumping off area for the next offensive, against Moscow.

The Soviet troops put up resistance all along the line. Step by step they slowed down the offensive of Army Group Centre and steadily counter-attacked. In order to divert the German forces from the Smolensk sector, an offensive by General Kuznetsov's 21st Army was launched in the direction of Bobruysk. The 20th Army, led by General Kurochkin, deeply enveloped on both flanks in front of Smolensk, tied down a number of German formations for several weeks.

The battle for Smolensk reached its climax between 21st July and 7th August. During this struggle the Red Army Supreme Command deployed several dozen additional fresh formations in three echelons in the western sector and established a new front, called the reserve front, in the rear of the western front.

The principal centres of fighting in this desperate battle were Smolensk, Yelnya, and Yartsevo. For several days troops of the 16th Army, led by General Lukin,

Top: Russian prisoners. Trapped by the German advance, 3,000,000 were captured in 1941 — few survived. In their camps they were just left to die of starvation and disease. Knowing their fate if captured, the Russians fought fanatically. Centre: German soldiers survey the ruins of a Russian village. Bottom: SS troops resting. The speed of their advance exhausted the German troops

Barbarossa:
the campaign

Leeb — **Army Group North**
XVIII Army Küchler
IV Panzer Group Hoepner
XVI Army Busch

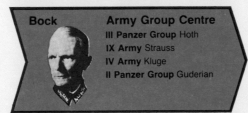

Bock — **Army Group Centre**
III Panzer Group Hoth
IX Army Strauss
IV Army Kluge
II Panzer Group Guderian

Rundstedt — **Army Group South**
VI Army Reichenau
I Panzer Group Kleist
XVII Army Stülpnagel
III Rumanian Army Dmitrescu
XI Army Schobert
IV Rumanian Army Ciuperca

Barbarossa was intended to occupy Russia well beyond Moscow by the autumn. But within two months it was clear that the plan was not going to succeed.

Army Group North: the first major obstacle was the Dvina River, but by 2nd July all of Leeb's armour was across, ready to tackle the next problem: the northern strongpoints of the Stalin Line. Smashing a Soviet armoured challenge, Leeb's Panzer units pressed on to the Luga, under 100 miles from Leningrad itself, which they reached on 14th July. Trapping 20,000 prisoners in the Luga pocket, the Panzers cleared out Estonia by the end of August and were preparing to storm Leningrad. But Hitler had already decided to fence off the city, and to concentrate on Moscow. On 17th September all of Army Group North's armour except for one Panzer corps was switched to the centre under Hoepner and the siege of Leningrad was taken over by infantry.
Army Group Centre had two Panzer Groups poised north and south of the Bialystok salient. The Soviet frontier forces were surrounded in large pockets around Bialystok on 30th June, and Minsk on 9th July. Fending off counterattacks from the south by Timoshenko, the Panzer forces loosely roped off another huge pocket of over 300,000 Russians by taking Smolensk on 16th July. Then Hitler switched Guderian's armour to the Ukraine to smash Budenny at Kiev, reprieving Moscow, and losing vital campaigning weeks. Operation Typhoon, the offensive against Moscow, began on 2nd October, with spectacular successes in the double battle of Vyazma/Bryansk. But within a week the mud of the Russian autumn and ever-stiffening Soviet resistance halted operations. A new offensive in mid-November, when the early frosts restored movement to the Panzers, took the Germans to within nineteen miles of Moscow, but they could do no more. Exhausted and badly equipped for the Russian winter, Army Group Centre now had to face Zhukov's counter-offensive which began on 5th December.
Army Group South: the target was Kiev and the Ukraine. Spearheaded by Kleist's Panzers, Army Group South battered through the southern Stalin Line forts by 9th July and the Rumanians moved on Odessa. Budenny, Soviet commander in the south-west, planned to concentrate at Uman and Kiev after the failure of his first counter-offensives. But Russian plans to defend the western Ukraine were shattered by the speed of the two German claws which pushed south-east between the Dniester and the Dnieper, sealing off the Uman concentration on 4th August and taking 100,000 prisoners. In the next three weeks Kleist pushed into the Dnieper bend. Then came the southward switch of Guderian's Panzers from Army Group Centre, which joined up with Kleist on 16th September. After the annihilation of the Kiev pocket in late September, in which over 500,000 were killed or captured, Rundstedt's forces drove for Kharkov and the Donets, trapping another 100,000 on 6th October. XI Army, now under Manstein, sealed off the Crimea and Kharkov fell on 24th October. The Moscow offensive by Army Group Centre was mirrored in the south by a drive on Rostov, which fell on 21st November; within a week the Wehrmacht suffered its first major defeat when the Russians recovered it.

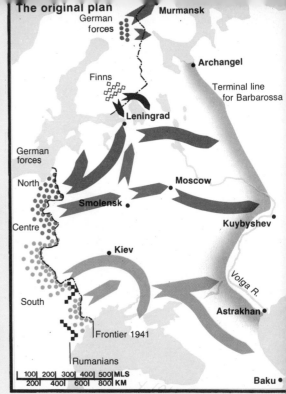

The original plan

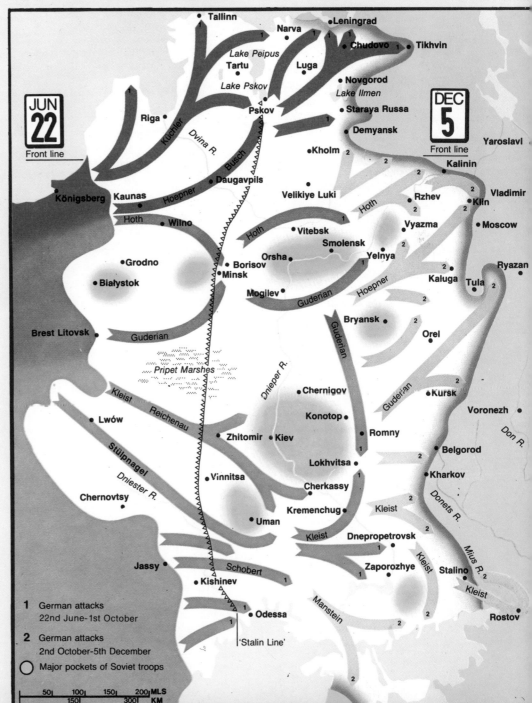

JUN 22 Front line

DEC 5 Front line

1 German attacks 22nd June–1st October
2 German attacks 2nd October–5th December
◯ Major pockets of Soviet troops

put up a stubborn resistance in Smolensk. An extremely intense struggle went on for many weeks without a break around Yelnya. Here the Nazis suffered such heavy losses that they called it 'the bloody furnace'. The battle for Yelnya was crowned with success for the Soviet troops, who drove the Germans out of the town and occupied it themselves. Near Yartsevo, tanks and infantry of Hoth's III Panzer Group were halted by General Rokossovsky's troops. Yartsevo, burning and in ruins, changed hands several times. German reports from the front commented on the fanatical Russian resistance; Halder was even beginning to doubt whether decisive victory was possible.

At the beginning of August a balance of forces was achieved on the western sector. The German armies were pinned down and obliged to go over to the defensive.

Within two months Army Group Centre had penetrated 170-200 kilometres to the east of the Dnieper, but this was not the progress that the German High Command had expected. Whereas in the first days of the war the German troops had advanced

on the average thirty kilometres in twenty-four hours, in July they had slowed down to six or seven kilometres. Smolensk, at the very centre of gravity of the German advance, had delayed the Blitzkrieg for two months and upset the schedule of Operation Barbarossa. Hitler was forced to change his plans, and, on 23rd August, rejected his generals' proposal to launch a concentrated attack on Moscow and made up his mind to attack the Ukraine and the Crimea. Economic factors obsessed Hitler; the wheatlands and industries of the Ukraine were of more importance than Moscow. And the Crimea, according to Hitler, was 'a Soviet aircraft-carrier for attacking the Rumanian oilfields'. Guderian's II Panzer Group was therefore transferred from the Smolensk-Moscow sector to the Ukraine.

At the same time there was fierce fighting in the other sectors of the Soviet-German front as well, namely, the north-western and the south-western sectors.

The Nazi leaders calculated that the capture of Leningrad, Kronstadt, and the Murmansk railway would result in the

Soviet Union losing the Baltic region and the far north, together with the Baltic Fleet. They also counted on acquiring a suitable area for a blow from the north-west at the rear of the Soviet forces protecting Moscow. Simultaneously, the Finnish army was to attack on the Karelian Isthmus and in the direction of Petrozavodsk. To the south of this they were to join up with the Germans who were attacking round Lake Ilmen, also in the Petrozavodsk direction. The XVIII Army was to occupy Estonia.

The Soviet people were determined to defend Leningrad. As early as the end of June a plan was drawn up for making defensive fortifications round the city, and this task was put in hand at the beginning of July. Around Leningrad a system of defences was established, comprising several zones. The city's inhabitants worked on these fortifications alongside the soldiers. No fewer than 500,000 people went out every day during July and August to take part in the digging. Weapons for the front were being forged in the works and factories of the city. Home guard battalions were formed.

On 10th July the Germans attacked Novgorod. In a stubborn battle lasting four days, near the town of Soltsy, Soviet troops annihilated part of the German Panzer corps commanded by General Manstein. Field Marshal Leeb, commanding Army Group North, found himself obliged to halt the offensive of IV Panzer Group for a time.

After re-grouping, the Germans reached Krasnogvardeysk, a town situated less than ten kilometres from Leningrad. Their XVIII Army occupied Estonia and arrived on the shores of the Gulf of Finland.

Before beginning to attack the defensive positions in front of Leningrad, the Germans subjected the city to a heavy artillery and air bombardment. Facing stiff opposition German troops got as far as the suburbs. From 8th September the city's communications with the outside world had to be kept up exclusively by air and across Lake Ladoga. However, the Germans' attempt to break into the city and link up with the Finnish army advancing over the Karelian Isthmus was decisively rebuffed by the Soviet forces directly defending Leningrad and those deployed along the

northern bank of the Neva. The Germans were unable to move one step further forward. Army Group North was forced to abandon the offensive. Hitler decided to take the city by blockade.

In the Ukraine in July 1941 the Soviet troops of the south-western front waged great defensive battles to the south of Polesye and before Kiev and Korosten. The southern front held the invading Germans and Rumanians in check in Moldavia.

Having great superiority of forces, German I Panzer Group, followed by VI Army, pressed towards Kiev, where they were halted. For seventy-two days the brave garrison of the Ukrainian capital defended the city, while to the south-west 5th Army, led by General Potapov, carried on a stubborn struggle, pinning down twelve German divisions and thereby easing the task of Kiev's defenders.

Farther south, the main forces of the south-western front were absorbed in great battles in right-bank Ukraine (the part of Ukraine to the west of the River Dnieper), which carried on until the first days of August 1941. Soviet 6th, 12th,

Soviet painting of an incident in the Crimea in 1941. A Black Sea sailor arms himself with grenades before throwing himself at a German tank

and 26th Armies inflicted heavy losses on German Army Group South. Kleist's I Panzer Group lost fifty per cent of its tanks. But by means of a deep turning movement at the beginning of August the Germans surrounded 6th and 12th Armies near Uman and thereby changed the general course of the battle in their favour.

In view of the grave situation, the Red Army Supreme Command ordered the armies of the south-western and southern fronts, commanded by Generals Kirponos and Tyulenev, to retire behind the Dnieper and stand on its left bank, while holding Kiev, Dnepropetrovsk, and a number of bridgeheads on the right bank of the river. The Soviet forces carried out this retirement in the last days of August, and military operations were transferred to left-bank Ukraine (Ukraine to the east of the Dnieper).

Now Guderian's II Panzer Group and II

Army were transferred from Army Group Centre near Smolensk to the Ukraine to help Army Group South encircle the Soviet armies near Kiev. Guderian's tank formations broke through the defence lines of the Soviet forces near Konotop and moved from the north into the rear of the main forces of the Soviet south-western front. Kleist's tank divisions pushed up from the south to meet Guderian, coming from the bridgehead on the Dnieper at Kremenchug. The two tank wedges met at Lokhvitsa. The four Soviet armies of the south-western front were now surrounded to the east of Kiev. On 18th September the Germans began to close in on the Kiev pocket of half a million trapped Red Army soldiers. On the next day the capital of the Ukraine fell to Hitler's armies. The battle of Kiev was the greatest disaster in the Red Army's history. The German forces advanced to the approaches to the Crimea.

At the same time Rumanian and German forces were blockading and besieging Odessa, one of the chief bases of the Black Sea Fleet. The city's inhabitants had constructed some defence lines around Odessa by the beginning of September. The enemy's attack on Odessa began on 10th August. The troops of the Special Black Sea Army and sailors of the Black Sea Fleet who were defending the city threw back the onslaught. Marine light infantry, supported by naval artillery, counter-attacked and smashed several Rumanian units.

On 20th August the enemy renewed the attack, with a five-fold superiority of forces over the defenders of the city. A bloody battle raged for a whole month. Very slowly, and with heavy losses, the attackers drew near the outskirts. Since the overall situation of the Soviet forces in the Ukraine and the Crimea in the autumn of 1941 had become extremely critical, the Supreme Command decided to evacuate the defenders of Odessa by sea and use them to strengthen the garrison of Sebastopol, the principal base of the Black Sea Fleet, which was also threatened.

By throwing in fresh reserves, the Soviet Supreme Command halted the German armies in the south in the late autumn. The Germans had suffered heavy losses. Nevertheless they were able, at the beginning of November, to get as far as Rostov, regarded as 'the gate to the Caucasus'. As a result, however, of transfers of Soviet troops to this area and a counter-offensive near Rostov, the shock force of Army Group South was smashed and thrown back from the town.

By the autumn of 1941 Hitler's plan for a

Left: *A man lies crushed in the wake of the advance.* **Top right:** *Reprisals.* **Bottom right:** *German machine-gunners*

On 5th December 1941 the Red Army counter-attacked the German armies threatening Moscow. Warmly-clad, well-equipped fresh troops from Siberia pounded the exhausted, ill-clad Germans in temperatures far below zero. The Germans retreated and Moscow was saved

Blitzkrieg against the Soviet Union had failed. Despite some resounding victories, Hitler and his strategists had proved unable to complete their eastern campaign before the autumn as they had hoped. The war was dragging on. The Soviet Union was still standing. The Red Army had repulsed the first and strongest blow of the aggressor, and had created the conditions for a turning point in the course of the war. This determined everything that followed. The main forces of Hitler's Wehrmacht were tied down for a long time on the Soviet-German front, and the danger of a Nazi invasion of Great Britain and of the Near East was finally dissipated.

Hitler and his generals had not achieved the victory they had expected. But the situation of the Soviet Union remained critical. The invaders were before the walls of Leningrad, were threatening Moscow, had occupied the greater part of the Ukraine, and held some of the most important economic areas of the country.

Hitler thought that victory over the Soviet Union was near. He now ordered the final blow against Moscow, so as to capture the Soviet capital and thereby terminate the eastern campaign.

The drive on Moscow was assigned to Army Group Centre, headed by Field Marshal Bock. Operation Typhoon, as it was called, envisaged the striking of three blows by tank and infantry groups in order to break up and surround the Soviet forces defending Moscow. After opening the road to the capital, Bock's forces were then to capture it by means of a headlong attack.

An army of a million men, comprising seventy-seven divisions (including fourteen tank divisions and eight motorized divisions with 1,700 tanks and assault guns) and 950 fighter aircraft assembled near Moscow. The preparations for the 'final blow' took more than a month.

The Soviet command entrusted the task of defending the approaches to Moscow to the troops of the western, reserve, and Bryansk fronts under the command of General Konev, Marshal Budenny, and General Yeremenko. The Nazis had twice as many tanks and guns as the defenders of the capital and three times as many aircraft.

The offensive began on 2nd October. The defenders were unable to repulse the attack. By 7th October the main forces of the western and reserve fronts were surrounded near Vyazma. The roads to Moscow were open.

Extraordinary efforts now had to be made and measures taken by the Soviet command in order to prevent the fall of the capital. Above all it was necessary to gain time. By their stubborn resistance the surrounded troops tied down twenty-eight German divisions for over a week. The Supreme Command and the new commander of the western front, General Zhukov, began to concentrate all available forces in the Moscow area. First, a rapid redeployment of the troops stationed nearby succeeded in covering the main roads leading to the capital from the west and in holding the German units which were advancing from Vyazma. Meanwhile, from Siberia, the Volga region, the Far East, and Kazakhstan troop-trains flowed in bringing fresh forces. Soon it was possible to throw another fourteen divisions, sixteen tank brigades, forty artillery regiments, and other units into the battle for Moscow. A new defensive front was formed, along the Mozhaysk defensive line prepared by the people of Moscow.

On 10th October the Germans reached this line and attacked it. Desperate fighting went on for many days and nights without a break. The Germans succeeded in breaking through on a few sectors, capturing Kalinin, Mozhaysk, and Volokolamsk. They reached the close approaches of the capital.

At the end of October and the beginning of November the German advance was halted, thanks to the tremendous efforts of the Soviet troops. The German armies, which had made a 250-kilometre dash in October 1941, were forced to go over to the

Russian peasants fleeing before the German advance on Moscow. By December 1941 70,000,000 people were living under German rule in Russia. The Nazi exploitation of occupied Russia was brutal. Millions were deported for slave labour, millions were arbitrarily executed

defensive along a line 70 to 120 kilometres from Moscow. There was a pause in the battle. The Soviet command had gained time for further strengthening of the approaches to the capital. The pause before Moscow enabled the Red Army Supreme Command to reinforce the western front with fresh troops and an anti-tank defence system was constructed in depth along the principal lines of approach to Moscow. In the first half of November the western front received an additional 100,000 men, 300 tanks, and 2,000 guns. The Muscovites dug defence-works in front of the entrances to their city.

The German command, after concentrating forces along the main roads leading to Moscow, began their second attack on the Soviet capital on 15th and 16th November. Again there was fierce and bloody fighting. Slowly, suffering heavy losses, the Germans drew nearer to Moscow, the capture of which they saw as their single and final aim, and their salvation. But the defences in depth held by the Soviet forces prevented them from penetrating the front. Guderian's II Panzer Army broke through to Tula, an important industrial centre and hub of communications. Numerous attempts to capture the town were successfully resisted by the troops under General Boldin, aided by detachments of Tula workers. Tula stood its ground, trans-

formed into the southern defence bastion of the western front. Then Guderian, leaving part of his forces to cover his right and left flanks, pushed on northwards with his main tank group, in order to come out to the east of Moscow and there join up with II and III Panzer Groups which were advancing from the north-west. The Germans were within a few kilometres of Moscow.

But the crisis of the German offensive had already come to a head. The staunch defence put up by the Soviet forces had worn out the shock troops of Army Group Centre. Having failed on the northern and southern approaches to Moscow, they tried to break through the defences in the centre of the western front. On 1st December the enemy succeeded in doing this in the sector to the north of Narofominsk (forty miles south-west of Moscow). Tanks and motorized infantry streamed along the highway as far as Kubinka, sixty kilometres from Moscow. But their further advance was held up by formations of 5th Army, commanded by General Govorov. After losing nearly half their tanks, the Germans turned eastwards into the area of Golitsyno station. Here the counter-blows of 33rd and 5th Armies descended upon them. The enemy's attempt to get through to Moscow had been frustrated. On 4th December, formations of these armies routed the Germans in fierce fighting and managed to

restore the front on the River Nara.

Thus concluded the last Nazi offensive against Moscow. The Soviet armed forces had won the defensive battle. The German shock groups had been bled white and deprived of power to continue their attack. Between 16th November and 5th December alone the enemy lost 55,000 dead and over 100,000 wounded and frostbitten.

The success of the defensive battle in front of Moscow was largely due to the fact that, at the most difficult period in the defence of the capital, Soviet forces went over to the counter-offensive south-west of Leningrad and in the Rostov area. The enemy was therefore unable to transfer forces from these areas to the Moscow sector. At the same time fresh Red Army reserves were assembled in the capital. The 1st and 20th Armies were deployed to the north of Moscow, and 10th Army to the south-west. The balance of forces gradually changed to the advantage of the Soviets.

On 5th December the Red Army began its counter-offensive before Moscow. The Germans were pushed back from the capital and were forced to assume the defensive, and were never again able to mount an offensive simultaneously along the entire strategic Soviet-German front. Their defeat at the walls of Moscow showed how much Hitler had under-estimated Soviet resistance.

3 THE RISING SUN

Challenge in the Pacific

The Japanese attack on the American fleet at Pearl Harbour was less an attempt to provoke the United States into a declaration of war than a final admission that war between the United States and Japan was bound to come. It signalled the end of a long period of increasingly embittered relations between the two powers. The struggle centred on Japan's ambitions for an unchallenged hegemony in the Far East, and these cannot be understood without at least a glance at the astonishing rise of Japanese power in the 20th century.

Unlike China, Japan did not resist the imported Western civilization introduced by the American Commodore Matthew Perry and his successors in the 19th century. Indeed, the Japanese showed an acute ability to adopt or to adapt all the inventive genius of America and Europe, and by the First World War her industrial revolution was well under way. She was greatly assisted by a sharply rising population and low wage scales—so much so that after the First World War other nations found it necessary to introduce trade barriers against unrestricted Japanese competition.

Although under the constitution of 1889 the Emperor, as a constitutional monarch, was to reign rather than rule, the military continued to occupy a place of unique privilege, beyond ordinary democratic controls familiar to Western democracies. Eleven years later an Imperial Ordinance stated that the ministers of war and navy must be serving officers. There was no civilian control over their departments

Left: Italian postcard shows Japan smashing the Allied Pacific fleets

and if either minister resigned over a disagreement with the government the service he represented could refuse to appoint a successor. In 1925 universal manhood suffrage was introduced but the government also introduced and saw enacted a bill enforcing a Peace Preservation Law providing ten years' imprisonment for those who sought to alter the national constitution or repudiate the system of private property. It helped break up and drive underground the Japanese Communist Party. By 1931 the rising tide of ultra-nationalism was manifesting itself in murderous conspiracy at home and unchecked aggression abroad. The Japanese occupation of Manchuria was inspired and carried out solely by the army. The government and cabinet were not so much defied as ignored.

American reactions to the seizure of Manchuria, which inspired a wave of patriotism among Japanese, might have been more forceful had not the United States embarked on an isolationist phase, with a consequent unwillingness to risk entanglements overseas. Nevertheless Japan's invasion of Manchuria presented a direct threat to the 'open door' policy which the United States, along with the other trading nations, had maintained towards China since the beginning of the century. This policy required that no power should claim any special or favourable commercial relationship with the vast Chinese market—least of all by territorial conquest. Japan had clearly offended this policy and the United States accordingly was bound to take notice. In the end, however, she did nothing positive, apart from

issuing public statements deploring the Japanese action and refusing to recognize the state of Manchukuo which Japan set up to replace Manchuria.

Emboldened by the seizure of Manchuria, Japan's ambition and adventurism soon turned to naval matters. The Washington Conference of 1921-22 had fixed the tonnage of capital ships among the three leading naval powers—Great Britain, the United States, and Japan—at a 5:5:3 ratio. Other treaties signed between the great powers, Japan among them, placed further restrictions upon Japan's naval construction programmes, as they also restricted the other powers. In December 1934, however, Japan demanded naval parity with the United States and when this was refused under the terms of existing treaties she abrogated the agreements and withdrew from the London Naval Conference in January 1936. Within a year, Japanese naval construction considerably exceeded that of France, Italy, Germany, or Russia, and building programmes promised to make her a formidable rival to the United States fleet in the Pacific.

Already Japan's leaders were declaring a policy of Japanese hegemony over Eastern Asia, and often alluded to a 'Japanese Monroe Doctrine'. They were aware of the new opportunities created in Asia as rumours of war occupied the attention of the colonial powers.

USS Panay *is sunk*
American policy was in a dilemma. The after-effects of the Depression and the initiation of the New Deal in consuming the national effort, coupled with the con-

tinued mood of isolationism in foreign affairs, were calculated to encourage Japanese ambitions. Although primarily designed to keep America out of European wars, the Neutrality Acts passed by Congress in 1935, 1936, and 1937 suited Japan's expansionists, just as President Roosevelt's declaration 'I hate war' in a speech in August 1936 must have fallen pleasantly on their ears.

Japan now sought to extend her interests on the Chinese mainland. In July 1937 Japanese forces extended her control over Inner Mongolia and northern China. Key ports on the coast of central and southern China were also seized and occupied. The American people sympathized with the Chinese, and public opinion called for something stronger than the moral gestures put forward by President Roosevelt. However, the President replied with no-

thing more forceful than his famous 'Quarantine' speech of October 1937. Observing that war was a disease and that the best thing would be to stop the contagion spreading, President Roosevelt suggested 'a quarantine of the patients in order to protect the health of the community against the spread of the disease.'

This was one of Roosevelt's least inspired addresses in the field of foreign affairs. In Great Britain, Neville Chamberlain, the Prime Minister, remarked of it: 'I read Roosevelt's speech with mixed feelings . . . seeing that patients suffering from epidemic diseases do not usually go about fully armed, there is something lacking in his analogy.'

In 1932 the League of Nations had condemned Japan for violating the Nine-Power Treaty and the Kellogg Pact in its invasion of China and proposed a meeting

of the signatories of the Nine-Power Treaty to discuss the situation. Japan had refused to attend the conference at Brussels which consequently had achieved nothing.

Thereafter the United States arranged to evacuate its nationals from Chinese territory. Once more, in 1937, Japanese militarists reacted to what they took to be a sign of weakness, and within a matter of weeks, on 12th December, the US gunboat *Panay* was bombed and sunk in the Yangtze River. The United States immediately protested, demanding reparations. Japan apologized promptly and paid indemnities. Whatever her territorial ambitions, at this stage Japan had no wish to find herself at war with the United States. But she did continue to expand her dominion over the Chinese mainland,

Emperor Hirohito inspects defences

bombing innocent civilians in a new and barbaric type of warfare which Europe was also to suffer during the next six years. By 1938, Japan had seized much of northern and central China: the only real opposition to her further control over the whole mainland came from Chinese Communists in the northern provinces and the Nationalist forces at Chungking.

Public opinion in the United States became more and more incensed at the Japanese methods of warfare and demanded at the very least an embargo on trade with Japan. In the summer of 1938 the American government urged manufacturers to place a 'moral embargo' on the shipment of aircraft and other engines of war. But in fact Japan's main purchases from the United States were oil, petrol, and huge quantities of scrap iron, so the 'moral embargo' hardly threatened her war potential.

Not surprisingly, perhaps, Japan's militarist leaders seized every opportunity to exploit the deepening crisis in Europe, and when Great Britain and France were drawn into war with Germany, Japan acted swiftly in the Far East. As Hitler marched into Prague in March 1939, Japan occupied the island of Hainan, controlling the Gulf of Tonkin. Then in 1940 she moved into French Indo-China, wringing concessions from the Vichy government as soon as France fell. The next step was to deny China supplies via the Burma Road by insisting that the British stop supplies to China along this vital route. Unable to gain any formal gesture of support from the United States, Great Britain was forced to close the road.

By now, there was sharp disagreement on United States policy towards Japan in American government circles, with the cabinet itself divided. Experienced diplomats and statesmen such as the secretary of the treasury, Henry Morgenthau, and the secretary for war, Henry L.Stimson, favoured some form of ultimatum to Japan. They were convinced that at all costs Japan was anxious to avoid a direct conflict with the United States but that, equally, her leaders were immune to the ordinary language of diplomacy. Others among President Roosevelt's advisers, however, urged caution, anxious not to provoke Japan into even wilder actions, such as an attack on the Dutch East Indies, now that the Netherlands were overrun.

In response to mounting pressure for some sort of deliberate action, President Roosevelt issued an order restricting the supply of strategic materials, especially petroleum products, and also ordered the United States fleet to Hawaii. This move met with strong opposition from the US Navy, who much preferred the home anchorage of San Diego in southern Cali-

fornia. Admiral Richardson, the fleet commander, protested that it was logistically unwise to have the fleet stationed at Pearl Harbour, so far from a home base. The admiral was overruled, however, and relieved of his command. The United States fleet was renamed the Pacific Fleet, and its main base became Pearl Harbour.

Greater East Asia Co-Prosperity Sphere

Japanese policy towards the United States had become double-edged. The diplomatic programme was to avoid provoking war with the United States whilst seeking to gain maximum concessions for Japanese expansionist aims in China and South-East Asia. At the same time, however, Japanese military experts were laying plans for an offensive war against the United States if the diplomatic programme failed.

On 27th January 1941 Joseph Grew, the American ambassador in Tokyo, sent a remarkable despatch to Washington which was ignored by State Department officials:

'My Peruvian colleague told a member of my staff that he had heard from many sources including a Japanese source that the Japanese military forces planned, in the event of trouble with the United States, to attempt a surprise mass attack on Pearl Harbour using all their military facilities. He added that although the project seemed fantastic the fact that he had heard it from many sources prompted him to pass on the information.'

The Chief of Naval Operations insisted that according to all the known data on Japanese naval forces, such a move could be discounted both then and in the foreseeable future. Nevertheless Japanese records show that in January 1941 Admiral Yamamoto began to prepare a careful study of the Pearl Harbour fortifications and stated that if war between Japan and the United States were to come, 'we will have no hope of winning unless the US fleet in Hawaiian waters can be destroyed.'

But there were also divided opinions within the Japanese government. The Prime Minister, Prince Konoye, favoured some sort of détente with the United States. On the other hand Yosuke Matsuoka, the headstrong nationalist foreign minister, favoured further expansion, including an attack on the Soviet Union now that Germany was engaging Russian armies in the west. Matsuoka's proposals were rejected in order to conserve Japanese forces for the thrusts into South-East Asia and the consolidation of Japanese gains there. Matsuoka continued to press his grandiose schemes on his colleagues, freely citing the German successes in Europe as the model for an expansionist Japan. But his belligerency eventually proved too much even for his cabinet colleagues and in July 1941 Prince Konoye reconstructed

his cabinet without including Matsuoka.

The US State Department still hoped for some agreement with Japan and took heart at this development. Moreover, Grew in Tokyo became more optimistic. But their optimism was short-lived, however, for it soon became clear that Japan intended to press on with her territorial ambitions, especially towards Indo-China now that France had fallen. President Roosevelt now recognized that positive action was needed from the American side if Japan was to be dissuaded. On 24th July the President made another attempt to reach an agreement when he proposed the neutralization of Indo-China. But Japanese forces were already on the move, and on 26th July Roosevelt issued an executive order freezing Japanese assets in the United States. Admiral Nomura, the Japanese ambassador in Washington, urgently telegrammed his government that the Americans 'meant business', and advised that some appeasement gestures be made promptly. The American action had, however, merely strengthened the convictions of the militarists, who urged that Japan must press on towards hegemony in Eastern Asia with all speed. Moreover Japan was now in acute need of oil and petrol for her war machine, and the rich deposits of the Dutch East Indies were ripe for pillage.

Prince Konoye, the Prime Minister, still hoped to avoid a direct confrontation with the United States, insisting that the overall policy of Japan was to set up a peaceful condominium of states, to be known as the Greater East Asia Co-Prosperity Sphere. Unfortunately for this pretence, American intelligence experts had succeeded in cracking the Japanese diplomatic code and knew a great deal more of Japan's expansionist aims than Prince Konoye realized. Nevertheless the wish to avoid war with the United States was genuine enough – if only because it was dictated by prudence and self-interest. Accordingly, Nomura in Washington sought to arrange a meeting between President Roosevelt and Prince Konoye – a proposal which Grew in Tokyo also favoured as he felt it would help strengthen the moderate elements in the Konoye cabinet, who were in danger of being overwhelmed by the militarists. On 29th September 1941 Grew sent a long despatch to Roosevelt urging a meeting and adding that failure to meet Konoye might well result in the fall of the government and its replacement by 'a military dictatorship with neither the temperament nor the disposition to avoid a head-on collision with the United States.'

Roosevelt's advisers differed sharply on the proposal. Some experts detected clear signs of Japan's willingness to scale down her territorial ambitions if American insistence were accompanied by a display

of military strength. Navy experts argued that Japan would not run the risk of engaging the Pacific Fleet. Other military experts pointed out that Japan was dangerously over-extended in Asia, and 'already more than half beaten'.

Roosevelt's diplomatic advisers, on the other hand, included those who strongly urged that a meeting with Konoye was the only way to avoid war with Japan, for the military leaders were pressing on with war plans in the event of a failure of diplomacy. One report stated that war plans were now being prepared for possible conflict at the end of October.

Faced with contradictory advice, Roosevelt played for time. In exchanges between the secretary of state, Cordell Hull, and Nomura, the American government asked for clear assurances that Japan would withdraw all military, naval, air, and police forces from China and Indo-China. Prince Konoye, caught between his own policies and those of the war leaders who watched his every move, was unable to supply the assurances demanded by Roosevelt.

The die is cast

When hopes of a meeting between Roosevelt and Prince Konoye vanished, the Konoye government soon collapsed. An assassination attempt on the Prime Minister failed, but by mid-October the cabinet submitted its resignation and General Tojo, war minister and army officer on the active list, took over with a new cabinet containing many military leaders. Although the Tojo cabinet continued diplomatic negotiations with the American government, reports from US Navy Intelligence pointed out that Japan's manpower was now being placed on a war footing, and that her naval forces were now fully mobilized 'for imminent action'.

A final effort at a modus vivendi was attempted on 20th November. Japanese diplomats presented a number of proposals whereby Japan would agree to withdraw her troops from Indo-China once peace had been restored in the Pacific area and normal trade had been re-established between the United States and Japan. A further requirement added that the United States should provide Japan with a required quantity of oil, and that the United States should refrain from any action 'prejudicial to the endeavours for the restoration of general peace between Japan and China.'

Not surprisingly, perhaps, the United

Left: Tojo, Prime Minister and army officer on the active list, addresses the House of Representatives in November 1941, the month before Pearl Harbour. Even after the war, he insisted: 'I believe firmly that it was a war of self-defence'

States found these proposals unacceptable. But intelligence sources also confirmed that Japan was now poised for war, and that these proposals were in fact Japan's final ultimatum. Roosevelt and Cordell Hull conferred carefully and decided once more to play for time. The American reply proposed a three months' period during which a certain amount of trade would be permitted in return for an end to Japanese hostilities in China and Indo-China. Messages intercepted by American intelligence disclosed that Tojo was not disposed to adopt the American proposals. The deadline for accepting the Japanese proposals was 29th November. 'After that,' the Japanese foreign minister informed his ambassador in Washington, 'things are automatically going to happen'.

Lulled by a decade of isolationist sentiment, neither America's leaders nor her people seemed able to accept that Japan would actually risk war with the United States. Certainly the balance of Roosevelt's policies implied that a conflict could be avoided and that reason and good sense would prevail in the Japanese cabinet. When, in late November 1941, the American cabinet accepted that war was now inevitable, secretary of war Stimson noted in his diary that the cabinet was now preoccupied with the question of 'how we should manoeuvre them [the Japanese] into the position of firing the first shot without too much danger to ourselves.' Rarely can a nation have approached a conflict so reluctantly.

Again, despite the hard evidence coming in from decoded cables and wireless messages in the Pacific, American military strategists seemed loath to take note of warnings that the first blow might come at Pearl Harbour.

With the American rejection of Japan's final proposals, and Japan's refusal to take up the American modus vivendi, the die was cast. On 5th December, Tokyo ordered members of the Japanese embassy staff to leave Washington. An intercepted message from Ambassador Nomura to his superiors in Tokyo read: 'We have completed destruction of codes . . .' On the morning of 7th December, even as Japanese diplomats kept up the farce of parleying in Washington, bombers took off from Japanese aircraft-carriers and swooped on Pearl Harbour, destroying a major part of the Pacific Fleet and killing over 2,300 American servicemen. Next day Congress declared war on Japan. The war which followed on sea and on land in the Pacific featured the ugliest and bloodiest fighting ever experienced by American forces. In calling for a declaration of war, President Roosevelt said of the attack on Pearl Harbour on 7th December 1941 that it was 'a date which will live in infamy'.

Pearl Harbour

America's decision to position her Pacific Fleet at a point covering Japanese lines of expansion was an event of great significance. Near Honolulu in the Hawaiian Islands, United States military authorities had dredged out a lagoon called Pearl Harbour, on which they located America's strongest outlying naval base before the Second World War and set up army and army air installations to protect it and the Pacific Fleet. Because of its location, Pearl Harbour came to be variously viewed as the Gibraltar of the Pacific, the defensive outpost of continental United States, a deterrent to Japanese aggressive intentions, or an encouraging inducement to Japanese to attack American forces and supplies situated in the East.

Launch edges up to blazing West Virginia to snatch a survivor from the water. In fact, most ships damaged and even sunk were restored to fighting condition

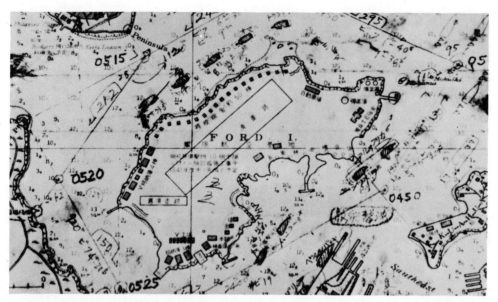

Japanese chart supplied to Pearl Harbour strike pilots marks the supposed position of US Navy vessels in the base. It was not very accurate

Pearl Harbour's destiny inevitably became involved in relations between Japan and the United States. These had been deteriorating badly since the previous year, as disagreements arose over Japan's southward expansion on the Asiatic continent. During the 1930's the United States had limited its objections to efforts to impose moral sanctions.

By 1940 both countries began to examine their relationships in the light of the war in Europe. The Japanese took advantage of Nazi successes to make new advances down the coast of China. The hard pressures of war forced the French to acquiesce in the movement of Japanese troops into northern Indo-China and the British to agree to close the Burma Road, the last important supply line into China from Lashio to Kunming. By imposing a limited check on the export of war materials to Japan, the United States emerged as the principal obstacle to Japanese advance.

In May 1940 President Roosevelt changed the Pacific Fleet's main base from San Diego, California to Pearl Harbour despite the opposition of its commander, thus making the force a pawn in the diplomatic manoeuvring between Japan and the United States.

But the Japanese had been making moves as well and in September 1940 secured a new alliance with Germany and Italy, known as the Tripartite Pact, which established spheres of influence, in effect giving Germany Europe, and Japan the Far East. In an obvious reference to the United States, the pact guaranteed mutual aid 'if attacked by a power at present not involved in the European war or in the Sino-Japanese conflict'.

Early in 1941, Japan fatefully started a dual course of action, one diplomatic and the other military, both aimed at removing American obstacles to Japanese expansion. The diplomats hoped to gain these ends peacefully by persuading the United States to stand aside. Meanwhile the militarists planned on war should the diplomats fail.

In January 1941 the American ambassador to Japan Joseph C.Grew reported a rumoured Japanese plan for a surprise attack on Pearl Harbour, but the report was discounted as 'fantastic'. Actually Admiral Isoroku Yamamoto was starting a study of the Pearl Harbour operation, convinced that the Pacific Fleet's destruction was essential to Japanese victory. In July, military and civilian leaders meeting before the Emperor decided to work for the 'establishment of the Greater East Asia Co-Prosperity Sphere and World Power', and declared that they would 'not be deterred by the possibility of being involved in a war with England and America'. The United States, too, hardened its position by freezing Japanese assets in the United States on 26th July 1941.

By this time the Washington government was being assisted greatly by intercepted and decoded messages. This 'Magic', as the decoding system was called, made it possible for the Americans, unknown to the Japanese, to be aware of Japanese diplomatic communications throughout the world. While it had limitations, including the fact that the information was diplomatic rather than military, the 'Magic' intercepts gave the American government at least an important diplomatic preview of things to come.

Another Japanese resolution on 6th September set in operation the advance to war. Only the successful achievement by diplomacy of three principal demands could halt the move. The United States and Great Britain should neither interfere with the settlement of the 'China Incident' nor strengthen their own forces in the Far East. Moreover, they should co-operate with Japanese efforts to obtain raw materials.

When a new, more militaristic government came into power in mid-October, the Japanese ambassador to the United States Kichisaburu Nomura felt out of touch and requested recall. Instead, the Japanese government sent Saburu Kurusu to Washington as a special emissary to work with Nomura.

On 5th November another Imperial Conference ordered one more diplomatic effort. If it failed, the question of war would go to the Emperor. Unable to persuade Tokyo to wait, its diplomats presented a new memorandum to Washington. Cordell Hull, the secretary of state, had no intention of accepting this proposal, which would have meant a reversal of the American position, but since he was under pressure from the military to delay, he and Roosevelt drafted a counter-proposal, including a short truce. They also learned through 'Magic' that Tokyo had set a final deadline for the diplomats—29th November. 'After that, things are automatically going to happen,' said the message.

Discouraged by British and Chinese opposition to the temporary proposal, Washington dropped it and presented a ten-point memorandum to the Japanese, restating its original position. Nomura and Kurusu 'argued back furiously' against the proposal but had to forward it when Hull remained 'solid as a rock'. Two days later Tokyo told Nomura that the memorandum was unacceptable and that negotiations would be 'de facto ruptured', although Nomura was instructed not to reveal this fact to the Americans.

Diplomatic efforts fail

After the war, Japanese leaders claimed that the American note forced Japan into war. True, the memorandum threatened Japanese expansion, but it did not menace Japan, its people, or its right to trade in the Far East. It challenged Japan's right to hold lands she had seized on the mainland but it did not threaten Japan in the sense that if Japan rejected the proposals the United States would declare war. The United States was not following a policy of dual initiative; it was not even planning

Right: Detail of illustration from American magazine Fortune, *published after Pearl Harbour, depicting (from left) a Japanese soldier, Prime Minister Tojo, Admiral Nagumo, who delivered the raid, and Emperor Hirohito*

The Rising Sun

to sever diplomatic relations. Nevertheless, Hull realized that the Japanese would not accept the proposals and that diplomacy was virtually at an end. On the 27th he told the secretary of war: 'I have washed my hands of it and it is now in the hands of . . . the Army and the Navy.'

Warnings had already been going out from time to time to outlying military commands. On 25th November, for example, Admiral Husband E. Kimmel in Hawaii heard that neither Roosevelt nor Hull 'would be surprised over a Japanese surprise attack'. On 27th November, military authorities decided to send new warnings to Admiral Kimmel and General Walter C.Short, the navy and army commanders in Hawaii. The note to Kimmel was the more explicit: 'Consider this dispatch a war warning.' It stated that diplomatic efforts had failed and that Japan might make an aggressive move 'within a few days'. Another message to Short on the same day, unfortunately, indicated sabotage as the principal threat, and he responded by issuing an alert, bunching aircraft against sabotage rather than dispersing them against air attack. Fortunately, no American aircraft-carriers were in Pearl Harbour on 7th December as the *Enterprise* and *Lexington* had been despatched to carry Marine fighter aircraft to Wake and Midway Islands.

Acting as if negotiations were still possible, the Japanese diplomats continued the farce, even while receiving orders to destroy codes and prepare to leave. On 6th December they received word that a fourteen-part memorandum was on the way, but were told, 'the situation is extremely delicate, and when you receive it I want you to keep it secret'.

The first thirteen parts of the memorandum were received first and, decoded by 'Magic', were ready for distribution about 9 p.m. on 6th December. When Roosevelt saw them, he reportedly said 'this means war', and discussed the matter with his confidential assistant Harry Hopkins, without mentioning Pearl Harbour. Knox, the secretary of the navy, and some high military officials also saw the message but acted as if it had no military significance. Moreover, the despatch was not sent to General George C.Marshall, Chief-of-Staff, although he was at his home.

The fourteenth part was available by 7.30 or 8 a.m. on 7th December. Seeing it about 10 a.m., President Roosevelt commented that it looked as if Japan would sever diplomatic relations, for this part stated that it was 'impossible to reach an agreement through further negotiations'.

Meanwhile, another intercepted message from Tokyo was ready for distribution about 9 a.m. Referring to the longer memorandum, it asked: 'Will the ambas-

sador please submit to the United States government (if possible to the secretary of state) our reply to the United States at 1 p.m. on the 7th your time.'

The officer in charge saw that the message was significant and got it to a presidential aide within twenty minutes. General Marshall returned late from a morning ride and did not read the message until almost 11.30 a.m. He immediately went into action and in longhand prepared a warning to key commands, including the Hawaiian Command:

'The Japanese are presenting at 1 p.m., Eastern Standard Time, today what amounts to an ultimatum. Also they are under orders to destroy their code machine immediately. Just what significance the hour set may have we do not know, but be on the alert accordingly.'

The message which went to Pearl Harbour met obstacles that appear almost comic in retrospect and did not arrive until after the bombs began to fall.

Target Pearl Harbour

In Washington, the diplomatic game came to an anticlimactic end. The Americans decoded the Japanese messages faster than did the Japanese embassy, which had to ask for a delay in meeting Secretary Hull, and the diplomats did not arrive until shortly after 2 p.m. On his way to meet them, Hull received a telephone call from President Roosevelt, who said, 'there's a report that the Japanese have attacked Pearl Harbour'. He added that the report

Pearl Harbour seen on Japanese film.
Top: Still shows hilarity with which pilots of Pearl Harbour Task Force, en route for their objective, greeted a broadcast by the unsuspecting Americans on Oahu.
Above: Carrier deck crews hold Zero fighters bound for Pearl Harbour until their engines have been revved up to take-off speed. Right: Oklahoma and West Virginia gush oil after the attack. Below right: Ford Island as the raid begins. A Kate peels off after scoring a direct hit on Oklahoma; the torpedoed Utah (arrowed) lists to port

had not been confirmed. Hull then went to meet the ambassador and Kurusu and read quickly through the fourteen-point memorandum which, unknown to the Japanese, he had already seen. Coldly furious, he told them that in his fifty years of public life he had never seen a document 'more crowded with infamous falsehoods and distortions on a scale so huge that I never imagined until today that any government on this planet was capable of uttering them'. He dismissed the diplomats and a few minutes later received confirmation of the Pearl Harbour attack.

All nations at this time had plans for possible war, and the United States was no exception. In 1924, American military planners prepared an 'Orange' plan in case of war with Japan. In the 1930's they replaced this with 'Rainbow 5' which envisaged war with the Axis, seeking particularly to enforce the Monroe Doctrine and protect the United States, its possessions, and its sea trade. By 1941 the United States had held discussions about the Far East with the British and the Dutch, but had not reached agreement. When war came each nation began fighting according to its own plan.

As war neared, American military leaders became increasingly concerned with fighting a defensive struggle in the Pacific against Japan and making the major effort in the Atlantic against Germany. Transfer of vessels from the Atlantic to the Pacific might 'well cause the United States to lose the battle of the Atlantic in the near future'. Consequently, the only plans recommended by General Marshall and Admiral Stark were 'to conduct defensive war, in co-operation with the British and the Dutch, for the defence of the Philippines and the Dutch East Indies'. Knowing that preparations were inadequate, they asked for more time.

Meanwhile, as we have noted, the Japanese had been carrying on their own war plans, in line with the policy of dual initiative. The nature of the nation's resources dictated a short conflict. Plans included early capture of oilfields in the East Indies, seizure of Singapore and the Philippines, and disabling the United States Pacific Fleet to keep it from interfering. Planners developed three phases of attack. First would be a blow at Pearl Harbour and an advance south in the Far East to seize lands and establish a perimeter extending from Wake Island through the Gilbert Islands, New Guinea, and the Dutch East Indies to Burma and the border of India. Second would be strengthening the perimeter, and third would be beating off attacks until the enemy tired of the effort. From the standpoint of the amount of territory to be occupied, the plan was aggressive and greatly expansionist. On the other hand, Japan apparently had no designs on either the United States or Great Britain.

Actual preparations for the Pearl Harbour attack began in August. The striking force consisted of six aircraft-carriers, screened by nine destroyers. A supporting force included two battleships, two cruisers, three submarines, tankers, and supply ships. Of the advance force of some twenty submarines, eleven bore small planes, and five were equipped with midget submarines, carrying two men and powered by storage batteries.

The battleships devastated

Leaving Japan in mid-November, the Pearl Harbour task-force rendezvoused in utmost secrecy at Tankan Bay in the Kurile Islands. On 26th November, it left the Kuriles to approach the Hawaiian Islands from the north. The weather probably would be rough and refuelling difficult, but the chances of avoiding detection were best by this route. On the morning of 7th December, the force reached its predetermined launching site, some 230 miles north of Pearl Harbour, and at 6 a.m. the first aircraft took off: forty Nakajima B5N2 ('Kate') torpedo-bombers equipped with torpedoes adapted for dropping in shallow water, fifty more Kates for high-level bombing, fifty Aichi D3A2 ('Val') dive-bombers, and fifty Zero fighters (Mitsubishi Zero-Sens, officially codenamed 'Zekes' by the Allies). The second wave consisted of fifty Kates, eighty Vals, and forty Zeros.

There was no significant advance warning. In the fleet a so-called 'Condition 3' of readiness was in effect, in which one machine gun in four was manned, but it was a peacetime 'Condition 3' in which main and 5-inch batteries were not manned and even manned machine guns had their ammunition in locked boxes to which officers of the deck had the keys.

The raid begins

At 7.30 a.m. a boatswain's mate saw twenty to twenty-five aircraft circling, but he did not identify them as enemy machines. At about 7.55 a.m. the Commander, Mine Force Pacific, on a minelayer in the harbour, saw an aircraft drop a bomb but thought it was an accident until he saw the crimson sun insignia on the machine. He immediately called General Quarters and had the signal hoisted: 'All ships in harbour sortie.' A few minutes later Admiral Kimmel heard of the attack, and Rear-Admiral Bellinger broadcast: 'Air raid, Pearl Harbour—this is no drill.'

Earlier, at 6.45 a.m., a midget submarine was detected and sunk, but the sole reaction was to send another destroyer to the area. Radar protection was primitive, poorly understood, and underrated. The one detection that was made by men practising on a radar set was disregarded by the watch officer as blips of approaching American bombers from the mainland.

Escaping detection and initial opposition, therefore, the Japanese aircraft swept in from over the sea. The first attack, starting at about 7.55 a.m., lasted for approximately half an hour. There were four separate torpedo-bomber attacks, with the first two directed at the main objectives, the battleships lined up in 'Battleship Row' on the south-east shore of Ford Island. The third attack was by a single aircraft on the

cruiser *Helena,* and the fourth struck at ships on the north side of the island.

The second major attack came at about 8.40 a.m., after a brief lull, and consisted of a series of high-level bombing runs across the targets. Dive-bombers and fighters followed with a half-hour attack, and at 9.45 a.m. the aircraft withdrew.

The results were devastating. Among the battleships, *West Virginia* was hit by six or seven torpedoes, and quick counter-flooding alone prevented the vessel from capsizing. *Tennessee,* moored inboard of *West Virginia,* was protected by it from torpedoes and suffered relatively little damage or loss of life from bombings and fires. *Arizona* was the hardest hit. Torpedoes and bombs caused explosions and fires, and the vessel sank rapidly, carrying to their deaths over a thousand men trapped below decks. Although sustaining at least five bomb hits and one torpedo, *Nevada* managed to get clear and avoid sinking or capsizing. *Oklahoma* took three torpedoes and capsized until her masts stuck in the mud of the harbour bottom. *Maryland* was saved from torpedoes by *Oklahoma* and suffered the least damage of the battleships. *California,* struck by torpedoes, sank into the water and mud until only the superstructure showed. Aircraft attacking the north-west shore inflicted heavy damage on the light cruiser *Raleigh,* damaged the seaplane tender *Curtiss* and capsized the old battleship *Utah* which had been converted to a target ship. Another light cruiser *Helena* was heavily damaged and *Oglala,* the minelayer alongside it, was sunk. Other vessels damaged included the light cruiser *Honolulu,* the destroyers *Cassin, Downes,* and *Shaw,* and the repair ship *Vestal.* The battleship *Pennsylvania,* in drydock, was hit but received no serious damage.

Although the battleships and other vessels were the prime targets, the Japanese did not forget airfields, and, relatively speaking, American airpower suffered more heavily than did sea power. The attackers strafed and bombed land-based aircraft and practically eliminated the seaplanes. Army Air Force aircraft at

Hickam Field, bunched against sabotage, proved a perfect target for Japanese attackers.

By the end of the day, 'a date which will live in infamy' as President Roosevelt called it, the Americans had suffered 2,403 deaths, of which, 2,008 were from the navy. Three battleships sank, and other vessels took varying degrees of punishment. The Japanese destroyed two-thirds of American naval aircraft and left only sixteen serviceable Army Air Force bombers. In contrast, Japanese losses were slight: besides five midget submarines only nine Zeros, fifteen Vals, and five Kates were lost out of an attacking force of 360 aircraft.

American reactions on the island ranged from an initial incomprehension through disbelief, shock, frustration, to displays of the utmost courage. Men fought back with all they had, in some cases successfully, as the twenty-nine downed planes attest, but more often against hopeless odds, at great personal danger or sacrifice, and with insufficient weapons.

A tremendous blunder

Nearby Honolulu suffered little damage. The fires which started were determined later to have stemmed mainly from misdirected anti-aircraft fire from Pearl Harbour. Over a local radio, the governor proclaimed a state of emergency, and at 11.41 a.m. the army ordered commercial broadcasting stations off the air. Radio silence and the suddenness of the attack gave rise to uncertainties among the civilian population and the spreading of many unfounded rumours. Radio stations occasionally broadcast important messages, such as the announcement at 4.25 p.m. that the island had been placed under martial law.

Viewed from the level of high political policy, the Pearl Harbour attack was a tremendous blunder. It is difficult to conceive of any other act which could have rallied the American people more solidly behind a declaration of war on Japan. Generally speaking, Americans were not neutral; they favoured and gave aid to the nations fighting the Axis. However, without an incident such as Pearl Harbour, there would have been strong opposition to open participation in the war. Many people remembered the unsatisfactory aftermath of the First World War and they questioned what the Second World War could accomplish. The Pearl Harbour attack ended all significant debate on such matters. The nation, in the eyes of Americans, had been attacked ruthlessly and without warning, and the only way out was to declare war on Japan.

The Japanese predicted American reactions but reasoned that strategic results would be worth it. Strategically, however,

Above left: At the height of the attack on Pearl Harbour. West Virginia *lies sunk but upright as a result of prompt counter-flooding. Inboard is the* Tennessee *which she protected from torpedoes and which consequently suffered relatively little damage.*
Above right: Marines at Ewa Field fire at attacking Japanese aircraft. Men fought back against hopeless odds, at great personal danger and sacrifice, and with insufficient weapons. Below: A scene of devastation at Pearl Harbour's Naval Air Station after the attack

Pearl Harbour

the Pearl Harbour attack was a blunder in that it was unnecessary. The Pacific Fleet could not have stopped or even checked the initial planned advance of the Japanese. American war plans envisaged defensive action by a slow penetration into the Pacific. The fleet would not have dared move within range of land-based enemy aircraft without the most careful preparations. The fate of the British ships *Repulse* and *Prince of Wales* early in the war is an indication of what would have happened.

Even tactically the Pearl Harbour attack was a blunder. Capital ships were no longer as effective a means of exercising sea power as aircraft-carriers, and the two carriers *Lexington* and *Enterprise* were out of harbour when the Japanese attacked. In fact, most of the ships that were damaged and even sunk were later restored to fighting condition. *Nevada,* for example, participated in the Normandy invasion and later helped bombard Iwo Jima. *California, Maryland, Pennsylvania, Tennessee,* and *West Virginia* all took part in the Philippines campaigns. It would have been more effective to blast permanent installations and oil supplies than ships. Destruction of the oil tanks would have delayed advance across the Pacific longer than damage to ships and aircraft. In fact, one of the reasons for surprise was the belief that the Japanese also recognized that such an attack would be unnecessary.

Pearl Harbour might have been more effective had it not been followed by a colossal blunder by Hitler. After the attack, Japan called on Germany to join in the fight against the United States. Had Hitler refused, the American administration would have been in a most difficult position. Its leaders viewed Germany as the principal enemy, but without any specific incident in the Atlantic they might have had difficulty gaining support for a declaration of war on Germany while launching into a struggle with Japan. Pressure would have been strong to fight the visible and open enemy and not deliberately to seek another foe. It is difficult to know what would have been the result in the Atlantic. One recalls that Marshall and Stark earlier had warned that withdrawal of American ships from the Atlantic might cause Great Britain to lose the Battle of the Atlantic. Fortunately for the American government, Germany forced the United States with a declaration of war. This action made it possible for the Allies to plan a coalition war that was world-wide.

Painting by Japanese artist M.Susuki of newly qualified pilots at a passing-out ceremony — part of the militaristic ritual which reinforced the self-sacrificial fighting spirit of the Japanese

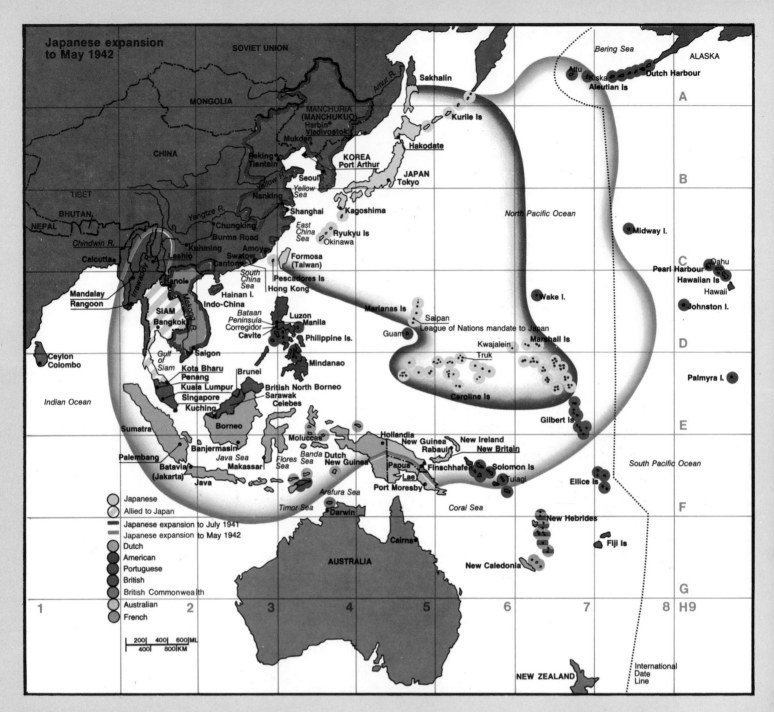

Japanese expansion
to May 1942

SOVIET UNION

MONGOLIA

CHINA

TIBET

BHUTAN
NEPAL

MANCHURIA
(MANCHUKUO)
Harbin
Mukden
Vladivostok

Peking
Tientsin

Nanking

Shanghai

Chungking

Burma Road

Kunming

Lashio

Calcutta

Mandalay
Rangoon

Hanoi

SIAM
Bangkok

Ceylon
Colombo

Indian Ocean

Sumatra

Palembang

Batavia
(Jakarta)

Java

Amoy
Swatow
Canton

Hong Kong

Hainan I.
Indo-China

Saigon

Kota Bharu
Penang
Kuala Lumpur
Singapore
Kuching

Banjermasin

Makassar

Sakhalin

Kurile Is

Hakodate

JAPAN
Tokyo

Kagoshima

Ryukyu Is
Okinawa

East
China
Sea

Formosa
(Taiwan)

Pescadores Is

South
China
Sea

Bataan
Peninsula
Corregidor
Cavite

Luzon
Manila

Philippine Is.

Mindanao

Brunei

British North Borneo
Sarawak
Celebes

Borneo

Moluccas

Java Sea

Flores
Sea

Banda
Sea

Dutch
New Guinea

KOREA
Port Arthur

Seoul

Yellow
Sea

Bering Sea

Attu
Kiska
Aleutian Is

ALASKA

Dutch Harbour

North Pacific Ocean

Midway I.

Pearl Harbour
Hawaiian Is

Oahu

Hawaii

Johnston I.

Wake I.

Marianas Is

Saipan

Guam

League of Nations mandate to Japan

Kwajalein
Truk

Marshall Is

Caroline Is

Gilbert Is

Palmyra I.

Hollandia
New Guinea
Rabaul
New Ireland
New Britain

Papua
Lae
Finschhafen
Port Moresby

Solomon Is
Tulagi

Ellice Is

South Pacific Ocean

Coral Sea

New Hebrides

Fiji Is

New Caledonia

Darwin

Timor Sea

Arafura Sea

Cairns

AUSTRALIA

Gulf
of
Siam

Irrawaddy R.

Chindwin R.

Mekong R.

Yangtze R.

Yellow R.

Amur R.

NEW ZEALAND

International
Date
Line

Japanese
Allied to Japan
Japanese expansion to July 1941
Japanese expansion to May 1942
Dutch
American
Portuguese
British
British Commonwealth
Australian
French

200 400 600 ML
400 800 KM

A
B
C
D
E
F
G
H9

1   2   3   4   5   6   7   8

The Risen Sun

America's introduction to total war came on 7th December 1941, with the greatest naval defeat suffered by a first-class power since the Battle of Trafalgar. In an age in which the battleship was still the index of maritime power, nothing experienced by the Germans in the First World War or by the Italians in the Second World War compared with the blows delivered on the United States Pacific Fleet by Admiral Chuichi Nagumo's naval aviators.

The catastrophe of Pearl Harbour was made possible on the Japanese side by a combination of superb training and re-markable duplicity, and on the American by culpable negligence in both Hawaii and Washington, aggravated by unsatisfactory communication between them. Perhaps it could be said that the Americans had made an even more direct contribution to their own defeat, as Nagumo's airmen followed a plan of attack based on that executed successfully against the same target by Vice-Admiral Ernest J.King during manoeuvres carried out by the Pacific Fleet in 1938. But there was some excuse for American negligence. All parties concerned fully appreciated in the last months

Japanese boys ape their soldier fathers. Young and old held the victorious military in great esteem in the early stages of the Pacific War

of 1941 that the Japanese were planning to attack the British and Dutch colonial empires in the Pacific. Few considered it rationally conceivable that they would add immeasurably to their difficulties by an attack on the United States at the same time.

Nor indeed did it prove to have been a rational decision. But there were certainly few signs during the first six months of the Pacific War that the Japanese had over-extended themselves. The assault on Pearl Harbour itself did not nearly exhaust their offensive capacity. Seven other attacks were launched almost simultaneously against British, Dutch, and American positions in the Pacific. These developed into an enveloping march of conquest unmatched in military history. No soldiers or sailors had ever before won such victories against such enemies. In terms of human achievement, nothing compares with Japanese triumphs in the Second World War except Japanese economic recovery after it. On 8th December forty-two American aircraft were destroyed on the ground in the Philippines, for the loss of only seven Japanese. Two days later, *HMS Prince of Wales* and *HMS Repulse,* observed rather than escorted by one antique and two veteran destroyers, and under the command of an admiral resolutely disbelieving in air power, made history by becoming the first capital ships to be sunk in open sea by aerial bombardment. But the Japanese were to establish a number of records at British expense during the next few months. Hong Kong surrendered on Christmas Day 1941 after a resistance which cost the attackers some 2,754 casualties but involved the total loss of its uselessly exposed garrison of 12,000 British and Commonwealth troops. Meanwhile a numerically superior Commonwealth army, inadequately trained and inappropriately deployed, was hustled through Malaya into Singapore by a Japanese force less than half its size, and forced to capitulate on 15th February 1942. 138,708 British troops had become prisoners or battle casualties in the greatest defeat and most humiliating surrender in British history. General Yamashita's invaders had lost only 9,824 killed or wounded. The catalogue of disaster rolled on. In two days of fighting in the Java Sea on 27th-28th February, a combined American, British, Dutch, and Australian fleet lost eleven of its fourteen vessels, without managing to sink a single Japanese warship. And in four dreadful days in the Indian Ocean Admiral Nagumo's veteran fliers sank a British aircraft-carrier, two cruisers, two destroyers, and a corvette, and drove British naval power helplessly back to the Arabian Sea. Even the RAF itself was unable to match the attackers.

In wild air battles over and around Ceylon, the British lost some forty-three aircraft, not counting those sunk with the carrier *Hermes,* against seventeen Japanese. And on 20th May the last British forces withdrew from Burma across the Indian border, after the longest retreat in British history, having suffered 13,463 casualties, against 4,597 Japanese.

The conquest of the Dutch East Indies presented the invader with even fewer problems. Borneo and Celebes were effectively overrun by 24th January; Ambon by the end of the month; Sumatra, Bali, and Timor by the third week of February; and Java by 9th March. The American colonies presented a rather different prospect, however. Almost undefended, Guam was overrun easily on 10th December. But Wake Island repelled a first attack and held out until 23rd December, by which time its garrison of 520 Marines had sunk two Japanese destroyers and killed or wounded about 1,150 of the enemy. And American resistance in the Bataan Peninsula and Corregidor Island actually set back the Japanese time-table for the conquest of the Philippines by a whole four months, and resulted in the disgrace of the unfortunate Japanese commander, General Homma. The heroic tenacity of his fighting men managed to obscure the fact that MacArthur's generalship in the Philippines was distinguished by errors of optimism at least as serious as those which General Percival had been guilty of in Malaya, and that the number of American and Filipino troops put out of action by General Homma was about the same as that of the British and Commonwealth forces routed by Yamashita. But due to the fact that Wake, Bataan, and Corregidor held out for longer than anybody expected they have entered American mythology as symbols of defiant and inspiring resistance, while Singapore has become associated with disgrace, and Hong Kong with tragic futility.

'Victory disease'

There was no disputing the sweep and rapidity of the Japanese conquests or the relatively slight losses with which they were gained. But they were not without features ominous for the victors themselves. The most serious one was that they had clearly not achieved their basic purpose. Japanese grand strategy required the establishment of an island barrier behind which the conquerors could enjoy the fruits of their conquest while meeting the inevitable American counter-attack. But this required that American offensive capacity should first have been effectively destroyed. And this had not been done at Pearl Harbour. The battleship force of the Pacific Fleet had certainly been put out of action. But the fast aircraft-carriers had

completely escaped the Japanese attack. *Saratoga* was still in California; *Lexington* was delivering Marine fighter aircraft reinforcements to Midway; and *Enterprise* was returning to Pearl Harbour from Wake Island having completed an identical mission there. This meant that the United States still possessed the means of striking against Japan with the same weapon of naval aviation which had been used so devastatingly against herself. Elementary prudence would thus have suggested that all the resources of the Imperial Navy should have been devoted to bringing the American carrier squadron to battle and destruction. But elementary prudence was the last quality to be considered in the Japanese plan of action. They, of course, had sufficient reason to be confident. Their fighting men had undoubtedly earned a reputation for invincibility; their only naval losses had been the five submarines lost at Pearl Harbour and the two destroyers sunk at Wake Island; and they still possessed a great numerical superiority in the air over the Americans, as well as in all classes of surface ships. But there was reason to believe that this invincibility was incomplete, and that the numerical advantage could easily be lost. Air losses had turned out to be about equal at the end of the Burma campaign, but in the brief air battles over Rangoon the Japanese had shown a disquieting inferiority to the veterans of the American Volunteer Group, who were shooting them down for a time at the rate of four or five to one. This at least suggested that the Japanese might need all the air supremacy they could get. And it was clear that Japanese strategic planning seemed to discount the basic principle of the concentration of force.

It was not merely the case that the Japanese and their supposed German allies were fighting totally separate and unrelated wars. So, frequently, were individual Japanese commanders in the field. Their tendency to go off on wild hunts after easy conquests unrelated to any overall strategic plan was categorized by the Japanese themselves as the 'victory disease'. It was accompanied and aggravated by what might

Right: 1 Lieutenant-General Sakai heads triumphant Japanese entry into Hong Kong, Christmas Day, 1941. 2 Japanese troops on a British gun emplacement in Hong Kong cheer news of the garrison's surrender. 3 Japanese paratroops are dropped to seize oil installations near Palembang, Sumatra, 14th February 1942. 4 Sinking of small British aircraft-carrier Hermes off Ceylon, 9th April 1942. Attacked by ninety bombers and fighters, she was sunk in twenty minutes. Orders to British fighters to give her cover failed to get through

similarly be termed the 'octopus complex'. This took the form of a predilection for enormously ambitious and complex plans of campaign which merely compounded the possibilities for human error in situations where rational military direction should surely have sought to minimize them.

The victory disease and octopus complex appeared in full bloom in the crucial campaigns of May and June 1942. Conflicting factions in the Imperial Navy were unable to agree either with themselves or with the army whether immediate priority should be assigned to seizing Port Moresby, so as to neutralize Australia; to attacking the Aleutian Islands, to divert American strength from the central Pacific; or to a thrust at Midway Island, to force the remainder of the Pacific Fleet to accept battle, as should have been done as soon as possible after Pearl Harbour. It was effectively decided to proceed with all three. Even this did not satisfy the determination of the Japanese High Command to make things difficult for themselves. The ships assigned to the Port Moresby campaign were divided into no less than six separate forces, performing two quite distinct operations. By contrast Admiral Chester W. Nimitz, Commander-in-Chief of the US Pacific Fleet, boldly concentrated every available ship to meet the Japanese in the Coral Sea. The result was that the opposing forces were not too disproportionate. When battle was actually joined on 7th May, two American aircraft-carriers with 121 aircraft and seven cruisers faced three Japanese carriers with about 180 aircraft and six cruisers. The odds were soon shortened in any case when bombers from both *Lexington* and *Yorktown* blew the carrier *Shoho* out of the water. *Lexington* was itself lost the following day, but in the meantime the Americans had put a further carrier, *Shokaku*, out of action.

The action in the Coral Sea might have seemed inconclusive as shipping losses were about equal and both fleets withdrew from the area, but in fact every advantage lay with the Americans. They had lost only eighty-one aircraft against 105 Japanese; the assault on Port Moresby was countermanded; and all the Japanese carriers had been immobilized, as the third, *Zuikaku*, had lost too many aircraft to be fit for action until its losses had been replaced. This weakening of the Japanese carrier strength at the Battle of the Coral Sea may well have determined the course of the Second World War.

It was not that the Japanese were even then seriously short of carriers. The enormous fleet available to Admiral Isoroku Yamamoto must have guaranteed him victory in any single enterprise he had committed it to. But Japanese naval power was dissipated in a futile attempt to confuse an enemy who could have been overwhelmed by a direct and concentrated attack. Yamamoto decided to proceed with the diversionary raid on the Aleutian Islands as well as the frontal assault on Midway, despite the failure of the Port Moresby bid. His plan of campaign resulted in the Japanese armada being scattered in ten separate groups all over the north and central Pacific. Two carriers were detached to cover the attack on the Aleutians, leaving the Midway force actually deficient in air power, although excessively strong in surface ships. Seven battleships, six heavy and light carriers, thirteen cruisers, and fifty destroyers challenged Nimitz's three carriers, eight cruisers, and fourteen destroyers. But Yamamoto brought with him only 325 aircraft, while Nimitz could assemble a motley collection of 348 land and sea-based machines. The Americans obviously could not offer battle at sea. Everything depended upon the prowess of the United States Naval Air Service — a glamourized body of fighting men, with their swashbuckling airborne admirals, their huge wooden-decked carriers, and years of experience in dive-bombing techniques.

And here two Japanese errors helped Nimitz decisively. The first was that Yamamoto still thought that two American carriers had been sunk in the Coral Sea engagement, and consequently quite underestimated the strike capacity of his opponent. The other was that the Japanese had not yet been forced to learn how to integrate their carrier squadrons with the rest of their fleet. The Americans had learned the hard way. Bereft of battleships, they had of necessity adopted their carriers as capital ships, and deployed their other craft as escorts around them. But the battle force which should have been in attendance to shield Nagumo's carriers with its anti-aircraft batteries was 400 miles distant when the assault on Midway commenced.

However the Japanese nearly won. The initial air battles between their naval aircraft and American land-based planes were wholly in their favour. They wrecked everything above ground on Midway and shot down thirty-three American aircraft for a loss of only six of their own. Then retribution came. Rear Admiral Raymond A. Spruance on board *Enterprise* ordered strikes by his torpedo and dive-bombers at a time deliberately calculated to reach the Japanese carriers while they were still refuelling their aircraft. The torpedo bombers arrived first and flew on to destruction, losing three-quarters of their number without scoring a single hit. But the death-flight of the old Douglas Devastators drew the attention of the Japanese away from the upper air where Spruance's Douglas Dauntless dive-bombers were assembling.

In less than five minutes three Japanese carriers, the *Kaga, Akagi* and *Soryu*, were on fire and out of action, and the great Pacific War had been won and lost. The surviving carrier *Hiryu* struck back, crippling *Yorktown*, but was itself destroyed by a further strike from *Enterprise*. By the end of the day, Yamamoto's air arm had been virtually eliminated. Twice on the following nights, he belatedly deployed his battle force in attempts to sink Spruance's carriers by gunfire. However, the Americans skilfully drew away at evening, returning with daylight to deliver more strikes, as a result of which a Japanese heavy cruiser was sunk.

Final casualty figures were four carriers, a cruiser, and 322 aircraft for the Japanese, against a carrier, a destroyer, and 147 aircraft for the Americans. The battle had been won on the American side by Spruance's almost faultless judgment and by the courage and technical skill of his aviators. It had been lost on the Japanese by the now familiar vices of over-confidence, over-complexity of planning, and unwillingness to concentrate on one objective at a time. This time they had been fatal. The margin of strength so brilliantly gained at Pearl Harbour had been squandered. The siege of the Japanese Empire had begun.

Victims of success

There can be little doubt that at any time between 7th December 1941 and 4th June 1942 the Japanese might have secured the victory of the Axis powers, if only they had got their priorities right and been content to do one thing at a time. An all-out search-and-destroy operation against American naval power after Pearl Harbour, culminating in an air and sea bombardment of California, would have made it virtually impossible for the Roosevelt administration to have maintained its policy of 'Germany First'. It would have certainly inhibited the transfer of American tanks and artillery to Africa which made possible the British victories at El Alamein, and thereby prevented the Germans from outflanking the Russian defences from the south. Even a headlong drive across India might have achieved the same end result. But the Japanese were the victims of their own military prowess. They had triumphed beyond all expectation. It was accordingly not surprising if they neglected the precautions necessary in a combat with an adversary whose economic capacity was some sixteen times as great as their own. But one need not be too critical of Japanese strategy. The outcome of the Pacific War, and effectively of the Second World War as a whole, was decided after all in less than five minutes over Midway. And there are many ways in which those minutes might never have happened.

Japanese arms in action

In the wave of conquest which followed Japan's strike southward, four actions were of special significance. A detailed examination of these is important for an understanding of the nature of the Japanese successes and why they should have had such a stunning effect on the world. Two of these were British disasters: the loss of *Prince of Wales* and *Repulse*, and the fall of Singapore; two were tough, fruitless defensive actions by Americans in Wake Island and the Philippines.

The nature of the Japanese offensive which disguised its central objective and dazed ill-prepared opponents was dictated by a number of important considerations. The need to continue the war against China and protect Manchuria from Soviet incursions together with the shortage of merchant shipping necessitated the employment of the same units in successive operations and precluded protracted fighting. Fast moving, surprise attacks, moreover, were essential if the considerable oil, rubber, tin, and bauxite (aluminium ore) resources of South-East Asia and the southwest Pacific were to be seized undamaged at an early stage in the hostilities, which Japan's Naval and General Staffs had timed to avoid the north-east monsoon in the South China Sea and the violent gales in the north Pacific.

Force Z detected

The first American possession to fall to a Japanese invasion force was Guam which capitulated on 10th December after half an hour's resistance. On the same day, the third of the Pacific war, the Japanese invaded the Philippines and seventy-five of their bombers from Saigon sunk the British capital ships *Prince of Wales* and *Repulse* seventy-five nautical miles south-east of Kuantan in eastern Malaya. At 1755 on 8th December the vessels, in company with the destroyers *Electra*, *Express*, *Vampire* and *Tenedos* under the command of Admiral Sir Tom Phillips, had slipped out of Singapore into the misty sunset to forestall further Japanese landings on the northeast coast of Malaya.

Later that evening at 2253, Phillips received a signal from Singapore informing him that fighter cover would not be available when he reached the area. The Japanese

Above: Seven of Wake Island's twelve Grumman Wildcats lie destroyed after a Japanese bombing raid on 8th December 1941. Left: An American soldier gives a dying Japanese captive a drink during bitter fighting on the Bataan Peninsula in the Philippines, March 1942. American and Filipino forces had withdrawn into the peninsula on Luzon for a last ditch stand

Survivors scrambling over the sides of HMS Repulse as she settles into the waters of the South China Sea after being bombed by Japanese aircraft off Malaya on 10th December 1941

had taken Kota Bharu airfield, thus depriving the fleet (code-named Force Z) of one of the basic conditions on which the successful execution of its mission depended. But the British force had the advantage of surprise and Phillips decided to proceed. The following day driving rain and thick, low cloud shrouded Force Z from Japanese air reconnaissance. But at 1700 the weather suddenly cleared to reveal three aircraft observing the fleet and Phillips, who had planned to alter course for Singora at nightfall to shell Japanese transports, was now robbed even of the advantage of surprise.

Although he was unaware that his ships had also been sighted by the Japanese submarine I 65 south of Poulo Condore at 1340, he promptly decided to abandon the mission and turn back. But to confuse the enemy he ordered Force Z, with the exception of *Tenedos*, to continue north until nightfall before altering course south. The heavy guns of the fleet, it appeared, would not be brought to bear on the vulnerable Japanese transports. But at 2400 as the fleet steamed for Singapore, *Prince of Wales* received a message which read: 'Enemy reported landing Kuantan, latitude 03 degrees 50 north.' Force Z, its commander hoped, would still have an opportunity of disrupting the Japanese landings in Malaya and fearful of sacrificing the element of surprise he once more enjoyed, Phillips maintained strict radio silence, assuming incorrectly that fighter cover would be provided when he reached his new objective.

At 0220 the following day, 10th December, a Japanese submarine, I 58, sighted Force Z and between dawn and 0930, seventy-five aircraft took off from Saigon in pursuit of the British fleet which had arrived off Kuantan at 0800 to discover it had answered a false alarm. The detonation of a number of mines in the vicinity of the town by straying water buffaloes had apparently prompted Indian troops to pass the information to Singapore that a Japanese landing was taking place.

Disappointed, Admiral Phillips ordered his fleet back onto a north-easterly course and proceeded to search for a suspicious tug and barges sighted earlier. Half an hour later *Tenedos*, which Phillips had ordered to Singapore when Force Z was discovered by Japanese reconnaissance aircraft, radioed that she was under air attack. Increasing their speed to twenty-five knots the ships of Force Z assumed first degree readiness and raced for base. But a patrolling Japanese reconnaissance aircraft sighted them and put out a general call.

At 1107 aircraft of the Japanese XXII Air Flotilla, which had strayed almost within sight of Singapore in quest of Force Z and which had bombed *Tenedos*, were sighted and at 1119 precisely the high angle guns throughout the fleet began firing at the attackers. Under a barrage of bombs and torpedoes *Repulse* sank at 1233 and as the eleven Buffalo fighters charged with the protection of Force Z arrived at 1320 in response to a belated distress call from Captain W.G.Tennant, commander of *Repulse*, *Prince of Wales* rolled over ponderously to port and sank with Admiral Phillips still on the bridge.

The loss of the two ships with 840 men on board sealed the fate of Malaya and confirmed Japan's command of the Pacific and Indian Oceans for the loss of three aircraft. 'Over all this vast expanse of water Japan was supreme, and we everywhere were weak and naked,' wrote Churchill. On the day after the action, a Japanese aircraft dropped a large bouquet of flowers over the sea in honour of the men who had died.

Wake spits back
There was no respite for the Allies. The exultant Japanese kept on hitting. But for two weeks the defenders of a lonely, treeless atoll in the central Pacific held a powerful invasion fleet at bay, subjecting the victory-flushed Japanese navy to its only defeat in the opening months of the war. Wake Island, annexed by the United States in 1899 and later developed as an aircraft staging post, belonged with Makin and Tarawa in the Gilbert Islands to a group of objectives Japan required if she was to secure the eastern boundary of her defence perimeter. On the outbreak of war, the island's occupants comprised seventy civilian employees of Pan American Airways, 1,146 civilians employed by contractors and a garrison of 449 marines, sixty-eight sailors, and five soldiers. Major James Devereux of the United States Marine Corps who effectively commanded the garrison had at his disposal six 5-inch coast defence guns, twelve 3-inch anti-aircraft guns, a number of machine-guns, besides twelve obsolete Grumman Wildcats of Marine Fighting Squadron 211 flown in from the *Enterprise* on 4th December. Not only did the island lack two-thirds of its garrison, it had no radar, fighter control centre, or fire control equipment. There were, moreover, no mines, no barbed wire, and no revetments for aircraft.

On 8th December, under cover of rain squalls, thirty-six Japanese bombers swept in over Wake and destroyed seven Wildcats on the ground. Air attacks continued on the following two days and on the 11th at 0500 the invasion forces composed of the light cruisers *Yubari*, *Tenryu*, and *Tatsuta* with six destroyers and accompanying vessels under the command of Rear-Admiral Sadamichi Kajioka steamed in, guns blazing to assault the island. Major Devereux held his fire. Contemptuous of the atoll's defences, Kajioka took his invasion fleet to within 4,500 yards of the shore. Suddenly, Devereux's 5-inch guns opened up and with their second salvo damaged the flagship *Yubari*. Within the first few minutes the island's 5-inch batteries sank the destroyer *Hayate* and damaged several other ships. Four of the five surviving Wildcats then took off to bomb and strafe the fleet, damaging the light cruisers *Tenryu* and *Tatsuta* and sinking the destroyer *Kisavagi*. It was one of the most humiliating reverses the Japanese navy had ever suffered and soon after 0700 Kajioka retreated to Kwajalein six hundred miles away to lick his wounds. Wake Island's few guns and aircraft had repulsed a powerful amphibious attack, sunk two destroyers, damaged several other vessels and inflicted some 700 fatalities on the invaders for the loss of two Wildcats.

Alarmed by this ignominious rebuff at Wake, Admiral Yamamoto, Commander-in-Chief of the Combined Fleet, ordered reinforcements to assemble for a second landing attempt and on 15th December Rear-Admiral Tamon Yamaguchi's II Carrier Division with the aircraft carriers *Soryu* and *Hiryu* escorted by four destroyers proceeded to a position north of the island. Accompanying the carrier force was Rear-Admiral Abe's VIII Cruiser Division with the heavy cruisers *Tone* and *Chikuma*. While the powerful invasion fleet assembled off Wake, the island was subjected to a series of attacks by land-based bombers and on the 21st aircraft from the carriers lent their weight to the bombardments. On the same day Kajioka again sailed from Kwajalein and before dawn on 23rd December, with no preliminary bombardment, substantially reinforced troops of the naval landing force began to pour ashore at points on which the American 5-inch guns could not be brought to bear. The only gun trained on the two antiquated destroyers, which had been beached with companies of the landing force, put fifteen shells into the nearest one, breaking its back. Without air support, its last two Wildcats having been shot down the previous day, the island's defences were pounded by aircraft and naval guns and at 0730, heavily outnumbered, the garrison surrendered. Fifty-two American servicemen, seventy civilians and 820 Japanese soldiers were killed during the bitterly contested landings, and 470 officers and men and 1,146 civilians were captured. The navy had vindicated itself for its initial

failure to take the island and the gallant American defenders, despite their defeat, earned the admiration of the world.

Singapore surrenders

Yet Wake might have been saved and a naval victory scored had Rear-Admiral Frank Fletcher's carrier-borne aircraft intervened while the Japanese invasion force was still disembarking equipment and supplies. Fletcher, who left Pearl Harbour for Wake on 17th December with a relief force which included the aircraft-carrier *Saratoga*, lost his chance of preventing the Japanese landings by pausing to refuel his destroyers. Although he could have caught the invasion fleet at a disadvantage he was ordered back to base for fear of risking his vessels in an encounter with those units detached from the Pearl Harbour Striking Force which were believed to contain two battleships.

While Wake defied the wrath of the Japanese navy, and American and Filipino troops were being driven into the Bataan Peninsula, the Japanese invasion of Malaya was proceeding swiftly. Its extent, once appreciated, spread demoralization among the confused British and Commonwealth forces. Without either command of the sea or air they fell back down the west coast of Malaya before Lieutenant-General Yamashita's XXV Army until they reeled into Singapore on 31st January. At 1810 on 15th February 1942, Lieutenant-General Arthur Percival, GOC Malaya, surrendered the town to Yamashita in a room in the Ford factory at Bukit Timah. It was the greatest disaster inflicted on the British Empire since Cornwallis surrendered Yorktown in the American War of Independence, and Churchill termed the fall of what was considered to be an impregnable fortress, 'the worst disaster and largest capitulation in British history'.

In the Malayan campaign, lost by the failure to provide adequate defence in the north, British, Indian and Australian forces lost a total of 138,708 soldiers of whom more than 130,000 were taken prisoner. The Japanese casualties in the seventy-three day campaign were 3,507 dead and 6,150 wounded.

It had been General Percival's misfortune, as James Leasor has written in *Singapore, The Battle That Changed The World*, to 'direct an ill-equipped and wrongly-trained army in a hopeless campaign; to defend a country for whose defence pre-war politicians influenced and activated by blind, petty motivations and crass ignorance, by indifference on the part of the voters who had elected them, had neglected to pay the insurance premium.' The humiliation of Great Britain at the hands of a numerically inferior Asiatic army that rode on bicycles and lived on rice was to have fateful consequences for the Far East.

The capture of Singapore, 'the bastion of the Empire' and the consequent premature collapse of Europe's hegemony in South East Asia after the war created a power vacuum which Communism struggled desperately to fill.

Bataan Death March

The fall of Malaya and Singapore led directly to the collapse of the Dutch East Indies. Burma was overrun within weeks and the Japanese tide swept on to the Indian frontier. For the United States, the military outlook was as bleak and on 6th May, after a desperate defence of the Bataan Peninsula and Corregidor Island, which humiliated General Homma's XIV Army and delayed Japanese victory for four months, American and Filipino resistance ended. Morale among the diseased, undernourished men had slumped when with the departure of General MacArthur, Commander-in-Chief United States Army Forces in the Far East, on 12th March, it became evident that reinforcements could not be expected. However, before handing over his command and leaving for Australia at Roosevelt's insistence, MacArthur promised the Filipinos that one day he would return to redeem the pledge of complete independence by 1946 which the American government had given eight years earlier. Just over a month after he left, the 64,000 Filipinos and 12,000 Americans who had surrendered on Bataan, began a fifty-five mile march from Mariveles to San Fernando. Because the Japanese had only expected to take some 25,000 prisoners, their arrangements for transporting and feeding the captives broke down. Between 7,000 and 10,000 men, including 2,330 Americans died of disease, starvation, exhaustion or brutality on what became known as the Bataan Death March.

It revealed the contempt the Japanese reserved for enemy soldiers who had not fallen in battle and foreshadowed the barbarous treatment Allied prisoners would receive at Japanese hands throughout the Pacific War.

Japan was everywhere victorious and the Allies everywhere in defeat or disarray. Yet prior to the outbreak of the Pacific War the strength of Japan's armed forces had been gravely underrated, ignored or even disbelieved. It was popularly supposed that, preoccupied with China, she was unable to mount military operations elsewhere. But although the allocation of forty divisions and 800 aircraft to the defence of Japan, Korea, Manchuria, and occupied China only left eleven divisions and some 700 first-line aircraft for the other theatres of war, Japan was able to reduce the whole vast south seas region. The myth of Japanese inferiority was promptly replaced by the myth of Japanese invincibility.

4 THE TIDE TURNS

Alamein

General Sir Claude Auchinleck, Commander-in-Chief Middle East Land Forces, took over personal command of 8th Army from Lieutenant-General Neil Ritchie on 25th June 1942. There is little doubt that Auchinleck had been ill-judged in February 1942 when he confirmed Ritchie in what had been a temporary command, despite evidence and advice that Ritchie lacked the experience and capacity to command an army. Equally it would have been well if Auchinleck, as Prime Minister Churchill had urged, had taken personal charge of the Gazala battles at an early stage. However, the Western Desert was only one among the commander-in-chief's several cares. It was not so simple a matter to go off and look after a single front. For although the Middle East Command had shed East Africa since Wavell's time, it was still responsible for support of Turkey, a neutral state, and for the defence of the Persian Gulf oilfields from attack from the north, through the Caucasus. Auchinleck had lived with this latter danger ever since the German invasion of Russia had reached the Don the previous autumn.

Auchinleck, therefore, unlike his predecessors or his successor, bore the double burden of an army commander and of a theatre commander-in-chief.

For this reason it was Auchinleck's belief as commander-in-chief that 8th Army must not be exposed to the risk of a final defeat, but must at all cost be kept in being,

Left: A German Hanomag half-track of the Afrika Korps rolls across the soft sand of the desert. The number plate prefix means 'Wehrmacht Heer', indicating an Army vehicle

in order to continue to defend the Gulf oil from Rommel. Whereas Ritchie had planned a do-or-die battle at Mersa Matruh, Auchinleck wished to retreat to El Alamein which would give him a little time to reorganize his forces and plan his own battle instead of fighting Ritchie's. But Rommel struck the day after Auchinleck assumed personal command. The Battle of Mersa Matruh (26th-28th June 1942), fought in decayed defences according to Ritchie's deployment, marked the climax of German moral domination in the desert. With handfuls of exhausted troops Rommel bluffed the British (including fresh, strong formations) into thinking they were broken through, surrounded, and beaten, while poor communications virtually cut Auchinleck off from the battle. As soon as he saw the compromised battle was lost, Auchinleck ordered the army back to Alamein. Both armies, units all mixed up, raced each other for the forty-mile-wide neck between the sea at Alamein and the impassable Qattara Depression. Alexandria lay only sixty miles beyond.

Although 8th Army narrowly won the race, the British still faced the possibility, in Auchinleck's words, of 'complete catastrophe'. 'No one,' he wrote later, 'least of all I, could say whether the Army could be rallied and re-formed soon enough to hold Rommel and save Egypt.' Auchinleck thus faced the greatest test of a general – the rallying of a beaten army and the redemption of a lost battle. Behind him in Egypt there was panic and defeatism. He told his soldiers: 'The enemy is stretching to his limit and thinks we are a broken army . . . He hopes to take Egypt by bluff. Show him where he gets off.'

In fact this was an accurate military appreciation. By failing to halt after Tobruk to allow Malta to be attacked, as agreed, Rommel had taken an immense gamble. For unless he managed to break through to the Delta very quickly, his army would be increasingly starved of supplies, reinforcements, and fuel, owing both to British naval action based on Malta and the length of his own communications. On 1st July, three days after Matruh, Rommel attacked 8th Army at Alamein.

The essential unity of all the fighting at Alamein from July to November 1942 has been obscured by the changes in the British command that took place in mid-August, when General Sir Harold Alexander replaced Auchinleck as commander-in-chief and Lieutenant-General B.L.Montgomery became the new 8th Army commander. It was one extended battle with pauses between the actions. It opened with Rommel's desperate attempts to shoulder his way past Auchinleck, his failure, and the failure in turn of Auchinleck to force him into retreat. This was the First Battle of Alamein (1st-26th July 1942). There followed a period of stalemate broken only by an unrealistic and vain second attempt by Rommel to break through: the Battle of Alam Halfa (31st August-3rd September). Finally came the British counter-stroke with massive fresh forces that swept Rommel out of Egypt. This was Montgomery's victory in the Second Battle of Alamein (23rd October-4th November 1942).

The commanding natural features of the Alamein battlefield (although so slight as to be discernible only to the military eye) were two east-west ridges, the Ruweisat

The Tide Turns

Ridge, and farther to the south and well to the east, the Alam Halfa Ridge. These were the tactical keys to the neck of land between the sea and the Qattara Depression. At no time in the Alamein battles was this neck solidly held by the British. In July Auchinleck had lacked the troops, and later he (and after him Montgomery) preferred to form a south-facing left wing that might entice Rommel into a trap.

Auchinleck's army at First Alamein was made up of survivors of the Gazala battles like 1st South African and 50th Divisions, survivors of Matruh like the New Zealand divisions and 9th Indian Brigade, together with fresh troops like 18th Indian Brigade from Iraq. Auchinleck was weakest in armour, for although 1st Armoured Division possessed 150 tanks, only two squadrons were Grants, and the division's skill, cohesion, and morale were not high. Nevertheless 8th Army heavily outnumbered Panzer Army Africa, now reduced to 60 German and 30 Italian tanks, some 5,000 Germans, and a similar number of Italians.

As a personal adviser and acting chief of staff in the field Auchinleck had brought with him from Cairo Major-General E. Dorman-Smith. He was not a member of the British army 'establishment' who had muddled the Gazala battles, but a man fertile in unorthodox ideas. These were reflected in some of the reforms Auchinleck attempted to carry out in the army's organization and tactics during First Ala-

mein. Auchinleck believed that the standard British infantry division was too large, cumbersome, and lacking in hitting power for mobile desert warfare. He therefore extemporized brigade-groups or smaller 'battle-groups' on the German pattern— trucked infantry escorting guns. Instead of manning the static defences of the Alamein perimeter, he kept the brigade-groups of 1st South African Division mobile in the open desert to the south. After the first day's fighting he also evacuated two 'boxes' in the centre and extreme south of the Alamein neck, in order to keep his army mobile and concentrated. (Boxes were strongpoints surrounded by wire and minefields.) At the same time the heavy and medium artillery was transferred from corps to army command to provide massed firepower. Auchinleck also tried to diminish the sluggishness and rigidity of the stratified British command organization by demanding the energetic local initiative and flexibility evinced by the enemy. The course of the First Battle of Alamein was to show that orders or instructions in this spirit failed to have much effect on minds habituated to another military tradition.

Although First Alamein was a highly complicated and shifting battle on the ground, it was essentially a struggle of will between the opposing generals. The struggle lasted for the first two weeks of July and ended with Rommel's surrender of the initiative to Auchinleck.

On 1st July Rommel tried to repeat his triumph at Mersa Matruh with a similar plan and similar audacity. He proposed to drive through Auchinleck's centre and turn outwards in a double envelopment of Auchinleck's wings. Both envelopments stuck under heavy flanking-fire from British battle-groups. On 2nd July Rommel reduced his plan to a single envelopment of the Alamein perimeter. This too failed. On 3rd July he tried again in the centre, made some progress, and stuck again, despite his own personal leadership of the attack. On 2nd and again on 5th July Auchinleck counter-attacked elsewhere, forcing Rommel to re-group, but 8th Army proved a slow and hesitant instrument. However, Rommel was forced to deploy Italian infantry for the first time since he attacked at Gazala. Nevertheless he decided to attack again on 10th July, after a brief respite, and try to break straight through eastwards into the Delta. Instead, on 9th July Auchinleck launched a major-counterstroke in the coastal sector: a bombardment that reminded some Germans of the Western Front in 1917, followed by an assault by Auchinleck's personal reserve, the fresh 9th Australian Division. The Italians collapsed, the hill of Tel el Eisa fell, and Rommel had to abandon his own

Wreckage of a German Junkers 52.
Rommel's supply planes were shot down
in droves crossing the Mediterranean

offensive in order to succour the Italians.

It was Auchinleck's plan (suggested by Dorman-Smith) to go for the Italians in one sector after another, thus forcing Rommel to run to and fro to their aid with his Germans. It worked brilliantly. Between 9th and 16th July six such attacks on Italians were launched, and Rommel only prevented the total collapse of his front by using his last German reserves.

On 21st-22nd July and 26th July Auchinleck attempted to turn Rommel's defeat into his destruction or retreat. These counter-strokes were a total failure. The cause lay yet again in the gulf of misunderstanding between British armour and infantry, which were incapable of the supple and intimate co-operation of the German troops who were trained together on common lines. A further cause lay in a breakdown of radio communication. Either the infantry was massacred by German armour because the British armour failed to come up in time; or the armour was massacred trying to 'charge' German defences that should have been carefully assaulted in conjunction with infantry.

Although Rommel had not been forced to retreat, First Alamein saved Egypt and the Middle East. It was one of the decisive battles of the Second World War.

It was Dorman-Smith's prediction, expressed in a strategic appreciation of 27th July accepted by Auchinleck, that Rommel even after reinforcement would not be strong enough to launch another offensive except as a gamble. Auchinleck therefore looked ahead to a set-piece British offensive in strength some time in September.

Meanwhile the British and American governments had taken a major strategical decision. Instead of an invasion of France in 1942, deemed a hopeless undertaking with the available troops and landing craft, the Allies were to invade French North Africa in the autumn, and, in conjunction with 8th Army, clear the entire North African coast. This operation would both re-open the Mediterranean to through sea traffic and appease Stalin with some kind of a 'second front' at not too great a risk of failure. The decision was made on 24th July, after Auchinleck had halted Rommel's offensive. It entirely changed the context of the war in the desert, for occupation of Algeria and Tunisia would directly threaten Rommel's own base at Tripoli and squeeze him between two armies.

Churchill visits the front

On 3rd August Churchill and the Chief of the Imperial General Staff arrived in Cairo. On 6th August, after visiting Auchinleck at 8th Army Headquarters, Churchill decided to replace Auchinleck and his immediate staff. General Sir Harold Alexander was appointed commander-in-chief, and Major-General W.H.E. Gott, a corps commander with a legendary though not altogether justified reputation, was appointed to command 8th Army. In these decisions personal political considerations undoubtedly played a large part. There was mounting public criticism of Churchill's leadership in Great Britain, and by-elections had gone heavily against the government. There had been a long run of disaster: the loss of the *Prince of Wales* and *Repulse,* the fall of Singapore, the loss of Burma, the loss of Tobruk, the Gazala battles. Churchill needed a resounding victory as quickly as possible to preserve his own position. There can be little doubt that Auchinleck therefore sealed his fate when he stubbornly refused to promise to attack before mid-September, arguing that this was the earliest that 8th Army could be re-organized and re-trained, and the new equipment run in.

Churchill instructed the new Commander-in-Chief Middle East, General Alexander, that his primary task was 'to take and destroy the German-Italian army commanded by Field-Marshal Rommel.' The commander-in-chief was relieved of anxiety about the German threat from the Caucasus (the German offensive in Russia poured across the Don into the Caucasus on 24th July, in the last days of First Alamein), for Iraq and Persia were transferred to a new command. Thus in the end all the vast existing resources of the Middle East base, and the immense reinforcements and supplies now flowing into Egypt had come to be devoted to the single purpose of fighting four somewhat neglected German divisions and their Italian allies. It was a measure of the success of the German diversion in North Africa, and also of the usefulness of the British Empire's contribution to ground fighting in the third year of the war. The Red Army was currently engaging some 180 German divisions, including twenty Panzer divisions.

Alexander's sole responsibility was therefore to support his 8th Army commander. On 7th August, however, Gott was killed, when the aircraft flying him to Cairo was shot down, and Lieutenant-General Montgomery was appointed commander of 8th Army. Montgomery was a man of legendary eccentricity and ruthless professionalism. He had not commanded in the field since 1940, had never commanded large masses of armour in battle, and was new to the desert. He compensated for these initial handicaps by a brilliant clarity of mind, iron willpower, and a bleak realism about the potentialities of individuals and units alike. He had an unrivalled power of piercing complex matters to the underlying simplicities. In August 1942 he enjoyed the advantage of the new broom, and he swept very clean indeed.

His first task was to meet the renewed German offensive which was expected soon. His plan, like that evolved by Auchinleck and Dorman-Smith, depended on forming a south-facing left wing along the Alam Halfa Ridge, and his main dispositions followed the existing defences and minefields. However, he brought up 44th Division, now available, to strengthen Alam Halfa. Although his general plan so closely resembled Auchinleck's, his style of fighting the battle was very different. He accurately took the measure of 8th Army's capabilities and enforced his own direct control right down to division level. It would be in his own words 'an army battle'. There would be no loose fighting, but a tight defence of tactical ground.

Rommel launched his offensive on 31st August 1942. It was, as Dorman-Smith had predicted in July, a gamble without much chance. Rommel had 203 tanks against 767 British; he himself and several senior officers were sick; and his army was so short of fuel that it had to make a tight turn up to the Alam Halfa Ridge instead of outflanking it to the east. After four days of vain effort to pierce the British defences while under violent air attack he slowly withdrew. An attempt by the New Zealand Division to endanger his retreat broke down in the usual 8th Army muddles and misunderstandings. Except for this failure Montgomery's first battle had been entirely successful. He was free to continue preparing his own offensive.

Alexander like Auchinleck was strongly pressed by the Prime Minister for an early offensive. He and Montgomery, with the advantage of being new men who could not be sacked, also refused. They, like Auchinleck, realized that an immense amount of training and preparation was needed before 8th Army would be fit to attack. In fact the Second Battle of Alamein opened on 23rd October, and even then 8th Army was by no means up to German standards.

The chronic problem lay in the inability of the British armour and infantry to work closely together. It originated in peacetime, when the British failed to evolve a coherent doctrine of tank warfare, but instead divided ground war into two separate compartments—the infantry battle of positions, and the (almost) all-tank mobile battle. Just before his departure Auchinleck had proposed to re-model the whole 8th Army into German-style mixed tank-infantry divisions. Co-operation would be secured under a single divisional command. Montgomery and his advisers instead decided to form a special wholly armoured corps (10th) in addition to the existing 30th and 13th Corps, charged with fighting a tank battle and then exploiting in pursuit. Thus co-ordination of armour and infantry would not now be secured by

The Tide Turns

divisional commanders, or corps commanders as hitherto, but by the army commander himself. The course of Second Alamein was to show that Montgomery also failed even by this scheme to solve the problem of armour and infantry.

Second Battle of Alamein

In planning his offensive Montgomery faced what was for the desert a novel problem. Rommel had created a continuous defence system across the forty-mile-wide neck between the sea and the Qattara Depression. It was of the standard German pattern dating back to 1917 — a maze of strongpoints and switchlines, protected by belts of wire, in minefields some 2½ to 4½ miles deep, and garrisoned by intermingled German and Italian infantry. Close behind lay the Panzer divisions. To this Western Front problem Montgomery produced a Western Front answer — a deliberate infantry attack under cover of a massive bombardment to drive a gap right through both the forward and main battle zones of the enemy defence system. The 10th Corps (armour) would then pass through this gap on to the enemy communications and fight and defeat the Panzer divisions. Montgomery recognized however that the skill and training of 8th Army was such that any 'mixing it' with the Panzer Army in the open would be risky. He therefore altered his plan to make it even more deliberate and methodical. The armour would merely defend the gap made in the enemy defences against counter-strokes, while behind its shield the defence system and its infantry garrison would be 'crumbled' away piecemeal. This Montgomery hoped would force the Panzer divisions to attack to try to save the infantry and expose themselves to defeat by British tanks and anti-tank guns fighting defensively.

For the battle Montgomery fielded 1,029 tanks against 496 (220 German); 1,451 anti-tank guns against 550 German and 300 Italian; 908 field and medium guns against 200 German and 300 Italian (plus 18 heavy howitzers); 85 infantry battalions against 31 German and 40 Italian. The overall odds were about two to one: 195,000 men against just over 100,000. For the first time the British anti-tank artillery was principally composed of powerful six-pounders, while the armour included 252 American Shermans, tanks at last really the equal of German equipment. The British enjoyed complete air superiority.

The Second Battle of Alamein fell into three phases. During 23rd-25th October the original plan of breaking clean through the German left centre failed. The infantry assault, instead of piercing the German defence system in one bound as ordered, spent its force in the German forward zone and stalled in the battle zone. Mont-

gomery ordered 10th Corps (armour) to force its own breakthrough, then modified his order to one armoured regiment; but the armour too became bogged down in the German defences. The super-imposition of two corps (10th and 30th) on the same sector caused much confusion. In the second phase of the battle (26th-31st October) Montgomery re-made his plan of operations and got a stalled offensive on the move again by sheer force of will. In this phase divisional attacks 'crumbled' the Axis defences away, while Rommel's counter-strokes (he had returned from a hospital bed in Austria to take command) foundered under air attack and anti-tank fire. In the third phase (1st-4th November) Montgomery (who had patiently re-created a reserve) launched a second massive breakthrough attempt. After fierce fighting and heavy loss the British this time succeeded. An order from Hitler to stand fast delayed the Axis retreat for twenty-four hours, and then the Panzer Army streamed west in defeat.

Second Alamein, like the battles of 1917, had turned on the size of reserves available to both sides. Although the Panzer Army had consistently inflicted a higher rate of loss on the British throughout the battle (the British lost more tanks than the original total German strength), the British superiority in resources proved just too great. Yet it had been a near-run battle for the exhaustion and confusion of 8th Army prevented immediate and effective pursuit.

Nevertheless the Panzer Army had been shattered: most of the Italian infantry were captured (some 26,000) and only 36 German tanks remained in action.

Because of the late pursuit, the British failed to cut off and destroy the remnants of Rommel's army. There followed a long pursuit and retreat back to Rommel's old bolt-hole of El Agheila characterized by bluff on Rommel's part and caution on Montgomery's—perhaps understandable in view of Rommel's reputation.

Meanwhile the Anglo-American landings in North Africa (Operation Torch) had taken place on 8th November. 'This,' wrote Rommel, 'spelt the end of the army in Africa.'

Left: 1 Montgomery, wearing Australian hat, discusses military situation with officers of 22nd Armoured Brigade in August 1942, soon after taking command of 8th Army. 2 Painting by British war artist Anthony Gross of desert casualties. 3 A barbed-wire fence is lifted to enable Rommel (striding ahead) to pass through to inspect units of the Afrika Korps. Rommel acquired a legendary reputation extending far beyond North Africa, among Germans and Allies alike

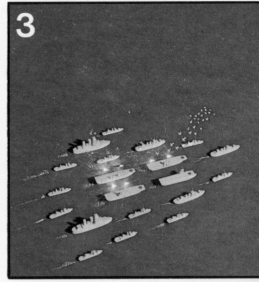

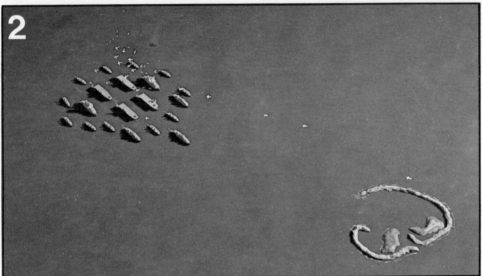

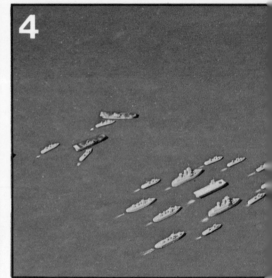

The course of the fleets

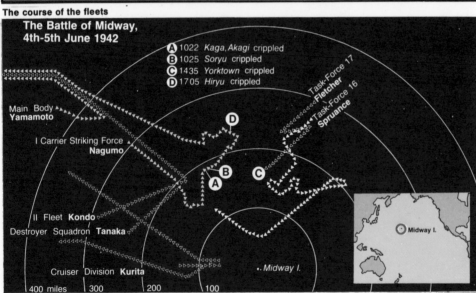

**The Battle of Midway,
4th-5th June 1942**

Ⓐ 1022 *Kaga, Akagi* crippled
Ⓑ 1025 *Soryu* crippled
Ⓒ 1435 *Yorktown* crippled
Ⓓ 1705 *Hiryu* crippled

Task-Force 17
Fletcher
Task-Force 16
Spruance

Main Body
Yamamoto

I Carrier Striking Force
Nagumo

II Fleet **Kondo**

Destroyer Squadron **Tanaka**

Cruiser Division **Kurita**

·. *Midway I.*

○ Midway I.

400 miles   300   200   100

For many years Japanese naval strategists had prepared for a 'decisive fleet action' with the Americans in the Pacific and at Midway in early June 1942 they hoped to destroy the surviving vessels of the US Pacific Fleet in such an encounter. Admiral Yamamoto, Commander-in-Chief of the Combined Fleet, was convinced that a threat to Midway, and therefore to Hawaii, would compel the weak enemy fleet to challenge overwhelming Japanese forces under whose guns and bombs, he imagined, it could not survive. He also planned to seize Midway as an advance air base and assault the western Aleutians to distract American forces from his central objective, that of eliminating US naval power in the Pacific.

But the Japanese were arrogant and over-confident, scattering their forces in a defective, diffuse, and over-complicated operational plan which, through a singular feat of code-breaking, was known to the US Navy. Moreover, they reckoned without the skill and self-sacrifice of a handful of American pilots.

1: At 0430, 107 Japanese torpedo-bombers, dive-bombers, and fighters are launched from the carriers *Kaga, Akagi, Soryu,* and *Hiryu* of I Carrier Striking Force. At 0634 they attack Midway. Of twenty-five fighters sent up to oppose them, only two survive.

2: Twenty-six Midway-based dive-bombers, torpedo-bombers, and bombers swoop on the Japanese carriers at 0705. They fail to score a single hit. Only nine aircraft return. A strike by eleven slower dive-bombers at 0817 proves similarly ineffective and costly.

3: Thirty-five dive-bombers led by Lieutenant-Commanders Leslie and McClusky from Task Forces 16 and 17 *(Yorktown* and *Enterprise)* pounce on *Akagi, Soryu,* and *Kaga* at 1025 and cripple them. The carriers, their decks crowded with aircraft, had not detected the approaching Americans as they had been pre-occupied with mauling a force of forty-one unescorted American torpedo-bombers.

4: At 1435 sixteen Japanese dive-bombers and fighters from *Hiryu* launch a second strike on *Yorktown* (Task Force 17), dooming it. Only seven aircraft survive the raid. Fire-racked *Akagi* and *Soryu* drift aimlessly.

5: Shortly after 1700 twenty-four dive-bombers from

Midway

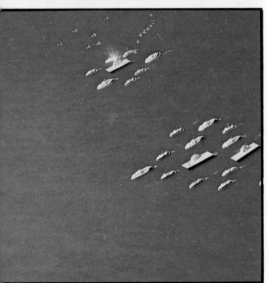

Task Force 16 attack *Hiryu*. Four bombs land near the bridge and cripple the carrier. *Yorktown*, dead in the water, is attended by her screening force.

The course of the fleets: fleet movement between 2400 on 3rd June and 2400 on 4th June. Apart from *Mikuma* of Kurita's Cruiser Division which was attacked by Midway-based bombers on 5th June, the remaining forces took no part in the action. Yamamoto's Main Body cruised hundreds of miles from the carriers, depriving them of anti-aircraft protection and him of any opportunity for night action. *Soryu* sank at 1913 and *Kaga* at 1925. *Akagi* was scuttled at 0455 on 5th June and at approximately 0915 *Hiryu* went down. *Yorktown*, which remained afloat, was torpedoed by a Japanese submarine on 6th June

After 1918 the Japanese navy regarded the United States as its most probable enemy, and consequently maintained an up-to-date and highly trained fleet. To a dispassionate observer, however, it was clear that Japan's geographical position, the size of her armed forces, and above all the disparity between her total resources and those of the United States gave her a poor chance of victory in any war with America.

But when war between the two countries became inevitable in 1941 the Japanese navy, for all its slender hopes of success, found itself in the front rank confronting the American navy.

The dilemma facing the strategists of the Imperial Japanese Headquarters was that until the occupation of the southern territories with their vast resources was completed they neither wanted to face an attack from the American fleet, nor entanglement in a protracted war. Although the Japanese navy and US Pacific Fleet were more or less evenly balanced in 1941, the Japanese had a greater number of aircraft-carriers, and because of the demands of the 'China Incident', the JNAF possessed pilots who were both experienced and highly trained. But it was certain that these advantages would promptly be nullified if America mobilized her massive productive strength and directed it to wartime production. What would happen, it was asked, if America was to wait until her crushingly superior forces were fully equipped, and then attempt to decide the issue with a single attack on Japan? To eliminate this possibility it was necessary, by a positive and continuous offensive, to force America into decisive battles at an early date, to destroy the main strength of her fleet, and to build up 'conditions for protracted warfare from an invincible position' by turning the resources of the southern territories to military purposes.

It was from this standpoint, too, that Admiral Isoroku Yamamoto, Commander-in-Chief of the Combined Fleet, planned the attack on Pearl Harbour in December 1941, and persuaded the Naval General Staff, who had opposed the plan as being too risky, to accept it.

Yamamoto stands firm
Possible future objectives the following year included Australia, Ceylon, Hawaii, Fiji, and Samoa but opinions differed as to the advisability of selecting targets among

Left: The course of the fleets during the Battle of Midway. The battle restored the balance between the American and Japanese navies in the Pacific

them. Moreover, the army was inclined to favour a withdrawal of land forces to Manchuria after the operations in the south in order to take the opportunity of combining with the German army in a double attack on Russia. Since it showed no enthusiasm for expanding the war on the Pacific front, and was hesitant about providing troops, plans for the second phase of the war had to be kept within the bounds of what naval forces alone could accomplish.

Yamamoto's plan for the Midway operation was put before the General Staff at the beginning of April, when discussions about strategy for the second phase of the war were already in their final stages. The primary object of the operation was to lure out and then destroy the US Pacific Fleet. This was to be achieved by attacking and occupying the solitary Pacific island of Midway, which served as an outpost for Hawaii, thus quickly forcing America into a major battle. At the same time it was planned to extend the defence perimeter in anticipation of American air attacks on the Japanese mainland by occupying the Aleutian Islands.

The Naval General Staff also accepted that it was desirable to involve the United States in a decisive battle as soon as possible, but it did not consider Midway, so close to Hawaii, an advantageous location for a major battle, or a suitable area into which to lure the American aircraft-carriers. It strongly advocated cutting the lines of communication between the United States and Australia by advancing on Fiji and Samoa which were about the same distance away as the Japanese outpost of Truk in the Caroline Islands. Nor were the Naval General Staff the only opponents of the Midway operation. II Fleet, which was to support the occupation forces, was opposed to it on the grounds that it was not ready; IV Fleet, which was to look after the logistical problems following the occupation, objected to it on the grounds that it could not be confident of fulfilling this role even if the operation was successful. In particular, I Air Fleet, which had arrived back in Japan in the middle of April following operations in the Indian Ocean, was anxious to postpone the operation so as to allow some time for rest and re-equipment.

But Admiral Yamamoto was firm in his resolution and the Naval General Staff eventually gave in to the Combined Fleet, as it had done before.

Just at this point, on 18th April, sixteen B-25 Mitchell bombers, led by Lieutenant-Colonel James Doolittle, took off from Vice-

1 Japanese Mitsubishi Zero fighter. During the Battle of Midway Zeros swept away attacks on their aircraft-carriers, slaughtering the lumbering Devastators of Torpedo Squadron 8. In the early part of the war the Zero was faster and more manoeuvrable than any opposing Allied aircraft. 2 Admiral Chester W.Nimitz, Commander-in-Chief US Pacific Fleet. He concluded correctly that Japan's objectives were Midway and the Aleutians and he decided to concentrate all his forces on the defence of Midway. 3 Devastators of Torpedo Squadron 6

Admiral Halsey's aircraft-carriers *Enterprise* and *Hornet* and carried out a surprise bombing attack on Tokyo. Damage was slight, but the psychological shock of this first air-raid on Japan itself was very great, and when the case for extending the defence perimeter to Midway and the Aleutians was again proposed, this time much more strongly, opposition to it melted away at once. Preparations for a major assault by almost the whole of the Japanese navy went forward with all speed, and the army, until now a mere onlooker, contributed one infantry regiment.

The second phase of the war was to proceed with the occupation of Port Moresby in early May, the occupation of Midway and the Aleutians in early June, and the occupation of New Caledonia, Fiji, and Samoa in July. On the 5th May Imperial General Headquarters ordered the occupation of Midway and the Aleutians.

Unlearned lessons

The forces taking part were almost the full strength of the Combined Fleet, including eleven battleships, eight aircraft-carriers, twenty-one cruisers and more than 200 other ships, together with 500 planes and 6,000 marines and soldiers. The plan was for this vast fleet to set out at different times and from different places in either nine or eleven groups with the

object of attacking and occupying Midway and the Aleutians.

From some points of view this plan was a subtle and artistic one, but at the same time it revealed characteristic shortcomings in the Japanese navy, and Admiral Chester Nimitz, Commander-in-Chief of the US Pacific Fleet, later criticized it for both attempting to lure the US Pacific Fleet into a decisive battle and seeking the occupation of Midway. He also criticized the multiplicity of divisions within the forces needed to execute it. Admiral Yamamoto, Commander-in-Chief of the Combined Fleet, who had overall command of the operation, was to be aboard the newly-constructed Combined Fleet flagship *Yamato*, the world's biggest battleship, in company with eight battleships drawn from the Main Body of the Main Force, the Main Force's Guard Force, and Rear-Admiral Abe's Support Group. They were to advance 600 nautical miles (this was later revised to 300 nautical miles) behind Nagumo's I Carrier Striking Force. As *Yamato* was obliged to maintain strict radio silence, it was hardly to be expected that there could be adequate leadership. Yamamoto was well-known as the foster-father of the Naval Air Corps, and had been quick to attach great importance to aircraft and aircraft-carriers. His foresight had already been proved by Japanese suc-

cesses in the opening days of the war. But now Yamamoto was compromising with the conservative advocates of the big ships and the big guns, possibly with the idea of letting the battleship fleet have some of the glory for the expected victory.

The main striking power undoubtedly lay with Vice-Admiral Nagumo's I Carrier Striking Force consisting of the aircraft-carriers *Akagi, Kaga, Soryu,* and *Hiryu* and whether or not the task-force was successful it seemed unlikely that there would be any opportunity to use the battleships' big guns, with their maximum range of forty nautical miles. In fact the young officers of Nagumo's force suggested sarcastically that the battleship fleet was going to hold a naval review in the Pacific. It is now accepted that, mainly due to the relaxed atmosphere resulting from Japan's string of initial victories and an underestimation of the enemy's strength, secrecy was not strictly maintained, intelligence reports were inadequate, instructions were not followed as carefully as they should have been, and tactical preparations in general were insufficient and left too late.

April's operations in the Indian Ocean together with the Battle of the Coral Sea in May had provided a number of valuable lessons about the weaknesses of reconnaissance work and aircraft-carrier vulnerability which should have been taken

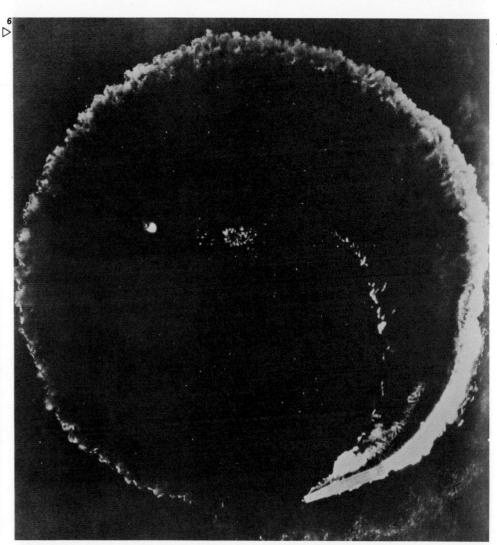

prepare to take off from Enterprise. *Only four came back. But the torpedo squadrons from* Yorktown *and* Hornet *suffered even greater losses.* **4** *Rear-Admiral Raymond A.Spruance, commander of Task Force 16. He decided to time his attack for the moment when the Japanese aircraft would have returned from Midway.* **5** *Admiral Isoroku Yamamoto, Commander-in-Chief Combined Fleet. By attacking Midway he wanted to lure out and destroy the US Pacific Fleet.* **6** Soryu *makes a full circle at high speed in an attempt to evade attack*

into consideration as a matter of course when the Midway operation was planned, but which, in fact, were largely ignored. A particularly interesting point was that the Battle of the Coral Sea was the first ever important battle in naval history in which aircraft-carriers opposed aircraft-carriers. The opposing forces, the Japanese V Carrier Division under Rear-Admiral Chuichi Hara containing the aircraft-carriers *Shokaku* and *Zuikaku,* and Task Force 17 containing the two American carriers *Lexington* and *Yorktown,* under the command of Rear-Admiral Frank Fletcher, were more or less evenly matched. Tactically speaking, it could be called a Japanese victory since the *Lexington* was sunk and the *Yorktown* damaged, but the Americans achieved their aim in preventing the occupation of Port Moresby. Moreover, although the Japanese carriers did make their way back to Japan, they had suffered such severe losses in combat-ready pilots that they were unable to take part in the battle of Midway, whereas the *Yorktown* returned quickly to Hawaii, underwent emergency repairs, and left again for the battle area. The Combined Fleet put down the 'unsatisfactory result' of the battle to the imperfect discipline of the recently-formed V Carrier Division, and did not attempt to analyse the nature of engagements between aircraft-carriers.

The US Navy had lost most of its battleship fleet at Pearl Harbour, but two large, fast aircraft-carriers had escaped. The traditional notion of battleship supremacy was no less firmly rooted in the US Navy than in the Japanese navy, but the former had lost their battleships and had been obliged to alter their tactics to make the aircraft-carriers the centrepieces of their strategy. From the beginning of 1942 two aircraft-carrier groups, under the command of Admirals Halsey and Fletcher, had carried out bold surprise hit and run attacks on Japan's peripheral defence-line timed to avoid confrontation with Nagumo's task-force. In February they had struck at the Marshall Islands, in March at Lae in Papua, and in May at Tulagi in the Solomon Islands.

The code-breakers
But the only aircraft-carriers Admiral Nimitz could muster for the defence of Midway were *Enterprise, Hornet,* and *Yorktown.* Their chances of successfully resisting a direct confrontation with the six large and four small Japanese aircraft-carriers, superior both in the power of their aircraft and the training of their crews, seemed slight. However, at the same time the US Navy had in its hands an invaluable weapon, which proved the key to victory—namely the expertise of their

intelligence service, and especially of their cryptographers. Before the outbreak of war the American code-breaking experts using their so-called 'Magic' system had succeeded in decoding the Japanese Foreign Ministry machine cypher, which proved of advantage to the Americans in conducting negotiations with Japan. In the spring of 1942 the code-breaking group from the Pacific Fleet, under the direction of Commander Rochefort, gradually, by dint of hard work, managed to break the main strategic code used by the Japanese navy. As a result they were able to alert Task Forces 11 and 17 just in time to frustrate the occupation of Port Moresby in the Coral Sea.

The first hints of the Midway operation began to appear in code messages in late April and early May, but until about 10th May Nimitz's headquarters were still tending to think that the next Japanese objective would probably be Fiji and Samoa. On 14th May Nimitz collated all his reports, which were based mainly on the decoded messages, and concluded correctly that Japan's objectives were Midway and the Aleutians. He decided to concentrate all his forces on the defence of Midway, and hurriedly ordered the strengthening of the island's garrison and additions to its defence facilities and fortifications. In addition, three submarine patrol arcs were set up at a distance of 100, 150, and 200 miles from Midway, with a total of twenty submarines on stations by 4th June. Moreover, Pacific Fleet Headquarters urgently ordered Task Forces 16 (grouped around *Hornet* and *Enterprise)* and 17 (including damaged *Yorktown)* to return at once to Pearl Harbour from the south-west Pacific. The defence of Dutch Harbour was to be the responsibility of a new fleet under Rear-Admiral Theobald.

Vice-Admiral William Halsey was now in hospital, and Rear-Admiral Raymond Spruance had replaced him as commander of Task Force 16, composed of *Enterprise, Hornet,* six cruisers, and nine destroyers, which sailed from Pearl Harbour on 28th May. Task Force 17, comprising *Yorktown,* whose damage was actually repaired in three days rather than in the estimated three months, plus two cruisers and five destroyers under the command of Rear-Admiral Frank Fletcher, left Pearl Harbour on 30th May. The two fleets met at 'Point Luck', about 325 nautical miles north-east of Midway, on the evening of 2nd June, and waited for the Japanese to attack. Since the end of May Catalina flying-boats, deployed at Midway, had been spreading a fine net of observation flights over a 700-mile radius around the island.

The attacking Japanese navy was also doing its best to collect reports. On 18th May a patrolling flying-boat spotted Halsey's two aircraft-carriers to the east of the Solomons archipelago, but thereafter no further reports of US aircraft-carriers were made. However, it was thought highly probable that they were in port at Pearl Harbour. On the basis of this supposition a second flying-boat reconnaissance was planned. An 'Emily' flying-boat, with its vaunted range of 4,000 nautical miles, was to take off from its base in the Marshall Islands, and, after stopping to refuel from a submarine at French Frigate Shoals, was to arrive over Hawaii during the night of 30th May. The mission had to be abandoned, however, when it was discovered that the shoals were already being used by the US Navy as a seaplane base. Moreover, submarines arriving at the north and south ends of the Hawaiian archipelago on 3rd June were too late to sight the two US aircraft-carriers.

On 26th May Nagumo's I Carrier Striking Force left the Bungo Strait and two days later the Main Body, the Midway invasion force Main Body, and the Guard Force followed. On 27th May the Transport Group sailed from Saipan towards the battle-area in the central Pacific. The whole fleet had maintained absolute radio silence, but immediately signs appeared which augured ill for its hopes of achieving a surprise attack. US submarines off the Bungo Strait and Saipan sent long radio code messages directly after the Japanese fleets had left these points, which were intercepted. Furthermore, two Japanese ships lost their way in fog and broke the radio silence, and it was assumed that their messages must have been picked up by the Americans. On 1st June the number of messages sent to the Hawaii area, including a good many urgent messages, increased sharply, and the commanding officers of the Combined Fleet decided that their movements were already known to the Americans. Rear-Admiral Ugaki, Combined Fleet Chief of Staff, noted in his diary: 'This should do us no harm. It will give us a bigger prize to fight for'. On the evening of the 3rd the cruiser *Tone* spotted 'enemy flying-boats', but the fighter aircraft sent up from the *Akagi* to intercept lost them in the clouds.

All these alarms were in fact no more than groundless fears originating with the Japanese themselves. The Americans had not in fact made any contact, and Nagumo's I Carrier Striking Force, which was hidden in the sense that it was out in front, was not spotted by American reconnaissance aircraft until early on the 4th June, the first day of the battle. Luck had not yet deserted the Japanese navy in the war.

The electrifying message
The final, decisive warning was sounded on 2nd June. On that date VI Fleet's interception unit on Kwajalein atoll detected messages being passed between what appeared to be two US aircraft-carriers, which suggested that the ships were at sea to the north-west of Midway Island. This information was passed on immediately to the whole fleet, but Nagumo's force, out in front, paid no attention. It, moreover, decided that the 'flying-boats' supposed to have been sighted on the evening of the 3rd had in fact been birds. I Carrier Striking Force still had confidence in its surprise attack scheduled for the following day.

The operation began on the morning of 3rd June with an aerial attack on Dutch Harbour by aircraft from II Carrier Striking Force under the command of Rear-Admiral Kakuta. To create a diversion and distract attention from Midway the Japanese navy arranged a simultaneous surprise attack on Sydney and Diego Suarez in Madagascar with special midget submarines, but as a result of reports extracted from decoded messages Admiral Nimitz was able to grasp almost every aspect of the Japanese plan.

On the same day a section of the Transport Group which had proceeded ahead of schedule was spotted by a patrolling Catalina plane, and the upshot was that one tanker was damaged in a torpedo attack the same evening.

At 0430 the following day, the 4th, Nagumo's I Carrier Striking Force arrived on schedule at a point 240 nautical miles north-west of Midway Island and the first attack wave, made up of thirty-six Nakajima B5N2s ('Kates'), thirty-six Aichi D3A2s ('Vals'), and thirty-six Zeros, took off to attack the island. The second attack wave, composed as the first, waited on the carriers' flight decks prepared for the appearance of enemy forces on the horizon.

As has already been stated, the chief purpose of the operation was to lure the American Pacific Fleet to destruction. But although I Carrier Division carried out a reconnaissance sweep that morning, there was a conviction that it would reveal no cause for uneasiness. This attitude of the General Staff, reflected in the movements of the reconnaissance planes, was a fatal weakness in the operation. At the same time as the first Midway attack set out, seven search aircraft took off to make a 300 nautical mile fan-shaped reconnaissance, but the heavy cruiser *Chikuma*'s seaplane which must have come close to passing directly above the US task-force at about 0630, not only failed to spot it, but also failed to report the important fact, indicating as it did the presence of an enemy aircraft-carrier, that the aircraft had encountered and engaged a Dauntless dive-bomber from the *Yorktown*. The *Tone*'s machine was assigned a course south of the *Chikuma*'s seaplane but because of a catapult fault its take-off was delayed for thirty minutes. However, at 0728 on its return flight it reported sighting 'what appears to be ten enemy surface ships'. This was Task Force 16, which had sent up aircraft at 0700 for an attack on Nagumo's I Carrier Striking Force after a Catalina plane had spotted it at 0534. But because of the clear visibility and the presence of enemy aircraft the *Tone*'s seaplane at first hesitated to move in close above the enemy fleet. It turned away, but at 0747 the General Staff of I Carrier Division demanded: 'Ascertain types of ships'. The seaplane flew in close and at 0807 radioed 'five cruisers and five destroyers'. Thirteen minutes later it sent the electrifying message: 'Enemy force accompanied by what appears to be aircraft-carrier bringing up the rear.'

But when the first message came in from the seaplane, Nagumo's force was being attacked by aircraft from Midway. However, without fighter cover the series of attacks by B-17s, B-26s, Avengers, Vindicators, and Dauntlesses of the army, navy, and marine corps were in vain. The aircraft were swept away by Zeros and failed to score a single hit.

Further evidence of the manoeuvrability of the Zeros was provided during the Midway strike between 0630 and 0710. The US defences, alerted by radar an hour before, sent up twenty-six Grumman Wildcats and Brewster Buffaloes to intercept the Japanese attackers. However, seventeen of the defenders were shot down, and a further seven damaged beyond repair. Japanese losses in the first wave attack were negligible. Three Kates and one Val were shot down by enemy anti-aircraft fire, and only two fighters failed to return. But Lieutenant Tomonaga, the leader of the attack, realized that the defences had been strengthened beyond what they had been led to expect and at 0700 radioed Admiral Nagumo: 'There is need for a second attack.'

There had been no report so far from the reconnaissance aircraft, so the General Staff, confident that there was no US fleet in the vicinity, decided that the second attack wave, which was waiting on the flight decks, should head for Midway, and at 0715 gave the order that the torpedo-laden Kates on *Akagi* and *Kaga* should be de-armed and re-loaded with bombs. After the seaplane's sighting of a US carrier a

Moment of impact on Yorktown. *The blast of a torpedo which has just crashed into her side hurls the port side catwalk into the air as a crewman crossed the deck*

message came by blinker signal from Rear-Admiral Yamaguchi, commander of II Carrier Division: 'Consider it advisable to launch attack force immediately'. Even though the torpedo-bombers were not yet ready, he wanted the dive-bombers dispatched immediately to bomb the US carrier. But Nagumo, who had witnessed the slaughter of the unescorted US bombers and torpedo-planes, decided on the advice of Commander Minoru Genda, of the aviation staff, to follow the orthodox line of recovering both the Midway strike aircraft and the second wave fighters which were now on combat air patrol and sending them as escort for the Kates and Vals.

Slaughter of the Devastators

At 0745 Nagumo ordered that the aircraft which had already taken on bomb loads should start exchanging them once again for torpedoes. In the small hangars maintenance crews worked desperately. If Nagumo had realized it would take two hours before the strike-force was ready, no doubt he would unhesitatingly have followed the timely advice given him by Rear-Admiral Yamaguchi. But misfortunes occurred one after another to retard the preparations. At 0830 the first attack wave

returned from Midway and began circling, waiting for permission to land. The landings were completed by 0918, and it was calculated that it would be 1030 before the attack squadron, now re-equipped with torpedoes, would have replaced the incoming aircraft on the flight decks and be ready for take-off.

At 0905 a message from the *Tone's* seaplane stated that a large fleet of US torpedo aircraft was on its way towards Nagumo's fleet. All the commanding officers of the I Air Fleet were on edge, but by now there was no time to regret taking the wrong decision. The only possible thing to be done was urgently to press on preparing the aircraft for take-off in time to meet the large fleet of US aircraft. The commanders turned their ships from a south-easterly course to a north-easterly one to meet the oncoming attack, and officers fiercely urged on their men.

When the news came through from a Catalina on the same morning that Nagumo's I Carrier Striking Force had been spotted, the two US task forces were 240 nautical miles east-north-east of the Japanese fleet. At that time the radius of activity of the US torpedo aircraft was not more than 175 nautical miles, so that 0900

The Tide Turns

Yorktown *listing heavily to port after attack by Japanese aircraft from* Hiryu. *She was finished off by a Japanese submarine, I-68*

was the earliest that the ships could reach their launching point. Rear-Admiral Spruance, however, knew that the Japanese had begun their bombing attack on Midway, and decided to time his attack for the moment when the Japanese aircraft would have just returned from their raid and would therefore be at their most vulnerable. He therefore launched his attack planes at 0700, two hours ahead of schedule. 116 aircraft took off from *Enterprise* and *Hornet* and an hour later an attack fleet of thirty-five aircraft took off from *Yorktown.*

The first to reach the target was Torpedo Squadron 8, from *Hornet,* led by the intrepid Lieutenant-Commander John Waldron. But his old-fashioned and unescorted Douglas Devastators were surrounded by a large number of Zeros and one after another they were shot down in flames. Every one of the fifteen aircraft was lost, and Ensign George H.Gay, who was picked up from the sea the next day by a navy Catalina, was the only man to be rescued.

The torpedo squadrons from *Enterprise* and *Yorktown* plunged into the attack after them, and they too were roughly handled. In the end only six aircraft survived out of the total force of forty-one, and they did not achieve a single hit. Nevertheless, their blood was not shed in vain. The low-altitude Devastators drew the Zeros down after them, and thus made possible a surprise attack by the Dauntless dive-bombers, which attacked from a high altitude. Lieutenant-Commander Clarence McClusky, of *Enterprise,* leading eighteen Dauntless dive-bombers, made straight for the estimated position of the fleet. He failed to find it, however, and after flying on westward for a short time, surmising correctly that Nagumo's task-force had altered

course, he turned north and continued the search. This was one of the most significant decisions of the battle. The thirty-four dive-bombers from *Hornet* found themselves in a similar position, but they turned south and did not find their target.

McClusky was extremely lucky. At 0955 he spotted the destroyer *Arashi,* followed it, and ten minutes later spotted Nagumo's fleet through a break in the clouds. At about the same time *Yorktown*'s dive-bomber squadron led by Lieutenant-Commander Maxwell F. Leslie, which had arrived by a different route, spotted their target. McClusky's aircraft began dive-bombing attacks on three of the Japanese aircraft-carriers at 1022. Three minutes later, when Leslie's squadron began their dive-bombing attack on the *Soryu,* the four carriers of Nagumo's task-force had almost completed their preparations, and were heading directly into the wind, ready for their aircraft to take off. Rear-Admiral Kusaka later bewailed the fact that, given just five more minutes, the aircraft would probably all have been in the air and moving in a great mass to attack the US aircraft-carriers. The whole shape of the battle altered in those few minutes. Four bombs struck *Kaga,* and as soon as it had gone up in flames, McClusky's squadron scored three direct hits on the *Soryu* and another on the *Akagi,* and a great cloud of black smoke went up from these three aircraft-carriers. In the normal course of events, bombs of between 550 and 1,100 pounds would damage the flight deck of an aircraft-carrier, but would hardly destroy the whole ship. In this case, however, the three carriers each had a full complement of aircraft loaded with fuel, torpedoes, and bombs, so that fires once started spread in a rapid series of explosions, and these, exacerbated by the fact that the damage control units were caught unprepared, were fatal to the three huge ships.

Hiryu *hits back*

Initially the *Hiryu* escaped damage and in a spirit of furious revenge sent up eighteen escorted Vals, seven of which eluded *Yorktown*'s combat air patrol and penetrated the anti-aircraft fire from the carrier's screening cruisers and destroyers to severely damage the vessel with three bombs. A second strike by ten escorted Kates scored two torpedo hits and doomed the carrier. Within fifteen minutes of the torpedoes crashing into her port side Captain Buckmaster ordered the crew to abandon ship, but the carrier was still afloat two days later when the Japanese submarine I-68 found her in the afternoon of 6th June and, penetrating her screen, sunk her. Meanwhile dive-bombers from Task Force 16 had crippled *Hiryu.*

Following the news of the destruction of

Nagumo's task force the staff of the Combined Fleet ordered all their forces to proceed to an attack on Midway Island. Kurita's Close Support Group of four heavy cruisers and two destroyers in the van was within ninety nautical miles of the island by the middle of the night and was preparing for battle on the following morning, but Rear-Admiral Spruance, wary of being caught in a night battle, for the Japanese navy specialized in night fighting, had begun to retreat eastwards in the evening. When Yamamoto learned of this he called off the whole operation, and ordered the withdrawal of the fleet.

The Battle of Midway is of particular interest in the history of naval warfare in that it marked the end of the transition period between the era of battleship domination and that of the aircraft-carrier. But the Battle of Midway, unlike Salamis, did not decide the outcome of the entire war in a moment. Unlike Jutland, Midway did not bring together the opposing forces in their entirety; unlike the battle of the Japan Sea it was not a conflict ending in the utter destruction of one of the two sides. If one considers the battles of the Pacific War from the point of view of their scale, then the Battle of the Philippine Sea and the Battle of Leyte Gulf were both greater than Midway. It can be said, indeed, that the Battle of Midway was the point in the Pacific War where the tide turned but, contrary to what is often stated, it was not the decisive battle determining the course of the entire war. Japan did lose four of her major aircraft-carriers, it is true, but this left *Zuikaku* and *Shokaku* besides six smaller carriers, which more or less matched America's fleet of three large carriers and a smaller one. At the same time Japan retained her superiority in battleships and heavy cruisers. In other words it can be said that the Battle of Midway broke Japan's superiority in the Pacific and restored the balance between the Japanese and American navies.

As is amply demonstrated by statistics, what really wore down the fighting power of the Japanese navy was the exhausting struggle for the Solomon Islands which began in August 1942. As compared to the Battle of Midway, where Japan lost 296 aircraft and 114 airmen, representing twenty per cent of the total number attached to Nagumo's task-force, in the battle for the Solomons the figures were as high as some 3,000 aircraft and 6,200 men.

No doubt the primary significance of the Battle of Midway lay in its psychological aspect. In the words of the naval historian Rear-Admiral Samuel Eliot Morison 'Midway was the first really smashing defeat inflicted on the Japanese navy in modern times.' But it had by no means been a foregone conclusion.

Stalingrad

It has often been said that Stalingrad was the decisive battle, and the turning point, of the eastern campaign. And indeed a glance at the map, with some hindsight of the German plans for the summer of 1942, would seem to make this the obvious site. Yet the irony is that neither side intended, or foresaw, that the fight to the death should be there.

At the beginning of 1942 both the German Armed Forces High Command (OKW) and the Stavka (the Supreme Command of the Red Army) projected planning for the summer that grossly over-estimated their own capabilities. In spite of the punishment they had sustained during the Soviet winter offensives of 1941 the Germans were confident that they could master the Red Army when the weather no longer impeded their mobility. And indeed there was some substance in this, for the terrible battles of the deep winter had been fought by a quite small proportion of the German strength which the extreme temperatures had isolated from manoeuvre or relief. More than sixty-five per cent of

Russians contest a few yards of rubble in the shattered streets of Stalingrad

the infantry had never been engaged in the winter fighting, and had spent the winter in training and re-equipment.

At the nadir of German fortunes there had been voices in the German Army High Command (OKH) which had favoured retreat to the line of the Dnieper and a suspension of offensive operations for a whole twelve-month period. But with the milder weather this caution evaporated (helped, no doubt, by the wholesale dismissals which Hitler had implemented in the new year) and planning proceeded apace for the summer campaign.

In fact it was the Red Army which got off the line first, staging three separate offensives immediately after the spring thaw. The Soviet intention was to relieve Leningrad and Sebastopol, and to recapture Kharkov – objectives more ambitious even than those of mid-winter, and set, moreover, in a context of German recovery and Russian exhaustion. In the result all three failed, and with crippling casualties. The Kharkov offensive in particular had most serious consequences as it ran head-on into a strong enemy concentration deployed to eliminate the Lozovaya salient, which had been established by the Red Army in January. The Russians lost over 600 tanks and in this critical area, where the Germans had decided to concentrate their summer offensive, the ratio of armour swung dramatically from five to one in the Russian favour to nearly ten to one against them.

For the Germans then, an initial domination of the battlefield was a certainty. How they would exploit this was less definite. At least three separate operational plans existed. The most conservative, naturally, was that formulated by the OKH staff, which envisaged advancing as far east as was necessary to safeguard the mineral resources of the Donets Basin. Stalingrad was suggested as a final objective but with the escape clause that if its seizure was not possible it would be enough to 'expose it to our heavy fire, so that it loses its importance as a centre of communications'. The OKW toyed with two schemes; the first anticipated swallowing Stalingrad in the opening weeks, wheeling north up the left bank of the Volga and outflanking Moscow; the second, only slightly less grandiose, also presumed the city's early fall followed by its tenure as a 'blocking point' to cover a *southward* wheel into the Caucasus where the Soviet oilfields lay. General von Kleist, commanding I Panzer Group, had been personally told by Hitler as early as April that '. . . I and my Panzers were to be the instruments whereby the Reich would be assured of its oil supplies in perpetuity. Stalingrad was no more than a name on the map to us.'

The southern offensive

Army Group South, commanded by Field-Marshal von Bock, launched its attack on 28th June. Three armies split the Russian front into fragments on either side of Kursk, and Hoth's eleven Panzer divisions fanned out across hundreds of miles of open rolling corn and steppe grass, towards Voronezh and the Don. Two days later the southern half of the army group went over to the attack below Kharkov, and Kleist took I Panzer Group across the Donets.

The Russians were outnumbered and outgunned from the start, and their shortage of armour made it difficult to mount even local counter-attacks. With each day the Russian disorder multiplied, their command structure degenerating into independent combat at divisional, then at brigade, finally at regimental level. Without even the protection of mass, which had characterized the Red Army's deployment in the Ukraine in 1941, or of swamp and forest, which had allowed small groups to delay the enemy in the battle of Moscow, these formations were at the German's mercy. Polarizing around the meagre cover of some shallow ravine or the wooden hutments of a *kolkhoz,* they fought out their last battle under a deluge of firepower against which they could oppose little save their own bravery. '. . . quite different from last year [wrote a sergeant in III Panzer Division]. It's more like Poland. The Russians aren't nearly so thick on the ground. They fire their guns like madmen, but they don't hurt us.'

Within a fortnight the Soviet command structure had disintegrated and on 12th July the Stavka promulgated a new 'Stalingrad front'. The title of this force (front was roughly equivalent administratively, though not necessarily in strength, to a German army group) showed that the Stavka, at least, appreciated where they must make their stand, and it was here that they were now directing their last reserves, which had been concentrated around Moscow. General Chuykov, who was to emerge as one of the vital personalities who inspired and directed the battle of Stalingrad, brought his reserve army of four infantry divisions, two motorized and two armoured brigades from Tula, a distance of 700 miles south-east. On his arrival Chuykov was given instructions so vague as to convince him that 'front HQ obviously possessed extremely limited information about the enemy, who was mentioned only in general terms'.

Chuykov has described how on his first day he was on a personal reconnaissance: 'I came across two divisional staffs . . . they consisted of a number of officers travelling in some three to five trucks filled to overflowing with cans of fuel. When I asked them where the Germans were, and where

they were going, they could not give me a sensible reply. It was clear that to restore to these men the faith they had lost in their own powers and to improve the fighting quality of the retreating units would not be easy.'

This was the moment which offered the Germans the best prospect of 'swallowing' Stalingrad as postulated in the wide outflanking plans of the OKW. In fact the Russian troops, though thrown into battle piecemeal as they arrived, proved just adequate to slow the German advance guard, now outrunning its supplies after an advance of 300 miles in three weeks. It took Paulus's VI Army five days to clear the Don bend, and he did not have the strength to eliminate every Soviet position in the loop of the west bank – an omission which was to have catastrophic consequences in November.

Stalingrad now began to exercise its magnetism over the whole of Army Group B (the northern section of Army Group South) and up along the chain of command to the Führer himself who moved his headquarters from Rastenburg to Vinnitsa (120 miles south-west of Kiev) on 25th August, where it remained until the end of the year. The Germans were committing themselves to the one kind of battle where their adversary held the advantage, forsaking their own enormous superiorities in firepower and mobility for a mincing machine of close combat. Hoth's Panzers were swung north, out of the steppe into the brick and concrete of the Stalingrad suburbs, and for nearly four months the city was wracked by continuous hand-to-hand fighting.

The nearest historical parallel is with the Battle of Verdun in 1916. But there are significant differences. At Verdun the contestants rarely saw one another face to face; they were battered to death by high explosives or cut down at long range by machine-gun fire. At Stalingrad each separate battle resolved itself into a combat between individuals. Soldiers would jeer and curse at their enemy across the street; often they could hear his breathing in the next room while they reloaded; hand-to-hand duels were finished in the dark twilight of smoke and brick dust with knives and pickaxes, with clubs of rubble and twisted steel. General Doerr has described how 'the time for conducting large-scale operations was gone for ever; from the wide expanses of steppe-land the war moved into the jagged gullies of the Volga hills with their copses and ravines, into the factory area of Stalingrad, spread out over uneven, pitted, rugged country, covered with iron, concrete, and stone buildings. The mile, as a measure of distance, was replaced by the yard. GHQ's map was the map of the city.

'For every house, workshop, water tower, railway embankment, wall, cellar, and every pile of ruins, a bitter battle was waged, without equal even in the First World War with its vast expenditure of munitions. The distance between the enemy's army and ours was as small as it could possibly be. Despite the concentrated activity of aircraft and artillery, it was impossible to break out of the area of close fighting. The Russians surpassed the Germans in their use of the terrain and in camouflage and were more experienced in barricade warfare for individual buildings.'

In the first week of September Hoth's tanks, operating in the southern sector, broke through to the Volga bank and split the Russians into two. A critical four-day period followed, with the defenders of the northern half outnumbered three to one, and the Germans got close enough to bring the central landing stage (where the Volga ferries landed supplies for the defending forces) under machine-gun fire. But the sheer tenacity and individual courage of the Russian foot-soldier was the deciding factor. General Paulus's offensive subsided, fought to a standstill.

It was now plain that a major strategic revision was called for. But the Germans were prisoners of their own propaganda, which had steadily been building up the importance of the battle. Any misgivings that Paulus himself may have felt were quietened by a visit from General Schmundt, formerly Hitler's adjutant and now chief of the Army Personnel Office. Schmundt strongly hinted that Paulus was being considered for 'a most senior post' (in fact the succession to Jodl as Chief of the Armed Forces Operational Staff), but that the Führer was most anxious first to see the Stalingrad operations 'brought to a successful conclusion'. Paulus's awareness of his own interests was, at all times, keener than his tactical abilities. This time he decided to strike head-on at his enemy's strongest point—the three giant edifices of the Tractor Factory, the Barrikady (Barricades) ordnance plant, and the Krasny Oktyabr (Red October) steel works, which lay in the northern half of the city, ranged one after another a few hundred yards from the Volga bank. This was to be the fiercest, and the longest, of the five battles which were fought in the ruined town, and that which finally drained the offensive strength from the German armies in south Russia. It started on 4th October and raged for nearly three weeks. Paulus had been reinforced by a variety of different specialist troops, including police batta-

1 The German advance. 2 The German assault on Stalingrad. 3 Red Army counter-attacks. 4 The crushing of VI Army

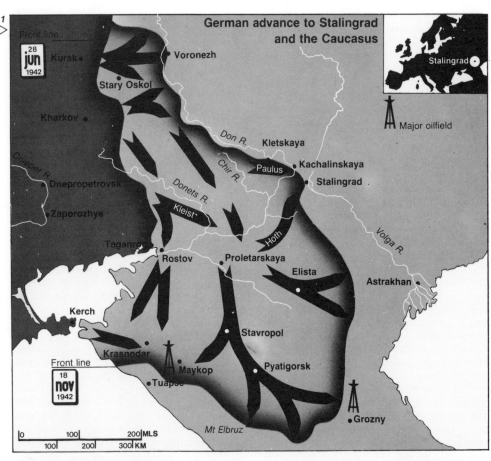

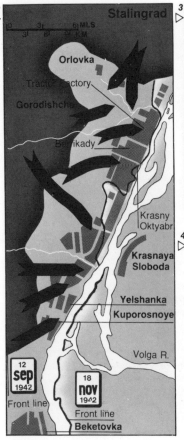

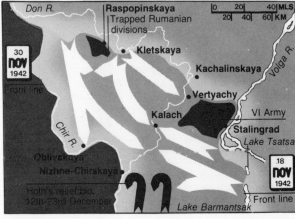

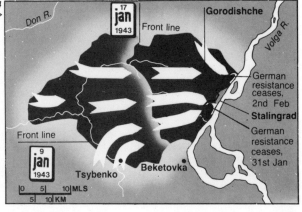

lions and engineers skilled in street fighting and demolition work. But the Russians, though still heavily outnumbered, remained their masters in the technique of house-to-house fighting. They had perfected the use of 'shock groups', small bodies of mixed arms—light and heavy machine-gunners, tommy gunners, and grenadiers usually with anti-tank guns, who gave one another support in lightning counter-attacks; and they had developed the creation of 'killing zones', houses and squares heavily mined, to which the defenders knew all the approach routes, where the German advance could be canalized.

Slowly and at a tremendous price the Germans inched their way into the great buildings, across factory floors; around and over the inert machinery, through the foundries, the assembly shops, the offices. 'My God, why have you forsaken us?' wrote a lieutenant of XXIV Panzer Division. 'We have fought during fifteen days for a single house, with mortars, grenades, machine-guns, and bayonets. Already by the third day fifty-four German corpses lay strewn in the cellars, on the landings, and the staircases. The front is a corridor between burnt-out rooms; it is the thin ceiling between two floors. Help comes from neighbouring houses by fire escapes and chimneys. There is a ceaseless struggle from noon till night. From storey to storey, faces black with sweat, we bombard each other with grenades in the middle of explosions, clouds of dust and smoke, heaps of mortar, floods of blood, fragments of furniture and human beings. Ask any soldier what half an hour of hand-to-hand struggle means in such a fight. And imagine Stalingrad; eighty days and eighty nights of hand-to-hand struggles. The street is no longer measured by metres but by corpses . . . Stalingrad is no longer a town. By day it is an enormous cloud of burning blinding smoke; it is a vast furnace, lit by the reflection of the flames. And when the night arrives, one of those scorching, howling, bleeding nights, the dogs plunge into the Volga and swim desperately to gain the other bank. The nights of Stalingrad are a terror for them. Animals flee this hell; the hardest stones cannot bear it for long; only men endure.'

By the end of October the Russian positions at Stalingrad had been reduced to a few pockets of stone, seldom more than three hundred yards deep, bordering on the right bank of the Volga. The Krasny Oktyabr had fallen to the Germans who had paved every metre of the factory floor with their dead. The Barrikady was half lost, with Germans at one end of the foundry facing Russian machine-guns in the extinct ovens at the other. The defenders of the Tractor Factory had been split into three.

Zhukov counter-attacks

But these last islets of resistance, hardened in the furnace of repeated attacks, were irreducible. Paulus's VI Army was spent, as exhausted as Haig's divisions at Passchendaele had been exactly a quarter of a century before. And all the time, to the north and west, a terrible storm was gathering. Early in September the Stavka had sent Zhukov—architect of their winter victory at Moscow—to the southern theatre and with him Zhukov had brought his colleagues Novikov and Voronov, the artillery specialist. For two months Zhukov carefully built up his reserves on the German flank and reinforced the Don bridgeheads against the Rumanians defending the German northern flank. Of twenty-two fresh infantry divisions created during this period only two were committed in Stalingrad itself. Virtually the entire autumn tank production was held back for use in the counter-offensive.

Paulus's Intelligence had warned him that something was afoot, but both Luftwaffe and army had grossly under-estimated its scale. The XLVIII Panzer Corps, VI Army's sole mobile reserve, consisted of ninety-two Czech light tanks, with Rumanian crews, and the remains of XIV Panzer Division refitting after five weeks continuous action in the rubble of Stalingrad. Against this, on 19th November, Zhukov threw six fresh armies, 450 new T34 tanks, and an artillery barrage from over 2,000 guns, in a pincer movement that converged on either side of the German salient whose tip was at Stalingrad.

The staff of VI Army went sleepless for two nights as they struggled to regroup the precious Panzers and pull back their infantry from the smoking maze of Stalingrad to protect the collapsing flanks. In the rear confusion was absolute: the western railway from Kalach had already been cut by Russian cavalry in several places; the sound of firing came from every direction, and periodically broke out between Germans going up to the front and ragged groups of Rumanians in leaderless retreat. The huge bridge at Kalach over which every pound of rations and every bullet for VI Army passed, had been prepared for demolition, and a platoon of engineers was on duty there all day on 23rd November in case the order to destroy the bridge should come through. At half past four that afternoon tanks could be heard approaching from the west. The lieutenant in charge of the engineers thought at first that they might be Russians but was reassured when the first three vehicles were identified as Horch personnel carriers with XXII Panzer Division markings; assuming that it was a reinforcement column for Stalingrad he instructed his men to lift the barrier. The personnel carriers halted on the bridge and

disgorged sixty Russian tommy-gunners who killed most of the engineer platoon and took the survivors prisoner. They removed the demolition charges and twenty-five tanks from the column passed over the bridge and drove south-east, where that evening they made contact with the southern claw of the pincer, 14th Independent Tank Brigade from Trufanov's 51st Army. The first tenuous link in a chain that was to throttle a quarter of a million German soldiers had been forged, and the turning point in the Second World War had arrived.

In the three days following their penetration of the Rumanian corps, the Russians had moved thirty-four divisions across the Don, twelve from Beketonskaya bridgehead and twenty-two from Kremenskaya. Their tanks had turned westward, defeating XLVIII Panzer Corps and probing dangerously into the confusion of stragglers, service and training units, and mutinous satellites who milled about in the German rear. Their infantry had turned east, digging with feverish energy to build an iron ring around VI Army. Zhukov kept the whole of the Stalingrad pocket under bombardment from heavy guns sited on the far bank of the Volga, but for the first few days he had exerted only a gentle pressure upon the surrounded Germans.

The Soviets' intention was to probe in sufficient strength to be able to detect the first signs of their enemy's actually striking camp, but to avoid any action which might precipitate this. For them, as for Paulus, these first hours were vital. All night on 23rd and during the morning of 24th November, men and tractors hauled and struggled with battery after battery of 76-mm guns across the frozen earth. By that evening Russian firepower on the west side of the pocket had trebled. Over a thousand anti-tank guns were in position in an arc from Vertyatchy, in the north, around to Kalach, then eastwards below Marinovka, joining the Volga at the old Beketonskaya bridgehead.

Field-Marshal von Manstein, the newly appointed commander of the German army group, set about preparing a relief operation, using the rump of Hoth's Panzers that had been left out of the encirclement, and some mobile units pulled back from the Caucasus. However, Russian pressure and administrative difficulties delayed the counter-attack (Operation Winter Tempest) until 12th December. Hoth's column was never strong enough to penetrate the Soviet ring on its own, and a simultaneous full-scale sortie by Paulus's force on the code signal *Donnerschlag*—'Thunderclap' —was to be vital to its success. When it came to the point Paulus refused to move, making a succession of excuses and finally referring Manstein to Hitler. Hitler, over the telephone, said he had to leave it to

Paulus. With the overall position deteriorating daily it was impossible to keep Hoth's column poised in the steppe for long and over Christmas it withdrew, carrying with it the last prospects of relief for the beleaguered army.

Stalingrad was the greatest single defeat suffered by German arms since the Napoleonic Wars. To this day it is impossible to make a final assessment of the failure to relieve the surrounded army because all the surviving participants are inhibited, for one or another reason, from giving an impartial account. Russian strength was, of course, a primary factor. Also contributory was the misrepresentation by the Luftwaffe of its ability to supply VI Army (incredibly Göring assumed that the He 111, which could carry 2,000 kilogrammes of *explosive* could as easily load 2,000 kilogrammes of *cargo*). But the real mystery is a strategic one. There was a widespread conviction that the Stalingrad garrison must stay where it was in order to cover the retreat of the rest of the army. Manstein himself is on record with the view that 'if the enemy siege forces had been released . . . the fate of the whole southern wing of the German forces in the East would have been sealed.' It was impossible to recommend that Paulus should be *sacrificed* to this end—easy to take comfort (as Paulus himself was doing) from the fact that many, weaker 'pockets' had held out through the previous winter until the thaw had brought relief.

At all events, the revictualling of so large a garrison was quite beyond the powers of the Luftwaffe even while its forward airfields were safe. Once these were lost to the Russian advance the garrison's life could be measured in weeks. VI Army rejected a surrender demand on 10th January and defeated the last Russian attack. On 2nd February the last remnants of the garrison were obliged by shortage of food and ammunition to surrender. Over 130,000 men went into the prison cages and German strength in the East was never to recover.

Russian soldiers emerge from hiding in a ruined house, October 1942. The stubbornness of the Russian defence baffled the Germans—and as they became tied down in the savage hand-to-hand fighting, they chose to regard it as a 'battle of attrition' in which the Red Army would be bled white. But it was the Wehrmacht which had failed to understand tactics as well as strategic reality; it was the German Army which was being exhausted and forced to throw in all its reserves, while the Russians built up their strength, committing only enough troops to deny the Germans any chance of a breakthrough

5 THE NEW ORDER

The Nazis at War

When Hitler ordered the attack on Poland on 1st September 1939, he thought he had only a localized campaign before him, yet he consciously risked its extension into world war. War for Hitler and the Nazi regime was not only a means to an end; with it was bound up the whole philosophy of Nazism. The Nazi dogma of the 'iron law' of struggle between races was nothing more than the naked spirit of warfare. And the preparation for the battle for 'Lebensraum' had defined all Nazi policy in Germany since 1933.

The First World War had shown what levels such a national fighting spirit was capable of reaching. Hitler consciously seized on this model. The desire to raise Germany from the 'disgrace' of 1918, the conviction that only treachery, stupidity, and weakness had caused defeat in the First World War, and the fanatical determination to resume once again – and this time more resolutely – the fight for Germany's greatness and her place in the world: all this was part of the special gospel of National Socialism. The Second World War was the decisive act of Hitler's regime. The total strength and the true nature of Nazism only came out fully in war, but so did its great weakness – its fanatical egocentricity, which was eventually to bring about its destruction.

Hitler's enormous military successes in the first years of the war – the eighteen-day war against Poland, the daring naval and air action to occupy Norway, and, above all, the swift victory over France

Left: Dutch civilians in a Gestapo jail

which inspired Mussolini to come into the war on Hitler's side – spread Germany's hegemony over almost the whole continent and created a readiness practically everywhere for the creation of a 'new Fascist order in Europe'.

The sensational triumphs in the military field and in foreign policy also strengthened the Nazi position in internal affairs and lent conviction to the belief that Hitler was not a dangerous gambler but a divinely endowed genius. Now National Socialist propaganda in Germany itself, conducted by its talented leader Joseph Goebbels, could pull out all the stops in the creation of national euphoria. This included special radio broadcasts linked by resounding military marches, newsreels glorifying German successes put out by the army's propaganda unit, the composition and broadcasting of more and more new battle songs, the award of higher and higher decorations for bravery, and the popularization of individual war-heroes. Hitler himself contributed to the creation of this mood with fifteen big speeches in the first two years of the war and so successful was Nazi 'education' that apparently only a minority in Germany preserved enough critical capacity to see the mania which spoke through Hitler's uncontrolled attacks.

It was true, however, that there was in the German population, as the confidential security service reports for 1940-41 show, an enduring and lively fear that Germany would, by over-extending her forces, run the risk of 'conquering herself to death'. But the full extent of Hitler's miscalcula-

tions, already visible in 1940, remained largely hidden. Thus only a few realized the importance of the RAF's success in the Battle of Britain and that Great Britain had by this time received the first reliable indication of active military support from the United States in the form of fifty destroyers.

But it was not only propaganda which served to conceal the seriousness of the situation. Food rationing, instituted in August 1939, guaranteed the nation a sufficient amount to eat in the first years of the war. Trusting in Hitler's Blitzkrieg strategy and the economic preparations for war which had been going forward since 1934, the Nazi regime thought that even in 1942 no radical switch in the economy to arms production was necessary and that it would be possible to preserve a relatively high standard of living for the civilian population. Nor did the military situation cause immediate alarm. The number of Germans killed in action up to the end of 1941 remained relatively low (about 200,000) and the RAF's night attacks, which had increased during 1940-41, did not at first cause great damage.

Military developments and Nazi propaganda also largely hid the changes in the state's power structure which were to have serious consequences in the future.

Although the army was potentially an important power-factor it had for some time shown itself to have feet of clay. The clearest signs of this were the forced resignations of Fritsch, the Commander-in-Chief of the Army, and General Beck, the Chief of the General Staff, and Hitler's

setting up in February 1938 of the High Command of the Armed Forces (Oberkommando der Wehrmacht, OKW) which was directly answerable to him under the command of General Keitel. These developments showed that after the consolidation of Nazi power Hitler was not prepared to allow the armed forces any significant influence in making political decisions. After the outbreak of war he pursued the suppression of the forces' political influence even more rigorously (for instance, by strangling the truth about the sinking of the *Athenia*). From the first day of the war, it was not the military commanders but the highest-ranking Gauleiters who were appointed Reich defence commissioners and entrusted with making the top decisions in all cases of civil emergency.

The army leaders took another fall — not without protests from individual generals — when in the autumn of 1939 commanding officers in occupied Poland tolerated the first systematic mass shooting of Poles and Jews by Special Action Units of the SS which claimed that they were acting under special secret orders from above.

The appointment of the Waffen-SS, under Himmler's supreme command, in the winter of 1939-40 also ended the army's monopoly as the only element allowed to bear arms, the monopoly which had been defended so successfully against the SA in 1934. The Waffen-SS, a direct rival to the army, amounted to only one division at the beginning of 1940, but towards the end of the war its numerous volunteer units comprised some 600,000 men.

As he had done on many different occasions since 1937 when he presented his expansionist aims, Hitler reproached the army leadership for being far too cautious and hesitant in applying his plan for the campaign in the West. This plan, which foresaw the violation of Dutch and

Belgian neutrality, led to further deterioration in his relations with top officers on the Army General Staff (for example with Halder, Chief of the General Staff, and Canaris, head of the Abwehr, the OKW counter-intelligence department). The first cells of military opposition formed.

The success of the campaign in the West, however, once again justified Hitler's judgement and increased his prestige to the detriment of that of the army leadership. In December 1941, after the first failures in Russia, Field-Marshal Brauchitsch resigned as Commander-in-Chief of the Army and Hitler took over this position himself.

As in Poland, moreover, Hitler took care to force the commanding army generals out of the administration of those occupied territories in which the Nazi regime was especially interested as soon as they had been overrun. Everywhere civilian rulers were installed. They were always high Party functionaries, usually Gauleiters, and all directly responsible to Hitler. There arose autocratically ruled satrapies in which control was wielded by Party favourites, the officials responsible for the carrying out of Göring's Four-Year Plan, and the security police and other SS organs under Himmler. It was this type of administrative irregularity that provided the basis for mass shooting, mass deportation, concentration camps, and ghettos, and finally, from 1941, the extermination camps — the means of achieving the 'final solution to the Jewish problem'.

Revolutionizing the law
The shift of power in the occupied territories into the hands of Party officials and the security police had its effect on the constitution of the Nazi regime itself. A variety of measures, caused directly by the war, but which were principally ideological and political, altered the division of power between the Nazi leaders to the advantage of the extremists.

This was particularly true of the law. Demands by Hitler and other Party leaders for stiff war-time penal laws led in the autumn of 1939 to the passing of a mass of new laws covering, for example, listening in to enemy radio broadcasts, economic sabotage of the war effort, 'disrupting the armed forces', and 'crimes of violence'. Crimes which carried the death sentence rose to forty-six by 1944. Statistics on death sentences passed by the civil courts rose from 43 in 1938, to 2,015 from January to August 1944. Hitler was however not content with the draconian increase in the severity of legal sentences. In the autumn of 1939 he had already authorized Himmler to use the security police for immediate execution without a court death sentence in cases of anti-national acts and sabotage which seemed particularly serious. The

The Nazis and German Youth.

Left: *A poster of the 1930's expressing the National Socialist ideal of the young Nazi. The rival youth organizations of the pre-Hitler years, the red-scarved communists and the socialists in berets flee with their decadent mentors from the vision of Aryan heroism. Goebbel's propaganda reached to the cradle.* **Right:** *A Hitler Youth at a hero commemoration ceremony. The Nazi grip on the young was total, from the Adolf Hitler Schools through the ranks of the Hitler Youth, training was for total obedience. Drafted into the Civil Defence early in the war, by 1945 twelve-year-olds went into the front line to face the advancing Russian tanks*

executions were mostly carried out in concentration camps. The SS and security police officials who undertook these killings received formal protection from inquiries by the state prosecutors by the introduction of special SS and police tribunals in October 1939. The total number of concentration camp prisoners in Germany between 1934 and 1938, when the Nazi regime was relatively moderate, was around 7,000 to 10,000, but after the beginning of the war the imprisonment of those from occupied countries suspected of opposition and the erection of new camps pushed the figure up to some 100,000 by 1942. But the highest numbers are to be found in the last war years (1944-45) when, under the forced labour scheme for armaments production, some half a million prisoners of all nationalities were crammed together in twenty main camps and 165 subsidiary camps.

From the start of the war, Hitler sought to link his fight against external enemies with the eradication of internal enemies and 'inferior' national elements. His aim was made quite explicit by his secret order of September 1939 to kill all the mentally ill. Under the euthanasia programme, for which a secretly selected commission of doctors was responsible, about 70,000 mentally ill were killed in hospitals in Bernburg, Hadamar, Hartheim, and elsewhere, until, in 1941, Hitler felt himself obliged to call a halt in response to various protests, especially from clergy.

Calculation and hate

The more extreme nature of the Nazi regime in 1941-42 was directly connected with the critical military situation. The combination of rational calculation and pathological hate, which increasingly dominated Hitler's decisions the more he was dominated by the idea of his role in history, was especially apparent in his decision to attack Russia.

This decision had no necessity other than as an escape from the military dead-end Hitler had reached in the West over Great Britain. It was also, however, an attempt to wage his own war, the war he had planned two decades before with the intention of conquering the Lebensraum of the East and destroying 'Jewish Bolshevism'.

His decision linked many elements: an obstinate determination to keep the initiative, if not against Great Britain, then against the last potentially dominant power on the continent, an impatient, half-blind impulse to take action (always a characteristic of Hitler and the Nazi movement as a whole), bitterness and anger that the Blitzkrieg strategy had not brought victory, increasing hate of the world-wide enemy, Jewry, on which he blamed his own

miscalculations, and an increasingly fanatical desire for destruction.

Thus, significantly, it was in connection with the preparations for the Russian campaign that Hitler issued the brutal secret orders which were later to acquire such terrible infamy in the Nazi war crimes trials: the order for the 'final solution of the Jewish problem', the order that captured Soviet commissars should be shot (an order which the Wehrmacht did not oppose), and the 'Night and Fog' decree of September 1941, which as a deterrent against sabotage in the Western occupied territories laid down that those suspected of opposition should be seized by police and whisked away to German prisons without any information being given to their families as to their fate.

At the same time, the German police introduced a mass of oppressive new measures against the churches, mostly the Catholic Church, with tighter bans on church demonstrations and the seizure of some 100 monasteries.

Failure and forced labour

The battle for Moscow during the winter of 1941-42 and the long drawn-out attacks of 1942 revealed what the battle of Stalingrad (October 1942 to February 1943) then confirmed: that victory in the East was no longer within reach. In the West, too, the initiative passed to the other side after the United States entered the war (December 1941). From 1942, 'area bombing' by the British and American air forces, which from 1943 possessed undisputed mastery of the air over Germany, had a disastrous effect on Germany's war economy and on the German population. Bombs killed some 400,000 civilians, and destroyed countless towns and industrial plants. The Anglo-American landing in Morocco and Algeria in November 1942 forced the capitulation of the Afrika Korps in May 1943. The Allied invasion of southern Italy in July 1943 also led to a German retreat. Mussolini's subsequent fall and the withdrawal of Italy from the Axis in August 1943 — which also brought into question the reliability of Germany's smaller allies (Hungary and Rumania) — threw the Nazi regime into its most severe political crisis to date.

This string of failures accelerated the growing extremism of Nazi policy inside Germany and caused further lasting changes in the Party's power structure in accordance with the 'total warfare' which had now been instituted. Symptomatic of this were the innovations in armaments production and labour allocation in March 1942. Particularly successful was the appointment of Albert Speer as Reich minister for armaments and production; the energetic and talented direction of

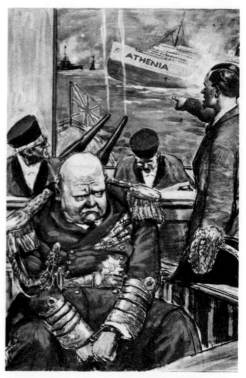

German cartoon of 1940 accuses Churchill of sinking the Athenia *to arouse anti-German feeling. The British liner was sunk a few hours after war started by a German U-boat, drowning 112 people, twenty-eight of them Americans. Mindful of how the sinking of the* Lusitania *helped bring America into the First World War, Hitler ordered a denial that a U-boat was involved and in October the official Nazi newspaper proclaimed: 'Churchill sank the* Athenia'. *The naval leaders who knew the truth were ordered to keep silent. Hitler had taken a further step towards total control of Germany and her people*

the former architect put Germany's armaments economy into high gear, and made possible a three-fold increase in arms production in 1943-44 compared with 1941, despite the Allied bombing raids. This brilliant technical and organizational feat was, however, closely bound up with the simultaneous massive extension of forced labour, for which responsibility was borne by Gauleiter Fritz Sauckel, named plenipotentiary general for the allocation of labour in March 1942, and — in the control of concentration camps — by Himmler. Millions of Russians — referred to derogatorily as *Ostarbeiter* (Eastern workers) — and Poles were forcibly brought to work in the Reich (as were French, Belgians, Dutch, Serbs, Czechs, Italians, and others). The building of the underground V-weapon production plant in the Harz mountains (transferred from Peenemünde after the RAF attack in 1943) was largely the work of 30,000 concentration camp prisoners. At least a quarter of them died of exhaustion before the end of the war.

Instruments of the police state

The fact that the regime had become more markedly a police state was also shown by the appointment of the former president of the Nazi People's Court, Otto Georg Thierack, as minister of justice in August 1942. Until then the department had been under the control of Franz Gürtner, of the German National People's Party (DNVP), and after his death in January 1941, of his state secretary, Schlegelberger. Both had repeatedly intervened to uphold fundamental legal principles and at least partly preserve the competence of the law, even if they were unable to prevent the law adapting in some form to Hitler's political and ideological standards. Thierack sought from the first a close understanding with Himmler and undertook on his behalf the sell-out of the legal system, for instance by his readiness to transfer some 10,000 state prisoners into SS concentration camps and to allow the prosecution of certain groups (Jews, Poles, Eastern workers) to be pursued wholly by the security police. His successor as president of the People's Court was Roland Freisler, who took office in the summer of 1942. Under his direction, this tribunal became an exemplary dispenser of Party justice after the manner of Stalin's show trials, most notably in the sentencing of the July Plot conspirators in 1944. In fact Freisler had become a fanatical Bolshevik as a prisoner of war in Russia in the First World War; he turned Nazi in 1924 but remained a warm admirer of Soviet terror. 'Freisler is our Vishinsky' (who was prosecutor during the Purge) exclaimed Hitler in one of the first conferences after Stauffenberg's attempt on his life.

An exotic Eastern court

Apart from Speer, who after 1942 replaced Göring as the leading power in economic policy (the Reichsmarschall's credit largely ran out with Hitler after the failure of the Luftwaffe), it was Goebbels, Himmler, and Bormann who held the most power and were the decisive influences from 1942-43. As Speer, the ablest and least corrupted member of Hitler's entourage, said: 'Relations between the various high leaders can only be understood if their aspirations are interpreted as a struggle for the succession to Adolf Hitler'. Hitler's last years reveal the steadily quickening breakdown of the machinery of government until his cabinet resembled an exotic Eastern court, with each vying with the other for the ruler's favours.

From 1942 onwards, Hitler tended to avoid public speeches and gatherings and seldom left his headquarters in East Prussia; the responsibility for the whole field of propaganda in the second half of the war thus fell increasingly on Goebbels. In contrast to the other Nazi officials, the propaganda minister, with an instinctive feeling for his job, saw that the turn of events after the first euphoric phase of the war demanded a completely new approach to propaganda. He knew that in the case of dire necessity, appeal to the suppressed readiness for self-sacrifice and participation, and to defiant national solidarity could be even more effective than delirious rapture. Thus Goebbels, in the famous demonstration in the Berlin Sportpalast on 18th February 1943, shortly after the Battle of Stalingrad was able even so to carry his listeners away into a fanatical affirmation of his own total commitment to sacrifice, an affirmation which later seemed merely to be an expression of mass hysteria.

In fact the attitude of a large part of the German population at this stage would be hard to understand without a knowledge of the psychological state of mind so successfully controlled by Goebbels. Certainly there was now growing doubt and criticism, and the war had brought considerable hardship—two million German soldiers dead by 1945. But recognition of the one who was truly responsible became more difficult the longer Hitler was relied upon and applauded. People managed to convince themselves that it was a precept of loyalty to hold out in the face of difficulties; they no longer really believed in 'final victory', but no-one dared think of defeat since in the present situation this would mean Russian victory and domination. This psychological mixture of panic, loyalty, self-pity, and self-deception also created a moral blindness to the spreading oppressiveness of the regime and the sufferings of the persecuted Jews, with whom contact had long been lost by discrimination and imprisonment in ghettos, even before the secret, but not unnoticed, deportations in 1941-42. It was the greatest failure that at this time those guardians of the nation who still held their posts—clergy, university professors, high-ranking officers—remained almost completely silent.

Goebbels' indispensability as propagandist of the total war effort greatly extended his influence in the last years. He remained true to the myth which he had served faithfully for so many years. At the end he had no thought of escape. He planned his death to mirror Hitler's. The high standing Goebbels won with the Führer was shown when Hitler appointed him future chancellor of the now non-existent Reich in his political testament dated 29th April 1945.

Himmler, too, had continually acquired new powers and responsibilities since the beginning of the war. Since 1936 joint SS-chief and head of the police, he was appointed Reich commissioner for the consolidation of German nationhood on 7th October 1939 and was given responsibility for the direction of the whole policy of deportation and Germanization of the East. Himmler's influence and that of individual SS departments spread increasingly to foreign policy through Himmler's control of relations with Germans living abroad, the enrolment of Germanic volunteers for the SS, and above all through his contacts with the security police and the intelligence services of allied and neutral countries. In addition, Himmler assumed control of the Reich Interior Ministry in 1943, and of the Reserve Army at home after the July Plot. Göring, Ribbentrop, Frick, and other formerly very influential ministers were unequivocally outmanoeuvred by Himmler from 1941 onwards.

Byzantine absolutism

Himmler's only competitor in the last years of the war was Martin Bormann, who was largely unknown even in 1939 but assumed the direction of the Party Chancery in May 1941 when Hitler's deputy Rudolph Hess flew to Great Britain on his peace bid. But what was more decisive for Bormann's rise was his position of confidence as Hitler's permanent attendant and secretary. He became the vital intermediary between Hitler and the outside world. He matched his master's eccentric hours and became the sole channel for his orders.

The more Hitler absented himself from Berlin, the more absolute his rule became. And, as it was impossible for his ministers to penetrate his headquarters for months on end, the more important became Bormann's position as king of the lobby, as executor and interpreter of Hitler's orders.

This Byzantine consequence of Hitler's absolutism was characteristic of the last phase of Hitler's rule; it meant that even Hitler's adjutants and the permanent representatives of the ministers in Hitler's headquarters became decisive figures. The almost permanent power struggle between personalities and groups for Hitler's favour and the increasing chaos in the definition of responsibilities—all this led to a process of growing self-destruction in the regime, which was only held together by more orders from the Führer. In the end, everyone who had the power to do so was playing the petty Führer to the full extent of his influence. With Hitler's suicide, dissolution was complete. Colossal energies had been unleashed, colossal crimes begun, colossal destruction risked—and nothing remained.

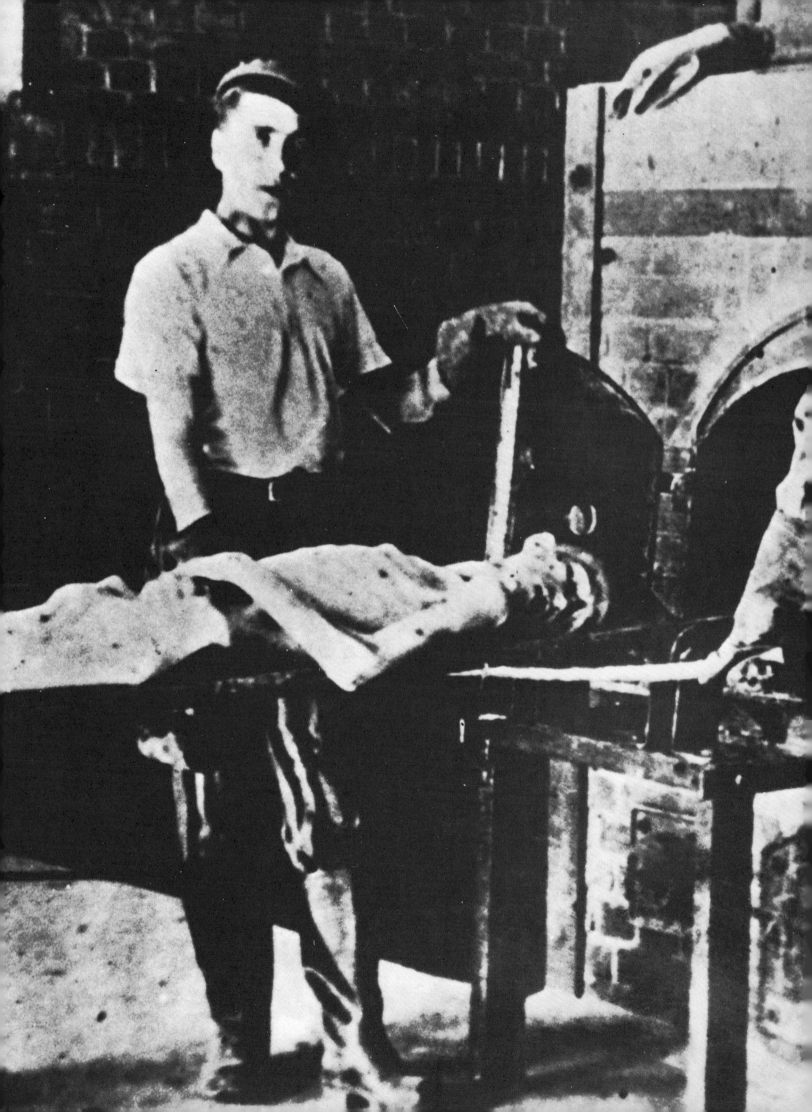

The Final Solution

Before the beginning of the war in Europe, the measures taken by Hitler against the Jews seemed essentially to be aimed at excluding them from all functions within German society. The result of this progressive isolation was that the majority of Jews decided to leave first Germany itself, and then post-Anschluss Austria, and the Protectorate of Bohemia-Moravia. But after the conquest of Poland more than three million Jews found themselves under German control and their number exceeded seven million after the extension of the Nazi hegemony of Western Europe, the Balkans, the Baltic countries, White Russia, and the Ukraine. Until October 1941 Jews were theoretically allowed to emigrate, but in fact only a few thousand privileged ones managed to escape those regions controlled by the forces of the Reich.

Three weeks after the German invasion of Poland, on 21st September 1939, the head of the Central Security Office of the Reich, Reinhard Heydrich, issued an order to keep the Polish Jews closely grouped together 'as a means to the final aim' *(als erste Voraussetzung für das Endziel).* This enigmatic phrase did not prove that the Nazi leaders were already envisaging the physical extermination of the Jews. On 23rd November 1939, the Polish Jews received the order to wear a distinctive sign — the yellow star. In April 1940, the Jews at Łódź were confined in a ghetto and in October of the same year it was the turn of the Jews at Warsaw to suffer the same fate. Soon, nearly all Polish Jews were imprisoned in ghettos containing populations ranging from several thousand to half a million in the Warsaw ghetto. The ghettos were separated from 'Aryan' quarters by high walls or barbed wire, guarded by both local and German police.

In the ghettos the administration of community affairs was allotted to 'Jewish councils', the *Judenräte,* whose authority was often considerable, backed up by an auxiliary Jewish police force. The role of the *Judenräte* has often been criticized, but the majority did what they could to alleviate the sufferings of the inhabitants of the ghettos. Nevertheless, from the winter of 1940-41, famine, cold, and epidemics caused tens of thousands of deaths.

After the beginning of the war, the fate of the Polish Jews was harshest, but that of the Jews who remained in the Reich was scarcely better. They were systematically submitted to the most humiliating and

Auschwitz camp oven for disposal of bodies. The Nazis saw the 'final solution' as an industrial problem, to be solved by industrial means

sadistic rules: they were forbidden to use public transport, to sit on park benches, to use public telephones, to own domestic animals, furs, or woollen clothes, typewriters, bicycles, spectacles, or electrical appliances. Converted Jews no longer had the right to attend religious services at the same time as 'Aryan' Christians. In the meantime, in the offices of the Wilhelmstrasse they were considering the possibility of deporting all European Jews to the island of Madagascar, which would become a sort of Jewish 'reserve' under the control of the German police. In fact the Madagascar plan came to nothing.

The fate of Jews in the Nazi-occupied countries of Western Europe differed vastly from one to another. In Denmark and Norway they were treated no differently from the rest of the community, but in Vichy France anti-Semitic laws were passed in 1941. Before long, thousands of foreign Jews were interned in special camps in both zones. In Holland, also, the plight of the Jews deteriorated rapidly: thus at the beginning of 1941 several hundred Jewish hostages were deported to the camp of Mauthausen where they were tortured to death: of the 618 who arrived in the spring of 1941, only eight survived to the beginning of 1942.

But a dramatic change in the Jewish situation took place with the preparations for the German attack on the Soviet Union.

When Adolf Hitler took the final decision to attack the Soviet Union, the conflict, within the sphere of political and strategic machinations, undoubtedly appeared to him as an apocalyptic struggle between the forces of good led by National-Socialist Germany and the forces of evil of which 'Jewish Bolshevism' was the supreme manifestation. It was then that Hitler decided to carry out what he had prophesied in a speech to the Reichstag on 30th January 1939: that a new world war would mark the extermination of the Jewish race in Europe....

It is not known exactly when Hitler gave the official order to exterminate all Jews under Nazi control, but he certainly gave this order orally to Göring and Himmler in March or April 1941. The commanders of the Special Action Units *(Einsatzgruppen),* who were made responsible for the liquidation of the Jews in occupied Russia, stated after the war that they had been informed of their mission by word of mouth in May 1941. On 31st July 1941, Göring gave Heydrich a written order charging him to take any steps necessary towards a 'general solution to the Jewish problem in the areas of German influence in Europe'. On 20th January 1942, Heyd-

rich put forward his plan at the so-called Wannsee Conference which brought together the leading functionaries of the principal German ministries: 'The final solution *(Endlösung)* to the Jewish problem in Europe', he declared, 'will be applied to about eleven million people . . . The Jews must be transferred to the East under close surveillance and there assigned to forced labour . . . It goes without saying that a great many of them will be naturally eliminated by physical deficiency. The remainder who survive this—and who must be regarded as the most resistant group—must be dealt with accordingly. Indeed, history has shown us that this natural élite carries within itself the seeds of a new Jewish renaissance . . .'

Mass-execution of the Jews began in Russia with the beginnings of the German occupation. The Special Action Units, mostly supported by the local militia and often aided by Wehrmacht units, sometimes organized temporary ghettos where the inmates were not liquidated until several months later. But their most frequent method was immediate mass-execution. During the first five months of the Russian campaign the Special Action Units massacred more than 100,000 Jews a month. Machine-gun executions were supplemented with executions by means of the carbon monoxide fumes of lorries. In all, nearly 1,400,000 Jews were executed in Russia by 3,000 members of the Special Action Units.

The deportation of German Jews to the ghettos and camps in the East began at the end of 1941. In the course of 1942 the Nazis systematically deported Jews from the various occupied and controlled countries in Western Europe. Depending on the country and the attitude of local authorities, the German action met with varying degrees of success. In Poland itself, where, in spite of famine and disease, more than two and a half million Jews were still living early in 1942, nothing could be done to halt the massacre.

The extermination of the Jews in Wartheland (that part of Poland which was annexed to the Reich) began in March 1942 at the Chełmno camp. There the gas chamber was most frequently used. Soon after it was the turn of the Jews from Lublin and Lwów who were taken to the Belżec camp, where carbon monoxide was the usual method. Systematic liquidation

Top: Himmler (left) is shown Mauthausen concentration camp. When he watched the extermination of Jews at Auschwitz it made him feel physically sick. Centre: Gestapo search for weapons during Warsaw ghetto raid. Bottom: Inspection of Warsaw Ordnungsdienst, those Jews responsible to the Germans for maintaining order in the ghetto

in the Warsaw ghetto began in July: hundreds of thousands of Jews from the ghetto in the capital were transferred in groups to the Treblinka camp. 'Operation Reinhard', so-called after Reinhard Heydrich, killed in June 1942 by Czech agents, swiftly engulfed the whole of Poland. Soon the immense installations of the Auschwitz-Birkenau camp (in German-controlled Upper Silesia) became the main execution site. Inspired by the 'experience' gained in 1940 and 1941 when euthanasia had been practised on the mentally ill, new methods of extermination were perfected, and from then on prussic acid (Zyklon B) replaced carbon monoxide from diesel engines. Extermination by means of Zyklon B took place in large gas chambers, each capable of holding up to 2,000 people, disguised as showers or disinfectant rooms. Those deportees who were not directly selected for the gas chambers soon died as a result of the forced labour to which they were submitted for the vast enterprises run by the SS within the camps or set up in close proximity by German industry (notably I.G.Farben). Others died by 'medical experiments' which included exposure to high-pressure, freezing, and vaccination with infectious diseases. The organization of deportation, forced labour, and immediate extermination of millions of people required the setting-up of a vast bureaucratic machine. This was primarily inspired by Hitler himself, but the actual responsibility fell to the Reichsführer SS, Heinrich Himmler. Himmler set the work in motion through many channels but primarily through the Central Security Office of the Reich, under the direction of Reinhard Heydrich and later Ernst Kaltenbrunner, and the Central Office of Economic Organization of the SS under the direction of Oswald Pohl. The hunt for Jews and their deportation to the camps was mainly carried out by the Central Security Office and particularly by Adolf Eichmann's office IV B4, while the actual supervision of the camps fell to Pohl's office. But the responsibilities in each of these domains remained imprecise, a situation which was further complicated by the delegation of special powers to the 'heads of police and of the SS' in certain zones.

The 'final solution' was only incidentally exploited to further the German 'war effort'. Certainly those who were forced to do hard labour contributed, but the essen-

Above: Member of a Judenrat, or Jewish council which administered community affairs in the Warsaw ghetto, counting the victims of starvation and disease whose emaciated corpses were piled into handcarts for removal and burial. **Right:** *A pile of human bones and skulls at Maidanek extermination camp in Poland*

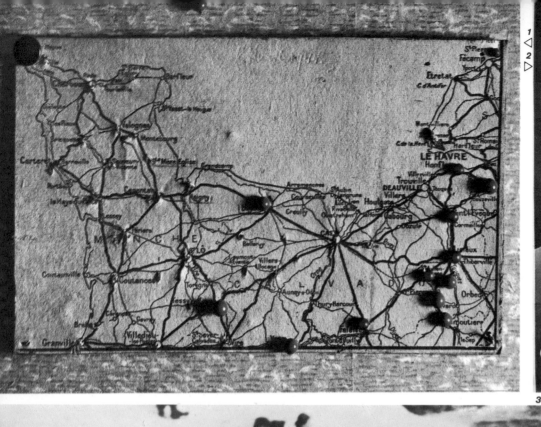

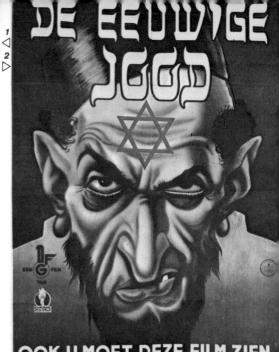

DE EEUWIGE JOOD

OOK U MOET DEZE FILM ZIEN

EEN DOCUMENTAIRE FILM OVER HET WERELD-JODENDOM.
NAAR EEN IDEE VAN DR. E. TAUBERT. SAMENSTELLING: FRITZ HIPPLER
MUZIEK: FRANZ R. FRIEDL

tial aim of the operation was to kill the Jews. Indeed during the last two years of the war, deportation hindered the war effort because the vehicles used to transport the Jews to camps were badly needed on the Eastern Front.

When at the beginning of 1945, this programme was about to end between five and six million Jews had died. (Himmler seems to have ordered an end to the 'final solution' in November 1944, but it was not followed.)

From 1943 the large-scale extermination of the Jews was a well-known fact in Germany, the neutral countries, and among the Allies. But protests were only sporadic and nothing was done to try to save those who still could be saved. In the occupied countries of the East, those Jews who managed to escape the Germans for a time were often killed by partisans or handed over to the Nazis by civilians.

When one takes this into consideration, it is easier to understand the strange 'passivity' of the Jews in Europe in the face of this massacre. The majority could not and would not believe that the Nazis had decided to kill them all. Others—who had understood—were exhausted both morally and physically to such an extent that they no longer had the strength to put up a resistance that was without hope. Many realized that they were in a hopeless position, caught between the barbarity of the Nazis and the general indifference of the 'spectators'. Only a few insignificant groups organized armed revolts in some ghettos and camps. The revolt in the Warsaw ghetto which flared up on 18th April 1943 is the best known. For several weeks, a few thousand Jews practically without arms and entirely without outside assistance held out against several German battalions. From the German point of view it was nothing but a minor anti-partisan affair and only a few dozen Germans were killed. But the revolt in the Warsaw ghetto became a symbolic turning point in the history of the Jews: 'It was,' as Reitlinger points out, 'the first national military combat undertaken by the Jews since the Bar Kochba revolt under the reign of the Emperor Hadrian, 1,800 years before.'

Left: 1 Map showing advancing Allies found in home of the Franks, a Jewish family in Amsterdam. In her diary Anne Frank left a moving account of Nazi persecution. 2 Dutch poster advertises The Eternal Jew, *a pre-war film shown widely in occupied Europe. 3 The gaolers confronted with their crime. SS wardresses transfer bodies to a mass grave after the British liberation of Belsen, April 1945.*
Right: 'The Prayer of the Killed' by Polish artist Bronisław Linke. A Jew, depicted surrealistically, prays amid the rubble of Warsaw

6 CLOSING THE RING

Russia Strikes Back

By November 1942 German forces were fighting on the banks of the Volga at Stalingrad, and in the foothills of the Caucasus. Hitler had not yet given up his plan to cut off central European Russia from the Caucasus and Central Asia and to seize the former's oilfields. In fact, by seizing this very rich and strategically important region he calculated on eliminating the Soviet Union the following summer, thus threatening the Middle East and India.

The predicament of the Soviet Union and its armed forces remained perilous. Leningrad was under blockade by German and Finnish troops and large forces of the enemy were still operating in the outer approaches to Moscow; the protracted and ferocious battle at Stalingrad was absorbing more and more forces; the main lines of communication with the Caucasus were cut and the Baltic Fleet was blockaded in the eastern end of the Gulf of Finland. But events had now passed out of German control. All those factors and circumstances which German Blitzkrieg strategy had failed to take adequately into account were making themselves increasingly felt. The turning point had been brought gradually nearer during the stubborn battles fought by the Red Army in 1941 and the summer of 1942, and as a result of the intense effort made by the entire country. The victory of the Soviet forces before Moscow between December 1941 and March 1942 served as a terrible warning to the enemy. Moreover, the failures suffered in the summer campaign of 1942 did not destroy the Red Army as a fighting force. By the autumn of that year it had made good its

Left: German painting shows a grenadier priming his weapon

losses and was no longer inferior to the enemy in strength. The front was stable along its whole length, from the Barents Sea to the foothills of the Caucasus.

The southern grouping of the enemy's armed forces was the most active and dangerous and it was necessary first and foremost to destroy this concentration. The very idea of a counter-offensive was conceived in the midst of defensive battles and as early as 13th September Marshal Zhukov wrote 'after studying all possible variants, Marshal Vasilyevsky and I decided to propose the following plan of action to Stalin: firstly to continue active defence in order to wear the enemy down and secondly to prepare a counter-offensive in order to deal such a blow to the enemy in the Stalingrad area as would radically change the strategic situation in the south of the country to our advantage.'

As a result of the Red Army's victory at Stalingrad, VI Army was annihilated and the strategic initiative passed, for good, to the Soviet Union. Soviet strategy was now faced with the question of how and in what order it should exploit the new opportunities arising out of victory on the Volga. At that time the Red Army had already achieved a certain numerical preponderance over the enemy, but this was not so significant that the simultaneous fulfilment of several strategic tasks could be contemplated. The Soviet Supreme Command wanted first and foremost to take advantage of the fact that the Voronezh, south-western, and southern fronts had achieved an ascendancy over the enemy. They could develop offensives in the direction of Rostov, into the rear of Army Group A in the northern Caucasus and towards the north-west into the rear of

Army Group B. Defeat of these forces would enable the Red Army to liberate important economic areas—the North Caucasus, the Donbas, Kharkov, Orel, Kursk, and other regions. The main forces of the Red Army were directed to these two objectives. In addition, the Supreme Command decided to lift the enemy blockade of Leningrad, and to destroy the Demyansk and Rzhev-Vyazma salients, from which the German forces might renew their offensive against Moscow if favourable circumstances should offer themselves.

After the destruction of German forces in Kotelnikovo the southern front command sent units towards the Donbas, and two armies towards Rostov. On 28th December Hitler was obliged to order Army Group A to fall back, destroying as it did so all railway lines and rolling stock. In mid-January two armies of the southern front reached the River Manych, where they encountered stubborn resistance from Army Group Don. On 3rd January the northern group of the trans-Caucasian front and the 11th Black Sea Group began offensive operations; but these Soviet forces lacked sufficient men, resources, and motor transport to make the pace of their offensive a rapid one. This fact enabled I Panzer Group to evade Soviet forces pursuing it, and one part fell back to Rostov while another joined XVII Army in the Taman Peninsula. On 12th February Soviet troops took Krasnodar and two days later Rostov. Although the offensive against the German XVII Army continued until the beginning of April, by mid-February the Red Army had liberated nearly all the north Caucasus, with its population of ten million.

In the second half of January the Voronezh front launched an offensive against Army Group B, resulting in the defeat, in the Ostrogozhsk and Rossosh areas, of the Hungarian II Army and the left wing of the Italian VIII Army.

At the end of January and the beginning of February 1943, a new and violent conflict erupted on the southern wing of the Soviet-German front. The Stavka (Soviet equivalent of Combined Chiefs of Staff) and the General Staff drew up a plan for a non-stop offensive by forces of the Voronezh, south-western and southern fronts in left-bank Ukraine (Ukraine to the east of the Dnieper), calculating that before the melting of the winter snows they would have reached the Dnieper along a front stretching from Chernigov to Kherson. In addition, it was planned to launch an offensive by the armies of the Kalinin, western and Bryansk fronts against Army Group Centre in mid-February.

The enemy strove to halt the Red Army's advance and, if unable to throw the Soviet forces back to the Don, then to stabilize the front and prepare to turn the tables when summer came. Hitler wanted, in any event, to hold on to the Donbas because of the importance of this area from the standpoint of war production. The reserves which had been concentrated in the south for the purpose of liberating Paulus's army were now assigned a different task, that of halting Red Army forces on the approaches to the Donbas and Kharkov and hurling them back. The forces of both sides exhausted themselves in ceaseless battles. With extremely extended lines of communication Soviet troops undertook a fresh offensive without adequate reserves, and without re-grouping. The Supreme Command had assumed that the enemy would retire. 'This idea,' General Shtemenko has written, 'which arose from an incorrect evaluation of the enemy's behaviour only seemed to correspond to the real situation. At that time, however, the General Staff and the Stavka were convinced of the correctness of their appreciations and calculations. The triumphant despatches from the fronts lulled the vigilance of both the Stavka and General Staff.'

At first the offensive on all fronts proceeded successfully. Voronezh front captured Kursk on 8th February and Kharkov on 16th February. Other centres of population followed. By mid-February the south-western front had cleared the enemy from the north-eastern Donbas and its forward divisions had reached the Dnieper at Dnepropetrovsk. The southern front had pushed between 90 and 150 kilometres to the west and arrived at the River Mius. By this time, however, the enemy possessed substantial advantages over the advancing Soviet troops. Owing to extremely extended lines of communication

both Soviet fronts were experiencing interruptions in the supply of munitions, fuel, and even food, whereas the enemy, in falling back, drew nearer to his main supply base.

The front stabilizes

While the Soviet forces were continuing their offensive towards the Dnieper, Manstein launched a counter-offensive towards Pavlodar with XLVIII Panzer Corps and towards Barvenkovo with XL Panzer Corps. Ferocious battles began in conditions unfavourable to the Soviet forces who continued to receive orders to advance. At last General Vatutin gave up trying to continue the offensive and began organizing defensive positions. The troops withdrew with heavy losses to the north part of the River Donets and at the beginning of March took up a firm defence line. At the same time, Manstein sent his Panzer Corps against the left flank of the Voronezh front which was still moving towards the Dnieper. The Soviet troops put up a determined resistance, but had to fall back under pressure of the superior German forces, abandoning Belgorod and Kharkov. Fighting continued in this sector until the end of March but the Germans were unable to advance any further and the front was stabilized, forming the Kursk bulge.

In order to stabilize the front in the south-western sector the Soviet Supreme Command was obliged in March to draw largely upon its strategic reserve. This meant that the offensive against Army Group Centre in the Smolensk sector had to be undertaken solely by troops of the Kalinin and western fronts. Within a fortnight they had smashed the Rzhev-Vyazma salient and advanced to the outer approaches of Smolensk.

In March 1943, after the siege of Leningrad had been partially lifted, a lull fell on the front. Every day for the next three months stereotyped communiqués reported that 'nothing important had happened at the front'. Behind this outward calm, however, intense preparations for the summer campaign were under way on both sides. The Soviet Union had achieved definite advantages over the enemy and during the year production of arms and military equipment increased considerably: the average monthly output of aircraft, for example, rose to 3,000 and that of tanks and self-propelled guns to 2,000. By the summer the strength of the operational army had grown to 6,442,000 while the enemy's comparable strength was 5,325,000. The operational section of the Red Army was equipped with 103,085 artillery pieces and mortars, the enemy with 56,250; our forces had 9,918 tanks and self-propelled guns as against the enemy's 5,850, and 8,357

fighter aircraft as against his 2,980. Inspired by their victories, the morale of the Red Army had risen, whereas that of the enemy had fallen. The Soviet troops had acquired a tremendous amount of battle experience and now knew both the enemy's strong and weak points. By the summer, the Soviet ground forces, the air force, the anti-aircraft defences, and the rear services of the Red Army had all been completely reorganized and in consequence the armed forces as a whole now possessed an organizational structure which was more flexible and better adapted to war conditions so that their striking power and mobility were enhanced. Besides restoring and reorganizing the front-line armies, the Supreme Command increased the number of reserve armies to ten.

At the end of March and beginning of April 1943 the problem on which the Stavka and the General Staff were working was where, when, and how to concentrate the forces they possessed so as to accomplish the main strategic tasks set for the summer. The views of the commanders who represented the Stavka in the operational armies were sought, and also those of some of the front commanders. After a thorough study had been made of intelligence about the state and disposition of the enemy's forces, all agreed that the centre of strategic operations during the summer should be the area of the Kursk salient. As regards the method to be followed, the first to express himself definitely on this question was Marshal Zhukov. In a letter he sent to Stalin on 8th April he wrote: 'I consider it inadvisable for our forces to go over to the offensive in the very first days of the campaign in order to forestall the enemy. It would be better to make the enemy first exhaust himself against our defences, and knock out his tanks and then, bringing up fresh reserves, to go over to a general offensive which would finally finish off his main force.' Four days later, Stalin convened a special conference at Supreme Headquarters to discuss the plan for the summer campaign. It was decided to concentrate the main effort in the Kursk area.

For operations along the 550-kilometre Kursk salient twenty-six per cent of the total manpower of the operational Red Army, twenty-six per cent of its artillery and mortars, thirty-five and a half per cent of its fighter aircraft, and over forty-six per cent of its tanks were concentrated. Meanwhile intensive operations for the summer campaign were also going on at Hitler's headquarters, the Wolfsschanze (Wolf's Lair) in East Prussia, in the German General Staff, and in the staffs of their armies and army groups. Hitler insisted that the positions won must be held. After careful inquiries and discussions, it was

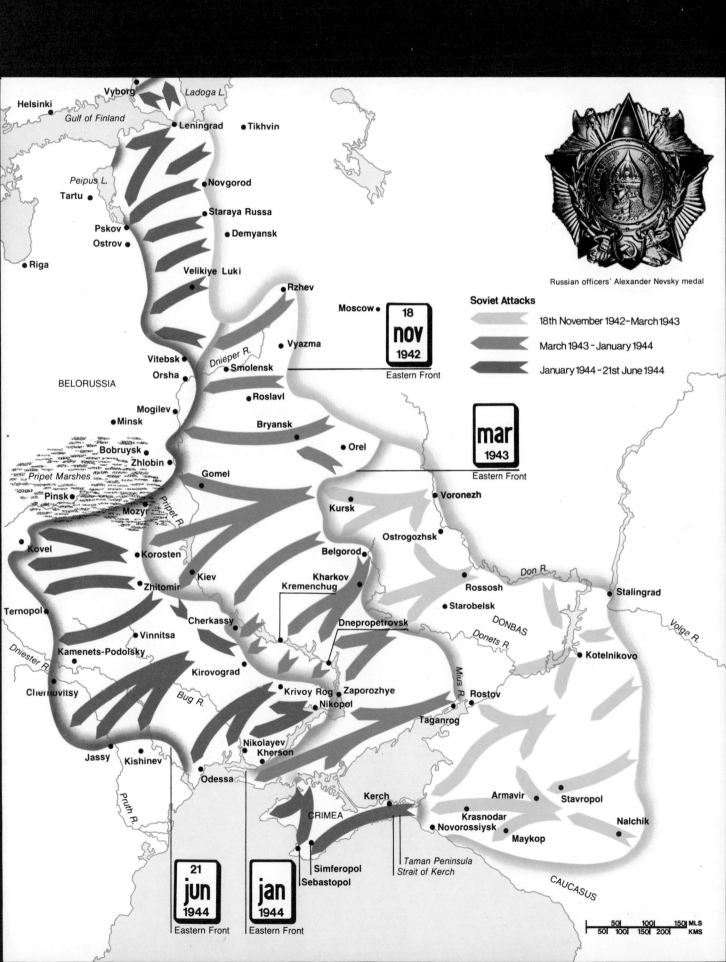

Russian officers' Alexander Nevsky medal

Soviet Attacks

18th November 1942–March 1943

March 1943 – January 1944

January 1944 – 21st June 1944

Helsinki

Gulf of Finland

Vyborg

Ladoga L.

Leningrad

Tikhvin

Peipus L.

Tartu

Novgorod

Staraya Russa

Pskov

Demyansk

Ostrov

Riga

Velikiye Luki

Rzhev

Moscow

18 nov 1942
Eastern Front

Vyazma

Vitebsk

Dnieper R.

Orsha

Smolensk

BELORUSSIA

Roslavl

Mogilev

Bryansk

Minsk

Orel

Bobruysk

Zhlobin

mar 1943
Eastern Front

Gomel

Pripet Marshes

Pinsk

Voronezh

Mozyr

Kursk

Pripet R.

Ostrogozhsk

Kovel

Korosten

Belgorod

Don R.

Kiev

Kharkov

Zhitomir

Kremenchug

Rossosh

Stalingrad

Starobelsk

DONBAS

Ternopol

Cherkassy

Dnepropetrovsk

Donets R.

Volga R.

Vinnitsa

Kamenets-Podolsky

Kirovograd

Mius R.

Kotelnikovo

Chernovitsy

Bug R.

Krivoy Rog

Zaporozhye

Rostov

Nikopol

Taganrog

Dniester R.

Nikolayev

Jassy

Kishinev

Kherson

Odessa

Kerch

Armavir

Stavropol

CRIMEA

Krasnodar

Pruth R.

Novorossiysk

Nalchik

Maykop

21 jun 1944
Eastern Front

jan 1944
Eastern Front

Simferopol

Sebastopol

Taman Peninsula
Strait of Kerch

CAUCASUS

| 50 | 100 | 150 MLS |
| 50 | 100 | 150 | 200 | KMS |

decided in mid-March to prepare and carry out during the summer an offensive code-named Operation Citadel, which should have the aim of surrounding and destroying the Soviet forces in the Kursk salient. After that, it was proposed to launch Operation Panther into the rear of the south-western front, which lay along the northern section of the River Donets. Hitler hesitated. Several times he put off the launching of the offensive. On 21st June he ordered its launching on 3rd July, later changing this date to 5th July.

The German offensive was tensely awaited in the Soviet camp. Stalin showed some irritation; Zhukov and Vasilyevsky stayed with the troops. All ranks at the front were kept in constant readiness for battle. And when on the morning of 5th July seventeen enemy Panzer divisions, with three motorized divisions and eighteen infantry divisions, moved from Orel and Belgorod towards Kursk, they met stubborn resistance from the central and Voronezh fronts. In five days the enemy's Orel force advanced only some nine to twelve kilometres and soon spent its offensive power. In the Belgorod-Kursk sector German forces did better, advancing between fifteen and thirty-five kilometres. Stalin approved the proposal made by Vasilyevsky and Vatutin to begin the Voronezh front's counter-offensive without waiting for the enemy forces to be brought to a halt. On 12th July five armies of this front, reinforced by one tank army and one general purposes army from the strategic reserve, delivered a counter-attack on the Germans while they were still continuing their advance. A bitter struggle began, especially in the Prokhorovka area, where about 1,100 tanks of both sides joined battle. The Soviet and German forces alike suffered great losses, but the German offensive was finally halted on the southern section of the Kursk salient.

On 12th July the western and Bryansk fronts launched Operation Kutuzov aimed at destroying the enemy's Orel forces. With difficulty they broke the long-sustained defence put up by the enemy on the edges of the Orel salient. Three days later the forces of the central front joined

Left: 1 January 1943 — village children near Stalingrad play with abandoned German weapons. The Germans were on the retreat, and in Stalingrad itself the remnants of VI Army were being bombarded, starved, and frozen into surrender. 2 Soviet infantry attacking. 3 Red Army patrol on the Volkhov front. 4 German soldiers captured by the Russians. The losses in manpower on the Eastern Front were enormous. By now young and old alike were drafted to fill the ranks

in the offensive. On 26th July the German commander, General Model, gave the order for his troops to withdraw from the Orel salient so as to avoid forming another cauldron. The Soviet forces pursuing them captured Orel on 5th August and within two days completely wiped out the Orel salient. As they retreated, the German forces burned down towns and villages, shot or drove away the local inhabitants, and destroyed the crops.

On 16th July, German troops in the Belgorod-Kharkov sector began to pull back to their start line. The troops of the Voronezh front, together with General Konev's troops of the steppe front, brought into the battle from the Stavka's reserve, reached the line held by the Soviet troops before the beginning of the defensive battle within a week and after re-grouping launched Operation Rumyantsev to smash German units in the Belgorod-Kharkov area on 3rd August. Belgorod was taken on 5th August,

and on 23rd August, Kharkov capitulated. Now Soviet forces began to advance towards the Dnieper. With the destruction of German forces at Kharkov the Battle of Kursk came to an end.

Having won the strategic initiative, the Red Army advanced along a 2,000-kilometre front from Velikiye Luki to the Black Sea. The troops taking part in this advance were carrying out an operation which has become known as the battle for the Dnieper.

On 13th August, the forces of the southwestern front, commanded by General Malinovsky, resumed the battle for the Donbas and forced their way across the northern section of the River Donets. Five days later, the southern front, commanded by General Tolbukhin, began to advance on Taganrog. The two fronts enveloped Army Group South from the flanks. In order to avoid encirclement, Manstein ordered his forces to retire across the Dnieper, applying scorched earth tactics as they went. Vigor-

ous pursuit by the Soviet forces prevented this plan from being fully realized, though the Donbas did suffer enormous damage.

In the second half of September, Soviet troops arrived on the banks of the Dnieper along a 700-kilometre front from the mouth of the River Sozh to Zaporozhye. After reaching the river they forced crossings at a number of points, besides utilizing those crossing places which had been captured and held by the partisans. Owing to the rapidity of the advance, the rear services had not been able to keep up the supply of engineering materials for bridging the river. By the end of the month, Soviet forces had won twenty-three bridgeheads on the right bank of the river, many of these being merely narrow strips of the

German prisoners with shaved heads being paraded through the streets of a Russian town – a ritual which underlined Russia's growing ability to seize the initiative

bank which were held until reinforcements could come up. Gradually, these bridgeheads were enlarged, and men and equipment assembled in them.

The offensive also proceeded in other directions. In August the Kalinin and western fronts undertook active operations in the direction of Smolensk, throwing back German forces and occupying the city. Although this offensive was not so successful as the southern one, it tied down fifty-five enemy divisions. Further south, the Bryansk and central fronts moved forward. By the beginning of October they had reached the borders of Belorussia and were fighting on the approaches to Vitebsk, Orsha, and Mogilev. On 10th September the forces of the North Caucasian front, commanded by General Petrov, began to advance on the Taman Peninsula. They destroyed this last German bridgehead in Caucasia, forced a crossing of the Strait of Kerch and seized a bridgehead for themselves in the Crimea.

In October the Soviet fronts were reorganized and renamed. On the foundation of the Bryansk front the 2nd Baltic front was formed, while the Kalinin front was renamed the 1st Baltic front, the central front became the Belorussian front and the Voronezh, steppe, south-western, and southern fronts were now called, respectively, the 1st, 2nd, 3rd and 4th Ukrainian fronts. The Ukrainian fronts waged an uninterrupted offensive battle right down to the end of the year. On 3rd November, two armies of the 1st Ukrainian front struck at the Lyutezh bridgehead, broke through the enemy front and on the evening of 5th November reached Kiev. By the next morning the city had been cleared of the enemy, and the troops of this front began to move on Zhitomir and Korosten. By the end of November they had established a strategic bridgehead extending 230 kilometres along the front and 150 kilometres in depth. The forces of the 2nd and 3rd Ukrainian fronts resumed their offensive from the bridgeheads they had won, captured the towns of Cherkassy, Dneprodzerzhinsk and Zaporozhye, and established a wide strategic bridgehead on the middle and lower course of the Dnieper. In September the 4th Ukrainian front smashed the German front on the River Molochnaya and came out on the lower reaches of the Dnieper and the Crimean Isthmus. Only at Nikopol did the Germans manage to retain a bridgehead on the left bank of the Dnieper.

The offensive continues

The onset of winter did not stop the Red Army's offensive in the Ukraine. And although the losses suffered by our operational forces were such as to make it impossible to restore and keep their strength at the level of summer 1943, an overall superiority over the enemy was maintained. As for the enemy, he had to fall back on the strategic defensive, hoping to be able to gain time to prepare to recover the initiative later on.

But the Stavka planned not only to continue the offensive but also to extend its front to the Baltic Sea. The main blow was to be struck in the south-western sector, in order to smash Army Group South and Army Group A in right-bank Ukraine and the Crimea. The Soviet forces operating in the north-western sector were assigned the tasks of smashing Army Group North, finally raising the blockade of Leningrad, and entering the approaches of the Baltic region. In the centre the task was to defeat Army Group Centre and clear a substantial part of the enemy from Belorussia. The implementation of this plan resulted in the liberation of nearly all Soviet territory.

On 14th January 1944 the forces of the Leningrad and Volkhov fronts went over to the offensive and within a week compelled the enemy's XVIII Army to begin withdrawing south-westward from its positions before Leningrad. In the other sector, troops of the Volkhov front smashed German forces before Novgorod and on 20th January recaptured this ancient Russian city. Subsequently the Leningrad front to which the greater part of the Volkhov front was subordinated, continued its advance, halting at the end of the winter at the approaches to Pskov and Ostrov. Meanwhile the 2nd Baltic front took Staraya Russa and an important road junction at Dno station. The result of the one-and-a-half-month offensive by the Soviet forces in the north-western sector was an advance of 220-280 kilometres and the complete raising of the blockade of Leningrad.

In the Ukraine, the Stavka planned an offensive along the entire front, from the River Pripet to the Black Sea. The first stage of this offensive was to finish finally with the enemy defences of the Dnieper and reach the southern section of the River Bug, and the second to cut the enemy's front in two, advance towards the Carpathians and reach a line from Lutsk through Mogilev Podolsky to the River Dniester. The four Ukrainian fronts were opposed by Army Group South under Field-Marshal Manstein and Army Group A under Field-Marshal Kleist. The German command thought that the Red Army would be unable to continue its advance immediately after the intense battle for the Dnieper.

The enemy's calculations were not confirmed by events. At the end of December 1943 and in the following January, the 1st Ukrainian front continued its advance towards Vinnitsa and the 2nd Ukrainian front its advance towards Kiro-vograd, deeply enveloping the flanks of the German VIII Army. At the end of January the forces of these two fronts surrounded the main German forces in the Korsun-Shevchenkovsky area and by the middle of February had annihilated them. The 3rd and 4th Ukrainian fronts, resuming their advance at the end of January, liberated Nikopol and Krivoy Rog, important industrial centres of the Ukraine.

By the beginning of March the Ukrainian fronts had been reinforced with men and equipment and possessed two and a half times as many tanks as the enemy. The Germans had also been reinforced and were strengthened by the arrival of fresh divisions transferred to the Soviet-German front from Germany, Yugoslavia, France, and Belgium. Nevertheless, overall superiority in men and material remained with the Soviet side. The Soviet forces continued their advance along the whole front from Polesye to the Black Sea. The offensive did not stop by day or by night. On 26th March the 2nd Ukrainian front arrived at the River Prut along an eighty-five kilometre stretch of bank and crossed into Rumanian territory. The 1st Ukrainian front advanced up to 350 kilometres westward and occupied Vinnitsa, Kamenets-Podolsky, Ternopol, and Chernovitsy. After forcing their way across the southern Bug, troops of the 3rd Ukrainian front took Nikolayev and Odessa. In mid-April they reached the Dniester. The 4th Ukrainian front and the Special Maritime Army, supported by the Black Sea Fleet and the Azov Naval Flotilla, began the liberation of the Crimea on 8th April. The operation proceeded successfully. Within only five days the administrative centre, Simferopol, was taken. By 12th May the Crimea had been completely liberated by the Red Army. The main forces of the 200,000-strong German XVII Army had been routed.

The advance proceeded less fortunately in Belorussia and the Baltic region. Down to the spring of 1944 battles continued along the whole front from Velikiye Luki to the River Pripet, but their outcome was successful only in the Kovel direction, where the Soviet forces reached Kovel and turned the southern flank of Army Group Centre.

The beginning of May saw a lull in the fighting. The Red Army had marched hundreds of kilometres, fighting fierce battles in which it had smashed dozens of enemy divisions. In the winter and spring it had freed 329,000 square kilometres of Soviet territory, inhabited by nineteen million people, re-established the state frontier of the USSR along 400 kilometres of its length, and entered Rumania. Favourable conditions had been created for the complete liberation of the Soviet Union and the final defeat of Hitler's Wehrmacht, the following year.

Resistance

Wherever men have exercised power there have been others to offer resistance. A greater number are usually prepared to collaborate, even in war. But in the Second World War collaboration became a dirty word and resistance acquired a new dimension, a new sense of tragic dedication. Hitler's conquest of Europe was no simple matter of armies crossing national boundaries. As the peculiar atrocities of the Nazis and the vicious doctrines of their perverted ideology became evident, they provided an indisputable reason against collaboration. It was the argument against selling one's soul to the devil. Those who aided their Nazi overlords soon reaped the scorn of all self-respecting men and, when liberation came, the most violent reprisals. It was not only patriotism but the need to defend human decency which impelled many men and women to risk capture by the Gestapo, to suffer brutal torture, and to give their lives in the cause of a free Europe.

As Hitler's Panzers rolled up to the western coast of Europe in the fateful summer of 1940, representatives of the governments of eight defeated nations withdrew across the Channel to Europe's last bastion of democracy, Great Britain. There they provided a focus for the loyalty of their now subject peoples and a base for continuing the fight against Nazism. Already in the lands they had left spontaneous resistance was growing. In Holland, for example, the introduction of anti-Jewish legislation led to long queues outside Jewish shops and crowded waiting-rooms in the surgeries of Jewish doctors. Clandestine newspapers and pamphlets began to play an important role in psychological warfare. The underground Press in Belgium became so highly organized that in November 1943 100,000 copies of a fake edition of the German-controlled *Le Soir* were sold on newstands throughout the country. But in the ultimate aim of freeing national territory the resistance was helpless without Allied aid.

In Western Europe this aid came from Great Britain, together with the émigré governments. Churchill showed an immediate interest in the European underground and, in keeping with his resolve 'to set Europe ablaze', he established in July 1940 the Special Operations Executive (SOE). Directed from a secret address in London, bankers, dons, lawyers, journalists, film directors, schoolmasters, wine merchants, and even women were trained to harass the enemy. This was to be done by setting up intelligence networks, organizing sabotage on a large scale, and training secret armies which would emerge when the Allied invasion of Europe was mounted. New per-sonalities were carefully fabricated, forged documents prepared, and special kits assembled. A whole new industry arose supplying false-bottomed suitcases and toothpaste tubes with special compartments. In 'Operation Lavatory' agents hid their radio sets in the cistern, set up a special chain as the aerial, and transmitted using codes in invisible ink written on men's shirt-tails and on women's pants and petticoats. There were new developments in sabotage: explosive 'coal lumps' destined for Gestapo offices, hand-painted explosive 'horse droppings' to be dropped in the path of German staff cars, and incendiary 'cigarettes'. Finally there was the 'L' pill which contained potassium cyanide. Held in the mouth during torture, its insoluble coating could be crushed between the teeth if the pain became too much for the agent to bear. Death would be almost instantaneous.

Agents were despatched to Hitler's Europe by parachute, by Lysander aircraft, submarine, or small fishing boat. The moment when they set off on their missions was likely to be the most solitary they had ever experienced. In the early days this was not purely subjective. The first agents were entirely on their own and 'parachuted blind', for British secret service links with all the occupied countries of Europe had virtually broken down. SOE therefore started from scratch, and by June 1941 little had been achieved and many lives tragically lost. It was the 'heroic' period of the resistance, characterized by lack of co-ordination, inexperience, and successful infiltration by V-men, informers working for the Nazis. But on 22nd June there was a turning point, for when Hitler attacked Soviet Russia Communists all over Europe ranged themselves wholeheartedly behind the Allies in a 'holy' war against Nazism. By the end of 1941 resistance was better organized and more efficient.

In Western Europe the Nazi tyranny never became as harsh as it was in Eastern Europe. Though exploiting to the full the occupied territories in the West, the Germans also attempted to win the allegiance of their new subjects. But even in partly German-speaking Luxembourg this policy failed. Everywhere resistance became the norm and in most countries proved its value in the struggle against Nazism. It was

Top: Fake issue of the Nazi military magazine Signal *printed by Belgian resistance, entitled: 'An outrage against humanity; after the Munich Putsch Mr Hitler was arrested.' Right: Fruits of resistance in Czechoslovakia. Freight train derailed by partisans in Moravia*

resistance which removed the possibility of a Nazi nuclear bomb. In March 1943 the Norwegian secret army, Milorg, co-operated with SOE in destroying the heavy water plant at Rjukan upon which the Nazi nuclear research programme depended. In Belgium, a vital staging-post for escape routes to Switzerland and Spain, underground engineers put all the high-tension lines in the country out of action simultaneously in January 1944, costing the Nazis vital man hours in repairs. In Denmark, however, resistance was slower to mature since the government, not officially at war with Germany, remained in Copenhagen. Until 1943, therefore, when the Nazis imposed direct rule, underground activity was hindered by the stigma of treason. And in Holland resistance suffered a catastrophe. The early capture by the Nazis of an SOE radio operator and the use of the secret code to deceive London condemned many Dutch agents to death and, by crippling the Dutch resistance, was ultimately responsible for the delayed liberation of the country after D-Day.

Radio, as the case of Holland suggests, was a vital element in resistance activities. It was underground Europe's chief contact with the outside world. On average two million words a week passed through SOE signals stations and on 5th June, the eve of D-Day, 500 signals were sent to alert agents and their secret armies. The German counter-measure was the Funkpeil Dienst (radio direction finding service) whose 'detection' vans constantly toured the darkened streets of occupied Europe in search of underground transmitters. The BBC had its own special war effort, broadcasting messages of hope and providing news for clandestine publications. Apparently meaningless sentences heard on overseas programmes, such as 'the cow will jump over the moon tonight', were in fact prearranged signals to herald the arrival of a new agent from London or to convince a sympathetic foreign banker of the *bona fides* of an agent in need of money.

Resistance was not only a revolt against Nazism; it was also a political movement. This was particularly true in France where the shattering of the Third Republic created a constitutional desert in which new institutions would have to be set up. As the dust settled, two architects appeared among the ruins. The first was the right-wing Marshal Pétain, victor of Verdun. To begin with the population rallied to his French State based on Vichy and collaboration became the order of the day. But as the Nazi tyranny became more oppressive the French turned to resistance—and therefore to Charles de Gaulle who as an unknown general had arrived in London in June 1940 as the self-appointed representative of the Free French. Progressively he established

himself as the leader of the new republic which was to be constructed.

The road to victory was not an easy one. It was marred by bad relations between the general's BCRA (Bureau Central de Renseignements et d'Action), established with British credits, and SOE whose French section under Colonel Maurice Buckmaster played a major part in organizing the resistance. In addition the Nazis infiltrated several important circuits. Through one such coup they were able to make full preparations to repulse the ill-fated Dieppe Raid in August 1943. However, after the union of disparate resistance groups under the National Resistance Council in November 1942, sabotage increased and by early 1944 100,000 underground fighters were organized to take part in the fight for liberation. With the founding of the French Forces of the Interior (FFI) the resistance war effort was linked directly to SHAEF (Supreme Headquarters, Allied Expeditionary Force) and played an important part behind the lines during the Allied landings in Normandy (Overlord) and Provence (Anvil). Alone the resistance could never have defeated the Nazis, but together with the Allied armies General Eisenhower considered that it 'played a very considerable part in our victory'.

Bearing the brunt of the worst Nazi barbarism, the peoples of Eastern Europe were quick to organize resistance. Help came from two sources, Soviet Russia and Great Britain, and it was to be politically motivated: once the Red Army was bearing down on Berlin, Stalin used the Communist elements of the resistance to install regimes congenial to himself. This pattern became evident in Czechoslovakia. President Beneš and his government in exile at first directed resistance operations from London. It was from London that the murder of 'Hangman' Heydrich, protector of Bohemia-Moravia, was arranged in co-operation with SOE in May 1942. But when Beneš saw that the Red Army would reach Prague before the Western powers, he established closer relations with Soviet Russia. Increasingly control passed from London to Moscow. The same occurred in Poland where the resistance, which ran the best radio communications system in occupied Europe, was at first directed by General Sikorski in London. But after the Warsaw Rising in August 1944, when Stalin stood by while the Germans ruthlessly crushed the uprising of the Polish Home Army and razed Warsaw to the ground, Poland fell under a Russian-directed Communist regime based on Lublin.

Resistance also brought Yugoslavia into the Communist camp, but for the less sinister reason that here the British supported the Communist partisans under Tito. But in Greece, where antagonism between the two

wings of the resistance verged on civil war, monarchist elements triumphed—because Churchill sent British troops to crush the Communists.

Resistance in the Axis countries and their satellites was by far the weakest. In these countries it was resistance by citizens against their own governments and therefore treason. Against traitors the Reich proved to have all the trump cards, and since the Allies seemed not to believe in the possibility of 'good Germans', resistance in Germany was deprived of outside help. It was therefore condemned to failure as the July Plot demonstrated, but it is as well to remember the words of Moltke, leader of the Kreisau circle, in a letter to an English friend: 'Never forget that for us there will be a bitter, bitter end to all this. When you are through with us, try to remember, however, that there are still a few who earnestly want to help you win the war and the peace.' In Italy the anti-Fascists succeeded in toppling Mussolini from power in July 1943, but this was more a matter of coincidental rather than concerted action. Once Mussolini was re-established at Salò, resistance was no longer treason for he was merely the puppet of an external power. In German-occupied Italy, therefore, resistance took much the same form as elsewhere in Europe: sabotage and assassinations. It was at the hands of Italian partisans that Mussolini met his death in April 1945.

Was resistance worth it? Compared with the victories of the Allied armies its achievements were modest. It could never have played more than a supporting role but as an ancillary force it had many successes. As an instrument of destruction it rivalled and on occasion surpassed Bomber Command. The continuous strain imposed by sabotage and assassination in the interior tied down many divisions that could otherwise have been employed on the front lines against Allied troops. As a medium of intelligence the resistance performed a vital service. And in France FFI units liberated five departments unaided.

But the achievements of the resistance were won at great cost. The murder of Heydrich was avenged by the destruction of Lidice and the massacre of 3,000 hostages in Prague and Brno. In France the disabling by FFI units of the SS Division Das Reich on its way to Normandy in June 1944 led to the murder of ninety-nine hostages in Tulle and the massacre of the entire population of Oradour-sur-Glane. In Russia anti-partisan operations often turned into orgies of murder and destruction.

For the many unsung heroes who fought in the secret war the reward was to know that they had played their part in the destruction of National Socialism. For those in Eastern Europe it was to see a new tyranny imposed. And for a great many it was death.

Victory in the Atlantic

By December 1941 the stage had been set for a decisive encounter on the Atlantic convoy routes between the convoy escorts, both surface and airborne, and the U-boats. The declaration of war on the United States by Germany on 11th December might, at first sight, have seemed to spell a huge access of strength to the escort forces, one which could tip the balance decisively in their favour. It was to prove, initially, quite the contrary.

Successive acts by the United States government since the President's declaration in July 1940 of a policy of 'all aid (to Great Britain) short of war' and the transfer of fifty over-age destroyers had clearly shown where American sympathies lay. In March 1941 'Lend-Lease' had been authorized and ten US coastguard cutters transferred to the Royal Navy. In July, when American troops relieved the British garrison in Iceland, US destroyers had begun to escort convoys to and from the island —convoys which ships of any nationality and ultimate destination could join. Two months later the US Navy had begun to take part in escort of transatlantic convoys during the western part of their voyages, on the grounds that ships for Iceland were included, and when five US destroyers were sent from Iceland to the aid of a convoy under attack in October, one of them, *USS Kearney,* had been torpedoed. A fortnight later *USS Reuben James,* escorting a convoy, was sunk with the loss of all but a handful of her crew.

Nevertheless, so long as the United States remained officially neutral, it had been German policy to avoid provocation. American declaration of a Defence Zone in the western half of the Atlantic had been respected to the extent that the great volume of merchant traffic thronging the sea route up the American east coast from the Caribbean and the Gulf of Mexico had been unmolested. Now, suddenly, it was open to attack.

This would not have been of vital consequence if effective protection for it had been prepared. Unfortunately, in spite of their own experience in the First World War and of more recent British experience, the fruits of which had been made freely available to them, the US Navy had taken no steps whatever to organize a convoy system. Shortage of escorts and the accepted dogma that inadequately escorted convoys were worse than none were given as the reasons, although in fact, some fifty per cent more surface craft and five or six times more aircraft were available than had been available to the British at the outbreak of the war.

An equally potent influence, as with the British in 1916 and, to some extent, in 1939 and 1940, was the unquestioning cult of the offensive, which demanded the employment of such forces as there were on 'search and patrol'. Leaving the stream of freighters and tankers to steam independently, warships and aircraft patrolled the route and dashed hither and thither in search of U-boats which betrayed their position by sinking merchantmen. They were, uniformly unsuccessful. Not one U-boat was destroyed off the American coast until April 1942, by which time more than 200 merchant ships and one of the patrolling destroyers had been sunk, many of them in sight of the shore.

Holocaust in American waters

The U-boat offensive began with only five boats, joined by three more before the end of January. Between 13th January and the end of the month they accounted for forty ships. Their easy success made Dönitz, the German Commander of Submarines, decide to deploy his whole available strength in American waters. Though frustrated by Hitler's insistence on retaining a number of U-boats in Norwegian waters and in the Mediterranean, he was able, by the use of supply U-boats, known as 'milch-cows', to loose his smaller, 750-ton boats, as well as the longer range 1,000 tonners in a simultaneous attack along the whole sea route from the Caribbean to New York.

The result was a holocaust. During February, sixty-five ships were sunk in American waters; in March eighty-six; a slight drop to sixty-nine in April was followed by a new 'high' in May of 111 ships. The Americans tried everything—except convoy—to stem the flow of Allied lifeblood. Ships were routed close in shore, the only result of which was to present an even denser stream of traffic to the attackers. Movements were restricted to daylight hours, ships sheltering in protected anchorages by night. Yet shipping losses continued to mount.

In May, at last, the Americans were convinced. A convoy system was instituted along their east coast. Sinkings in that area immediately ceased. The U-boats moved

Grand-Admiral Karl Dönitz, Commander of Submarines throughout the war and Commander-in-Chief of the German Navy from 1943. He succeeded Admiral Raeder, the exponent of surface ships. Nominated as Hitler's successor, Dönitz was head of the German state at the time of Germany's surrender

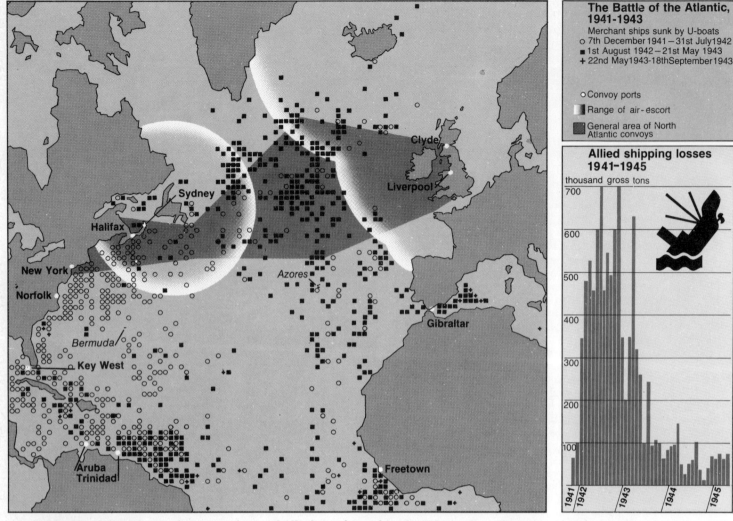

Map of Battle of the Atlantic showing sinkings of Allied merchant ships by U-boats from December 1941 to the Allied victory in 1943. The area in mid-Atlantic not covered by air-escort is the 'Black Gap'. The table of Allied shipping losses shows the U-boats' 'Happy Time' from December 1941 to June 1942. The heavy losses of November 1942 were during the Allied Torch landings in North Africa

south to the Gulf of Mexico and the Caribbean, however, where the stream of 'independents', many of them valuable tankers, continued to flow. June saw the highest score of all, with 121 ships sunk in those waters. Nevertheless, conversion of US naval thought when it came was nothing if not whole-hearted. The Commander-in-Chief of the US Navy, Admiral King, had stated the view in March that 'inadequately escorted convoys were worse than none'. Now he went on record as saying that 'escort is not just one way of handling the submarine menace; it is the *only* way that gives any promise of success. The so-called patrol and hunting operations have time and again proved futile.'

By the end of June the Gulf of Mexico and the Caribbean were being incorporated into a comprehensive convoy system with sea and air escort. Sinkings there likewise ceased. In July five U-boats were destroyed in American waters. The second 'Happy Time' for U-boats was over. Once again the U-boat commanders sought for the weakest portion of the convoy chain. They found it in the 'Black Gap' in mid-Atlantic where air escort was still almost non-existent.

In the meantime both sides had grown stronger. U-boat losses had been few during the previous six months; the construction programme was in full swing. But the escorts had also greatly increased in numbers and efficiency. They had been formed into regular groups composed usually of

two destroyers and four corvettes, the former having been modified to give them more anti-submarine weapons and devices at the expense of gun armament. The majority had received intensive individual and group training. Except for one or two groups in which American coastguard cutters led a mixed flotilla of American, British, and Canadian escorts, about half the groups were British and half Canadian.

Improved equipment

Most escorts and anti-submarine aircraft had received the new ten-centimetre radar which enabled them to detect surfaced submarines at considerable ranges. Some ships were equipped with High Frequency Direction Finders (HFDF) by means of which the bearing and to some extent the range of a unit transmitting on short wave radio could be determined. The existence of these two devices was unknown to the Germans. The latter enabled the escort commander to send an escort ship or aircraft probing for any U-boat making the signals essential to the concentration of a wolf-pack. The former could then cause the U-boat to be surprised on the surface at night or in low visibility. When they then submerged they were hunted with greatly improved asdics and attacked with larger salvos of more powerful depth-charges.

So that escorts could remain with their convoys for the whole of the long voyage,

tankers from which they could refuel under way were included in the convoys. To avoid the need to distract escorts from the task of driving off and hunting down the attackers, rescue ships specially equipped to pick up and give medical aid to survivors of sunken merchant ships were also attached.

Where the improved equipment and well-led and trained groups combined, the U-boats were detected and foiled. Either for this reason or because of skilful diversions based on the information gathered in the U-boat tracking room in the Admiralty, the majority of convoys got through without loss. But in the rapid expansion of the escort force, particularly the Canadian element which had grown out of a tiny prewar navy, there were bound to be groups lacking experience and ships in which provision of up-to-date equipment had been delayed. When convoys with such less effective escorts were located by the U-boats, scenes of earlier times were repeated with the defence swamped by the concentrated attack.

The primary antidote to such massed attacks was close air escort which, either by patrolling round the convoy or by flying along the bearings obtained by HFDF in the surface escorts, could force the U-boats to dive and so virtually immobilize them until the convoy had passed. Equipped with radar and, after more than two years of war, with effective depth-charges, these aircraft were the greatest dread of the U-

A U-boat surfaces after being hit by a depth-charge fired by a British convoy escort vessel in the North Atlantic. Oil painting by Norman Wilkinson. On the deck of the escort in the foreground are torpedoes, usually used against enemy surface vessels but sometimes for sinking a torpedoed and burning merchant vessel which might give away the location of a convoy to a prowling U-boat

boat commanders, allowing them no relaxation or opportunity to surface and recharge their batteries in peace by day or night. It was in the mid-Atlantic gap, therefore, that they preferred to operate, where so long as Coastal Command of the RAF was denied the very long-range Liberator aircraft they needed, only scanty air escort could be given.

It was to fill this 'Black Gap' in air cover that escort aircraft carriers, converted from merchant ships, were being constructed in American and British yards. The first four were in commission by the late summer of 1942; but it was then decided that they were required to give fighter cover to the forthcoming Anglo-American landings in North Africa. None could yet be spared for Atlantic convoy protection, though one of them, *HMS Avenger,* played a decisive part in fighting a convoy through to north Russia against a concentrated air and submarine attack in September.

So it was principally between the surface escorts and the U-boats in the 'Black Gap' that the battles round the Atlantic convoys were fought out. German ability to read coded messages between the Admiralty and the escorts enabled them to place U-boat patrol lines across the convoy routes. Where wolf-packs were able to concentrate, they inflicted some heavy losses. In August a slow convoy with a make-shift escort-force lost eleven ships in a six-day running

fight. Two of the U-boats were destroyed. In the next month the U-boats sank nine ships from an outward-bound convoy without loss to themselves. Similar disasters to convoys continued to occur at intervals during the autumn and winter months.

In October an outward-bound convoy lost seven of its number as well as the destroyer *Ottawa* of its Canadian escort, and four more freighters were torpedoed and damaged without any loss to the wolf-pack. But in another convoy similarly beset, the loss of seven ships was offset by the destruction of two U-boats and several more damaged a rate of exchange the U-boats could not afford. Had Dönitz been given his head to deploy his whole force in the Atlantic, the crisis in the Battle of the Atlantic would probably have developed at this time, perhaps with fatal consequences to the Allies; fortunately Hitler still insisted on maintaining a large U-boat strength in the Mediterranean and the Arctic. So the outcome hung in the balance while in the savage North Atlantic winter each side was as much occupied in fighting the wild weather as the enemy.

Climax of the battle

It was true that merchant ships were still being sunk, worldwide, at a rate greater than they could be replaced; but the American shipyards were swinging into full production. Furthermore the majority of merchant ship casualties were among

the independently-sailing vessels; these would get fewer and harder to find as the convoy system was being steadily extended. U-boat losses were by no means insupportable as yet and the number of operational boats was growing fast. But their opponents were gaining daily also in numbers and efficiency. Thus a climax in the Atlantic was approaching.

From the Allied point of view, as the storm-imposed winter lull was passing, three features of the situation made prospects for the spring of 1943 bright. At long last the Prime Minister's Anti-U-boat Committee, delivering a judgment of Solomon between the rival claimants for allocation of very long-range Liberator aircraft, reached a compromise which raised the number in Coastal Command from ten to forty, allowing about thirteen to be operational at any one time. By increasing the size of individual convoys and so reducing their frequency, enough escorts would be released to form independent support groups which could be used to reinforce threatened convoys. And, finally, the long-awaited escort carriers were at last to be employed in the task for which they had been conceived.

Yet March 1943 was to prove one of the most disastrous of the war in terms of merchant shipping lost. The more experienced escort groups had a well-founded confidence that they were a match for the wolf-packs; U-boats which encountered them paid

heavily for any sinkings they achieved. But it was not always possible to give convoys top quality protection; then disaster set in. Thus, while the well-trained veteran escorts of the mixed British, Polish, and Free French group were fighting a homeward-bound convoy through a dense U-boat concentration, destroying two of the enemy at the cost of four ships of the convoy and the escort commander's ship, another inexperienced group lost thirteen of their convoy without exacting any retribution.

Then two convoys, a fast and a slow, homeward bound, each beset by a large wolf-pack, came together to make one huge, widespread chaotic struggle in which twenty-one merchantmen were lost and, though one U-boat was finally sunk and Dönitz was to record that 'nearly all the other boats suffered from depth-charges or bombs and two were severely damaged', viewed from the Admiralty the scale of disaster was appalling. For a while the validity of the convoy system came in question.

The loss of morale was brief, however, being restored by the safe arrival of the next two convoys in spite of their being similarly threatened by several wolf-packs. In fact the elements which were to ensure the defeat of the U-boat were now present for the first time. The escort carrier, *USS Bogue,* and a support group of British destroyers gave these convoys cover through the danger area. By the end of March five British support groups were ready for operations, one of them centred on the escort carrier *HMS Biter.*

U-boats checked

At the same time a stream of fresh U-boats from Germany and the Biscay bases, no less than ninety-eight during April, was setting out for mid-Atlantic for what was to be the decisive battle. Convoys were duly located; yet somehow, inexplicably to the Germans, the well-tried techniques for gathering the wolf-packs failed. Hardly had the U-boat making contact flashed his radio message to headquarters when there would be seen the sharp stem and frothing bow wave of a racing destroyer following up the bearing obtained by her HFDF set or a Liberator plane directed by the escorts diving to the attack. Often it was the last object in the outside world the U-boat crew would see. The first signal would be the last; at U-boat headquarters another U-boat lost would be chalked up. At best, the submarine would be forced to stay submerged, blind and reduced to a crawl,

Left: Allied convoy in the North Atlantic
Right: German propaganda designed for Holland shows torpedo-boat and Dutch man-of-war sailing against England

STEEDS DEZELFDE VIJAND

1673
1943

while the convoy slipped through the patrol line to safety.

In the last week of April five U-boats were destroyed round the convoys for an almost negligible loss of merchant ships. However Dönitz did not yet concede victory. During May his force was deployed in massed attacks against the convoys. Sixty U-boats fought an eight-day battle with the escorts of an outward-bound convoy in the first week of that month. By the end of the month twelve merchant ships had been sunk; but it had cost the attackers eight of their number with many others severely damaged.

As the losses became known and the tales of narrow escapes by the survivors spread through the U-boat fleet, the nerves of the submarine crews cracked. Redirected on to other convoys they refused to press home their attacks and even so they were detected and surprised on the surface by air and surface escorts. A number were sunk; the convoys steamed on unscathed. During May forty-one U-boats were sunk, twenty-five of them by the air and surface escorts, seven more, on passage in the Bay of Biscay, were surprised on the surface by aircraft equipped with new radar. At last Dönitz accepted defeat, at least for the time being, and withdrew all U-boats from the North Atlantic convoy routes.

Allied victory
It is generally accepted that May 1943 marked Allied victory in the Battle of the Atlantic. To quote from Captain Roskill's official history, *The War at Sea*: 'After forty-five months of unceasing battle of a more exacting and arduous nature than posterity may easily realise, our convoy escorts had won the triumph they so richly merited.'

Nevertheless, though Dönitz was forced to abandon his efforts against the transatlantic convoys, he has recorded in his memoirs his conclusion at that time that 'the U-boat campaign must be continued with the forces available. Losses, which bear no relation to the success achieved, must be accepted, bitter though they are.' Furthermore, new weapons were under development which could tip the balance back in his favour.

Having started the war equipped with a torpedo which was unreliable in its depth-keeping, his U-boats had been forced to limit their attacks to deep-draught vessels and could not strike back at the escorts. Now, however, a torpedo was under trial which, by means of an acoustic device in its head, would 'home' on to the propeller noises of a ship. With this, a hunted submarine could turn the tables on its attacker.

When Holland was overrun, Dutch submarines had been captured which had an ingenious device, a *Schnörkel* or breathing tube through which a submerged submarine could draw air to enable it to run its diesel engines to propel it, as well as to recharge its electric storage batteries. The Germans now adopted this; U-boats when fitted with it would no longer need to come to the surface, exposing themselves to radar detection. The menace from the air would then be largely overcome. Finally a new U-boat with greatly increased battery power, the Type XXI which would be able to make as much as 18 knots submerged, was being designed.

U-boats' last hope
The knowledge that these several improvements were in the offing kept hope alive. Meanwhile the U-boats were redeployed in the hope of finding more profitable and less dangerous areas. In the Caribbean and off the coast of Brazil there were still some independently sailing ships to be found; but there were convoys, too, and in attacking them eight U-boats were destroyed by the air escorts. Once again the survivors were withdrawn.

Another group had been sent to an area south-west of the Azores to intercept United States to Mediterranean convoys. They found themselves harried by aircraft from American escort carriers. In June *USS Bogue*'s group sank two U-boats. In the next month the *Bogue, Core,* and *Santee* destroyed six more; not a single merchant ship was sunk.

But in the meantime the work of re-equipping the U-boats had pressed ahead — acoustic torpedoes to strike back at surface escorts, increased anti-aircraft armament, an improved radar search receiver, and a radar decoy to reduce the threat from the air. On 13th September Dönitz announced 'all the essentials for a successful campaign are to hand'. Once again they were launched against the main transatlantic convoys. They found them even more effectively guarded than before.

The target they first assailed comprised a conjunction of two convoys, a fast and a slow, which being fairly close to one another when the threat developed, had been ordered to unite. The total of sixty-five merchant ships thus had no less than fifteen escorts as well as a merchant aircraft carrier (MAC-ship), one of a number of tankers and grain ships which had been equipped with a flight deck from which four Swordfish aircraft could operate.

Emboldened by the possession of acoustic torpedoes, the U-boats fought their way through the screen by night, sinking three escorts in the process. Heavy casualties resulted from the loss of one of these which had embarked the survivors from another. Six merchant ships were torpedoed; two U-boats were destroyed and two more severely damaged. The Germans believed they had sunk many more escorts and were pleased with their new offensive tactics.

The sudden revelation of the new weapon was certainly a blow to the morale of the escort crews; but it was quickly countered by towing a noise-maker at a distance astern — a device known as a 'foxer' — which diverted the acoustic torpedo away from its target. With this, the escorts' ascendancy was re-established. A second massacre of U-boats round the North Atlantic convoys followed, and by November the U-boat command was seeking fresh remedies, including a renewal of co-operation by long-range aircraft.

In the face of the combined air and surface escort now available to convoys and of support groups, often operating with escort carriers, ever poised to intervene when a convoy was threatened, nothing availed. In February 1944 the most successful of the support groups, 2nd Escort Group commanded by Captain F.J.Walker, during a three-week patrol accounted for six U-boats in the vicinity of the three convoys it assisted. At the end of March the Germans again conceded victory on the North Atlantic convoy routes; U-boats were transferred to independent cruises in southern waters.

The submarine dominated
A feature of these was the necessity to refuel in mid-Atlantic from milch-cows. And here, time and again, US escort carrier groups, aided by good intelligence, surprised and destroyed them. Compelled to abandon mid-ocean refuelling, the U-boats' time on patrol became so restricted that their operations were uneconomical and ineffective. The submarine had been completely dominated.

The Battle of the Atlantic could finally be seen to have been won by the Allies. The fruits of the victory gained in May 1943 were now to be gathered as the anti-submarine forces went over to the offensive. Although the U-boats continued to fight with a dogged and desperate courage, their expectation of survival was reduced to one and a half sorties each; though equipment with the *Schnörkel* device greatly reduced the danger from air attack and of being surprised on the surface by night while re-charging their batteries, the U-boat threat was nevertheless reduced to negligible proportions from this time onwards. Never again were they seriously to threaten the vital life-line between Europe and America.

How near the campaign had come to achieving victory for the Germans can perhaps best be judged from the wry admission by Winston Churchill: 'The only thing that ever really frightened me during the war was the U-boat peril.'

Malta: The Island Fortress

The two-and-a-half-year struggle for the Mediterranean from the fall of France in June 1940 to the Allied landings in North Africa in November 1942 was an increasingly desperate one, for on it depended the safety of the convoy routes to North Africa and thus the outcome of the North African campaign. The action increasingly centred on Malta as both Axis and Allies came to see the importance of the island as the key to control of the Mediterranean. The conflict reached a climax in the first months of 1942 with the concentrated bombing attacks by the Axis on Malta and the convoys, all but starving the island into surrender. Its endurance and ability to hit back played a major role in Allied victory.

On Italy's declaration of war on 10th June 1940, Mussolini with typical flamboyance called for 'an offensive at all points in the Mediterranean and outside'. Within hours, Italian aircraft dropped their first loads of bombs on Malta.

For the first three weeks, Malta's only protection came from three Gloster Gladiators which had been removed from their crates and assembled on the island. The three, known as Faith, Hope and Charity, won a permanent name as symbols of Malta's resistance, forcing the Italians to bomb from a higher level and thus lose accuracy, but they could scarcely hope to hold off full-scale bombardment.

The poor state of Malta's defences was the result of pre-war decisions that Malta was indefensible, and should not be defended. Now, reinforcement had to start almost from scratch. By the end of the year, Malta had only fifteen Hurricanes and twenty-eight bombers. It was hardly surprising that Italy lost less than three per cent of the 690,000 tons of shipping running the convoy route to North Africa in 1940.

In the wider context of the Mediterranean war, both sides were evenly matched in surface vessels. But Italy had a huge advantage in submarines and aircraft, and the British suffered from having to cover both the Suez Canal (with the Mediterranean Fleet under Admiral Sir Andrew Cunningham) and Gibraltar (with Force H under Vice-Admiral Sir James Somerville).

They were helped by the timidity of the Italian naval leaders, who held to the need to maintain 'a fleet in being'. This meant attacking only when circumstances were clearly favourable. They appeared never favourable enough: this uncertainty led to Italy's failure to seize the initiative even in 1940 when her fleet could have gained Malta and control of the Mediterranean.

With the Italians unwilling to engage, it was clear that air-power was going to be the decisive factor, and its importance was brought home dramatically to the Italians by two actions—in Taranto and off Cape Matapan—before the Allied withdrawal from Crete in April 1941 focused Axis attention finally on Malta.

In October 1940 three Glen Martin Maryland reconnaissance planes arrived in Malta. They allowed Cunningham to keep watch on the Italian fleet and gave him a chance to realize a plan he had long dreamed of: an attack on that fleet in harbour.

All six Italian battleships were together in Taranto as the British approached on the night of 11th November. Italian reconnaissance reports had been so confused that the Italian commander, Campioni, remained in harbour, vainly waiting for information. In a very short space of time, the twenty-one Swordfish torpedo-bombers, dipping and weaving to avoid the hawsers of barrage balloons and the storm of tracer shells, reduced Italy's serviceable battleships to two, the *Vittorio Veneto* and the *Cesare*, for the loss of two aircraft. After Taranto, the mere presence of a carrier was enough to make an Italian naval commander nervous of any engagement.

Four months later, on the night of 27th-28th March, the Italian navy, under German pressure, set out to break the British convoy route to Greece. Iachino, who had replaced Campioni after Taranto, expected Luftwaffe support. None came. Instead, he was taken by surprise by aircraft from the carrier *Formidable*. The cruiser *Pola* was damaged, and two other cruisers returning to help her were picked up on British radar and sunk within five minutes. The crew of the *Pola*, meanwhile, having abandoned ship, found she was not sinking after all, climbed back on board and set about warming themselves—with alcohol. When the British boarded, the Italians were in no state to offer any resistance. They were taken prisoner and the *Pola* too was sunk.

By this time the Germans had already seen the need for full-scale support in the Mediterranean. By January, about 100 bombers and 25 fighters of X Fliegerkorps had arrived in Sicily from Norway to bring the Axis forces there up to 150 bombers and 100 fighters. The Germans signalled their arrival on 10th January with a dive-bomber attack on the carrier *Illustrious*.

The *Illustrious* limped into Malta, and over the next fortnight the Germans launched what are still known as the 'Illustrious raids' to knock out the carrier and the airfields. The exhausted ground crews on Malta were only able to put some ten fighters in the air at any one time against perhaps eighty German aircraft, but the

Clearing the streets of rubble in Valletta after the Opera House had been hit by German bombs

One of Malta's rock-shelters; people would sometimes stay underground for days on end

Closing the Ring

Illustrious was hit only once. She sailed on the 23rd bound for America for repairs.

Malta now stood in immediate peril of subjection by the Luftwaffe. From February to May 1941 only thirteen ships got through, with some 100,000 tons of supplies.

There was little Malta's bombers could do to prevent the Italian supplies for the Afrika Korps getting through. The Italians even got one of their few congratulatory messages from the Germans for their efforts. With Rommel's successes in March and the German advance down Greece and into Crete, Malta's position seemed more and more hopeless.

Reprieve

But in June Hitler removed aircraft from the Mediterranean to strengthen his attack on Russia, and Malta was given a chance to recover. By mid-August aircraft strength rose to about 130, including 69 Hurricanes.

The second half of 1941 saw an immense improvement in the Allied position. The Axis forces in North Africa needed some 50,000 tons of supplies a month, but in September they lost a quarter en route and in November a staggering sixty per cent. The speed of Auchinleck's Crusader offensive in November was due largely to Malta's domination of the Mediterranean.

But Malta's real test was still to come, and the end of 1941 saw the pendulum swing once more against the Allies. In November, the carrier *Ark Royal* was torpedoed. In December, Force K, a four-vessel reinforcement from Force H, was almost totally destroyed by mines off Malta.

Also in December Hitler redeployed II Fliegerkorps from the Russian front to Sicily and North Africa. Together with X Fliegerkorps, which was responsible for the eastern Mediterranean, it formed Luftflotte 2 under Field-Marshal Kesselring, who could soon call on 500 Stukas, up to 300 Me 109s, and a mass of heavy bombers.

George Cross Island

The Axis once more had a free hand from Crete, Libya, and Sicily to bomb the Allied convoys, and Italian vessels could provide Rommel with the supplies he needed to take the offensive and press on into Egypt.

In February, Malta's serviceable aircraft were down to eleven and the island was reeling under the impact of ten raids a day. Malta had to have more fighter cover and supplies if it was not to be starved into surrender. But any success seemed to call forth increased Axis efforts.

On 23rd March, two freighters, *Talabot* and *Pampas*, the survivors of a four-vessel convoy, came steaming through bomb splashes to a delirious welcome from Malta's inhabitants thronging the harbour walls. Kesselring, however, had assured Hitler he would 'wipe Malta off the map' and he directed over 300 bombers to destroy the two freighters. In three days of ceaseless attack, they succeeded. Only 5,000 of the 20,000 tons which had left Alexandria with the convoy was unloaded before the *Talabot* and *Pampas* were sunk in harbour.

The idea of reinforcement seemed hopeless, and Malta was slowly starving. A soldier on active service was supposed to get 4,000 calories a day; in Malta the average was now half that, with a bread ration of ten ounces. Communal—or 'Victory'—kitchens were set up in which goat stew became the staple diet.

It was in recognition of the island's spirit of endurance and defiance that on 15th April a simple message arrived for the governor of Malta: 'To honour her brave People I award the George Cross to the Island Fortress of Malta to bear witness to a Heroism and Devotion that will long be famous in History. George R.I.'

The pendulum began to swing finally against the Axis on 9th May when sixty Spitfires landed from the carriers *Wasp* and *Eagle*. The next day, just when Kesselring was reporting the neutralization of Malta, his raiders were met by a superior force for the first time in months.

But there had to be aid from outside. In June a massive double operation from both ends of the Mediterranean set out to end Malta's permanent fuel and food crisis. Five freighters and a tanker were to come from the west (Operation Harpoon) and eleven freighters from the east (Operation Vigorous). Its tragic results showed how hopeless was the task of running convoys with inadequate air cover.

The convoy from the east was an utter failure. Movement and counter-movement in 'Bomb Alley' between Crete and Africa took their toll of ammunition, and the whole convoy had to turn about and return to base, with the loss of several freighters and warships. But the Italian admiral, da Zara, misjudged the path of the western convoy and two freighters escaped the devastating Axis air attacks to deliver their 15,000 tons of supplies to Malta. Without them, Malta would undoubtedly have fallen. Of the seventeen supply ships loaded for Malta, covered by eighty-two warships, just two had got through and six had been lost.

But by July, the siege was nearing its end. Fighters shot down sixty-five Axis aircraft for the loss of only thirty-six Spitfires. The submarines returned, and seven Axis supply ships were sunk.

The failure of the Axis powers in the siege can be ascribed to lack of consistent planning. It was never clear whether the island was to be subdued by bombardment, by assault, or by starvation. Too frequently policies were changed and other demands intervened allowing the Allies to recover.

A landing had in fact been tentatively planned for July by the Axis, but by this time the operation would have involved enormous losses. Malta's coasts were defended with thickets of barbed wire and three lines of concrete strong points had been built inland. Rommel's successes in North Africa seemed to make a landing unnecessary and it was postponed.

By August, the Allies were beginning to dominate the Mediterranean theatre. Thirty-eight per cent of all Rommel's supplies were being lost en route. But Malta had only enough fuel and food to last a month; the time had come for a final effort to raise the siege. By 10th August, Operation Pedestal was ready: fifty-nine warships were to escort fourteen merchant ships from Gibraltar to Malta. Lying in wait for the convoy were twenty-one Axis submarines and some 800 aircraft.

The first blow was the torpedoing of the carrier *Eagle*, which sank within eight minutes taking 200 of her crew with her. The heavy ships turned back as planned on the 12th, and immediately a night of chaos began. Axis MTBs surged to within fifty yards of their prey, sweeping decks with automatic fire, while Allied vessels steamed in all directions to avoid torpedoes as best they could. By morning on the 13th there were just seven merchantmen left. One of them was the tanker *Ohio*, lying dead in the water with her vital 11,000 tons of fuel, awaiting a tow over the last ninety miles to Valletta. The following day two more freighters were sunk, but four of the scattered fleet arrived in Malta. The Italian navy, deprived of air cover by the German demand that fighters should accompany the Luftwaffe bombers, was deterred from any attacks by a massive display of air strength from Malta.

It took forty-eight hours to tow the sinking *Ohio* to Grand Harbour, and having discharged her cargo she lay immovable in the harbour until she was expended as an RAF gunnery target in 1946.

Stocktaking after Pedestal showed that Malta could hold out until December, at a pinch. But even with the Allied victories of October and November in North Africa, there was no sign of relief, and discussion started on how the island's surrender was to be made known. It was not until 17th November that the last convoy, codenamed Stoneage, sailed from Port Said. It entered Malta on the night of 19th-20th November without interference, and the siege was finally over. The balance of power had passed to the Allies, now pouring troops into the western Mediterranean following the Torch landings, and Malta was free to back the invasion of Sicily in July 1943.

Rommel had prophesied in February 1941: 'Without Malta, the Axis will end by losing control of North Africa.' He had now been proved right.

Desert Victory

Even before Italy entered the war in June 1940, the Mediterranean and the Balkans to the north had loomed large in British strategic thinking. In addition to the great importance of keeping the Mediterranean open as a route to India and the Far East, it was recognized that a hold on the Middle East was vital to the retention of Persian oil; while the Balkans, which provided an important part of German oil imports, was an area which should be denied to the enemy as soon as possible. Thus the encouragement of subversion in the Balkans and the retention, at the least, of Turkish neutrality were among the first objectives of British policy. On the American entry into the war, this strategy was confirmed at a conference at Washington in December 1941, code-named 'Arcadia', when it was decided that one of the primary aims should be to 'close and tighten the ring around Germany', the southern sector of which was to run along the North African coast, from where attacks across the Mediterranean were to be launched. While the American military authorities agreed with this strategy, they were critical of what they believed to be a leisurely British

approach to the ultimate invasion of north-western Europe and the defeat of Germany, and they looked upon operations such as those projected in the Mediterranean as politically motivated diversions from the main objective. Possibly the British, with memories both of the Somme and Passchendaele and of defeat in France in 1940, were slow and unenthusiastic, but they were realists and the American suspicions were not fully justified.

In November 1942 the first effective steps to occupy the whole of the North African shore and thus complete the southern sector of the ring around Germany were taken, in the east by 8th Army under Montgomery, which after ten days hard fighting broke through the Axis lines at El Alamein on 4th November and in the west by 'Operation Torch', the Allied invasion of north-west Africa which was launched on 8th November. In the centre, Malta still hung on precariously—four ships out of a convoy of fourteen (Operation Pedestal) had reached the island in August—while the bases in Egypt and Gibraltar were secure. There were fears of a German attack on Spain as a result of Operation

Men of US 1st Division disembark in Morocco from Royal Navy landing craft. All Allied forces landed quickly in the face of only slight Vichy French resistance

Closing the Ring

Torch and the ensuing neutralization of Gibraltar, but General Franco preserved his neutrality and Gibraltar was able to handle the vast mass of ships, stores, and aircraft needed for the operation.

Operation Torch had been forced on the reluctant Combined Chiefs of Staff by Roosevelt and Churchill who were determined that their pledge to Stalin of a 'second front in 1942' would be redeemed. The US Joint Chiefs of Staff never lost their dislike for the operation which they regarded, rightly, as likely to delay the invasion of north-west Europe until 1944; the British chiefs of staff, however, soon became enthusiastic supporters. An American, Lieutenant-General Dwight D.Eisenhower, was placed in supreme command with a British naval commander, Admiral Sir Andrew Cunningham, under him. The air forces, contrary to all experience up to date, were split into national components, each under its own commander, while the commanders of the land forces for all three initial landings were to be American generals until their forces, once ashore, combined to form 1st Army under Lieutenant-General Sir Kenneth Anderson. Major-General Mark Clark, an American, was appointed deputy commander.

An American task force was to attack Casablanca, while combined Anglo-American task forces were to attack Algiers and Oran. At the latter American troops were to land first as it was thought that the French would welcome the Americans and resist the British. The British chiefs of staff believed that the Bône-Bougie area should have been the target of one of the task forces rather than Casablanca, but caution prevailed; indeed, at one stage, the American planners envisaged landing only in Morocco and fighting their way eastwards overland, because of the dangers of passing the Straits of Gibraltar.

In the event French resistance was spasmodic, the chance presence of Admiral Darlan, the Commander-in-Chief of the French Armed Forces, proving a strong influence in favour of capitulation. All three task forces landed quickly with few casualties or material losses, despite the lack of training and experience of many of those engaged, and by 11th November an armistice had been signed and preparations for the move east towards Bizerta and Tunis under way.

The landings came as a complete surprise. Only one submarine attack was made on the vast fleets and the Italian surface ships were 'grounded' by lack of fuel, but the German reaction was quick and effective. Troops moved into the unoccupied zone of France early on 11th November and simultaneously strong forces were flown to Bizerta where the airfield had been occupied on 9th November while Italian

troops advanced from Tripolitania. So, despite the landing of a British brigade at Bougie on 11th November and the capture of Bône airfield by British paratroops the following day, the Germans with remarkable efficiency and flexibility, and, aided by the weather and the terrain, were able to stabilize a line in the mountains west of the Tunisian plains in early December. Allied hopes of capturing Tunis and Bizerta by Christmas were thus frustrated.

The Mareth Line

The stalemate was doubly disappointing as 1st Army had been so close to victory. But much had gone well. The intricate organization required had been effective and it had proved possible to form integrated staffs of American and British officers. Spain had not interfered, and French troops, re-armed with Allied equipment, were fighting the Germans. That a little more boldness in the original concept of the operation would almost certainly have allowed the capture of Tunisia by the new year must not mask the quick and competent German reaction to the landings which surprised the intelligence experts. One unexpected side effect had been the scuttling of the French fleet at Toulon on 27th November 1942, but this tragedy at least ensured, as Darlan had always promised, that the ships would not fall into the hands of the Germans.

Meanwhile Rommel had been conducting a well organized fighting retreat from Alamein, harried by impossible directives from Hitler which if obeyed would have meant the destruction of his army. A succession of well-known names filled the newspaper headlines, places which had often changed hands more than once such as Mersa Matruh, Sidi Barrani, Bardia, Tobruk, Derna, Benghazi, Agedabia, and finally El Agheila, where Rommel made his first serious stand on 12th December. All attempts to cut off the Afrika Korps during the long chase across the desert failed and Rommel's skilful disengagements retained his forces almost intact. The pursuit was vigorous, but most of the British, Australian, New Zealand, and Indian troops had been there before and some were looking over their shoulders for the Rommel magic which would cut them off and send them reeling back. But when Montgomery broke through at El Agheila, it was clear that this time there would be no recovery. Logistical problems made the pursuit difficult and the whole of one corps had to be withdrawn from the line to help with the transport of supplies. Ports were quickly reopened and supplies started to flow by sea, but the pace of the advance was determined as much by logistics as by enemy resistance. Rommel withdrew from El Agheila on 18th December and the

retreat continued, with checks at Buerat, on the Homs-Taruna line, and outside Tripoli, which fell to Montgomery on 23rd January 1943. By 24th February the Afrika Korps had withdrawn behind the formidable Mareth Line on the boundary between Tunisia and Tripolitania, detaching some formations to counter-attack successfully the American troops that were threatening its rear.

Throughout January and February 1943, the Germans in Tunisia under the command of Colonel-General Dietloff Jürgen von Arnim were building up to a strength of 100,000 men and continued doggedly to counter-attack the Allied forces. The Allied command was unsatisfactory; the French refused to take orders from the British, and Anglo-American co-operation was not good. None of the lessons of the use of tactical aircraft in the land battle which had been learned at such cost in the desert were being applied in Tunisia and it was only when 8th Army and the desert air force joined in that land-air co-operation became satisfactory. Moreover, the training and experience of most of the troops was inferior to that of the Germans. By early February, Rommel, with his main force behind the Mareth Line, took a hand in the Tunisian battle, bringing with him a strong detachment of the Afrika Korps. On 14th February Rommel and Arnim launched a major attack, from the southeast and east respectively. It had considerable initial success, capturing a number of important features, including the Kasserine Pass. On 19th February, General Alexander, who had been placed in command of both 8th and 1st Armies, found a most confused situation and took over personal command of all the Allied forces in Tunisia. After some bitter fighting, the Allied line held and Rommel's dream of cutting off 1st Army by a thrust to the coast faded. But the battle had been close and had shattered Allied complacency.

The end in North Africa was now inevitable. Between 20th and 28th March, 8th Army fought the Battle of Mareth against tenacious opponents who managed to withdraw in good order. On 6th April, 8th Army crossed the Wadi Akarit after another tough fight and by 28th April it had attacked the Afrika Korps at Enfidaville without success. It had now joined up with 1st Army and the ring around Tunis and Bizerta was complete. Alexander had been watching a series of unco-ordinated attacks by both armies and now stepped in, halting the attack at Enfidaville and then, on 30th April, transferring two of the best divisions in

Right: General George Patton, the brash American tank expert who broke on to the scene after the landings in North Africa

Closing the Ring

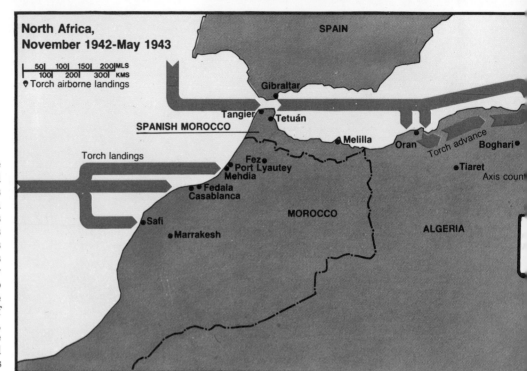

8th Army to join in the attack from the centre of the line opposite Bizerta and Tunis. The effect of this concentration was immediate. On 7th May, Tunis and Bizerta were captured and with the end of Axis resistance on 13th May, Alexander was able to report to Churchill: 'We are masters of the North African shore.' The Germans who had fought so bitterly to the end now surrendered meekly, most of those who escaped being destroyed at sea by the Royal Navy which obeyed its task of executing Cunningham's signal: 'Sink, burn, and destroy. Let nothing pass.' Some 240,000 German and Italian prisoners had been taken with great stores of weapons and equipment. On 20th May, a convoy reached Alexandria and one of the main Allied objectives, that of opening the Mediterranean, had been achieved.

The next move

Since the autumn of 1942, a continual debate had been carried on between the British and American planners on the next step after the capture of the North African shore. Many possibilities had been canvassed — ranging from landings in the south of France, the capture of Crete and the Dodecanese, landings in the Balkans, to the establishment of a stabilized 'defensive encircling line' and the transfer of the main forces to Great Britain to prepare for an invasion of north-west Europe in 1943. Generally, the Americans, supported by Churchill, who wanted to keep up the pressure in the Mediterranean and Middle East, were pressing for invasion in 1943 while the British chiefs of staff believed that it would not be possible to mount a successful invasion that year and that momentum in the Mediterranean must be maintained by further attacks to the northwards. The differences were serious and there was a danger that the Americans would divert forces to the Pacific, thus ignoring the 'Germany first' principle. Indeed, fifteen groups of aircraft destined for the British theatre of war were sent to the Pacific and the build-up of land forces in Great Britain slowed down.

However, at the Casablanca Conference in January 1943 it was agreed to attack Sicily in the summer and from then on, although nothing else was agreed and the Allied chiefs of staff did not want to land on the mainland, the Italian campaign became inevitable.

Above: The end in North Africa. Allied forces advancing from Morocco, Algeria, and Egypt roll up the Axis. But final victory was not gained until bitter German resistance in Tunisia had been overwhelmed. Below: Operation Torch. In a painting by Richard Eurich the vast invasion fleet steams for its objectives

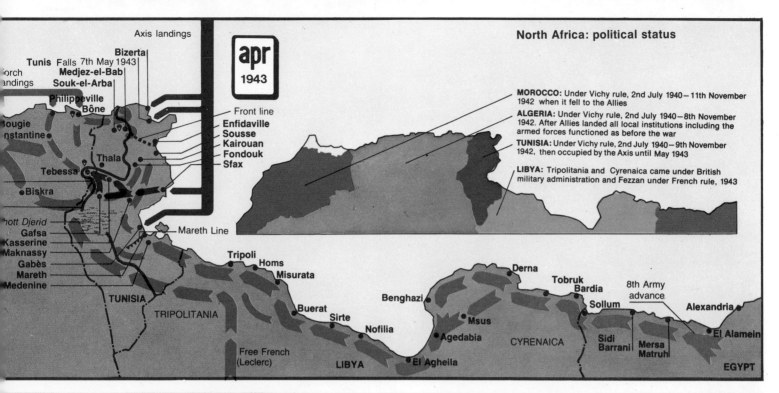

Axis landings

Bizerta
Tunis Falls 7th May 1943
orch **Medjez-el-Bab**
landings **Souk-el-Arba**
Philippeville
Bône
Bougie
Instantine

Thala
Tebessa

Biskra

Shott Djerid
Gafsa
Kasserine
Maknassy
Gabès
Mareth
Medenine

TUNISIA

Mareth Line

Front line
Enfidaville
Sousse
Kairouan
Fondouk
Sfax

North Africa: political status

MOROCCO: Under Vichy rule, 2nd July 1940 — 11th November 1942 when it fell to the Allies

ALGERIA: Under Vichy rule, 2nd July 1940 — 8th November 1942. After Allies landed all local institutions including the armed forces functioned as before the war

TUNISIA: Under Vichy rule, 2nd July 1940 — 9th November 1942, then occupied by the Axis until May 1943

LIBYA: Tripolitania and Cyrenaica came under British military administration and Fezzan under French rule, 1943

Tripoli Homs
Misurata
TRIPOLITANIA
Buerat
Sirte
Nofilia
Free French
(Leclerc)
LIBYA El Agheila

Benghazi
Msus
Agedabia

Derna
Tobruk
Bardia
Sollum

CYRENAICA

Sidi
Barrani

8th Army
advance

Alexandria

El Alamein
Mersa
Matruh
EGYPT

Italy: The Hard Underbelly

The Italian campaign was born of compromise, continued in discord, and ended in controversy. From its beginning in July 1943 to its end in May 1945, it was the pawn between opposing British and American concepts of war. The Americans, confident in their immense material resources and true to their own military tradition, favoured frontal attack. If war was the science of military victory, then Germany should be attacked by the shortest and most direct route: across the Channel. Overlord therefore came first on the list of American priorities in Europe; Italy was regarded as a tiresome division.

The British, forced to rely on smaller resources and schooled by long experience as a naval power, preferred a more indirect approach. Churchill believed that Italy, the 'soft underbelly of the Axis', was the ideal target. An Allied military presence there would be the best way of maintaining a threat to the Balkans and causing Hitler to disperse his forces. But there is evidence Churchill also looked beyond the moment of victory for the direction which military planning should take during the war. Fearing post-war Soviet domination of South-East Europe, he saw Austria and the Balkans as the ultimate objectives of the Italian campaign.

These strategic differences at the highest level dictated the course of the whole campaign. They became clear at the Casablanca Conference between Churchill and Roosevelt and their staffs which began on 14th January 1943. This has become celebrated as the moment when the words 'unconditional surrender' entered the Allied war vocabulary. More significant were its strategic decisions. Now that victory in North Africa was in sight, an answer had to be found to the question: what next? The answer was to invade Sicily. This was no easy decision. The Americans were brought to it unwillingly, and then only as a strategic conclusion to the North African campaign, with the aim of clearing the Mediterranean sea route. Eisenhower argued that if the aim was to invade Italy in strength, the proper objectives were Sardinia and Corsica. But no agreement could be reached about Italy, and therefore no commitment was made to move beyond Sicily for the time being. However, while the Americans intended to stop there, the

British, on the other hand, hoped to go on.

The invasion of Sicily (Operation Husky) was a thoroughly well-planned operation. The planning began in February, but without the direct supervision of the commanders, who were still engaged in North Africa. The Supreme Commander was to be an American, General Eisenhower, but direct conduct of the fighting was assigned to the British. General Alexander became commander of 15th Army Group, consisting of 7th US Army and 8th British Army; Admiral Cunningham was the naval commander, and Air Chief Marshal Tedder the air commander. When they were finally able to pay more attention to Husky in April, a number of changes were made to the provisional plan. There were two reasons for this. First General Montgomery, commander of 8th Army, buttonholed General Bedell Smith, Eisenhower's chief of staff (in a lavatory), and persuaded him of the superiority of his own plan. Second, and more decisive, was the emergence of the DUKW, a six-wheeled amphibious lorry, and the LST (landing ship for tanks). These were now available for the first time, and their specifications convinced Alexander that he could rely on maintenance over open beaches—in defiance of the orthodox doctrine of amphibious warfare. He therefore adopted a plan which he had originally favoured himself and which was the same plan as that proposed so assiduously by Montgomery. This envisaged a concentrated attack by 7th and 8th Armies on the south-eastern end of the island.

Husky was the largest amphibious attack mounted by the Allies in the Second World War. Eight divisions were put ashore during the initial assault compared with only five during the same phase of the Normandy landings eleven months later. Nearly 3,000 ships and landing-craft took part, starting from places as far away as Suez, Tunisia, Algiers, and even Scotland. One division came direct from the United States, staging only at Oran. Malta served admirably as army and navy headquarters, and its airfields were packed with as many aircraft as they could absorb. On the night of the invasion, 10th July 1943, a storm blew up and seemed to threaten the success of the operation. In fact, apart from making them seasick, it proved a positive advantage to the seaborne invaders, for it caused the Italian coastal divisions to relax their vigil. The troops achieved complete surprise and mostly landed unopposed. But the airborne assault, intended to capture certain key road junctions and bridges, suffered considerably from the bad weather. More than a third of the gliders landed in the sea,

*Left: Americans in Tunis with their prisoner, a Luftwaffe officer. Victory in North Africa was the jumping-off stage for the invasion of southern Italy. **Right:** Troops of the British 8th Army wade ashore in Sicily*

and American parachute troops were scattered all over southern Sicily.

The plan now was for Montgomery to drive to Messina at top speed in order to cut off the two German and nine Italian divisions on the island from their escape route into the toe of Italy. This danger was not lost on the Axis garrison, and although he quickly captured Syracuse, Montgomery was soon held up in the malarial plain of Catania by strong German reinforcements. He therefore transferred his main thrust to a left hook round Mount Etna, the active volcano which dominates the eastern end of the island. Meanwhile, US 7th Army was making good progress further west. Palermo fell on 22nd July and by the beginning of August General Patton was advancing along the northern coastal road towards Messina at high speed. This, combined with Montgomery's left hook round Mount Etna, quickly led to the evacuation of the German garrison (most of the Italians had surrendered by the end of July) and on 17th August Patton's forces entered Messina. Montgomery arrived from the south shortly afterwards. The island had been taken in only thirty-eight days.

Italy knocked out of the war
Further up the Italian peninsula these dramatic events had been having repercussions. Plots against Mussolini had begun to hatch as early as November 1942. Now they gathered momentum. On 24th July, at an extraordinary meeting of the Fascist Grand Council, the Duce received a stunning vote of no confidence. The next day the King had him arrested and driven away in an ambulance. Marshal Badoglio, one of the chief conspirators, took over the government and declared his intention to continue the war. Few people took him seriously. Already on 15th August the first official peace feeler was extended. Unfortunately for the new government, the Germans had moved in quickly to take control of the country, and a capitulation augured ill for their own safety. The negotiations therefore centred on the arrangement of an Allied attack to coincide with the announcement of surrender.

The successful operations in Sicily and the fall of Mussolini encouraged those who favoured an all-out campaign in Italy. At the Quebec Conference (code-named 'Quadrant') in August the Americans agreed to a landing in Italy, but at a price. The priority of Overlord was re-affirmed and the British were forced to agree to a landing in southern France. Soon after the conquest of Sicily, the hard realities of life in a secondary

High in the Apennines, two German soldiers watch an Italian farmhouse burn. The mountain ranges of Italy provided defensive positions of great strength

theatre began to dawn. Eight of the best divisions, four American, four British, were ordered back to Great Britain in preparation for Overlord, and Eisenhower was informed that he could expect the number of landing craft at his disposal to dwindle. The forces remaining in the theatre were assigned the role of containing the maximum number of German divisions. In fulfilment of this aim, the next objectives were to be the airfields of Foggia, from which the bombing of Germany could be stepped up, and the port of Naples.

On 3rd September an entirely new phase of the Italian campaign opened. Operation Baytown was launched and Montgomery slipped unobtrusively across the Straits of Messina to Reggio on the toe of Italy. This was the first time an Allied army had set foot on the continent since Dunkirk. 'It is a great day,' wrote Montgomery to Sir Alan Brooke. But privately he was less enthusiastic. He had been told of no master plan for Italy, and indeed there was none. From now on, in comparison with Husky, operations were conducted off the cuff. Montgomery began to push on up the mountainous toe of Italy.

Meanwhile, negotiations with the Italians had been maturing, though for a moment there seemed to be danger of a hitch. On 8th September at 6.30 p.m. General Eisenhower announced the surrender of Italy over Algiers radio. Badoglio was due to broadcast at the same time, but Rome radio continued to play operatic selections. There were fears of a double-cross, but finally about an hour later the expected announcement was made and Italy was out of the war. However, the Germans in Italy quickly took over control, disarmed the Italians, and prepared for a defensive campaign.

The Allies now staged their part of the surrender agreement: Operation Avalanche. On 8th-9th September US 5th Army under General Mark Clark landed on the beaches of Salerno. Having just heard the news of the armistice, the troops expected little resistance. But Field-Marshal Kesselring, the German commander, deployed his forces with lightning rapidity. For eight days the Allied army fought with its back to the sea against heavy counter-attacks. Reinforcements were hurriedly brought in, but the most notable part of the Allied recovery was the success of naval gunfire against troops. Admiral Cunningham ordered in the battleships *Warspite* and *Valiant*, and their 16-inch salvoes proved highly effective against the Germans. By the 15th the leading elements of Montgomery's 8th Army were only fifty miles away and the Allied bridgehead was firmly secured. The Germans fell back.

Simultaneously with Avalanche another operation had been launched against the heel of Italy. This was Slapstick, the invasion of Taranto. British 1st Airborne Division was transported in Admiral Cunningham's battle fleet straight into Taranto harbour. This unorthodox action was a success, though a cruiser with more than 200 men aboard was sunk by a mine. The Allies were now firmly ashore at three points in southern Italy: Reggio, Salerno, and Taranto. By 1st October both Foggia and Naples were in Allied hands and the first major objectives of the Italian campaign had been achieved. Corsica and Sardinia had been evacuated. The Italian fleet had surrendered and Admiral Cunningham had sent his famous signal to the Admiralty: 'Be pleased to inform their Lordships that the Italian fleet is anchored under the guns of the fortress of Malta.'

On 12th September there occurred a dramatic event. Mussolini was rescued from the hotel which served as his prison in the Gran Sasso d'Italia. On Hitler's orders Captain Otto Skorzeny of the Waffen SS landed by glider with a force of shock-troops and after a daring escape flew the Duce to Munich. Here Mussolini received his orders from Hitler and returned to Italy as the ineffective puppet leader of the Salò Republic. Although a few Italian divisions continued to serve by the side of Germany, Mussolini's rump Fascist state posed no real threat to the Allies.

Hitler reacts
The consensus of opinion at the Cairo Conference in November was that only modest objectives should now be attempted in Italy. The desirability of reaching the Po during the winter was acknowledged, but to achieve this, it was agreed, would mean withholding so many troops and so much equipment that the cross-Channel operation would not be possible in the spring of 1944. Therefore the shipment of troops and equipment to England continued.

At about this time, apart from the onset of winter, another event occurred which ensured a slower pace in Italy. This was Hitler's sudden decision to appoint Kesselring rather than Rommel Commander-in-Chief South-West and to stop withdrawing up the leg of Italy. Instead Kesselring was to make a stand south of Rome.

The German's winter position, the Gustav Line, was a formidable barrier, and the most formidable part of its defences was Monte Cassino, crowned with a famous sixth-century Benedictine monastery. Until Cassino had been forced, the Liri valley which was the key to Rome was denied to the Allies, and Cassino defied every attempt to blast it into submission. While Clark's US 5th Army struggled across the Volturno and moved up towards Cassino, the western bastion of the Gustav Line, Montgomery's British 8th Army prepared to assault the eastern defences on the River Sangro. In late

Closing the Ring

November he pushed across the river against fierce resistance and in bad weather. Heavy rain turned streams into torrents, roads into mud. The cold became intense. Montgomery's assault was soon held up and by Christmas Day 1943 the Allies were halted along the length of the Gustav Line.

At that time a new amphibious operation came under discussion. Rather than crawl up the leg of Italy 'like a harvest bug', in Churchill's phrase, the obvious tactic was to mount amphibious hooks along the vulnerable flanks of the peninsula. Here a direct conflict arose with Overlord, for such operations depended on landing craft earmarked for the Normandy landings. However, a landing at Anzio was now proposed and in Tunis Churchill managed to persuade Eisenhower, newly appointed to command the Normandy landings, to postpone the departure of this shipping.

At Anzio, complete tactical surprise was achieved. The first the Germans knew of the operation was the report on 22nd January from a fighter pilot that a full-scale invasion was in progress. This was six hours after the first landings by 6th Corps. However, this initial advantage was lost by the failure of the commander, General Lucas, to strike out of the bridgehead. Equally, Kesselring was once again quick in throwing together reinforcements. When Lucas eventually did strike out, he was held up, and on 3rd February subjected to a heavy counter-attack. Anzio convinced Hitler that the Allies meant business in Italy. His reaction, to send two new divisions to eliminate the bridgehead, was a success for the official Allied intention to tie down as many German forces as possible in Italy. General Truscott replaced General Lucas just in time to parry a major counter-offensive, imposing a heavy defeat on the Germans. However, this was not until 6th March, more than six weeks and 19,000 Allied dead after the first landings. Even then there was no breakout until 23rd May.

Meanwhile, renewed attacks on Cassino had failed. The Air Force now offered to help out by dropping 1,100 tons of high explosives on the monastery which was wrongly believed to be occupied by the Germans. In fact it was still occupied by the abbot and his monks who were inside when bombing began. The monastery was reduced

Right: Three stages in the Italian campaign. 1 Salerno, 9th September. Infantry of US 5th Army dash onto the beaches during Operation Avalanche. A tough, bitter fight awaited them. 2 Cassino, end of May. Allied mopping-up patrol clears all that remains of the town. 3 Rome, 5th June: Lieutenant-General Clark (left), commander US 5th Army, and Major-General Truscott, Commander US 6th Corps, arrive at the Capitol to take over the city

The Allied advance up Italy, July 1943 – May 1945

FRANCE
SWITZERLAND
St Tropez
St Raphael
Cannes
Nice
Aix
AUSTRIA
Digne
Turin
Alessandria
Milan
Bolzano
Pavia
Trento
Genoa
15 aug 1944
dec 1944
Verona
Parma
Modena
Argenta
Venice
Anvil'
Gothic Line
Cavalaire
Bologna
Pisa
Imola
Livorno
Ravenna
Florence
Forli
CORSICA
Rimini
Pesaro
sep 1943
Perugia
Ancona
Axis evacuation
Terni
Civitavecchia
SARDINIA
Rome
ITALY
Pescara
Anzio
Ortona
Sangro R.
dec 1943
Gustav Line
Cassino
Garigliano R.
Volturno R.
Termoli
Caserta
Campobasso
Naples
Foggia
Salerno
Potenza
Bari
Marsala
Palermo
Taranto
Mt Etna
Messina
Brindisi
Pizzo
Licata
Enna
SICILY
Catanzaro
Catania
Gela
Ragusa
Syracuse
Reggio
aug 1943

20 40 60 MLS
40 80 KMS

7th US Army
(later 5th)

8th Army

The map shows the general lines of advance by the Allies in Italy. The first two rounds ended with winter stalemates, and the third in victory. In the first, the Allies captured Sicily and drove the Germans back to their winter position south of Rome, the Gustav Line. By this time Corsica and Sardinia had been evacuated. In the second round the Allies broke the Gustav Line, took Rome, and drove swiftly on until the loss of forces to Anvil and the onset of winter halted their advance half-way across the Gothic Line. The third round saw the rapid pursuit and defeat of the German armies

to powder, but Cassino still held out.

It was impossible to break out from Anzio because there were no longer any landing craft available to bring in necessary reinforcements. They had returned to England for Overlord. Another attempt had to be made in the Cassino area. Alexander therefore thinned out the forces on the Adriatic front, bringing the bulk of 8th Army temporarily over to the west, and built up formidable forces between Cassino and the sea. Their presence was carefully camouflaged. After successfully persuading Kesselring that he intended to launch an amphibious attack on Civitavecchia, on 11th May Alexander threw thirteen divisions, consisting of both 8th and 5th Armies, against the unsuspecting Germans. On 17th May Monte Cassino was finally evacuated and 8th Army rolled forward up the Liri valley. On the 23rd Truscott broke out of the Anzio bridgehead and joined up with 5th Army two days later. X and XIV German Armies, retreating before 8th Army, were now threatened with envelopment, but instead of attempting to cut them off, Clark drove straight for Rome which he entered triumphantly on 4th June, two days before the D-Day landings.

For the Allies there seemed to be every chance of driving over the Apennines and across the Po before the summer was out. Alexander hoped to be into Hungary or Austria by autumn, an achievement which would have had profound effects on postwar Europe. However, it was now time for the Allies to fulfil their pledge to mount an invasion of southern France. This was Anvil, later named Dragoon. Seven divisions, three American and four French, were withdrawn from Alexander's Italian front at a time when operations there held out every promise of success. Kesselring was given a vital breathing space. Anvil went in on 15th August, meeting very little resistance. Strategically it had little effect, except to accelerate the arrival of the German Riviera garrison in front of Eisenhower's forces attacking from Normandy.

At the same time that Alexander was losing seven divisions Kesselring was gaining eight. Soon the Allied advance beyond Rome would have to slow down. Once established in the formidable Gothic Line, astride the Apennines, Kesselring could look south with confidence.

The Allied plan for assaulting the Gothic Line demanded that 5th Army should strike in the centre towards Bologna while 8th Army would make for the flat ground on the other side of the Apennines. The attack opened on 25th August. Four days later 8th Army was sweeping through the eastern defences. But Kesselring, as always, acted swiftly, bringing up reinforcements from the centre. He was aided by two days of torrential rain. On 8th September, however,

5th Army mounted an attack in the denuded centre simultaneously with a further attack by 8th Army on the right. 8th Indian Division succeeded in breaking the line and came within ten miles of Imola. 8th Army also broke the line and debouched on to the plain of the Romagna, entering Rimini on 20th September.

On the 20th the rains began. Rivers turned into brown torrents, roads and bridges disappeared. Infantry and armour foundered in a sea of mud. In addition, ammunition became scarce. The Allied armies had lost momentum, and once more faced a winter stalemate. 5th Army came to halt in the mountains just south of Bologna at the end of October, 8th Army in December with the capture of Ravenna and Forli.

The winter stalemate lasted until April 1945. The final battles in Italy were a fine example of strategic skill. During the winter Alexander had lost five more divisions to northern Europe and now had only seventeen against twenty-three German and four Italian. Yet on 9th April 8th Army launched an attack in amphibious vehicles across Lake Comacchio, to the east of Argenta, and by 23rd April both 5th and 8th Armies were across the Po and pursuing the remnants of Vietinghoff's X Army northwards. Two days later the Italian partisans rose in general insurrection as the Germans were already beaten. On 28th April Mussolini was executed and the following day the German forces in Italy signed an instrument of unconditional surrender at Caserta. Resistance ceased on 2nd May. This unilateral capitulation is generally considered to have shortened the war in Europe by several weeks.

But this was only a minor contribution to the Allied victory in Europe. Was there also a more significant contribution? It is often believed that because the Western powers did not beat the Russians to Vienna—Churchill's dream—the Italian campaign failed. This is not so. Such an outcome would have been a bonus to what was essentially a holding operation. The most that can be claimed for the Italian campaign is that had it not taken place German strength on the Channel front would have been even greater. On a broader perspective, of the 127 German divisions covering the long arc from Norway to Greece twenty-two, scarcely more than a sixth, were directly held down by operations in Italy at the time of D-Day. The thirty Allied divisions employed to do this represented an expensive investment with a relatively poor return.

But this should not obscure the achievement of the Allied armies which fought with such determination during the long struggle in Italy, receiving the first surrender of a great German army group on the continent.

D-Day

To uninitiated Frenchmen the second half of a verse by Verlaine transmitted by the BBC at 2115 on Monday 5th June 1944 meant nothing. But to the resistance *'Blessent mon coeur d'une langueur mono-tone'* concealed a message they had longed to hear: more than three and a half million Allied troops were poised to invade and liberate France in one of the greatest amphibious operations in history.

Although Stalin had urged the creation of a second front in France ever since the German invasion of the Soviet Union, proposals for an attack on Brest or Cherbourg in 1942 and the liberation of France in 1943 never developed. In fact planning for a mighty cross-Channel assault on Hitler's *Festung Europa* (Fortress Europe) did not begin until the Casablanca Conference in January 1943 when it was resolved to set up a joint Anglo-American staff to attend to the multiplicity of problems involved in such a massive and hazardous venture. The conception of a full-scale invasion of France was confirmed at the Washington Conference in May 1943 and code-named 'Operation Overlord', it was set for 1st May 1944.

Three months later Lieutenant-General Sir Frederick Morgan, who led the Allied team with the designation Chief of Staff to the Supreme Allied Commander (COSSAC), submitted a tentative plan to the Quebec Conference, and although Churchill suggested a twenty-five per cent increase in the forces employed, its proposals were approved. At the end of the year the appointment of General Dwight D.Eisenhower as Supreme Allied Commander for Operation Overlord was announced. Within the space of one year a relatively unknown chief of staff of an American army training in Texas, whose promotion had been consistently slow, had become the Allied commander-in-chief of a daunting military array charged with striking into the heartland of Germany and destroying her armed forces. It was an inspired choice. The Supreme Commander may not have been a great soldier but the great soldiers of his day willingly served him. Universally trusted, he won the affection, respect, and loyalty not only of his men but of political and military leaders alike. But his greatest contribution to victory undoubtedly lay in his very real ability to allay inter-Service rivalry and

international prejudice among the forces under his command. It was a gift that enabled him to weld together the Allied armies in the field and forge a weapon which the Germans, distracted by their mortal struggle in the east, were unable to deflect.

The remainder of Eisenhower's team was speedily selected. Air Chief Marshal Sir Arthur Tedder was appointed as his deputy, and General Walter Bedell Smith became his chief of staff, with General Sir Frederick Morgan as his deputy. Admiral Sir Bertram Ramsay, the mastermind of Dunkirk and Air Chief Marshal Sir Trafford Leigh-Mallory had been appointed earlier as the commanders-in-chief of the Allied naval and air forces respectively. There was no parallel appointment of commander-in-chief for Allied land forces and although Eisenhower expressed a preference for General Alexander, 'a friendly and companionable type', Churchill felt he could not be spared as Commander in Chief Allied Armies in Italy and consequently Sir Bernard Montgomery handed over command of the 8th Army to assume command of the British 21st Army Group with operational control of all land forces during the initial phase of Operation Overlord. When he was first shown the COSSAC plan for the invasion of France and asked for his comments by Churchill, Montgomery replied that he considered the initial assault forces too weak and the proposed frontage of assault too narrow. The Supreme Commander thus requested the dynamic, and supremely confident general to make his first task the revision of the plan in co-operation with Ramsay, Leigh-Mallory, and Bedell Smith.

COSSAC had proposed the area between Grandcamp and Caen in the Bay of the Seine for the assault. The choice of location, confined by the effective range of the Spitfire to the coast between Flushing and Cherbourg, had to possess harbours capable of handling an immense concentration of men and matériel besides beaches across which the assault forces could be reinforced before ports could be captured. Although the Pas de Calais area offered many obvious advantages such as good air support and a quick turn round for shipping it was formidably defended and offered poor opportunities for an expansion out of the lodgement area. On the other hand, the relatively lightly defended Caen sector afforded a sheltered coastline and offered good terrain for airfield construction. In addition the region was suitable for the consolidation of the initial bridgehead and discouraged the development of

Men of the 1st South Lancashire Battalion help wounded comrades ashore during their comparatively easy landing on Sword beach, 6th June 1944

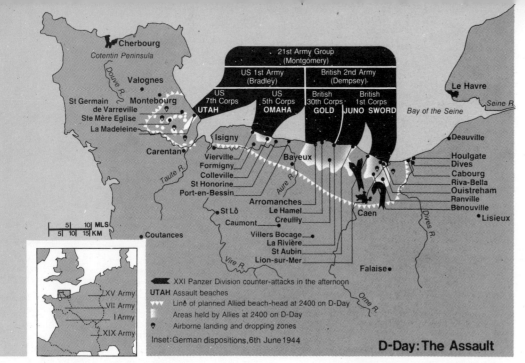

D-Day: The Assault

Map legend:

XXI Panzer Division counter-attacks in the afternoon
UTAH Assault beaches
Line of planned Allied beach-head at 2400 on D-Day
Areas held by Allies at 2400 on D-Day
Airborne landing and dropping zones

Inset: German dispositions, 6th June 1944

armoured counter-attacks. COSSAC's plan, limited as it was by resources, proposed the invasion of Normandy with three seaborne divisions and two airborne brigades in the assault, and although Montgomery accepted its proposals, he considered that the assault should be mounted in greater strength and on a wider front.

He therefore recommended the dropping of two, or, if possible, three airborne divisions before a seaborne assault on a five-divisional frontage. But it was easier to recommend these increases than to find the means of implementing them. While Air Chief Marshal Leigh-Mallory envisaged no difficulties, Admiral Ramsay reported that the Admiralty was uncertain whether it could even meet COSSAC's demands for 'Operation Neptune' (the cross-Channel assault phase of Overlord) which called for 3,323 landing-craft (a generic term embracing landing-ships), 467 warships, and 150 minesweepers. Montgomery's amended plan would double the number of minesweepers and require a further 240 warships and 1,000 landing craft. The central problem was the provision of these craft and although a quantity could be obtained from other theatres of war, Ramsay and Montgomery proposed that the invasion should be postponed until early June to enable an additional month's factory production to be utilized. However, even with this extra production it was discovered that there would still be insufficient craft for the undertaking and it was suggested that additional resources be apportioned Overlord from the Mediterranean. Ever since the Casablanca Conference an invasion of southern France code-named 'Operation Anvil' had been under consideration. By the end of 1943 the Combined Chiefs of Staff decided that both assaults on France were to be 'the supreme operations for 1944'. But although Eisenhower regarded Anvil as an important adjunct to Overlord he advised the Combined Chiefs of Staff that he regarded Overlord as the first priority and that if insufficient naval resources were available for both operations, Anvil should be postponed or reduced. Therefore, despite the fact that he would have preferred to launch the invasion of Normandy in May, to obtain the longest campaigning season, he recommended to the Combined Chiefs of Staff

Left top: The Normandy landings, 6th June 1944. With the exception of Omaha, where the Americans were delayed at the cost of 1,000 dead and 2,000 wounded, the Allies landed swiftly. Centre: Rommel (left) inspects the Atlantic Wall, January 1944. He was given command of the two armies holding the most important sector of the invasion coast. Bottom: Eisenhower briefs paratroopers before take-off

that Overlord should be postponed for a month. They agreed to this on 1st February and at the same time General Eisenhower informed them that the exact date of the assault would depend on a detailed study of moonlight and tidal conditions prevailing during the first week of June. On 24th March the American chiefs of staff, who had opposed any interference with Anvil, agreed to its postponement so that the landing craft of one division could be used for the invasion of Normandy. The craft for a further division would be obtained by the postponement of Overlord. As for the additional forces, Great Britain and the United States would each contribute one division to bring the total to five.

Apart from the question of shipping, the postponement of Operation Overlord afforded a longer period for the strategic bombing of Germany which had been accorded highest priority at the Quebec Conference and for the destruction of bridges and railways which had to be severed if German communications into the invasion area were to be disrupted. Moreover, weather conditions at the end of May would be more likely to favour the launching of a large-scale Russian offensive in conjunction with Operation Overlord.

The broadening and strengthening of the assault was only a partial solution to the problem of breaching the German Atlantic Wall. It was to take specialized equipment and new techniques to break out from the beaches and establish a lodgement. Fortunately the COSSAC planners and the War Office had paid close attention to lessons of the disastrous Dieppe raid which taught that a far stronger and closer fire support for the assaulting troops together with tank support from the moment of disembarking would be required of any future attempt to land in France.

The débâcle had a profound effect on the planning of Overlord and in March 1943 General Sir Alan Brooke, Chief of the Imperial General Staff, ordered the conversion of 79th Armoured Division into Specialized Armour and ordered its commander, Major-General Sir Percy Hobart, to devise and develop specialized armour and equipment for the invasion of France. As a brigadier, Hobart had commanded 1st Tank Brigade, evolv-

Right top: Picture by Robert Capa, who went in with the first wave of troops, shows a GI struggling through the surf to land on Omaha, the bloodiest of the landing-areas. Assault troops landed cold, sodden, cramped, and weakened by sea-sickness. Centre: American forces land on Omaha after dogged assaults and naval bombardment had breached the defences. Bottom: Survivors of a wrecked landing-craft are helped ashore on Utah

ing tactics and doctrines of armoured warfare which the Germans had eagerly assimilated. In 1938 he had created the celebrated 7th Armoured Division (the 'Desert Rats') but in the process so outraged orthodox thinkers with his pioneering concepts that he was relieved of his command and, driven into premature retirement in 1940, he became a corporal in the Home Guard. Happily he was rescued from oblivion on Churchill's personal intervention but it was not until Brooke became convinced of the need for specialized armour to eliminate beach obstacles that his exceptional ingenuity received full rein. By early 1944, despite numerous frustrations, he was able to reveal a range of vehicles to his brother-in-law, General Montgomery, and to the Supreme Commander, General Eisenhower. Tagged 'The Funnies', Hobart's creations presented a bizarre spectacle. There were Crabs, Sherman tanks fitted with flails to beat pathways through minefields; Bobbins, track-laying Churchill tanks; Churchill AVREs (Armoured Vehicles, Royal Engineers), bridge-laying tanks; Churchill Crocodiles, flame-throwing Churchill tanks; Churchill AVREs which could hurl explosive charges against blockhouses; armoured bulldozers, and most significantly of all, amphibious or Duplex-Drive (DD) tanks which could swim ashore under their own power. Although the latter were the brainchild of Nicholas Straussler, a Hungarian-born engineer, Hobart's contribution was to adapt the canvas screen attachment, which enabled the tanks to swim, from obsolete British Valentines to American Shermans. Montgomery immediately recognized the significance of Hobart's 'Funnies' and while Eisenhower appreciated the value of the DD tanks, requesting a brigade's worth, he left the choice of other vehicles to General Omar Bradley, commander of the American assault forces. With fateful consequences, Bradley rejected the devices.

'Occupied England'

The Dieppe raid had made it clear that no major port could be captured quickly or intact and before Cherbourg could be cleared of mines and repaired, Overlord forces would have to be supplied across open beaches. The upshot was the production of two prefabricated harbours known by their code names as Mulberry A and Mulberry B which would be towed across the Channel and sunk or anchored in position off the Normandy coast northwest and north-east of Bayeux. However, only one was brought into use as the harbour on the American sector near Vierville was destroyed in a violent storm from the 19th-22nd of June.

Faced with the inevitable destruction of port facilities, the provision of adequate fuel for vehicles and aircraft was another problem that had confronted COSSAC planners. Their solution was 'PLUTO' or Pipe-Line-Under-The-Ocean along which fuel was pumped first from the Isle of Wight to Cherbourg and later from Dungeness to Ambleteuse near Boulogne. But the pipe-line only began functioning forty-one days after the invasion and by that time the Allies were moving through Belgium.

By the spring of 1944 all southern England had become a gigantic air base, workshop, storage depot, and mobilization camp. On 1st January American forces in Great Britain numbered three quarters of a million and in the following five months they increased to over one and a half million. While British and Canadian troops assembled in south-eastern England, the Americans gathered in the western and south-western coastal belt. Between Dorset and Cornwall, Sir Basil Liddell Hart observed wryly, lay 'occupied England'.

While the massive invasion force trained and rehearsed its tasks, constant reconnaissance, often involving daring landings

Flail tank for clearing minefields. Had General Bradley provided such tanks on Omaha, assaulting American forces would not have suffered so grievously

on the enemy beaches, provided vital information on off-shore rocks, the geological formation of the beaches, beach obstacles, tidal conditions, and changes in the seabed. Great pains were moreover taken to persuade the enemy that the blow was to fall in the Pas de Calais. This was done by simulating concentrations of troops in Kent and Sussex, assembling fleets of dummy ships in south-eastern ports, staging landing exercises on nearby beaches, stepping-up wireless activity, and dropping more bombs on the Pas de Calais than in Normandy. Furthermore, the SD and Abwehr were deliberately swamped with 'secret information' which convinced them that the invasion was scheduled for July in the Pas de Calais. And they were no better served by the Luftwaffe. Its reconnaissance aircraft seldom managed to penetrate the formidable defences which ringed southern England from Falmouth to Harwich. The Germans were almost completely deceived—only Hitler guessed the correct location for the invasion and he was reluctant to back his hunch. The larger part of the German forces were thus deployed east of the Seine and even after D-Day, the Germans believed that the real attack was still to come.

In the last few months before the invasion, security dictated a severe restriction on civilian movement. Coastal areas from the Wash to Land's End were banned to visitors and innumerable ammunition dumps, airfields, camps, and vehicle parks became prohibited areas. Nothing was left to chance. The delivery of letters was postponed and foreign embassies were forbidden to send cipher telegrams. Even their diplomatic bags were delayed.

'The whole mighty host was tense as a coiled spring,' wrote Eisenhower in *Crusade in Europe,* 'and indeed that is exactly what it was—a great human spring, coiled for the moment when its energy should be released and it would vault the English Channel in the greatest amphibious assault ever attempted.' Immense force had been assembled: 1,200 warships, 4,000 assault craft, 1,600 merchant vessels, 13,000 aircraft, and over three and a half million men. They would shortly be pitted against the Atlantic Wall.

For several years the Germans had been developing this coastal defence complex, primarily concentrating on the defence of ports and the Pas de Calais, and although by the end of 1943 a quarter of a million men, conscript workers, and garrison troops were toiling at its construction, it was only approaching completion between Antwerp and Le Havre. Field Marshal Gerd von Rundstedt, Commander in Chief West, had no faith in forts. He was acutely aware of the wall's weaknesses, observing after the war that it had been nothing but

'an illusion fostered by propaganda to fool the Germans as well as the Allies'. Committed to defending 2,000 miles of French coastline, Rundstedt believed that an actual landing could not be prevented and he planned, therefore, to hold strongly only key ports and the most vulnerable sections of the coast. By these tactics the Commander-in-Chief West hoped to delay any Allied build-up long enough for counter attacks to drive small bridgeheads back into the sea.

Throughout the winter of 1943 Rundstedt had appealed repeatedly to OKW for reinforcements; but instead of the men he badly needed, Hitler sent him the hero of North Africa, Field Marshal Erwin Rommel. Initially appointed to inspect defences between Denmark and the Spanish border in November 1943, he was given command of the two armies holding the most important sector of the invasion coast from the Zuider Zee to the River Loire— VII and XV Armies—three months later. Rommel predicted that Allied air power would disrupt the movements of Rundstedt's reserve and that once Allied forces had secured a lodgement they would inevitably break out. He therefore insisted that the invasion would have to be broken on the beaches if it was to be broken at all.

The differing theories of how best to counter the invasion were to lead to a fatal compromise. While the armoured reserves were generally kept well back, the majority of the infantry divisions were committed to strengthening the coastline. In the event the Panzer divisions were forced into action prematurely and found it impossible to concentrate in order to deliver a co-ordinated blow until too late.

In February 1944 Rommel, who had come to share Hitler's view that Normandy would be the main Allied target, instituted an elaborate scheme for obstructing the coastline with underwater obstacles. It was hoped that the 'Czech hedgehogs', concrete tetrahedrons, and mined stakes would impale, cripple, or destroy landing-craft before they reached the beach minefields and that steel 'Belgian grilles' and 'Maginot portcullises' would disable any tanks that landed. To obstruct airborne assaults all open areas within seven miles of the coast were to be sown with booby-trapped stakes. In addition, low-lying areas were to be flooded and gaps between them mined. It was Rommel's intention that heavy coastal batteries immune to air attack should engage the Allied armada at sea. As they raced for the beaches the assault waves would be met by direct fire from fortified machine and anti-tank gun emplacements and from the indirect fire of inland mortars and artillery. Rommel believed that those craft which survived such a devastating concentration of fire

and the forest of lethal underwater obstacles would shatter themselves on the mined beaches. Any troops or tanks which landed would have to contend with additional minefields, barbed-wire, anti-tank ditches, and the withering blast of flame-throwers. Immediately behind this belt Rommel proposed to deploy all armoured divisions so that they could pour their fire onto the foreshore. It was imperative, he maintained, that the maximum force should oppose the invasion on the very day of the landings. 'The first twenty-four hours,' Rommel averred, 'will be decisive.'

The considerable variation in the quality of the sixty German divisions in the West gave Rommel further cause for concern, for while the equipment, training, and morale of the SS and Panzer divisions was superb, the infantry formations contained many low-quality, static, coast-defence troops. Many were too young or too old and many more were Armenian, Georgian, Azerbaijanese, and Tartar 'volunteers' who had elected to wear a German army uniform rather than face a slow death in a prison camp. Rommel had few illusions about his task. The German armies in the West, deprived of training, transport, and their essential radar installations and harassed continually from the air, could only wait for the blow to fall. It was perhaps fortunate for the Allies that the dynamic hero of North Africa had not been appointed earlier and that his plans were neither wholeheartedly supported by his superiors nor thoroughly executed by his subordinates.

In essence, Allied mastery of the air (won by the introduction of the Mustang long-range escort fighter in December 1943) ensured the success of Operation Overlord, but the interdiction of road and rail communications into the battle area was not achieved without prolonged and acute inter-Allied wrangling. The 'Transportation Plan', as the massive air offensive was code-named, concentrated on the scientific destruction of those control, repair, and maintenance facilities which were vitally necessary for the operation of railways in northern and western France, the Low Countries, and western Germany. By mid-May the German armies in France were cut in two for lack of communications.

On 17th May Eisenhower selected Monday 5th June as the tentative D-Day. A final decision would depend on the weather. But the weather was not favourable. Gales and high seas lashed the fog-bound Normandy beaches on Sunday 4th June and the Supreme Commander decided that the invasion would have to be postponed. At 4 a.m. the following day, promised a short period of good weather, Eisenhower announced 'OK, we'll go', and within two hours a mighty armada began emerging into a stormy Channel from Falmouth,

Fowey, Plymouth, Salcombe, Dartmouth, Brixham, Torbay, Portland, Weymouth, Poole, Southampton, Shoreham, Newhaven, and Harwich. It was almost four years to the day that the BEF had escaped by the skin of its teeth at Dunkirk. Now with powerful Allies the British were going back to avenge their humiliation and liberate France.

Meanwhile Allied aircraft had been maintaining diversionary attacks on gun emplacements and beaches in the Pas de Calais and that evening the impression created by these attacks was reinforced. It was essential that the enemy should not discover the course of the invasion fleet and accordingly those radar stations between Cherbourg and Le Havre which had survived air attacks were jammed, while those between Le Havre and Calais were persuaded that the fleet was moving towards this section of the coast. As ships of the Royal Navy towed barrage balloons and produced 'big ship echoes' on the operative German radar sets, bombers circled nearer and nearer the French coast jettisoning bundles of metal foil known as 'Window' which appeared to German radar operators as a large convoy crossing the Channel.

On D-Day, 6th June 1944, the long months of preparation and planning for the most momentous amphibious operation in history came to an end. As the silent column of ships surged towards the Bay of the Seine through ten swept channels, waves of aircraft roared over them and at 0020 the first Allied troops to reach French soil, a *coup de main* force of the British 6th Airborne Division, landed by glider with extreme accuracy near Bénouville to seize the bridges over the Canal de Caen and the River Orne. Half an hour later 3rd and 5th Brigades began to drop east of the Orne to silence the Merville battery, destroy the bridges over the River Dives, and clear an area north of Ranville so that seventy-two gliders carrying guns, transport, and heavy equipment could land at 0330. While 6th Airborne Division was securing the eastern flank of the beachhead, the US 101st and 82nd Airborne Divisions had landed in the south east corner of the Cotentin Peninsula near Ste Mère Eglise and Vierville to carry out the same task on the western flank. Despite losses and confusion arising out of the scattered nature of the landings they forced the enemy on the defensive and succeeded in capturing the causeways across the inundated areas behind the western-most landing area.

While the airborne landings were in progress, over 1,100 British and Canadian bombers attacked coastal batteries between Le Havre and Cherbourg and at daybreak, during the half hour before the first waves hit the beaches, a massive naval and air bombardment was delivered against coastal defences in the target area. The Germans were confident they could not be surprised, but blinded by the bombing and jamming of their radar installations they failed to intercept the airborne forces and only detected the invasion fleet when it was close enough to be heard.

At 0630 Force U, comprising the US 4th Infantry Division of the 7th Corps of the US 1st Army spearheaded by 8th Regimental Combat Team, made a swift and painless landing at the eastern base of the Cotentin Peninsula near the village of La Madeleine, on a beach code-named Utah. Through a navigational error the force had been deposited a mile too far south in a surprisingly weakly defended area and this fortunate error, together with the fact that late launching of the DD tanks ensured the survival of twenty-eight out of thirty-two, accounted for the ease of the landing achieved at the cost of only twelve dead.

Bloody Omaha

Force O, however, landing between Vierville and Colleville on Omaha beach, was not to breach the Atlantic Wall with similar impunity. The plan on this beach provided for the US 1st Infantry Division of 5th Corps of the US 1st Army to assault with two regimental combat teams, supported by two battalions of the DD tanks and two special brigades of engineers. At 0300 the force boarded its assault craft and was lowered into heavy seas twelve miles offshore. Almost at once ten small craft were swamped and others were only kept afloat by troops who baled vigorously with their helmets. As the assault battalions lurched towards the shore beneath a protective barrage, limited in its effectiveness by poor visibility, twenty-seven prematurely-launched DD tanks foundered. There were no dry landings. The apprehensive men, cold, sodden, cramped, and weakened by sea-sickness, disembarked awkwardly to be raked with mortar shell and machine-gun fire. Three hours later the foreshore was littered with burning vehicles, shattered craft, dead, exhausted, and terrified men. For some hours the position on Omaha hung in the balance. Yet the outcome need never have given rise to such anxiety or the battle claimed so many lives had the commander of the American assault forces, Lieutenant-General Omar Bradley, utilized more of Hobart's menagerie of specialized armour. As a consequence of his rejection of the Crabs, Crocodiles, and AVREs, Omaha rapidly became a bloodbath where the Americans suffered 1,000 dead and 2,000 wounded. Although they met a degree of resistance from a spirited infantry division whose presence they had discounted, their cruel losses from gunfire and mines would have been infinitely fewer had Crabs been available to flail the necessary exits. The failure to land the DD tanks—which Bradley had only grudgingly accepted—in advance of the infantry and the ineffectiveness of the naval and air bombardment left the infantry at the mercy of strongpoints they were expected to storm. Only a combination of sustained and accurate naval bombardment and dogged assaults broke the crust of the defences and prevented a local disaster from becoming a major crisis.

If it had not been for the specialized armour and the policy of preceding all British units by special assault teams of Hobart's 79th Armoured Division, progress on the British beaches, code-named Gold, Juno, and Sword, might have been as agonizingly slow and costly as it was on Omaha. But Forces G, J, and S, comprising British and Canadian troops of 1st and 30th Corps of the British 2nd Army under the command of Lieutenant-General Sir Miles Dempsey, landed swiftly between Le Hamel and St Aubin, and Lion-sur-Mer and Riva-Bella.

'Apart from the factor of tactical surprise, the comparatively light casualties which we sustained on all beaches, except Omaha, were in large measure due to the success of the novel mechanical contrivances which we employed and to the staggering moral and material effect of the mass of armour landed in the leading waves of the assault,' the Supreme Commander stated in his report, adding, 'it is doubtful if the assault forces could have firmly established themselves without the assistance of these weapons.'

By nightfall on 6th June 1944, 156,000 Allied troops had landed in Normandy and, although Caen had not been carried in the first onslaught as was planned, the vaunted Atlantic Wall had been breached on a front of thirty miles between the Vire and the Orne at the cost of 11,000 casualties of whom not more than 2,500 lost their lives.

With no reserves behind the thin beach defences and no heavy artillery to challenge the naval bombardment squadrons, Rommel had failed to smash the invasion on the beaches and by 9th June, despite an attack by XXI Panzer Division, the Allied bridgeheads had been safely consolidated. The previous year Churchill had expressed hopes for the liberation of France 'before the fall of autumn leaves'. The liberation had not come and the Germans scattered green paper leaves in French streets bearing the mocking inscription: 'I have fallen, Oh Churchill! Where are your soldiers?' They were here now. Rommel had insisted that the first twenty-four hours of the invasion would be decisive. They had been.

Science at War

Science has made a vital contribution to the defence of nations since the advent of gunpowder, but it took two world wars to make it vital to national survival. Just as a Chinese firework became an arbiter of power, the most obvious examples of how science was harnessed with devastating effect in the Second World War—radar, rockets, and the atom bomb—were forged from basic scientific discoveries made before the war began. The impact of science was due to the incentive the war provided for its technological exploitation; the greatest war ever fought produced a commensurate effort in the laboratories. But it was not as simple as that. To take the products of research, mass-produce them and transfer them to the battlefield required as much a political as a scientific insight, and it was here the Allies had the edge. The Allies developed, in varying degrees, a new climate of co-operation between scientists and servicemen at all levels and a comparable co-operation between science and industry. Nazi Germany on the other hand, for all the political debt it owed to technology, failed to realize where science and politics parted company.

The story of science and the Second World War is of how effectively the brilliance and invention of the individual was realized in the field. Allied victory in the scientific war was dictated by superior organization at this stage, providing speedy answers to the most simple and the most complex of problems. The basic situation has been outlined. To every advance the enemy made counter measures had to be devised, tested, and mass-produced and this called for the greatest flexibility and constant operational liaison. For each new weapon, teams of operators had to be quickly trained, and their knowledge—together with the unfamiliar new weapons—had to be passed on to millions. New theatres of war brought new challenges, whether it was malaria in New Guinea, or wrecked harbours in France —and a rapid answer had to be found in every case.

The war years themselves produced massive challenges to which massive research programmes were one answer; but the basic discoveries, often the work of an individual starved of resources, which allowed the development of an atom bomb, radar, the jet engine and the rocket, had been made before 1939. German scientists, drawing on the lessons of 1914-18 when Germany's war-machine had been run on a siege economy, had invested much effort in material science. Germany not only had a healthy synthetic rubber industry but a plastics and

hydrogenated petrol programme based on coal. These plants became primary targets in the USAAF precision bombing offensive. The same was true in metallurgy. When I.G. Farben scientists first produced magnesium alloys for aircraft construction and engine castings they made a technological gap which British and American scientists launched crash programmes to close.

Before the war, however, Great Britain alone had taken the trouble to organize cadres of scientists to be ready to assist the services. This is ironic when one considers how much the political climate of appeasement in Britain and France during German re-armament was born of a popular fear of the scientific unknown. The prospects of strategic bombing, the distortedly high estimates of deaths per 'bomb tonnage' and the vision of aeroplanes raining lethal gas on London or Paris sapped the will to prepare for war in the West. The popular press was full of death-rays; the film of H.G. Wells' *Shape of Things to Come* saw a Europe flattened by super-bombs and ravaged by germ warfare. And there had been a revolution in communications too. It had already altered the face of politics. Now the rival propagandists had, in mass broadcasting and the cinema, the instruments to instantly reach their populations. Marconi's idealistic hope that radio might go some way to averting the 'evils of war' was turned on its head in the Second World War.

Just as the major areas of research had been opened before the war, the war itself ended with a series of 'might have beens' precursing the age of the nuclear umbrella. Basic research on nerve gases had been implemented in the course of German insecticidal research before the war. By 1945, 'tabun', 'sarin' and 'soman' had been stockpiled by the Germans in vast quantities. Toxic gases had been used operationally by the Japanese in China; botulinum toxin, the deadliest agent of biological warfare, was under test in the United States in 1943. Long-range rocket bombardment

Top: Barnes Wallis—British bomb designer. He invented the bouncing bombs used to attack the Möhne, Sorpe, and Eder dams in the Dambuster raid. Centre: Sir Henry Tizard, chairman of the Aeronautical Research Committee from 1933 to 1942. The Tizard Committee was responsible for first developing radar in Britain. Bottom: Sir Alexander Fleming whose discovery, penicillin, was developed in America during the war and was used to treat sepsis of wounds which had caused huge loss of life in all previous wars

of London and Antwerp was carried out by the Germans in an attempt to reverse the tide of the war. The German A-9 rocket and the *Laffarenz-projekt*, on the drawing board in 1945, were the ideas from which the ICBM and the Polaris submarine were developed; Above all, the atom bomb had been dropped on two Japanese cities.

The developments in mathematical science, computing systems and instrumentation could ensure new accuracies and prediction of effects. Thus the delivery systems existed; the weapons of total destruction existed. The story of science and the Second World War, underwriting Allied victory, is not only the story of an arms race; it tells of how new weapons were used, and also why some new weapons were never used at all.

Even before 1936, Great Britain was aware that scientific research was a most integral part of national defence, faced as she was with the prospect of a massive hostile bombing force negating the two historic advantages in British defence—the Channel and the Royal Navy. In March 1935 the Tizard Committee on Air Defence discovered that the only instrumental aid for providing warning of the approach of hostile aircraft was the telescope. If there was any hope at all, it lay in Admiralty research into the possibilities of locating hostile ships and aircraft by their heat radiation, or the Air Defence Experimental Establishment's work on sound location. In the pre-Munich period, British air defence had rested on biplane fighters and immovable concrete sound-mirrors with a ten-mile range—and they were placed facing France, not Germany. By July 1939, however, an operative system of radio location was in existence.

By 1936, it had been realized in several countries that an aircraft reflects radio waves. Radar was in operation in Britain first, because the brilliance of the individual scientist was backed up by foresight and faith at the committee stage; the Treasury's release of funds through the initial efforts of A.P. Rowe and H.E. Wimperis at the Air Ministry, through the Tizard Committee led to the construction of a coastal radar chain with an ability to measure range and plot the position of hostile aircraft approaching Britain—to a

Left: The radar plotting room aboard a US aircraft-carrier in the Pacific. Working on information provided by radar, the men plot the positions of hostile and friendly surface vessels and aircraft. Above right: Painting by J. S. Baker of a train transporting V2s bombed by the RAF. Travelling at speeds up to 3,000 mph, V2 rockets were almost impossible to intercept, unlike their predecessors, the V1s, whose maximum speed was 400 mph.

range of 100 miles and more. British industry was becoming geared to the new technology, a pool of specialist operators had been established, and Fighter Command group headquarters and fighter stations linked early warning by high-frequency radio-telephony to the eight-gun 350 mph monoplane designs of Camm and Mitchell —the Hurricane and the Spitfire.

The operative lessons of radar research had a wider relevance. A.P. Rowe's Telecommunications Research Establishment at Bawdsey developed a system of operational liaison between scientists and services which allowed prototype testing in action and post-design, in which parties of scientists were sent to squadrons actually using the new radar equipment to find out just how well (or indeed badly) it worked. Operational Research—the subjection of military operations to quantitative analysis —largely began in the British Air Ministry, though it was later brought to a high pitch of perfection by the Americans. It came into being through the need to improve the technique of interception by radar direction, a problem which the Germans failed to satisfactorily resolve until comparatively late in the war. The demands made by such militarized technology on manpower justified the compilation of that central register of qualified men devised by Professor Hill and Dr Goodeve in 1938. Two months before the war it contained the names of 5,000 scientists in 'reversed' occupations, thus separating the 'boffins' and operators—each to his alloted task. This made good sense, in direct contrast to the woeful German

experience of 1939 when academics were indiscriminately drafted to handle rifles in the infantry or to be sergeants in command of a signals platoon.

'The sleeping giant'

Scientific organization in the United States between the wars was not so pressured by the immediate prospects of national defence. Remembering that the American Expeditionary Force of 1917 had been given its aeroplanes, gas masks, steel helmets, tanks, even its automatic weapons by Britain and France, the wartime development of weapon science, other than production techniques, had little prominence. In 1939 America was the world's largest industrial producer. If its plant was not tuned to munitions production, the slack in the economy and the ample labour supply, both legacies of the Depression, made America both militarily and industrially a 'sleeping giant'. The war which began for America with the blip on an untrusted and primitive radar scanner above Ford Island ended with the dropping of the atom bomb from the stratosphere. Meanwhile, American technology had established its ability to overcome any problem of logistics and terrain—from the spot-welding of 'Liberty ships' to the mass-production of DDT and penicillin: above all, it had proved its ability to develop, test and implement new devices, new answers to new problems. Take as examples the whole range of amphibious vehicles designed for the Pacific Campaign, or the long-range bomber escort which arrived in quantity to affect materially a deteriorating military situation for which existing technology had until then proved inadequate.

The American scientific effort depended on the immediate assimilation of as much British material as possible and the avoidance of the mistakes of departmentalism and misdeployment of resources. In the summer of 1940, the British government approved the despatch of a scientific mission to the United States led by Sir Henry Tizard. The great research facilities and manufacturing power of the US overruled any security considerations. Due to this mission, 16 months before they entered the war, the Americans were in possession of the most important findings of British research to date: the Kerrison anti-aircraft gun predictor, solid-propellant rockets, the proximity fuse, asdic, RDX explosive, shipborne radar and especially the cavity magnetron.

This last device allowed the second revolution in radar. Its transformation from an early-warning screen to an airborne, seaborne, high- or low-level instrument of acute long-range perception depended on the generation of shorter radio wavelengths. Two devices seemed to have potential: the 'Klystron' developed by the Varian brothers at Stanford University, California, and an American invention of 1921—the magnetron itself. Two British scientists, Professor J.T. Randall and Dr H.A.H. Boot, applied a simple resonator principle to this last device, producing by February 1940 a wave-length of 9 cm at a power of 400 watts. The valve had made centimetric radar possible. Reducing redundant information echoing from the landscape, it closed a blind spot which prevented low-flying aircraft from escaping detection, and proved of vital importance in the Battle of the Atlantic and the strategic bombing of Germany.

The revelation of the cavity magnetron allowed American radar research to make a quantum jump forward. Karl T. Compton, chief of the Radar Division National Defence Research Committee, had long foreseen the importance of micro-waves. He appreciated the prediction of Sir Charles Wright that the side which developed power on the shortest wave-length would win the coming war. The Americans significantly put the project into a civilian laboratory, establishing a short-wave research laboratory at the Massachusetts Institute of Technology. American military research relied heavily on the resources of the universities and of industry. This was largely because the Office of Scientific Research and Development, established in 1940 under Vannevar Bush, felt itself to be pressed for time. The OSRD reported directly to President Roosevelt and received funds from Congress by direct appropriation, either administering them by negotiating contracts

with private or industrial laboratories.

The National Defence Research Committee's work was split into 19 divisions, each responsible for a particular area, such as radar or rocketry. The Committee for Medical Research was responsible—among other things—for the manufacture of penicillin and plasma. There were, however, organizational gulfs within the American scientific effort which went some way to impairing its efficiency. The Military Establishments, particularly the Army Service Forces under Lieutenant-General Sommervell, placed the army's semi-independent technical services under a single close control, but they never approached the degree of operational liaison current in Great Britain. Sommervell's sprawling empire included Quartermaster, Ordnance, Signal, Engineer, Medical, Chemical warfare and Transportation departments. Each department conducted research and development and placed contracts for procurements, functions which overlapped yet remained isolated from the sub-committees of the NDRC. And the sub-committees were themselves compartmentalized, relying on sheer weight of resources to produce results. The products of American science therefore —the Manhattan Project aside, unique in its scale, organization and funding—tended to have a distinct technological bias, characterized by the capacity for series development and volume production. The Americans excelled in such simple war-winning innovations as the amphibious truck, the DUKW, which allowed rapid turnaround at an invasion beachhead, the bazooka which could knock out a Tiger Tank, and the armoured bulldozer which cleared airstrips under fire in the Pacific island-hopping campaign.

Weapons of revenge

The German scientific effort during the Second World War was the one that most excited popular imagination. Certainly, the spectacle of long-range rocket bombardment, jet and rocket aircraft, Mach 10 wind tunnels, helicopters, assault rifles, infra-red devices, true 'submarines' running on hydrogen peroxide, influence warheads and nerve gases made it possible to imagine the most ingenious and deadly arsenal which science could put at man's disposal. Why, therefore, was the German scientific effort constantly baffled and rendered ineffective by the Allies? The ability of the Third Reich actually to produce new weapons capable of deciding the issues of war was not only greatly overestimated by its enemies (a misapprehension not without significance for the scientists who worked on America's atom bomb), but remains so by those who look only at the products of science—and forget the significance of their implementation. Germany's pro-

gramme of technological development was a programme characterized not by organization but by chaos.

The post-war investigation by the Allies showed that at the outbreak of war, the German leaders believed they could achieve final victory with the weapons they already had. In the crucial years of 1939–43, basic research on radar had been halted on Hitler's orders. German scientists had rejected centimetric radar as impractical until an H_2S set with its magnetron-core was recovered from a crashed RAF night-bomber. No scientist was asked to advise effectively on the U-boat war until the end of 1943, and the advantage held by the Allies was by then so great there was no chance of reversing it. The most significant area of research, the Army's A-4 rocket project, capable of delivering a ton of high explosive at a 200-mile range, was advanced in preference to the development of the guided anti-aircraft missiles capable of blasting the four-engined Allied bombers out of the sky.

The *Enzian* and *Wasserfall* AA rocket programmes could, with coherent direction, have interdicted German airspace to the very bombers pounding all *Vergeltungswaffen* (the 'revenge weapons' V1, V2 and V3) installations. But coherent direction was lacking. Partisans of rival schemes fluttered about Hitler's court until a project was rejected or approved, given a highest priority stamp, millions of cubic tons of ferro-concrete allocated (this always found particular favour with the Führer) and labour mobilized. The *Führerprinzip* worked in two ways. A dubious project such as the Coender 'high-pressure pump gun' (the V3) was given a priority far beyond its proven ability, whereas a potentially vital development such as the Me 262 jet fighter was diverted by Hitler himself to a highly unsuitable bomber role, against the pleadings of Luftwaffe experts. During the war there was not one single German agency, let alone one individual, which controlled the vast number of overlapping projects. Only the intervention of a powerful political initiative could ensure the durability of a research programme. The increasing infiltration by the SS into the Army's rocket project and its transfer from Peenemunde to Blizna in Poland shows how completely the political monoliths inside the Third Reich intervened in weapons programmes without imposing the coherence that a 'totalitarian system' may presuppose.

In these ways the undesirable brilliance of individual German scientists was cauterized and grotesquely framed in the Aryan vision of science which denounced Einstein's relativity theory as being Jewish, and saw medical experiments on concentration camp prisoners as legitimate. The division of scientific effort between the universies, industry, the Wehrmacht and the SS was never reconciled. Reflecting the National Socialist emphasis on practical technology rather than pure science with its *Untermensch* tinge, it was the engineer who could command attention and funds and who was amply rewarded and cosseted by the state—such men as Ferdinand Porsche, designer of the Volkswagen and Tiger tank, Wernher von Braun, the 'interplanetary travel enthusiast' and guiding light of the German rocket programme, or Kurt Tank, designer of the Fw 190 fighter. This emphasis on the engineer coupled with the Nazi distrust of the natural scientist had, long before 1939, already prejudiced their efforts in the field of nuclear technology.

There was never a 'race' for the ultimate deterrent, the atom bomb; the Germans

never got near it. Apart from the efforts of the Allied sabotage offensive, the manufacture of heavy water at the Rjukan plant in Norway had never taken place in anything approaching industrial quantities. Germany's uranium production came to a dead halt with the bombing of the Degussa plant in 1943. However, German atomic science was already foredoomed by the usual disadvantages of poor organization and inadequate recognition by the Reich leadership. Another contributory factor to their slow development in this field was the absence of those physicists driven into exile by Nazi racial and ideological policies, such men as Einstein, Born, Peirils, and Haber, and the Italian refugees from Fascism— Fermi, Pontecorvo and Gullicini. Again, the Germans had insufficient technical equipment, machine tools, telemetry and computers for so vast a project. And finally, in contrast to the rocket lobby who had managed to overcome Hitler's initial indifference by their sheer enthusiasm and got their 'V-weapons'—if not a means to land on the moon—the atomic scientists themselves did little to overcome the authorities' incomprehension of the importance of such research and technical development. Only Göring at the Air Ministry, an agency which proved consistently fecund in its research programmes, saw its potential—but too late. The last V-2, the ideal delivery system for atomic warfare, had already been launched, while a German nuclear reactor, let alone a bomb, had never been tested.

The key to victory
The American atom bomb was, however, not destined for Germany. A highly complex technological war waged by America, Britain and Russia had already defeated the Third Reich. The lesson of that war, in the terms of operational experience, was that finely balanced scientific ingenuity needed political and military scope to use it; it had to ensure the right weapon was in the right place at the right time. But however subtle the 'secret war' may have been, it was often a simple technological factor that swung the outcome of a battle. The elegance of the Allied anti-submarine effort

Above: The indicator of the ASV (air to surface vessel radar) Mark II. Operational from 1940, this meter equipment enabled bombers to detect and home on surfaced U-boats. Left: Laying a supply pipe-line across the English Channel. Code-named PLUTO, the Pipe-Line-Under-The-Ocean carried fuel from England to France for the Allied forces in Western Europe. Although not functioning until forty-one days after D-Day, in the final stages of the war PLUTO was capable of delivering a million gallons of fuel a day

in the Atlantic for example, using High-Frequency direction finding, H_2S airborne radar and ahead-throwing weapons might have been negated had *Schnörkel*-equipped U-boats appeared earlier. Similarly, the RAF night-bombing offensive had by 1944 exhausted all the technical subtleties in its armoury. Oboe and Gee, its navigational aids, H_2S and 'Window', the anti-radar device which showered metal foil into the beams of the German electronic defences, had been rendered largely ineffective by German electronic counter-intelligence and new night-fighter tactics. However, the appearance of the P-51 Mustang long-range escort fighter equipped with droptanks in the day-time skies over Germany gave the USAAF bombing effort an absolute advantage. Similarly, the great battle on Germany's Eastern Front was materially turned in 1942 by the appearance of the Russian T-34 tank, with its sloped armour, 75-mm gun, and high standard of durability. It made obsolete the bulk of Germany's tank and anti-tank arsenal at a stroke. Chronologically, at least, jets, rockets, perhaps even the bomb itself were an afterthought in the story of science and the Second World War, the prototypes heralding an unfought new age of warfare. Where the scientist, technologists, doctors and engineers held the key to victory was in providing devices as simple yet as subtle as a tank that could swim up a beach, an engine filter that might resist the dust of the desert and a spray that would kill malarial mosquitoes. The fact that the German scientific war effort failed to produce the mundane but effective weapons in preference to the spectacular is a factor that largely contributed to the Allied victory in the Second World War. And just as important, war experience had made it apparent that science itself had a vital role to play not only on the battlefield, but in maintaining the social fabric of both war and peace.

7 WAR AT THE TOP

The Strains of Alliance

The surprising thing is not that the Grand Alliance of Great Britain, the United States, and the Soviet Union began to fall apart as soon as Nazi German forces surrendered in May 1945. The surprising thing is that it lasted as long as it did. All the cards were stacked against it. There had been the thirty-year-old feud between Soviet Communism and British liberal democracy, Soviet mistrust of British appeasement policies in the 1930's, and British revulsion against the Nazi-Soviet Pact which had made war inevitable in 1939. Russia had unsatisfied territorial claims in Eastern Europe and the Far East, whereas Great Britain had entered the war in 1939, in part at least, to defend an East European state against aggression, and the United States had a traditional aversion for territorial changes without the consent of the people concerned. In relations between Great Britain and America, there was suspicion on the American side, symbolized in the person of President Roosevelt, that Great Britain was once more using a war for the liberation of mankind in order to shore up the British Empire, on the British side that Americans intoxicated themselves with high-flown language while misunderstanding political realities. In relations between America and Russia, there was the deep-seated fear and mistrust of the capitalist giant on the Soviet side; on the American, ignorance of Russia's security requirements in Eastern Europe, quickly followed by repugnance when these became known.

What held the Big Three together was

Left: The Big Three at Yalta, February 1945. Churchill, Roosevelt and Stalin

the common struggle against Germany and her allies in Europe; Anglo-American dependence on the continuing exhaustion of German forces by the Red Army on the Eastern Front and on a Soviet entry into the war against Japan after Germany's defeat; Soviet reliance on aid from the Western powers and Stalin's wish not to alienate President Roosevelt while Soviet paramountcy in Eastern Europe was still being established; and the genuine belief among the three allies that conflict between them in the post-war world could, without exaggeration, tear the world apart.

Inter-Allied differences arising from the actual conduct of military operations and the terms and manner of the enemy's surrender were inextricably linked with the wider political issues of the war. This was especially true for Churchill and Stalin owing to the long experience of both their countries of European wars and politics. Churchill was keen to reach an understanding with Stalin about Russia's post-war territorial claims in Europe almost as soon as Germany invaded Russia on 22nd June 1941, while Russia was still dependent on Western military aid, rather than later when she might be able to dictate an East European settlement from the basis of her own strength. Stalin, too, sought Western consent to Soviet territorial claims while the struggle on the Eastern Front wavered to and fro. Roosevelt, however, with a more doctrinaire distinction between war and peace, clung to Germany's overthrow as the prime object: territorial issues should await the peace conference. Hence it was owing to American influence that territorial agreements

were not included in the twenty-year Anglo-Soviet treaty signed on 26th May 1942 and that Churchill's argument was not accepted, when German resistance was collapsing in the spring of 1945, that Anglo-American forces should strike as deep as possible into Eastern Europe in order to limit Soviet freedom to prescribe the post-war settlement there.

Nevertheless, the military struggle left its mark, psychologically at least, on the later development of political differences. The first and major military discord concerned the opening of a second front in Europe by the two Western powers. Stalin, with Nazi forces rolling deep into Russia in 1941, called insistently for an attack on Germany from the west, insinuating that Great Britain and America were afraid of taking on German might and suspecting that they were hoping to see Nazism and Communism destroy one another while keeping their own strength intact. The United States was keener on attacking Western Europe than Great Britain was. As early as 11th June 1942, following the visit of the Soviet foreign minister Molotov to Washington, the White House stated, more definitively than Churchill wished, that understanding was reached 'with regard to the urgent tasks of creating a second front in Europe in 1942'.

Bitter feelings

This intention was revised at the Anglo-American summit meeting in Casablanca in January 1943, when the decision was reached to attack Sicily. Stalin conveyed his bitter feelings about this to Roosevelt on 15th March 1943 and again on 11th June, when he condemned the decision to attack Italy and charged his allies with bad faith.

Another source of East-West conflict over the actual waging of the war was the British decision in July 1942 temporarily to suspend convoys of supplies to Russia's northern ports owing to losses inflicted by German aircraft and submarines. Again there followed Soviet charges of British faint-heartedness countered by Churchill's indignant defence of British seamen.

A further military controversy with strong political overtones which sprang up between Russia and the West concerned the conditions and manner of the enemy surrender. The question was how the three Allies were to be represented at the surrender of enemy forces and on the control commissions to administer conquered enemy territory. The general principle was adopted that each ally should be responsible for receiving surrender offers on fronts on which its own forces were mainly engaged, but the Italian surrender in 1943, because of the special nature of the case, raised special problems.

Stalin had already complained about not being kept informed about political affairs in North Africa, where a regime under the French admiral, Darlan, was installed by British and American forces, to be succeeded by General Giraud after Darlan's assassination in December 1942. In August 1943 Stalin first objected to not being informed about the Italian offer to surrender and then demanded a say in the Italian settlement; these differences became critical at the three-power foreign ministers' conference in Moscow in October 1943. From this dispute emerged a three-power advisory council for Italy, but it was evident that the Soviet representative on this would have as little real say as the British and American representatives on the control commissions created for the four ex-enemy states of Bulgaria, Finland, Hungary, and Rumania, which the Red Army subdued. This was in accord with the famous 'spheres of influence' agreement reached by Churchill at his Moscow meeting with Stalin in October 1944, when Rumania was ceded to ninety per cent and Bulgaria to seventy-five per cent Soviet influence and Greece to ninety per cent British, with Yugoslavia and Hungary shared equally between Russia and Great Britain. Roosevelt never accepted this kind of bargain over the fate of nations and clung to the idea that, as in the Atlantic Charter of August 1941, the wishes of the people should be the principal factor in deciding their political fate.

Anglo-American co-operation in settling military as well as political issues of the alliance was naturally more intimate than that between the two Western powers and Russia. Geographical situation, ideological affinities, cultural and sentimental bonds, together with the peculiar relationship which sprang up between Churchill and Roosevelt, on one side, and Soviet secretiveness, on the other, had much to do with this. All told, Churchill had five major private meetings with Roosevelt during the war with Germany—at Placentia Bay, Newfoundland, in August 1941; in Casablanca in January 1943; in Washington (the 'Trident' Conference) in May 1943; in Quebec (the 'Quadrant' Conference) in August 1943; in Cairo in November and December 1943, where they also met Generalissimo Chiang Kai-shek; and again in Quebec in September 1944. The two also met briefly at Malta in February 1945 before the Yalta Conference. Churchill only went twice to the Soviet Union alone, once in August 1942 and again in October 1944. Roosevelt never saw Stalin alone except for short exchanges during the three-power Tehran and Yalta meetings in November 1943 and February 1945, though he vainly proposed a two-power meeting in May 1943. The Big Three met together only three times: in Tehran in November 1943, Yalta in February 1945 and Potsdam—where the United States was represented by President Truman, Roosevelt having died on 12th April—in July and August 1945.

The comparative rarity of tripartite talks was largely due to Stalin's unwillingness to leave Russia while personally directing military operations. At the same time, Churchill did his utmost to ensure that Roosevelt and Stalin did not get too close together for fear that this might be at Great Britain's expense, while Roosevelt often shunned Churchill's private approaches lest Stalin suspect that they were 'ganging up' against him. In addition to heads-of-government meetings, the foreign ministers of the three powers held an important conference in Moscow in October 1943 and all three states were represented at the Dumbarton Oaks and San Francisco Conferences of August-October 1944 and April-June 1945 respectively for finalizing agreement on the United Nations Charter.

The first inter-Allied political difference emerged over the Atlantic Charter signed by Churchill and Roosevelt on 12th August 1941. Churchill himself dissented in the House of Commons on 9th September 1941 from the Rooseveltian conception of the charter when he insisted that Article 3, asserting the rights of all peoples to choose the form of government under which they live, could not apply to the British Empire. Later, at the Yalta Conference, he protested 'Never! Never! Never!' against a Soviet-American wish that all dependent territories be placed under international trusteeship. The Russians, on the other hand, who had not been consulted about the Atlantic Charter though they adhered to it, wished to reach an agreement with their allies about Article 2–'no territorial changes that do not accord with the freely expressed wishes of the peoples concerned'—so as to legalize their territorial acquisitions in 1939-1940 during the operation of the Nazi-Soviet Pact of 1939. When the British foreign secretary Anthony Eden visited Moscow in December 1941 Stalin pressed for immediate incorporation into the Soviet Union of the three Baltic states, Soviet acquisitions from Finland as a result of the Winter War of 1939-40, eastern Poland as far as the Curzon Line, and Bessarabia. Stalin promised in return Soviet support for the acquisition of British military bases in western Europe.

Great Britain was not hostile to these demands but had reservations about the Soviet claim to Lwów which, in Churchill's, though not Stalin's, view lay west of the Curzon Line. Churchill was more interested then, as he remained throughout the war, in the independence of the Polish political regime to be left in the new Polish territory, which was to include former German territory in the west as compensation for the area of eastern Poland to be ceded to the USSR. The United States, however, was hostile and not until Eden visited Washington in March 1943 did the Americans express their agreement to Soviet territorial demands. Even so, at the tripartite foreign ministers' conference in Moscow in October 1943 the United States was still standing out for plebiscites in eastern Poland and the Baltic states. When the Big Three met at Tehran in November 1943, however, agreement was reached on the main lines of the territorial settlement in Eastern Europe and, in very broad outline, of a Polish settlement, too.

The Big Three meet
Some progress had also been achieved on three other major questions before the Yalta Conference in February 1945. First, with regard to the post-war treatment of Germany, differences arose between. Churchill and Roosevelt at their Quebec meeting in August 1943. Roosevelt favoured the dismemberment of Germany into weak provinces, a policy his spokesman pursued at the foreign ministers' conference in October, while the British delegation was cautious, mindful of the consequences of creating an economic and power vacuum in the heart of Europe. At Tehran in November 1943, the first Big Three meeting, no decisions were reached about post-war Germany; Roosevelt again advocated its division into five separate states, whereas Churchill called merely for the splitting of Prussia and the south German states from the rest of Germany and the organization of the

An Italian propaganda postcard shows Churchill and Roosevelt as Chicago-style gangsters, 'liberators' of a Europe that Allied bombers have devastated

latter as part of a larger Danubian federation. Stalin opposed this as a threat to Russia. By the time Churchill and Roosevelt met for their second Quebec conference in September 1944 British views had moved a shade nearer the tougher American attitude. Both leaders tentatively accepted the notorious Morgenthau Plan which involved the destruction of German industry and the conversion of the country into a weak pastoralized state. But the Morgenthau Plan was no sooner adopted than it was dropped. The two Western leaders went to their Yalta encounter with Stalin with only the vaguest ideas about the post-war treatment of Germany. They wanted time to think out a policy.

Secondly, ideas moved forward on the post-war settlement in the Far East. When Churchill and Roosevelt met Chiang Kai-shek in Cairo in November 1943, they agreed that Japan should be stripped of all the Pacific islands which it had seized or occupied since 1914, and that all the territories Japan had taken from China, such as Manchuria, Formosa, and the Pescadores, should be restored; Korea, ruled by Japan since 1910, was to be free and independent. Then, at the Tehran Conference a month later, Stalin made clear that if, after Germany's defeat, the Soviet Union took part in the Far Eastern war, she would expect her reward in the form at least of access to a warm-water

port in the Pacific, the southern half of Sakhalin, and the Kuriles.

As for the third of these issues, progress towards the shaping of a future world security organization, Eden had listened in Washington in March 1943 to the view of Roosevelt that it should be dominated by America, Great Britain, China, and Russia. Roosevelt then believed, unlike Churchill, that France was incapable of playing the role of a world leader; not until 26th August, two months after the Allied landing in northern France, was General Eisenhower authorized to accept General de Gaulle's Committee of National Liberation as the de facto authority in France. In Quebec in August 1943 Churchill and Roosevelt agreed that the new world organization must be based on the principle of sovereign equality and that the Soviet Union must be a dominant member after Germany's defeat. The agreed intent to form a world security organization was further elaborated at the three-power foreign ministers' meeting in Moscow in October 1943, when the two basic principles were laid down: firstly, that the organization, founded on the concept of sovereign equality and open to all 'peace-loving' states, should be formed 'at the earliest practicable date'; and, secondly, that, 'pending the re-establishment of law and order and the inauguration of a system of general security,' they–the Big Three– would 'consult with one another and as occasion requires with other members of the United Nations with a view to joint action on behalf of the community of nations'. The broad framework of the world

security organization was drawn up at the Dumbarton Oaks Conference in October 1944 but four major questions still remained to be answered by the Big Three: the principle of representation for the great powers; the rules governing enforcement action by the new organization; the powers of the General Assembly representing all member-states; and the position of France.

The meeting of Churchill, Roosevelt, and Stalin at Yalta in the Crimea (4th-11th February 1945) represented the high tide of Allied unity. But this was largely due to the exhilaration arising from the imminent total German collapse and because many key questions were glossed over by fair-sounding compromises which reality destroyed in the following months before the Potsdam meeting in July and August. On the position of France, Stalin–and to a lesser extent Roosevelt–remained hostile notwithstanding the signature of a Franco-Soviet mutual assistance pact on 10th December 1944. It was chiefly due to Churchill's pressure that France was granted an occupation zone in defeated Germany, to be formed out of the proposed British and American zones, and invited to be a fourth member of the Allied Control Council for Germany. On Germany itself, it was agreed that supreme authority in the country would pass to the three and that its exercise would include the 'complete disarmament, demilitarization, and dismemberment of Germany'. But agreement was reached neither then nor afterwards on how uniformity was to be attained in the government of the occupation zones, the borders of which were being worked out by

'I like waiting' – German cartoon of 1943 mocks Churchill who was not present at private talks between Stalin and Roosevelt during the Tehran Conference

a three-power European Advisory Commission sitting in London, or how, if ever, independent German political life was to be revived.

On the vexed question of reparations, the general principles were laid down that removals were to take place from the national wealth of Germany within two years of the end of the war so as to destroy its military potential; that there should be annual deliveries of goods from current production in Germany 'for a period to be fixed'; and that German labour should be used in the reconstruction of war-devastated lands. A detailed plan to implement these principles was to be drawn up by a three-power Allied Reparations Commission sitting in Moscow, though this was never able to reconcile the conflict between the Soviet determination to milk Germany dry in order to make up Russia's war losses and British and American reluctance to pump assistance into western Germany to keep life going there while reparations went out on the other side to Russia. However, in the teeth of British resistance, Stalin secured in the Yalta accords the phrase that the Reparations Commission 'should take in its initial studies as a basis for discussion the suggestion of the Soviet government that the total sum of reparations . . . should be twenty billion dollars and that fifty per cent should go to the USSR'. Was this a definite commitment to

that sum split in that ratio? Russia later said it was. Britain and America denied it.

Then came the crucial accord over Poland. Stalin's achievement at Yalta, the fruit of Russia's overwhelming military presence in Poland, was to secure Churchill's and Roosevelt's agreement to take the 'Provisional Government now functioning in Poland' – that is, the handpicked Communist group based on Soviet patronage in Lublin – as the core of a reorganized regime with the inclusion of 'democratic' leaders from Poland and Poles abroad. This reorganization was to be effected by a three-power commission in Moscow, the Lublin regime, and other Poles, including the exiled leaders in London. The new Provisional Government of National Unity was pledged to 'the holding of free and unfettered elections as soon as possible on the basis of universal suffrage and secret ballots'. As to Poland's new boundaries, the eastern frontier would follow the Curzon Line 'with digressions from it in some regions of five to eight kilometres in favour of Poland' which would receive in recompense 'substantial accessions of territory' from Germany in the north and west.

It is hard to know whether Churchill or Roosevelt really believed that the new Polish government would ever be anything but a projection of the Soviet state, or that Western and Soviet differences over the definition of 'democracy' could ever render meaningful the Declaration on Liberated Europe which the three also signed at Yalta. This committed them to European reconstruction by processes which would enable the liberated peoples 'to destroy the last vestiges of Nazism and Fascism and to create democratic conditions of their own choice'. Two months later Russia arrested fifteen of the sixteen Polish resistance leaders who had gone to Moscow to discuss the agreed broadening of the Lublin regime and on 21st April concluded a treaty of alliance with a virtually unmodified Lublin administration, now recognized as the provisional government of Poland. Meanwhile, on 6th March a Soviet-nominated government had been installed in Soviet-occupied Rumania. The most Churchill and Roosevelt could claim was that they had secured certain paper pledges from Stalin which could later be used in the war of words as East and West went their separate ways. But the brutal facts were that Russia exercised dominant military control in Eastern Europe and was determined that never again would that region act as a corridor through which German forces could march into Russia.

Had differences not developed between the three Allies over the future regimes in Germany and Eastern Europe, the Yalta accords on the post-war United Nations Organization might have fared better. All

three agreed that the five permanent members of the proposed Security Council – Great Britain, China, France, the Soviet Union, and the United States – should be unanimous when enforcement action to keep the peace was envisaged and that parties to a dispute, including the great powers, should refrain from voting when pacific means of settlement were under discussion. But Stalin's reluctance to allow the Security Council even to inquire into an issue in which enforcement might have to be resorted to, except on the basis of great-power unanimity, foreshadowed later East-West conflict over the organization's right of intervention to maintain peace.

The same applies to the secret Yalta accords on the Far East, disclosed only after Roosevelt's death, to which Great Britain was little more than an observer. Stalin demanded as Russia's price for entering the war against Japan recognition of the status-quo in Outer Mongolia, South Sakhalin, the Kuriles, a lease of the Manchurian naval base, Port Arthur, and participation in the Manchurian railway to Dairen, and the internationalization of Dairen. Roosevelt undertook to secure China's agreement to this deal. But it was struck before the power of the atomic bomb to secure a quick Japanese surrender was known and when Mao Tse-tung's Communists were far from securing their final victories in China. It was only later, when Stalin cashed his Yalta cheque after two weeks' fighting against the Japanese in Manchuria and helped the Chinese Communists with arms, that the Yalta accords on the Far East became the symbol of appeasement in America.

The break-up of the alliance

In the interval between Yalta and Potsdam unity between East and West followed a downward path. The surrender of German forces in May destroyed the most vital bond between them; the Reparations Commission in Moscow made no progress; the Lublin regime, undiluted by non-Communist elements of any significance, became for Russia the Polish government and was recognized, because they had no alternative, by Great Britain and America in July; Communism was entrenched in Rumania and the Greek government was barely able to keep afloat during the Communist disturbances supported by Tito's Yugoslavia. By the time the Potsdam meeting convened in July to hammer out methods of securing four-power agree-

Right: 1 Molotov, after his arrival in Great Britain in May 1942 to discuss the Anglo-Soviet alliance. 2 Painting by Charles Pears of British Arctic convoy. 3 Soviet troops in Manchuria after Russia's attack on the Japanese

ment on the treatment of Germany and to finalize the accords on the new East European territorial arrangements, it was clear that ideological differences, together with fear on both sides about the future balance of power in Europe, would result in little more than agreements to differ all along the line. When President Truman was notified at Potsdam that the atomic bomb worked, some of his advisers, notably George Marshall, urged him to use it as a threat to compel Stalin to respect his pledges of self-determination in Eastern Europe. Whether American opinion would have tolerated this is doubtful, but the fact that the proposal was made testifies to the extent to which the rift had grown.

On 29th April Churchill had written his famous letter to Stalin summing up his feelings on relations between the Allies. 'There is not much comfort,' he wrote, 'in looking into a future where you and the countries you dominate plus the Communist parties in many other states are all drawn up on one side and those who rallied to the English-speaking nations and their associates are on the other. It is quite obvious that their quarrel would tear the world to pieces and all of us leading men on either side who had anything to do with that would be shamed before history.'

With the advent of the détente in East-West relations since about 1962, Western historians, especially in the United States, have revised their views on the origins of this celebrated international rift. More attention is now paid to the weakened Soviet condition in 1945 and the unlikelihood of any Soviet attack, as was feared after Potsdam, on Western Europe; to the natural Soviet fears of a German revival; and to a great power's inevitable demand to have a friendly sphere of influence adjacent to its borders. Moreover, the East-West rift did not, as Churchill feared, 'tear the world to pieces'; it led to a hard-headed recognition on both sides of the suicidal character of armed conflict in the nuclear age. Above all, though Eastern Europe has been denied the freedoms promised at Yalta, as the tragic Czechoslovak experience shows, the de facto division of Europe which sprang from the great-power discords of that time led, paradoxically, to greater order in Europe than it had seen since the 20th century began.

Above: Roosevelt and Churchill with Chiang Kai-shek and Madame Chiang in Cairo, November 1943. Centre: Truman (left) Churchill (centre) and Stalin (right) in conference at Potsdam, 1945. Below: The Big Three, now Attlee, Truman and Stalin, at Potsdam, July 1945. Roosevelt had died on the 12th April, Churchill lost the British general election during the conference

Roosevelt and Stalin

The Japanese attack on the American naval base at Pearl Harbour which brought the United States into the Second World War put a sudden end to a long period in which the United States under the leadership of President Roosevelt had increasingly involved itself in measures directed towards sustaining the countries at war with Germany and Italy in Europe, and with Japan in the Far East. Some American writers observing this undoubtedly un-neutral course, have seen President Roosevelt as deliberately contriving a situation which should leave the United States no option but to go to war. It has even been hinted that the warnings that were available as to the proposed Japanese onslaught were deliberately concealed so as to make the provocation more deadly. The latter charge can be dismissed; the former contains an element of truth in the sense that the United States was putting curbs on Japan's forward march and that it was always likely that a point would come at which Japan would prefer to put the issue to the test of force.

The ambiguity about Roosevelt's intentions and hopes in the pre-Pearl Harbour period is not an isolated problem. Throughout his career as President his objectives and policies were subject to divergent interpretations, and it is not surprising that his allies as well as his enemies did not always find them easy to fathom. In foreign as well as in domestic affairs, Roosevelt eschewed binding commitments and clear-cut positions. Among his own advisers he gave his confidences fully to no-one, and preferred to make use of several channels for making his wishes known and his desires felt. His approach to each subject was primarily that of the politician — concerned with the total effect of his actions upon the situation and in particular upon his position with the American electorate rather than with individual goals.

It is hard to say that he had a definite philosophy of foreign affairs or a fully thought out view of where America's interests lay. He had come into politics as a follower of Woodrow Wilson and had campaigned for the League of Nations. But during the decade in which he was out of national politics — through his illness and later his absorption in New York state affairs — he had come to accept the general tenets of the prevalent isolationism. Roosevelt's return to the national arena had

Roosevelt — he placed great reliance on personal contact with Stalin, believing he was open to amicable persuasion

placed him among those who believed that economic recovery, the nation's prime need, could best be attained by action on the home front, rather than through attempts to rebuild the tattered structure of international credit and finance. Much of the early New Deal was isolationist in spirit and Roosevelt found little to quarrel with in this attitude.

He had, it is true, been concerned both with the Japanese encroachments upon China from 1931 onwards and with the increasing aggressiveness of Nazi Germany and Fascist Italy, and his recognition of the Soviet government in 1933 was in response to developments in the Far East as well as to the hope that a market in Russia for American business might provide an important way out of the Great Depression. By 1937 Roosevelt was warning the American people that their own lot would not be comfortable in a world where aggression was allowed to go unchallenged. But the lack of response was enough to prevent him following these warnings up with any suggestions for concrete action which might conceivably involve the United States in political commitments.

After the outbreak of war in Europe, he had managed to get the neutrality laws relaxed and through the device of Lend-Lease to make the United States in his own words, 'the arsenal of democracy'. But it was only the submission of France and the possibility of the British fleet falling into German hands that galvanized him into more positive action directed towards sustaining the British war effort. And his policies in this respect were still justified — as during his successful campaign for re-election in the autumn of 1940 — by the argument that they would help keep America out of war. After Hitler's attack on Russia in June 1941, Roosevelt had extended material aid to the Soviet government as well. To do this it was necessary to face the strong anti-Communist sentiment still powerful in the United States, and enhanced by the failure of relations to live up to the expectations placed on the 1933 agreement as well as by the activities of the American Communist Party and its sympathizers, particularly after the Nazi-Soviet Pact.

For this reason, although from the summer of 1941 the United States was a non-belligerent associate of both Great Britain and the Soviet Union and from December 1941 their partner, relations between these three great powers were neither simple nor symmetrical. Roosevelt now had to deal not with American politicians, most of whom were no match for him

Stalin—to him the war was another round in the conflict between the 'imperialist' and Communist halves of the world

in political skills and none of whom could command equal popular support, but with two veteran statesmen, Josef Stalin and Winston Churchill, each the unquestioned leader of a major power and each with ideas of his own about the nature of the contest and its desirable outcome. From 1941 until Roosevelt's death in April 1945, two interconnected problems monopolized his energies—the waging of war against the Axis and the laying of the foundations of a permanent peace.

While Stalin, like Churchill, was deeply involved in the day-to-day running of the military campaigns and in the detailed problems of supply, Roosevelt was prepared to delegate his powers to a much greater extent, particularly on the military side where his professional advisers played a more independent role than did their British and Russian counterparts. The main strategic decision to concentrate upon the defeat of Germany before embarking on the final overthrow of the Japanese was implicit in American thinking before the United States entered the war, and was confirmed over naval opposition afterwards. Most of the other strategic decisions followed from this one.

Roosevelt was thus somewhat freer than his allies to consider the political consequences of the war, and what America's aims would be in an ultimate settlement. On the other hand, he suffered from two limitations upon his freedom of action. In the first place, the American military took the view that there was no direct connection between the course taken by the campaigns and the position of the armies at the end of hostilities and an ultimate settlement. Moreover they strenuously objected to any suggestion that political as well as military considerations should enter into decisions respecting actual operations. In the second place, there was always the nagging possibility that the Russians if too hard pressed might make a separate peace—and the Nazi-Soviet Pact was there to dispel any claim that differences of ideology might make this impossible. And this meant that in any dispute with the Soviet Union there was always some reluctance to push the matter to extremes. Nor did this only affect policy in Europe where until the summer of 1944, it was the Soviet Union that was still engaging by far the largest part of Germany's military might. The toll of the island-hopping campaigns in the Pacific convinced the Americans that Russian help would be required if the Japanese were to be defeated in their Manchurian vassal-empire and in the Japanese home islands. Even the small group privy to the secret could not rely upon the atomic weapon coming in time or being effective enough to preclude the necessity of a sea-borne invasion, so it was still necessary to keep the Soviet Union in line.

A further handicap, of lesser though not negligible significance, was that Roosevelt had public opinion to contend with (as of course did Churchill) while Stalin did not, and once the Americans and the Russians became allies, it was necessary to persuade American opinion that the Russians were no longer the Communist bogey-men of earlier years but Russian patriots only concerned with the defence of their fatherland. Pro-Soviet propaganda was thus given a free hand and prospered by it to the extent that Roosevelt himself became its victim, in that he did not perceive fully that the Russians made no distinction between the military and the political and that the war they were fighting, defensive though it might be in immediate origin, was nothing more in their eyes than another round in the inevitable conflict between the 'Communist' and the 'imperialist' halves of the world. Nor, believing this, could the Russians take seriously the Americans' protestations of political neutrality in respect of other countries. When any military decision was taken which did not suit their book, they assumed that it showed that their allies were still hankering after a compromise peace and had no real interest in relieving the Russian front.

The relations between Roosevelt and his principal allies were thus curiously paradoxical. Outwardly the intimacy was far greater between the Americans and the British than between either and the Russians. Their service and supply personnel worked in relations of mutual confidence and at many levels; the personal rapport that developed between Roosevelt and Churchill through personal encounters and continuous correspondence was paralleled lower down. The British had no hesitation about admitting their indebtedness to the Americans or their hopes that the partnership would be prolonged into the peace. They were prepared, in order to get the necessary results, to transfer to North America the work on atomic weapons which had made its first crucial strides on British soil.

On the Russian side everything was different. Help was asked for, and even demanded, but no accounting was given and no information as to Russia's own plans and resources was ever proffered; the Russian people were insulated as far as possible from the knowledge of the American (and British) contributions to their defence. Roosevelt and Stalin met only twice. Nevertheless, it was the American

belief that fundamentally Americans and Russians were fighting for the same ends and looking forward to the same kind of post-war world while the British were interested in objectives which were alien or antipathetic to American opinion. It was for a long time Roosevelt's clear desire not to do anything which could suggest that he and Churchill were making plans from which Stalin was excluded, and his clear belief that Stalin would be open to the kind of amicable persuasion that had been so successful an instrument of his domestic policy.

Roosevelt's illusions
The principal reasons why Roosevelt cherished such illusions—illusions encouraged by his highly unsuitable and poorly qualified ambassador in Moscow, Joseph E. Davies—could be found in three very abstract ideas which figured largely in Roosevelt's thinking but which had quite a different meaning from the ones that the Russians attached to them. In the first place he believed that the British—and Churchill in particular—were 'imperialist' and that both the Russians and the Americans were 'anti-imperialist'. That is to say he was worried lest Churchill try to influence the grand strategy of the war in ways which would be conducive to the defence of Britain's imperial possessions, or the recovery of those that had been lost, to the detriment of a more rapid overall victory. He did not perceive that the Russians attached quite another meaning to anti-imperialism and were by no means averse to using their power to spread the bounds of the Communist empire. In the second place, Roosevelt believed that Americans and Russians both stood for 'democratic' government while the British hankered after preserving or restoring monarchies and other non-democratic forms of government for instance in Italy and Greece. It was only towards the very end of his life, when Russian intentions in Poland could no longer be overlooked, that Roosevelt came to understand the interpretation that Stalin put upon democracy. Finally, Roosevelt shared the antipathy of his former leader Woodrow Wilson for the notion of the balance of power, imagining that the post-war world could be managed by an amalgam of the wartime Grand Alliance with the principle of national self-determination and the equality of states, the whole given institutional form in what became the United Nations Organization. He was thus averse to any consideration in advance of how the peace settlement could be assured of sufficient support against future revisionism. And this again separated him from Churchill, since, while the Russians could accept with equanimity Roosevelt's assumption that

once victory was won, American forces would rapidly be withdrawn from Europe, Churchill had to consider how British security could be safeguarded in such circumstances.

The practical consequences of the last of these attitudes revealed themselves particularly in respect of two other countries, China and France. Roosevelt believed that once Japan had been defeated China would become a great and friendly power deserving of a permanent seat in the Security Council of the United Nations, and was influenced in his assessment of the Asian scene by Chinese opinion. Churchill was much more sceptical about the Chinese regime and its future. He, again, was very conscious of Britain's need for a restored and strengthened France as an essential component of the new Europe. Having early decided that General de Gaulle and his movement was the most likely vehicle for France's recovery of her independence, Churchill gave the de Gaulle movement a considerable degree of material and moral support. Roosevelt on the other hand first took longer to despair of the Vichy government and then, after the liberation of North Africa, did his best to avoid handing over the political reins there to de Gaulle. Later on he tried to avoid installing de Gaulle's authority in France itself and to plan for some form of temporary Allied military occupation until the French could choose their own form of government. At both stages the strength of de Gaulle's position was such that Roosevelt's objectives were frustrated. Finally, Roosevelt and Stalin were at one in minimizing France's importance and in being unwilling to allow the de Gaulle government to share in the occupation and control of Germany and it was left to Churchill to make the running in favour of France's claims—this time successfully, partly perhaps because of a temporary Franco-Russian rapprochement.

Fundamentally—though the personal antipathy of Roosevelt and of his narrow and limited secretary of state, Cordell Hull, for de Gaulle had something to do with it—the point was that Roosevelt believed that France's major role in world politics was at an end and was indifferent to France's claims. He was also hostile to the continuation of France's overseas empire and his successor, in conjunction with the Chinese, was able to hold up the re-imposition of French authority in Indo-China after the Japanese defeat. Churchill did not hold these opinions but realized the extent to which Great Britain depended upon American goodwill and could never afford ultimately to defy the Americans for the sake of the French. Thus while the British were in fact doing what they could for de Gaulle, they gave the French the impression that they were wholly committed to the same attitude as the Americans – and this helped to foster de Gaulle's strong feelings about the 'Anglo-Saxons'.

For although Roosevelt played down the role of power in the post-war world so long as the war lasted, he was very ready to use American power to make sure that he got his way. But this realism could go the other way as well. His desire to see the Russians enter the war against Japan gave them the means of extracting concessions from the Americans at China's expense. In fact the Americans did not need Russian aid; the atomic bomb was enough. And the Russians did not need bribing to enter the war in the Far East since they had their own territorial and political aims to fulfil, nor did they require anyone's permission to do so. For the Russians it was never the same war as the one Roosevelt thought he was fighting.

But it would be a mistake to try to view the history of wartime diplomacy and policy-making in terms of 'Cold War' origins as is sometimes done. The lines of conflict between the Soviet regime and the West had been defined between 1917 and 1919 and had not changed in essentials. What happened during the period between 1941 and 1945 was a partial suspension of the conflict because of the mortal danger in which the Soviet Union found itself and because of the greater immediacy for the Western powers of the threat from Nazi Germany. For most of the war Roosevelt like his allies had to concentrate on the planning and winning of the campaigns against the immediate enemy. It is only in retrospect that one can see how the unresolved issues in the Soviet Union's relations with the rest of the world had their effects upon what was done.

The Americans were slower than the British in pledging support to the Soviet Union after Hitler's attack in June 1941 and shared British scepticism as to the ability of the Russians to carry out a prolonged resistance. But the visit of Roosevelt's confidant Harry Hopkins to Moscow set in train the process of supplying the Russians out of the now rapidly increasing war production of American industry.

The main issue was the Russian demand for a 'second front' against Germany: that is to say a landing as soon as possible on the mainland of Europe by Anglo-American forces so as to draw off part of the German land forces from the Russian front. This pressure began with a letter from Stalin to Churchill on 18th July 1941 and it was against Great Britain that the main pressure was directed. It was clear, however, that any such landings would have to involve American forces and the American military were indeed convinced that this strategy would be the most effective way of defeating Germany quite irrespective

of Russian needs. They were suspicious that Churchill's unwillingness to press forward with this policy and his interest in alternatives were due to an excessive concern about possible losses, and to a nostalgia for the 'indirect approach' exemplified in the Gallipoli operation of the First World War. On the other hand, in contrast to the Russians, the Americans were fully aware of the immense difficulties of making an amphibious assault on a heavily defended coastline and were unwilling to attempt such a thing until all the technical preparations had been made. Meanwhile they came round to relying for the time being upon the strategic air offensive against Germany itself and upon the Mediterranean operations which began in November 1942.

Uncertain alliance

The degree to which the Russian war was still considered as something separate is illustrated by the absence of the Russians from the meeting between Roosevelt and Churchill at Placentia Bay, Newfoundland, in August 1941 at which the policy to be adopted towards Japan was discussed and at which the Atlantic Charter, with its promise of joint action after the war in the setting up of a new and more peaceful world system was promulgated. It remained the case that relations with Japan with which Great Britain and the United States were at war from December 1941 was something from which the Russians deliberately held aloof, since they were unwilling to add Japan to the number of their enemies before they came in to seize their share of the spoils of Japan's defeat in August 1945. The Grand Alliance which was embodied in the United Nations Declaration of 1st January 1942 was thus of necessity ambiguous about the enemy against which it was directed.

Subsequently relations between Roosevelt and his principal two allies were for some time carried on on a triangular basis by means of bilateral discussions. And this may partly explain the ambiguities about the promises to invade Europe made in the summer of 1942. When it came to the North Africa landings which the Russians had perforce to accept as a substitute, the political issues of the future began to show themselves. In North Africa, the Americans took the lead, first in making a deal with the Vichy commander Admiral Darlan, and subsequently in endeavouring to promote General Giraud in preference to General de Gaulle and who had the support of the British and of the French resistance movement including the Communist elements and so might be expected to commend himself to the Russians.

An attempt was made to clear up the political and military difficulties in the

Mediterranean theatre in a meeting between Roosevelt and Churchill at Casablanca in January 1943. Stalin, who was invited, declared himself unable to leave Russia. It was here that the principle of 'unconditional surrender' was agreed upon; and Stalin later approved it.

In fact the phrase was not a very meaningful one since the important thing was the decisions that would be taken in handling the problems of the liberated territories and ultimately those of Germany, Italy, and Japan. Roosevelt was opposed in theory to the division of spheres of influence between the victors; but in practice there was no real alternative. The Soviet Union did not take part in the negotiations leading to the surrender of Italy, and its ultimate reappearance in October 1943 as an Allied co-belligerent; and the Russians were given after protest only a formal share in the running of Italian affairs. Events were to follow the same course in Greece where Great Britain, by agreement with the Russians, took the lead; and on their side, the Russians were ultimately to exclude all Western influence from the rest of Eastern Europe.

This was the reality against which one had to measure the work of the tripartite conferences which were the focus of the last phase of the conflict: the meeting of the three foreign ministers at Moscow in October 1943 and between the leaders themselves at Tehran in November-December 1943 and Yalta in February 1945. The Americans were too concerned to secure Russian co-operation in the setting up of a world security organization which was agreed upon in principle at the Moscow conference and in getting agreement on general principles for co-operation in the handling of a defeated Germany to worry overmuch about the precise nature of the political settlements arrived at. It was the loose diplomacy of this period and the refusal of the Americans to entertain the doubts which Churchill now began to express about Russia's future intentions, or to let the military operations take such doubts into account, that were typical of these final stages of the war in Europe. And it was in these circumstances that the ambiguous agreement over Berlin and access to it was allowed to go forward with all the future problems that this entailed.

But it would be an error to think that had Roosevelt lived there would have been a very different attitude towards relations with Russia from that which developed under President Truman. Towards the end of his life, the Russians' behaviour, particularly in respect of Poland, was already causing Roosevelt deep anxiety and had he lived the same decisions as fell to be made by Truman would almost certainly have been made by him.

8 THE DEFEAT OF THE AXIS

The Bombing of Germany

At the outset of the war in September 1939 Bomber Command went into action with such stringent instructions to avoid causing civilian casualties that there was even doubt about the advisability of attacking German warships at their bases in case civilian dock staff should be on or near them. Less than three years later, in May 1942, Bomber Command launched a thousand bombers against the centre of Cologne. In late July and early August 1943 about 40,000 German civilians were killed in a series of Bomber Command operations against Hamburg. In February 1945 even greater casualties were caused by a catastrophic attack on Dresden.

In September 1939 Bomber Command was small in size, inadequate in equipment, and defective in technique. For operations against Germany it could muster about 280 aircraft. Bomber Command was not only much smaller than the corresponding German force but it was also equipped with less reliable high explosive bombs than the German equivalents. In addition, Bomber Command, surprisingly, had no proper system of navigation.

By the end of the war Bomber Command could regularly despatch more than 1,500 aircraft on a single operation. More than a thousand of these were four-engined Lancasters which, with their great range, their huge bomb loads of up to ten tons, and their remarkable durability, were, as heavy bombers, internationally in a class of their own. Of the rest, some 200 were Mosquitoes which, owing to their performance, had a versatility perhaps exceeding that of any

other aircraft which saw service in the Second World War. The bombs available ranged from the 4lb incendiary which chiefly accounted for the firestorms in Hamburg and Dresden, to the 22,000lb Grandslam designed by Dr Barnes Wallis which, with the smaller version, the 12,000lb Tallboy, brought down the Bielefeld viaduct.

Nor was this the whole, or even in terms of numbers of aircraft the greater part, of the bomber forces which, in the last year of the war, could be brought to bear upon Germany. Other than Great Britain, the United States was the only power which before the war had evolved a doctrine of strategic bombing and during it had worked up a force to carry it out. This working up began in 1942 when US 8th Air Force, having established bases in the United Kingdom for its B-17 Flying Fortresses and B-24 Liberators, both of which were four-engined bombers, began experimental daylight operations against targets in France and other parts of German-occupied Europe. In January 1943 these operations were extended to Germany but it was not until the end of the year that 8th Air Force had enough bombers to mount regular operations from 600 to 700 strong.

Meanwhile, another US bomber force, the 15th, was formed on Italian bases and in January 1944 these two formations were placed under unified command to compose the United States Strategic Air Forces in Europe. By June 1944 the American bomber forces so combined could despatch more than 1,500 aircraft on operations in a single day. Thus, within two years of their initial bombing attacks in August 1942

involving only a dozen aircraft, the Americans were ranging over all Europe from England and Italy in greater strength than RAF Bomber Command.

Because their aircraft carried lighter loads than the British, the Americans were in the last year of the war still inferior to the British in bombing power. All the same, American 8th and 15th Air Forces were in some other respects more significant fighting formations than Bomber Command. In particular, the Americans made a more important contribution to the winning of command of the air than the British, and command of the air was decisive in making bombing a really effective and ultimately conclusive way of waging war.

This paradox arose from the different bombing policies which the two forces followed. In the last three years of peace, when the bombing offensive was planned, and in the first year of the war, when it began to be attempted, the main idea of the British was the selection of key points in the German war machine such as power stations, oil plants, railway junctions and marshalling yards, dams, and other sensitive points destruction of which would impede or even dislocate the German war effort. This policy, to be effective, depended upon accurate intelligence since the whole idea of 'key point' attack would only work if the target really was a key point. It also depended upon a high degree of bombing accuracy and destructiveness.

Marching with this selective key point theory was another which owed its origin not only to its own merit but also, perhaps, to a fear in anticipation that key point bombing might be hard to realize in prac-

tice. It was that bombing, even if it lacked the accuracy and destructiveness to dispose effectively of key points, might, through its moral effect upon the people who lived and worked in their neighbourhood, nevertheless achieve important and possibly even decisive effects upon the enemy's capacity to continue the war. After all, the bombing of London in June 1917 by a mere handful of primitive Gothas had caused a panic. The merit of this idea was that it could seemingly be realized with a considerable bombing inaccuracy, such as for example would be produced in night operations, and by a force lacking the power to destroy major installations like concrete dams. The difficulty was that it might be considered improper to attack towns rather than installations and there had, indeed, been a furore about the bombing of people rather than things in the Spanish Civil War.

By Christmas 1939 Bomber Command had sufficient experience of war to know that it could not carry on major operations against Germany in daylight. The reason was simply that an aircraft able to go the distance and carry a worthwhile load of bombs could not achieve the performance to survive in combat with an enemy fighter which could do its work with a much smaller load and duration. By the autumn of 1941, Bomber Command had proved photographically that oil plants and even large railway marshalling yards were much too small to be found and hit in night operations against defended areas.

Area attack on major cities

Thus, at the end of 1941, Bomber Command was presented with the alternatives of being withdrawn from its strategic offensive against Germany or of concentrating upon much larger targets. At a time when British arms on land and at sea were defeated almost upon appearance, at a time when the Germans were advancing rapidly into the heart of Russia, and the Japanese, having struck down the American fleet at Pearl Harbour, were on the verge of the conquest of an empire, it is not to be wondered at that the British, despite some disagreement in their inner councils, refused to put Bomber Command into voluntary liquidation. Instead the policy of area attack upon major German cities was instituted as the prime one to be followed.

Though this did not initiate area bomb-

Above: *Veteran Lancaster bomber about to make its 100th operational trip, May 1944. The base commander watches as the ground crew write a message on an 8,000-lb bomb to be loaded on the aircraft*
Left: *Flares illuminate German V1 flying bomb launching site for RAF Halifax bomber, July 1944. V1s killed some 6,000 people, mainly in London*

ROTTERDAM
PARIJS - ANTWERPEN

Les femmes et les enfants d'Europe accusent!

C'est l'Angleterre qui a jeté les premières bombes le 12 janvier 1940 sur la population civile

ing, which had already been practised both by the British and the Germans, it did make it the main theme of the Bomber Command offensive, which it remained for the duration of the war. From this, and in particular from an important directive of February 1942, there flowed the great offensive of 1942-45 embracing the Battles of the Ruhr, Hamburg, and Berlin.

This was not wanton or indiscriminate bombing. It was an organized attempt to destroy German military power, which nothing else seemed able to check, through the systematic destruction of its greatest industrial and administrative centres. But to be effective, area bombing had to be concentrated, sustained, and very heavy. In the Thousand Bomber attack upon Cologne in 1942 only about 400 Germans were killed and this attack was only made possible by calling into action the whole front line of Bomber Command and the whole of its operational training organization as well. Clearly Bomber Command had to be greatly expanded and its operations had to be made much more concentrated.

This latter requirement found expression in the creation of the Pathfinder Force and accompanying techniques and equipment ranging from marker bombs to radar devices for navigation and target finding. By these means more and more bombers were brought over smaller and smaller areas in shorter and shorter times and in 1943 Bomber Command became more and more able to 'rub out' towns. These greater concentrations of bombers which emitted more and more radar emanations and pyrotechnics, however, offered the German night-fighter force easier targets for interception and the bombing offensive at night became a grim race between the destruction of towns by Bomber Command and the destruction of Bomber Command by the German night-fighter force.

In the summer of 1943 when the Battle of Hamburg was over, Albert Speer, the German minister for armament and war production, thought that six more blows on that scale would end the war. In the four and a half months of the Battle of Berlin from November 1943 to March 1944, Bomber Command lost the equivalent of the whole of its front line, mostly to German fighters, and it became obvious that a continuing offensive on that scale would end, not the war, but Bomber Command.

*The Allied bombing of enemy cities gave the Germans good material for propaganda. Between 1939 and 1945 nearly 600,000 German civilians were killed in bombing raids. The total British civilian losses for the same period were 65,000. **Above:** Posters issued in Holland and Belgium stress civilian suffering. **Right:** Germans salvage belongings after an air raid*

The Defeat of the Axis

As the fortunes of Bomber Command and the German night-fighter force see-sawed with each tactical shift and technical innovation, the constant factor was the inability of Bomber Command to deal directly with its scourge. Lancasters could not fight Junkers 88s or even Messerschmitt 110s. Their only hope was to dodge them. Nor could they bomb their airfields and factories. The area bombing offensive, for all its destructive and terrifying powers, could only achieve incidental or indirect effects against 'key' targets. Whatever else it may have done in diverting German effort and pinning it down, area bombing up to March 1944 had not resulted in a significant reduction in essential German war production nor had it prevented the German armed forces from continuing their operations in Russia and Italy or against Bomber Command itself.

The Americans had expected as much. They had refused to be diverted by British warnings from their plan of daylight precision attacks against selected key point targets. Throughout 1942, however, they had not felt strong enough in numbers to carry their determination into operational effect over Germany. In 1943 they began to do so. Believing that night area bombing was a blunt and ineffective tactic and possessing aircraft unsuitable for and crews untrained in night-flying, they massed their Flying Fortresses and Liberators in tight highly-disciplined formations and operated at very high altitudes. At high altitude they hoped to escape the worst of the flak and in their formations they hoped to bring such concentrated fire-power to bear that the formations would successfully fight their way to and from their targets in daylight.

One difficulty was that at altitude over Germany the bombers often found themselves over dense cloud so that the best they could do was to deliver approximate or area attacks. Another was that the formations were regularly shot to pieces by the German fighters. The Americans therefore gave higher priority to bombing Germany's aircraft industry. But the aircraft industry in Germany was divided into small units, well dispersed, and often at extreme range from England. So the Americans were given no alternative to the policy of seeking to make a dangerous and difficult task possible by undertaking a more dangerous and more difficult one. The result was disaster. Two-thirds of a force despatched to Schweinfurt on 14th October 1943 was destroyed or damaged. Within six days and from four attacks the Americans lost 138 bombers.

This was comparable to, and indeed, even more decisive than the fate which at that time was approaching Bomber Command in the Battle of Berlin and in incurring it the Americans had done much less damage to Germany than the British had achieved. So in the winter of 1943-44 it seemed that the strategic air attack on Germany had been a costly failure. The indications, however, were misleading. The break-through in the air was imminent and the heavy bombers of Great Britain and America were on the verge of achievements which were not only important but decisive for the war.

The reasons for this, one of the most extraordinary and abrupt changes in military fortune in the Second World War, are chiefly to be found in three singular developments: first, the introduction of an effective long-range fighter, secondly, the advance of Allied armies across France, and thirdly, the development by Bomber Command of heavy precision-bombing techniques.

After Schweinfurt, the Americans realized that their survival depended upon the introduction of a machine with the range of a bomber and the performance of a fighter. The answer was found in the hybrid P-51 Mustang, a North American aircraft with a Rolls Royce engine and hitherto chiefly in service with the RAF, which, with droppable long-range tanks, was rushed into action with US 8th Air Force from December 1943. By March 1944, it had developed the capacity to fight over Berlin from British bases. Moreover, it could take on any German fighter in service on at least equal and, in most respects, superior terms. These aircraft swept into action in such force — 14,000 were produced before the end of the war — and to such effect that the day-fighter force of Germany in the air was rapidly smashed and the way opened for a major resumption of the daylight bombing offensive. From February 1944 onwards 8th and 15th Air Forces seized their opportunity with growing confidence and rapidly diminishing casualties. The command of the daylight air over Germany and German Europe passed from the Germans to the Americans. In May 1944, the Americans began an offensive against German synthetic oil production.

To prepare for the invasion

During this period, Bomber Command still had to face severe casualties in maintaining what it could of the area offensive against Germany and in conducting a night precision offensive against the French railway system. The latter was to open the way for the invasion of Europe by the American and British armies. And it did. So accurate and so destructive were these Bomber Command attacks that the Germans lost the sovereign advantage which had previously made ideas of invasion academic, namely, an efficient interior system of communications which would enable them rapidly to concentrate a superior force against whatever invasion areas were selected.

The Bomber Command attacks, however, did even more than that. They showed the way to heavy precision bombing. They were the link between the vast destructive power which the needs of the area offensive had demanded and generated and the almost surgical accuracy of the Möhne Dam raid of May 1943. In June 1944, Bomber Command began to reinforce the American attacks on German oil plants. By September the Germans were confronted with an oil crisis so serious that they were compelled to restrict flying and the Allied air superiority became even more pronounced. As the armies advanced towards the German frontier, greatly aided by this superiority, the Germans lost the forward bases of their fighter defences and the Allied bomber forces were able to push their radar transmitters nearer the German targets upon which a greater and more and more accurate rain of bombs therefore descended.

Differences of opinion as to the best targets, together with weather and tactical considerations, divided the aim of the bombers between support of the armies, the oil offensive, the destruction of communications, naval bombing, and the continuing area offensive. But in late 1944 and early 1945, the huge destructive power of bombing was liberated by the attainment of command of the air. The great German synthetic oil plants were ruined beyond repair and the oil crisis became a famine. The communications system of Germany was rendered chaotic and eventually unworkable to the point where administration began to break down.

As the German armies retreated from the East and the West, they fell back not upon a heartland but upon a national disintegration which proved incapable of mounting even an underground resistance. The British and American bombers played a vital role in assisting the advance of the armies. They also produced a situation in the interior of Germany which guaranteed the collapse of the war machine.

The surviving paradox of the final triumph of strategic bombing is this: if the British had not adopted the policy of night area bombing, which in itself produced disappointing results, it is difficult to see how the power of heavy destruction of 1944-45 could have been generated. If the Americans had not persisted with the policy of daylight self-defending formation-bombing tactics, which produced poor results and terrible casualties, it is hard to see how command of the air could have been won. It was, in the last resort, the combination of command of the air and very heavy bombing which made a critical contribution to Germany's defeat.

From Normandy to the Baltic

The Allied liberation-invasion of Normandy, in June 1944, was the most dramatic and decisive event of the Second World War. The cross-sea move of the Anglo-American expeditionary force, based on England, had been delayed by bad weather. It was launched when the wind was still strong enough to make the move hazardous—but also unlikely. General Eisenhower's decision to take the risk was not only justified by the outcome of the Normandy invasion but contributed to its surprise effect.

The Allied landings were made on the morning of 6th June in the Bay of the Seine between Caen and Cherbourg and were immediately preceded by the moonlight dropping of strong airborne forces close to the two flanks. The invasion was prepared by a sustained air offensive of unparalleled intensity, which had been particularly directed against the enemy's communications, with the aim of paralysing his power of moving up reserves.

Although many factors had pointed to this sector as the probable scene, the Germans were caught off their balance—with most of their reserves posted east of the Seine. That was due partly to the ingenuity of the plans for misleading them, and partly

Troops of Cheshire Regiment land on east bank of the Rhine during opening phase of 21st Army Group's drive across the Rhine towards the heart of the Ruhr, March 1945

to an obstinate preconception that the Allies would come not only direct across the Channel but by the shortest route. The effect of this miscalculation was made fatal by the action of the Allied air forces in breaking the bridges over the Seine.

By deductions drawn from the lay-out of the Anglo-American forces in England prior to the invasion, and contrary to the views of his military staff, Hitler had, in March, begun to suspect that the Allies would land in Normandy. Rommel, who was put in charge of the forces on the north coast, came to the same view. But Runstedt, who was commander-in-chief in the West, counted on the Allies landing in the narrower part of the Channel between Dieppe and Calais. That conviction was due not only to the Allies' past fondness for maximum air cover, and the effect of their present deception plans, but even more to his reasoning that such a line was theoretically the right line since it was the shortest line to their objective. That was a characteristic calculation of strategic orthodoxy. Significantly, it did not credit the Allied command with a preference for the unexpected, nor even with an inclination to avoid the most strongly defended approach.

The invaders' actual plan secured more than the avoidance of the best prepared defences. In choosing the Normandy route, the Allied command operated on a line which alternatively threatened the important ports of Le Havre and Cherbourg and was able to keep the Germans in doubt until the last moment as to which was the objective. When they came to realize that Cherbourg was the main objective, the Seine had become a partition wall dividing their forces, and they could only move their reserves to the critical point by a wide detour. The movement was lengthened by the continued interference of the Allied air forces. Moreover, when the reinforcements reached the battle-area, they tended to arrive in the sector farthest from Cherbourg—the Caen sector. The British lodgement here became, not only a menace in itself, but a shield for the development of the American operations farther west, in the Cotentin Peninsula. That double effect and alternative threat had a vital influence on the success of the invasion as a whole.

The vast armada achieved the sea-passage without interference, and the beaches were captured more easily than had been expected, except where the American left wing landed, east of the Vire Estuary. Yet the margin between success and frustration, in driving the bridgehead deep enough, was narrower than appeared. The invaders did not succeed in gaining control of the keys to Caen and Cherbourg. Fortunately, the wide frontage of the attack became a vital factor in redeeming the chances.

Dutch SS poster predicts end of European culture from brutalized US 'liberators'

The Germans' natural concentration on preserving these keys on either flank left them weak in the space between them. A quick exploitation of the intermediate landings near Arromanches carried the British into Bayeux, and by the end of the week the expansion of this penetration gave the Allies a bridgehead nearly forty miles broad and five to twelve miles deep between the Orne and the Vire. They had also secured another, though smaller, bridgehead on the east side of the Cotentin Peninsula. On the 12th, the Americans

pinched out the intermediate keypoint of Carentan, so that a continuous bridgehead of over sixty miles span was secured.

General Montgomery, who was in executive command of the invading forces as a whole, under Eisenhower, could now develop his offensive moves more fully.

The second week brought a marked expansion of the bridgehead on the western flank. Here American 1st Army developed a drive across the waist of the Cotentin Peninsula, while British 2nd Army on the eastern flank continued to absorb the bulk of the German reinforcements by its pressure around Caen.

In the third week, having cut off Cherbourg, the Americans wheeled up the peninsula and drove into the port from the rear. Cherbourg was captured on 27th June, though not before the port itself had been made temporarily unusable. Around Caen, British thrusts were baffled by the enemy's skilful defensive tactics in country favourable to a flexible defence, but their threat continued to distract the German command's free use of its reserves.

Under cover of this pressure, the build-up of the invading forces proceeded at a remarkably rapid rate. It was aided by the development of artificial harbours, which mitigated the interference of the weather and also contributed to surprise—by upsetting the enemy's calculations.

July was a month of tough fighting in Normandy, with little to show for the effort except heavy casualties. But the Germans could not afford such a drain as well as the Allies could, and behind the almost static battle-front the Allied resources were continually growing.

On 3rd July American 1st Army, having regrouped after the capture of Cherbourg, began an attempted break-out push southward towards the base-line of the peninsula. But the attackers were still short of room for manoeuvre, and progress was slow. On the 8th, General Dempsey's British 2nd Army penetrated into Caen, but was blocked at the crossings of the Orne. Successive flanking thrusts were also parried. On the 18th a more ambitious stroke, Operation Goodwood, was attempted—when a phalanx of three armoured divisions, one behind the other, was launched from a bridgehead north-east of Caen—through a narrow gap created by a terrific air bombardment by 2,000 aircraft on a three-mile frontage—and drove across the rear of the Caen defences. A break-through was momentarily in sight, but the Germans were quick in swinging a screen of tanks and anti-tank guns across the path. After that missed opportunity, fresh British and Canadian attacks made little headway. But they kept the enemy's attention, and best troops, fixed in the Caen sector. Seven of the eight Panzer divisions were drawn there.

At the western end of the Normandy bridgehead, the American forces under General Bradley advanced their front five to eight miles during the first three weeks of July. Meantime, General Patton's American 3rd Army had been transported from England to Normandy, in readiness for a bigger thrust.

Operation Cobra

Operation Cobra was launched on 25th July, initially by six divisions on a four-mile frontage, and was preceded by an air bombardment even heavier than in Operation Goodwood. The ground was so thickly cratered that it aided the sparse and dazed defenders in putting a brake on the American drive. On the first two days only five miles was covered but then the breach was widened, and progress quickened—towards the southwest corner of the peninsula. The decisive break-out took place on 31st July. It was helped by a sudden switch of the weight of British 2nd Army from east of the Orne to the central sector south of Bayeux, for an attack near Caumont, the previous day. While the enemy were reinforcing this danger-point with such troops as they could spare from Caen the Americans forced the lock of the door at Avranches, near the west coast of the Cotentin Peninsula.

Pouring through the gap, Patton's tanks surged southward and then westward, quickly flooding most of Brittany. Then they turned eastward and swept through the country north of the Loire, towards Le Mans and Chartres. The cramped seventy-mile front of the bridgehead had been immediately converted into a potential 400-mile front. Space was too wide for the enemy's available forces to impose any effective check on the advance, which repeatedly by-passed any of the road-centres where they attempted a stand.

The one danger to this expanding torrent was that the enemy might bring off a counter-thrust to cut the Avranches bottle-neck, through which supplies had to be maintained. On Hitler's insistence, the Germans attempted such a stroke on the night of 6th August, switching four Panzer divisions westwards for the purpose. The approach, chosen by Hitler on the map at his remote headquarters in the east, was too direct, and thus ran head-on into the Americans' flank shield. Once checked, the attack was disrupted by the swift intervention of the Allied air forces. And when the thrust failed, it turned in a fatal way for the Germans—by drawing their weight westward just as the American armoured forces were sweeping eastward behind their rear. The American left wing wheeled north to Argentan, to combine in a pincer move with General Crerar's Canadian 1st Army, pushing down from Caen upon Falaise. Although the pincers did not close in time to cut off completely the two armies within their embrace, 50,000 prisoners were taken and 10,000 corpses found on the battlefield, while all the divisions which got away were badly mauled. Their vehicles were even worse hit than their men by the continuous air-bombing they suffered in an ever-narrowing space. The Germans' losses in the 'Falaise Pocket' left them without the forces or movement resources to meet the Allies' continued easterly sweep to the Seine, and past the Seine.

The rapidity of this wide flanking manoeuvre, and its speedy effect in causing a general collapse of the German position in France, forestalled the need of the further lever that was inserted by the landing of General Patch's American (and French) 7th Army in southern France on 15th August. The invasion was a 'walk-in', as the Germans had been forced to denude the Riviera coast of all but a mere four divisions, of inferior quality. The subsequent advance inland and up the Rhône Valley was mainly a supply problem, rather than a tactical problem. Marseilles was occupied on the 23rd, while a drive through the mountains reached Grenoble the same day.

On the 19th, the French Forces of the Interior had started a rising in Paris, and although their situation was critical for some days, the scales were turned in their favour by the arrival of Allied armoured forces in the city on the 25th. Meantime Patton's army was racing towards the Marne, north-east of Paris.

The next important development was an exploiting thrust by British 2nd Army, which crossed the Seine east of Rouen, to trap the remnants of German VII Army, which were still opposing Canadian 1st Army west of Rouen. Dempsey's spearheads reached Amiens early on the 31st, having covered seventy miles from the Seine in two days and a night. Crossing the Somme, they then drove on swiftly past Arras and Lille to the Belgian frontier—behind the back of German XV Army on the Pas de Calais coast. To the east, Hodges' American 1st Army had also leapt forward to the Belgian frontier near Hirson.

Farther east, Patton's army made an even more dazzling drive through Champagne and past Verdun, to the Moselle between Metz and Thionville, close to the frontier of Germany. And although it had begun to lose impetus through the difficulty of maintaining adequate petrol supplies and its armoured spearheads were halted by lack of petrol, its strategic importance was increasing daily. For Patton's army was hardly eighty miles from the Rhine. When they received sufficient fuel to resume their advance, opposition was stiffening. Patton's thrust had produced a decisive issue in the Battle of France, but the supply position checked it from deciding the Battle for Germany in the same breath. The strategic law of overstretch re-asserted itself, to impose a postponement. On this sector it proved a long one, as Patton became drawn into a direct approach to Metz, and then into a protracted close-quarter battle for that famous fortress-city to the forfeit of the prospects of a by-passing manoeuvre.

In the early days of September the pace grew fastest on the left wing, and it was

The Defeat of the Axis

thither that a bid for early victory was now transferred. British armoured columns entered Brussels on the 3rd, Antwerp on the 4th, and then penetrated into Holland. By this great manoeuvre, Montgomery had cut off the Germans' remaining troops in Normandy and the Pas de Calais—their principal force in the West. American 1st Army occupied Namur and crossed the Meuse at Dinant and Givet.

German recovery

At this crisis the executive command of the German forces in the West was taken over by General Model, who had gained the reputation on the Russian front of being able 'to scrape up reserves from nowhere'. He now performed that miracle on a bigger scale. On any normal calculation it appeared that the Germans, of whom more than half a million had been captured in the drive through France, had no chance of scraping up reserves to hold their 500-mile frontier from Switzerland to the North Sea. But in the event they achieved an amazing rally which prolonged the war for eight months.

In this recovery they were greatly helped by the Allies' supply difficulties, which reduced the first onset to a lightweight charge that could be checked by a hastily improvised defence, and then curtailed the build-up of the Allied armies for a powerful attack. In part, the supply difficulties were due to the length of the Allies' own advance. In part, they were due to the Germans' strategy in leaving garrisons behind to hold the French ports. The fact that the Allies were thus denied the use of Dunkirk, Calais, Boulogne, and Le Havre, as well as the big ports in Brittany, became a powerful indirect brake on the Allies' offensive. Although the Allies had captured the still greater port of Antwerp in good condition, the enemy kept a tenacious grip of the estuary of the Schelde, and thus prevented the Allies making use of the port.

Before the break-out from Normandy, their supplies had to be carried less than twenty miles from the base in order to replenish the striking forces. They now had to be carried nearly 300 miles. The burden was thrown almost entirely on the Allies' motor transport, as the French railway network had been destroyed by previous air attacks. The bombing that had been so useful in paralysing the German counter-measures against the invasion became a boomerang when the Allies needed to maintain the momentum of their pursuit.

In mid-September a bold attempt was made to loosen the stiffening resistance by dropping three airborne divisions behind the German right flank in Holland, to clear the way for a fresh drive by British 2nd Army up to and over the lower Rhine. By dropping the airborne forces in successive layers over a sixty-mile belt of country behind the German front a foothold was gained on all four of the strategic stepping-stones needed to cross the interval—the passage of the Wilhelmina Canal at Eindhoven, of the Meuse at Grave, of the Waal and Lek (the two branches of the Rhine), at Nijmegen and Arnhem respectively. Three of these four stepping-stones were secured and passed. But a stumble at the third forfeited the chance of securing the fourth in face of the Germans' speedy reaction.

This check led to the frustration of the overland thrust and the sacrifice of 1st Airborne Division at Arnhem. But the possibility of outflanking the Rhine defence-line was a strategic prize that justified the stake and the exceptional boldness of dropping airborne forces so far behind the front. 1st Airborne Division maintained its isolated position at Arnhem for ten days instead of the two that were reckoned as the maximum to be expected. But the chances of success were lessened by the way that the descent of the airborne forces at these four successive points, in a straight line, signposted all too clearly the direction of 2nd Army's thrust.

The obviousness of the aim simplified the opponent's problem in concentrating his available reserves to hold the final stepping-stone, and to overthrow the British airborne forces there, before the leading troops of 2nd Army arrived to relieve them. The nature of the Dutch countryside with its 'canalized' routes, also helped the defenders in obstructing the advance, while there was a lack of wider moves to mask the directness of the approach and to distract the defender.

After the failure of the Arnhem gamble, the prospect of early victory faded. The Allies were thrown back on the necessity of building up their resources along the frontiers of Germany for a massive offensive of a deliberate kind. The build-up was bound to take time, but the Allied command increased its own handicap by concentrating, first, on an attempt to force the Aachen gateway into Germany, rather than on clearing the shores of the Schelde to open up a fresh supply route. The American advance on Aachen developed into a too direct approach, and its progress was repeatedly checked.

Along the rest of the Western Front the efforts of the Allied armies during September and October 1944 amounted to little more than nibbling. Meantime the German defence was being continuously reinforced—with such reserves as could be scraped from elsewhere, with freshly raised forces, and with the troops which had managed to make their way back from France. The German build-up along the front was pro-gressing faster than that of the Allies, despite Germany's great inferiority of material resources. The Schelde Estuary was not cleared of the enemy until early in November.

In mid-November a general offensive was launched by all six Allied armies on the Western Front. It brought disappointingly small results, at heavy cost; and continued efforts merely exhausted the attackers.

Allied differences

There had been a difference of view between the American and British commanders as to the basic pattern of this offensive. The British advocated a concentrated blow, whereas the Americans chose to test the German defences over a very wide front. After the offensive had ended in failure, the British naturally criticized the plan for its dispersion of effort. But closer analysis of the operations suggests that a more fundamental fault was its obviousness. Although the offensive was wide in the sense of being distributed among several armies, it was narrowly concentrated within each army's sector. In each case the offensive effort travelled along the line where the defender would be inclined to expect it. For the attacks were directed against the natural gateways into Germany. Moreover, the main attacks were made in flat country that easily became water-logged in winter.

In mid-December the Germans gave the Allied armies, and peoples, a shock by launching a counter-offensive. They had been able to hold the Allied autumn offensive and slow it down to a crawl without having to engage their own mobile reserves. So from the time when the chances of an American break-through waned, the risk of a serious German riposte might have become apparent—and the more so, in view of the knowledge that the Germans had withdrawn many of their Panzer divisions from the line during the October lull, to re-equip them with fresh tanks. But the Allies' expectations of early victory tended to blind them to the possibility of any counter-stroke, so that this profited by unexpectedness in that respect.

The German command also profited by treating the problem of suitable ground in a way very different from their opponents.

The liberation of France. **Top:** *Civilians kick and jeer at German soldiers in Paris. As the Allied forces approached the city, resistance to the occupiers came out into the open.* **Centre:** *Jeering townsfolk escort a woman collaborator, marked by her shaved head, out of a village near Cherbourg after that area's liberation in July 1944.* **Bottom:** *Crowds greet General de Gaulle as he walks down the Champs Elysées from the Arc de Triomphe on 26th August 1944, the day after Paris's liberation*

*Dropping forces behind the front at Arnhem, September 1944, was part of a bold plan to outflank the Rhine defence-line. The gamble failed and hope for an early victory faded. **Left:** British Horsa glider used to land troops. **Right:** American paratrooper at Arnhem*

They chose for the site of their counter-offensive the hilly and wooded country of the Ardennes. Being generally regarded as difficult country, a large scale offensive there was likely to be unexpected by orthodox opponents. At the same time, the thick woods provided concealment for the massing of forces, while the high ground offered drier ground for the manoeuvre of tanks. Thus the Germans might hope to score both ways.

Their chief danger was from the speedy interference of Allied air-power. Model summed up the problem thus: 'Enemy No. 1 is the hostile air force which, because of its absolute superiority, tries to destroy our spearheads of attack and our artillery through fighter-bomber attacks and bomb carpets, and to render movement in the rear impossible.' So the Germans launched their stroke when the meteorological forecast promised them a natural cloak, and for the first three days mist and rain kept the Allied air forces on the ground. Thus even bad weather was converted into an advantage.

High stakes on limited funds

The Germans needed all the advantage that they could possibly secure. They were playing for high stakes on very limited funds. The striking force comprised V and VI Panzer Armies, to which had been given the bulk of the tanks that could be scraped together.

An awkward feature of the Ardennes from an offensive point of view was the way that the high ground was intersected with deep valleys, where the through roads became bottle-necks. At these points a tank advance was liable to be blocked. The German command might have forestalled this risk by using parachute troops to seize these strategic defiles. But they had allowed this specialist arm to dwindle and its technique to become rusty since the coup that captured Crete in May 1941. Only a few handfuls were used.

The aim of the counter-offensive was far-reaching—to break through to Antwerp by an indirect move, cut off the British army group from the American as well as from its supplies, and then crush the former while isolated. V Panzer Army, now led by Manteuffel, was to break through the American front in the Ardennes, swerve westward, then wheel north across the Meuse, past Namur to Antwerp. As it advanced, it was to build up a defensive flank-barricade to shut off interference from the American armies farther south. VI Panzer Army, under an SS commander, Sepp Dietrich, was to thrust north-west on an oblique line, past Liège to Antwerp, creating a strategic barrier astride the rear of the British and the more northerly American armies.

Aided by its surprise, the German counter-offensive made menacing progress in the opening days, creating alarm and confusion on the Allied side. The deepest thrust was made by Manteuffel's V Panzer Army. But time and opportunities were lost through fuel shortages, resulting from wintry weather and growing Allied air-pressure, and the drive fell short of the Meuse, though it came ominously close to it at some points. In that frustration much was due to the way in which outflanked American detachments held on to several of the most important bottle-necks in the Ardennes, as well as to the speed with which Montgomery, who had taken charge of the situation on the northern flank, swung his reserves southward to forestall the enemy at the crossings of the Meuse.

In the next phase, when the Allied armies had concentrated their strength and attempted to pinch off the great wedge driven into their front, the Germans carried out a skilful withdrawal that brought them out of the potential trap. Judged on its own account, the German counter-offensive had been a profitable operation, for even though it fell short of the objectives, it had upset the Allies' preparations and inflicted much damage at a cost that was not excessive for the effect—except in the later phase, when Hitler hindered the withdrawal.

But viewed in relation to the whole situation, this counter-offensive had been a fatal operation. During the course of it, the Germans had expended more of their strength than they could afford in their straitened circumstances. That expenditure forfeited the chance of maintaining any prolonged resistance to a resumed Allied offensive. It brought home to the German troops their incapacity to turn the scales, and thereby undermined such hopes for victory as they might have retained.

Since the summer of 1944 the main Russian front had been stationary along a line past Warsaw through the middle of Poland. But in mid-January 1945 the Russian

American column delayed whilst moving up to meet the German retaliation in the Ardennes, December 1944. The German counter-offensive inflicted some damage but it cost the Germans the chance of maintaining any prolonged resistance to a resumed Allied advance

armies launched another and greater offensive, making longer bounds than ever before. By the end of the month they reached the Oder, barely fifty miles from Berlin, but were there checked for a time.

A new Anglo-American offensive
Early in February 1945, Eisenhower launched another offensive by the Anglo-American armies, aimed to trap and destroy the German armies west of the Rhine before they could withdraw across it. The opening attack was made by Canadian (and British) 1st Army on the left wing, wheeling up the west bank of the Rhine to develop a flanking leverage on the German forces that faced American 9th and 1st Armies west of Cologne. But the delay caused by the enemy's Ardennes stroke meant the attack was not delivered until the frozen ground had been softened by a thaw. This helped the Germans' resistance. They improved their dangerous situation by blowing up the dams on the River Roer, thus delaying for a fortnight the American attack over that waterline. Even then it met tough opposition. As a result the Americans did not enter Cologne until 5th March. The Germans had gained time to evacuate their depleted forces, and much of their equipment, over the Rhine.

But the Germans had been led to throw a high proportion of their strength into the effort to check the Allied left wing. The consequent weakness of their own left wing created an opportunity for American 1st and 3rd Armies. The right of 1st Army broke through to the Rhine at Bonn, and a detachment was able to seize by surprise

an intact bridge over the Rhine at Remagen. Eisenhower did not immediately exploit this unexpected opening, which would have involved a switch of his reserves and a considerable readjustment of his plans for the next, and decisive, stage of the campaign. But the Remagen threat served as a useful distraction to the Germans' scanty reserve.

A bigger advantage was gained by 3rd Army's breakthrough in the Eifel (the German continuation of the Ardennes). 4th Armoured Division—once again the spearhead as in the break-out from Normandy—dashed through to the Rhine at Koblenz. Patton then wheeled his forces southward, over the lower Moselle into the Palatinate and swept up the west bank of the Rhine across the rear of the forces that were opposing Patch's 7th Army. By this stroke he cut them off from the Rhine, and secured a huge bag of prisoners, while gaining for himself an unopposed crossing of the Rhine when he turned eastward again. This crossing was achieved on the night of the 22nd, between Mainz and Worms, and was quickly exploited by a deep advance into northern Bavaria. That unhinged the Germans' whole front, and forestalled the much-discussed possibility that the enemy might attempt a general withdrawal into their reputed mountain stronghold in the south.

Assault on the Rhine
On the night of the 23rd the planned assault on the Rhine was carried out, far downstream near the Dutch frontier, by Montgomery's 21st Army Group. The great

river was crossed at four points during the night, and in the morning two airborne divisions were dropped beyond it, to loosen the opposition facing the newly gained bridgeheads. The Germans' resistance began to crumble everywhere, and this crumbling was soon to develop into a general collapse.

When the British advance developed, much the most serious hindrance came from the heaps of rubble created by the excessive bombing efforts of the Allied air forces, which had thereby blocked the routes of advance far more effectively than the enemy could. For the dominant desire of the Germans now, both troops and people, was to see the British and American armies sweep eastward as rapidly as possible to reach Berlin and occupy as much of the country as possible before the Russians overcame the Oder line. Few of them were inclined to assist Hitler's purpose of obstruction by self-destruction.

Early in March Zhukov had enlarged his bridgehead over the Oder, but did not succeed in breaking out. Russian progress on the far flanks continued, and Vienna was entered early in April. Meanwhile the German front in the West had collapsed, and the Allied armies there were driving eastward from the Rhine with little opposition. They reached the Elbe, sixty miles from Berlin, on 11th April. Here they halted.

On the 16th, Zhukov resumed the offensive in conjunction with Konev, who forced the crossings of the Neisse. This time the Russians burst out of their bridgeheads, and within a week were driving into the

suburbs of Berlin—where Hitler chose to remain for the final battle. By the 25th the city had been completely isolated by the encircling armies of Zhukov and Konev, and on the 27th Konev's forces joined hands with the Americans on the Elbe. But in Berlin itself desperate street by street resistance was put up by the Germans, and was not completely overcome until the war itself ended, after Hitler's suicide on 30th April, with Germany's unconditional surrender.

In Montgomery's 21st Army Group the advance across the Elbe by British 2nd Army began in the early hours of 29th April. It was led by 8th Corps, employing DD (swimming) tanks, while the infantry were conveyed in amphibian vehicles, as in the crossing of the Rhine. On its right it was also aided by US 18th Airborne Corps (of three divisions) operating on the ground, which crossed the Elbe on the 30th. Progress now became swift, and on 2nd May British 6th Airborne Division, also operating on the ground, meeting no opposition, occupied Wismar on the Baltic coast after a forty mile drive. (A few hours after its arrival Russian tanks appeared and made contact with the British troops.) British 11th Armoured Division entered the city of Lübeck, on the Baltic, without opposition, after an exploiting drive of thirty miles. The American troops on its right likewise made rapid progress. Meanwhile, British 12th Corps had passed through 8th Corps' bridgehead with the task of capturing Hamburg, but the German garrison commander came out to surrender the city, and the British troops entered it without opposition on 3rd May.

The war in Europe came to an end officially at midnight on 8th May 1945, but in reality that was merely the final formal recognition of a finish which had taken place piecemeal during the course of the previous week.

Left: 1 German soldier during the Ardennes counter-offensive. 2 Moment of weariness for US soldier in Bastogne, Belgium, one of the vital bottlenecks which held out against the German assault. Bastogne was weakly defended until the US 101st Airborne Division ('the Screaming Eagles') raced in from Reims one day ahead of the Germans. On 22nd December the German commander demanded surrender. McAuliffe, commanding the 101st, replied with just one word: 'Nuts!' 3 Painting by Canadian Alex Colville of infantry near Nijmegen, Holland
Right: 1 Poster issued by SS in Belgium depicts profit-hungry Roosevelt riding to prosperity in war, exploiting efforts of Churchill and Stalin. 2 The vice tightens. Map shows the armies of the Allies advancing into Germany

1 △ 2 ▽

Russian and East
European forces

1 Malinovsky
2 Tolbukhin
3 Rokossovsky
4 Konev
5 Zhukov
6 Chernyakhovsky
7 Zakharov

Western Allied
forces

1 Montgomery
2 Bradley
3 Patton
4 Patch
5 De Lattre
6 Devers

Yugoslav partisan
forces, Tito

1937 boundaries

New Guinea and the Philippines

'The President of the United States ordered me to break through the Japanese lines and proceed from Corregidor to Australia for the purpose, as I understand it, of organizing the American offensive against Japan, a primary object of which is the recovery of the Philippines. I came through and I shall return.' So spoke General Douglas MacArthur on his arrival in Australia in March 1942 to assume command of the meagre Allied forces in the Southwest Pacific. At the beginning of American participation in the war, Roosevelt and Churchill had agreed that the Pacific area, including Australia, should be under American command—with the Middle East and India remaining under British control, and Europe and the Atlantic coming under joint Anglo-American direction. The command in the Pacific was further divided between MacArthur's Southwest Pacific Command and the Central Pacific Command of Admiral Chester Nimitz. Each was in control of the land, sea and air forces in his zone except that Nimitz had, in addition, the direction of the amphibious operations in his rival's command.

For almost 40 years the American Navy had expected war with Japan and, now that war had finally come, was determined that the Navy was to have the pre-eminent role in the Pacific. Nimitz and the Naval Chiefs of Staff headed by Admiral Ernest King did not want any naval forces under Army command and hence decided to launch a purely naval campaign west from their big base at Hawaii towards Japan, while the commander in the Southwest Pacific was to stay on the defensive. MacArthur, however, was too strong a personality and his ideas about the way to defeat Japan were too firm for him to accept this role, and he launched his own campaign north from Australia towards Japan. Having been driven out of the Philippines by force of arms, MacArthur felt strongly that the only way for the United States to regain control of the islands was by the same means, otherwise she would never be able to reassert her pre-war authority.

MacArthur believed that the Western Allies, having been defeated so disastrously by the Asians, must prove their superiority again, a factor he felt it was folly not to take into consideration when planning the Pacific strategy against Japan. For MacArthur the only road to Tokyo which took account of American interests in Asia lay through the Philippines.

Thus Nimitz and MacArthur were to compete against each other to see which of them could defeat Japan first. Fond of this sort of confrontation, Roosevelt approved the divided command in the hope of using the natural rivalry between the Army and Navy to produce faster results. MacArthur thought it was incredible that the Navy could allow inter-service rivalry to determine the course of the war and later wrote, 'Of all the faulty decisions of the war, perhaps the most inexpressible one was the failure to unify the command in the Pacific.' Through the insistence of Admiral King, however, the commands of Nimitz and MacArthur remained separate throughout the war, despite a general realization in Washington that this was not the best of arrangements.

MacArthur was indeed a controversial figure. He had been in conflict with Roosevelt since before the war and remained so throughout. The politics and personalities of the two men were in total contrast. The situation was exacerbated by the fact that MacArthur was a thoroughgoing conservative whom some Republicans on the home front promoted as a candidate for the presidency against Roosevelt. MacArthur was also in conflict with Army Chief of Staff George Marshall and the Army establishment on a number of issues, but mainly over the 'Europe first' policy against which MacArthur repeatedly protested. This conflict was perhaps less serious as the Army was glad to have a strong and popular figure like MacArthur, however much it itself disliked him, to uphold its role in the Pacific against the pretensions of the Navy.

When MacArthur arrived in Australia, he found his new command short of manpower, poorly equipped and quite deficient in air power. He also found Australian morale shattered by the Allied *débâcle* in Asia and especially by the fall of Singapore, which had been regarded by Australians as the keystone of their security; hence his first task was to infuse the Australians with an offensive spirit and his own sense of confidence. New Guinea was to be the first priority, as it was from there

Left: Painting of American marines landing on Bougainville in the Solomon Islands, 1st November 1943 by W. F. Draper. **Right:** *An American transport, its decks crammed with supplies, including petrol and trucks, heads for Cape Gloucester in New Britain where Allied forces landed on 26th December 1943. Rabaul, the key Japanese base on New Britain, was virtually encircled and isolated by thrusts through the Solomons and Bismarck Archipelago*

that the Japanese were threatening Australia, which was the main American base in the South Pacific. To make Australia secure the Japanese would have to be evicted from New Guinea. Since a large part of New Guinea was Australian territory a strong offensive there would do wonders for Australian morale; it was as important to the Australians to reconquer New Guinea by force of arms as it was to Mac-Arthur to re-occupy the Philippines

the same aggressively convincing manner.

In organizing his staff, however, Mac-Arthur refused to appoint Australian and Dutch officers to senior positions and indeed brought most of his senior officers with him from the Philippines. It was not until General George Kennedy took command of the air forces in the Southwest Pacific that his breezy ebullience unlimbered Mac-Arthur's stiff personality and brought him out of this close circle of intimates and into

closer and warmer contact with the remainder of his subordinates, hence also closer to current information and intelligence. MacArthur soon developed a highly efficient team which played a major role in his coming success. A further invaluable asset for MacArthur was the discovery of Commander Long of the Australian armed forces, organizer of the superb intelligence network of coastwatchers whose information made the difference in many opera-

tions. Within three months of his arrival, MacArthur was able to start on the road back to the Philippines.

The pressure of their original offensive launched in December 1941 had carried the Japanese forces to the chain of coral islands to the north of Australia but energy had flagged when the islands were only half occupied. The Japanese held the Solomons but the object of their next offensive was the remainder – New Hebrides, New Caledonia

and Port Moresby in Papua. It was with this in view that men and ships were first concentrated for a seaborne move against Port Moresby. This expedition was turned back in the carrier action of 5th-8th May in the Coral Sea, the first fought entirely by airplanes and in which the ships of the opposing forces never sighted each other. A month later a powerful Japanese thrust across the central Pacific was turned into smashing defeat by Admiral Nimitz's ships

58/59 Australian Infantry Battalion storm Japanese strong-point ('Old Vickers') on Bobdubi Ridge, Salamaua, New Guinea, 28th July 1943. Painting by Ivor Hele

at Midway, after which Japanese attention again shifted to the Southwest Pacific. Suffering from what a Japanese admiral later called 'victory disease', and against all the dictates of sound strategy, the Japanese laid plans to enlarge their already over-extended position. The new Eighth Fleet under Admiral Mikawa was to spearhead a fresh advance from Rabaul with its newly enlarged airfields with the object of seizing the islands of Tulagi and Guadalcanal in the Solomons, and Port Moresby, the latter to be attacked by land over the Owen Stanley Mountain Range. By these moves the Japanese sought to gain mastery of the Coral Sea.

'Don't come back alive'

Having already broken the Japanese codes before the war, the Joint Chiefs of Staff were aware of the Japanese plan and formulated 'Operation Watchtower' to counter it. The goal of Watchtower was to remove the Bismarck Archipelago as a barrier to the recovery of the Philippines and to an assault on Japan itself. MacArthur was to seize the Solomons and the north-east coast of New Guinea, followed by the big Japanese base at Rabaul on New Britain and adjacent positions in and around New Guinea and New Ireland. This was the origin of what came to be known as the 'island-hopping campaign'. The Japanese had just occupied Tulagi and Guadalcanal, whence their bombers could menace the entire Allied position in the Southwest Pacific, so in August Operation Watchtower began with a Marine assault on both islands. In a hard-fought campaign from August 1942 to February 1943, American troops finally ousted the Japanese after seven major naval engagements and at least ten pitched land battles.

MacArthur began the campaign to clear Papua and New Guinea by increasing the garrison of Port Moresby which ultimately attained the strength of 55,000 American and Australian troops. The Japanese move over the Owen Stanley Range was, however, pushing back the Australian forces while on 25th August 2,000 Japanese marines made a landing near Milne Bay airstrip. The Australian defenders managed to hold for ten days and then began to push the enemy back, but a lengthy contest ensued. About the same time, the Japanese advance over the Owen Stanley Range was halted. The Japanese High Command then decided to de-emphasize the Papuan campaign and throw all their resources into the struggle for Guadalcanal. The Papuan campaign was being waged with considerable acrimony on the Allied side. MacArthur was not satisfied with Australian progress and considered these troops inferior to his Americans, yet his Americans were also coming in for some cogent criticism from the Australians, criticism which MacArthur knew had more than a little truth to it.

In October a new all-out offensive was launched, but progress was still slow. Finally MacArthur put General Robert Eichelberger in command, ordering him to take Buna, admittedly a tough nut to crack, or 'don't come back alive'. Leading his American and Australian troops through a stinking malarial jungle and reinforced by a fresh Australian brigade, Eichelberger did take Buna and successfully concluded the Papuan campaign by mid-January. But by 4th January it was already known that the Japanese command had decided to abandon both Papua and Guadalcanal, since by then control of air and sea had passed to the Allies and it was no longer possible to supply and reinforce the troops there.

With the victories in Papua and Guadalcanal, the offensive in the Southwest Pacific had definitely passed to the Allies. MacArthur was now arguing with his superiors in Washington, and not increasing his popularity in the process, that the best route to Japan lay along the 'New Guinea-Mindanao Axis'. Nimitz and the Navy argued cogently that a route through the Gilbert, Marshall, Caroline and Mariana Islands was not only shorter but necessary to protect the New Guinea-Mindanao Axis from air attacks staged from these islands. Thus the Nimitz-MacArthur race continued, although MacArthur now had greater resources as increased supplies and equipment flowed to his command. He was also aided by the appointment in October 1942 of Admiral William F. Halsey as commander of the naval forces in the Southwest Pacific. Like MacArthur, Halsey had a well deserved reputation for leadership, confidence and aggressiveness.

MacArthur now turned his attention to the rest of New Guinea and his main objective of Rabaul in New Britain. As first steps, the undefended Trobriand Islands, Finschhafen and Nassau Bay, were occupied. The Air Force sent a massive hundred-plane raid against Wewak, the principal Japanese base in New Guinea, while paratroops seized the Japanese airstrip at Nadzab in a daring attack. Australian forces took Lae and Salamaua. Finally in October 1943, another hard-fought and lengthy campaign was launched against Bougainville, a large island in the Solomons whose possession was necessary for the coming attack on Rabaul. The Bougainville fighting dragged on until March 1944. MacArthur was closing in on Rabaul but it was becoming apparent that island-hopping was too costly in time, hence 'leap-frogging' was substituted. This meant bypassing the stronger Japanese positions, sealing them off by air and sea and leaving them to 'wither on the vine' or as one of the more baseball-minded members of MacArthur's staff put it, 'hitting 'em where they ain't'. The Quadrant Conference at Quebec in August 1943 directed MacArthur and Halsey to bypass Rabaul and occupy Kavieng in New Ireland and the Admiralty Islands instead. This was surely a wise decision as Rabaul contained 100,000 defenders under a tough and resourceful general with ample supplies left from expeditions which had come to nought. An assault on Rabaul would have delayed the Allied advance by many months. So the occupation of the Admiralties was begun in February 1944 and completed in April. With the fall of Bougainville to the south, Rabaul was now sealed off and left to 'die on the vine'.

MacArthur now planned to leap-frog the 50,000-strong Japanese garrison at Wewak and in four operations arrive at the northwest point of New Guinea. Supported by Halsey's Seventh Fleet, MacArthur's forces pushed rapidly along the New Guinea coast in a series of amphibious operations. Wakde, Biak, Noemfoor and Sansapoor all fell to troops from a flotilla of 215 assorted LST's and LCT's, Biak being a particularly tough fight because the Japanese had prepared a skilled defence in depth. On 30th July, the capture of Sansapoor completed Allied control of New Guinea and was the last stop on that island on MacArthur's road back to the Philippines. There were still mopping-up operations and many bypassed Japanese troops to be watched, but now MacArthur could look across the Celebes Sea towards Mindanao.

The strategy question was still unresolved at this point. The Naval Chief of Staff, Admiral Ernest King, led the Navy school of thought which wanted to bypass the Philippines, invade Formosa and set up a base on the Chinese mainland or in the Ryukyu Islands for the final assault on Japan. MacArthur's position was based on the liberation of the Philippines and use of Luzon as a base for the final assault. Loyal Luzon could be sealed off by Allied air and sea power far more successfully than hostile Formosa which Japan could easily reinforce from the Chinese mainland. He also insisted that the United States had a compelling moral duty to liberate the Philippines which had been nourishing the Filipino resistance movement, and where the troops he had left in 1942 were still imprisoned. At a conference at Pearl Harbour in July, MacArthur converted Nimitz and Roosevelt to his 'Leyte then Luzon' strategy which was then formalized by the Joint Chiefs of Staff. MacArthur and Nimitz were to continue their advances and converge on Leyte in December. But then the fast carrier forces of Halsey, spearheaded by the new *Essex* class carriers, demonstrated graphically Japan's great weakness in air power, so the date of the Leyte assault was moved forward two months to 20th October.

By way of preparation, Morotai and Saipan were seized as staging air bases against Leyte. The action at Saipan brought about a massive air battle in which the

Japanese lost 300 irreplaceable planes and pilots—the 'great Marianas turkey shoot' as American pilots called it. On 12th-15th October Allied Task Force 38 knocked out a further 500 planes based on Formosa, leaving Japan denuded of her naval air force. A powerful fleet was detached from the Central Pacific Command to assist Halsey in protecting MacArthur's 700 transports and auxiliaries carrying 174,000 troops. These forces landed on schedule the morning of 20th October in the Gulf of Leyte in the central Philippines.

The Japanese High Command chose to regard the Leyte operation as a major crisis. If the enemy succeeded in occupying the Philippines, the supply lines of Japan would be fatally obstructed. The High Command decided that the issue of the war hung on its ability to defend the Philippines, so it gathered its Navy to turn the American threat into a Japanese victory with one decisive blow. Now that Japan's naval air force had been virtually eliminated, however, the attack would have to rely on the battleship fleet led by the awesome *Yamato* whose 18-inch guns made it the most powerful ship afloat. The Japanese were also well supplied with cruisers and destroyers, but these would go into battle alongside the capital ships without air cover and with no way of striking at the enemy other than with gunfire and torpedoes. The Japanese Chief of Naval Staff, Admiral Soemu Toyoda, devised a complex plan to use a decoy force to draw off MacArthur's protective fleet of battleships and carriers under Halsey, after which two strong fleets would move in and attack the American forces while they were unprotected and in the highly vulnerable process of disembarkation. Toyoda counted on his forces making unimpeded contact with the enemy, free from air attack, and destroying the American transports and army by sheer gun power. Thus Toyoda laid his plans for what was to become the largest sea battle in history, a battle which if successful would have had the impact of a second Pearl Harbour and kept Japan in the war for at least another year.

On 23rd October the battle opened on a successful note for Toyoda as Halsey withdrew his entire force to chase the decoy force and never did get into serious action with his powerful fleet, a fact for which he was subsequently heavily criticized. The smaller Japanese attack force, led by two battleships supported by cruisers and destroyers, was ambushed by the remnants of the American fleet under Admiral Kinkaid in a hot night action from which only

Right: End of a Kamikaze off the Philippines, June 1945. Under the guns of an American carrier a suicide bomber is transformed into a fireball

one Japanese destroyer escaped. Spearheaded by five battleships, the larger Japanese attack force appeared soon after but bumped into a weak force of American escort carriers and a few destroyers. These delayed the Japanese for hours with a heroic fight while reinforcements were mustered. After learning of the annihilation of his sister force, the Japanese commander withdrew as he was coming under heavier air attack and was uncertain of the strength of his opposition. The decoy force escaped completely. The Battle of Leyte Gulf was the final action of the war for the Japanese Navy, which was so heavily battered that it was reduced to an auxiliary role. The great naval lesson of Leyte Gulf was that battleships without air cover are helpless in a modern sea battle; Toyoda's plan was defeated mainly by Japan's lack of planes and to a lesser extent by bad intelligence and a lack of co-ordination among his commanders.

As it was, Halsey had left MacArthur dangerously exposed and, had the Japanese decided to press home their second attack, the lack of co-ordination between the Navy and Army surely would have resulted in the stunning disaster for the Allies envisaged by Admiral Toyoda. In the event, however, the assault on Leyte was successful and after the first wave was ashore, MacArthur followed with Sergio Osmena, now President of the Philippines after the death of Manuel Quezon. Standing on the beach, MacArthur made the broadcast to the people of the Philippines for which he had been waiting two and a half years: 'People of the Philippines, I have returned. By the grace of Almighty God, our forces stand again on Philippine soil—soil consecrated by the blood of our two peoples.' The broadcast made a tremendous impact on the Philippines, and there on the beach MacArthur scribbled a note to Roosevelt urging him to grant immediate independence to the islands.

Although Japan had suffered a shattering defeat on the sea at Leyte Gulf, there were still 60,000 Japanese troops on Leyte under the tough and determined command of General Yamashita. Ever since their defeats in Papua and Guadalcanal, the Japanese had followed a policy of selling their territory as dearly as possible and Yamashita continued to do so on Leyte. MacArthur was forced to commit a quarter of a million troops to its capture. Progress was slow as American troops, largely conscripts, tended to bog down in the jungle and relied on artillery fire power to clear the way. When the battle for Leyte was over, the Japanese had lost an estimated 48,000 killed, as against 3,500 for the Allies.

Back to Corregidor

The strategy debate had continued right

up to the assault on Leyte. MacArthur wanted to land on Luzon as soon as possible while Nimitz was still arguing for Formosa. Admiral King was all for bypassing Luzon in favour of Japan itself. By mid-September the others had come around to MacArthur's point of view, except for the adamant Admiral King. MacArthur informed the Joint Chiefs of Staff that he could land on Luzon on 20th December, and finally on 3rd October received a directive to do so. At the same time, Nimitz was ordered to attack Iwo Jima in January 1945 and Okinawa in March, so the two-pronged assault leading to Japan was to continue. MacArthur was understandably relieved at the final demise of the Formosa plan as it made little sense to attack in the direction of ally China rather than enemy Japan. The order to land on Luzon also meant that now he had authority to liberate all of the Philippines instead of only parts of them. It was a job he relished as he intended to eradicate all traces of the Japanese presence.

As the Japanese had done three years before, MacArthur decided to land on Luzon at Lingayen Gulf. With Halsey and the Third Fleet for cover, he would, after landing at Lingayen, secure both banks of the Agno River and then thrust southwards towards Manila. He was operating on the assumption, soon proved correct, that Yamashita would defend the Cagayan River and the Sierra Madre Mountains in northern Luzon to the end. The heavy fighting on Leyte, however, delayed the landing until 9th January. The Japanese offered little opposition to the landings, but their retreat north was slow and tedious. The fighting around Clarke Field, the major air base in the islands, was especially fierce. On 3rd February American troops entered Manila and after two weeks of hard fighting had secured control of the city, though Japanese diehards continued to hold out in the old quarter until March 3rd. Under MacArthur's personal supervision, XIV Corps sealed off the Bataan Peninsula at the end of January while XI Corps landed at Subig Bay, the major naval base on Luzon. The island fortress of Corregidor, last

Right: Top: Two highly romanticized views of the Pacific war. 1 'Fighter in the Sky' by Tom Lea. A grimly determined American pilot in combat with Japanese Zeros. On 19th June 1944, 891 American aircraft shot down 330 aircraft out of a 430-strong Japanese force. It was dubbed 'the Marianas turkey shoot'. 2 In a painting by T.Ishikawa American and Japanese carrier-borne aircraft duel over the south Pacific. 3 Chinese unloading ammunition from Dakotas at Kweilin in south China painted by Samuel D.Smith. The aircraft supplied the American 14th Air Force based there

The Defeat of the Axis

American position to surrender in 1942, took weeks to capture as it was defended almost to the last man, only 26 of its 5,000-man garrison, being taken prisoner.

These were highly emotional days for MacArthur who had been enthusiastically welcomed by the Filipinos and who was now reconquering territory which he had been unsuccessful in defending in 1942. As the prison camps were liberated, the ragged, half-starved inmates wept at the sight of him and came running to touch him. These were the men for whom he had felt so strong a need to return. On 27th February MacArthur reintroduced constitutional government and insisted on the Philippine Commonwealth having the same autonomy as it had before the war.

The main objectives on Luzon had now been taken, but it remained to deal with Yamashita in the north. By April the sea route through the Visayas had been cleared while by June, under strong American pressure, Yamashita's 40,000 men had been reduced to several fiercely defended pockets in central Luzon and its north-east coast. When Japan capitulated in August, there were still about 50,000 Japanese holding out on Luzon. The Japanese defence had been admirably resolute, stalling the Ameri-

can re-occupation for months, and requiring large numbers of troops. Luzon in fact became the largest land campaign of the Pacific theatre, involving 15 American divisions and substantial numbers of Filipino troops as well. This was the most difficult and stubborn jungle fighting that MacArthur's troops had seen since Papua and Guadalcanal, with the Japanese soldier at his defensive best. The Allied task on Luzon was made easier, however, by the strong Filipino guerrilla movement which provided valuable intelligence and harassed the retreating Japanese.

MacArthur and his staff had been planning the re-occupation of the Netherlands East Indies and the invasion of the Japanese home islands when the use of the atomic bomb by President Truman removed the latter need. The last operations of the Southwest Pacific Command were the despatch of some Australian units to Borneo.

The road from New Guinea to the Philippines had been a long and hard fought trip, usually against superior enemy forces. In New Guinea, MacArthur had had to overcome the arts of the Japanese in defensive warfare in territory favourable to the defenders, yet he had inflicted enormous losses in manpower on them. In the Papuan

campaign, for example, 13,000 of 20,000 Japanese participants were killed as against 3,000 Allied losses. In the Philippines, MacArthur faced a similar situation, except that he had far greater forces at his disposal during that campaign. As he once told Roosevelt, 'The days of frontal attack should be over. Modern infantry weapons are too deadly. . . . Good commanders do not turn in heavy losses.' MacArthur's battles were won by sheer artistry, by bringing his usually inferior force to bear on the enemy in places and at times when his opponent was off balance, so that his attack could succeed with minimum loss. Rather than assaulting the Japanese fortresses like Wewak and Rabaul directly, MacArthur's tactic was to envelop them by attacking their lines of communication until they were isolated and 'died on the vine'. MacArthur later wrote that this tactic was 'the ideal method for success by inferior in number but faster-moving forces . . . I determined that such a plan of action was the sole chance of fulfilling my mission.' By contrast the island-hopping campaign in the Central Pacific by Nimitz relied much more on simply overwhelming the enemy with a superior force, often resulting in appallingly high casualties.

The Pacific Island-Hopping Campaign

The achievements of the Imperial Japanese Navy between Pearl Harbour and the Battle of Midway rank as one of the classic campaigns of naval history. Following Admiral Yamamoto's meticulous strategic plan, Japanese naval air power knocked out the United States' surface fleet, and their ground, sea and air forces, and then bundled the British, Dutch and Americans out of the East Indies, the Philippines and Malaya in a matter of weeks.

The resulting 'island chain' of forward bases was intended to act as a defensive perimeter to protect the new Japanese conquests from any Allied counter-stroke. That counter-stroke was sure to come, for despite their humiliating losses the Allies had not been totally disabled. The American aircraft carriers were still untouched and, despite the loss of Singapore, the British could still muster troops and warships to defend both Australia and India.

The problem for the Japanese was that their impressive victories had not given them the secure perimeter that they needed. They wanted bases in the Indian Ocean if they were to keep the British from making a counter-attack and they needed New Guinea if they were to pose a serious threat to Australia. To meet this latter threat the US Navy took over responsibility for the Southwest Pacific, and it was in this theatre that the first big battle between the Japanese and American carriers took place. The Battle of the Coral Sea, 5th-9th May 1942, was in the material sense no more than a draw, but it checkmated the Japanese attempt to gain control of the Coral Sea and to capture Port Moresby in New Guinea.

The next move by the Japanese was an attack on the Aleutians and an attempted invasion of Midway Island, which they knew to be the 'sentry for Hawaii'. The Battle of Midway which ensued gave the Japanese a fleet action, but not the kind that they wanted. The opposing aircraft carriers struck at one another over a distance of 200 miles. As mentioned in an earlier chapter, losses in ships and aircraft were heavy on both sides, but by the early hours of 5th June 1942, after 24 hours of bitter fighting, it was clear to the Japanese that they had lost their chance of taking Midway.

Midway was the end of the Japanese Navy's dominance in the Pacific, for the ships and aircrew were never fully replaced, whereas the American losses were replaced many times over. Nor was the counter-attack long in coming, but the question was, where to strike? Although there were two schools of thought about how to defeat the Japanese in the Pacific, there was fortunately total agreement that the Solomon Islands in the Southwest Pacific were to be the objective. This was because the area dominated New Guinea and Australia, and once in Allied hands it would make a good springboard for further operations, while removing the threat of a Japanese invasion of Australia. The Japanese, however, with the same advantages to themselves in mind, drew up their own plans to capture the Solomons. As a result they were moving powerful forces into the area at the same time as the Americans.

Death before surrender

The American landing on Guadalcanal, one of the largest of the southern group of the Solomons, and a simultaneous landing on the lesser island of Tulagi, were bitterly opposed by their Japanese garrisons. After a day of fierce fighting, however, all the major objectives were taken and by 8th August 1942 everything seemed to be going according to plan. Only one disquieting feature came to light: the defenders of Tulagi had been prepared to fight to the last man rather than surrender.

The Japanese naval commander at Rabaul, who been reinforced for a landing in the same area, was able to launch a rapid counter-attack. A cruiser squadron under Admiral Mikawa was sent to destroy the landing forces, and this group of five heavy and two light cruisers inflicted a severe defeat on the Allied naval forces in the Battle of Savo Island. In a disastrous night action the Australian *Canberra* and the American *Quincy*, *Vincennes* and *Astoria* were sunk without being able to reply. Mikawa does not seem to have grasped how close he had come to destroying the entire expedition, and just when he should have pressed on to attack the transports he retired rapidly.

Between August and December 1942 the battle over the Solomons raged, both on land and sea. The US Marines were locked in a struggle to the death with an enemy better trained and equipped to cope with the enervating heat and jungle conditions, who fought with fanatic courage for every yard of ground. At sea the fighting was less intense on a personal scale, but still distinguished by a ferocity unequalled any-

Right: Architect of the attack on Pearl Harbour: Admiral Yamamoto, C-in-C Combined Fleet. Left: A painting of Kamikaze *suicide pilots by S. Awata. The Japanese first resorted to the use of these fliers, who dived their explosive-laden aircraft on to American warships, in January 1945 in the Philippines.* Kamikaze *or 'Divine Wind' was a reference to the typhoon that destroyed an invading Mongol armada in 1281*

The Defeat of the Axis

where else during the war. By day American air and sea power gave them control of the vital 'Slot', as the waters between the north-eastern and south-western islands were known; at night the Japanese had virtually a free hand to run in supplies, land men, or even bombard shore positions.

Fortunately the Allies had radar, and this gave them a chance in the night actions, but even so their forces were roughly handled during this period. After the Battle of Santa Cruz on 26th October the US Navy was left with only one damaged carrier, the *Enterprise*, although luckily she was able to fight on. In an action on the night of 14th

November the battleship *South Dakota* was badly knocked about, but the Japanese battleship *Kirishima* was sunk. This must be accounted the first Allied victory of the campaign, but just over a fortnight later a force of five cruisers was defeated by only eight Japanese destroyers, which sank the USS *Northampton* and damaged three others. Eventually the Allies were able to clear the 'Slot', and early in 1943 the Japanese defenders of Guadalcanal were evacuated.

As the remaining Japanese forces in the eastern part of New Guinea had been driven out by the end of December 1942, the way

was now clear for the prosecution of Admiral Nimitz's drive across the Pacific. As we know, the Army under General MacArthur wanted to recapture the Philippines, whereas the Navy wanted to strike with its far-ranging aircraft-carrier task forces straight across the Pacific to the heart of Japan. In the event, both strategic

Allied forces – largely American, but including Australian units in the south-west Pacific – bound towards Japan in an island-hopping campaign which began with landings on Guadalcanal on 7th August 1942 and ended in June 1945 on Okinawa

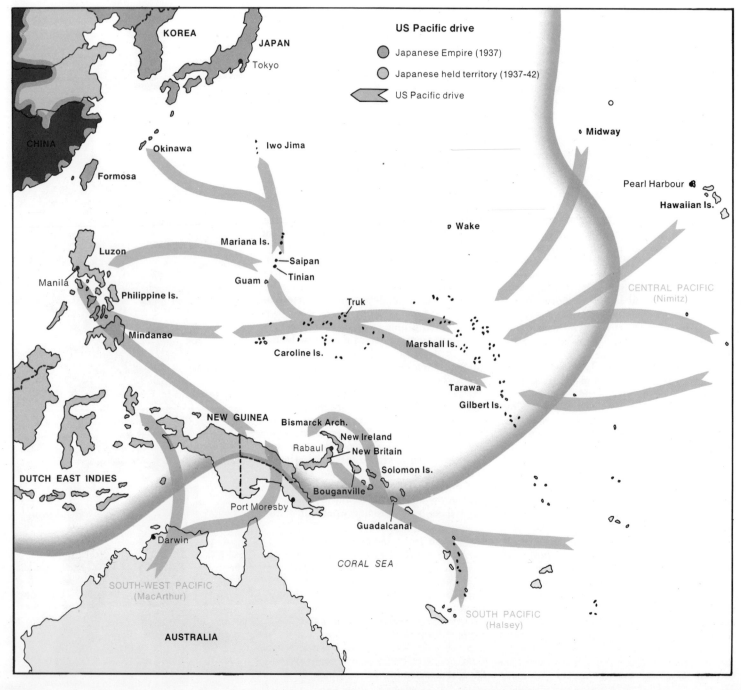

plans were followed to some extent, but the logic of the naval plan seems to have been both simpler and more economical. No matter how many Japanese garrisons were scattered across the Pacific, the Japanese mercantile marine was nowhere near adequate to keep them supplied.

On 29th March 1943 new directives were issued by the US Chiefs of Staff to the Army and Navy to clear the Solomons of Japanese forces and to attack New Britain. In February a small force of 9,000 men had captured the small Russell Islands, just north of Guadalcanal, and had shown how successful surprise attacks could be. Accordingly, assaults were planned against New Georgia and the Trobriand Islands, and the first moves were made to expel the Japanese from the Aleutians.

By the middle of 1943 the losses of the Guadalcanal campaign had been made good, and the new forces were better trained and equipped than those of a year before. The strategic aim was to break through the so-called Bismarck Barrier of island bases in the Bismarck Archipelago. To distract and bluff the Japanese about the main direction of the thrust, Admiral Nimitz was ordered to launch an offensive against the Marshall and Caroline Islands well to the north. The main Japanese fleet base was at Truk in the Carolines, and it was here that the weight of American carrier air-strikes would fall.

Against such an array of strength the Japanese could do little. Like the Germans all over Europe, they were trying to hold an impossibly large number of strongpoints. A new Combined Fleet under Admiral Koga at Truk was hoping to defend a perimeter stretching from the Aleutians down to the Andaman Islands in the Indian Ocean, but even that plan collapsed. Late in June 1943 nearly the whole of the Combined Fleet was withdrawn to protect the homeland against a fancied threat from Russia. The underlying reason for this was a chronic shortage of trained aircrew, carrier pilots who had been lost in the Coral Sea and Midway battles, or frittered away in attacks on heavily defended bases in the Solomons.

Although the Combined Fleet was allowed to return to Truk in July, some of its carriers still lacked crews for their aircraft. When the combined thrust from Nimitz at Pearl Harbour, and Halsey and MacArthur from the Solomons, began at the end of June 1943 they were ill equipped to cope. First came a successful move against the north-western coast of New Guinea, then came the landings in New Britain. The New Guinea landings were timed to coincide with Halsey's landing in New Georgia, so that the Allies now had six airfields around the southern Solomons to enable them to give air cover to all their ground forces.

Nimitz strikes

As the Japanese were now reduced to relying on sending their striking forces a distance of 400 miles from Rabaul, there was little they could do. But their ships still showed outstanding ability in fighting night actions, and once again the night battles raged in the 'Slot'. In two costly actions in July and August they showed that their night-fighting skill was only just matched by radar, and even then the slightest error by their opponents was punished heavily. Only after a year of fighting around the Solomons was there any sign of the Japanese weakening.

The first true example of 'island-hopping' came in August 1943, when Admiral Halsey switched from an attack planned against Kolombangara Island to one against Vella Lavella. This latter island was not only closer to Rabaul, but its possession also made the capture of Kolombangara redundant. Accordingly, a combined Allied amphibious force took Vella Lavella, and although the garrison took six weeks to capitulate, it proved an easier target than the original objective.

From Vella Lavella Halsey moved on to Bougainville, and although this large island north of New Guinea was strongly defended, the central part around Empress Augusta Bay promised an easier landing. It caught the Japanese on the wrong foot, with their Combined Fleet watching for a thrust by Nimitz against the Marshall Islands. For the whole of October 1943, therefore, Halsey's forces had no attacks from enemy carrier aircraft. Even when land-based aircraft attacked in November, the American carriers proved that they could stand up to them better than anyone had believed possible. Indeed, until then the risk had been thought unacceptable.

Nimitz was preparing to strike at the Marshalls, but he was aiming first at the Gilbert Islands. To gauge what this means in the context of the vast areas of the Pacific, it must be remembered that Pearl Harbour was over 2,000 miles from the west coast of the United States, and the same distance from the Gilbert and Marshall Islands; the Solomons were 3,000 miles from the Australian bases, and over 9,000 miles from the United States, and yet forces were fed, ammunitioned and maintained.

The islands attacked by Admiral Nimitz were Tarawa and Makin, as the Chiefs of Staff had decided that their garrisons dominated the Marshalls. At his disposal he had a fleet of battleships and aircraft carriers almost equal to the pre-war strength of the US Navy and, despite the presence at Truk of the giant battleships *Yamato* and *Musashi*, Admiral Koga was badly outclassed. Therefore there was almost no Japanese naval activity when Makin and Tarawa were attacked, but the 5,000 defenders of Tarawa inflicted 3,000 casualties on the Americans before they could be subdued; only 150 prisoners surrendered.

To the soldiers and marines who fought their way from Guadalcanal to Tarawa the whole campaign must have seemed a futile sacrifice of lives to wrest a string of useless coral atolls from the Japanese, but this was not the case. What was unfolding was a planned advance across the Pacific towards the Japanese homeland. The way was now clear for an even greater offensive in 1944.

The Japanese had decided late in 1943 to do what they should have done a year earlier; they drew up a more modest defensive perimeter, running from the Mariana Islands through Truk and Rabaul down to northern New Guinea and Timor. Behind this line they planned to deliver counter-attacks on the Allies, but they nevertheless allowed garrisons to remain outside the perimeter with a view to tying down and harassing the enemy.

The American assault on the Marshalls showed great boldness. On 31st January 1944, 40,000 troops landed on Kwajalein and Majuro, right in the heart of the islands. With small losses they took their objectives, and bases for heavy bombers were immediately set up. The larger islands were left alone, and although they remained in Japanese hands until the end of the war, their garrisons were almost annihilated by disease and starvation. Not all garrisons could be bypassed like this, but from now on the rule was to outflank and starve out isolated islands and bypass obstinate garrisons.

Following a highly successful carrier strike against the Marianas in February, the decision was made to leap-frog Truk and go straight on to land in the Marianas. This chain of islands in the central Pacific contains four whose names stand out: Saipan, Tinian, Rota and Guam. In a three-day air battle the carrier pilots of Admiral Mitscher's Fast Carrier Task Force destroyed the defending air forces in the famous 'Marianas turkey shoot'. This time the landings prodded the Japanese fleet into action, and the Battle of the Philippine Sea was the result. Again Japanese losses were heavy, particularly among their dwindling reserve of carrier pilots, and three more carriers had been sunk.

This highly mobile campaign was yielding ever better results, not only in terms of Japanese losses, but also in growing American skill in the techniques of shore bombardment and inter-service co-operation. The invasion of the Philippines reflected the skill developed in two years' constant campaigning. There was also the bonus of the great Battle of Leyte Gulf in October 1944, in which the Imperial Japanese Navy made its last attempt to defeat the Ameri-

cans in open battle, and was destroyed as an effective fighting force.

Epic on Iwo Jima

The last phase came in April 1945, when large forces attacked Okinawa, only 800 miles south of the Japanese mainland. It was needed as a forward base to assemble shipping for the eventual assault on Japan itself, and also as a bomber base. At the same time, it was decided to seize the little island of Iwo Jima, somewhat closer to Japan, to eliminate its fighter aircraft which were causing bomber casualties, and also to provide an emergency landing strip for damaged B-29s on their homeward run. As there were not enough ships to carry out both landings simultaneously, Iwo Jima was chosen as the first objective in the hope that it would prove the easier.

The epic of Iwo Jima was remarkable for the ferocity of the fighting on both sides. Despite a crushing bombardment from the naval forces, the defenders emerged from their underground bunkers and fought with such tenacity that the Americans suffered 21,000 casualties; that figure was only 1,000 less than the casualties inflicted on the Japanese. By comparison the landing on Okinawa was less costly, but this time the naval forces were heavily punished by Kamikaze attacks—suicidal dives by aircraft onto ships, which frequently turned them into a flaming shambles.

The fall of Okinawa on 21st June 1945, after nearly three months of fighting, marked the end of the island-hopping campaign. From the rebuilt airstrips bombers could now fly round-the-clock raids against Japanese cities, and carrier task forces were close enough to maintain a complete blockade of Japan. Operations continued against outlying garrisons, particularly in Borneo, and carrier aircraft methodi-

Above: Rather death than dishonour: a dead Japanese soldier lies in the sand of Namur islet, Kwajalein, in the Marshalls after squeezing the trigger of his rifle with his foot. Although Namur received a heavy preliminary bombardment, marines who assaulted the islet met stiff resistance from an intricate system of blockhouses. Left: US marine on Guadalcanal in the Solomons. Although landings on the island were unopposed, the Japanese soon reacted violently, and for nine months Guadalcanal was the scene of bitter battles.
Right: 1 Incendiary bombs rain from the bellies of American B-29s over Yokohama, Japan, May 1945. Forty per cent of the built-up area of more than sixty Japanese cities and towns was destroyed in these incendiary raids. 2 Kobe receives its third incendiary bomb raid on 5th June 1945. 3 View of railway yards near Osaka after American air raid

cally eliminated the surviving units of the Japanese Navy. Without fuel for ships or aircraft the Japanese were now helpless, and the end was a matter of time.

On 26th July the Allies issued the Potsdam Declaration, which stipulated unconditional surrender for the Japanese armed forces, though not for the Emperor or his government. It was hoped that this formula would allow the Japanese to 'save face', but when no clear reply was received the Allies set in motion plans for the final destruction of the country. The choice lay between the atomic bomb, terrible but costing no Allied soldiers' lives, or a gigantic invasion of the land, with the likelihood of one million casualties.

The choice of the bomb was inevitable, but in strictly military terms it was not necessary. The three-year campaign waged across the Pacific by the US Navy had brought Japan to its knees, and by July 1945 the mainland was 'besieged' by naval forces which enjoyed almost complete immunity. Battleships were shelling industrial targets in daylight, and air strikes could hit whenever and wherever they chose. It is hard to see how much longer the Japanese military authorities could have maintained any defence in the face of starvation and the collapse of civilian morale caused by a truly horrific scale of air raids.

The island-hopping campaign was primarily an exercise in sea power, both in attack and defence. It could only be waged by highly mobile task forces of aircraft carriers, supported by tankers and supply ships. Conversely it could only have worked against a maritime empire, for it was the deadly onslaught against the Japanese supply lines which made it so hard for them to launch any counter-attacks. But it also needed the fullest inter-service co-operation, and the land-based air forces and ground troops were all vital to the victory.

Left: Top: Marines burn out Japanese resistance with a flame-thrower, Guam, July 1944. Centre: Marines hug the beach after landing on Iwo Jima in the Bonin Islands, 19th February 1945. During the month that it took to break organized resistance on the formidably fortified island the Americans suffered 26,000 casualties of whom 6,800 were killed and when all resistance ceased on 26th March the 21,000-man garrison had been virtually annihilated. By the end of the war emergency landings had been made on the island by 2,251 B-29s which might otherwise have been forced to ditch in the Pacific. Bottom: Jubilant marines with a souvenir of war, Leyte Island, Philippines, December 1944. Right: Ecstatic Allied prisoners-of-war at a camp near Yokohama celebrate their liberation by American forces, August 1945

The Russians Reach Berlin

The last year of the Second World War was a year of decisive battles, the results of which affected the fate of many peoples. The thunder of the battles of the winter of 1943-44 died away and summer drew near. The belligerents surveyed the lessons of the campaign just over and began working on new plans. The Germans had much to think about, for the time when the course of the war on the Eastern Front was decided by Hitler's HQ and the German General Staff was past. The initiative now lay exclusively in the hands of the Soviet armed forces.

'We cannot win the war by military means,' wrote Jodl to Hitler in February 1944. A number of other German generals and statesmen shared his view, and there were serious grounds for holding it. Germany had failed in every military campaign from the hard-fought Battle of Stalingrad on suffering heavy losses. The country's economy was finding increasing difficulty in coping with the demands of war. The July Plot to assassinate Hitler was a reflection of Germany's worsening situation. The political, economic, and military superiority of the USSR over the Third Reich was obvious by summer 1944.

In 1944 the Soviet Union achieved great new successes in economic development and consequently a mighty advance in war production: 29,000 tanks and self-propelled guns, over 40,000 aircraft, and about 122,000 pieces of artillery. The Soviet rear ensured the supply to the front of an ever-increasing quantity of trains loaded with arms, equipment, and food. There was also an improvement in the quality of the guns, tanks, and aircraft produced, and new types of weapons, equipment, and shells made their appearance. All this led to an increase in the striking-power and mobility of the Red Army.

It should be mentioned that the war production of Germany and her allies also increased down to the second half of 1944. In the summer of that year German output of armaments and military equipment reached its highest level for the entire war. Yet the Nazi leaders were unable to raise their war economy to the level attained by the economy of the USSR and they were incapable of replacing the losses suffered by the German forces on the Soviet-German front. Then in the autumn of 1944 there was a serious decline in German war production. The chief cause of this

The end of Hitler's Thousand-Year Reich, Berlin, May 1945. Russian soldiers hoist the Red Flag above the Brandenburg Gate

decline was the victorious advance of the Red Army, which deprived Germany of numerous sources of strategic raw materials. The ever-increasing shortage of labour also had a considerable effect.

By the summer of 1944 Germany's position had become hopeless. This was the result not only of the decisions taken by Roosevelt, Churchill, and Stalin at the Tehran Conference of November 1943 but also of the Allied invasion of northern France. This huge, well-organized landing operation evoked a feeling of satisfaction in the Soviet Union but unfortunately the slow pace of the Allied advance failed for a long time to confirm the hopes aroused by the operation.

Meanwhile in the occupied countries of Europe popular liberation movements developed on a wider scale, and in the countries of the Nazi coalition—Finland, Rumania, Hungary—anti-war feeling and the desire to end association with Germany increased.

Military plans

Despite its heavy losses in previous campaigns, the German army was still, at the beginning of June 1944, strong in numbers and well-equipped. On the Soviet-German front it maintained, including the armies of Germany's allies, 228 divisions and 23 brigades, with over 4,000,000 men, 49,000 guns and mortars, 5,250 tanks and assault guns, and about 2,800 aircraft. In the West, in France, Belgium, and Holland, the Germans had at this time only 61 divisions.

The fundamental idea of the German plan for the further conduct of the war was set out in a report by Field-Marshal Keitel at a conference at Sonthofen on 5th May 1944. It was to employ the bulk of Germany's forces to maintain the defence of the Eastern Front while using the remainder to resist invasion from the West. The great hope of the Germans was to prolong the war and bring about a split between the Allies.

To make his defence line firmer Hitler had already ordered, in March 1944, that a system of fortresses and strong-points be constructed on the Eastern Front. He thus hoped to 'pin down as many Soviet troops as possible'. The generals appointed to command these fortresses were men who could be relied upon, it was considered, to hold them to the end, even if they should be surrounded. 'Only the army group commander personally may, with my approval, remove a fortress commander from his post and assign him to other tasks,' said the order.

The Defeat of the Axis

At the start of the summer offensive the Red Army's operational forces amounted to 6,425,000 men, with 92,500 guns and mortars, 7,750 tanks, and over 13,400 aircraft. The plan for the Soviet offensive envisaged the delivering of a sequence of powerful blows in different directions aimed at routing the enemy's principal groupings on Soviet territory, and the transferring of military operations on to enemy territory. The main blow was being prepared for the centre of the Soviet-German front, in Belorussia and the western regions of the Ukraine.

Stalin told Churchill about the plans of the Soviet Supreme Command for the summer of 1944. 'The summer offensive of the Soviet forces, organized in accordance with the agreement made at the Tehran Conference, will begin in the middle of June on one of the important sectors of the front,' he wrote on 6th June. 'Our general offensive will be developed in stages by the successive involvement of the armies in offensive operations. At the end of June and during July, offensive operations will be transformed into a general offensive by the Soviet forces.'

In their estimate of the intentions of the Soviet Supreme Command the Nazi leadership committed an irrevocable mistake. At a conference of Eastern Front army commanders in May 1944 Keitel reported: 'Given our information on the regrouping of the enemy forces and the overall military and political situation, it must be reckoned that the Russians will probably concentrate their main forces on the southern sector of the front. They are not now in a position to give battle in several main directions at the same time.' This false assumption by the German General Staff was skilfully exploited by the Soviet Supreme Command.

The summer offensive begins
The task of beginning the summer offensive of 1944 fell to the forces on the Karelian and Leningrad fronts, commanded by Generals Meretskov and Govorov. Despite the strong fortifications confronting them, and the forested, marshy, lake-covered terrain, unfavourable to offensive

February 1945: Soviet infantry march through Kraków, the ancient former capital of Poland

operations, the forces of these fronts made considerable progress on the Karelian Isthmus and in Karelia. Field-Marshal Schörner's Army Group North was forced back to the Finnish Frontier, suffering heavy losses and abandoning the towns of Vyborg and Petrozavodsk. The Kirov railway and the White Sea-Baltic canal, of great importance as transport arteries, were cleared of German troops. Influenced by these military developments, Finland's President Riuti, one of Germany's most fervent supporters, resigned his office. On 4th September Finland broke off relations with Germany, and, although German troops continued to hold positions in the north of Finland, a fortnight later an armistice agreement was signed between the Finnish and Soviet governments.

The offensive in Karelia was in full swing when the Red Army began operations on the central sector of the Soviet-German front. On 23rd and 24th June, 1st Baltic front and the three Belorussian fronts, commanded by Generals Bagramyan, Chernyakhovsky, Zakharov, and Rokossovsky, began their offensive. This offensive in Belorussia was disastrous for the Germans. Army Group Centre, commanded by General Busch, was routed. Large concentrations of German forces were surrounded and destroyed before Vitebsk and Bobruysk, to the east of Minsk, and around Brest Litovsk and Wilno. On 17th July 57,000 German prisoners-of-war captured in the Soviet offensive were marched round Moscow's ring road. The Belorussian Republic, a considerable part of Poland, most of Lithuania, and part of Latvia were liberated from German occupation. Soviet forces reached the frontiers of East Prussia and the Rivers Narew and Vistula. Favourable conditions had been created for the final liberation of Poland and the invasion of Germany but the offensive potential of the Soviet forces operating in this direction was for the time being exhausted.

The tragic events which occurred in Warsaw can still be keenly felt. Polish reactionary circles irresponsibly encouraged the inhabitants of the city to launch an ill-prepared uprising without prior agreement with the Soviet military command. The result was the killing by the Germans of many thousands of people and the complete destruction of Warsaw.

The success of the Belorussian offensive facilitated the Red Army's operations elsewhere. To the north, in the middle of July, 2nd and 3rd Baltic fronts went over to the offensive, and by the end of August liberated a substantial part of the Baltic region. To the south, 1st Ukrainian front, commanded by Marshal Konev inflicted a major defeat on General Harpe's Army Group North Ukraine. Konev's forces reached the banks of the Vistula and the foothills of the Carpathians. Almost the whole of the Soviet Ukraine and the south-eastern parts of Poland were now freed. A large bridgehead was established on the far side of the Vistula in the region of Sandomierz, and this, together with bridgeheads to the south of Warsaw conquered by Rokossovsky's forces, created favourable conditions for a further advance westward. The total losses of the German armies on the Eastern Front between 1st June and 31st August were, according to German figures, some 917,000 men. German losses in the West in the same period came to 294,000 men.

Offensive in the south

The German command believed in the summer of 1944 that the Red Army had its hands full with operations against Army Groups North and Centre and that consequently a big offensive against Army Group South Ukraine was 'improbable' in the near future. They were mistaken.

Early in the morning of 20th August, 2nd and 3rd Ukrainian fronts, under Generals Malinovsky and Tolbukhin, began a powerful new offensive on the southern wing of the Soviet front in the region of Jassy and Kishinev. On the fifth day of the offensive Soviet forces surrounded the main forces of Army Group South Ukraine. The total losses suffered by Army Group South Ukraine exceeded half a million men. Between 20th August and 3rd September alone the Soviet forces took 208,000 prisoners including twenty-one generals.

Malinovsky's forces went on, by the end of September, to liberate almost the whole of Rumania and reach the frontiers of Hungary and Yugoslavia. During the next three months they continued to strike blows at Army Group South, freed the northern part of Transylvania, took Debreczen, crossed the Tisza on a wide front, and opened the road to Budapest.

Meanwhile Tolbukhin's forces cleared the northern Dobruja and crossed the Bulgarian border. By the end of September Bulgaria had been completely cleared of German troops. Then, together with the People's Liberation Army of Yugoslavia, Tolbukhin's troops liberated the eastern part of Yugoslavia.

The liberation of the Ukrainian areas of Transcarpathia was also completed in this period. By the end of October, 4th Ukrainian front under General Petrov had cleared the Germans from the towns of Mukačevo and Užhorod.

The end of October saw the start of the Budapest operation and on 26th December troops under Malinovsky and Tolbukhin encircled the 188,000 enemy troops in the Hungarian capital. The subsequent warding off of the enemy's several attempts to relieve the besieged troops went on until their eventual destruction by Soviet forces in mid-February 1945.

These operations in the south were distinguished by their speed, flexibility, and great scope. One operation led to another without any lengthy pauses for the preparation of a new advance. The Red Army showed great ability in surrounding and destroying large forces of the enemy in a wide variety of circumstances – in open country, in large cities, along the seashore. There was skilful co-operation between the fronts and the air arm, the Black Sea Fleet, the Danube Flotilla, and the Soviet anti-aircraft defences.

The successful offensive of the Red Army on the southern wing of the Soviet-German front brought the people of South-Eastern Europe liberation from Nazi rule and enabled them to re-establish their independence. Anti-Nazi governments came to power in Rumania on 24th August and Bulgaria on 8th September. In Hungary the Provisional National Assembly, opened in Debreczen in the second half of December, elected a new government, so giving legislative form to the overthrow of the fascist regime. Under their new governments these countries did not merely cease to fight on Germany's side, they declared war against their former ally and their troops fought alongside those of the Red Army.

The strategic situation on the Soviet-German front continued to improve. Soviet forces entered the eastern part of Czechoslovakia, and took up suitable positions for advancing further into Czechoslovakia, Austria, and southern Germany.

Successes in the north

The successes achieved on the central sector of the front and on the southern wing made it possible to undertake the final liberation of Soviet territory in the Baltic region and within the Arctic Circle.

On 14th September the forces of 3rd, 2nd, and 1st Baltic fronts, commanded by Generals Maslennikov, Yeremenko, and Bagramyan, moved into action to liberate Riga, while the troops of the Leningrad front, commanded by Marshal Govorov, aided by the Baltic Fleet, struck at Tallinn. Soon the flag of free Estonia was raised on Tallinn's ancient tower of Toompea. On 15th October Soviet forces drove the German forces out of Riga, and by the end of October all Latvia had been freed.

The operations in the Baltic region resulted in the rout of a large strategic grouping of enemy forces, the release of a large number of Soviet forces for other tasks, and the capture of naval bases for the Baltic Fleet. The Red Army reached the Baltic Sea along a wide front.

On the northern flank of the Soviet-

The Defeat of the Axis

German front the troops of 14th Karelian front, commanded by General Meretskov, with the help of the Northern Fleet, commanded by Admiral Golovko, spent three weeks of October 1944 in smashing German XX Mountain Army and liberating the Petsamo region. Soviet forces entered Norway and began the liberation of that country from the Nazis.

The year 1945 had begun. The Red Army had been victorious on all fronts and the Anglo-American forces had also had considerable success, driving the Germans out of northern Italy, France, and Belgium. Germany was being squeezed between two fronts, east and west. The Soviet General Staff saw the strategic situation as one in which Germany could be completely crushed in the very near future. 'Essentially, the Soviet army and the Anglo-American forces had won positions from which they could proceed to a decisive offensive against Germany's vital centres,' wrote General Shtemenko, former head of the Operations Department of the Soviet General Staff. 'It was now a matter of making a final vigorous thrust and finishing off the enemy in a short time.'

The Nazi leaders still had no intention, however, of acknowledging their defeat. They were still striving to prolong the war, to bring about a split between the Allies, and to make a separate peace with the West. The greater part of the Wehrmacht was concentrated on the Soviet-German front. Here there were over 179 German and 16 Hungarian divisions. These forces amounted to over 3,000,000 men, 28,000 guns and mortars, about 4,000 tanks and assault guns, and 2,000 aircraft. Between the Vistula and the Oder the Germans had equipped seven defence lines, which it was hoped would halt the Soviet advance. At this time 107 German divisions were fighting in the West against the forces of Great Britain and the United States.

'Fanaticization' of the struggle
To strengthen the resistance put up by their forces on German soil, the German command issued an order for the 'fanaticization' of the struggle. 'In the zone of military operations,' said this order, 'our fight must be carried on with the utmost stubbornness, and every able-bodied man must be used to the fullest extent. Every bunker, every quarter of every German town, and every German village must be turned into a fortress where either the enemy will be drained of blood or the garrison will perish in hand-to-hand fighting and be buried under the ruins. There can

German soldiers captured by the Russians. The signpost, in Russian, points forty-two kilometres to Berlin

be no alternative but defence of one's position or annihilation.'

The Red Army's operational forces at this time were very strong, amounting to about 6,000,000 men, with 91,400 guns and mortars, about 11,000 tanks and self-propelled artillery mountings, and 14,500 aircraft.

So as to break the German's resistance once and for all and force them to surrender, the Soviet Supreme Command decided to destroy the largest concentrations of German troops and finish the war victoriously along with the Allied armies. The main blow was to fall on Berlin. At the Yalta Conference, held in February 1945, Roosevelt, Churchill, and Stalin agreed on and planned in detail 'the timing, scale, and co-ordination of fresh and even more powerful blows to be struck at the heart of Germany . . . from east, west, north and south.'

The Red Army's offensive in the final campaign was planned for 20th January 1945, but at the request of the British Prime Minister, in connection with the setbacks suffered by the Allied forces in the Ardennes, it was brought forward by eight days. Simultaneously, five fronts struck at the enemy along a line 750 miles long, stretching from the Baltic Sea to the Carpathians. After the first breakthroughs, large tank formations rushed deep into the rear of the enemy defence.

On 17th February the British Prime Minister sent congratulations to Moscow on the gigantic offensive that had begun. It was followed next day by a message from President Roosevelt who wrote that the heroic feats of the Soviet soldiers and the efficiency they had already shown in their offensive gave grounds for hoping that the Allied forces would soon be winning victories on all fronts.

The successes achieved were indeed tremendous. The Germans were defeated in East Prussia and Pomerania. On the main line of the offensive Soviet troops reached the Oder at the beginning of February. In March they cleared the enemy from the whole of the right bank of the Oder and widened their bridgehead on its western bank in the Küstrin area. The Baltic ports of Danzig and Gdynia were also liberated in March, and Soviet troops south of the Carpathians repulsed a German offensive near Lake Balaton.

It is sometimes asked whether the Rus-

*Top: Street fighting in Berlin, April 1945. Red Army machine-gun emplacement. Centre: Marshal Zhukov, the conqueror of Berlin, on the steps of the Reichstag. Russian soldiers have scratched their names on the columns. **Bottom:** Eastern Front meets Western Front, April 1945*

The Defeat of the Axis

'Death to the German invaders!' Soviet poster of 1945. The Red Army thrusts at the heart of Nazi Germany—Berlin

sians could not have taken Berlin by storm immediately after their arrival on the banks of the Oder in February 1945. Careful analysis shows that they could not. In their impetuous advance westward the fronts had left their rear services lagging behind and the troops were experiencing shortages of munitions and fuel. 1st Belorussian front was greatly weakened by its previous advance of more than 250 miles and the main forces of the front had been sent to the north where, as Keitel said after the war, the German High Command intended 'to launch a counter-offensive against the forces advancing on Berlin, utilizing for this purpose the Pomeranian bridgehead'. In addition the Germans were reinforcing their already considerable forces between the Vistula and the Oder, and concentrating new forces on Hungarian territory, hoping to thrust Tolbukhin's troops back across the Danube. To have attempted to capture Berlin by storm in such circumstances as these would have been highly dangerous. By eliminating the danger on the flanks and by making thorough preparations for the advance on Berlin, the Russians were able to ensure that the operation, when it came, was really crushing.

The struggle for Berlin

The Red Army went on to occupy East Prussia and Pomerania, to liberate Poland and a substantial part of Czechoslovakia, to complete the liberation of Hungary, and to enter Austria. The powerful Soviet offensive forced the German command in January 1945 to send against it the bulk of the forces which had been until then

fighting the Allied troops in the Ardennes. In February and March the Anglo-American forces pushed the enemy back to the Rhine and seized a number of bridgeheads on its east bank.

Berlin was now the Red Army's next objective. The Germans were ready to defend their capital 'to the last man and the last bullet'. One million men had been concentrated in the Berlin sector, with 10,400 guns and mortars, 1,500 tanks and assault guns and 3,300 aircraft. The Berlin garrison amounted to more than 200,000 men. The defence consisted of an outer belt of minefields, outer and inner defence zones, and the defended area itself. The underground railway and the network of drains were to be used for defending the city. Railway and road bridges, and other large installations were prepared for demolition in the event of Soviet troops getting through. Blocks of flats and reinforced concrete structures were transformed into fortified strong points. An order by General Reimann, the commandant of Berlin, demanded that every quarter of the city be defended at all costs, and likewise every house, every storey, every fence, and every shell-hole. 'The struggle for Berlin can decide the outcome of the war,' was the watchword inspiring the defenders of Germany's capital.

The Soviet Supreme Command assigned 2nd and 1st Belorussian fronts and 1st Ukrainian front, commanded by Marshals Rokossovsky, Zhukov, and Konev, to take part in the historic battle for the German capital. These fronts numbered 2,500,000 men, with more than 42,000 guns and mortars, over 6,200 tanks and self-propelled guns, and 8,300 aircraft.

Not long before the operation began—on 12 April 1945—President Roosevelt died. The death of the leader of one of the Allied states was viewed by the Nazis as the possible start of a new political situation. But such hopes were vain. On 16th April the Russians began their massive assault on Berlin.

Tens of thousands of guns and mortars began a mighty barrage just before dawn. After this artillery preparation assault troops, supported by aircraft, moved to the attack. A fierce conflict developed. Despite the stubborn resistance put up by the Germans, the Oder-Neisse defence line was broken and attempts to hold lines behind this one also ended in failure. On the night of 21st April Soviet troops broke into the outskirts of Berlin. Bloody battles took place in the streets of the city. On 25th April the armies of Zhukov and Konev linked up to the west of Berlin and completed the encirclement of the city. On the same day one of Konev's divisions encountered forward units of American 1st Army in the Torgau area, an event marked by

mutual greetings and firm handshakes. The day before, German IX Army had been surrounded to the south-east of Berlin. By a decisive blow from the Soviet divisions the opposing German forces were surrounded and cut into two parts, each of which was then destroyed separately.

On 30th April Soviet soldiers broke into the Reichstag building and on the same day Hitler killed himself. As the hour of reckoning drew near, his close assistants fled in all directions, like rats from a sinking ship. Only two days earlier Hitler's fellow dictator Mussolini had been arrested and shot by Italian partisans who had discovered him attempting to flee.

Berlin falls

On the morning of 1st May, the Red Flag was hoisted over the statuary which rises above the columns of the main entrance to the Reichstag building. This was a banner proclaiming that the road to peace, freedom, independence, and social progress had been opened. On 2nd May the German garrison of Berlin headed by General Weidling surrendered. On 8th May at Karlshorst plenipotentiaries of the German High Command, headed by Keitel, signed a document of unconditional surrender in the presence of representatives of the USSR, Great Britain, the USA, and France. The war in Europe had ended in complete victory for the Allies.

The German people had paid dearly for Hitler's crimes. Germany's total losses in the Second World War amounted to 13,600,000 men of whom ten million fell on the Soviet-German front. During the war the Soviet armed forces destroyed or took prisoner more than 500 German divisions and 100 divisions of Germany's satellites. On the Soviet-German front Germany lost the bulk of her artillery and tanks, seventy-five per cent of her aircraft, and 1,600 warships and transport vessels. The Allied forces defeated 176 enemy divisions in Western Europe, North Africa, and Italy.

The Russians reached Berlin after overcoming very grave ordeals and winning many battles on a grand scale. It took them 1,418 days to reach the German capital and win victory. It was a thorny path, demanding unprecedented efforts and enormous sacrifices. Out of the total of fifty million people killed in the Second World War, twenty million were Soviet citizens, and of these about fifty per cent were civilians and prisoners-of-war, killed or tortured to death on occupied Soviet territory.

The fall of Berlin and the arrival of the Allied armies on the Elbe showed the inexhaustible possibilities possessed by the United Nations when their efforts are directed in common toward the attainment of just aims.

The Fall of the Dictators

During the evening of Sunday, 29th April 1945, the short-wave receiver in Adolf Hitler's underground shelter in Berlin—the 'bunker'—picked up a broadcast from Radio Stockholm reporting the death of Benito Mussolini, struck down the previous day near Milan by Italian partisans. A few minutes later the text of the broadcast was shown to Hitler. It was in this way that the Führer learned of the death of the Duce, the man he had never ceased to admire. When he read this report, Adolf Hitler's decision had already been taken. Next day he would join his old comrade, in death.

On 17th April Mussolini had left his villa at Salò, near Gargnano, on the shore of Lake Garda. Abandoning Rachele, his wife, he had decided to go to Milan. After Otto Skorzeny had rescued the Duce from captivity on the Gran Sasso in September 1943, Mussolini was still full of hope. When he met Hitler after his escape, the latter had confided in him that secret weapons were about to change the course of the war. But then the Allies had landed in Normandy. The Russian advance had become a flood. In Italy the Americans, British, and French had crossed the Apennines and turned Kesselring's retreat into a rout. For Mussolini as for so many others the hour had struck for an end to illusions. Physically he was now no more than a shadow of himself. When his mistress Claretta Petacci rejoined him beside Lake Garda she found him, as she said later, 'flacco, debilitato, svagato'—weakened, debilitated, ravaged. In fact Mussolini suffered from a stomach ulcer which his grave worries had considerably aggravated.

When, on 17th April, Mussolini decided to leave for Milan, the neo-Fascist governmental institutions set up after his escape no longer existed except in theory. The Committee of National Liberation had decreed that the Fascist leaders could be executed without trial.

Mussolini as the ill, ageing head of the puppet Salò Republic just before his final flight in April 1945

Everything that Mussolini did at this stage shows that he realized he was no longer able to control his fate. He said: 'I am close to the end . . . I await the epilogue of this tragedy in which I no longer have a part to play. I made a mistake, and I shall pay for it, if my life can still serve as payment.'

On 21st April news of the capture of Bologna reached Milan; on the 23rd the fall of Parma was reported. Mussolini's entourage asked the Germans for an aeroplane, in order to enable the Duce to escape to Spain. Mussolini himself had not been consulted on the matter. In any case, the occupying authorities refused to provide the aeroplane.

On the morning of the 24th Mussolini received his last message from Hitler. It told that the Soviet forces had entered Berlin. That same day Gian-Riccardo Cella, an industrialist, asked to meet Mussolini. When he was in the Duce's presence, Cella revealed that he was a member of the Committee of National Liberation. He wished to spare Milan the horrors of civil war. Since the defeat of Fascism was an accomplished fact, why should not Mussolini hand over his powers to the resistance? Mussolini replied calmly that it was an interesting proposal. He required, however, to be given guarantees for himself, his people, his entourage. During the afternoon Cella reported to the committee on his interview with Mussolini and its outcome. The committee proposed to Mussolini a meeting on the following day, at 5 pm, at the residence of the Archbishop of Milan, Cardinal Schuster. Mussolini agreed. 'At this moment,' we are told by those who had dealings with him then, 'he showed no irritability, only great fatigue.'

'The Germans have betrayed us'

Next day, at the time arranged, the meeting took place. It lasted an hour. With Cardinal Schuster as chairman, Mussolini, Marshal Graziani, the Fascist ministers Barracu and Zerbino, and the prefect of Milan, Bassi, faced General Cadorna, the advocates Marazza and Arpesani, and the engineer, Lombardi. Mussolini asked what guarantee could be given to Fascists who surrendered, and to himself. The reply was: 'The ordinary guarantees given to prisoners-of-war.' Mussolini then asked in whose name the undertaking would be given and was told: 'In the name of the Committee of National Liberation and of the Allies.'

It was proposed that the Duce spend the night at the Archbishop's house. There he would be regarded as a prisoner-of-war and kept in hiding until the Allies arrived. Marshal Graziani broke in roughly: 'We will not make an agreement behind the

The bodies of Mussolini and Claretta Petacci strung up in Milan. Mussolini's face was horribly distorted, but many were struck by Claretta's look of peace

Germans' backs, because fidelity to an ally is a sign of honour and justifies our attitude in the past.'

General Cadorna replied ironically: 'This concern for the Germans seems misplaced. They have been negotiating with us for a long time now, behind your backs.' Cardinal Schuster confirmed this, producing evidence of secret negotiations carried on between the Wehrmacht and the Italian resistance. Mussolini stood up, flushed with anger, and shouted: 'They have always treated us like dogs, and in the end they have betrayed us!'

Turning towards the members of the committee, he said, more calmly: 'Very well. I accept all your conditions. First of all, though, I want to see the Germans . . . I mean to throw this premeditated treason in the face of these people who, for so many years, have been calling us traitors. As soon as I have done that I shall come back here and sign whatever you want.' Then he left, saying that he would be back in an hour. When he went out the time was 7.15 pm.

He did not return. When he got back to the prefecture of Milan he encountered the German general in command there. He went straight up to him and insulted him: the Germans were, he said, 'traitors and cheats'. After that, he appears to have been called on by Milan's prefect of police, who implored him vehemently not to go back to the Archbishop's house. The prefect of police did not believe that the Committee of National Liberation was in a

position to honour its promises. Mussolini would not be handed over to the Allies but to a people's tribunal, and everyone knew what that would mean. Perhaps this explains why Mussolini did not return to the Archbishop's house. Perhaps he had never intended to do so. What is certain is that on 25th April 1945, at 8 pm, Mussolini had given up the idea of negotiating with the resistance. At that hour he left Milan in his open Alfa-Romeo, escorted by a line of cars occupied by panic-stricken Fascist dignitaries. The column was preceded by a German detachment made up of ten cars and two armoured cars, together with an Italian detachment. In one of the private cars was Claretta Petacci, Mussolini's mistress. The rear of the column was brought up by trucks loaded with fifty-six suitcases, large and small, containing state papers and the Republic's 'treasury' – amounting to two thousand million present-day lire or about a million pounds. As the column emerged on to the Como motorway, explosions rent the air. The first battles between partisans and Fascists had begun in the suburbs of Milan.

At 9 pm the column arrived at the prefecture of Como where Mussolini stayed seven hours. During the night he wrote a last letter to his wife: 'Here I am, on the last lap of my life, at the last page of my book.' He told her he was going to make for the Valtellina with some Fascist partisans. He advised his wife and children to try to get to Switzerland, or else to give themselves up to the Allies. 'I ask your forgiveness for all the harm I have done you without wishing to. But you know that you are the only woman I have really loved.' A little later that night, Mussolini managed to contact Rachele by telephone. 'There is no-one left. I am alone . . . Rachele, you will start a new life, but I must follow my destiny.'

At dawn the column set off again, now much reduced. In front was the German car occupied by Lieutenant Birzer, entrusted with Mussolini's 'security'. Then came Mussolini's own car, followed by an SS van and a car belonging to the SD (Security and Intelligence Service of the SS). The Duce was obviously now a mere prisoner – the prisoner of his former allies. Apparently Mussolini did not know where he was going. That evening they halted at Menaggio, not yet having left Lake Como. There it was that Claretta found Mussolini again, after having done everything she could to rejoin him. Next day they continued their journey. Mussolini said no more about the Valtellina redoubt. The Fascist partisans whom he had summoned to his side for this 'last stand' had failed to turn up – another disappointment. And so they drove on northward, towards the Swiss frontier. Though the Swiss had announced officially that they would not allow Mussolini to enter their country, it seems likely that the Duce wished to attempt this as a last resort. In the previous few days he had several times remarked: 'I am a Freeman of the city of Lausanne.'

After leaving Menaggio the column met up, by chance, with a German Luftwaffe convoy going north—about twenty trucks—and decided to merge with it. Towards noon, just before reaching the village of Dongo, the column came to a halt, its way suddenly blocked by barricades. The partisans of 52nd Garibaldi Brigade were stopping the convoy. The partisan leaders came forward. Their names were Bellini Della Stelle, nicknamed Pedro, and Costatina Lazzari, who preferred to be called Bill. They explained that they had been ordered to let the Germans through but to stop the Italian Fascists escaping. Accordingly they had to check the cars and trucks. The German major agreed to this inspection. The partisans made Claretta Petacci and her brother Marcello get out of the car they were in. They examined the first two trucks but found nothing of interest. In the third, amid a seated group of six German soldiers, the partisans noticed a man crumpled up against the driver's cabin, wearing a Wehrmacht sergeant-major's greatcoat. A young German lieutenant explained: 'He's drunk.'

Mussolini's flight is checked

Two partisans, Ortelli and Peralli, then noticed that the man was wearing boots of good-quality leather, and also that he had sun-glasses on, although the sun was not shining. They ordered him to get out. He obeyed, jumping to the ground. Someone removed his glasses. There was a cry of astonishment: it was Mussolini.

They took him to the municipal offices. The villagers gathered round, amazed, unable to believe their eyes. Calmly, Mussolini drank a cup of coffee. He was asked questions about the war and about his government, and he replied to them. He was coping with the situation, very much at his ease. That evening he was taken to the customs-officers' barracks at Germasino. It was raining. At 11 pm, after eating a meal, Mussolini lay down on a camp bed which had been prepared for him. He was not left to sleep for long. Shortly after 1 am on the morning of 28th April he was awakened. Apparently the resistance leaders feared intervention by the partisans of the extreme Left and had therefore decided to take Mussolini to the residence of the industrialist Cademartori, four miles from Como, on the lake shore. Concealed in this place of refuge the Duce would be safe until the Americans arrived. At 1.35 am a car drove away with Pedro and his prisoner. As it left the village of

Cover of post-war novelette about Mussolini and Claretta. Their affair preserved an aura of romance despite the violent reaction against Fascism

Dongo this car passed another one, containing Claretta Petacci. Once more, Benito and Claretta had found each other; they were not to be separated again. During the night major decisions had been taken in Milan. The Committee of National Liberation, which had hitherto favoured turning the Duce over to the Americans, had changed its mind. Cadorna tells us: 'I imagined the consequences for Italy of the capture of Mussolini by the Allies and the spectacular trial that would inevitably ensue, which would become a trial of Italy's political life during the past twenty years—whereas silence was now needed regarding facts and circumstances in which it would be hard to distinguish between the responsibility of the nation and that of its leader... In any case, I would never of my own free will have undertaken to arrange for Mussolini to be handed over to the Allies, to be judged and executed by foreigners.'

A certain Walter Audisio, a Communist partisan who used the name 'Colonel Valerio', came to see Cadorna. He told him that he had instructions to 'go and find Mussolini and execute him'. It seems clear that the general did nothing to hinder this 'mission'. He even dictated a document which looked like a grant of full power.

Valerio set off at once, at full speed, along the Como road. Pedro has told how, as he was driving towards Como with Mussolini, he heard a sound of shooting. On the advice of one of his companions, Captain Neri, he decided to take Mussolini and Claretta Petacci into the house of a peasant

patriot at Bolzanigo, above Azzano. There it was, in this little isolated house, in a tiny room with whitewashed walls, scantily furnished with a double bed, a dressing-table with a washbasin, and some straw-bottomed chairs, that Mussolini and his mistress spent the rest of the night, and also the morning and the first part of the afternoon of the day. At mid-day their peasant hosts, the De Maria family, gave them polenta with milk, and some bread and sausage, which the prisoners ate in silence. There was water to drink.

At 4 pm, a civilian in a raincoat, accompanied by two men in khaki uniform, burst into the room. It was Colonel Valerio. He told Mussolini he had come to release him. The Duce's eyes at first showed great amazement, then lit up with joy: 'I will give you an empire!'

Claretta dressed hurriedly and Mussolini put on his greatcoat. They left the house and got into a black Fiat 1100, which set off towards Lake Como. The driver, who had been conscripted for the job by Valerio, later told Bandini: 'I could see the couple in the driving mirror. They were sitting close together, their heads touching. Mussolini was pale, the lady seemed calm. They didn't appear to me to be particularly frightened.'

The car stopped before the gate of the Villa Belmonte, one of those fine residences of which there are so many along the shores of Lake Como. Valerio said to Mussolini and Claretta: 'Get out.' He pushed them towards a low wall two yards away. He spoke a few words very quickly, talking of an order and a sentence of death. 'Mussolini did not stir, it was as though his thoughts were elsewhere,' the driver recalls, 'but Claretta suddenly showed great energy. She clung to Mussolini and looked from Valerio to him and back again. "No, you can't, you can't do that!" Her expression was terribly strained, her voice was shaky, her eyes were wild. In a dry tense voice Valerio exclaimed: "Get out of the way or I'll shoot you as well." But Claretta remained pressed against Mussolini as if she had not heard.'

Valerio pulled the trigger of his weapon. It failed to go off. One of the other partisans handed him his sub-machine-gun. Mussolini clutched his greatcoat, opened it and said in a loud voice: 'Aim at my breast.'

'At that very moment,' the driver tells us, 'Claretta was standing on Mussolini's left, partly protecting him. Valerio fired the fatal burst—I think there was only one, continuous burst. The first to be shot was Claretta, who fell to the ground with a dull thud. She neither screamed nor groaned; and I had the impression that she had fallen before the bullets hit her. Mussolini fell almost immediately after her, but his fall was hindered by the wall, against which he slid slowly to the ground. He was in a bent position, his right shoulder against the wall, and he reached the ground as though sitting down on his legs as they folded under him, almost squatting. . . . Mussolini's throat rattled for several seconds, sepulchrally, and this affected me deeply. He seemed to be breathing hard. Valerio pulled out his revolver, went forward, checked where Mussolini's heart was, and fired a coup de grâce. Mussolini's body gave a last convulsion and then moved no more.'

A little later, Valerio presided at Dongo over the execution of fifteen Fascist army officers who had been arrested along with Mussolini. The bodies of Mussolini and Claretta were added to the fifteen bodies thrown on to a truck. Next day all seventeen were taken to a yard in front of a garage at a corner of the Piazza Loreto in Milan. A noose was pulled tight around Mussolini's feet and he was hoisted up to the roof of the garage porch, so that his head hung six feet above the ground. Beside him they hung Claretta, also by the feet. Then a great silence fell on the jeering crowd. 'It was as if,' said a man who was there, 'we had all in those few seconds shared in the realization that there had been a time when we would have given his dead body the honours due to a hero, and the prayers worthy of a saint.'

Death of Adolf Hitler

All that now remained of Hitler's empire was a narrow corridor in the middle of Germany and a few pockets of resistance in the south. On 16th April 1945, at 5 am, Marshal Zhukov's offensive had begun, with the Soviet forces attacking on a front nearly 250 miles long. The Battle of Berlin had begun; it was to end on 2nd May, at 3 pm, with the city's fall.

Adolf Hitler had lived through this battle under fifteen yards of concrete, in his underground shelter in the Reich Chancellery. Berlin was dying. Crushed beneath bombs and shells, the city was burning down. Who could doubt, in this situation, that the defeat of the Third Reich was inevitable? It was no longer anything but a matter of days, or even of hours. The extraordinary feature of this unprecedented tragedy was, however, that one man in Berlin did still believe a Nazi victory to be possible. That man was Adolf Hitler.

In these days Captain Gerhardt Boldt, General Guderian's aide-de-camp, was taken aback by the wretched physical state of the Führer. 'His head sways slightly. His left arm hangs down as if paralysed, the hand trembling all the time. His eyes shine in an indescribable way, suggesting almost inhuman anguish. His face and the pockets under his eyes show how tired he

is, and how exhausted. He moves like an old man.' Hitler's hair was now almost white, and he walked with a stoop.

On 20th April he celebrated his fifty-sixth birthday. This was the last official ceremony of the Third Reich. The dignitaries came to the bunker to offer their good wishes to the dictator: Göring, Himmler, Goebbels, Ribbentrop, Bormann, Arthur Axmann, leader of the Hitler Youth, Admiral Dönitz, Field-Marshal Keitel, General Krebs, and General Karl Koller, Chief of Staff of the Air Force. We must picture these visitors lined up in the concrete central corridor, and Hitler walking down the line, shaking their hands and thanking them. The survivors of the occasion have recorded how their hearts were wrung by the sight of this tattered remnant of a human being. But that did not stop propaganda minister Goebbels from proclaiming on the radio: 'I can assure you that the Führer is in the best of health. As always, he is at the head of his troops, bringing them encouragement and inspiration.'

Himmler had come from his headquarters in the north, Göring from his in the south. These two men had only one thing in common: they both knew all was lost. There was only one hope, that a separate peace might be made with the Western Allies. Himmler was already preparing through Count Bernadotte, of the Swedish royal family, to negotiate on his own behalf. That day he dared, for the first time, to implore Hitler to stop the fighting. Hitler refused. Himmler then urged him at last to leave Berlin. Hitler again refused, reiterating his confidence in victory. In his view the Soviet forces had taken a risk in attacking Berlin. It was still possible to defeat them outside the city. On the morning of 21st April, Hitler ordered an offensive to be launched. General Steiner of the SS would take command of some of the troops defending Berlin and attack in the suburbs of the city. This attack by XI Army would sound the knell of the Soviet adventure. Next day at 3 pm, when the routine military conference began, the Führer immediately asked for news of XI Army. No-one spoke. 'I demand a reply! Has Steiner attacked?' General Krebs did not dare reply. It was General Jodl who spoke up. The fragments of units stationed in Berlin were so disorganized that it had not been possible to bring them together into a single force. XI Army had remained a fantasy, a dream in the brain of Adolf Hitler alone. Worse still, in order to create Steiner's army, units had been withdrawn from the front north of Berlin, and the Russians, finding themselves facing abandoned positions, had immediately attacked there. As Jodl was speaking, the Soviet troops were entering Berlin.

Then Hitler burst into one of those frightful rages that terrified those around him: 'I have been betrayed by the SS! This is something I should never have expected! By the SS!'

He went on shouting for a long time, denouncing everybody and everything. All the same, he had not yet accepted defeat. During the night of 22nd-23rd April he sent Keitel to see General Wenck, commanding XII Army, located fifty miles west of Berlin. Wenck was an excellent general. Keitel told him Hitler's orders – to march at once on Berlin and relieve the capital. This was in fact, Hitler's last idea. In the next few days he was to follow on the map the advance of Wenck's army, declaring himself confident that Wenck, in a lightning counter-offensive, would drive back 'the Asiatic invader'.

What did Wenck's army really amount to? Made up of remnants of various formations, reinforced by boys of the Hitler Youth and veterans of the First World War – the Volkssturm – it dragged itself along broken roads to obey Hitler's command. At a point ten miles south of Potsdam Wenck's force linked up with General Busse's 40,000 men, who were as worn out as they were and had no ammunition left. Frenzied orders kept coming from the bunker. Wenck's army was called upon to attack forthwith. In the midst of such a catastrophic situation, orders like this took on a sinister, nightmarish quality. Busse and Wenck put their heads together. These soldiers, who had up to that moment always been slaves to discipline, decided for the first time in their lives to disobey orders. A man who gave such orders at such a moment was no longer worthy to be the leader of the German people. Wenck and Busse resolved to fall back and lead their men towards the American lines, so as to spare them the fate of being taken prisoner by the Russians.

The strong concrete revetment of the bunker protected its inmates from bombs and shells. Those fifteen yards of concrete seem to have cut them off from reality as well. In the central corridor of the bunker Hitler presided every day over a general staff meeting. One door, to the left, led to the series of six rooms which constituted the quarters of Hitler and Eva Braun, the discreet partner of his days of glory, and now of misfortune.

'My orders are that Berlin be relieved at once. Where is Heinrici? What is Wenck's army up to? What is happening to XI Army? When are Wenck and Busse going to link up?' This was the message that Keitel received from Hitler: a message woven out of anguish. And, naturally, Keitel gave back no answer. After further demands, the answer so intensely awaited was given, at about 8 pm on the 28th. It did not bear Keitel's signature—he was obviously terrified. It merely reported, in very few words, that Wenck's army had ceased to exist.

Eye-witnesses tell us that when Hitler read this message he said nothing, but withdrew into his room. The Soviet forces were now only a few hundred yards from the Chancellery. And only now did Adolf Hitler concede his defeat. During that evening of 28th April Hitler told his orderly officer Heinz Linge that he was going to marry Eva Braun—to marry her before he died. Goebbels was instructed to summon to the Chancellery an official competent to solemnize the marriage. Extremely scared, the registrar Walter Wagner arrived at the bunker not knowing what he was expected to do. On 29th April, about half past midnight, he married Adolf Hitler to Eva Braun. Stammering, he asked the Führer to state whether he was of Aryan extraction. With complete seriousness the Führer replied that he was, as also did Eva Braun. When they had exchanged their vows, they each signed the register. The bride began by writing 'Eva B. .', then struck out the B and wrote: 'Eva Hitler née Braun.'

Hitler and Eva Braun. He rewarded her empty-headed devotion by marrying her, on the last day of his life. She had no desire to survive him and they died together

In the next few hours Hitler dictated his last will. There was not the slightest self-examination or conflict of conscience. He had always been right, only he had seen clearly. 'It is false,' he declared in this will, 'that I wanted or that anyone in Germany wanted war in 1939. The war was sought and provoked exclusively by international politicians belonging to the Jewish race or working for the Jews. The numerous offers that I made to disarm are there to testify before posterity that responsibility for the war cannot be ascribed to me. I said often enough, after the First World War, that I had no desire at all to fight Great Britain. Nor did I want war with the United States. In times to come the ruins of our cities will keep alive hatred for those who bear the real responsibility for our martyrdom: the agents of international Jewry.'

The dictation of this will was briefly interrupted for a reception to be held, at which Hitler and Eva received the congratulations on the occasion of their marriage, of those who had remained loyal to them to the last. When saying goodbye, Hitler remarked suddenly: 'National Socialism is dead. We have lost the game. All that remains is for us to die worthily.' Heinz Linge reports that he spoke 'in a calm and steady voice'. When Hitler withdrew to his quarters, everyone felt sure that they would never see him alive again.

However, 29th April passed without Hitler seeming to have varied his usual routine in any way. At noon he held, just as on any other day, a conference on the military situation. He held another one at 10 pm, when the Soviet troops were only 300 yards from the Chancellery.

On 30th April, at 2 am, Hitler received, at his own request, all the women who were in the bunker—secretaries, cooks, and chambermaids. He wished while still alive to hear their condolences on his death. Then he went back into his own quarters.

Adolf Hitler's last day had begun. At 10 am according to Linge's account, Hitler came out of his room wearing a new uniform decorated with his gold Party badge, his Iron Cross, and his medal for wounds received in the First World War. At his command, Linge asked the telephone switchboard for the latest news. When he returned to the Führer's side he reported: 'All resistance has ceased nearly everywhere. The Russian vice gripping Berlin is unbreakable. The Russians will be here tomorrow, at the latest.'

The leader of the Hitler Youth, Axmann, broke in vehemently: 'I still have 200 Hitler Youth and a tank. Let us try to get you out of here.' Hitler refused with a shake of his head, and mumbled: 'No, no, it's useless. I must die.'

Linge records that the Führer lunched with Eva Braun: 'they had a frugal meal,

The Defeat of the Axis

Fallen hero: Norwegian SS newspaper of 5th May relays Hamburg radio's announcement of 1st May that 'Hitler, fighting to the last breath against Bolshevism, fell for Germany in his operational headquarters in the Reich Chancellery'

for we were short of provisions.' Once again, farewells were said to the most faithful comrades. Standing before Frau Goebbels, Hitler showed emotion. He had just learned that she and her husband had decided to kill themselves, together with their six children. Hitler unpinned his gold Party badge and fastened it on Frau Goebbels's dress, kissing her as he did so.

Then Hitler and his wife went to their quarters. 'I had left in there, as I had been ordered,' states Linge, 'two revolvers which I had loaded myself. One was a Walther PP 7.65-mm, as used by the police. The other, of smaller calibre, a 6.35-mm, was for Eva Braun to use, or to take the place of the other weapon should it not work properly. Suddenly we heard a shot. It was about 3.35 pm. There was no second shot, and when I felt sure about this, approximately a quarter of an hour later, I went into the Führer's quarters. He was sitting on the couch. He had fired a 7.65 bullet into his right temple – not into his mouth, as has often been said. The revolver had fallen at his feet and his blood had poured onto the carpet. Beside him, half-lying on the couch, was his wife: she had preferred to take poison.'

Hitler had asked that his body and that of Eva be burned. He did not want them to become playthings for the Soviet soldiers. On Bormann's instructions, Erich Kempka, head of the transport service of the Chancellery, had managed with difficulty, to get together 180 litres of petrol.

Bormann, Dr Stumpfegger, the doctor of the bunker, Linge, Kempka, and Günsche, the Führer's aide-de-camp, climbed the thirty-nine steps that led up to the armoured door of the bunker carrying the two bodies and went out into the garden. They found themselves amid a storm of fire and steel. Never before, perhaps, had the bombardment been so heavy. At every moment the ground was ploughed up by shell splinters. Hastily they laid the bodies down, three metres from the door. Kempka, helped by Linge, poured the petrol over the bodies, can by can. Linge set fire to them, using a paper towel soaked in petrol.

An hour later it was possible to ascertain that the bodies had not burned at all well. The petrol had been absorbed mainly by the wrappings and the earth. Accordingly, Linge, so he says, gave an order for the bodies to be buried in a bomb crater near the place where they had tried to burn them, and this was duly done.

Many disputes have arisen over the actual circumstances of the Führer's death. There has been an attempt to create a 'mystery of Hitler's end'. Some sensational newspapers published articles after the war was over trying to prove that Hitler had succeeded in escaping from Berlin at the last moment. It must be said that the Soviet authorities did much to confer credibility on these legends. On 9th June 1945, during a press conference in Berlin, Marshal Zhukov, the Soviet commander-in-chief, said, regarding Hitler's death: 'The circumstances are very mysterious. We have not identified Hitler's body. I can say nothing for certain about his fate. He may have got away from Berlin by air at the last moment. The state of the runway would have made that possible.'

Then Colonel-General Berzarin, military commandant of Berlin, spoke: 'We have found several bodies, among which one may be Hitler's, but we cannot state definitely that he is dead. I think Hitler is hiding somewhere in Europe, probably in Franco's Spain.'

On 26th May 1945 Stalin told Harry Hopkins, the US envoy, that, in his opinion, 'Bormann, Goebbels, Hitler, and probably Krebs got away and went underground'. On 6th June Stalin repeated to Hopkins that 'he was convinced that Hitler was alive'. On 17th July the Soviet leader said at the Potsdam conference that he believed Hitler to be alive, 'probably in Spain or the Argentine'.

These statements did not reflect reality in any way. When these Soviet spokesmen gave them utterance the remains of Hitler and Eva Braun had long been found. Professor Trevor-Roper has suggested that this was on Stalin's direct orders to prevent any chance of Hitler's death being interpreted as heroic and thus acting as a

cult round which a revival of Nazism could flourish. It was only very recently – in 1968 – that the Russians decided to publish their material on the subject. A Soviet historian and journalist, Lev Bezymensky, has published a book entitled *The Death of Adolf Hitler*. He quotes all the records of the investigations, exhumations, and autopsies carried out. On 4th May 1945 Lieutenant-Colonel Klimenko, head of the counter-espionage unit of the Red Army's 79 Corps, found the bodies of Hitler and Eva Braun buried in a shellhole in the garden of the Chancellery.

Identification and autopsy

Subsequently, the bodies were shown to German prisoners and formally identified. The jaw of Hitler's body, which was intact, corresponded very exactly to the mouth-chart drawn by the Führer's own dentists. The autopsy made possible the discovery of traces of cyanide. 'No sign of a wound or of fatal disease was found in this body, which had been badly distorted by fire. The presence of fragments of a crushed glass phial in the mouth, as in the mouths of the other bodies, the pronounced smell of bitter almonds given off the body, and the forensic-medical examination of the internal organs, in which cyanide was found, all permit the commission to conclude that, in this case, death was due to poisoning with cyanide.' These were the actual words of the report completed on 8th May 1945.

This is a revelation of great significance. The survivors of the bunker, notably Günsche and Linge, asserted that Hitler had killed himself with a revolver bullet. It is odd, however, that Günsche spoke of the right temple and Linge of the left, while other accounts, collected by Trevor-Roper, indicate the mouth as the target of the fatal shot. The Soviet autopsy report puts an end to all these legends. Hitler died by cyanide poisoning.

It should be mentioned that the Soviet investigators gave particular attention to the statements of Major-General-SS Mohnke. According to him, Hitler had indeed swallowed the cyanide, but Linge was assigned the responsibility of giving him the coup de grâce when he came into the room. Another German prisoner in Soviet hands, Major-General-SS Rattenhuber, confirmed Mohnke's testimony.

In spite of everything said to the contrary, the doctors who carried out the autopsy maintain their view. Over twenty years later, Dr Shkaravisky, who presided over the 1945 autopsy, told Lev Bezymensky: 'The fact of poisoning is irrefutable. Whatever may be said nowadays, our commission found no trace of a bullet on 8th May 1945. Hitler poisoned himself.'

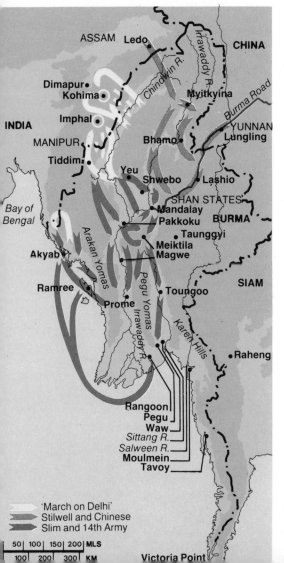

Victory in Burma

Even before Singapore fell on 15th February 1942, the Japanese XV Army under General Iida had crossed the Burma frontier from Siam and pushed beyond the river Sittang. Opposing him he found 1st Burma Division and 17th Indian Division and, as he had expected after the Japanese experience in Malaya, these kept retreating whenever his columns made hooks through the jungle to get behind them. There would be no major battle, he anticipated, until he reached the capital, Rangoon. In fact, when he reached here on 8th March it was to discover to his amazement that the city had been abandoned; and he knew that his campaign had virtually been won.

From the British viewpoint, the war in the Far East had been developing like an ugly dream. The Empire seemed to be falling apart. And now in the spring of 1942, with Malaya and the impregnable bastion of Singapore lost to the enemy, the loss of Burma had to be faced also. In Burma, General Sir Harold Alexander took over as General Officer Commanding Burma, soon to be joined by Lieutenant-General William Slim, of the Indian Army, as General Officer Commanding 'Burcorps', as the land forces were now designated. But even these two soldiers of proven ability could not halt the retreat; by 23rd March the last of the RAF units had been forced to retire to India, and Japanese X Air Brigade dominated the sky; by the end of March it became evident that the defensive line on the Irrawaddy could not be held; and on 26th April Alexander decided that Burma was lost and his main object must be the defence of India. A few months later he returned to Europe.

It must be mentioned that not only British and Indian troops took part in the opening battles for Burma. Under the American Lieutenant-General Joe Stilwell, Chinese 5th Army marched south and fought a spirited action near Toungoo. Prickly and temperamental, though not without military talent, Stilwell wielded his Chinese forces effectively, but, denied air cover—like the British and Indians of Burcorps—was forced to retreat back to China. Here he reorganized and later on was to take part in the advance from the north in 1944 which reopened the Burma

Above left: Japanese invasion, December 1941 to May 1942. Left: Allied reconquest February 1944 to August 1945. Starting with the defeat of the Japanese 'March on Delhi', the Burma campaign was fought in some of the most difficult conditions in the world, showing in the end that Commonwealth troops could beat the Japanese in jungle warfare

road, the vital supply line to China.

Japan's immediate object in going to war in December 1941 had been to break out of the stranglehold which the United States was maintaining over her supplies of raw material. Her declared political object was to set up a Greater East Asia Co-Prosperity Sphere, dominated by herself and comprising the Philippine Islands, the Netherlands East Indies, and Malaya. Burma was to be captured for strategic reasons, to form a protective flank for the conquered areas, and also as a source of vital supplies, especially oil and rice. The long-term consequences of occupying a country contiguous with India do not seem to have been thought out in any detail; but there was a facile assumption on the part of some generals that with Malaya and Burma gone the British would have as much as they could do to hold down the Indian nationalist movements. Even if the Indian Army should remain loyal, they did not consider it a force of any great consequence.

The field of battle

But what lay between Burma and India? Here it is necessary to enter into some geographical details, for without them the campaigns may appear somewhat incomprehensible. They were, in fact, incomprehensible at the time, even to the Combined Chiefs of Staff, who on one occasion asked why the fighting should be characterized by so many battalion and company actions. Briefly then, Burma occupies about a quarter of a million square miles, and if placed on the map of Europe would cover Belgium and France together. To the west, east, and north it is flanked by great mountain barriers, largely covered by thick jungle. On the west (towards India) the mountains run 600 miles from the Himalayas to the sea in a succession of chains some 200 miles across. Within these ranges lie the small countries of Assam and Manipur, at this time forming part of British India. Linked to this barrier, and running parallel to the coast, lie the Arakan Yomas; they separate Burma proper from the coastal regions. To the east lie more ranges, forming the borders with China, Yunnan, and Siam. As the mountains run from north to south, so do Burma's great rivers, the Irrawaddy (with its tributary the Chindwin), the Sittang, and the Salween. Even in 1941 these remained great highways of communication, for away from the large cities roads were few, and there was only one main railway line from north to south. Burma is not solidly covered with jungles, as the popular imagination sees it; large areas of

the central plain are, in fact, devoted to cultivation of rice. To the south, however, the Pegu Yomas, a wooded range of hills, lie between the Arakan Yomas and the Karen Hills.

The climate of Burma runs to extremes. In the plains the heat can be almost unbearable and in the hills the rainfall often exceeds 200 inches. In Assam 800 inches have been known. The heat and the damp encourage blood-sucking leeches and all manner of insects which sting or bite or infect; and malaria, scrub typhus, dysentery, and even cholera are endemic. Away from the towns, Burma is an uncomfortable country to live in, and it is hell to fight in, especially during the monsoon. By the end the troops would be called upon to endure no less than three monsoons.

The British had completed their annexation of Burma in 1885 and since that date generations of civil servants and soldiers had laboured to bring the benefits of civilization. To their efforts the Burmese, an independent and highly xenophobic race, reacted with indifference. The only loyalty towards the British, as the Japanese invasion would show, developed among the hill tribes, especially the Karens and Kachins. In 1937 the British government separated the administration of Burma from that of India, and the country received a measure of self-government. This, however, did not satisfy certain political groups who announced their intention to fight for freedom. Some of their leaders even visited Japan to enlist support. While these political moves were developing, the British tried to make up their minds how Burma should be defended, and who should be responsible. As she lay between India and Malaya, it was felt at Westminster that her defence should come under the Commander-in-Chief Far East. But in Delhi another view prevailed; as Burma lay on the north-east frontier of India, it was argued, GHQ Delhi should take over her defence. Despite many conferences, no agreement was reached, and the whole matter was given a low priority. Even in August 1940, the chiefs of staff recorded their opinion that the Japanese invasion of Burma remained a threat too remote for serious consideration. Only with the fall of Singapore did reality assert itself, and by then it was far too late.

When Slim's bedraggled forces retreated over the border from Burma in the summer of 1942, most of them made for Imphal, the capital of Manipur, which lies some 2,600 feet up in the mountain barrier, to the south of Assam. The town itself lies on a plain, known as the Imphal Plain, which extends forty miles by twenty and originally formed the bed of a lake. It is a fertile area, growing all manner of fruit and crops and is inhabited by the Mani-

puris, a clean, prosperous people, with a love of song and dancing. Slim's men had little but the clothes they marched in and their weapons; and they were bitter with defeat. They had made the longest retreat in British military history, over difficult terrain, and during the last stages, through the monsoon. Their only blessing was that since the Chindwin there had been no pursuit. Slim has said 'the Japanese army seemed as little prepared as we were to advance in the monsoon and we might reasonably look forward to a breathing space. . . .' In fact, Colonel Hayashi, a staff officer, was already arguing that Imphal should be captured before the British could organize it as their forward base, but though his views found favour in Tokyo, Iida wanted to rest his division. For the moment the frontier seemed safe, and for the rest of 1942 the Chindwin saw nothing but patrol activity.

1943 was a year of frustration. Quite obviously, before any lost territory could be regained, a new army must be built up; and before this army could advance, communications (both road and rail) would have to be improved, forward airfields would have to be built, and a considerable stock-pile of war supplies achieved. Also, there were some formidable medical problems to be solved, for doctors examining the troops of Burcorps as they filtered back to India were horrified at their condition. Malaria and amoebic dysentery had taken an enormous toll, and had in fact caused a hundred times more casualties than the enemy. Equally important was the question of morale, for with their rapid conquests the Japanese began to take on the role of supermen. Could British and Indian troops ever defeat them in jungle warfare? Could their tactics be countered successfully? These matters were discussed at every level, and a good deal of uninformed nonsense was talked. One man, however, was convinced that given proper training, good leadership, and effective air cover, the Anglo-Indian forces could win. He was General Slim.

For the moment he did not have the chance to put his ideas into practice. The campaign in the jungles of the Arakan in early 1943, though launched by part of 15th Corps, which he commanded, was directed by his superiors in Eastern Army. It proved abortive and costly, and tactically

Three of the men who forged the Allied victory in Burma. 1 Major-General Orde Wingate (right), a strange, unorthodox soldier, he hit the Japanese behind their own lines. 2 Lieutenant-General Joe Stilwell, 'a prickly American, not without military talent'. 3 Lieutenant-General Sir William Slim—his genius broke the Japanese onslaught

it achieved nothing. However, it did demonstrate convincingly that the long chain of command, running from GHQ Delhi via Eastern Army to the battle front, was quite impractical. A new command structure and new leaders were needed.

Before this change came about there took place a minor operation which must be mentioned: Major-General Orde Wingate's first Chindit operation, which took place in February and March 1943 ('Chindits' was the name given to his jungle groups). Wingate was a strange unorthodox soldier of great intellectual power, and for some time had been preaching the gospel of what he called 'long range penetration'. Briefly he planned that his brigade, specially organized into columns, should march into enemy territory, disrupt communications, gather intelligence, and be ready to take any opportunity to damage plant

and installations. The guerrilla columns would have no line of communications, but would be supplied from the air. Wavell's original intention was to co-ordinate the operations with an advance by the Chinese American forces from the north, but when this was cancelled, Wingate was still able to persuade him that the LRP operation, was worthwhile. In fact, it achieved very little in military terms,. but the publicity it gained was enormous. The fact that 3,000 men could operate hundreds of miles behind the enemy lines and the vast majority get back, gave the Allied armies a tremendous boost. In terms of morale alone, the gamble had paid off.

It was in August 1943 at the first Quebec

Conference that the new command structure was created. It was called South-East Asia Command and its task was to take over the conduct of the war in this theatre. The supreme commander was to be Admiral Lord Louis Mountbatten, and under him would be three commanders-in-chief for the three services. All British Commonwealth land forces in the war zone would come under Sir George Giffard's 11th Army Group and the strike force on the Burma borders would be designated 14th Army, under General Slim. The rapidity and extent of the changes brought about by these new commanders was remarkable. At Imphal 4th Corps under Scoones built up a vast forward base and patrolled forward to the Chindwin, and in the Arakan 15th Corps under Christison prepared for a new offensive. But the rail link from India, cut by the Brahmaputra River, was still inadequate and limited the build-up. From the Brahmaputra it ran to the railhead at Dimapur, where a supply base had been set up and from here supplies had to be loaded on to trucks for the hundred-mile journey through the mountains, via

Kohima and Maram to Imphal. Never had a front presented such logistical problems, and as Mountbatten saw at once, his only hope of maintaining the troops already in Assam and the Arakan, let alone building up an effective strike force, lay in air supply. One of his many preoccupations now and throughout the campaigns to come, would be borrowing transport aircraft.

The Japanese had also improved their command structure. Based on Rangoon, the Burma Area Army Headquarters was formed, with a cautious general called Kawabe as its commander. Under Kawabe came Hanaya's XXVIII Army in the Arakan, Renya Mutaguchi's XV Army in central Burma, and various formations facing Stilwell and the Chinese in the north, which were later to be incorporated into Honda's XXXIII Army. Kawabe was cautious, but Mutaguchi was completely his opposite: thrusting, ambitious, and ruthless. A defensive role was not to his taste, and by the early autumn of 1943 he was urging his superiors to launch an offensive against Imphal. This, he believed, would prevent an Allied counter-offensive, and would cause the Indian people to rise in rebellion. Privately, he saw no reason why the Japanese should not keep advancing till they reached the plains of India; and he even had daydreams (as he confessed later) 'of riding through Delhi on a white horse'.

After a good deal of argument his plan was accepted, though the objectives were limited to 'the strategic areas near Imphal and in north-east India'. The plan was that Hanaya should attack in the Arakan, forcing Slim to commit his reserves; and when these had been committed, Mutaguchi should advance on Imphal and Kohima. Kohima was a strong tactical position north of Imphal, on the road to Dimapur; and once this had been captured, Imphal itself would be cut off. In three weeks, Mutaguchi hoped, his troops would break through the mountain barrier and come streaming down on to the Imphal plain. And the British front would automatically collapse.

By January 1944 the British had got wind of the coming offensive and Slim, following Mountbatten's personal directions, made his plans accordingly. When it came under attack in the Arakan, 15th Corps would not retreat, but stay where it was, supplied by air drops. Two divisions of 4th Corps, then in forward positions towards the Chindwin, would retreat back to the Imphal Plain and fight the battle on its perimeter. Slim, it must be mentioned, had already made a great impression on his new army; officers and men alike realized that at long last they had the commander they needed.

The 'March on Delhi'

The Japanese offensive in the Arakan was launched on 4th February, led by Lieutenant-General Sakurai of LV Division. Soon he had moved round the flank of the leading divisions of 15th Corps and mounted a series of ferocious attacks from the jungle. 15th Corps held firm, as Slim had planned, but he was forced to commit his reserve, 5th Indian Division. Receiving the news, Mutaguchi launched his army over the Chindwin on 15th March and the 'March on Delhi' had begun. What he did not realize was that Mountbatten would be able to call on new formations from India, notably 2nd British Division which was soon moving by road and rail to Dimapur. But Mutaguchi was also able to spring a surprise: Sato's XXXI Division was heading across the mountains towards Kohima and making rapid progress.

(It may be mentioned here that Mutaguchi was advised by Tazoe, the Commander of III Air Division, to postpone his advance till he had dealt with Wingate who had now mounted a second and more ambitious campaign. But he refused, a decision he would live to regret.)

The twin battles at Kohima and Imphal raged from March to June and were undoubtedly the decisive battles of the Burma campaign. The territory was thick and mountainous; the slopes were steep and once the monsoon set in, the conditions under which the troops were asked to fight became a nightmare of rain and mud. By mid-April Sato had taken all but the central ridge of Kohima and the garrison was nearing exhaustion. Stopford's 33rd Corps, moving up the road from Dimapur, were having to fight every inch of the way over terrain which presented appalling difficulties. From the start it was obvious that the battle for Kohima would be a long one. Meanwhile, Scoones's forward divisions had been caught on their way back from the Chindwin and Cowan's 17th was having to break through a series of road blocks. The order to retreat had been given too late; and the battle was starting untidily.

However, Cowan was an excellent soldier; he not only got his divisions back to the Imphal Plain, but dealt his opponent Yanagida such a savage blow that the latter lost faith in the campaign and was later dismissed. By mid-April Scoones's 4th Corps was concentrated and ready for the concerted attack to come. Meanwhile Mountbatten had received confirmation that ninety-nine transport aircraft would be lent him from Mediterranean Command, and with these Imphal could be supplied.

Though he remained confident, Mutaguchi was unable to capture Imphal in three weeks as promised; and on 23rd April he learned that at Kohima General

The Defeat of the Axis

Sato had gone over to the defensive. From now on events swung against Japan and though Mutaguchi moved forward to take command in the field, he could do nothing to prevent this. On 1st June Sato began retreating from Kohima against orders, hotly pursued by 33rd Corps. On 22nd June, the road to Imphal was opened and supplies and reinforcements poured in; from a beleaguered fortress, Imphal was transformed into a base for offensive operations. For Mutaguchi and the Japanese, disaster followed disaster. Sakurai's men had already come back defeated in the Arakan; and now the remnants of the XI Army streamed back towards the Chindwin, thousands dying from disease and starvation (Mutaguchi's ramshackle line of communications had collapsed) and attacked from the air by the RAF. This was the greatest disaster suffered so far by any Japanese army in the field.

Though the monsoon was now at its height, swamping roads and jungle alike, Mountbatten took the decision to fight on; and such was the morale of 14th Army that the troops responded. Rapidly the Japanese were pushed back over the Chindwin, and then hounded towards the Irrawaddy. Once his armies had debouched from the jungle, Slim planned to deploy his tanks on the central plain, where they could operate to maximum effect. The days of 'thrashing around in jungles', as Churchill had described the early operations in the Arakan, would be over.

It was in the early months of 1945 that the battle for central Burma developed. Slim, whose army now included West African and East African formations, apart from his veteran Indian and British divisions, now struck at Kimura (Kawabe's successor) who was defending the Irrawaddy line. In February Slim secured bridgeheads south of Mandalay, then captured Meiktila, to the south-east. In this swift and carefully prepared move, Slim had tricked Kimura, who now found his communications with Rangoon cut off, and his armies isolated from each other. Honda, whose XXXIII Army had been retreating before a combined offensive by Stilwell's forces and the Chinese, was rushed to take command at Meiktila. But though he threw in his forces in a series of ferocious actions it was to no avail. The remnants of his army were forced to retreat to the southeast, with XV Army on its right flank being rapidly cut to pieces.

The race was now on for Rangoon, and Slim's forces moved south in two great columns, Stopford's 33rd Corps down the Irrawaddy valley, and to the east, 4th Corps (now under Messervy) along the Toungoo/Pegu railway route. Slim had decided that the enemy would not be able to hold him on both routes but, because of transport problems, had to concentrate his main thrust on the left. This route was the shorter of the two and, if Messervy's thrust was successful, vast numbers of Japanese would be cut off from their escape routes to the Sittang. Though, as the days of April went by, his advance gained momentum, Slim was in a difficult position. His land communications now stretched over a thousand miles, and could not survive the monsoon which was due in May. Somehow Rangoon must be taken before it broke. Fortunately, as he knew, an amphibious hook was being mounted from Akyab, now in Allied hands, and from Ramree, an island on the Burma coast, and if this were successful his task would be considerably eased.

Naturally, however, each division in 14th Army wanted to be the first to enter Rangoon, and none wanted this honour more dearly than Cowan's 17th Division, the only formation still in action which had taken part in the retreat back in 1942. Japanese XV Army was now little more than a rabble retreating through the Shan States and Honda's XXXIII Army, now desperately trying to reach the Sittang estuary, was being carved to fragments by Cowan's armoured columns. Town after town fell in rapid succession, and by 25th April Toungoo airfield had been secured. The fall of Rangoon could not be far away.

Decisive victory

In fact, it fell on 3rd May and the race was won by the troops on the seaborne landing, who were soon able to link up with their comrades coming from the north. The capital was found to be unoccupied. Now began the last phase of the Burma campaign. 15,000 men, the remnants of Sakurai's XXVIII Army, were trapped in the Irrawaddy valley and the Pegu Yomas to the east of it. Their only alternatives were to strike east or starve, and action could not long be delayed. On 11th May small parties began feeling their way forward, but found no escape route. Slim had ordered 4th Corps to cover the tracks leading from the Pegu Yomas, and 33rd Corps to clear the Irrawaddy Valley; he was determined that not one enemy soldier should escape. Though cornered, the Japanese still fought with their accustomed ferocity and time and again brought their mortars into action with great effect. On 3rd July Honda made a diversionary attack on Waw, hoping to help Sakurai by thinning Slim's line in the centre, but the attack petered out in the paddy fields. The monsoon had begun at the beginning of May and was unusually heavy. By July the Japanese were trying to slip round the flanks of the 14th Army positions in small groups but even those who reached the banks of the Irrawaddy found themselves hounded night and day. As to those who tried to cross, Slim has recorded: 'They were surprised as they launched their rafts, shot as they swam and drifted across on logs, or swept away by the rapid current to drown.' Many who survived the passage of the Irrawaddy were cut down further east or drowned in the Sittang. In July 11,500 bodies were counted. And on 4th August no more Japanese came. There were none left to come. The Burma campaign was over.

How is one to sum up this extraordinary and unique episode of war in the 20th century? How was it that the Japanese won the first two rounds, but lost the third so decisively? Undoubtedly the weight of armament and manpower that Great Britain was able to summon from her Indian empire was an important factor; and the seizure of complete air superiority was vital. Moreover, from the spring of 1944 the British, Indian, and Gurkha soldiers were able to demonstrate that man for man they could outfight their enemy, and by the end their morale was superb. But troops are no good without the right leaders, and in Mountbatten and Slim, SEAC had two of the finest leaders ever produced by Great Britain. Arriving in India, Mountbatten had to overcome not only massive prejudice and inertia, but administrative and logistical problems of immense complexity; yet he succeeded through sheer professional ability, character, and integrity. As for Slim, he may be regarded by history as the greatest English general since Marlborough. Under him 14th Army was forged into a striking force of immense power. Quiet and courteous in manner, resolute but never too proud to take advice, even from private soldiers, he grew in stature as each month went by. And his vision, his prophecies, and his tactical plan were vindicated, for he gained one of the most complete and decisive victories in military history, destroying three entire armies in the field.

Of the Japanese it can be said that no soldiers ever fought harder or at greater sacrifice. Every unit fought to the last man; and, except for a few individuals, surrender was unknown throughout the whole campaign. Though restricted by the rigidity of Samurai code, the Japanese generals were men of considerable skill and energy. Mutaguchi came within an inch of success in the 'March on Delhi'; Sakurai made a great impression in the Arakan; and Honda was superb, even in defeat. If one has to select a single factor which swayed the balance it is Slim. The fury of the Japanese onslaught in 1944 was broken by his genius. And what came afterwards was inevitable.

The Bomb

The history of the birth of the atomic bomb has something to offer everyone. To the nuclear physicist, it is a tale of scientific research on an unprecedented scale, completed successfully in spite of appalling handicaps imposed by secrecy and wartime shortages of men and materials. To the engineer it is an epic of technological enterprise, in which 1,400 million dollars worth of productive resources were staked on four largely untested industrial processes, each one of which came perilously close to failure. To the political historian, it is a saga of machinations in the corridors of power, set against a backcloth of international hostility and suspicion. To the moral philosopher it is a study in conflicts of loyalty—the competing claims made upon a scientist or politician by his own instincts and ambitions, his

The fateful mushroom cloud billows up over the Japanese city of Nagasaki. It was here that the second atomic bomb was dropped on 9th August 1945

friends, his country, and mankind. To the man in the street it is like other stories of war – a drama at once thrilling and disgusting which is played by an enormous cast, with characters ranging from the most dedicated patriot to the most perfidious secret agent.

How do nuclear weapons work? The basic facts of nuclear physics had been established by 1940. To explain briefly, the nuclei of atoms consist of a mixture of protons and neutrons. The number of protons can be anything from one to 101 and this number determines the chemical element of the atom. Thus hydrogen nuclei have one proton, iron 26, uranium 92, and plutonium 94. The number of neutrons is variable, and nuclei differing only in the number of neutrons are called 'isotopes'. Thus there are three known isotopes of hydrogen with zero, one, and two neutrons, known colloquially as hydrogen, deuterium, and tritium respectively, and fourteen isotopes of uranium, of which the most abundant on earth are U^{235} and U^{238} with, respectively, 143 and 146 neutrons. The existence of these isotopes, and the non-existence of other isotopes with different numbers of neutrons, is a consequence of the rather peculiar laws governing the forces which hold nuclei together. Roughly speaking, protons and neutrons attract each other strongly when very close together and otherwise ignore or (in the case of protons) repel each other. Nature has had some difficulty in building stable units with this rather uncompromising material, and it turns out that the only viable combinations are those in which the nucleus has more neutrons than protons, but not many more. The most stable nucleus is that of iron (with 26 protons and 32 neutrons), and as a rule any nuclear reaction (that is a re-arrangement of protons and neutrons to form a new nucleus or nuclei) which leads to a nucleus in which the number of protons is closer to 26 than previously, results in a release of nuclear energy. Consequently one can obtain nuclear energy either by fusing together two nuclei which are much lighter than iron (for example, deuterium and tritium which both have one proton) or by fissioning (splitting into two roughly equal halves) nuclei which are much heavier than iron (for example, uranium 235 which has 92 protons). The hydrogen bomb is based on the former option, the atomic bomb on the latter.

Fortunately for the stability of the material world, both fusion and fission only occur under exceptional circumstances. Fusion only occurs when nuclei collide very violently, and until recently the temperature required (around 100 million degrees Centigrade) could only be reached on earth with the help of an atomic bomb.

Fission, on the other hand, is an exceptional phenomenon only because the universe is many millions of years old, and during its evolution most of the nuclei capable of spontaneous fission have already done so, and the few that are left (for example radium) fission so slowly as to be useless as sources of energy. However, since certain heavy nuclei are only just stable, the addition of one more neutron is sufficient to tip them over the edge. The uranium isotope U^{235} and plutonium are examples of this. Since each fission releases two or more neutrons, it is possible to induce a chain reaction: a first neutron is captured by a heavy nucleus which fissions, releasing two neutrons which are captured by two more nuclei and so on.

Such a chain reaction can be thought of as a population explosion in neutrons, and it leads to the enormously rapid release of nuclear energy which occurs in every atomic explosion. However, like all population explosions, it depends upon maintaining a 'reproduction rate' of more than one neutron per neutron captured. Two adverse factors can prevent this. First, if the lump of material containing the fissile nuclei is too small, too many neutrons can escape from its surface, rather than undergo capture by other nuclei within it and thus lead to fission. Second, if the nucleus which captures a neutron is of the wrong kind, it may not undergo fission at all, or not fast enough. The first factor is not crucial – it simply shows that the lump of material must exceed a certain critical size, and atomic bombs are in practice ignited by bringing together two lumps of uranium, each slightly less than the critical size. However, the second factor is crucial, for uranium 238 is not fissile. Thus even a fairly small proportion of U^{238} in a lump of U^{235} is sufficient to prevent an explosive chain reaction from occurring within it. In fact, natural uranium consists of 99·3% of U^{238} and a mere 0·7% of U^{235}, so before U^{235} can be used as a nuclear explosive it is necessary to separate it from a much larger quantity of U^{238}. The other fissile material, plutonium, does not exist in nature at all; however, if one bombards U^{238} with *slow* neutrons (obtained by passing fast neutrons through a 'moderator' made of heavy water or graphite in a nuclear reactor) it slowly becomes transmuted into plutonium which can then be separated off and used as an explosive. The first option (U^{235}) was used in the bomb exploded at Hiroshima, the second at Nagasaki.

Virtually all the physical ideas described above were familiar to the nuclear physicists of all nations by September 1939, and it is hardly surprising that every scientifically advanced country took steps to explore the military potential of nuclear energy.

But progress in the various countries concerned was very uneven. In France nearly all work stopped with the German occupation and most of the principal nuclear physicists fled to England (and later transferred to Canada); including two who were to make a considerable impact, Halban and Kowarski. In the Soviet Union the Academy of Sciences formed a 'special committee on the uranium problem', but its plans were frustrated by the German invasion which led to the evacuation of the bulk of Soviet industry and research establishments beyond the Urals. This delayed their nuclear programme until the end of 1942, by which time they were already receiving regular communications about the British and American work from their agent Klaus Fuchs. But it seems they did not give high priority to producing their own bomb until 1945.

In Germany, work was impeded from the outset by the loss of many of the most gifted nuclear physicists during the anti-Jewish purges of the academic community immediately before the war, and by factional disputes among those who remained. Nevertheless, by mid 1940 a powerful group of physicists, including Bothe, Weizsäcker, and Heisenberg, had set up a research institute in Berlin which was given the code name 'The Virus House'. Until about 1942 their work was at a level roughly comparable with that of America. However, in April 1942, an Anglo-Norwegian sabotage team wrecked the heavy water plant at Rjukan, upon which their programme heavily depended, and from then on their fortunes declined. Nevertheless, the possibility of an imminent German weapon continued to serve as a spur to Allied physicists until the discovery of Weizsäcker's papers in Strasbourg (captured in 1944) revealed how far behind they then were.

In Great Britain, most of the nation's scientists were initially occupied in other war work and in the early months the nuclear effort depended largely upon refugees who were prevented by their nationality from being incorporated into secret military projects! Nevertheless, during the early years, Great Britain made most of the main contributions to nuclear weapons development. The first serious indication that it was possible to build an atomic bomb was given in February 1940 by Professors Peierls and Frisch, then working at Birmingham University. In their outstanding *Memorandum* (which has since been published) they set out in three pages the main problems in designing a bomb, and the possible solutions. They pointed out for the first time that it was vital to separate U^{235} from U^{238} and indicated a method by which this could be done – 'thermal diffusion'. They calculated the 'critical mass' of U²³⁵ and obtained a figure of 600 grams, an answer which was subsequently revised upwards to nine kilograms as more accurate nuclear measurements were made. The resulting explosion, they estimated, would be equivalent to about 1,000 tons of TNT, and they commented on the lethal effects of the radiation which would be produced.

With the stimulus provided by the Peierls-Frisch memorandum, research on isotope separation was given steadily increasing support during 1940, chiefly under the direction of Professor Simon at Oxford University. By the end of the year it was clear that a different separation process—gaseous diffusion—was better than thermal diffusion and that a plant capable of separating enough U²³⁵ for a bomb would cost over five million pounds and would require materials for its construction which only considerable research and development effort could produce. In the meantime, the French physicists Halban and Kowarski, who had joined Cambridge University, had shown that a slow chain reaction could be maintained in natural uranium, producing plutonium, provided that heavy water was used to moderate the speed of the neutrons, and their colleagues Bretscher and Feather suggested that the plutonium could indeed be used as a nuclear explosive. Finally, at Birmingham University, Oliphant was working on a third technique for separating isotopes—the electromagnetic method. However, neither this approach nor the Cambridge plutonium approach appeared very hopeful at this stage, and when the Maud Committee (set up by the Air Ministry to investigate nuclear weapons) finally reported in mid-1941, it came down in favour of the gaseous diffusion method.

By this stage, it was clear to most British scientists that the larger scale work which was now required could only be carried out in America where the necessary productive resources were still available. Until 1942, the American effort had been less intense, and less successful, than the British; indeed they had repeatedly pressed for closer co-operation with Britain. By the summer of 1942, however, as a result of the impact of Pearl Harbour and the strongly favourable report by the Maud Committee on the feasibility of nuclear weapons, the American effort had at last acquired momentum. Their programme, which for security reasons was known as the 'Manhattan Project', was now put under the control of the army, in the person of the formidable General Groves, and expenditure which had hitherto been measured in thousands of dollars was now to be measured in millions. The timing of this major expansion was such that Great Britain graciously consented to co-operate with

America in a development programme at precisely the moment when the American scientific leaders Conant and Bush had decided they were no longer dependent upon British help. The resulting breakdown in co-operation was a disastrous episode in Anglo-American relations, and the resentment and suspicion on both sides were only slowly removed even after the quarrel had been officially resolved by direct discussions between Churchill and Roosevelt which led to the Quebec agreement in August 1943. In the meantime, work progressed in America on all the approaches described above—gaseous diffusion isotope separation under Urey and Dunning at Columbia University, electromagnetic separation under Lawrence at California, thermal diffusion separation under Abelson at Anacostia, and plutonium breeding with slow neutrons under Fermi at Chicago. The fluctuating fortunes of these four approaches were the despair of General Groves and his scientific advisers. The gaseous diffusion method required the manufacture of literally acres of 'membrane'—thin metal sheets with millions of fine holes in them through which uranium hexafluoride gas diffused—and the construction of a vast industrial plant consuming enough electricity to supply a large city. This plant, at Oak Ridge, Tennessee, was largely completed (at a cost of 280 million dollars) by July 1944 but technological difficulties with the 'membrane' were still proving so formidable that there was a serious possibility that the entire investment would be wasted. The electromagnetic method depended on scaling up a delicate laboratory instrument to industrial dimensions. The electromagnet used in Lawrence's early experiments had measured a few inches across: in the electromagnetic separation plant (also at Oak Ridge) it was a massive 122 feet long and 15 feet high with electrical windings made of 86,000 tons of pure silver, borrowed from the Treasury bullion reserves for the purpose. Here again there were repeated setbacks: the plant began to operate in February 1944, but by July it was clear that there was no hope of relying upon this method alone to produce enough U²³⁵ before the end of the war. The thermal diffusion process proved useless as a means of enriching U²³⁵ by a large amount, though good for small improvements. Finally there was the plutonium approach, which appeared very hopeful after the success of Fermi's first experimental pile, built in Chicago in December 1942. This pile, which was the brilliant forerunner of all subsequent nuclear reactors, led to the construction of several enormous plutonium breeding reactors at Hanford on the Columbia river. The first of these was set into action by Fermi in September 1944, but

within a few hours it shut itself down, as a result of a totally unexpected 'nuclear poisoning' phenomenon.

In the end, all four approaches were used. The thermal diffusion method was used to raise the U²³⁵ content of uranium from 0·7% to 0·9%. This slightly enriched material was then fed into the gaseous diffusion plant, which took it up to about 20% U²³⁵, and finally the electromagnetic plant was used to produce material with over 90% U²³⁵. As a result, enough U²³⁵ for a weapon was available by August 1945 at a total cost of about 1,000 million dollars. Plutonium production proved more difficult to plan, since the amount required to produce a weapon remained uncertain until the last minute, and there were doubts at one stage whether it could be made to work at all. For this reason, it was decided to test a plutonium weapon as soon as enough became available. This test was carried out in the Alamogordo desert in New Mexico on 17th July 1945, under the scientific direction of J.Robert Oppenheimer, the physicist who was responsible for the top secret weapon design laboratory at Los Alamos. The explosion, which comfortably exceeded the calculations of the theoreticians, had an impact which was not to be measured only in kilotons equivalent of TNT. For a number of the scientists who witnessed the test, the horror of the experience convinced them that the weapon must never be used against men. However the majority (at least of the senior scientists whose voices carried weight in government circles) had no serious doubts that nuclear weapons should be used against Japan if by so doing the war could be shortened. In spite of strenuous protests by Szilard and other leading scientists, the final decision to use it was taken by Truman, with the concurrence of Churchill, and the bombs were dropped on Hiroshima on 6th August and on Nagasaki on 9th August. The Japanese Emperor communicated his decision to surrender on the 10th. How events would have developed if the bombs had not been dropped is one of the great unresolvable uncertainties of history. A strong though not watertight case can be made that the Japanese would shortly have surrendered in any case, without further major bloodshed. At a different level it has been argued that the use of the weapons then has given them the credibility upon which their role as deterrents to world warfare now depends. It is impossible to be certain about such imponderables: what is certain is that the events of August 1945 initiated a debate about the morality and efficacy of these weapons of destruction which will continue at least until general and complete disarmament has become a practicable means of ordering human affairs.

Balance Sheet of Second World War

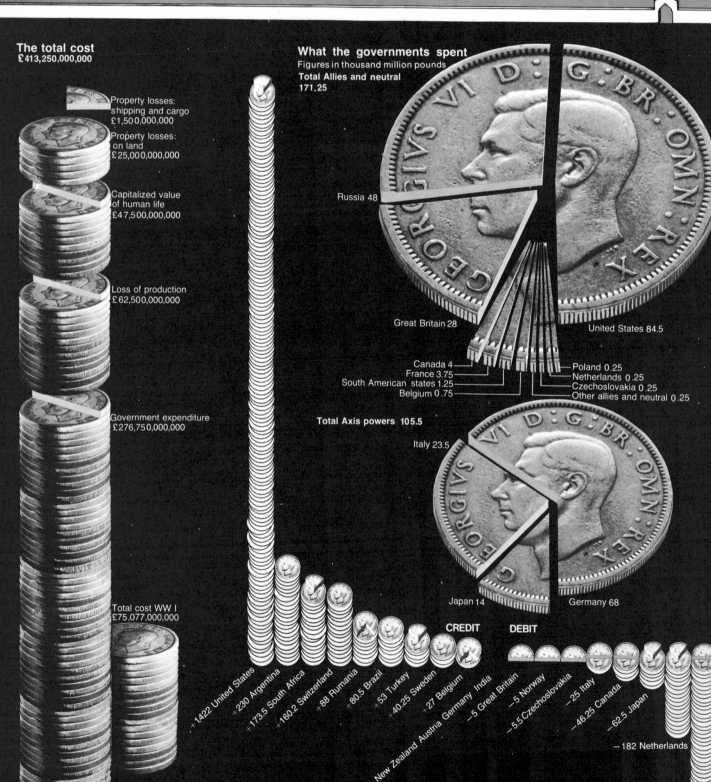

The war dead

1914-18

1939-45

WW I 17,000,000

Russia 20,000,000

The total cost
£413,250,000,000

Property losses:
shipping and cargo
£1,500,000,000

Property losses:
on land
£25,000,000,000

Capitalized value
of human life
£47,500,000,000

Loss of production
£62,500,000,000

Government expenditure
£276,750,000,000

Total cost WW I
£75,077,000,000

What the governments spent
Figures in thousand million pounds
**Total Allies and neutral
171.25**

Russia 48

Great Britain 28

United States 84.5

Canada 4
France 3.75
South American states 1.25
Belgium 0.75

Poland 0.25
Netherlands 0.25
Czechoslovakia 0.25
Other allies and neutral 0.25

Total Axis powers 105.5

Italy 23.5

Japan 14

Germany 68

CREDIT   **DEBIT**

+1422 United States
+230 Argentina
+173.5 South Africa
+160.2 Switzerland
+88 Rumania
+80.5 Brazil
+53 Turkey
+40.25 Sweden
+27 Belgium
0 New Zealand Austria Germany India
−5 Great Britain
−5 Norway
−5.5 Czechoslovakia
−25 Italy
−46.25 Canada
−62.5 Japan
−182 Netherlands
−335 France

Who gained : who lost   Changes in gold reserves   Figures in
millions of pounds

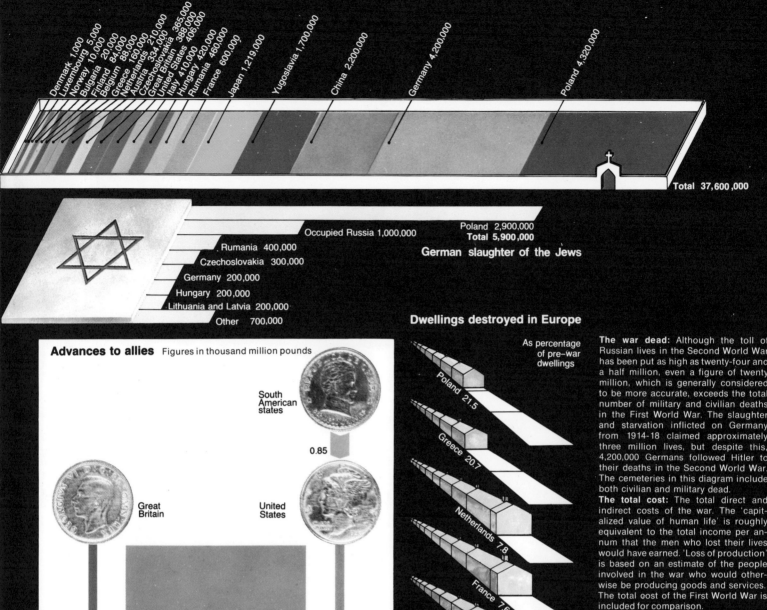

Denmark 1,000
Luxembourg 5,000
Norway 10,000
Bulgaria 20,000
Finland 84,000
Belgium 88,000
Greece 160,000
Netherlands 210,000
Austria 334,000
Czechoslovakia 365,000
Great Britain 388,000
United States 406,000
Italy 410,000
Hungary 420,000
Rumania 460,000
France 600,000
Japan 1,219,000
Yugoslavia 1,700,000
China 2,200,000
Germany 4,200,000
Poland 4,320,000

Total 37,600,000

Occupied Russia 1,000,000
Poland 2,900,000
Total 5,900,000
Rumania 400,000
Czechoslovakia 300,000
Germany 200,000
Hungary 200,000
Lithuania and Latvia 200,000
Other 700,000

German slaughter of the Jews

Dwellings destroyed in Europe

As percentage of pre-war dwellings

Poland 21.5
Greece 20.7
Netherlands 7.8
France 7.6
Great Britain 6.5
Belgium 6.2
Italy 4.9
Hungary 3.9
Norway 3.6
Czechoslovakia 3.4

Advances to allies
Figures in thousand million pounds

South American states

0.85

Great Britain

United States

Great Britain and British Empire 7.9

0.30 Russia 2.78

0.30 France 0.11

1.2 USA

China 0.40

0.1 Other countries 0.40

The war dead: Although the toll of Russian lives in the Second World War has been put as high as twenty-four and a half million, even a figure of twenty million, which is generally considered to be more accurate, exceeds the total number of military and civilian deaths in the First World War. The slaughter and starvation inflicted on Germany from 1914-18 claimed approximately three million lives, but despite this, 4,200,000 Germans followed Hitler to their deaths in the Second World War. The cemeteries in this diagram include both civilian and military dead.

The total cost: The total direct and indirect costs of the war. The 'capitalized value of human life' is roughly equivalent to the total income per annum that the men who lost their lives would have earned. 'Loss of production' is based on an estimate of the people involved in the war who would otherwise be producing goods and services. The total cost of the First World War is included for comparison.

What the governments spent: Direct expenditure by governments on the war, excluding loans to allies. Not all of this should be regarded as loss. It includes military pay and the creation of assets like merchant ships.

Who gained, who lost: Some significant changes in gold in reserve and in circulation between the end of 1938 and the end of 1945, indicating some nations who profited from the industrial demands of the war, such as the USA, the 'arsenal of democracy', and minerally-rich South Africa and Brazil.

German slaughter of the Jews: The decimation of Polish Jewry is self-evident. Only 100,000 survived the extermination camps. 'Other' comprises Denmark, Holland, Belgium, France, Italy, Bulgaria, Yugoslavia, Austria, and Greece. Some Jews saw the danger in time: 280,000 left Europe for the United States, South America, Great Britain, and Japan from 1933-40.

Advances to allies: Loans by the United States and Great Britain to their allies. British advances to the United States were termed 'reciprocal aid' and consisted of raw materials.

Dwellings destroyed in Europe: For some countries—including Russia and Germany—there are no exact figures. Rough estimates put the dwellings destroyed or damaged in these areas at about 7,500,000.

Index

Index

Index

Index

Acknowledgments

This book has been compiled from material contained in the *History of the 20th Century* partwork published by BPC Publishing Ltd. Pictures were obtained from the following sources:

Herman Axelbank; Chris Barker; Bavarian Army Museum, Munich; Derek Bayers; Earl Beatty; Berliner Illustrierte; Bibliothek für Zeitgeschichte, Stuttgart; Bibliothèque Nationale, Paris; Bradford City Library; Brown Brothers; Commando 1a Divisione; Carabinieri Pastrengo, Milan; Camera Press; Culver Pictures; Coll. René Dazy; Domenica del Corriere; Will Dyson/Odhams Ltd; E. C. Armées; Editions Rencontre; Fine Arts Publishing Co. Ltd; Martin Gilbert; Hartingue/Viollet; Heeresgeschichtliches Museum, Vienna; Historical Research Unit; Robert Hunt Library; Huntingdon Hartford; L'Illustration; Illustrazione Italiana; Imperial War Museum; Das Interessante Blatt; International Institute of Social History; Kladderadatsch; Photothèque Laffont; Leach Heritage of the Air Collection; London Express; Lords Gallery; Mansell Collection; Moro, Milan; George Morrison; Musée de l'Armée, Invalides; Musée de la Guerre, Paris; Museo Aeronautico Caproni di Taliedo; Museo Bersagliere, Rome; Museo di Storia Contemporeanea, Milan; Museo Storico dei Granatieri, Rome; Museo Storico Italiano Della Guerra, Rovareto; Musée Royal de l'Armée, Brussels; National Army Museum, Sandhurst; National Gallery of Canada; National Museum of Ireland, Dublin; National Portrait Gallery; Nerbini; New Ireland Assurance Co; New York Public Library; Novosti; Gerard Oriol; Paul Popper; Press Association; Princip Museum Sarajevo; Radio Times Hulton Picture Library; S.C.R. Photo Library; Simplicissimus; Smithsonian Institute, Washington (Henry Beville); Snark International; Alan Spain; SPB Prague; Sphere; Staatsbibliothek, Berlin; Strato Maggiore Aeronautica, Rome; Südd-Verlag, Munich; Syndication International; Tate Gallery; Oscar Tellgmann; Topix; Tretyakov Gallery, Moscow; Ulk/Tasiemka; Ullstein; USIS; US Navy Dept; Vhú Prague; Roger Viollet; Der Welt Spiegel; Wehrgeschichtliches Museum, Rastatt.

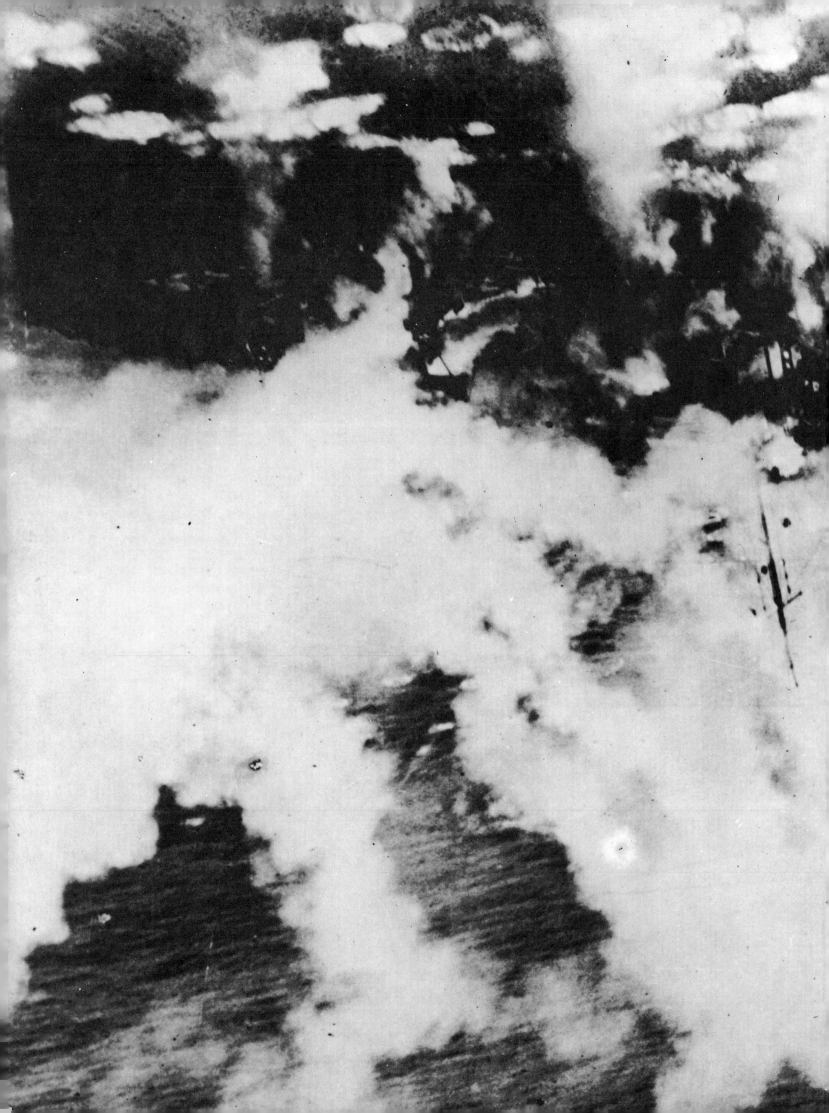